Cost Accounting in Anglophone Subsidiaries

MÜNSTERANER SCHRIFTEN ZUR INTERNATIONALEN UNTERNEHMENSRECHNUNG

Herausgegeben von Peter Kajüter

Band 11

Zu Qualitätssicherung und Peer Review der vorliegenden Publikation

Die Qualität der in dieser Reihe erscheinenden Arbeiten wird vor der Publikation durch den Herausgeber der Reihe geprüft.

Notes on the quality assurance and peer review of this publication

Prior to publication, the quality of the work published in this series is reviewed by the editor of the series.

Moritz Schröder

Cost Accounting in Anglophone Subsidiaries

Empirical Evidence from Germany

PL ACADEMIC RESEARCH

Bibliographic Information published by the Deutsche Nationalbibliothek
The Deutsche Nationalbibliothek lists this publication in the Deutsche Nationalbibliografie; detailed bibliographic data is available in the internet at http://dnb.d-nb.de.

Zugl.: Münster (Westfalen), Univ., Diss., 2014

Library of Congress Cataloging-in-Publication Data
Schröder, Moritz, 1985-
Cost accounting in anglophone subsidiaries : empirical evidence from Germany / Moritz Schröder.
pages cm
Includes bibliographical references.
ISBN 978-3-631-65537-5 – ISBN 978-3-653-04996-1 (ebook)
1. International business enterprises–Germany. 2. Subsidiary corporations–Germany. 3. Cost accounting–Germany. 4. English-speaking countries.
I. Title.
HD2859.S35 2014
657'.420943–dc23

2014034446

D 6
ISSN 1868-7687
ISBN 978-3-631-65537-5 (Print)
ISBN 978-3-653-04996-1 (E-Book)
DOI 10.3726/978-3-653-04996-1

Peter Lang – Frankfurt am Main · Bern · Bruxelles · New York · Oxford · Warszawa · Wien

This publication has been peer reviewed.

www.peterlang.com

Preface

Since the industrialisation in the 19th century, cost accounting has developed into one of the key management accounting tools in practice. As a consequence, it has also become an important topic in education and a relevant research object for management accounting scholars. However, cost accounting has not delevoped uniformly across countries, but has rather been shaped by various institutional forces such as national culture, education and financial accounting systems. As a result, specific national cost accounting traditions have emerged and still prevail today despite a trend to global standardisation of management accounting practices. Broadly speaking there are two main traditions: German and Anglophone cost accounting. Companies from Germany are known for their very detailed and refined cost accounting systems, whereas firms from Anglophone countries such as the USA or UK generally have less complex systems in place. Such national particularities naturally evoke the question how multinational firms design their cost accounting systems. Whereas from a corporate perspective, standardised cost accounting systems seem to be very appealing, subsidiary companies may favour their local cost accounting traditions over a corporately induced standard.

Even though there is fragmented research on the design of cost accounting systems in international groups, little is known about the actual consequences of cross-national differences of cost accounting for multinationals. *Do these companies indeed transfer their home country's cost accounting traditions in their foreign subsidiaries and if so, what are the consequences for the use of cost information in subsidiaries?* Continuing my interest in management and cost accounting practices around the world, I gladly supervised Moritz Schröder's PhD thesis, which is devoted to the exploration of these research questions.

Moritz Schröder investigated cost accounting in subsidiaries of Anglophone multinationals in Germany. He explored the complexity of these companies' cost accounting systems and the use of cost information by the subsidiaries' board members. Given the relatively small population of only 500 small to medium sized Anglophone manufacturing companies in Germany and an equally sized German control group, Moritz Schröder carefully developed a dyadic research design and collected an acknowledgeable empirical data set of roughly 200 questionnaires on the design of cost accounting systems and about 100 questionnaires on the use of cost information.

The empirical results reveal that the subsidiaries of Anglophone multinationals in Germany are indeed characterised by Anglophone cost accounting traditions. Moritz Schröder can attribute these results to coercive institutional determinants such as parent companies' cost accounting standards as well as voluntary institutional determinants (e.g. further trainings by professional institutes of management accountants) and economic effects (e.g. the diversity of the subsidiary's products). Similar determinants affect the cost accounting systems in the domestic German subsidiaries.

Remarkably, Moritz Schröder finds that cost information, despite all corporate effects, is used by the subsidiaries' top management for both decision facilitating and decision influencing. Although the parent companies appear to foster these usage types in both the Anglophone and the German subsidiaries, the former seem to work around their parent companies' standards more extensively than the latter. This finding seems to be associated with the existence (and absence) of cross-national differences in cost accounting. Also, the avoiding or defying reaction of subsidiaries can be aligned with an unfavourable relationship between subsidiaries and their parent companies.

Based on these findings, Moritz Schröder aligns both the design of cost accounting systems and the use of cost information with the performance of cost accounting in subsidiaries. He can reveal that both management accountants and managers in the Anglophone companies base their performance evaluations on the design of cost accounting systems and the use of cost information. Both, however, seem to prefer to deviate from a parent company's cost accounting standard. In the domestic German firms, management accountants and managers also assess cost accounting systems similarly. Remarkably, though, they seem to compromise their parent company's involvements and other institutional and economic determinants during the design of their cost accounting systems.

By explicating the relevance of cross-national differences in cost accounting for multinationals, Moritz Schröder's work contributes considerably to current management accounting research. Throughout his thesis, Moritz Schröder provides profound insights into the design of cost accounting systems and the use of cost information in international groups. Moreover, he derives various practical recommendations for cost accounting in such organisations. Given this importance for both management accounting scholars and practitioners, I wish that this thesis will be as highly respected in management accounting research and practice as it deserves to be.

Münster, June 2014 Prof. Dr. Peter Kajüter

Acknowledgements

During my time as a research assistant and PhD student at the Chair of International Accounting of the University of Münster, I have explored the cost accounting systems of Anglophone groups in Germany. The Münster School of Business and Economics accepted this thesis, in which my research project resulted, as a dissertation in April 2014. Undoubtedly, my aspirations to meet challenges, my curiosity to explore and my commitment to the task helped realising this PhD project. However, I am convinced that I would not have completed this thesis as satisfactory if it was not for all the people that accompanied the different stages of my project. I will try to express my deep appreciation for their support, encouragements, patience and distractions in the following words.

First, I would like to thank my supervisor Prof. Dr. Peter Kajüter very sincerely. Without his advice, guidance and comments, I would not have completed this PhD project. I also very much appreciate the contributions of Prof. Dr. Wolfgang Berens and Prof. Dr. Johannes Becker who reviewed my work as a second and third examiner. Moreover, I would like to thank Prof. Dr. Max Albert and Prof. Dr. Mark Houston for their doctoral seminars at the University of Münster. Their comprehensive visions of the philosophy of science and the development of questionnaire items were very helpful. Equally supportive were the experiences I made in the 2012 ACMAR Doctoral Coloquium and the 2012 ERMAC. Without naming all faculty members, coaches and participants of these events, I would like to express my gratitude to all these people for their inspiring insights.

Having honoured my academic teachers, I would like to thank my colleagues at the Chair of International Accounting for accompanying the development of this work. My deepest gratitude goes to my cell- and wallmate Max Saucke. He proofread part of my draft thesis, helped me to become clear-headed in numerous occasions and became a real friend. I am equally thankful for the support of my former colleagues Dr. Christina Voets, Dr. Daniel Blaesing and Dr. Matthias Moeschler. They did not tire of listening to me conceptualising my ideas, even though the thoughts did not always lead somewhere. My sincere appreciations also go to Daniela Peters, Marcel Baki, Julius Hannemann, Friedrich Kalden, Florian Klassmann, Martin Nienhaus and Alexander Schulz for proofreading parts of my draft thesis and for supporting my theoretical, statistical, conceptual and nonsensical questions. I really enjoyed working, socialising, partying and working-out with all these folks. This holds equally true for my fellow PhD students Stephanie Eckert, Dr. Kristian Bachert, Gregor Hagemann, Stefan Hannen, Dr. Thomas Poplat, Dr. Martin Merschdorf, Dr. Christian Reisloh and Rodrigo Paiva Souza as well as our secretary Leila Prousch.

In addition, I wish to thank my student assistants Theresa Jording, Ina Gährken, Mareike Schlöter, Michael Huth and Jonas Pöhler. Without their reliable and independent work, data collection would not have been as successful. Even though I have not always been explicit about my appreciation, I really value their help. The same holds true for all the additional assistants that helped transcribing the expert interviews, which preceded my questionnaire investigation (Laura Spiske, Robert Beukmann, Christoph Mauritz, Robert Seidel and Martin Vogelpohl).

Besides extolling the people linked to my alma mater, I also wish to thank my dear cousin Agnetha Duddeck and my precious friends Henning and Johanna Marquardt. They confronted the demanding task of proofreading my thesis and truly helped streamlining my work. Moreover, I would like to express my gratitude to my friends and former fellow students Mario Englert and Sebastian Hohenberg from the University of Mannheim. Their selfless willingness to help really supported my work. Finally, I take this opportunity to thank all the business experts that provided their company's and personal insights to support this project. The people that participated during the development of the questionnaires, the expert interviews as well as the survey investigation made this thesis possible.

I dedicate this work to my father Frank, my mother Susanne and my sister Julia. Without their unswerving support, patience, confidence, sympathy, encouragement and love during my personal development and my academic career, I would have been unable to write these words. Thank you very much!

São Paulo, June 2014 Moritz Schröder

Contents overview

Contents

List of figures

List of tables

List of appendices

List of abbreviations

ABC	Activity-based costing
Angl.	Anglophone subsidiaries
AU	Australia
cf.	compare
centr.	Centralised
coeff.	coefficients
CIMA	Chartered Institute of Management Accountants
CND	Variable: Cross national differences
e.g.	for example
E.S.	expected sign
ERP	Enterprise resource planning (software)
esp.	especially
et al.	et alii
FA	Financial accounting
f.	and the following one
ff.	and the following
$f(x_i)$	function of variable x for respondent i
GE	General Electric
Ger.	Domestic German subsidiaries
GM	General Motors
GPK	Grenzplankostenrechnung
ibid	ibidem
ICV	International Controller Association
i.e.	that is
IMA	Institute of Management Accountants
incl.	including
Instr. / concept. use	Instrumental / conceptual usage type
IT	Information technology
KMO	Kaiser-Meyer-Olkin criterion

MA	Management accounting
max.	maximum
MCS	Management control system
min.	minimum
MNC	Multinational company
N/A	Not applicable
Neg.	negative
NIS	New institutional sociology
No.	number
NZ	New Zealand
OIE	Old institutional economics
p.	page
per.	perceived
PLS	Partial least squares
P/L	Profit and loss
Pos.	positive
R&D	Research and development
RCA	Resource consumption accounting
resp.	respective
RQ	research question
RR.	Response rate
TDABC	Time-driven activity-based costing
TEA	Dynamic theory of economic actors
UK	United Kingdom
US	United States
USA	United States of America
VIF	Variance inflation factor
vs.	versus

List of symbols

*	10 % significance level
**	5 % significance level
***	1 % significance level
#	10 % significance level (for variables with an unexpected sign)
##	5 % significance level (for variables with an unexpected sign)
###	1 % significance level (for variables with an unexpected sign)
%	per cent
<	smaller than
≤	smaller or equal than
>	larger than
≥	larger or equal than
✓	accepted
(✓)	conditionally accepted
X	rejected
(X)	conditionally rejected
±	unexpected 'quasi significant' result

1 Introduction

1.1 Motivation and research questions

> *"Comparative management research consistently reports that organizations within one national setting can exhibit similarities not shared by enterprises in other countries."*[1]

Despite tendencies towards international convergence,[2] there are remarkable national particularities of management accounting practices.[3] This holds especially true for **cost accounting**,[4] the source of modern management accounting.[5] Since the establishment of cost accounting during the industrialisation in the 19th century,[6] its development is especially attributable to German-speaking and Anglophone researchers and practitioners.[7] Hence, it is not surprising that German and Anglophone[8] cost accounting is characterised by unmistakable particularities. Whereas German cost accounting is particularly sophisticated and refined, Anglophone cost accounting traditions tend to be considerably less detailed.[9]

> *"Companies may implement home-country practices in subsidiaries located in countries where the home-country practice will be ineffective."*[10]

Such cross-national differences in cost accounting imply a tension for **multinational companies**[11] (subsequently MNCs or multinationals). To ensure the efficiency of their cost accounting systems, multinationals need to choose between a company-wide alignment of cost accounting systems with their home country traditions (ethnocentric design) or worldwide best practices (geocentric design) and the approval of diverging cost ac-

---

1 *Bhimani* (2005), p. 250.

2 Cf. *Granlund/Lukka* (1998), p. 170; *Macintosh* (1998), p. 498; *Shields* (1998), p. 506; *Chow et al.* (1999), p. 455; *Jones/Luther* (2006), p. 8.

3 For reviews of comparative management accounting research, cf. *Endenich et al.* (2011), p. 365ff., and *Moeschler* (2012), p. 52ff.

4 For associated reviews, cf. *Brierley et al.* (2001), p. 218ff.; *Blake et al.* (2003), p. 181f.; *Krumwiede/Suessmair* (2007a), p. 2ff.; *Kajüter* (2011), p. 89ff.; *Moeschler* (2012), p. 64ff. and 343f.

5 Cf. *Vellmann* (1990), p. 549; *Küpper* (1990), p. 11; *Weber/Schäffer* (2011), p. 3.

6 *Dorn* (1961), p. 23ff., and *Pfaff* (1993), p. 24f., trace cost accounting back to the late 18th century. Yet, the rise of the field is generally attributed to industrialisation (cf. *Dorn* (1961), p. 23ff.; *Garner* (1976), chapter 1; *Kaplan* (1984), p. 391; *Littleton* (1988), p. 321; *Pfaff* (1993), p. 24ff.; *Zirkler* (2002), p. 34; *Bhimani/Bromwich* (2010), p. 2f.; *Weber/Schäffer* (2011), p. 3).

7 Cf. *Boons et al.* (1992), p. 97; *Bungenstock* (1995), p. 354f.; *Sheridan* (1995), p. 288; *Bjørnenak* (1997), p. 367; *Hopper et al.* (1999), p. 73; *Amat et al.* (2000), p. 8f.; *Währisch* (2003), p. 71; *Ewert/ Wagenhofer* (2006), p. 1050; *Kilger et al.* (2012), p. 60.

8 This terminology refers to the USA and five Commonwealth countries which are commonly covered in international research and have German affiliates (Great Britain, Australia, New Zealand, Canada and South Africa). For a similar aggregation of Anglophone firms cf. e.g. *Hoffjan et al.* (2009), p. 116f.

9 Cf. section 2.2 for a comprehensive review.

10 *Portz/Lere* (2010), p. 45.

11 This term is not restricted to the identical terminology by *Bartlett/Ghoshal* (1989), p. 49ff., in this study but embraces *Bartlett/Ghosal*'s international, multinational, global and transnational firms. Similar to *Macharzina* (1981), p. 44f., or *Berens et al.* (2000), p. 16, the terminology thus describes companies with cross-border operations more generally.

counting systems for each legal entity (polycentric) or certain regions (regiocentric)[12]. As such, national particularities in cost accounting introduce alternative options for the design of cost accounting systems in MNCs.[13] These options, however, also imply a tremendous potential for conflicts. On the one hand, cost accounting systems in subsidiaries tend to be disregarded for local decision-making if it is too heavily influenced by a parent company.[14] On the other hand, foreign subsidiaries may lobby for their national cost accounting traditions or strive for a certain level of local adaptiveness.[15] Therefore, foreign subsidiaries of MNCs[16] provide a unique research opportunity to analyse the consequences of cross-national differences in cost accounting.[17]

During such an analysis, the above insights reveal that it is not only relevant to look at the prevalence of a parent's cost accounting traditions in the design of a subsidiary's cost accounting system but it is also necessary to consider the actual use of cost information for decision-making. Both affect the performance of cost accounting systems in subsidiaries.[18]

This far, the **current state of knowledge** on the effect of cross-national differences in cost accounting for subsidiaries in multinationals is scarce. To this point, there is no research which describes and explains the design of cost accounting systems and the use of cost information in subsidiaries and simultaneously looks at these systems' performance. This holds particularly true for affiliates of Anglophone companies in Germany (hereafter Anglophone subsidiaries). Given the cross-national differences of Anglophone and German cost accounting traditions and the recently evolving interest of Anglophone researchers and practitioners in German cost accounting,[19] the negligence of this research perspective

---

[12] For this differentiation of a multinational according to the "the orientation toward 'foreign people, ideas and resources' in headquarters and subsidiaries" (*Perlmutter* (1969), p. 11), cf. *Perlmutter* (1969), p. 9ff.; *Heenan/Perlmutter* (1979), p. 17ff.

[13] Cf. *Amat et al.* (2000), p. 20; *Van der Stede* (2003), p. 279f.; *Kellermanns/Islam* (2004), p. 43ff.; *Endenich et al.* (2011), p. 365.

[14] Cf. section 3.3.2.2.

[15] Cf. *Meyer* (1988), p. 53ff.; *Bhimani* (2003), p. 523ff.

[16] *Roth/Kostova* (2003), p. 894ff., motivats researchers to use multinationals as a research site to look at the standardisation of management practices. Similarly, *Shields* (1998), p. 512, reveals the importance of MNCs for the international convergence of management accounting practices.

[17] Cf. *Wullenkord* (1995), p. 56–58. Also, a subsidiary perspective can best reflect the level on which cost information of MNCs is accumulated (cf. *Währisch* (1998), p. 55, 61; *Pfaff* (2003), p. 32; *Wolfsgruber* (2011), p. 251) and reflects that inadequatly designed systems tend to be delinked from decision-making in (foreign) subsidiaries.

[18] Cf. *Kellermanns/Islam* (2004), p. 46, or similarly *McMann/Jr. Nanni* (1995), p. 333; *Jones et al.* (1998), p. 212; *Cruz et al.* (2009), p. 113; *Portz/Lere* (2010), p. 45.

[19] Cf. *Keys/van der Merwe* (1999), p. 2ff.; *Keys/van der Merwe* (2002), p. 41ff.; *van der Merwe/Keys* (2002), p. 31; *Sharman* (2003b), p. 42ff.; *Sharman* (2003a), p. 30ff.; *Lynn/Todd* (2003), p. 20ff.; *van der Merwe* (2004), p. 1ff.; *Clinton/Webber* (2004), p. 21ff.; *Webber/Clinton* (2004), p. 1ff.; *White* (2004), p. 6f.; *Grasso* (2005), p. 12ff.; *Sharman/Vikas* (2004), p. 28ff.; *Smith* (2005), p. 36ff.; *Friedl et al.* (2005), p. 56ff.; *Zayer* (2005), p. 322ff.; *Mackie* (2006), p. 33ff.; *MacArthur* (2006), p. 10ff.; *Vikas* (2006), p. 27ff.; *Krumwiede et al.* (2007), p. 1ff.; *Krumwiede/Suessmair* (2007b), p. 5ff.; *Krumwiede/Suessmair* (2007a), p. 1ff.; *White et al.* (2008), p. 5ff.; *Portz/Lere* (2010), p. 45ff.; *White et al.* (2011), p. 38; *White* (2009), p. 63ff.

is very surprising. Consequently, the study at hand poses the following **research questions**:

RQ (1a)	Are there differences with respect to the design of cost accounting systems in Anglophone and domestic subsidiaries in Germany?
RQ (1b)	How do Anglophone and domestic subsidiaries in Germany use their cost information for managerial decision-making?
RQ (2a)	What determines the design of cost accounting systems in Anglophone and domestic subsidiaries in Germany?
RQ (2b)	What determines the use of cost information for managerial decision-making in Anglophone and domestic subsidiaries in Germany?
RQ (3a)	How can Anglophone and domestic subsidiaries in Germany improve the design of their cost accounting systems?
RQ (3b)	How can Anglophone and domestic subsidiaries in Germany improve the use of cost information in managerial decision-making?

These six questions comprise three **research objectives** which are followed by this study. First, descriptions of the design of cost accounting systems and the use of cost information in subsidiaries of Anglophone MNCs and domestic companies in Germany are provided. Second, this study aims to provide explanations for the design of cost accounting systems and the use of cost information in subsidiaries of Anglophone MNCs and domestic companies in Germany. Thereafter, the study attempts to derive practical recommendations on how to improve the cost accounting systems in subsidiaries of Anglophone MNCs and domestic companies in Germany.

By pursuing these research objectives through an empirical research strategy, this study **contributes** considerably to international management accounting literature and provides fruitful insights for practitioners. From an **academic perspective**, the study takes on the debate of accounting system's cross-national 'travel' and potential local resistance to or avoidance of diffused accounting systems.[20] It, as such, bridges the demand for more international management studies on MNCs[21] and management accounting research. Thereby, the inclusion of the actual use of cost information does not only reflect continuous calls for more accounting research on the use of information[22] but also enables to reveal whether local resistance to corporate cost accounting initiatives is more present for the design of management accounting instruments or their application for decision-making. Above all, the study can assess whether the knowledge on cross-national differences in management accounting is of actual relevance for the analysis of MNCs. The study, hence, contributes to the call for more comparative management accounting informed research.[23] For **practitioners**, the study is especially relevant for two reasons. First, the inclusion of the performance of cost accounting can lead to revelation of pathways how to improve cost accounting systems in subsidiaries. Second, the comparative character of the study provides practitioners with the ability to learn about cost accounting prac-

20 Cf. *Baxter/Chua* (2003), p. 109; *Merchant et al.* (2011), p. 640.

21 Cf. *Roth/Kostova* (2003), p. 894ff.

22 Cf. *Küpper* (1993), p. 614; *Brierley et al.* (2001), p. 239; *Chung et al.* (2002), p. 124; *Brown et al.* (2004), p. 354.

23 Cf. *Hopwood* (1999), p. 378; *Brierley et al.* (2001), p. 240.

tices in companies of different national origin. If e.g. there were some German cost accounting traditions in Anglophone subsidiaries in Germany, the study may uncover whether Anglophone companies can learn from their German subsidiaries in terms of cost accounting systems[24] to improve their domestic cost accounting system.[25]

1.2 Structure of the study

Figure 1-1 illustrates the structure of this study. Fundamental to any research project is a clear statement of its philosophical and theoretical assumptions.[26] Consequently, section 1.3 points out how this study is positioned with respect to ontological and epistemological issues. Theoretical positions are postponed to chapter 4. Thereby, the insights of previous researchers on the issue of cost accounting systems in foreign subsidiaries can be taken into account.

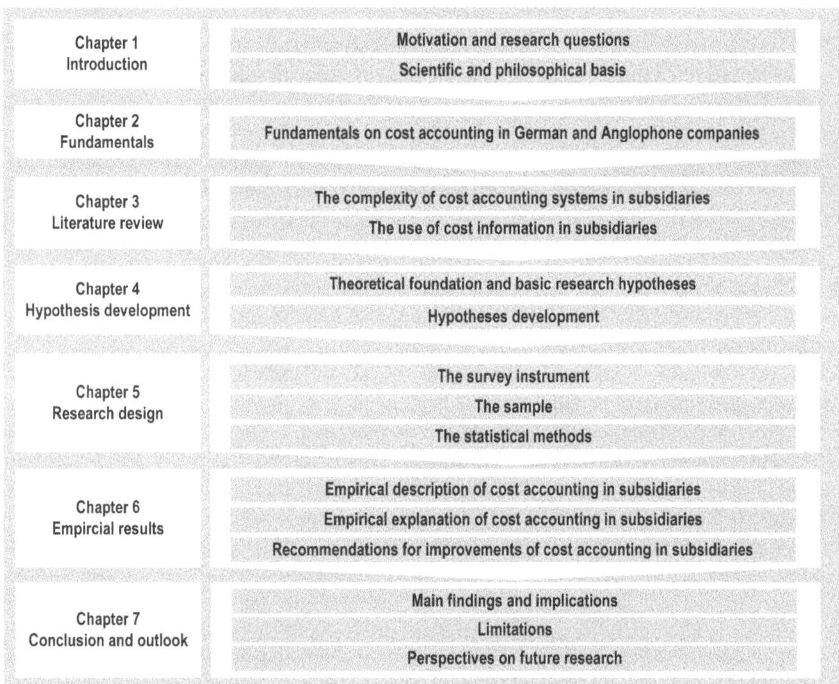

Figure 1-1: Outline of the study

---

[24] *Krumwiede/Suessmair* (2007b), p. 55, identify the lack of knowledge on German cost accounting as a key drawback for its application in non-German companies. In line, *Portz/Lere* (2010), p. 51, suggest that the applicability of GPK varies for different nations.

[25] *Clinton/White* (2012), p. 53, reveal a wish for detailed cost information in Anglophone companies.

[26] Cf. *Hopper/Powell* (1985), p. 429.

In order to pursue the research questions and accomplish the research objectives, section 2 introduces the fundamentals on cost accounting in Anglophone and German companies. Subsequently, section 3 presents the current state of research on the design of cost accounting systems (3.2) and the use of cost information (3.3) in subsidiaries. Building on the scientific and philosophical positioning as well as the literature review, section 4.1 identifies business theories for the analysis of subsidiaries' cost accounting systems and will translate these into basic hypotheses. These basic hypotheses are refined in section 4.2 by establishing this study's hypotheses.

This study answers its research questions on the grounds of a large sample of Anglophone subsidiaries and a domestic German control group. The samples as well as the survey instruments are introduced throughout sections 5.1 and 5.3. After an introduction of the statistical methods in section 5.4, section 6 will present this study's empirical results. Thereby, research questions (1a) and (1b) are targeted in sections 6.1.1 and 6.1.2, respectively. The explanatory analysis for research questions (2a) and (2b) is included in sections 6.2.1 and 6.2.2. Recommendations on how to alleviate the performance of cost accounting systems in subsidiaries (research questions (3a) and (3b)) are discussed in section 6.3. In the closing chapter 7, the main findings are summarised and critically evaluated.

1.3 Scientific and philosophical positioning

Science strives for a contribution to knowledge development which enables humans to complete their life-task.[27] This striving can be subdivided into general **scientific objectives.**[28] The *descriptive objective* involves defining a real phenomenon to be regarded and describing this construct with respect to its empirical validity. The *theoretical objective* is based on the fundamental goal of describing phenomena but exceeds it by explaining the described observations (Explanandum) on the grounds of certain antecedents (Explanans). Making use of the connections between an explanandum and its explanans for practical decisions and shaping practical activities is known as the *pragmatic objective.* Alternatively, science can strive for a *normative objective.* This objective comprises the discourse of norms that should underlie peoples' behaviour. While the former three objectives are reflected in the research questions introduced in section 1.1, this study does not pursue a normative objective.

Pursuing the introduced research objectives requires choosing an adequate **research strategy**. Business research can pursue three different research strategies.[29] *The normative conceptual strategy* involves deriving recommendations for actions based upon plausibility and speculation. It lacks systematic empirical considerations which are key to *the empirical strategy.* This strategy, despite being able to provide real-descriptive evidence, strives for a systematic collection of experience in order to assess certain expectations about practical phenomena (empirical-cognitive assertions). On the contrary, *the formal-analytical strategy* involves modelling certain phenomena for theoretical and rational problem solving. As

[27] Cf. *Wild* (1966), p. 22.

[28] For this and the following, cf. *Kosiol* (1964), p. 745; *Wild* (1966), p. 22ff.; *Grochla* (1976), p. 633; *Schweitzer* (1978), p. 3ff.; *Chmielewicz* (1994), p. 17f.

[29] For this and the following, cf. *Grochla* (1976), p. 634.

real-descriptive and empirical-cognitive assertions about subsidiaries' cost accounting systems are targeted in this research, an empirical research strategy is most appropriate.

The persuasion of research strategies is highly influenced by researchers' considerations about the existence of a research object (ontology) and their methodological assumptions on how to obtain knowledge about real life phenomena, i.e. the truth (epistemology).[30] In this regard, business research in general as well as management and cost accounting research in particular is influenced by *Popper/Albert's* critical rationalism and the methodological constructivism as introduced by *Lorenzen* and the *Erlangen School*.[31] Both are discussed in this section with respect to their ontological and epistemological assumptions to align this study purposefully with a philosophical position.

Critical rationalism is, due to its roots in realism, mainly based on the ontological assumption of reality (or the research object) being existent independently of the researcher's perception. A research object is assumed to be predetermined with respect to its structure, elements and interrelations.[32] Hence, existent logics, which determine the development of phenomena in an objective reality, are assumed to be predetermined.[33] From an epistemological point of view, critical rationalism is based upon both neo-positivism (an advancement of empiricism) and rationalism.[34] The former stressed the essence of experience for knowledge creation and highlights induction (i.e. generalisation of the observed), which is assumed to be verifying, as the primary possibility of cognition.[35] Rationalism, on the other hand, is based on the assumption that irrevocable knowledge can be obtained logically through consciousness and reasoning, thus emphasising that intuition and deduction are essential for knowledge creation.[36] Since induction is argued to be unable to serve as a mean for generalisation,[37] in critical rationalism, knowledge can be obtained through deduction only.[38] Thus, rationalistic elements are embraced.[39] Due to the fallibility of the consciousness, however, such knowledge is not regarded to be irrevocable but hypothetic instead.[40] As such, knowledge merits critical validation (i.e. ultimately empirical testing). Thus, neo-positivistic elements are included as well.[41] In contrast to neo-positivism, however, testing cannot serve for verification in critical rationalism. Non-dogmatically, a successful empirical test underlines the current non-rejection of knowledge which the tested (non-falsifiable) hypothesis was based upon.[42] The possibility

---

[30] Cf. *Burrell/Morgan* (1979) and *Quattrone* (2000), p. 132f.

[31] Cf. *Fülbier* (2005), p. 23, and section 3 for the mere amount of cost accounting studies based upon contingency theory, which is, according to *Elsik* (2004), p. 803, and *Scherer* (2006), p. 32, heavily reliant upon the former line of thought.

[32] Cf. *Scherer* (2006), p. 25.

[33] Cf. *Cappallo* (2006), p. 25; *Scherer* (2006), p. 44ff.

[34] Cf. *Scherer* (2006), p. 26.

[35] Cf. *Kornmeier* (2007), p. 38; *Scherer* (2006), p. 24f.

[36] Cf. *Albert* (1980), p. 21ff.

[37] Cf. *Chmielewicz* (1994), p. 89.

[38] Cf. *Popper* (1973), p. 3ff.

[39] Cf. *Fülbier* (2005), p. 22.

[40] For this and the following, cf. *Popper* (1973), p. 47ff.

[41] Cf. *Fülbier* (2005), p. 22.

[42] Cf. *Popper* (1973), p. 8.

to assess knowledge's ultimate correctness is denied (i.e. fallibism).[43] Hence, despite principally assuming an objective reality, critical rationalists acknowledge that such constructs are only as 'true' as they cannot be falsified through the latest deductively derived thoughts.[44]

Methodological constructivism roots ontologically on the relaxed assumption of practise (or the research object) being predetermined by certain structures, thus it stressed that practise cannot persist without theory.[45] Thereby, the associated *Erlangen School* criticised realism as incorporated into critical rationalism because it differentiates the research object and subject[46] by assuming a rather objective reality. According to the *Erlangen School*, reality shall rather be understood to be something that is defined as well as agreed upon in a consensual process.[47] Epistemologically, methodological constructivism is primarily concerned with knowledge (especially theory) creation.[48] Due to its roots within rationalistic traditions, it stresses deduction and non-empirical argumentation as the main source of (rather more dogmatic) knowledge, though recognising consciousness' fallibility and as such the inability to find a final evaluation about knowledge.[49]

Methodological constructivism shall not be mistaken for radical constructivism. By being the counterpart of realism,[50] radical constructivism reflects an ontological position (i.e. relativism) which discharges any objective reality.[51] It is stressed that radical constructivism cannot provide information apart from "projections of human imagination".[52] Therefore, radical constructivism is criticised for being ultimately unable to serve for any (objective) knowledge provision because reality is purely constructed by a research subject.[53] Puzzlingly, though radical constructivism is seen as the ontological counterpart of realism, which are both generally kept separate from epistemological positions,[54] radical constructivism is sometimes argued to reflect a positivistic, i.e. empirical epistemological point of view.[55] An analysis of the origin of these apparent contradicting arguments is out of the scope of this study. It appears linked to the underlying given-up distinction between the research object and the research subject's knowledge about the research object, however.

This study cannot be based thoroughly on either of these two positions. On the one hand, the empirical research strategy is somewhat in contrast to methodological constructivism. On the other hand, cost accounting is not assumed to be naturally given (i.e. of objective

---

43 Cf. *Albert* (1996), p. 5.
44 Cf. *Scherer* (2006), p. 27.
45 Cf. *Elmar* (1979), p. 205f.; *Cappallo* (2006), p. 25; *Scherer* (2006), p. 44.
46 Cf. *Cappallo* (2006), p. 23.
47 Cf. *Raffée/Abel* (1979), p. 6f.; *Steinmann/Wolfram* (1979), p. 195f.; *Scherer* (1995), p. 305f.
48 Cf. *Scherer* (2006), p. 44.
49 Cf. *Albert* (1996), p. 5; *Fülbier* (2005), p. 23.
50 Cf. *Kornmeier* (2007), p. 32f.; *Cappallo* (2006), p. 23.
51 Cf. *Lattmann* (1993), p. 217.
52 *Morgan/Smircich* (1980), p. 492.
53 Cf. *Kornmeier* (2007), p. 35.
54 Cf. *Kornmeier* (2007), p. 31.
55 Cf. *Zitterbarth* (1991), p. 10.

reality) as it would have to fit *Popper/Albert*'s position strictly. Hence, the idea of social constructivism is incorporated at this point.

Similarly to the ontological position in radical constructivism, *Berger/Luckmann (2004)*[56] assume reality to be something socially constructed.[57] These authors gave rise to a line of thought known as **social constructivism**.[58] They assume that "*knowledge [in terms of ontology as well as epistemology*[59]*] (...) is inter-subjective - constructed of statements which are socially accepted as facts*".[60] As such, it is particularly similar to the ontological position in methodological constructivism as well. But, other than in methodological constructivism, it is regularly assumed that such a socially constructed reality is of (apparent) objective existence.[61] Thus, social constructivism appears to compromise rationalistic and radical constructivistic ontological positions.[62] Due to its intersubjective existence, reality as defined by the ontological point of view of social constructivism appears combinable with epistemological positions included in critical rationalism, i.e. deducting theoretical constructs which (empirically) hold true as long as they cannot by falsified.[63]

In this study, cost accounting's conceptual design and its application for decision-making is understood to reflect social constructs. These are assumed to be formed e.g. by organisation's employees, who derive their information, e.g. from academic textbooks; which in turn contain constructed (normative) recommendations how to design a cost accounting system. Therefore, the philosophical position of social constructivism is applied in this study. Thereby an explicit attempt is made to avoid an assumption of cost accounting reflecting some sort of natural law alike objective reality, as it appeared necessary if this

---

56 The first version of their book was published in 1966.

57 Cf. *Cappallo* (2006), p. 23.

58 For this and the following, cf. *Jones* (1995), p. 257f.; *Quattrone* (2000), p. 150.

59 In constructivistic positions, the duality of the research object (i.e. reality) and the research subject (i.e. researcher and his knowledge) is abdicated (cf. *Cappallo* (2006), p. 23). According to *Tinker* (1982), p. 169 esp. footnote 5, and *Neimark/Tinker* (1986), p. 374, knowledge in this context thus concerns the creation of the world itself as well as a picture of it. This enables to argue that it involves ontology as well as epistemology. Note that, e.g. *Johnson* (1995), p. 492, links social constructs to epistemology rather than ontology.

60 *Jones* (1995), p. 258.

61 Cf. *Lukka* (1990), p. 245; *Jones* (1995), p. 258. Similarly *Scott* (1987), p. 495f.; *Neu* (1992), p. 229; *Quattrone* (2000), p. 147; *Nielsen* (2001), p. 505.

62 Cf. *Morgan/Smircich* (1980), p. 494; *Johnson* (1995), p. 485ff. The former regard social constuctivism in its "most extreme version (...) – *ethnomethodology* - " (cf. *Jones* (1995), p. 257). The social construtivism pursued in this study is situated ontologically more towards these authors' objectivist approach on their objectivist - subjectivist continuum of social science.

63 Since this line appears to embrace different ideas about how to balance the two compromised ontological positions (Cf. *Morgan/Smircich* (1980), p. 493ff.; *Jones* (1995), p. 257; *Kornmeier* (2007), p. 39), it is essential to stress that a moderate understanding of social constructivism is applied here. This ensures the intended empirical analysis to become an effigy of socially constructed cost accounting system rather than the researchers' subjective impression only.

study were unreflectedly aligned within a strict interpretation of *Popper*'s critical rationalism.[64]

Lukka highlights the particular usefulness of this philosophical position as opposed to critical rationalism and methodological constructivism in the context of cost accounting system research among affiliates of MNCs by stating that

> *"the adoption of social constructivism seems to offer a potentially fruitful ontological basis for increasing the understanding of (...) the fundamental nature of accounting concepts in their various uses."*[65]

Though *Lukka* explicitly aligns social constructivism with ontology only, the chosen social constuctivistic position appears combinable with the epistemological position as reflected by *Popper/Albert*'s critical rationalism due to the assumption of social constructs being of apparent objective existence rather than relativistic with respect to a researcher's cognitive ability. Despite being constructivistically informed, the chosen philosophical basis is, in contrast to methodological constructivism, thus capable to pursue the chosen empirical research strategy.

As such, this project compromises the ontological and epistemological positions reflected in the philosophies of science which dominate international business research. This compromise is made in order to avoid the totality regarding the "objectivism and the relativist quagmire of subjectivism"[66] rather reflected in either one of these positions.[67]

---

64 Interpreting objective reality in critical rationalism less strictly as some god-alike natural laws, makes social constructs well includable into the ontological position of *Popper*'s position. From such an interpretation, the taken philosophical position corresponds to critical rationalism.

65 *Lukka* (1990), p. 246.

66 *Johnson* (1995), p. 491.

67 As such, this research is in line with *Johnson* (1995), p. 490ff., who argues such compromises to be a pragmatistic middle position between *Burrell/Morgan* (1979)'s strict subjectivistic and objectivistic philosophical positions.

2 Cost accounting in Germany and Anglophone countries

2.1 Introduction

Internationally, cost accounting refers to the measurement, analysis and reporting of the use-up or sacrifice of organisational resources in monetary terms (i.e. costs), which is induced by production of goods and services (i.e. a specific goal) in a certain period.[68] Cost accounting's core is to provide information that facilitates or influences decision-making[69] during the management process.[70] As such, it is linked to internal planning and control (incl. plan execution) activities.[71]

Cost accounting in organisations can be regarded with respect to the determination of the value of resources used and sacrificed as well as the inclusion of yielded cost information in decision-making.[72] The former comprises the determination of costs itself, i.e. their accumulation and assignment to organisational units, goods and services, as well as cost classification according to certain categories. The latter subsumes the use of information derived from a cost accounting system. In this study, technical aspects of cost determination will be labelled as cost accounting system design (A). The use of cost information will be labelled accordingly (B). This differentiation is equivalent to the distinction of (A) macro/mezzo and (B) micro levels of management accounting research.[73]

The national differences of cost accounting which motivate this study are especially evident for cost accounting systems' designs. These differences are introduced in section 2.2. There is only preliminary evidence that cost information tends to be used differently across-nations. Hence, it is introduced in this section, what is commonly researched as the 'use of cost information'. Similarly, the section also comprises an introduction of common themes describing the performance of cost accounting systems. Since according considerations were shown in section 1.1 to be interwoven with both macro/mezzo and micro level cost accounting research, they shall not be assigned to either of these two categories, though.

---

68 Cf. *Schweitzer/Küpper* (2010), p. 13–15; *Horngren et al.* (2012), p. 26 and 49.

69 Cf. *Demski/Feltham* (1976), p. 8.

70 The process of management summarises a company's internal planning and control activities. Cf. e.g. *Kaplan/Atkinson* (1989), p. 1; *Garrison et al.* (2006), p. 4; *Langfield-Smith et al.* (2006), p. 18f.; *Anthony/Govindarajan* (2007), p. 7; *Hilton* (2007), p. 4f.; *Horngren et al.* (2008), p. 12; *Drury* (2012), p. 6f.; *Horngren et al.* (2012), p. 33.

71 Though cost information is derived for documentation as well (cf. e.g. *Schweitzer/Küpper* (2010), p. 27)- this purpose shall, in accordance with *Dellmann* (1984), p. 279, be attached to control.

72 Cf. *Weber* (2005), p. 4f.; *Hoitsch/Winter* (2005), p. 32; *Horngren et al.* (2012), p. 49.

73 Cf. *Granlund/Lukka* (1998), p. 153f.; *Kajüter/Moeschler* (2010), p. 4; *Moeschler* (2012), p. 24f.

2.2 Design of cost accounting systems

2.2.1 Three components of cost accounting systems

Internationally, cost accounting systems consist of three components.[74] **Cost type accounting** comprises the accumulation of all costs incurred, categorised by their very nature (e.g. costs of material X and material Y).[75] **Cost object accounting** describes the calculation of all costs, assignable to a specific object such as a product, service or customer. Since some cost types, however, are directly traceable to an object (i.e. direct costs) while others are not (i.e. indirect costs or overheads), an approach for indirect cost allocation is necessary. **Cost centre accounting** provides such a possibility for cost allocation. Indirect costs generally occur at a specific organisational unit. Thus, by regarding that unit's impact on the cost object under consideration or by forming an aggregated allocation rule, indirect cost can be allocated to a specific cost object. Figure 2-1 illustrates the interplay of these components of cost accounting systems.

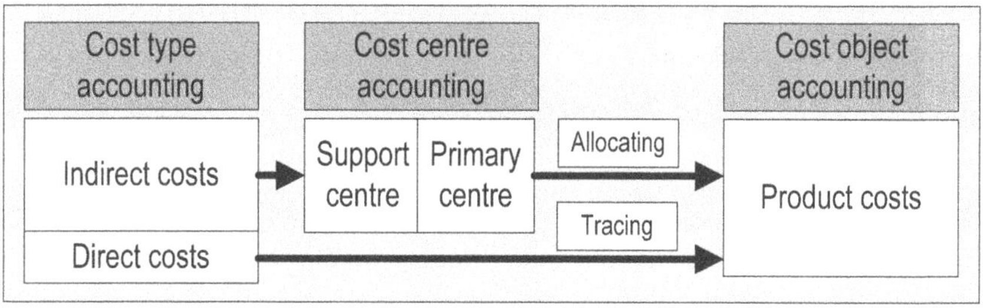

Figure 2-1: The three components of a cost accounting system

Despite these similarities with respect to the three components of cost accounting systems, substantial national particularities prevail with respect to their conceptual design.[76]

2.2.2 Cost type accounting

Regarding cost type accounting, three interlinked particularities display cross-national differences. These are (1) the number of cost types included in a cost accounting system, (2) the recognition of imputed costs and (3) the separation of costs from financial accounting oriented expenses.

---

[74] Cf. *Horngren et al.* (2012), p. 51, for Anglophone countries and *Küpper* (1990), p. 11, for Germany. Note, however, that in Anglophone literature cost-centre and cost-object accounting tends to be summarised as cost assignment, (cf. *Schweitzer/Küpper* (2010), p. 52; *Horngren et al.* (2012), p. 51). Besides, the chosen wording of cost centre reflects a German understanding as will become obvious in section 2.3.

[75] For this and the following, cf. e.g. *Schweitzer/Küpper* (2010), p. 50-53 and 79f.; *Coenenberg et al.* (2012), p. 67ff.; *Friedl et al.* (2013), p. 62ff.

[76] German-speaking literature does not regard the three components itself as part of a cost accounting system but rather their specific design (cf. e.g. *Schweitzer/Küpper* (2010), p. 60; *Coenenberg et al.* (2012), p. 68; *Friedl et al.* (2013), p. 24f.). This definition is followed here.

(1) Number of cost types

Anglophone companies distinguish substantially less **primary cost types** than German firms do.[77] A primary cost type represents the consumption of externally obtained resources.[78] This difference thus suggests a greater disaggregation of costs in Germany.

(2) Recognition of imputed costs

Imputed costs are costs which reflect neither actual cash flows nor do they fulfil financial reporting requirements.[79] They are computed particularly for cost accounting purposes to express the use of a company's resources. Literature on this issue suggests that Anglophone companies tend to disregard **imputed costs.**[80] In contrast, imputed interests or replacement-costs based depreciation are regularly found in German companies. Yet, as will be seen for aspect (3), German firms are increasingly interested in the Anglophone general ledger concept. Hence, the traditional strong focus on imputed costs is subject to ongoing changes.

(3) Separation of costs from financial accounting oriented expenses

In Anglophone companies, the general ledger concept, i.e. the integration of databases for management and financial accounting, is applied extensively.[81] In contrast, costs are generally separated from financial accounting oriented **expenses** in Germany by maintaining different datasets. Peculiarly, recent empirical studies in Germany reveal that there is an increasing interest in a more intensive alignment management and financial accounting in German firms as well.[82] Since these alignments centre on corporate accounts or concerns corporate decision-making only,[83] this trend does not alter the strong emphasis on **costs** in German companies, however.[84]

Aspect of cost accounting		German	Anglophone
(1)	Number of cost types	German companies differentiate substantially more cost types than Anglophone ones	
(2)	Recognition of imputed costs	Common, ongoing changes	Rather uncommon
(3)	Separation of costs and expenses	Traditionally very common, ongoing changes	Rather uncommon

Table 2-1: Differences between Anglophone and German cost type accounting

77 Cf. *Krumwiede/Suessmair* (2007a), p. 7. Limiting such a comparison to primary rather than secondary costs (cf. section 2.2.3), accounts for the dependence of the latter on, e.g. the sub-division of a company's production processes.

78 Cf. *Schweitzer/Küpper* (2010), p. 77. Accordingly, a secondary cost type is created during a company's value creation processes (e.g. work in progress). Primary costs can be of both direct and indirect character (cf. section 2.2.3).

79 Cf. *Coenenberg et al.* (2012), p. 89, for an overview of imputed costs.

80 For this and the following, cf. *Becker* (1984), p. 104; *Küpper* (1993), p. 610; *Busse von Colbe* (1996), p. 417; *Scherrer* (1996), p. 105; *Ahrens/Chapman* (1999), p. 43; *Zirkler* (2001), p. 17; *Währisch* (2003), p. 101ff.; *Jones/Luther* (2006), p. 14; *Krumwiede/Suessmair* (2007a), p. 6; *Wolfsgruber* (2011), p. 96; *Moeschler* (2012), p. 247f.

81 For this and the following, cf. *Drury/Tayles* (2000), p. 60; *Zirkler* (2002), p. 19ff.; *Brierley et al.* (2007), p. 672; *Luther et al.* (2010), p. 20f.; *Schweitzer/Küpper* (2010), p. 18.

82 Cf. *Jones/Luther* (2005), p. 188f.; *Friedl et al.* (2009), p. 114; *Heimel et al.* (2012), p. 58ff.

83 Cf. *Weißenberger* (2003), p. 206ff.; *Trapp* (2010), p. 309.

84 Cf. *Friedl et al.* (2009), p. 114.

Table 2-1 summarises the cross-national differences in Anglophone and German companies' cost type accounting.

2.2.3 Cost centre accounting

The international particularities of **cost centre accounting** are more diverse than those for cost type accounting. The differences stem from (1) the rationale for cost centre formation, (2) the number of cost centres and (3) the distinction of cost centres into primary and support cost centres and (4) the classification of costs in cost centres. Furthermore, the employment of cost centres for overhead cost allocation (5) among cost centres and (6) from cost centres to cost objects can reveal cross-national differences. The latter two aspects can be split into (a) conceptual considerations of cost allocation, (b) the number of allocation bases and (c) the applied types of allocation bases.

(1) Rationale for cost centre formation

In Germany, cost centres are formed for reasons of responsibility accounting as well as to allocate overhead costs. This becomes obvious by the elaborated recommendations (or **rationales**) for cost centre formation which can be found in the German literature.[85] Accordingly, only those organisational, functional or spatial areas are summarised as cost centres which, among others, do not differ significantly with respect to impact on (overhead) cost incurrence and which have a clear responsibility structure, i.e. only one person is responsible for a centre. Given these restrictive *rules*, German companies are generally divided into numerous cost centres.[86] The differentiated cost centre structure facilitates the identification of areas of cost incurrence as well as cost planning and control or cost allocation.[87] In the Anglophone countries, the **terminology cost centre** regularly refers to the field of responsibility accounting.[88] Though in Germany such issues of responsibility appear intertwined with the identification of multiple cost centres, Anglophone companies differentiate relatively few cost centres, only. Moreover, these regularly reflect wider areas of responsibly such as entire plants.[89] For the purpose of a more refined cost allocation, so-called **cost pools** appear to be common for Anglophone cost accounting.[90] Despite these being informed by the assumption of common cause of costs in one cost pool,[91] they do not necessarily uphold to this assumption but may reflect a bare summary

---

85 For this and the following, cf. e.g. *Kilger* (1979), p. 71ff.; *Seicht* (1990), p. 616f.; *Keys/van der Merwe* (1999), p. 4; *Grasso* (2005), p. 16; *Kilger et al.* (2012), p. 255f.

86 Cf. *Ewert/Wagenhofer* (2006), p. 1049; *Jones/Luther* (2006), p. 14f.; *Friedl et al.* (2009), p. 112; *Moeschler* (2012), p. 249f.

87 Cf. *Schweitzer/Küpper* (2010), p. 122; *Kilger et al.* (2012), p. 251ff.

88 Cf. *Boons et al.* (1992), p. 104; *Lere* (2009), p. 111.

89 Cf. e.g. *Keys/van der Merwe* (1999), p. 4; *Krumwiede/Suessmair* (2007a), p. 7; *Brierley* (2008b), p. 71ff.; *Lere* (2009), p. 12; *Portz/Lere* (2010), p. 104; *Horngren et al.* (2012), p. 221; *Lanen et al.* (2013), p. 464.

90 Cf. *Langfield-Smith et al.* (2006), p. 296; *Horngren et al.* (2012), p. 122 and 566; *Lanen et al.* (2013), p. 47.

91 Cf. *Christensen/Demski* (1995), p. 17; *Mastilak* (2011), p. 1712f.

of several overhead costs instead.[92] Such bare summaries appear to prevail empirically due to few cost pools identified in applicable studies.[93]

(2) Number of cost centres

Regardless language discrepancies, which impede a clear-cut differentiation between cost centre and cost pool by their purpose,[94] it remains empirically unclear to argue that Anglophone companies are less subdivided for both the purpose of cost allocation as well as aspects of responsibility accounting. For the reason of clarity, it has to be stressed that in this study, the terminology cost centre is applied here to refer to constructs which facilitate cost allocation and describes cost incurrence.

(3) Distinction of cost centres into primary and support cost centres

Besides the mere number of cost centres, there are different types of cost centres in German cost accounting. In conceptual considerations[95] and empirical findings,[96] an identification of cost centres for areas of both direct (**primary cost centres**) and indirect impact[97] (**support cost centres**) on products/services is common. It is argued that support cost centres account for the most cost centres in German companies.[98] They become necessary to facilitate the detailed overhead cost allocation that typically characterise German companies (see (5a/6a)).[99] Thus, the identification of numerous support cost centres in Germany appears to allow for a more refined description of the introduced difference regarding the differing number of cost centres among German and Anglophone companies.[100]

The explicit distinction into support and primary cost centres[101] with the particular importance attributed to support cost centres is rather underrepresented in Anglophone companies.[102] Possible explanations appear to be a mere lack of explicit differentiation of

---

92 Cf. *Langfield-Smith et al.* (2006), p. 296; *Mastilak* (2011), p. 1712f.; *Horngren et al.* (2012), p. 122; *Lanen et al.* (2013), p. 47.

93 Cf. e.g. *Abernethy* (2001), p. 268ff.; *Drury/Tayles* (2006), p. 414; *Al-Omiri/Drury* (2007), p. 414.

94 There are Anglophone studies which use both phrases interchangingly (cf. *Drury/Tayles* (2005), p. 80; *Al-Omiri/Drury* (2007), p. 411; *Brierley* (2008b), p. 64, esp. footnote 4).

95 Note that German textbooks sometimes distinguish cost centres of (in)direct product impact (*Hilfs- and Hauptkostenstellen*) from cost centres whose costs are (in)directly assignable to cost objects (*Vor- and Endkostenstellen*). Cf. *Schweitzer/Küpper* (2010), p. 125f. or *Coenenberg et al.* (2012), p. 119; *Friedl et al.* (2013), p. 118ff. Yet, the latter differentiation cannot be expressed to be typical for German literature. There are textbooks which apply these definitions synonymously (cf. *Kloock et al.* (2005), p. 123) or disregard an according distinction (cf. *Hoitsch/Lingnau* (2007), p. 84). According to *Götze* (2010), p. 79, this ambivalence is due to minor differences among the two definitions, which are especially identifiable for material cost centres. Following the latter author, no explicit distinction is made here.

96 Cf. *Weber* (1993b), p. 260; *Jones/Luther* (2006), p. 15.

97 Indirect product impacts comprise both manufacturing (e.g. maintenance department) and non-manufacturing (e.g. general administration) value chain activities (Cf. *Schweitzer/Küpper* (2010), p. 125f.).

98 Cf. *Coenenberg et al.* (2012), p. 119.

99 Cf. *Kloock et al.* (2005), p. 123; *Hoitsch/Lingnau* (2007), p. 84; *Götze* (2010), p. 79; *Schweitzer/Küpper* (2010), p. 125f.; *Coenenberg et al.* (2012), p. 119; *Friedl et al.* (2013), p. 118ff.

100 Cf. *Kajüter* (2011), p. 104f. for such an argumentation.

101 Cf. for this wording *Krumwiede/Suessmair* (2007a), p. 6.

102 Cf. e.g. *Zirkler* (2001), p. 17.

primary and support cost centres or the (academic) tendency to disregard non-manufacturing areas when normatively describing support and primary cost centres.[103] Whether the absence of support cost centres can fully explicate the lower number of cost centres in Anglophone companies, however, remains empirically unclear.

(4) Classification of costs in cost centres

In German and Anglophone cost centres, cost types tend to be classified differently. In the US, a distinction between **product and period** costs is common. This distinction reflects costs' inventoriablity[104] and as such a financial reporting focus.[105] Germans are more concerned with **primary and secondary costs.** This distinction subsumes whether a cost type in a cost centre reflects an externally obtained resource or has been transferred in from another cost centre.[106] An according focus is in line with the strong reliance on primary and support cost centres as well as the extensive overhead allocation procedure (see (5) and (6)). Additionally, there is general evidence for German companies to avoid subsuming different cost types (or differently classified costs) in cost centres to a greater extent than their US counterparts.[107] This finding is mirrors the higher number of cost types in German firms.

(5a/6a) Conceptual considerations of cost overhead cost allocation

In Germany, the conceptual design of overhead cost allocation both among cost centres (hereafter (5) **first stage allocation**) and from cost centres to cost objects (subsequently (6) **second stage allocation**) is closely related to the design of cost centres.[108] With respect to the conceptual considerations of overhead allocation, German researchers favour causality relationships (i.e. cause and effect or means-end relations) for overhead cost allocation, in order to establish a reality reflecting overhead allocation[109] and to facilitate decision-making.[110] Therefore, in Germany, allocation bases are recommended to be associated with (both support and primary) cost centres' work (direct allocation bases).[111] From an academic perspective, averaging overheads or allocating indirect costs in accordance with a product's sales volume (i.e. bearability) is sometimes argued to be only acceptable if the former relationships are unachievable.[112] Some researchers even wish to avoid overhead allocation in order to avoid any arbitrary allocation.[113] Though the latter aspect is

---

[103] For this latter aspect, cf. e.g. *Langfield-Smith et al.* (2006), p. 300; *Blocher et al.* (2010), p. 234f.; *Horngren et al.* (2012), p. 565.

[104] Cf. *Clinton* (2007), p. 28; *Keys/van der Merwe* (1999), p. 7f.; *Kajüter* (2011), p. 104.

[105] Cf. for this focus *Sheridan* (1995), p. 289; *Clinton* (2007), p. 28, or section 2.3.

[106] For this and the following, cf. *Keys/van der Merwe* (1999), p. 4; *Hoitsch/Lingnau* (2007), p. 148ff.; *Kajüter* (2011), p. 104.

[107] For accordingly identified cross-national differences in German and US firms, cf. e.g. *Krumwiede/Suessmair* (2007a), p. 7.

[108] For the differentiation of first and second stage allocation, cf. *Langfield-Smith et al.* (2006), p. 300, and similarly *Blocher et al.* (2010), p. 234f.

[109] Cf. *Fandel et al.* (2009), p. 33.

[110] Cf. *Weber* (2005), p. 4; *Schweitzer/Küpper* (2010), p. 54.

[111] Cf. *Hoitsch/Lingnau* (2007), p. 84–88.

[112] Cf. *Hoitsch/Lingnau* (2007), p. 71; *Schweitzer/Küpper* (2010), p. 59.

[113] Cf. *Riebel* (1959), p. 213ff., or the discussion by *Weber/Weißenberger* (1997), p. 281–287.

underrepresented in German practice,[114] causality relationships are of particular importance in German cost accounting. These are, e.g. reflected in the rules for cost centre formation stressed under aspect (1).

(5b/6b) Number of allocation bases and **(5c/6c) Applied types of allocation bases**

German cost allocation is rather sophisticated. Firms tend to regard a variety of overhead cost types and apply a **variety of different allocation bases.**[115] Allocation bases in Germany include e.g. measures of time, space, weight and activities performed as well as physical measures such as kWh.[116] These physical measures are recommended to be identified in accordance with an allocating cost centre's output. Apart from these quantitative measures, monetary bases such as direct labour or direct material costs are well known in Germany as well. The detailed overhead cost allocation procedures reflect a strong influence from engineering professionals on German cost accounting,[117] and can be aligned to the introduced causality considerations. Anglophone companies, on the contrary, rather apply simple overhead allocation bases (such as direct labour hours or direct costs) and often adopt a single overall overhead cost centre and/or a single allocation basis.[118] Accordingly, overhead allocation is perceived to be an important source for cost distortions.[119] These findings correspond to the broad definition of cost pools/centres. Also, such causality neglecting tendencies are linkable to a financial reporting focus of Anglophone cost accounting,[120] which tends to abort overhead allocation based on transactional (i.e. physical) data.[121] In contrast to these general whispers, however, there is some evidence for rather small numbers of cost allocation bases in German firms[122] as well as differentiated allocation procedures in Anglophone companies.[123] Such contradicting findings might be due to insufficiently specified research. According to a recent comparison of

---

[114] *Riebel*'s 'Generic Direct Costing' is uncommon in German companies (cf. *Weber/Weißenberger* (1997), p. 277f.).

[115] Cf. *Becker* (1984), p. 118f.; *Jones/Luther* (2006), p. 15; *Krumwiede/Suessmair* (2007a), p. 7; *Kilger et al.* (2012), p. 258ff.

[116] For this and the following, cf. *Hoitsch/Lingnau* (2007), p. 84ff.; *Schweitzer/Küpper* (2010), p. 132; *Kilger et al.* (2012), p. 258ff.

[117] Cf. *Sheridan* (1995), p. 289; *Schweitzer/Schweitzer* (2008), p. 166.

[118] Cf. *Howell et al.* (1987), p. 37ff.; *Kim/Song* (1990), p. 28f.; *Shields et al.* (1991), p. 64; *Jones et al.* (1993), p. 122; *Al Chen et al.* (1997), p. 424; *Drury/Tayles* (1997), p. 269; *Brierley et al.* (2001), p. 223f.; *Lamminmaki/Drury* (2001), p. 338–341; *Garg et al.* (2003), p. 4; *Hughes/Paulson Gjerde* (2003), p. 25; *Al-Omiri/Drury* (2007), p. 413; *Brierley* (2008b), p. 71.

[119] Cf. *Clinton/White* (2012), p. 51.

[120] For a strong importance of inventory valuation for cost accounting in Anglophone companies, cf. *Karmarkar et al.* (1990), p. 368; *Jones et al.* (1993), p. 122; *Joseph et al.* (1996), p. 79 and 90; *Drury/Tayles* (2000), p. 60f.; *Dugdale et al.* (2006), p. 81; *Clinton* (2007), p. 27; *White et al.* (2011), p. 41. Yet, such a primacy of external tasks is partially challenged for the UK by *Scapens* (1996), p. 3ff and 153f., and *Drury/Tayles* (1997), p. 269.

[121] Cf. *White et al.* (2011), p. 42 and similarly *Williams et al.* (1991), p. 150f.

[122] Cf. *Schehl* (1994), p. 260f.; *Krumwiede/Suessmair* (2007a), p. 6.

[123] Cf. *Jones* (1991), p. 35; *Abdel-Kader/Luther* (2006), p. 15; *Drury/Tayles* (2006), p. 412.

German and Japanese cost accounting, altering details of first and second stage allocation procedures might explain the identified contradictions.[124]

The issue of broad overhead cost allocation (aspects 5 and 6) was recognised to impinge internal decision-making in Anglophone companies in the late 1980s.[125] It facilitated the development of **activity-based costing** (subsequently ABC).[126] In ABC, (manufacturing) overhead cost allocation is refined through an initial attribution of costs to multiple activities. Thereby, costs can be allocated based on the utilisation of an activity (i.e. means-end relations).[127] Efforts to base overhead allocation on the duration of activities rather than their accomplishment per se, lead to a refinement of ABC, known as **time-driven activity-based costing** (subsequently TDABC).[128] ABC and TDABC rather correspond to the German overhead allocation traditions (i.e. focussing on the work of a cost centre to allocate overhead costs).[129] Instead of functionally oriented cost centres, however, (TD)ABC forms (possibly cross-functional) activities.[130] Nevertheless, ABC cannot be argued to have improved Anglophone overhead allocation procedures considerably. The moderate adoption rates of (TD)ABC[131] rather underline Anglophone tendencies to rely on simple overhead allocation procedures.[132] Thus, it is little surprising to find the unrefined overhead

---

[124] Cf. *Moeschler* (2012), p. 252ff.

[125] Cf. *Miller/Vollmann* (1985), p. 142ff.

[126] For this and the following, cf. *Cooper/Kaplan* (1988) and *Kaplan/Cooper* (1998), p. 79ff.

[127] ABC is not merely applicable for product costing, but emerged as a tool to improve organisational performance through activity analysis and resource management (cf. *Jones/Dugdale* (2002), p. 126ff) as well. Since the application of activity analysis for performance improvements does not necessarily require the refinement of cost allocation through ABC, there are activity-based techniques that map the resource flow in organisations, irrespectively the costing purpose (cf. *Gosselin* (1997), p. 106).

[128] Cf. *Kaplan/Anderson* (2003), p. 1ff.; *Kaplan/Anderson* (2004), p. 131ff.; *Kaplan/Anderson* (2007), p. 7ff.

[129] Cf. *Kloock* (1992), p. 186; *Schildbach* (1997), p. 274; *Friedl et al.* (2005), p. 60; *Grasso* (2005), p. 17; *Ewert/Wagenhofer* (2006), p. 1049. *Kloock/Schiller* (1997), p. 314, highlight that despite these similarities with respect to cost allocating rationales, the total amount of costs assigned via GPK (see p. 20ff) and ABC differ substantially.

[130] *Grasso* (2005), p. 17, highlights that activities in ABC summarise multiple cost centres as defined in German cost accounting. Thereby, ABC allocates costs more broadly than German cost accounting because costs of different causes are allocated conjointly (cf. similarly *Kloock* (1992), p. 182ff.). By incorporating time equations, it is argued that costs allocated through one actitivy cost pool can reflect omore diverse causalities of cost incurrence than traditional ABC (cf. *Kaplan/Anderson* (2007), p. 27ff.). Hence, if the duration of output creation was the reason for cost centre differentiation in a German cost accounting system, TDABC would be capable to integrate different areas, which are split into multiple cost centres in a German cost accounting system, without relaxing the idea of linking cost centre output and cost incurrence.

[131] Internationally, ABC adoption does rarely exceed 40 % (cf. *Askarany/Yazdifar* (2012), p. 432. Since some surveys include 'considering ABC' as adoption (cf. *Brierley* (2008a), p. 58), the actual application of ABC might actually be considerably lower.

[132] Cf. *Groot* (1997), p. 24; *Nguyen/Brooks* (1997), p. 10; *Krumwiede* (1998), p. 243; *Clarke et al.* (1999), p. 450; *Hopper et al.* (1999), p. 76; *Hoque* (2000), p. 143; *Innes et al.* (2000), p. 352; *Ittner et al.* (2002), p. 714; *Kidwell et al.* (2002), p. 64; *Al-Omiri/Drury* (2007), p. 413; *Bhimani et al.* (2007), p. 14; *Brierley* (2008a), p. 66; *Askarany/Yazdifar* (2012), p. 436.

cost allocation to hinder the decision usefulness of cost information in Anglophone firms.[133]

	Aspect of cost accounting	German	Anglophone
(1)	Rationales for cost centre formation:		
	- Existence of detailed formation 'rules'	Yes	No
	- Dominant criteria for centre formation	Responsibility accounting Overhead cost allocation	Responsibility accounting
	- Size of organisational areas summarised as cost centres	Rather small	Rather large
(2)	Number of cost centres	High	Low
(3)	Differentiation of primary and support cost centres	Common	Uncommon
(4)	Classification of costs in cost centres	Primary and secondary costs, Variable and fixed costs[134]	Inventoriable and period costs
(5)/(6)	Overhead cost allocation between cost centres and from cost centres to cost objects:		
(a)	- Rationale beyond cost allocation	German companies strive for causality relation for overhead cost allocations	Causality relation are rather underrepresented in Anglophone companies
(b)	- Number of allocation bases	Multiple bases common	Rather few bases common
(c)	- Types of overhead cost allocation bases	Tendency to regard physical, transactional and durational information. Direct costs based allocation is not uncommon	Tendency to focus on labour hours or direct labour and direct material costs for overhead allocation Tendency to disregard physical data. Transactional and durational bases rather uncommon (ABC and TDABC)
	- Treatment of unused capacity	Allocation bases reflect the available capacity to determine the costs of unused capacity	Determination of costs of unused capacity uncommon

Table 2-2: Differences between Anglophone and German cost centre accounting

Despite these differences, in the light of (5c/6c) another international difference prevails, which is associated with the treatment of unused capacity. German firms tend to identify the costs of **unused capacity**.[135] They reflect costs of a cost centre which are associable to provided but not consumed capacity.[136] This implies that theoretically available capacity rather than actually used capacity is applied as a basis for overhead cost allocation.[137] Such an approach is less common in Anglophone companies,[138] even though there are similar recommendations in the conceptual (TD)ABC literature.[139] According to some authors, this is a consequence of the rather simple overhead allocation on the grounds of volume

133 According arguments can be found in the literature on RCA (cf. e.g. *Krumwiede et al.* (2007), p. 1ff.; *Krumwiede/Suessmair* (2007b), p. 5ff.; *Krumwiede/Suessmair* (2007a), p. 1ff.; *White et al.* (2008), p. 5ff.; *White et al.* (2011), p. 38).

134 Cf. section 2.2.4.

135 Cf. *Küpper* (1983), p. 171 and 174; *Jones et al.* (1993), p. 112; *Sopariwala* (2004), p. 5; *Krumwiede/Suessmair* (2007a), p. 6.

136 Cf. *Kilger et al.* (2012), p. 385.

137 For a refinement of provided capacity into theoretical, practical and normal capacity, cf. e.g. *Hertenstein et al.* (2006), p. 65.

138 Cf. *Jones et al.* (1993), p. 112; *Sopariwala* (2004), p. 5; *Krumwiede/Suessmair* (2007a), p. 6.

139 Cf. *Kaplan/Cooper* (1998), p. 127; *Kaplan/Anderson* (2003), p. 8f.

bases (e.g. direct labour costs), which hide away idle capacity.[140] Remarkably, the Anglophone interest in German cost accounting and RCA that motivates this study popularises considerations on idle capacity in the Anglophone cost accounting literature. This already led to a stronger focus on cost of idle capacity in some Anglophone companies.[141] This focus may spread in the future; there are current tendencies in US (financial) accounting to emphasise 'unused fixed costs'.[142]

The differences of Anglophone and German cost centre accounting practices are summarised in Table 2-2.

2.2.4 Cost object accounting

Regarding cost object accounting in Anglophone and German firms, there are various differences as well. On the one hand, there are cost object specific findings for (1) the types of differing cost objects, (3) the design of contribution margin accounting, and (4) the distinction of internally and externally oriented profitability analyses. On the other hand, there are several differences that can be linked to the classification of costs on cost objects such as (2) the costs allocated to cost objects, (5) the time reference of (cost object) costs and interlinked with the latter, (6) the extent of cost variance analysis. Obviously, such classifications require a categorisation by cost types. Furthermore, companies categorise costs in cost centres in order to decide which costs to assign to cost objects.[143] Hence, these classifications are relevant for the cost centre level, too. Nevertheless, these categories are explicated at this point though multiple references will have to be made to the sections on cost type and cost centre accounting.

(1) Types of differing cost objects

With respect to the **different cost objects** the knowledge on cross-national differences is scarce. On the one hand, there is no evidence for a different emphasis attributed to products or product lines in Anglophone and German companies. On the other hand, there are two potential sources for cross-national differences. First, it remains to be explored whether the diverging reliance on ABC (section 2.2.3) is accompanied by a diverging focus on customer profitability analysis in Anglophone and German firms.[144] Second, a newly risen interest in the costs of spoilage and emissions, which characterises the Japanese literature,[145] may enable a differentiation of the cost objects regularly regarded in German and Anglophone cost accounting. Preliminary evidence shows that these analyses are not unknown for German[146] and Anglophone companies.[147] It remains to be discovered whether there are cross-national differences in this regard, however.

---

[140] Cf. *Tse/Gong* (2009), p. 42.
[141] Cf. *Lynn/Todd* (2003), p. 21ff.; *Clinton/Webber* (2004), p. 25.
[142] Cf. *Bettinghaus et al.* (2012), p. 1ff.
[143] Cf. *Schweitzer/Küpper* (2010), p. 64.
[144] For the association of ABC and customer profitability analysis cf. exemplarily *Drury* (2012), p. 259ff.
[145] Cf. *Nakajima* (2004), p. 2; *Kokubu et al.* (2009), p. 15ff.; *Crönertz* (2010), p. 213; *Wagner et al.* (2010), p. 200ff.; *Nakajima* (2010).
[146] Cf. e.g. *Küpper* (1983), p. 176.

(2) Costs allocated to cost objects

The 'costs allocated to cost objects' describes whether the sum of all costs recorded or only a proportion of these are assigned to cost objects.[148] It is labelled as *product costing* hereafter. Though such proportions can refer to direct and indirect costs as well, it generally describes the distinction of **fixed and variable costs**. Variable (product) costs are those that differ over the short run in function of a certain cost driver, being regularly the number of manufactured products.[149] The total amount of fixed product costs on the other hand does not vary during a certain period in function of a certain cost driver, also being regularly the number of manufactured products.[150] If the degree of cost allocation comprises variable costs only, the terms variable or marginal costing are used, while allocating both variable and fixed costs is referred to as full or absorption costing.[151]

In Germany, a prominent variable (product) costing system is known as *Grenzplankostenrechnung* (subsequently GPK).[152] This cost accounting system is academically well established[153] as well as applied in its various facets in German firms.[154] Despite spotlighting the necessity of variable cost information on a cost object level, in a GPK context considerations of alternative reference points with respect to costs' variability are important. Accordingly, it is crucial to consider whether the costs accumulated on a cost centre depend in absolute height on that cost centre's output.[155] Especially in support cost centres, the performed tasks rarely concern a final product in a direct sense and the centres' output measures deviate from the final output of a company. Nevertheless, the protagonists urge to split these cost centres' costs into variable and fixed proportions. This implies an un-

---

[147] Cf. *Dugdale et al.* (2006), p. 95.

[148] For this and the following, cf. e.g. *Schweitzer/Küpper* (2010), p. 63f.; *Coenenberg et al.* (2012), p. 71f.

[149] Cf. e.g. *Hoitsch/Lingnau* (2007), p. 51f and 429.

[150] Cf. e.g. *Hoitsch/Lingnau* (2007), p. 51f and 418.

[151] Cf. e.g. *Schweitzer/Küpper* (2010), p. 64f.

[152] The differentiation of variable and fixed costs is of major concern for GPK (cf. e.g. *Kloock/Schiller* (1997), p. 229, or *Smith* (2005), p. 36). The focus on variable and fixed costs distinguishes GPK from other cost accounting contributors dominantly discussed in literature such as Laßmann or Riebel (cf. *Kilger* (1979), p. 86 and *Kilger et al.* (2012), p. 89). Therefore, GPK is stressed in the light of variable and full costing though the concept comprises additional particularities.

[153] Cf. *Plaut* (1953a), p. 347ff.; *Plaut* (1953b), p. 402ff.; *Kilger* (1976), p. 679ff.; *Kilger* (1979), p. 71ff.; *Kilger et al.* (2012), p. 76ff.

[154] For empirical evidence on a German tendency to differentiate variable and full costs, cf. e.g. *Küpper* (1983), p. 171; *Weber* (1993b), p. 261; *Friedl et al.* (2009), p. 112f; *Moeschler* (2012), p. 255f. Moreover, other particularities of German cost accounting are also attributed to GPK. Following *Kilger* (1979), p. 72; *Schildbach* (1997), p. 265f.; *Sharman* (2003a), p. 31f., or *Bohr/Obermeier* (2004), p. 589f., the cost centre formation *rules* stem from GPK considerations. Moreover, *Krumwiede et al.* (2007), p. 34 link the refined overhead cost allocation procedures in German firms to GPK. Whether these procedures are purely attributable to GPK, which can be seen to refuse the allocation of fixed cost to cost objects (cf. *Kilger et al.* (2012), p. 91), remains a matter of argumentation. In line, *Christensen/Wagenhofer* (1997), p. 257, argue that "German practice (…) [is] a mixture of the pure systems advanced in textbook literature". Therefore, a clear-cut attribution of the particularities of German cost accounting to the multiple contributors is neglected at this point.

[155] For this and the following, cf. e.g. *Hoitsch/Lingnau* (2007), p. 151ff.; *Schweitzer/Küpper* (2010), p. 428 and 431ff.; *Kilger et al.* (2012), p. 251ff.

conventional understanding of costs' variability because their dependence on a measure other than the final output is taken into account (e.g. kWh).

Despite the greater presence of the determination of costs of **unused capacity** in German firms as compared to the Anglophone companies, it remains empirically unclear to what extent GPK's refined understanding of variable costs can be found in German companies. The presence of variable cost centre costs[156] indicates an implementation of such practices. Moreover, it is rather indisputable to identify above discussion as a particularity of German cost accounting research and practice.[157] Interestingly, the analysis of variable and fixed costs in accordance with a cost centre's output recently finds its way into Anglophone costing systems through resource consumption accounting.[158]

Regarding the issue of marginal and full costing in Anglophone companies, there is some UK evidence for the application of a costing system which relies on direct costs for the purpose of cost object cost determination.[159] These, however, are generally supplemented by the allocation of overhead costs.[160] Additionally, some US companies distinguish fixed and variable cost object costs on a regular basis as well.[161] In general, however, Anglophone companies tend to be characterised by a great emphasis on full costing (i.e. little emphasis on variable costing) to determine the costs of a cost object.[162] This can be contrasted to the arguable importance of variable product costs in Germany as exemplified above.[163] Similar to Anglophone practices, however, variable product costs are not the only product costs determined by German companies. Rather, German companies generally supplemented variable costing systems by the allocation of fixed costs to products.[164] Even in the context of GPK, extensions are made to allow for supplementing full cost calculations. Accordingly, costs which do not vary in accordance with a cost centre's output, but are still transferred to other cost centres (or cost objects) are sometimes labelled ter-

---

[156] Cf. *Küpper* (1983), p. 171; *Becker* (1984), p. 129ff.; *Lange/Schauer* (1996), p. 206; *Scherrer* (1996), p. 103; *Jones/Luther* (2006), p. 13; *Friedl et al.* (2009), p. 112f.

[157] Cf. *Keys/van der Merwe* (1999), p. 3ff.; *Krumwiede* (2005), p. 28.

[158] Cf. *Keys/van der Merwe* (2002), p. 44; *Webber/Clinton* (2004), p. 4ff.; *White* (2009), p. 67ff. Despite acknowledging the existence of fixed and variable cost centre costs, however, RCA rather deviates from GPK's strictness to disregard the assignment of fixed cost centre costs (cf. *van der Merwe/Keys* (2002), p. 33ff., or *Webber/Clinton* (2004), p. 4ff.). Interestingly, above definition of idle capacity as included in Kilger's textbook, also informed the development of RCA (cf. e.g. *Keys/van der Merwe* (1999), p. 3).

[159] Cf. *Abdel-Kader/Luther* (2006), p. 15; *Drury/Tayles* (2006), p. 412; *Al-Omiri/Drury* (2007), p. 413.

[160] Cf. *Drury/Tayles* (2006), p. 412; *Al-Omiri/Drury* (2007), p. 413.

[161] Cf. *Bhimani/Bromwich* (2010), p. 19, who interpret *Ernst & Young* (2003), p. 13, accordingly.

[162] Cf. *Shields et al.* (1991), p. 64; *Lamminmaki/Drury* (2001); *Drury/Tayles* (2006), p. 412; *Al-Omiri/Drury* (2007), p. 413; *White et al.* (2011), p. 41, or similarly *Clinton/White* (2012), p. 59.

[163] For empirical evidence on a German tendency to differentiate variable and full costs, cf. e.g. *Küpper* (1983), p. 171; *Becker* (1984), p. 129ff.; *Weber* (1993b), p. 261; *Lange/Schauer* (1996), p. 206; *Scherrer* (1996), p. 103; *Jones/Luther* (2006), p. 13; *Friedl et al.* (2009), p. 112f.; *Moeschler* (2012), p. 255f. These authors regularly stress that variable and fixed cost are separated for cost objects as well as cost centres, though the extent to which variable and fixed costs are separated for the different components of cost accounting differs.

[164] Cf. *Küpper* (1983), p. 171; *Becker* (1984), p. 129; *Weber* (1993b), p. 261; *Scherrer* (1996), p. 103; *Friedl et al.* (2009), p. 112; *Moeschler* (2012), p. 255f.

tiary costs.[165] Moreover, fixed cost allocation tends to be rather detailed in Germany as compared to Anglophone companies as can be explicated the application and design of contribution margin accounting.

(3) Contribution margin accounting

German companies emphasise the determination of contribution margins (defined as price less variable costs).[166] Rather than deriving one contribution margin only, however, German companies tend to derive various contribution margins by allocating fixed costs in a multiple staged procedure.[167] Such a refined fixed cost allocating system assigns fixed costs to the cost object level, on which the costs are incurred (e.g. product level, product group level or departments). Thereby, the stepwise fixed cost deduction facilitates the derivation of different **layers of contribution margins**.[168] Exemplarily, after having deduced product prices by products' variable costs, German companies tend to subtract product level fixed costs to derive a *contribution margin II* and thereafter, e.g. product group fixed costs to derive a *contribution margin III*.[169]

In Anglophone countries, contribution margin accounting is similarly established as it is in Germany.[170] Despite the somewhat diverse picture in country specific literature presented below, contribution margin accounting tends to be applied less regularly in Anglophone companies if compared to German practices.[171] More remarkably, contribution margin accounting in Anglophone companies tends to neglect multiple level contribution margins.[172] This reflects recommendations from **direct costing**,[173] which has been rather influential for the development of Anglophone cost accounting. Peculiarly, there is some normative Anglophone literature which stresses multiple staged fixed costs allocations systems as the ones outlined by German researchers.[174] Moreover, contribution margins are less clear-cut defined as selling price less variable costs in Anglophone literature. Rather,

---

165 Cf. *Hoitsch/Lingnau* (2007), p. 163. Note that in this context, secondary costs of one cost centre reflect only those costs of an allocating cost centre which vary in accordance with the latter centre's output (cf. *Hoitsch/Lingnau* (2007), p. 151).

166 Cf. *Kosmider* (1992), p. 28; *Lange/Schauer* (1996), p. 207; *Scherrer* (1996), p. 103; *Homburg/Karlshaus* (1999), p. 75; *Schäffer/Steiners* (2005b), p. 322; *Becker et al.* (2013), p. 61.

167 Cf. *Küpper* (1983), p. 171; *Becker* (1984), p. 136; *Jones/Luther* (2006), p. 13; *Rautenstrauch/Müller* (2007), p. 1825; *Friedl et al.* (2009), p. 113; *Luther et al.* (2010), p. 85; *Moeschler* (2012), p. 257f.

168 Cf. *Agthe* (1959), p. 407ff.

169 Cf. e.g. *Schweitzer/Küpper* (2010), p. 573ff.

170 Cf. *Kim/Song* (1990), p. 30; *Zirkler* (2002), p. 290; *Drury/Tayles* (2006), p. 412f.; *Dugdale et al.* (2006), p. 73f.; *Krumwiede/Suessmair* (2007b), p. 52.

171 For direct comparisons of German and Anglophone companies cf. *Zirkler* (2001), p. 18 or *Krumwiede/Suessmair* (2007b), p. 52.

172 Cf. *Zirkler* (2002), p. 290 or *Drury/Tayles* (2006), p. 413.

173 Cf. *Harris* (1936), p. 503ff., who criticised the application of a standard cost based accounting system by illustrating the effect of fixed cost allocation on a company's profits.

174 Cf. *Marple* (1967), p. 6ff., and the discussion of his work by Böer at the 1989 Annual Meeting of the American Accounting Association (published as *Robinson* (1990), p. 24ff.). Similarly, the recommendations for ABC by *Cooper/Kaplan* (1991), p. 88f., to add costs to products, batches and product lines, are reasoned to allow for the derivations of multiple level contribution margins (cf. *Kaplan* at the 1989 Annual Meeting of the American Accounting Association (published as *Robinson* (1990), p. 5ff.).

they are also computed as selling-price less direct costs.[175] Though such an alternative definition reflects the German cost accounting system by *Riebel*,[176] it remains unclear, whether this is not merely an example of imprecise language in Anglophone management accounting.[177]

From a German point of view, direct costs, in contrast to variable costs, do not describe whether costs' absolute height depends on a level of production but whether costs can be attributed to a single cost object.[178] This terminological clarification is essential, as it can explicate another potential cross-national difference with respect to (4) the design of product costing. Anglophone companies tend to disregard the allocation of non-manufacturing overhead costs (indirect costs) to products.[179] Such product costs, reflecting **manufacturing costs** only, are known as '*Herstellkosten*' in German cost accounting. In excess to Anglophone practice, these are regularly supplemented by an allocation of **non-manufacturing** overhead costs to derive the so-called '*Selbstkosten*' in Germany. The Anglophone segregation of manufacturing and non-manufacturing costs is also linked to the Anglophone focus on inventoriable and non-inventoriable costs.[180] As such, it remains explorable to what extent the differentiation of manufacturing and non-manufacturing costs can actually depict a cross-national difference in Anglophone and German cost accounting.

(4) Operating income statements

The analysis of contribution margins essentially reflects complementing measures for a products' profitability for short-term decisions. Reflecting their importance in Germany, German companies traditionally rely on management accounting information summarising the economic performance. This information supplements financial accounting information. In particular, German cost accounting is associated with the derivation of operating income statements. These assess a company's economic situation from an internal perspective. Thereby, such statements can deviate (substantially) from external accounting informed profit and loss statements (subsequently P/L statements) in terms of content and structure.[181] In Anglophone companies, cost based profitability analyses are known, too.[182] Other than in Germany, however, there is no clear picture on the application and design of operating income statements in Anglophone companies. This appears attributable to two explanations. On the one hand, there is a lack of accordingly focussed research. On

---

[175] Cf. *Drury/Tayles* (2006), p. 411f.

[176] Cf. *Riebel* (1959), p. 213ff., or the discussion by *Weber/Weißenberger* (1997), p. 281–287.

[177] Such terminological issues may have evoked *White et al.* (2011), p. 40, to call for a standardisation of language used in cost accounting.

[178] Cf. *Schweitzer/Küpper* (2010), p. 79f.

[179] Cf. for the following *Garrison et al.* (2006), p. 36ff.; *Stratton et al.* (2009), p. 33; *Kajüter* (2011), p. 106.

[180] Cf. *Garrison et al.* (2006), p. 36ff.; *Kajüter* (2011), p. 104.

[181] For textbook examples, cf. *Ewert/Wagenhofer* (2008), p. 677ff.; *Coenenberg et al.* (2012), p. 183ff. For the application of operating income statements and their deviance from P/L statements in small as well as large German companies, cf. *Friedl et al.* (2009), p. 113; *Moeschler* (2012), p. 255f., or *Becker et al.* (2013), p. 61.

[182] Cf. *Jones* (1991), p. 34; *Drury/Tayles* (2006), p. 412f.

the other hand, the distinction between financial and management accounting is less clear-cut in Anglophone companies (section 2.2.2). Especially the dominance of financial over management accounting remains a highly disputed topic in Anglophone countries.[183]

(5) Time reference of cost accounting

The application of multiple contribution margins and the derivation of operating income statements underline the diversity of profitability figures in Germany. Additional emphasis for such diversity can be revealed by the time references in cost accounting. Typical time references in cost accounting are **planed/standard, actual or normal** (i.e. average) **costs.**[184] Furthermore, **target costs**' forward-looking market oriented character can be contrasted to the forward looking but technology driven character of standard costs.[185] Thus, target costs, which reflect an amount of resources that can be sacrificed to meet customers' willingness to pay and a company's profit expectation,[186] can be summarised under this category. Standard costing is widely used in Anglophone companies.[187] Given a focus on planned costs in GPK, standard costs are regularly computed in German companies as well.[188] Preliminary evidence suggests, however, that Anglophone companies apply standard cost for more decision problems than German companies do.[189] Moreover, there is some evidence about target costing to be more common in German than in Anglophone companies.[190] Other than that, however, little distinctive patterns exist with respect to time reference of cost accounting since actual costs are rather common for both regarded geographical areas. Nevertheless, the time references of cost accounting are essential at this point because of their close link to variance analysis, which proves to exhibit a remarkable cross-national difference between German and Anglophone companies.

(6) Cost variance analysis

Cost variance analysis describes the comparison of, e.g. actual costs with another cost reference (e.g. planned/standard, normal or target costs). Linked to the prevalence of GPK and the detailed cost centre accounting, refined **analyses of cost variances** are extensively discussed in conceptual German cost accounting works.[191] In line, cost variances are analysed extensively for both cost objects *and* cost centres in German companies.[192] Despite

[183] For the influence of financial accounting on management accounting, cf. e.g. *Joseph et al.* (1996), p. 90; *Dugdale et al.* (2006), p. 81.

[184] Cf. *Coenenberg et al.* (2012), p. 70f.

[185] Cf. *Hiromoto* (1988), p. 24; *Guilding et al.* (1998), p. 570.

[186] Cf. *Coenenberg et al.* (2012), p. 555.

[187] Cf. *Karmarkar et al.* (1990), p. 377; *Shields et al.* (1991), p. 67; *Drury et al.* (1993), p. 35; *Lyall/Graham* (1993), p. 42; *Scapens* (1996), p. 24 and 145; *Guilding et al.* (1998), p. 580ff.; *Jones/Luther* (2006), p. 16; *Dugdale et al.* (2006), p. 89.

[188] Cf. *Scherrer* (1996), p. 103; *Krumwiede/Suessmair* (2007a), p. 6 or *Friedl et al.* (2009), p. 112.

[189] Cf. *Krumwiede/Suessmair* (2007a), p. 6.

[190] For a review, cf. *Kajüter* (2013), p. 90. In line with *Kajüter* and respectively cited authors, *Yazdifar/Askarany* (2012), p. 388, and *Clinton/White* (2012), p. 60, provide consistent evidence for Anglophone and *Schäffer/Steiners* (2005b), p. 322f., for German companies.

[191] Cf. *Kloock/Schiller* (1997), p. 316ff.; *Küpper* (2008), p. 227ff.; *Kilger et al.* (2012), p. 64ff.

[192] Cf. *Krumwiede/Suessmair* (2007a), p. 6, or *Moeschler* (2012), p. 249f., for detailed findings for cost variance analysis on cost centres and *Währisch* (1998), p. 42ff., and 164ff., for refined findings for both

variance analysis being discussed in early Anglophone cost accounting articles[193] as well as major Anglophone textbooks[194] and studies on RCA,[195] it is rarely under consideration in empirical research.[196] Preliminary results suggest that variance analysis of cost centre costs is rather intensively applied in Anglophone companies, but still falls behind the German practices.[197] It remains unclear whether this comparative difference is particular for cost centre accounting or prevails for cost object accounting, for which variance analysis is also common in Anglophone companies.[198]

The cross-national differences of German and Anglophone cost object accounting are summarised in Table 2-3.

	Aspect of cost accounting	German	Anglophone
(1)	Type of cost objects	There are little particularities in this regard. Potential differences with respect to customer profitability analysis and cost of spoilage.	
(2)	Extent of costs allocated to cost objects	There is a stronger tendency to separate variable and fixed costs of a cost object in German companies.	
		Determination of cost variability with respect to cost centre output. Allocation of manufacturing and non-manufacturing costs.	Particular focus on manufacturing costs for cost object accounting.
(3)	Design of contribution margin accounting	Determination of multiple CMs	Determination of a single CM
(4)	Distinction of internally and externally oriented profitability analyses	Rather common	Disguised evidence
(5)	Time reference of costs	There are little particularities in this regard. Most remarkably, Anglophone companies appear to emphasise standard costs, whereas German companies tend to rely more strongly on target costs.	
(6)	Extent of cost variance analysis	Rather detailed variance analysis for cost object *and* cost centres	Disguised evidence for the cost object level. Rather broad variance analysis for cost centres.

Table 2-3: Differences between Anglophone and German cost object accounting

2.2.5 Summary

The differences and similarities illustrated above will facilitate the analysis of cost accounting in Anglophone subsidiaries in Germany and the comparison with domestic German companies. Figure 2-2 summarises the areas of particularities of cost accounting. Thereby, variance analysis is included twice. Rather than being a peculiarity of cost object accounting systems, the particularities of variance analyses apply for the cost centre level as well.

---

cost objects and cost centres. For complementing though less differentiated findings see *Küpper* (1983), p. 172; *Weber* (1993b), p. 260; *Lange/Schauer* (1996), p. 204; *Becker et al.* (2013), p. 61.

193 Cf. *Harris* (1936), p. 505ff.

194 Cf. e.g. *Garrison et al.* (2006), p. 435ff.; *Drury* (2012), p. 431ff.; *Horngren et al.* (2012), p. 248ff.

195 Cf. e.g. *Keys/van der Merwe* (2002), p. 144.

196 For exceptions, cf. *Dugdale et al.* (2006), p. 94ff.; *Krumwiede/Suessmair* (2007b), p. 53, and *Krumwiede/Suessmair* (2007a), p. 6.

197 Cf. *Zirkler* (2001), p. 18; *Krumwiede/Suessmair* (2007a), p. 6.

198 Cf. *Dugdale et al.* (2006), p. 94ff.

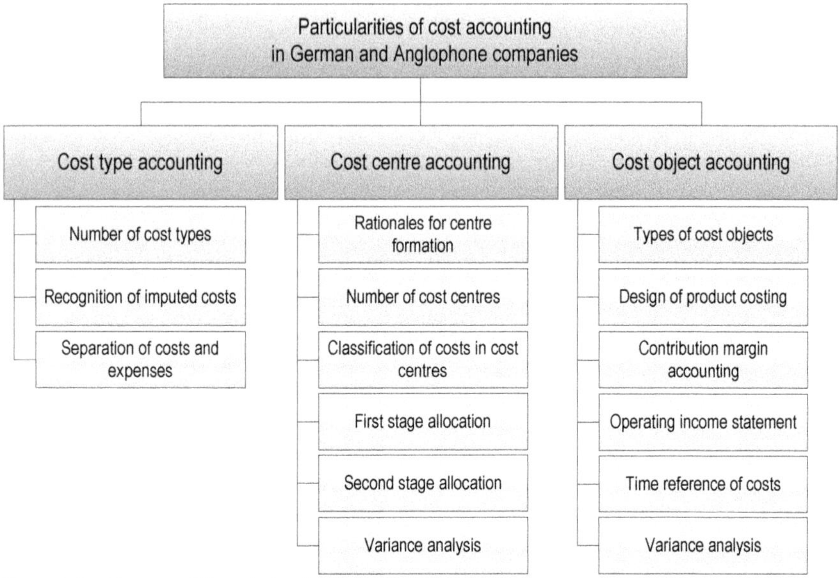

Figure 2-2: Elements differentiating Anglophone and German cost accounting

2.3 Use of cost information

2.3.1 Introduction

There is no single way to describe the use of cost information.[199] Two concepts dominate the prior literature on this issue.[200] The **types of use** explicate how decision makers or accountants incorporate cost information into the process of management. The **extent of use** is applied to describe adoption rates of cost accounting systems and the extent to which cost accounting systems are applied for day-to-day decision-making by different management areas.[201] Moreover, it is applied to measure how intensively certain cost accounting objectives are pursued.

---

[199] Cf. e.g. *Ansari/Euske* (1987), p. 551; *Hunold* (2003), p. 75ff. For similar arguments for the use of management information more generally, cf. *Menon/Varadarajan* (1992), p. 54; *Schäffer/Steiners* (2004), p. 378ff.

[200] For the following, cf. *Menon/Varadarajan* (1992), p. 54; *Diamantopoulos/Souchon* (1998), p. 113f.; *Hunold* (2003), p. 75ff., or implicitly *Weber/Hunold* (2002), p. 39, and p. 42.

[201] For this perspective, cf. *Anderson* (1995), p. 5–7; *Krumwiede* (1998), p. 242; *Krump* (2003), p. 189ff.; *Brown et al.* (2004), p. 342, or *Pike et al.* (2011), p. 67f., who apply a model to evaluate the implementation of information systems introduced by *Cooper/Zmud* (1990).

Figure 2-3 summarises the multidimensionality of the construct 'use of cost information'. The figure illustrates the discussion of the following two sections and serves as a reference point throughout the section.

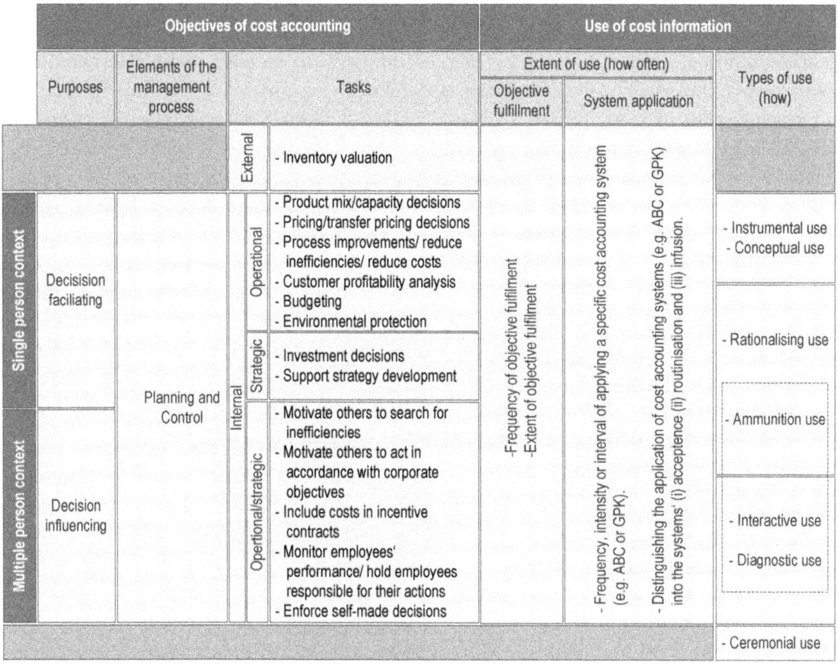

Figure 2-3: Conceptual alternatives to research the use of cost information

Though the extent of use explicitly refers to the *use* of cost accounting, its strong emphasis on adoption rates and cost accounting objectives can be contrasted to the focus on cost information which characterises the research on different usage types. Thus, the extent of use cannot be differentiated conclusively from studies on the application of cost accounting systems (i.e. a macro perspective). In contrast, different types of cost information use complement the analysis of a conceptual design of cost accounting (i.e. a mezzo level of analysis) by considerations on *how* cost information is actually used in the process of management. Hence, this perspective is regarded in this study.

Yet, the types of cost information use cannot be regarded irrespectively of cost accounting objectives. Hence, the extent of use is briefly introduced hereafter with respect to common cost accounting objectives.

2.3.2 Cost accounting objectives

The objectives of cost accounting tend to be researched with respect to the general purposes of cost accounting, specific tasks (i.e. decisions) associated with these purposes as well as the elements of the management process.

The **general purposes** of cost accounting are facilitating and influencing managerial decisions.[202] The former assumes information to be provided to a single decision maker, who acts in accordance with the overall organisational goals, prior to a decision to be made.[203] The latter explicitly recognises that there are several decision makers in organisations, who decide simultaneously. Since these decision makers potentially strive for differing goals, their decisions are often directed by ex-post information to align their actions with a company's overall goals. These two basic purposes can be concretised by linking them to the **management process**. Hence, cost information shall facilitate and influence managerial decisions during planning or control activities. Typically, in German research, the management is relevant when focussing on the decision facilitating purpose of cost accounting only.[204] The decision influencing purpose is discussed separately. However, since cost information can serve decision facilitating as well as decision influencing during the entire management process,[205] this differentiation cannot be found in Figure 2-3. The **tasks** of management accounting describe specific strategic and operational actions, which can be supplemented by cost information.[206] As illustrated in Figure 2-3, such tasks are pricing, production planning and process improvements as well as the application of cost information to influence employees' behaviour (e.g. motivate them to act in accordance with a firm's strategy). Moreover, externally (i.e. financial accounting) oriented inventory valuation can be regarded as a task which is regularly based on cost information.

Complementing the above perspectives, the **time period** for which a cost-based decision is made, often structures the cost accounting objectives. Academics typically link cost accounting to short-term or operational decisions since it is applied in a context of given capacity.[207] Considerations which are essential for strategic decisions such as, e.g. opportunity costs are not generally reflected in cost information. Nevertheless, the studies researching cost accounting objectives regularly find the application of cost information for strategic or long-term decisions as well.[208] Despite theoretical deficiencies,[209] it becomes evident that companies use cost information for both operational and strategic objectives. Figure 2-3 reflects this additional perspective describing cost accounting objectives.

Information on some common cost accounting objectives in **Anglophone and German companies** will facilitate the understanding of the usage types to be discussed hereafter. Since these are not at the core of this study, however, only a brief introduction is presented at this point.

---

202 Cf. *Demski/Feltham* (1976), p. 8.

203 For this and the following, cf. *Aust* (1999), p. 56f.; *Schweitzer/Küpper* (2010), p. 32.

204 For this and the following, cf. e.g. *Aust* (1999), p. 44–63; *Weber* (2005), p. 39–44; *Schweitzer/Küpper* (2010), p. 27–36.

205 Cf. *Kaplan/Atkinson* (1989), p. 1; *Friedl et al.* (2013), p. 3ff.

206 For a summary of tasks which can be fulfilled by cost accounting, cf. *Hummel/Männel* (1986), p. 22–40.

207 Cf. for this and the following *Kloock et al.* (2005), p. 16ff.; *Ewert/Wagenhofer* (2008), p. 59ff.

208 Corresponding citations can be found in the the next paragraph.

209 For a discussion of the applicability of cost accounting for strategic decisions, cf. *Küpper* (1985), p. 26ff., or *Hax* (2002), p. 762ff.

Empirically, the four perspectives which describe cost accounting objectives are regularly studied conjointly.[210] Thereby, different foci and aggregations prevail. These various aggregations inhibit a profound comparison of commonly pursued cost accounting objectives in Anglophone and German companies.[211] Nevertheless, some restricted national particularities are identifiable. For German companies, it is generally stressed that decision facilitating has a longer tradition than decision influencing.[212] In contrast, Anglophone firms are already known for a longer period to employ cost information for both decision facilitating and influencing purpose.[213] Moreover, Anglophone firms are generally stressed to pursue external tasks more extensively,[214] whereas internal tasks dominate in German speaking firms.[215] In addition, the emphasis on standard (i.e. planned) cost for various decision-problems in Anglophone firms is remarkable in this context.[216] It shows the importance of cost information for planning activities. Yet, it remains empirically unclear whether this characteristic also hints that cost accounting is less important for control activities in Anglophone companies. In contrast, it is sometimes stressed that cost information is traditionally more intensively applied for control than for planning activities in German firms.[217] Despite these differences, however, specific tasks associated with cost accounting are regularly found to prevail similarly in comparative management accounting research.[218]

---

[210] Cf. e.g. *Küpper* (1983), p. 173; *Weber* (1993b), p. 257ff.; *Innes/Mitchell* (1995), p. 144; *Shields* (1995), p. 156; *Geiger/Ittner* (1996), p. 556; *Lange/Schauer* (1996), p. 204; *Foster/Swenson* (1997), p. 114; *Groot* (1997), p. 30; *Nguyen/Brooks* (1997), p. 9; *Homburg* (1998), p. 34f.; *Währisch* (1998), p. 81; *Clarke et al.* (1999), p. 455; *Drury/Tayles* (2000), p. 45ff.; *Frank* (2000), p. 99; *Hoque* (2000), p. 147; *Innes et al.* (2000), p. 355; *Karlshaus* (2000), p. 110; *Cagwin/Bouwman* (2002), p. 19; *Cotton et al.* (2003), p. 70; *Garg et al.* (2003), p. 31; *Hunold* (2003), p. 146; *Krump* (2003), p. 231; *Chenhall* (2004), p. 31 and 40; *Krumwiede/Suessmair* (2007a), p. 5; *Friedl et al.* (2009), p. 112; *Schoute* (2009), p. 215; *Stratton et al.* (2009), p. 34; *Wolfsgruber* (2011), p. 248; *Moeschler* (2012), p. 237.

[211] Similarly, *White et al.* (2011), p. 39, recommends to differentiate objectives and purposes of cost accounting more clearly.

[212] For examples, cf. *Küpper* (1993), p. 616; *Weber* (1994), p. 99f.; *Pfaff* (1996), p. 151 or *Schweitzer/Küpper* (2010), p. 27–36.

[213] For this and the following, cf. e.g. *Zirkler* (2002), p. 55ff.; *Schweitzer/Küpper* (2010), p. 610ff.

[214] Cf. *Karmarkar et al.* (1990), p. 368; *Jones et al.* (1993), p. 122; *Joseph et al.* (1996), p. 79; *Drury/Tayles* (2000), p. 60f.; *Clinton* (2007), p. 27; *White et al.* (2011), p. 41. Accordingly, *Krumwiede/Suessmair* (2007a), p. 3, finds dissatisfaction with cost accounting for internal decision-making. Yet, a primacy of external tasks is partially challenged for the UK by *Drury/Tayles* (1997), p. 269, and *Scapens* (1996), p. 3ff and 153f.

[215] Cf. *Währisch* (1998), p. 79ff.; *Luther et al.* (2010), p. 85f.; *Wolfsgruber* (2011), p. 248f.

[216] Cf. *Guilding et al.* (1998), p. 580ff.; *Karmarkar et al.* (1990), p. 377; *Shields et al.* (1991), p. 67; *Drury et al.* (1993), p. 35; *Lyall/Graham* (1993), p. 42; *Scapens* (1996), p. 24 and 145; *Jones/Luther* (2006), p. 16 or *Dugdale et al.* (2006), p. 89.

[217] Cf. *Küpper* (1993), p. 610.

[218] For a comparison of Germany and Japan, cf. *Moeschler* (2012), p. 238. Similarly, international research does not reveal major differences with respect to commonly prevailing cost accounting objectives (cf. *Küpper* (1983), p. 173; *Weber* (1993b), p. 257ff.; *Innes/Mitchell* (1995), p. 144; *Shields* (1995), p. 156; *Geiger/Ittner* (1996), p. 556; *Lange/Schauer* (1996), p. 204; *Foster/Swenson* (1997), p. 114; *Groot* (1997), p. 30; *Nguyen/Brooks* (1997), p. 9; *Homburg* (1998), p. 34f.; *Währisch* (1998), p. 81; *Clarke et al.* (1999), p. 455; *Drury/Tayles* (2000), p. 45ff.; *Frank* (2000), p. 99; *Hoque* (2000), p. 147; *Innes et*

Having introduced cost accounting objectives, the following section can now broach the issue of different types of cost information use. Thereby, special attention will be directed to the conceptualisation of these usage types. Also, empirical evidence on the prevalence of different usage types in international literature will be provided.

2.3.3 Types of cost information use

The analysis how cost information is incorporated in the process of management (i.e. the analysis of different usage types) is a field of research which is scarce in cost accounting research.[219] Nevertheless, several similar, yet complementing typologies exist.[220] For this study, the four typologies by *Pelz* (1978), *Burchell et al.* (1980), *Ansari/Euske* (1987) and *Simons* (1995a/b) are relevant because they prevail in previous cost accounting literature[221] as well as international business research[222] and can embrace the opposition of subsidiaries to corporately induced cost accounting initiatives.

Pelz differentiates the instrumental, conceptual and symbolic use of information.[223] Following the author, the **instrumental use** describes that a decision is directly informed by (cost) information. It refers to a situation in which a decision maker deliberately solves a due decision-problem on the grounds of a certain piece of (cost) information. In contrast, the **conceptual use** captures that a decision is facilitated indirectly by (cost) information. It describes that a decision maker gains experiences for future decisions by deliberately or unconsciously looking at (cost) information irrespectively any due decisions. The term

---

al. (2000), p. 355; *Karlshaus* (2000), p. 110; *Cagwin/Bouwman* (2002), p. 19; *Cotton et al.* (2003), p. 70; *Garg et al.* (2003), p. 31; *Hunold* (2003), p. 146; *Krump* (2003), p. 231; *Chenhall* (2004), p. 31 and 40; *Krumwiede/Suessmair* (2007a), p. 5; *Friedl et al.* (2009), p. 112; *Schoute* (2009), p. 215; *Stratton et al.* (2009), p. 34; *Wolfsgruber* (2011), p. 248).

219 Cf. *Küpper* (1993), p. 603ff.; *Weber* (2005), p. 56.

220 Cf. *Simon et al.* (1954), p. 24; *Caplan et al.* (1975), p. 17ff.; *Rich/Caplan* (1975), p. 239ff.; *Knorr* (1976), p. 171ff.; *Knorr* (1977), p. 175; *Rich* (1977), p. 200f.; *Weiss* (1977), p. 7ff; *Pelz* (1978), p. 349ff.; *Weiss* (1979), p. 427ff.; *Burchell et al.* (1980), p. 13ff.; *Earl/Hopwood* (1980), p. 8f.; *Feldman/March* (1981), p. 175ff.; *Ansari/Euske* (1987), p. 553ff.; *Menon/Varadarajan* (1992), p. 54ff.; *Hirst/Baxter* (1993), p. 191ff.; *Simons* (1995b), p. 6ff.; *Vandenbosch* (1999), p. 79ff.; *Schäffer/Steiners* (2004), p. 385f. or *Henri* (2006a), p. 80ff. and the reviews in *Diamantopoulos/Souchon* (1998), p. 112f.; *Sandt* (2004), p. 156–161; *Schäffer/Steiners* (2004), p. 378ff.; *Henri* (2006a), p. 80–82; *Jais* (2007), p. 10–27.

221 Cf. *Homburg et al.* (1998), p. 36ff.; *Aust* (1999), p. 94ff.; *Frank* (2000), p. 157ff.; *Karlshaus* (2000), p. 111ff.; *Reitmeyer* (2000), p. 74f.; *Hunold* (2003), p. 145ff. For a comprehensive review of this research, cf. *Weber* (2005), p. 56.

222 *Menon/Varadarajan* (1992), p. 54, identified these conceptualisations to be the most widely applied internationally.

223 *Pelz* (1978), p. 349ff., derives instrumental and conceptual use from *Caplan et al.* (1975), p. 17ff.; *Rich/Caplan* (1975), p. 241f., and *Rich* (1977), p. 200f., whose research project consider the use of social science information by policy makers in the US public sector. The symbolic use stems from considerations of *Knorr* (1977), p. 175, and *Weiss* (1977), p. 14f. *Knorr* published her results for the use of social science research in Austrian federal and municipal government agencies previously as *Knorr* (1976). Moreover, *Weiss* (1977), p. 14f., argues that social science research can be used as 'political ammunition' by governments and governmental units seek support for their opinions.

symbolic use describes the conscious use of (cost) information to legitimate[224] personal decisions (ex-post). In a similar vein, *Burchell et al.* differentiate answering, learning, ammunition and rationalisation machines.[225] Information is seen as an **answering machine** if it is used as "algorithms, formulae and rules (...) to solve problems by computation".[226] **Learning machines** are used to refer to the provision of assistance through accounting systems through "*ad hoc* analysis, what-if models and sensitivity analysis"[227]. The other two constructs refer to the promotion of personal interests (**ammunition machine**) and the ex-post justification, legitimation and rationalisation of a personally taken decision (**rationalisation machine**).[228]

Despite difficulties with respect to a clear attribution, authors argue that the answering machines are similar to *Pelz*'s instrumental use, while learning machines reflect the conceptual use.[229] The ammunition and rationalisation machines are generally stressed to differentiate what *Pelz* previously summarised as the symbolic use of information.[230]

In this study, the instrumental, conceptual and rationalising use of information is distinguished. The ammunition use will be refined in the next paragraphs. The phrase symbolic use will be maintained in order to refer to the rationalising and the refined ammunition use conjointly. Table 2-4 summarises this integration of *Pelz*'s and *Burchell at al.*'s typologies.

Authors	Differentiated types of information use			
Pelz (1978)	**Instrumental use**	**Conceptual use**	Symbolic use	
Burchell et al. (1980)	Answering machine	Learning machine	**Rationalising machine/use**	Ammunition machine

Table 2-4: Usages types by Pelz (1978) and Burchell et al. (1980)

These types of use share particularities with the primary purposes of cost accounting. Since the instrumental and the conceptual usage types are especially concerned with the considerations of cost information prior to a personal decision, they can be aligned with the purpose 'decision facilitating'.[231] Using cost information in a rationalising manner

224 *Pelz* (1978), p. 351 also stresses that the symbolic use embraces the provision of information to pretend that something is done about a problem, despite no actual decision being taken. This argument reflects according points in *Knorr* (1976), p. 81 and 93ff., and *Knorr* (1977), p. 171ff. In *Pelz's* forthcoming examples, however, the author especially stresses legitimating aspects only. As will be seen in the next paragraphs, the revealed aspect shall not be seen as an integral part of the symbolic use of information in this study since 'feigning' is explicitly included in an additional type of use in this study.

225 Cf. *Burchell et al.* (1980), p. 14f., whose discussion can almost literally be traced back to *Earl/Hopwood* (1980), p. 8ff.

226 *Earl/Hopwood* (1980), p. 8; *Burchell et al.* (1980), p. 14.

227 *Burchell et al.* (1980), p. 15, emphasis in the original.

228 For this and the following, cf. *Burchell et al.* (1980), p. 17f., and *Earl/Hopwood* (1980), p. 10f.

229 For the comparability of these concepts, cf. *Aust* (1999), p. 74; *Karlshaus* (2000), p. 38; *Sandt* (2004), p. 160; *Jais* (2007), p. 26. For difficulties with respect to a clear cut attribution of *Burchell et al.*'s constructs to *Pelz*'s usage types cf. *Schäffer/Steiners* (2004), p. 385f.

230 Cf. *Aust* (1999), p. 74; *Karlshaus* (2000), p. 38; *Sandt* (2004), p. 160; *Schäffer/Steiners* (2004), p. 387ff.; *Jais* (2007), p. 26.

231 Simiarly arguments are put forward by *Hunold* (2003), p. 215f.

includes the (retroperspective) inhibition of personal decisions against others' as well as personal perceptions. Its link to ex-post information reasons for a link with the decision influencing purpose. However, the simultaneous focus on single and multiple decision makers hinders such a clear-cut attribution. Similarly, the use of cost information for the promotion of interest (i.e. ammunition machine) may merely reflect the influence of decisions to be made by others during the decision-making process (i.e. decision influencing). At the same time, the usage type comprises a striving of an individual to clarify personal interests in a joint decision-making process (i.e. decision facilitating). Thus, both of these types of use cannot be clearly attributed to either one of the primary purposes of cost accounting. Figure 2-3 pictures these (non-) ambiguous attributions by a box bridging the decision facilitating and decision influencing purposes.

As also revealed in Figure 2-3, the types of use by *Pelz* and *Burchell et al.* do not fully expound how cost information can be used for decision influencing purposes. Rather than explicating conclusively how cost information can be used to influence subordinates' decisions, the conceptualisations centre on personal decisions.[232] As a consequence, the adapted control system typology by *Simons* can complement the definition of different types of use.[233]

Based on practical managerial applications of control systems,[234] *Simons* distinguishes four systems (or levers) of control.[235] Each system refines one of the four constructs that *Simons* assumes to be core for strategy implementation (core values, risks to be avoided, critical performance variables and strategic uncertainties).[236] Accordingly, the latter two constructs are managed through the **diagnostic and the interactive** control systems respectively.[237] *Simons* explicitly stresses that these systems are "*use[d]* in different ways".[238] As such, it becomes evident that this control system typology is easily adaptable to a (cost) information use context.[239] In such a setting, the interactive use describes situations in which managers apply cost information to "personally involve themselves in the decision making activities of subordinates"[240]. To be interactive, this involvement is argued to be

232 To *Schäffer/Steiners* (2004), p. 385ff., the types of use do not fully explicate the use of information for decision facilitating (rather comparable to 'learning' perspectives in those authors words) purposes either. The authors argue that neither post decision control nor non-decision-directed information scanning is included. As the build-up of experience, (i.e. *Pelz*'s conceptual use) might include both aspects, however, the decision influencing purpose is assumed to be fully captured by *Pelz* in this study.

233 This extension can also be found in *Sandt* (2004), p. 160f.; *Jais* (2007), p. 26, and *Schäffer et al.* (2010), p. 312.

234 Cf. *Bisbe et al.* (2007), p. 795.

235 Cf. *Simons* (1995b), p. 6; *Simons* (1995a), p. 81.

236 Cf. *Simons* (1995b), p. 6.

237 Cf. *Simons* (1994), p. 170f.; *Simons* (1995b), p. 6; *Simons* (1995a), p. 81ff and 86ff. According to Simons, belief systems and boundary systems shall control the other two constructs. These two systems cannot be found in studies applying Simons' ideas to an information use context. Therefore, they are excluded at this point.

238 *Simons* (2000), p. 304, emphasis in the orginial.

239 Cf. *Sandt* (2004), p. 156ff., for an equivalent application.

240 *Simons* (1994), p. 171.

rather inspirational or empowering than intervening.[241] Furthermore, interactive use also includes the use of information to understand competitive dynamics and internal competencies that facilitate the management of a business.[242] Diagnostic use on the other hand describes the use of cost information to track subordinates' performance and to provide feedback for motivational and goal-achievement purposes.[243]

Given these definitions, *Simons'* descriptions can explicate *Pelz's* symbolic and *Burchell et al.*'s ammunition use of information. A diagnostic and interactive use of information explicates[244] how cost information can be used for decision influencing purposes.[245] Hence, Table 2-5 (p. 34) includes *Simons'* typology as an explication of *Burchell et al.*'s ammunition machine. Moreover, this explication is pictured by the dotted-line in Figure 2-3. Above all, from the perspective of the purposes of cost accounting, a combination of *Pelz's, Burchell et al.'s* and *Simons'* typologies of information use can describe the use of cost information rather comprehensively.

Alongside the introduced usage types, which can be linked to the primary purposes of cost accounting, *Ansari/Euske* explicate an additional type of cost information use that they label the 'institutional model'.[246] According to *Ansari/Euske*: "The technical-rational model would assert that a cost system (...) would provide data for the efficient allocation of resources. It would see efficiency and decision needs as the primary variable driving the system. The socio-political model would predict that information would be used to influence perceptions and behaviors of organizational participants. Finally, the institutional

241 Cf. *Bisbe et al.* (2007), p. 798.

242 Cf. *Bisbe et al.* (2007), p. 797f.

243 *Simons* (1995b), p. 59f.

244 *Schäffer/Steiners* (2004), p. 386, adduce that the impact on other peoples' decisions is partly included in *Pelz*'s 'symbolic use' category but actually entirely captured by *Burchell et al.'s* ammunition aspect. This is because the involvement of persons in the decision-making process of others (interactive use) or the use of control for motivational purposes (diagnostic use) might reflect a promotion of interests (ammunition machine). As such, despite the clear-cut differentiations by *Sandt* (2004), p. 160f., or *Jais* (2007), p. 26, the interactive and diagnostic use of information cannot be disjunctively differentiated from the formerly discussed ammunition machine. This cross-over of different typologies with respect to the use of cost information to impact subordinates' decisions is depicted in Figure 2-3.

245 Note that according to *Simons* (1995b), p. 59f., diagnostic control systems are arguably including the documentation of management accounting information, regardless of any influence on subordinates' decisions. Since documentations can be applied for direct decision-making or the build-up of experience as well, this perspective shares similarities with instrumental and conceptual use as well. This lack in discriminatory power is recognisable in earlier usage typologies, such as the one by *Simon et al.* (1954), too. The author stresses management accounting information to be used for score-carding or attention-directing purposes. These usage types are considered similar to *Simons*' diagnostic and interactive use (cf. e.g. *Vandenbosch* (1999), p. 79ff., or *Sandt* (2004), p. 160). In line with the perceived lack in discriminatory power, *Schäffer/Steiners* (2004), p. 385, stress that the usage type(s) by *Simon* (1954) require subsequent actions taken by decision makers to respond to identified comparisons of planned and actual outcomes. Thus, the authors rather link *Simon* (1954) and as such implicitly *Simons* (1995) to decision facilitating rather than decision influencing. Such difficulties in discriminatory power are similarly identifiable in *Hirst/Baxter* (1993), p. 191; *Abernethy/Brownell* (1999), p. 191; *Tuomela* (2005), p. 301; *Henri* (2006a), p. 80ff.; *Widener* (2007), p. 760, and *Abernethy et al.* (2010), p. 5. These concerns are considered in this study by operationalising these usaget types very carefully.

246 Cf. *Ansari/Euske* (1987).

model would see a system (...) as a vehicle for gaining legitimacy with an organization's external constituencies."[247]

Comparing *Ansari/Euske*'s definitions with *Pelz* and *Burchell et al.* reveals that the technical rational use embraces both the instrumental and the conceptual use of cost information.[248] The socio-political use rather resembles the symbolic use of cost information. This latter similarity is explicitly emphasised by *Ansari/Euske.*[249] Given the overlapping definitions, the socio-political usage cannot be clearly distinguished from the diagnostic and interactive use either. In contrast, the institutional use highlights a new perspective on the use of information. It describes the implementation of cost accounting systems irrespectively of any links to the process of management. As such, the institutional use cannot be linked to any of the types of use discussed so far.[250] In line with this argument, it was explored that for-profit organisations adopt (cost) accounting systems to fulfil certain coercive requirement (e.g. a parent company's directive) rather than making actual use of it during the management process. Therefore, authors differentiate such a **ceremonial adoption of cost accounting** from the actual internalisation of (cost) information.[251] The terminology 'ceremonial use' by *Burns/Scapens* (2000) is applied here for *Ansari/Euske*'s institutional use to avoid misinterpretations attributable to institutional theory which will be introduced in chapter 4.

Authors	Differentiated types of information use					
Pelz (1978)	**Instrumental use**	**Conceptual use**	Symbolic use			
Burchell et al. (1980)	Answering machine	Learning machine	**Rationalising machine/use**	Ammunition machine		
Simons (1995)				**Interactive use**	**Diagnostic use**	
Ansari/Euske (1987)	Technical rational use		Socio-political use			**Ceremonial use**

Table 2-5: Usage types differentiated in this study

[247] *Ansari/Euske* (1987), p. 556.

[248] A similar argument can be found in *Sandt* (2004), p. 160.

[249] Cf. *Ansari/Euske* (1987), p. 552.

[250] By explicitly separating *Ansari/Euske*'s institutional use from other types of use, this study does not follow *Knorr* (1976), p. 81 and 93ff.; *Knorr* (1977), p. 171ff.; *Pelz* (1978), p. 351; *Feldman/March* (1981), p. 177f.; *Sandt* (2004), p. 160; *Jais* (2007), p. 26, and in tendency *Burchell et al.* (1980), p. 18; *Diamantopoulos/Souchon* (1998), p. 113; *Henri* (2006a), p. 81. To these authors, institutional use is rather reflected within the ammunition/rationalisation machine, i.e. the symbolic usage type. Since the institutional use does not involve information use within the management process, however, a more disaggregated categorisation appears more appropriate for the purpose of this study. A differentiation similar to the one applied in this study prevails in *Weiss* (1977), p. 15; *Hirst/Baxter* (1993), p. 192, footnote 5, or *Schäffer/Steiners* (2004), p. 388f.

[251] Cf. *Kostova/Roth* (2002), p. 217ff. *Hopper/Major* (2007), p. 66 and 88, present similar findings. They, however, label this tension as 'resistance and institutionalisation'. *Burns/Scapens* (2000); *Yazdifar et al.* (2008), p. 408ff., and *Soin et al.* (2002), p. 254ff., distinguish ceremonial adoption and instrumental adoption to describe similar patterns. All of these authors are linked to the definitions of 'decoupling' by *Meyer/Rowan* (1977), p. 356ff., and 'ceremonial conformity' by *Oliver* (1991), p. 164.

Table 2-5 summarises the different types of cost information use which were conceptually distinguished in this section. The types to be studied hereafter are marked in bold.

Having explicated these usage types from a conceptual perspective, the current state of knowledge on their presence in Anglophone and German companies can be provided at this point. Given a lack of according cost accounting research, such considerations must embrace research on the use of more general management accounting information.

Prior research on *Pelz's* and *Burchell et al.*'s types of information use in Germany indicates that cost information tends to be used for decision influencing (i.e. **symbolically**) as well as for decision facilitating (i.e. instrumentally or conceptually). Regarding the latter two types, it is used slightly more for direct decision-making (i.e. **instrumentally**) than for gaining experiences (i.e. **conceptually**).[252] Interestingly, these findings are somewhat contrastable to the use of unspecified management accounting information in German companies. In tendency, these appear to be used rather symbolically, followed by the conceptual usage type. Mere instrumental use tends to lack behind.[253] These results can be linked to the introduced traditions of cost accounting's application for decision facilitating in Germany, which does not appear to hold universally true for general management accounting. With respect to these usage types, little comparison can be drawn to cost information use of Anglophone companies due to a lack of direct comparisons as well as a lack of comparable similar studies from these countries.[254] Insights into Anglophone companies stem from a more general control and executive support system research. Despite differences among individual studies, on an aggregated basis, a dominance of symbolic use over conceptual and instrumental use can be identified for these geographical areas as well.[255] Since these studies neither conceptualise nor operationalise the types of use equivalently but similarly only, both the Anglophone results for the use of management control information and the findings from Germany in this regard, cannot be assessed conclusively with respect to the existence of a cross-national difference in the use of cost information. Rather, they represent tendencies only. Also, they may not hold universally for other pieces of information, such as costs. Section 3.3 regards the use of cost information more conclusively in the context of subsidiaries.

Despite one study which highlights that cost information is used interactively and diagnostically for new product developments in a sample of US and European companies,[256] no cost accounting study was identified to include *Simons'* typology. Nevertheless, *Simons'*

[252] Section 3.3.2.1 includes a more detailed review of this cost information specific research.

[253] Cf. *Schäffer/Steiners* (2004), p. 385f.; *Sandt* (2004), p. 160; *Schäffer/Steiners* (2005a), p. 216ff. Since *Bauer* (2002), p. 204ff and 237ff., does not report the individual scores for the types of use, his work is excluded at this point.

[254] *Schäffer/Steiners* (2005a), p. 216, argue that there is a lack of relevant research.

[255] Cf. *Simon et al.* (1954), p. 24; *Hirst/Baxter* (1993), p. 201ff.; *Vandenbosch/Huff* (1997), p. 90; *Vandenbosch* (1999), p. 87; *Diamantopoulos et al.* (2003), p. 26; *Henri* (2006a), p. 91; *Jais* (2007), p. 158f.

[256] Cf. *Davila* (2000), p. 396f. Note that the author measures the use of cost information on a scale ranging from diagnostic use to interactive use. However, he does not report whether cost information is used rather interactively or diagnostically. Yet, he reports that the level interactive use increases with the detail of cost information and the frequency, cost information is updated with (on p. 397 *Davilla* reports a large Chronbachs alpha for these three aspects).

considerations prevail in the more general management control literature.[257] One study of German managers' use of key performance indicators reports a dominance of the **interactive over the diagnostic** usage type.[258] Another study in a German context regards the use of budgets and finds these to be used rather diagnostically than interactively.[259] This latter finding reflects the results generally found in Anglophone countries. A Canadian research project and a US study find executives to use their information systems rather more diagnostically than interactively.[260] In line, *Jais*' study of the subsidiaries of a US MNC reports the diagnostic use to dominate the interactive use (as well as the instrumental/conceptual and symbolic use).[261] Interestingly, despite differing magnitudes, the study identifies this to hold true in German and US subsidiaries of a US financial investor. Though all these findings can be contrasted to the evidence from domestic German companies, this does not imply a home-country effect for *Simon*'s usage types. The above findings for Anglophone countries are in sharp contrast to another study identifying a more interactive use of executive support systems in US and Canadian companies.[262] Also, they do not correspond to UK case evidence indicating the simultaneous prevalence of both usage types[263] and Australian evidence on the dependence of these two types on the prevalence of current strategic change initiatives.[264] Because all these studies rather regard the use of different pieces of information, interpreting the results in favour of a home country effect with respect to diagnostic and interactive information use is to rigid. Unfortunately, further international studies provide little additional insights since these do rather focus upon the interactive use only,[265] summarised both types into one measure of use[266] or do not report results for Anglophone or German companies.[267] In essence, very little is known with respect to the prominence of the diagnostic and the interactive use of cost information in Anglophone and German firms.

The **ceremonial use** of information has not been extensively compared cross-nationally. Hence, no insights can be provided for this type of use with respect to cross-national differences. The empirical analysis by *Ansari/Euske* found the ceremonial use to dominate the symbolic and instrumental/conceptual use of cost information in a US public sector setting.[268] Also, there is some additional evidence for the ceremonial use of cost information

[257] For an introduction, cf. *Mundy* (2010), p. 504.

[258] Cf. *Sandt* (2004), p. 172ff.

[259] Cf. *Hofmann et al.* (2012), p. 175.

[260] Cf. *Henri* (2006b), p. 541, for the Canadian evidence and *Widener* (2007), p. 772, for the US evidence. Interestingly, *Henri* (2006a), p. 91, reports these two usage types to be more prevalent in his Canadian sample than usage types similar to the instrumental/conceptual ones (strategic decision making) and the rationalising one (legitimisation) distinguished in this study.

[261] Cf. *Jais* (2007), p. 158f.

[262] Cf. *Vandenbosch* (1999), p. 87.

[263] Cf. *Marginson* (2002), p. 1025.

[264] Cf. *Abernethy/Brownell* (1999), p. 198.

[265] Cf. *Bisbe/Otley* (2004), p. 709ff.; *Tuomela* (2005), p. 308ff.; *Bisbe/Malagueño* (2009), p. 371ff.; *Dossi/Patelli* (2010), p. 508; *Abernethy et al.* (2010), p. 5.

[266] Cf. *Bisbe/Malagueño* (2009), p. 23.

[267] Cf. *Naranjo-Gil/Hartmann* (2006), p. 31; *Schäffer et al.* (2010), p. 312.

[268] For this and the following, cf. section 3.2.2.2.

in both German and US companies. These empirical studies do not stress the ceremonial use of cost information to be a particularity of Anglophone or German firms, however. Rather they identify a significant dependence of this usage type on corporate directives that explicate the design of cost accounting system. Because according considerations are at the core of the literature review, these studies will be discussed more conclusively in section 3.

Above all, the empirical evidence reveals a difficulty to identify cross-national differences with respect to the six usage types included in this study. Hence, common whisper on cross-national differences with respect to the use of cost information[269] seems to be based on other conceptualisations of use and requires clarification. Because the inclusion of the usage types into this study is motivated by their ability to shed light on the response of subsidiaries to corporate directives on the design of cost accounting systems, however, this does not dilute the relevance of the above considerations for this study.

2.4 Performance of cost accounting systems

The practical relevance of this study is enlarged through its pragmatic research objective, i.e. the derivation of recommendations on how design a well performing cost accounting system. Thereby, pathways for improvements of the design of cost accounting systems and the use of cost information are disclosed. To accomplish this objective, it is necessary to evaluate the cost accounting systems of subsidiaries. Hence, despite merely introducing the design of cost accounting systems and the use of cost information, it is essential to provide fundamental insights how to appraise a cost accounting system.

In this study, corresponding assessments will be referred to as the *performance* of cost accounting systems.[270] Throughout this section and the literature review in section 3, however, the label '*success*' of cost accounting will be applied synonymously to acknowledge a notation which is often applied in cost accounting research.

> *"(T)he definition of the most desirable type of cost accounting system has yet to be established (...)"*[271]

Lee (2003) emphasises that a cost accounting system's performance is an unclear construct which merits **conceptual consideration**. To restrict the length of the following discussion,[272] the section will centre on the explication of commonly regarded conceptualisations. Thereby, it is ensured that the discussion is based on measures which are of the prima facie relevance and significantly supported in literature.[273] The study of *Foster/Swenson* (1997) is a particularly good starting point for the due introduction. The authors critically review how to assess the implementation of ABC. Yet, their compendium

[269] Cf. *Granlund/Lukka* (1998), p. 170 or *Shields* (1998), p. 507.

[270] Cf. *Moeschler* (2012), p. 170ff., for a similar application.

[271] *Lee* (2003), p. 49.

[272] For a detailed review of previous research on the measurement of the performance of management accounting/management accountants cf. e.g. *Sill* (2009), p. 38ff.; *Weber et al.* (2010b), p. 322ff.

[273] *Brown et al.* (2004), p. 335, recommend these criteria for the selection of research objects and their operationslisation.

of alternative performance measures also mirrors the performance measures applied in non-ABC specific international cost accounting research.

According to *Foster/Swenson*, there are four ways to evaluate a cost accounting system.[274] The researchers label these measures as the (1) use of cost information, (2) decision actions taken based on cost information, (3) dollar improvements resulting from cost information and (4) general management evaluation.

The **use of cost information** measure is based on the assumption that a cost accounting system is the more 'successful', the more extensive the provided cost information is used.[275] In accordance to the above introduction of the 'extent of use', such measures reflect the extensive use of a cost accounting system in general or with respect to particular cost accounting objectives. The measure is widely applied in international cost accounting research.[276] Yet, the criticism of the extent of use being rather similar to measures of system application (cf. section 2.3.1) dilutes measuring the performance of cost accounting as its use.

The measure '**taken decision actions**' generally determines changes or improvements of managerial decision-making which follow a modification of a cost accounting system (e.g. the implementation of ABC).[277] Such measures can be expressed financially and non-financially. They appear particularly applicable for studies of cost accounting change. In contrast to the former conceptualisation, the measure is applied rarely in cost accounting research.[278]

Despite not being clearly distinguishable from the latter conceptualisation of the previous measure, **monetary improvements** attributable to cost accounting are regularly found in international research. Since the determination of cost accountings' contribution to a company's financial 'success' cannot be isolated easily,[279] monetary improvements are approximated by management assessments or by stock returns.[280] The application of this measure is further impeded by suggestions that dollar improvements attributable to cost accounting (changes or decision actions taken) shall actually be contrasted with the implementation expenditures of such systems for the purpose of construct validity.[281]

---

274 For the following, cf. *Foster/Swenson* (1997), p. 110.

275 For this and the following, cf. *Foster/Swenson* (1997), p. 110.

276 Cf. *Khandwalla* (1972), p. 275ff.; *Swenson* (1995), p. 172ff.; *Foster/Swenson* (1997), p. 110; *Brewer* (1998), p. 252f.; *Krumwiede* (1998), p. 248; *Anderson/Young* (1999), p. 537; *Stoi* (1999), p. 191; *Pizzini* (2006), p. 192; *Schoute* (2009), p. 215; *Stratton et al.* (2009), p. 32ff.; *Pike et al.* (2011), p. 69ff.; *Moeschler* (2012), p. 173.

277 Cf. *Foster/Swenson* (1997), p. 110.

278 Cf. *Krump* (2003), p. 245ff.; *Innes/Mitchell* (1995), p. 146; *Friedman/Lyne* (1999), p. 8; *Pike et al.* (2011), p. 69.

279 Cf. *Schoute* (2009), p. 208.

280 Cf. *Kennedy/Affleck-Graves* (2001), p. 19; *Ittner et al.* (2002), p. 714f.; *Shields* (1995), p. 154; *Foster/Swenson* (1997), p. 110; *Karlshaus* (2000), p. 169ff.; *Hunold* (2003), p. 217ff.; *Frank* (2000), p. 227ff.; *Chenhall* (2004), p. 29; *Friedman/Lyne* (1999), p. 9; *Moeschler* (2012), p. 174.

281 Cf. *Lee* (2003), p. 40; *Dopuch* (1993), p. 615ff.; *Pike et al.* (2011), p. 69.

Management evaluations are most widely applied in international research.[282] Since some researchers merely ask for 'success ratings',[283] it is argued that these measures tend to be unspecified with respect to their 'success' definition.[284] Nevertheless, there are rather precise definitions such as the 'perceived accuracy',[285] the 'satisfaction with cost accounting system'[286] or assessment of a systems' decision usefulness.[287] Moreover, such evaluations are researched for the design of cost accounting systems in general as well as specific purposes or the implementation of a new costing system such as ABC. Remarkable, corresponding results, despite being considerably diverse, depend upon respondents' position in an organisation.[288] Thus, it is essential to distinguish preparers and users of cost information if considering a 'success' evaluation.

The provided information reveals a considerable diversity with respect to measuring a cost accounting system's performance. Hence, *Foster/Swenson* suggest to include scores consisting of multiple 'success' measures because these can increase the validity of a study.[289] In contrast, others prove that different success measures are rather intertwined. *Cagwin*, for example, finds the extent of use to influence changes in financial performance.[290] Similarly, authors link an overall satisfaction rating of a cost accounting system statistically to measures reflecting the extent of cost accounting system use.[291] Others apply the accuracy of cost accounting systems as an antecedent of an overall success rating.[292] Therefore, a multidimensional assessment as well as the aggregation of different measures into a single score is not necessarily superior due to potential interrelations.

---

282 Cf. *Howell et al.* (1987), p. 41ff.; *Innes/Mitchell* (1995), p. 144; *Shields* (1995), p. 153; *Swenson* (1995), p. 167; *Foster/Swenson* (1997), p. 110; *McGowan/Klammer* (1997), p. 217; *McGowan/Klammer* (1997), p. 230; *Krumwiede* (1998), p. 268; *Währisch* (1998), p. 198; *Anderson/Young* (1999), p. 537; *Aust* (1999), p. 155ff.; *Friedman/Lyne* (1999), p. 9f.; *Frank* (2000), p. 134ff.; *Innes et al.* (2000), p. 354ff.; *Karlshaus* (2000), p. 158ff.; *Cagwin/Bouwman* (2002), p. 19; *Cotton et al.* (2003), p. 70; *Hunold* (2003), p. 200ff and 217ff.; *Chenhall* (2004), p. 29f.; *Pierce/Brown* (2004), p. 44; *Pizzini* (2006), p. 205ff.; *Krumwiede/Suessmair* (2007a), p. 4; *Schoute* (2009), p. 211; *Moeschler* (2012), p. 173ff.

283 Cf. *Innes/Mitchell* (1995), p. 144; *Shields* (1995), p. 153; *Währisch* (1998), p. 198; *Innes et al.* (2000), p. 354ff.

284 Cf. *Foster/Swenson* (1997), p. 110.

285 Cf. *Pike et al.* (2011), p. 69; *Moeschler* (2012), p. 174.

286 Cf. *Howell et al.* (1987), p. 41ff.; *McGowan/Klammer* (1997), p. 230; *Schoute* (2009), p. 215; *Moeschler* (2012), p. 174.

287 Cf. *Pizzini* (2006), p. 192; *Moeschler* (2012), p. 173. Despite being rather implicit in their studies, these authors combine mere application based measures (use of cost information for particular objectives) with an assessment of the ability of the cost accounting system to fulfil these objectives.

288 Cf. *Malmi* (1997), p. 495ff.; *McGowan/Klammer* (1997), p. 234; *Bhimani* (2003), p. 539ff.; *Major/Hopper* (2005), p. 223; *Pierce/O'Dea* (2003), p. 258ff.; *Dietz/Snyder* (2011), p. 38, and *Walker et al.* (2012), p. 15ff., for the differing perceptions on the performance of management accounting by users and preparers of management accounting information.

289 Cf. *Foster/Swenson* (1997), p. 128ff.

290 Cf. *Cagwin/Bouwman* (2002), p. 24f.

291 Cf. *Foster/Swenson* (1997), p. 127ff.; *Innes et al.* (2000), p. 357; *Friedl et al.* (2009), p. 116; *Schoute* (2009), p. 218.

292 According to *Wang/Strong* (1996), p. 16, accuracy measures are reflecting information systems' quality. Such quality measures were researched as an antecedent of the management assessment of cost accounting systems' contribution to financial performance (cf. *Frank* (2000), p. 229).

The **international research** on the performance of cost accounting systems derives considerably diverse results. Whereas some researchers find positive performance effects of cost accounting, others reveal a negative effect of cost accounting on performance or even find insignificant effects. In the light of **comparative management accounting research**, there is one peculiarity which is essential to be stressed at this point. One measure of *Foster/Swenson*'s compendium prominently identifies cross-national differences in comparative cost accounting research on the performance of cost accounting systems in German and Anglophone companies. German cost accountants are rather more satisfied with their cost accounting systems if compared to their US counterparts.[293] Also, Anglophone accountants perceive their cost accounting to provide information that cannot be applied for the intended purposes.[294] Looking at these two measures can potentially extract whether Anglophone firms in Germany perceive issues with respect to the information usefulness and the satisfying performance of their cost accounting systems. As such, management evaluation on the satisfaction with cost accounting and a cost accounting system's ability to fulfil its objectives appear most appealing for this study.

293 Cf. e.g. *Krumwiede/Suessmair* (2007a), p. 4.

294 Cf. e.g. *Howell et al.* (1987), p. 41; *Sharman* (2003b), p. 44, or *Clinton/Webber* (2004), p. 22, for summaries on respective US-evidence. *Yazdifar/Askarany* (2010a), p. 4, provides alike evidence from the UK, Australia and New Zealand.

3 Review of prior research

3.1 Introduction

A multinational's corporate cost accounting system is generally formed by the accounts of their subsidiaries.[295] Nevertheless, subsidiaries have rarely been chosen as a research object in cost accounting studies. Essentially, this lack of research can be traced back to the separation of functional and organisational aspects of management accounting research,[296] or more generally the split-up of business disciplines concerning organisational behaviour and management accounting.[297] Hence, despite this study's focus on subsidiaries, this section reviews research on cost accounting in both legal and economic organisational sub-units. In order to avoid misconceptions about such organisational structures, they are briefly introduced at this point.

Legal structures describe the different legal entities in a multinational and their interrelations with respect to share property, control agreements or profit transfer agreements.[298] In research, legal structures facilitate the identification of research objects. Yet, these provide little information with respect to managerial authority or reporting obligations in MNCs.[299] These authorities, however, also affect the design of management and cost accounting systems in multinationals.[300] Thus, various studies in international cost accounting research are focussed on **economic structures**. Typically, these studies look at business units, i.e. divisions of a MNC which are responsible for all value chain activities with respect to different products, regions or customers.[301] In addition, there is some research on functionally specialised units of MNC such as different production sites.[302] In functionally specialised companies, top-level departments reflect different value chain activities, such as procurement, production, sales or administration. Both legal and economic structures are potentially affecting the cost accounting systems in subsidiaries. They are conjointly referred to as **affiliates** hereafter.[303]

The relevant studies on cost accounting in affiliates were identified through a profound **snowballing-based literature review**. This selection approach was applied since there is

---

[295] Cf. *Währisch* (1998), p. 55, who had difficulties in analysing his survey with respect to subsidiaries due to data quality.

[296] Cf. *Aust* (1999), p. 40.

[297] Cf. *Littkemann/Derfuß* (2004), p. 693.

[298] Cf. *Holtbrügge/Welge* (2010), p. 228; *Kutschker/Schmid* (2011), p. 595ff.

[299] Cf. *Holtbrügge/Welge* (2010), p. 228.

[300] Cf. *Weber/Schäffer* (2011), p. 454ff.; *Holtbrügge/Welge* (2010), p. 410ff., or section 3.2.

[301] Cf. *Scherm/Süß* (2001), p. 165ff.; *Kreikebaum* (2002), p. 118ff.; *Schreyögg* (2008), p. 106ff.; *Kieser/Walgenbach* (2010), p. 87ff.; *Kutschker/Schmid* (2011), p. 494; *Perlitz* (2013), p. 374f.

[302] For this and the following, cf. *Scherm/Süß* (2001), p. 165ff.; *Kreikebaum* (2002), p. 118ff.; *Schreyögg* (2008), p. 106ff.; *Kieser/Walgenbach* (2010), p. 87ff.; *Kutschker/Schmid* (2011), p. 494; *Perlitz* (2013), p. 374f.

[303] For the purpose of this review, subsidiaries, joint ventures (cf. e.g *Perlitz* (2013), p. 405ff. for a definition) and economic organistational sub-units are labeled 'affiliates'. Thereby, an economic rather than a legal definition of affiliation is applied (cf. *Littkemann* (2001), p. 1287).

no established strand of literature on the particular issue of cost accounting in affiliates, which would have legitimated a more sophisticated study selection.[304]

As briefly introduced in section 2, cost accounting research can be grouped according to its **level of analysis**. Accordingly, there are studies analysing a macro, mezzo or micro level of cost accounting systems.[305] Macro level studies focus on the general adoption (rate) of cost accounting systems such as ABC or GPK. Mezzo level research is concerned with the conceptual design of cost accounting systems. As such, it focusses on, e.g. the number of cost drivers or the number of cost centres. Macro and mezzo level research on cost accounting in organisational sub-units can be found in section 3.2. Micro level research explores the use of cost information. Associated research projects are discussed in section 3.3.

A difficulty inherent to the differentiation of these levels of analysis is the classification of cost accounting objectives and the performance of cost accounting.[306] As stressed in section 1.2.2, the use of cost accounting systems, i.e. micro level analysis, regularly involves cost accounting's objectives. However, as **objectives** per se do not involve actual use, they appear assignable to the mezzo level, too.[307] Similarly, the performance of cost accounting systems proved intertwined with the use of cost information in section 2.4 but might also involve mere evaluations of a system's design. Since cost accounting objectives are argued to be rather similar for different organisational levels,[308] they are not reviewed at this point. Several studies on the macro, mezzo and micro level of cost accounting, on the other hand, also comprise considerations of the **performance** of cost accounting in affiliates. As such, these studies are not reviewed independently but will be considered throughout the analyses in the section on the design of cost accounting systems and the use of cost information.

The following review will be subdivided according to studies' scientific strategies (cf. section 1.3). Since no formal-analytical research project on the issue of cost accounting in affiliates could be identified, this research strategy cannot be found hereafter.

3.2 Design of cost accounting systems in affiliates

3.2.1 Normative conceptual research

Normative or conceptual considerations on the design of cost accounting systems in affiliates are rare in international management accounting research. Essentially, two contradicting strand of research exist in this respect. Whereas the first one emphasises the necessity for ethnocentric cost accounting systems in multinationals, the second reveals the relevance of local adaptiveness.

---

[304] Cf. *Lamnek* (2010), p. 175, for this reasoning.

[305] Cf. *Granlund/Lukka* (1998), p. 153f., for the macro and micro level perspective. The mezzo level is introduced by *Kajüter/Moeschler* (2010), p. 4, and *Moeschler* (2012), p. 24f.

[306] Cf. *Granlund/Lukka* (1998), p. 153, for a similar expression.

[307] Cf. *Kajüter/Moeschler* (2010), p. 4, and *Moeschler* (2012), p. 24f.

[308] Cf. *Kirsch* (1998), p. 210, or *Franz* (2003), p. 9.

The authors from the first strand consider the necessity for **cost accounting in groups** (*Konzernkostenrechnung*).[309] Describing this stream of research in detail would not contribute to this study's objectives because these publications centre on the calculatory particularities of cost accounting consolidation.[310] Thus, only subsidiary and **uniformity**[311] related aspects are discussed in the following.

Three general alternatives for the design of cost accounting systems in groups are identified in the discussion.[312] First, cost accounting systems can be unified throughout a group. Second, cost accounting systems can be specific for each affiliated company. These non-unified systems have then to be consolidated by offsetting and reconciliations. Finally, groups can have affiliate-specific cost accounting systems and simultaneously another cost accounting system in the parent company.

From a parent company's point of view, the ease of applicability and low complexity of the first alternative is stressed.[313] Recognising the necessity to regard cost accounting systems in multinationals from both the parent company's and the affiliates' perspectives, the second alternative encompasses a potentially higher level of local managers' acceptance for the local cost accounting system. From a parent company's point of view, the increased complexity and inability to consolidate information stand out. The third alternative is recommended as an intermediate possibility only (e.g. after merger and acquisition transactions) due to its high complexity. From a parent company's or group's point of view,[314] the favourability of the first alternative is emphasised in the literature on *Konzernkostenrechnung*.[315] This recommendation is surprisingly simple. It does not reflect the variety of factors which are also argued to be relevant for the choice of a group's cost accounting system. On the one hand, it is revealed that such a choice must account for the cost information needs on the corporate and the subsidiary level.[316] On the other hand, the authors also highlight the necessity to consider different production processes, a subsidiary's

---

[309] Cf. *Kajüter* (2003), p. 18ff., for a comprehensive list of associated authors and their main contributions and *Wolfsgruber* (2011), p. 32ff., for a respectively updated list.

[310] Cf. *Kajüter* (2003), p. 21f.

[311] This terminology is applied to reflect whether equivalent cost accounting systems are present in all legal entities of a MNCs (cf. *Ziener* (1985), p. 136). The terminology 'standardisation' is neglected since it embraces the consideration whether to adjust corporate management control systems to the peculiarities of subsidiaries such as varying economic conditions (cf. *Ziener* (1985), p. 136f.; *Hoffjan/Weide* (2006), p. 391; *Hoffjan/Weber* (2007), p. 27f, 38; *Hoffjan* (2009), p. 267ff.; *Modell* (2002), p. 659). Thus, it is linked to a focus on parent companies which does not characterise this study.

[312] For this and the following, cf. *Währisch* (2003), p. 77. Similarly, though only focusing on cost types and centres, *Amshoff* (2003), p. 250ff., distinguished the former two possibilities. Additionally he proposes a compromising possibility which consists of the application of parent companies' cost types for core types but allows for diverging types as well. In line with Währisch and Amshoff, Steinbichler also expresses the necessity for unified cost accounting systems, particularly with respect to cost type accounting as this allows for a conglomerate wide consolidation of cost figures (cf. *Steinbichler* (1990), p. 146).

[313] For this and the following, cf. *Währisch* (2003), p. 77ff.

[314] Cf. *Währisch* (2003), p. 79.

[315] Cf. *Franz/Hieronimus* (2003), p. 6ff., for an introduction of the special research group, which established according considerations in Germany.

[316] Cf. *Pfaff* (2003), p. 36.

strategic role or internal interdependencies in a group to be relevant for a subsidiary's cost accounting system.[317] By the negligence of these aspects, this normative strand of research explicitly accepts that the cost accounting systems in groups are not equally useful for all group companies.[318]

With respect to the three components of a cost accounting system, uniformity among cost type accounting and rules for the allocation of indirect costs are regarded as particularly import because they affect the consolidation of cost accounting systems.[319] As such, above authors implicitly assume that uniformity should be achieved with respect to the parent company's national tradition,[320] though global differences in cost accounting systems are explicitly recognised.[321] Thereby, the normative considerations of *Konzernkostenrechnung* neglect conceptual and empirical differences in, for example, Anglophone and German cost accounting systems. The implicit suggestion that parent companies should diffuse their local costing systems does not reflect the complexity of the issue whether or not cost accounting in subsidiaries can be unified and which national cost accounting traditions would be most appealing for the cost accounting system(s) in international groups. Though this stream of research strives for a pragmatic research objective by attempting to explicate how cost accounting systems in groups should be designed (mezzo level), it yet remains inconclusive. The affiliates' point of view is disregarded vastly.

In contrast to the first strand, other normative studies find the design of cost accounting systems to depend on other **organisational and environmental variables** than a parent company's influence only.[322] By revealing the importance of a company's context for the design of its cost accounting system, these conceptual studies considerably contribute to an understanding of cost accounting in affiliates. The studies centre on influential factors stemming from within a company rather than, e.g. a company's parent. These *internal* factors dominantly include the organisational processes and products, which cost accounting is picturing, as well as factors reflecting the information usefulness of costs and more general factors on organisational structures (e.g. the size of a company). Also, two authors indicate an impact of corporate guidelines and one stresses the importance of external macroeconomic conditions for the design of companies' cost accounting systems.

---

317 Cf. e.g. *Küting/Dusemond* (1994), p. 247; *Wullenkord* (1995), p. 250f. or *Dusemond* (2000), p. 59.

318 Remarkably, it is explicitly recognised that a unified cost accounting system may require some subsidiaries to adopt a more complex system than necessary while others cannot fully picture their specifics by the system (cf. *Dusemond* (2000), p. 59).

319 Cf. *Müller* (2001), p. 10f. or *Pfaff* (2003), p. 36. Similarly, *Dent* (1996), p. 258f., stress that a database which allows for multi-dimensional analysis to regard a MNC by market region or function may be a powerful tool to takle the challenges of MNCs with respect to cost accounting. As such, he implicitly stresses the importance for a unified cost accounting, which may serve the diverse needs of parent and affiliate companies.

320 Cf. *Küting/Dusemond* (1994), p. 245ff.; *Wullenkord* (1995), p. 237ff.; *Kajüter* (2003); *Währisch* (2003), p. 77.

321 Cf. *Währisch* (2003), p. 72ff.

322 Cf. *Cooper* (1990), p. 2271ff.; *Brink* (1992), p. 172ff., or *Krieger* (1995), p. 119ff. Similarly, *Merchant/Shields* (1993), p. 77ff., and *Weber* (2005), p. 9ff., highlight a number of potential influencing factors. These authors, however, base their discussion at least partly on previous empirical investigations or anecdotal evidence.

All these authors regard cost accounting on a mezzo level of analysis. They essentially reveal that cost accounting in subsidiaries must be regarded in the light of both contextual factors and a parent company's influence. Thereby, they implicitly suggest that a unified cost accounting system would only be beneficial for a MNC if the organisational context (e.g. production technology, products, competitive strategy) is similar in the whole MNC. Though the studies centre on the revelation of variables which are potentially relevant for the design of affiliates' cost accounting systems, they do not provide a theoretical explanation for the relevance of these variables. Hence, these studies remain descriptive in nature. They do not contribute to a theoretical explanation of cost accounting in subsidiaries.

The normative publications reviewed in this section[323] yield two **contradicting results**. On the one hand, uniformity with respect to parent companies' cost accounting traditions is suggested for cost accounting systems in subsidiaries. On the other hand, it is suggested that these latter systems must reflect their organisational context. This suggests that uniformity is inappropriate in some situations. Since none of the studies reveals a theoretical viewpoint to explain their suggestions, these twofold results can neither be explained nor can they be linked to one another.

Mirroring the two strands of normative research, *Kellermanns/Islam* (2004) describe thoroughly how MNCs should handle alternative national cost accounting traditions. The authors expect that German management accountants favour German cost accounting systems (German ABC[324]), while their American colleagues favour American systems (American ABC) due to differing perceptions on the 'ease of use' of these systems.[325] At the same time, the authors suggest that in the context of MNCs, such preferences cannot come into play due to mandatory effects of a parent company on its subsidiary. A US firm, for example, may prohibit a German affiliate to apply German ABC. Surprisingly, the authors emphasise that the application of the US system is to be favoured in all companies operating in both the USA and Germany. Whereas for US companies, this argument builds on the ease of use of the system, for German companies it is derived from avoided resistance of US employees. Thereby, *Kellermanns/Islam* ultimately reflect the German debate on *Konzernkostenrechnung* for the US-firms. Both uniformity and the diffusion of home-country constructs are underlined. Yet, for German companies they deviate from according suggestions because the American system is recommended for conflict minimisation. As such, *Kellermanns/Islam*'s macro level recommendation essentially re-

[323] It is not claimed that the list of the reviewed studies is exhaustive.

[324] During the emergence of ABC in the late 1980s, a related refinement, known as *Prozesskostenrechnung* emerged in German research. (cf. *Horváth/Mayer* (1989), p. 215ff., and *Horváth* (1993), p. 15ff., for English references cf. *Gaiser* (1997), p. 38ff., or *Kellermanns/Islam* (2004), p. 33ff.). In contrast to the Anglophone ABC, which was concerned with a refinement of cost accounting in both manufacturing and non-manufacturing departments, the German development particularly focussed on non-manufacturing areas (cf. *Horváth/Mayer* (1995), p. 59f.). A detailed discussion on the communalities and differences between the German and Anglophone approaches is disregarded at this point due to convincing publications on this matter (Cf. *Horváth/Mayer* (1995), p. 59ff.; *Gaiser* (1998), p. 65ff., or *Kellermanns/Islam* (2004), p. 33ff.).

[325] For this and the following, cf. *Kellermanns/Islam* (2004), p. 43f.

flects the diverse picture derived above and thereby underlines the need for further research on this issue.

3.2.2 Empirical research

3.2.2.1 Introduction

To enable the analysis of the broadened focus on affiliates, the literature review will be sub-dividend in accordance with the results of the reviewed literature. These results reflect the diverse picture highlighted in section 3.2.1. On the one hand, there is research including evidence that cost accounting in affiliates is influenced heavily by a corporate levels' involvement (i.e. **ethno- or geocentric cost accounting systems**). For simplicity reasons, these studies will also be labelled as evidence on the uniformity of cost accounting systems in affiliates. They are analysed in section 3.2.2.2. On the other hand, there are research projects which find affiliates to oppose corporate cost accounting initiatives or which disregard organisational hierarchies during the analysis of cost accounting in affiliates (i.e. **regio- or polycentrism**). According publications can be found in section 3.2.2.3. They will be referred to synonymously as evidence on the non-uniformity of cost accounting systems in affiliates. To avoid redundancy, research projects that provide evidence for both perspectives (uniformity and non-uniformity) are reviewed separately in section 3.2.2.4. These studies are labelled as 'mixed evidence' studies.

The review will centre on four particular topics. With respect to the content of the studies, the review explicates (1) whether cost accounting in organisational sub-units reflects the parent company's traditions. Thereby, (2) it will be explored whether previous empirical research considered the national particularities of cost accounting in the light of organisational sub-units. In addition, (3) the review explores the empirical consideration of the contextual factors summarised by the studies from section 3.2.1. From a methodological perspective, the review shall assess (4) the theoretical positions and research strategies applied by previous researchers.[326]

3.2.2.2 Research on ethno- and geocentric cost accounting systems

Brewer (1998) provides case study evidence on the implementation of ABC in a Malaysian and three domestic subsidiaries of a US manufacturing company. Since the implementation of this Anglophone informed cost accounting tradition is reported to be headquarter-initiated, *Brewer*'s findings can be interpreted as evidence for ethnocentric overhead cost allocation in the researched company. This interpretation, however, must be emphasised to hold for the macro level only. Through a micro-level reflecting analysis, *Brewer* reveals that the site-accountants in Malaysia derive more data from their ABC system and use the system more extensively for decision-making than the site-accountants in the US. Intertwined, he finds the performance enhancing capabilities of ABC to be assessed higher in Malaysia than in the US. Despite these differences in the use of ABC, *Brewer* does not provide evidence on dissimilarities in the systems' designs but actually stresses the compa-

---

[326] For survey studies, evidence on the response rate (subsequently RR) is provided.

rability of the ABC implementation process for all subsidiaries (e.g. centralised project team or comparable levels of training). Hence, *Brewer*'s well-structured, coding-using descriptive[327] case study is interpreted to be rather suggestive for a uniform design of cost accounting in the regarded multinational.[328] Brewer aligns his findings conceptually with differences in the Malaysian and the US-American culture. He contributes to this research by providing early evidence on the ethnocentric design of cost accounting systems in affiliates of Anglophone multinationals.

Smith (2005) provides anecdotal evidence for an ethnocentric cost accounting system at the German chain saw manufacturer STIHL. Accordingly, the company forced its US manufacturing and distribution affiliate into the application of GPK. The associated German cost accounting traditions, it is argued, are applied in the parent company and the domestic German subsidiaries as well. In line with *Brewer*, *Smith* highlights that a profound implementation process and the applied information technology (namely SAP) facilitated a successful implementation. Regardless corporate objectives, the authors find local managers' satisfaction with the imposed system. They link this finding to the imposed GPK system's applicability for decision-making in the US subsidiary. Despite being purely anecdotal and regardless the absence of theoretical considerations, *Smith*'s descriptive macro level study reemphasises a tendency for ethnocentrism in German multinationals.[329]

Similar to *Smith*, *Kemper/Rau* (2007)[330] report that the German manufacturing multinational *Phoenix Contact* unified its cost type accounting and overhead allocation procedures in one Chinese subsidiary. Narratively, the protagonists involved in the unification process report that the company implemented their German cost accounting traditions in the Chinese subsidiary (e.g. imputed interest and depreciation or detailed allocation of overhead costs). *Kemper/Rau* identify an intended comparability of cost data as the driving force for this ethnocentrism. From their experience, the authors identify cultural differ-

---

[327] *Brewer* chooses the subsidiaries' national culture (measured by *Hofstede*'s taxonomy) to explain differences in the systems' application. Though expressing that usally regarded contingencies such as the environment, technology or organisational factors are similar in all four regarded sites and, as such cannot underly the identified differences, the author does not provide a profound theoretical derivation why culture can serve as an explanatory variable for differences in the use of ABC. Also, the analysis remains rather inconlusive because the Malaysian ABC team is experienced in cross-functional work, an element identified to be relevant for ABC use and success (cf. e.g. *Anderson/Young* (1999), p. 528). Hence, *Brewer*'s study is assessed as being rather descriptive, especially with respect to the macro level uniformity.

[328] Similarly, *Pike et al.* (2011), p. 65ff., reports the implementation of ABC in three business units of a South East Asian telecommunication company. The authors find 16 ABC systems which were implemented in the business units under the impact of a corporate management group. As such, their findings are suggestive of uniform cost accounting systems in the researched company. Since the design of the systems is not explicitly highlighted in this study on the use and performance of cost accounting systems, however, *Pike et al.* is not explicitly reviewed.

[329] Similar anecdotal evidence prevails for the German car manufacturer Porsche (cf. *Lochner et al.* (2007), p. 145ff.), the German telecomunication company Telekom (cf. *Knoop et al.* (2006), p. 150ff.) and the German consumer goods producer Beiersdorf (cf. *Balke/Eberenz* (2006), p. 105ff.).

[330] Cf. *Hoffjan/Weber* (2007), p. 41–49, for their report.

ences, language problems, external reporting requirements, legal requirements and expertise as important factors if striving for the unification of cost accounting systems. Moreover, information technology is emphasised to enable a uniform design of cost accounting systems. Also, the presence of employees sent from the parent company to the Chinese affiliate (i.e. expatriates) is highlighted as a facilitating explanans for the unification. The authors' descriptive mezzo level anecdotal evidence cannot be statistically generalised due to the single case character. Because the findings underline *Smith's* evidence, however, they are to be acknowledged at this point.

In line with the former two, *Wolfsgruber* (2011) provides evidence on the macro-level uniformity of cost accounting systems in internationally operating Austrian groups. The author yields 28 analysable questionnaires from a cross-sectional survey. She finds a unified cost accounting system in 11 companies of her sample. Similarly, 11 companies report to have non-unified cost accounting systems. Of the latter, eight companies plan uniforming actions, while only three deny such plans. No dissimilarities in this respect are found for the three components of a cost accounting system. The study is based on contingency theory. Yet, only few differentiating or control variables (e.g. size or internationality) are regarded to explicate the reported level of uniformity. Unification is reported to be (planned to be) achieved through group standards as well as software integration. Remarkably, the holding structure of the groups does not affect whether or not cost accounting systems are unified. With respect to potential national particularities of the unified systems, there is no explicit evidence in *Wolfsgruber's* work. But, she reports that several companies have a SAP system. Since the management accounting module of SAP incorporates the design of German cost accounting,[331] this indicates that the cost accounting systems in some of the researched companies is actually ethnocentric.[332] Overall, *Wolfsgruber*'s descriptive study[333] indicates unified cost accounting systems in subsidiaries of Austrian multinational companies. Due to the few responses and the relatively simple statistics, however, her work remains far from being conclusive.[334]

Table 3-1 summarises the above reviewed studies.

---

[331] Cf. *White* (2004), p. 6; *Vikas* (2006), p. 36; *Kilger et al.* (2012), footnote 137 in chapter 1, and p. 389.

[332] Because management accounting research in German language does not emphasise differences in cost accounting of Austrian and German companies, above finding is interpreted as ethnocentrism.

[333] Even though contingency studies usually strive for an explanation of their findings by highlighting the statistical relevance of contextual variables, this approach is classified as descriptive rather than as theoretical. This is because contingency theory in general is criticised for its lack of theory and (thus) the unlimited number of potential contingencies (cf. e.g. *Picot* (1991), p. 157; *Homburg* (1998), p. 67; *Bhimani* (1999), p. 416; *Granlund* (2001), p. 145; *Modell* (2001); *Bhimani* (2004), p. 581 or *Major/Hopper* (2005), p. 225, and section 4.1.2). Accordingly, contingency theory is also known as the contingency approach (cf. *Kieser* (2006), p. 215).

[334] In a broadly documented research report of a sample of "almost 200" multinational firms operating in a German context, *Heimel et al.* (2012), p. 58ff., report similar evidence. The companies want to unify their cost type accounting and overhead allocation procedures. 74 % have already achieved an intended level of uniformity on the cost type level. The authors stress that commercial managers rather wish to simplify their cost accounting systems. Because of the unspecified character of their work, *Heimel et al.* (2012) shall not be reviewed explicitly in this study.

Author/s	Contribution to the study	Countries	Theoretical basis	Level of analysis	Research method	Sample size
Brewer (1998)	Example of 4 subsidiaries of an US MNC with uniform ABC systems. The systems are used and perceived differently successful in the 4 companies, however.	USA/Malaysia	Cultural contingency theory (implicit)	Descriptive/ theoretical, esp. macro	On-site survey/ interviews/ observation	1 MNC, 4 subsidiaries
Smith (2005)	Example of a U.S subsidiary of a German MNC which is urged to implement German cost accounting traditions (GPK). By being able to apply GPK for decision-making in the subsidiary, this ethnocentric unification is successful.	Germany/ USA	None made explicit	Descriptive macro	Anecdotal evidence	1 MNC, 1 subsidiary
Kemper/Rau (2007)	Example of a Chinese subsidiary, whose cost type and cost centre accounting is unified with respect to its German parents' cost accounting traditions.	Germany/ China	Cultural contingency theory (implicit)	Descriptive/ theoretical mezzo	Anecdotal evidence	1 MNC, 1 subsidiary
Wolfsgruber (2011)	Cost accounting in subsidiaries of Austrian MNCs is rather unified. Moreover, unification appears to be characterised by ethnocentric structures.	Austria	Contingency theory	Descriptive/ theoretical macro	Survey/ questionnaire	28 MNC [RR: 25.7 %]

Table 3-1: Studies on the ethnocentrism of cost accounting in multinationals

Apart from these studies that allow for an assessment of the national cost accounting traditions being reflected in a unified cost accounting system two additional cost accounting studies are regarded hereafter. Both identify the importance of a parent company's involvement for the design of subsidiaries' cost accounting systems. Yet, they disregard the nationality of the parent companies.

As *Brewer*, *Clarke et al.* (1999) study the adoption of ABC on a macro level. Based on a survey of 204 Irish manufacturing firms, they find Irish subsidiaries of MNCs to be using ABC more often than domestic Irish companies. Their rather descriptive evidence, however, does not provide any theoretical or empirical explanations for these uniformity-suggestive findings. Narratively, the observations are associated with parent companies' involvement, the transfer of employees (e.g. expatriates) or knowledge transfers between subsidiaries. *Clarke et al.* do not distinguish the home countries of regarded foreign affiliates. Hence, no insights into the diffusion of home country cost accounting systems can be derived. Their contribution for this project is the result that the importance of parent companies for subsidiaries' cost accounting systems can be shown in statistical terms. The identification of differences among cost accounting systems of foreign and domestic companies in Ireland merits future verification for a German setting.[335]

Similar to *Clarke et al.*, *Malmi* (1999) investigates the adoption of ABC in 104 domestic Finnish and foreign-owned business units from four Finish manufacturing industries. Single business units are researched because large companies are assumed explicitly to have

[335] Similar results are provided by *Pierce/Brown* (2004), p. 41. The authors also report ABC in domestic and foreign companies in Ireland to be applied to an (insignificantly) different extent. Other than Clarke et al., however, they find ABC to be less often implemented in subsidiaries of foreign MNC in Ireland than in domestic Irish companies. An equally scarce description of the foreign companies origin disables a conclusive attribution of these apparent differences to alternative home countries of foreign companies in *Clarke et al.*'s and *Pierce/Brown*'s work.

several cost accounting systems. The results show that 18 % of the sample firms were forced into the application of ABC by their parent companies and another 9 % implement ABC after a previous positive experience in a sister affiliate. Despite not being the primary motives for ABC adoption, these results reveal a certain level of uniformity with respect to overhead allocation in these organisational units.[336] Because *Malmi* does not specify the home countries of the ABC adopting units, his results cannot be interpreted with respect to national cost accounting particularities. Despite the imprecise results, *Malmi*'s macro-level study is included at this point because it relies on neo-institutional sociology (subsequently NIS)[337] as a theoretical basis.[338] Hence, other than the previously reviewed studies, *Malmi*'s work is characterised by a theoretical research objective. From the applied perspective, *Malmi* stresses above findings to reflect coercive isomorphic pressures of headquarters and mimetic pressures stemming from other unit's experience. As such, *Malmi*'s work introduces a theoretical viewpoint into this study which may facilitate a later theoretical explanation of cost accounting in subsidiaries. From a descriptive perspective, of course, *Malmi*'s findings remain rather inconclusive and to some extent contradicting.

These additional studies on the importance of a parent company's involvement for the design of subsidiaries' cost accounting systems are summarised in Table 3-2. Besides these studies which explicitly regard cost accounting systems, the literature on management control systems in multinationals provides further evidence for uniform cost accounting systems in MNCs as well as their ethnocentric character.

Author/s	Contribution to the study	Countries	Theoretical basis	Level of analysis	Research method	Sample size
Clarke et al. (1999)	ABC adoption in foreign and domestic companies in Ireland deviates. Thus, cost accounting in foreign subsidiaries must be seen to be substantially influenced by parent companies.	Ireland	None made explicit	Descriptive, macro	Survey/ questionnaire and interviews	208 manufacturing firms, thereof 73 % subsidiaries [RR: 41 %]
Malmi (1999)	Parent company influences and sister affiliates' experiences are among the motives for ABC adoption. NIS is a potential theoretical pathway to explain cost accounting in subsidiaries.	Finland	NIS	Theoretical macro	Survey/ questionnaire and interviews	592 subsidiaries /business units [RR: 40 %]

Table 3-2: Studies on the unifying effect of corporate involvements in affiliates' cost accounting systems

Firth (1996) studies which influences Western companies have on the management accounting practices (incl. cost accounting) in their Chinese joint ventures. Also, he regards their effect on the management accounting function of their Chinese venture partners. His findings are based on a questionnaire sent to joint ventures, the Western and the Chinese venture partners as well as a Chinese control group. He obtains 361 matched

---

336 These findings are rather in contrast to *Malmi*'s intention to study business units for the purpose of potentially non-uniform cost accounting systems.

337 Cf. section 4.1.2.

338 The applied framework of *Abrahamson* (1991) is based on NIS; which shall thus be included here.

triads[339] and results from 348 control companies. Based on a diffusion index, *Firth* summarises the diffusion of the Western partner's management accounting system into the Chinese joint venture (and the Chinese partner). Through regression analysis, *Firth* highlights that US partners affect their joint ventures' management accounting systems to the strongest extent, followed by European and Japanese companies.[340] *Firth* does not provide disaggregated results for the diffusion of the cost accounting systems. Nevertheless, the relative frequencies reported with respect to, for example, absorption costing, multiple overhead cost pools and multiple allocation bases indicate their diffusion by the Western venture partners. *Firth's* results do not reveal whether they rather indicate ethno- or geocentrism. Nevertheless, his descriptive[341] study is included in this review because it is the only mezzo level study that provides generalisable evidence for a certain *home-country* effect for MNCs' cost accounting.

Noack (2000) describes the management accounting function in a German manufacturing MNC. His report of the responsibilities on the parent company and the subsidiary level reflects the previous evidence for German multinationals. *Noack* highlights that indirect costs of all subsidiaries are managed by the parent company. Combined with a centrally administrated pool of locally collected (cost) information and the existence of a common chart of accounts, this hints at a unified cost type accounting. In addition, *Noack* stresses minimum company-wide standards for cost centre and cost object accounting and highlights cost allocation and tracing to be rather unified in his case company. In addition, *Noack* points out that subsidiaries are expected to establish cause-and-effect (causality) relationships for cost allocation purposes. Because such relationships are a particularity of German cost accounting,[342] *Noack* hints at ethnocentric cost accounting systems in the researched company. His mezzo level anecdotal evidence is included at this point because it provides an example of a uniform cost object accounting. None of the previously reviewed studies reports evidence of the uniformity of this component of a cost accounting system. Since the field report remains descriptive, it cannot add to the understanding of explanatory alternatives for cost accounting in subsidiaries, however.

Groot/Merchant (2000) implicitly uncover the relevance of cross-national differences in cost accounting for the design of cost accounting systems through their analysis of three joint ventures. In a joint venture between a Swedish company, the Netherlands and a Japanese company, the authors find overhead allocation procedures to be under continuous discussion between the venture partners from Sweden and Japan.[343] Because cost accounting traditions in Scandinavian countries as well as the Netherlands are similar to the Ger-

[339] 40 of which have an international venture partner from Europe, 179 from Hong-Kong, 49 from Japan and 66 form the USA. Besides, 27 other countries are included.

[340] *Firth* expresses his finding for the Chinese venture partner. An index which indicates differences between the Chinese partner's and the joint venture's management accounting elements, however, is indicative for an influence on the joint venture's management accounting system as well.

[341] Despite his focus on *explications* of the diffusion index, the implicit focus on contingencies serves as a differentiation of the results rather than as a theoretical explanation of the occurred diffusion.

[342] Cf. section 2.2.3.

[343] The Dutch partner is a state-owned entity only.

man ones[344] and since the Japanese venture partner only recently joined the venture, a German-like costing system in the joint venture is very plausible. German cost accounting, however, deviates considerably from Japanese cost accounting traditions.[345] Since the Japanese venture partner tried to compare product costs continuously to the ones in Japan and strived for an application of Japanese costing traditions, the disputed overhead allocation can be linked to the venture partners' differing national understandings about how to allocate costs. *Groot et al.* report similar conflicts regarding the cost accounting system in a joint venture of a Dutch and a Japanese partner. This finding supports the above interpretation. Different cost accounting traditions may lead to conflicts on how to design cost accounting in joint ventures. For the third joint venture, the authors do not highlight any such conflicts. Both partners are US companies[346], who are likely to share a common cost accounting tradition. Hence, the absent conflicts also support the above interpretation. These insights are very light shedding for this study. On the one hand, it appears plausible to interpret *Groot/Merchants* research as evidence that Dutch, Japanese, Scandinavian and US multinationals favour ethnocentric cost accounting systems. On the other hand, the study reveals that a striving for ethnocentrism in affiliates can lead to conflicts if the involved parties do not share a common understanding of cost accounting. This is very likely to be the case in Anglophone firms in Germany. Nevertheless, because the mezzo level findings in *Groot/Merchant's* case study have to be interpreted considerably, the above insights remain indicative only.

By looking at acquired firms' (management) accounting systems, *Busco et al.* (2006)[347] report the consequences of being taken-over by General Electric (hereafter GE) and Nestlé respectively. The authors report that GE aligns accounting systems, including the cost accounting[348] of newly acquired companies with its 'GE Way' of management. Describing the example of an acquired Italian company, the authors complement previous examples about Anglophone firms' tendency to unify their cost accounting systems. Other than above, the study explicates that the 'GE Way' is comprised of worldwide best practice solutions rather than Anglophone traditions only. Thereby, *Busco et al.'s* work expands this chapter's evidence on a dominance of ethnocentric characteristics at the presence of a unified cost accounting by an example of a geocentric structure. In addition, *Busco et al.* reveal that Nestlé had virtually different cost type accounting systems until the 1990s because the company consisted of regionally organised autonomous subsidiaries. The authors express that these differences were reduced after a change towards a product-oriented management. Thereby, the authors show that the presence of a unified cost accounting system can be associated with the economic organisation of a MNC. Despite this information, *Busco et al.* provide rather limited insights for this study. Their macro

[344] Cf. *Boons et al.* (1992), p. 103ff.; *Bjørnenak* (1997), p. 380; *Segelod/Carlsson* (2010), p. 327ff. The latter argues that Swedish cost accounting was complemented by other ideas than Germans as well.

[345] According to *Moeschler* (2012), p. 252ff., these are significantly German cost accounting traditions, particularly with respect to overhead treatment.

[346] The joint venture was a European family business before the take-over by venture partner A and A's inclusion of venture partner B. The business had week accounting systems, which were strengthened and updated by A's emphasis on cost control and a new ERP system.

[347] Slightly extended, this article is also published as *Busco et al.* (2007).

[348] Cf. *Busco et al.* (2006), p. 33.

level analysis remains purely descriptive and provides its evidence merely in an anecdotal manner.

Yazdifar et al. (2008) look at the management accounting systems in a UK company (hereafter *Sub*) after the company is sold to another owner. Case study based, the authors report that the new UK-based parent (hereafter *Parent2*) imposes its management accounting system on *Sub* (including cost accounting). The new system substitutes an old one which was perceived unsuitable for decision-making by *Sub* but had to be applied since it stemmed from the former parent (subsequently *Parent1*[349]). It becomes clear that the cost accounting system that is imposed by *Parent2* comprises Anglophone cost accounting traditions.[350] As such, *Yazdifar et al.'s* case can be interpreted as an example for an ethnocentric cost accounting system in a British multinational. Their mezzo level study is of theoretical nature. Based on old institutional economics (OIE)[351], NIS and a concept of power[352], the authors explain that both parents impose coercive pressure on *Sub*. Alongside the overcome dissatisfaction with the former system, the authors highlight that *Parent2*'s implementation process ensured that their system is implemented successfully. Accordingly, the disempowerment of opposing actors was very important in this regard. As such, *Yazdifar et al.* reveal that ethnocentrism can be ensured if a corporate involvement overcomes local resistance (i.e. local power). Their single case, despite adding an example to the list of uniform cost accounting systems, highlights theoretical perspectives which can help to explain cost accounting in subsidiaries.

Anecdotally, *Gerlach (2009)* summarises the striving of KS, a domestic sub-unit of a German manufacturing company, to ensure an ethnocentric design of its worldwide cost accounting systems. Similar to *Kemper/Rau,* the author highlights that KS implemented cost centre accounting and overhead allocation procedures in a newly formed joint venture in China. These procedures reflected KS's German cost accounting traditions. The author emphasises the importance of an expatriate manager for this implementation. On the one hand, this employee helped to overcome Chinese resistances against the new control system. On the other hand, he helped to take cultural differences (as expressed by *Hofstede*'s taxonomy) into account which hampered KS's striving for uniformity. Despite disregarding any theoretical basis and reporting purely anecdotal evidence, *Gerlach*'s experiences complements *Yazdifar et al.*'s finding that there is an interaction effect between local resistance and the effect of parent companies on their affiliates. Other than the former, he finds expatriate managers to be important in this respect. This will re-emerge from a theoretical perspective in section 4.1. Also, *Gerlach* underlines findings from Table 3-1. Yet, since his work neglects a discussion of the involvement of KS's parent company or the joint venture character of the regarded affiliate, *Gerlach*'s mezzo level field report remains superficial.

---

349 Parent1's origin remains disguised.

350 Their results report Sub's cost object accounting to be characterised by the application of standard costing to compute contribution margins, which are defined as sales less material costs.

351 For an introduction, cf. *Scapens* (2006), p. 14.

352 For an introduction, cf. *Hardy* (1996), p. 3ff.

Author/s	Contribution to the study	Countries	Theoretical basis	Level of analysis	Research method	Sample size
Firth (1996)	Statistically sound and rather generalisable evidence on the dependence of foreign affiliates' cost accounting systems on their parents' involvement is provided in a joint venture context.	China/ USA, Europe, Hong Kong, Japan	Contingency theory (implicit)	Descriptive/ theoretical mezzo	Survey/ questionnaire	361 triads of joint ventures & the venture partners [RR: 30-40 %]
Noack (2000)	Example of an ethnocentrically designed cost accounting system in a German MNC. Presents evidence for ethnocentrism of all three components of a cost accounting system.	Germany	None made explicit	Descriptive mezzo	Anecdotal evidence	1 MNC & its subsidiaries
Groot/ Merchant (2000)	Example of three joint ventures highlighting that parallel confrontation of organisations with different cost accounting traditions may be associated with conflicts on how to design cost accounting systems.	Netherlands, Sweden, Japan, USA	None made explicit	Descriptive mezzo	Case study	3 joint ventures
Busco (2006)	Example of a geocentric cost accounting system of a US multinational and the dependence of uniformity considerations on the economic organisational structure of MNCs	USA/ Italy and France	None made explicit	Descriptive macro	Anecdotal evidence	2 MNC, several subsidiaries
Yazdifar et al. (2008)	Example of a British affiliate which is forced to apply a corporate cost accounting system. The study emphasises that local acceptance is associated with information usefulness and the disempowerment of resistances.	United Kingdom	OIE, NIS and a concept of power mobilisation	Theoretical, mezzo	Case study	1 subsidiary, its current & former parent company
Gerlach (2009)	Example of a German/Chinese joint venture which is forced to apply German cost accounting traditions. The study highlights that affiliates' resistance against corporate involvement is reducible by expatriates.	Germany/ China	Cultural contingency theory (implicit)	Descriptive/ theoretical mezzo	Anecdotal evidence	1 subsidiary of a MNC, its joint venture in China
Yazdifar/ Askarany (2010b)	The application of ABC and target costing in Anglophone firms can be aligned with their affiliation to a parent company and sister affiliates' costing experiences.	Australia, New Zealand, UK	Especially NIS	Theoretical macro	Survey/ questionnaire and interviews	584 (in)-dependent companies [RR: ~30 %]

Table 3-3: Studies on management control systems indicating the uniformity of cost accounting systems

Yazdifar/Askarany (2010b) report results for management accounting innovations adapted in independent and dependent (i.e. subsidiary) companies. The results are based on a questionnaire returned from 310 Australian, 142 New Zealand and 132 UK companies and subsequent interviews conducted in about 10 % of the companies. The authors rather focus on the (apparently domestic) subsidiaries. They find the adoption of ABC as well as target costing in subsidiaries to be particularly influenced by parent companies' and sister affiliates' prior experience with these concepts.[353] Only 13 % of these adoptions occur independently of prior experiences in their groups. Interestingly, they find both ABC and target costing to be more sophisticated if these are implemented voluntarily rather than coercively by a parent company. Despite not providing any evidence whether the adoption in the subsidiaries reflects the general cost accounting system design in the associated

353 Similarly, *Ferreira/Otley* (2010), p. 12 and 42, could statistically align the design of control systems in Portugese companies with a foreign ownership structure. Because their applied measure captures both foreign ownership and being a family business, however, these results remain inconclusive.

group, *Yazdifar/Askarany's* macro level study is interpreted to stress cost accounting to be rather unified due to the prevailing influence of parent and sister companies.[354] In contrast to previously reviewed studies, this especially NIS informed project indicates that Anglophone companies also acknowledge international practices (i.e. target costing) with respect to the analysis and optimisation of costs (i.e. geocentrism). Despite formulating their theoretical interpretations on absolute and relative frequencies and distribution tests only, *Yazdifar/Askarany* provide important insights to this study by being among the only researchers, who centre their research effort on the fact that the design of cost accounting could depend on a company's affiliation to another organisation. Their reliance on Anglophone companies reveals considerable potential for future research in this regard.

Despite the various studies reviewed in this section, which univocally highlight that affiliates' cost accounting systems are affected by their parent companies and especially reflect these companies' national cost accounting traditions, this evidence is far from conclusive (cf. Table 3-3 for a summary). As will be elaborated in the following section, there is equally much evidence on the non-uniformity of cost accounting systems in affiliates of MNCs.

3.2.2.3 Research on regio- and polycentric cost accounting systems

The non-uniformity reflecting research projects can be divided into two broad streams of research. First, there is evidence for locally designed cost accounting systems at the absence of corporate directives as well as evidence on affiliates' opposition to corporate cost accounting initiatives.[355] Second, there are studies that look at cost accounting in affiliates rather irrespectively of the underlying organisational hierarchy. Both streams indicate that affiliates' cost accounting systems are characterised by the cost accounting traditions of the country in which the organisations operate. Yet, they seldom allow for a differentiation of poly- and regiocentrism. These characterisations will, thus, only be mentioned if they are clearly distinguishable.

Anecdotally, *Meyer* (1988) reports on the adoption of German cost accounting traditions (GPK) in a German IBM plant. The plant perceived the application of these German traditions superior to the previously applied corporate directive. The implementation became possible after IBM relaxed this costing directive which had previously fully unified the cost accounting systems in the group. Despite dating back to 1988[356] and being purely anecdotal, *Meyer's* evidence of non-uniform cost accounting systems at IBM is particularly fruitful for this project. It provides the only empirical evidence about cost accounting in an Anglophone subsidiary in Germany. Remarkably, this example is one of non-

---

354 *Yazdifar/Tsamenyi* (2005), p. 190, reemphasise this interpretation by highlighting that in a similar sample of dependent UK organisations, management accounting change is perceived to be more strongly driven by factors stemming from the affiliation to a global parent than in independend UK companies.

355 The latter studies will be reviewed in section 3.3 since they are more concerned with the micro-level application of cost information.

356 The study by *Mouritsen* (1995) (cf. section 3.2.2.4) indicates that IBM returned to ethnocentric cost accounting systems in the 1990s.

uniformity and it can be linked to cross-national differences in cost accounting. As such, *Meyer*'s anecdote underlines the discussion on *Groot et al.*'s and *Kellermanns/Islam*'s works. Cross-national differences in cost accounting are indeed important for companies which are confronted with various national traditions. Other than suggested by *Kellermans/Islam*, however, US companies which neglect German cost accounting traditions when operating in Germany do potentially need to consider local subsidiaries' dissatisfaction with a costing system. Of course, *Meyer*'s anecdote cannot be generalised to today's Anglophone companies in Germany. Nevertheless, the mezzo level study, which lacks any theoretical explanations, is rather exceptional. Not only does *Meyer*'s work affirm the importance of corporate directives for the analysis of cost accounting in subsidiaries, but also a potential tendency of German practitioners to prefer their cost accounting traditions over the Anglophone ones.

Somehow similar to *Meyer*, there are German field reports on the non-uniformity of cost accounting at Siemens. Conjointly, two Siemens managers stress that their group accepts differing charts of accounts in their German and US affiliates. This indicates differing cost type accounting practices in the company.[357] Additionally, the design of subsidiaries' cost object accounting is not subject to central regulation to allow for recognition of the peculiarities of the various business areas of the group.[358] These findings must be seen in the light of Siemens' abandonment of cost accounting for management purposes at the corporate level in the early 1990s.[359] Despite corporate abandonment, alarmed management accounting scholars did not hesitate to stress that cost accounting survived in the company.[360] Cost information, however, is derived for affiliates' purposes. Overall, this evidence provides an example of poly- or regiocentric cost accounting in a German MNC. Remarkably, the study is not contradicting the findings from section 3.2.2.2. Rather, the importance to consider parent company directives, which were present in the majority of uniformity suggestive studies, is underlined as their absence can lead to non-uniform cost accounting systems. Yet, the authors' mezzo-level field reports do not reveal any theoretical explanations for the design of cost accounting systems in affiliates. Nevertheless, the Siemens anecdotes complement the studies reviewed this far. They explicate that business units can be a reasonable research object in management accounting research in large MNCs. In such a context, cost accounting might be rather specific to business areas than legal entities.

Associated with the former, *Bhimani* (2003) reports on the introduction of a new cost accounting and cost management system in a business-unit of Siemens' semiconductors group in 1995. The new system pictures the production processes better than the former system and has a market perspective (target cost orientation). Thereby, it reflects the business-unit's information needs to a greater extent. Because the implementation is restricted to one business-unit, *Bhimani* provides evidence underlining the non-uniformity of cost

[357] Cf. *Baumann* (1986), p. 432.
[358] Cf. *Ziegler* (1992), p. 308.
[359] Cf. *Ziegler* (1994), p. 177f. As will be seen in the next paragraph, there is evidence for accordingly designed cost accounting systems. The importance of cost accounting at the corporate level of Siemens today could not be uncovered.
[360] For this and the following, cf. *Pfaff* (1994), p. 1075, or *Währisch* (1998), p. 3.

accounting systems at Siemens.[361] Moreover, *Bhimani* complements the list of variables affecting the non-uniform design of cost accounting systems. He provides evidence that an affiliate specific cost accounting system can increase the local usefulness of cost information if it is possible to adopt a cost accounting system to an affiliate's specific context and local objectives.[362] Following *Bhimani*, local information usefulness may require taking on cost accounting traditions from other geographical areas than a parent company's home-country. As such, the author questions the relevance of ethnocentric cost accounting systems for affiliates. *Bhimani*'s mezzo level study lacks a theoretical basis. It cannot contribute towards theorising affiliates' cost accounting systems. Yet, the study's explicit focus on an affiliate's perspective contributes considerable to this review. *Bhimani* highlights the necessity to regard affiliates' cost accounting systems in the context of local particularities, local information needs, as well as a parent company's involvements.

In addition to these findings on non-uniform cost accounting systems at IBM and Siemens (cf. Table 3-4 for a summary), there is a second stream of research which suggests that affiliates' cost accounting systems are not reflecting the systems of their parent companies. These, however, are rather focussing on organisational sub-units other than subsidiaries.

Author/s	Contribution to the study	Countries	Theoretical basis	Level of analysis	Research method	Sample size
Meyer (1988)	Provides an example that management accountants at an Anglophone company in Germany prefer German cost accounting traditions to Anglophone informed cost accounting directives.	Germany, USA	None made explicit	Descriptive, mezzo	Anecdotal evidence	1 subsidiary of a MNC
Ziegler (1992 & 1994) and Baumann (1986)	Cost accounting at Siemens is not applied for corporate decision-making. (Therefore), organisational sub-units at Siemens are rather free to choose their cost accounting system.	Germany, USA	None made explicit	Descriptive, mezzo	Anecdotal evidence	1 MNC
Bhimani (2003)	Provides an example that sub-units at Siemens can adjust their cost accounting systems to their information needs. Complements previous research by revealing that such ability is associated with positive perceptions by sub-unit employees.	Germany	None made explicit	Descriptive, mezzo	Case study	1 business unit of a MNC

Table 3-4: Studies on non-uniform cost accounting systems at the absence of corporate directives

Bhimani/Pigott (1992) conduct a case study on the implementation of ABC in one out of three manufacturing sites of a British Pharmaceutical company. The authors reveal that the implementation occurs when both the corporate accountants and the site accountants perceive the old standard absorption costing system to provide inaccurate cost information. *Bhimani/Pigott* report that implementation leads to cost information which re-

361 The author argues that this unit had a costing system in-line with the "Siemens-wide accounting procedures" (p. 532 and 534) prior to the introduction. The introduction followed an autonomy granting project initiated at Siemens in 1993. As such, *Bhimani*'s findings can be linked to the introduced abandonment of costing at Siemens' corporate level.

362 For this purpose, *Bhimani* makes use of a questionnaire returned from 33 employees of the affiliate.

flects the manufacturing process at the case site in a better way. Hence, both the site and the corporate level accountants are satisfied with the new cost allocation procedure. *Bhimani/Pigott*'s report complements this review by revealing that the implementation of a costing initiative which meets its objectives is subsequently assessed a success. Acknowledging that the case company is affiliated to a UK group shows that *Bhimani/Pigott* provide another example that subsidiaries' ability to design their cost accounting systems with respect to their requirements can be an antecedent of a subsidiary's favourable attitude towards their cost accounting system.[363] With respect to the theoretical explanation of cost accounting in subsidiaries, however, no insights can be drawn from *Bhimani/Pigott*'s macro-level descriptive study. Also, their study's focus on one site must be seen as indication for a potentially restricted applicability of ABC. This limits the conclusiveness with which *Bhimani/Pigott*'s study presents an example of a non-uniform cost accounting system.

Abernethy (2001) explore the cost accounting systems in three divisions of a manufacturer of healthcare products (A) and two divisions of a textile producer (B). Their explorative case study is based on semi-structured interviews (8 in A and 7 in B) and observations. *Abernethy et al.* find two different cost accounting systems in the three divisions of A. The two divisions of B have non-uniform cost accounting systems as well. In their grounded theory based and contingency theory informed study the authors find less sophisticated cost accounting systems[364] to be implemented and perceived adequate in units of lower product diversity and simple production process (A1, A2 and B1). Sophisticated systems are implemented (B2) or perceived necessary (A3) in times of high product diversity and complex production processes. Also, advanced manufacturing technologies reduce the need for sophisticated systems (B2). As such, the authors provide descriptive evidence for non-uniform cost accounting systems in two presumably Anglophone companies.[365] Moreover, the study indicates that the design of cost accounting systems in affiliates depends on the characteristics of the implementing units' products and production processes. The disregarded influence of cross-border operations and the limited number of observations, however, limit the conclusiveness of *Abernethy et al.*'s mezzo level study.

---

[363] Similarly, *Briers* (1997), p. 81ff., and *Briers/Chua* (2001), p. 237ff., report of an research project in a domestic business unit of an Australian mining company. The author highlights the implementation of ABC to be driven by the BU's management, its accountants, management accounting seminars and external consultants. The author identifies an organisational sub-unit to have taken the initiative of cost accounting change. Other than *Bhimani/Pigott*, however, *Briers* (1997), p. 60ff., and *Briers/Chua* (2001), p. 240ff., apply actor network theory and stress the importance of non-economic reasons for accounting system change. Despite providing an additional theoretical background, however, the research project provides only incremental insights for this study and, therefore, is not explicitly reviewed.

[364] A sophisticated cost system is defined as one with cost pools being reflective of activities rather than areas of responsibility. Moreover, such systems are urged to require costs drivers which link costs not only to products but to, e.g. batches or the company as a whole as well. As such, the study focusses on ABC rather than general cost accounting systems.

[365] Following the Australian origin of the authors, both companies seem to be Anglophone and all five divisions appear to be domestic. Yet, the study excludes any evidence on the origin of (A) and (B).

Based on 400 questionnaires returned from the largest companies in Canada, France, Germany, Italy, Japan, the USA and the UK, *Bhimani et al.* (2007) analyse the adoption of ABC. Their findings indicate that only French firms implemented overhead allocation based on ABC in the majority of their units. In all other countries, researched firms implemented ABC in some units or a pilot unit, if at all.[366] As such, *Bhimani et al.* provide macro-level descriptive evidence for cost accounting being rather non-unified with respect to overhead allocation procedures in multinationals of various origins. The reported evidence, of course, is only indicative for polycentric cost accounting systems in multinationals. Companies might merely doubt the usefulness of ABC or tend to test ABC before implementing it.[367] Nevertheless, *Bhimani et al.'s* evidence is relevant for this review since it highlights that there are differences among the cost accounting systems of affiliates in multinationals.

Table 3-5 contains a summary of these three research projects.

Author/s	Contribution to the study	Countries	Theoretical basis	Level of analysis	Research method	Sample size
Bhimani/ Pigott (1992)	Provide an example for a successful ABC system, which is implemented selectively by an initiating subsidiary.	UK	none	Descriptive, mezzo	Case study	1 manufacturing site of a subsidiary
Abernethy et al. (2001)	Provide an example of cost accounting systems in sub-units of two Anglophone companies. The systems, which are adapted to the units' characteristics, are perceived a success by the units.	Australia	Grounded theory, contingency theory	Descriptive/ theoretical, mezzo	Case study	5 sub-units of 2 companies
Bhimani et al. (2007)	ABC is rarely applied throughout entire companies but tends to be implemented in selected affiliates.	Canada, France, Germany, Italy, Japan, USA, UK	None made explicit	Descriptive, macro	Survey/ questionnaire	400 companies [RR: 10-20 %]

Table 3-5: Studies on affiliate specific cost accounting systems

In addition, there are various studies on the context contingent design of cost accounting in economic sub-units which contribute to the understanding of cost accounting in affiliates.

Ittner et al. (2002) address the association between ABC, a company's context and manufacturing performance by studying 2.789 US production plants. Thereby, the authors (implicitly) assume that overhead allocation varies in US companies because it is rather plant specific. By highlighting that ABC is less often used in plants that do not have a discrete production process and more often used if the plant has a variety of products, a

366 A similar argument can be found in *Scapens* (1996), p. 32, who summarise his findings of several case studies in UK companies. In line, *Kim et al.* (2002), p. 609, find that in 75 % of the researched US companies the adoption decision for target costing is made at an affiliate's rather than corporate level. Little surprisingly, they thus find that only 19 % apply target costing throughout the whole firm.

367 Similar results are found for Germany by *Stoi* (1999), p. 153, for the UK by *Innes et al.* (2000), p. 353, and for the UK, US and France by *Yakhou/Dorweiler* (1995), p. 119f. The latter two, however, report of ABC adoption in company's *areas or parts*. These studies do not clearly allow to assess whether organisational sub-units or simply manufacturing and nonmanufacturing areas are addressed.

high percentage of new products and advanced manufacturing technology,[368] the authors implicitly confirm such assumptions.[369] According to *Ittner et al.*, enabling affiliates to design their cost accounting system in accordance with their context can also increase these units' manufacturing performance.[370] Despite providing explanatory variables for the application and performance of ABC, the authors' macro level study is not exclusively theoretical due to its (implicit) reliance on contingency theory. Moreover, it must be reasoned that the conclusiveness of *Ittner et al.*'s analysis remains unclear. It cannot be assessed whether the identified contextual factors would have been equally relevant for ABC and its success in the plants if the authors had acknowledged corporate involvements.[371] Nevertheless, *Ittner et al.*'s work complements the other research projects summarised throughout this section. On the one hand, they reveal additional context factors, which can be relevant for the analysis of cost accounting in affiliates. On the other hand, their reliance on economic choice reflecting contingency factors and the highlighted criticism emphasises the necessity to acknowledge both conventional contingency factors as well as parent company influences during the analysis of cost accounting in subsidiaries.

Other than *Ittner et al.*, *Baird et al.* (2004) assume that activity management (including ABC) is likely to differ across the business units of a firm explicitly. The authors regard the application of ABC through the analysis of 184 questionnaires from Australian business units. Regression-based, the authors find this application to be positively dependent on a business unit's size, the decision usefulness of cost information and the business unit's *culture* (measured as innovation and outcome orientation and its locus of control). The effects of a business unit's size and innovation orientation are of little robustness. As such, *Baird et al.* provide evidence for their assumption that cost accounting systems are likely to be non-uniform on a macro level in Australian firms.[372] *Baired et al.*'s study is included at this point since they underline the necessity to consider contingency theory informed variables during the analysis of sub-units for another Anglophone country. Their findings, however, are subject to the same criticism as *Ittner et al.*'s study.

In line with *Baired et al., Drury/Tayles* (2005) decide to research cost accounting systems in UK business units because entire companies have numerous cost accounting systems.[373] They yield 187 usable responses from domestic and foreign business units in the UK. In

---

368 Only statistically significant variables are reported here.

369 Non-incremental evidence for another sample of US business units is provided by *Krumwiede* (1998). Despite being the younger study, *Ittner et al.* is included at this point to due their inclusion of performance effects.

370 By making use of the yielded regression to explain ABC implementation and comparing its suggestion for each company against actual implementation, the authors find that companies which should not use ABC, but do and companies that should use ABC but do not have lower performance in terms of return on assets.

371 According to *Van der Stede* (2003), p. 279f, such context factors are likely to be overruled if corporate involvements were accounted for. A similar argument is included in *Jones* (1985), p. 321. The review of *Gosselin* (1997) in section 3.2.2.4 suggests this to hold true, too.

372 Similar evidence can be found in *Brown et al.* (2004) for another sample of Australian business units.

373 *Drury/Tayles* also reported their findings as *Drury/Tayles* (2000) and *Drury/Tayles* (2006). Because these two studies do not align cost accounting to the business units' contexts, however, the 2005 publication is cited here.

line with their expectation, they find the cost accounting systems in business units to depend on these units' internal and external contextual factors. Exemplarily, the number of cost pools and cost drivers in business units are determined by product diversity, the sales volume of business units as well as the sector which a unit operates in. As such, the authors implicitly emphasise that cost accounting in organisations with various business units can be rather diverse. *Drury/Tayles* underline the findings by *Ittner et al.* and *Baired et al.* for a sample of UK companies.[374] Their findings, however, are subject to the same criticism as the former two studies.

Table 3-6 summarises these three studies.

Author/s	Contribution to the study	Countries	Theoretical basis	Level of analysis	Research method	Sample size
Ittner et al. (2002)	The authors find the application of ABC in organisational sub-units to depend on these units' organisational context. Moreover, if ABC is applied in accordance with contextual factors this increases a unit's manufacturing performance. The study disregards influences of organisational hierarchies, however.	USA	Contingency theory (implicit)	Descriptive/ theoretical, macro	Survey/ questionnaire	2789 US production plants [RR: 11 %]
Baired et al. (2004)	The application of ABC in organisational sub-units reflects these units' organisational context. The study disregards influences of organisational hierarchies, however.	Australia	(Cultural) contingency theory (implicit)	Descriptive/ theoretical, macro	Survey/ questionnaire	246 business units [RR: 61.50 %]
Drury/Tayles (2005)	Organisational sub-units overhead allocation procedures reflect these organisational units' contextual factors. The study disregards influences of organisational hierarchies, however.	UK	Contingency theory	Descriptive/ theoretical, mezzo	Survey/ questionnaire	187 business units [RR: 30.10 %]

Table 3-6: Studies on non-uniform cost accounting systems disregarding corporate directives

As can be seen by the evidence in sections 3.2.2.2 and 3.2.2.3, there is various evidence which unambiguously reveals whether affiliates are characterised by their parent company's cost accounting system (i.e. ethno- and geocentrism) or not (i.e. poly- and regiocentrism). In addition, there are several research projects which do not provide a univocal picture whether or not cost accounting in affiliates is dominantly affected by a corporate level. Rather, these 'mixed evidence studies' provide simultaneous evidence for both the uniformity and non-uniformity of cost accounting systems in MNCs. They are introduced hereafter.

3.2.2.4 Mixed evidence studies

Anderson (1995), *Anderson/Young* (1999) and *Anderson et al.* (2002)[375] provide evidence for the implementation of ABC at General Motors (GM) and Chrysler. In line with *Bhimani et al.* (2007), they describe that GM first tested ABC at some local plants. ABC then

[374] Similarly, *Brierley* (2008a), p. 58ff., finds non-incremental results by researching 280 operating companies in the UK.

[375] The studies were conjointly published as *Anderson/Young* (2001).

emerged into a corporate GM policy, which was only implemented in the North American operations, however. Part of this policy was a striving for the "commonization" of ABC with respect to activities and cost drivers. This common design, however, could not be achieved to 100 %. *Anderson et al.* (2002) report substantial differences with respect to the number of activities, as well as the first and second stage allocation bases. As such, the cost accounting systems at GM appear regionally unified on a macro level but remain non-unified on a mezzo level of analysis. Similarly, *Anderson/Young* (1999) described Chrysler to have a company-wide policy for ABC. They also report that the ABC models converge over time, thus expressing Chryslers' tendency to unify overhead cost allocation. This tendency is confirmed by *Anderson et al.* (2002) since the number of activities, as well as first and second stage allocation bases differ less extensively than the figures for GM do. The macro level study by *Anderson* (1995), her (1999) micro level and the (2002) mezzo level study provide evidence for non-uniformity at GM despite a corporate implementation policy while stressing uniformity at Chrysler. In the two younger studies, the findings are explicated by a context contingency of ABC. Accordingly, the interplay of parent involvement, the subsidiaries' local environment as well as the implementation process can explain the results. In line with these non-incremental insights, the studies explicatory attempts are little revealing for the issue of cost accounting in affiliates. The studies (implicitly) rely on contingency theory only. Yet, this research project is very interesting for this review due to its early analysis of a potentially non-uniform overhead allocation at GM and Chrysler. Also, the studies find parent company's top management involvement to be more important for the success of an ABC implementation than a subsidiary's management support.[376] Such varying effects remained concealed in the previous sections.

As introduced during the discussion of *Meyer* (1998), *Mouritsen* (1995) explores management accounting at two multinationals with different organisational structures. Based on interviews with managers at IBM and Superfos (a Danish MNC) the author provides evidence for different cost accounting systems in these two companies. *Mouritsen* highlights that IBM, a centrally governed company, has globally unified (cost) accounting systems. Superfos, a rather decentralised company, is characterised by non-uniform cost accounting. Exemplarily, he provides evidence that one of Superfos business units employs a standard costing system while a project-oriented division is indicated to rely more on actual costing only. Despite lacking a theoretical basis and being rather imprecise about his case study approach, *Mouritsen*'s work contributes to this review. Accordingly, the uniformity of cost accounting systems in affiliates with respect to a parent's (national) cost accounting traditions depends on the centralisation (i.e. the level of corporate involvements) of a MNC and the activities of the subsidiary.

Focusing on subsidiaries in the US, *Al Chen et al.* (1997) analyses product costing, cost planning and cost control procedures of Japanese multinationals. The authors evaluate their cross-sectional evidence from 47 small- to medium-sized subsidiaries through a

[376] Cf. *Anderson/Young* (2001), p. 127.

comparison with two former studies.[377] *Al Chen et al.* provide evidence that direct labour hours served as the primary overhead allocation base in regarded affiliates. Similarly, they observe the application of variable costing in the US subsidiaries. By a comparison with *Howell* and *Scarbrough*, these findings are interpreted to indicate ethnocentric cost accounting systems in the researched affiliates. The authors reemphasise this interpretation by their findings on Japanese-informed cost management approaches (target costing and value engineering). Accordingly, the Japanese affiliates in the US reflect their parents' cost accounting/management systems. Neglecting the methodological deficiencies of the authors, *Al Chen et al.*'s interpretation of ethnocentrism must be weakened for two reasons. First, the authors find the adoption of ABC in the researched US affiliates to exceed the adoption rate *Scarbrough* reports for Japan. Second, the cost accounting systems are overwhelmingly developed locally rather than being strongly infused by parent companies. As such, their study rather reveals that subsidiaries compromise the cost accounting traditions of their home and host countries. *Al Chen et al.* do not stress any variables or theoretical positions which could explain their findings. Hence, their study cannot further the understanding of explanatory alternatives for cost accounting in subsidiaries. Reviewing their mezzo-level study explicitly at this point is motivated by younger evidence on Japanese affiliates that underlines the diverse picture found by *Al Chen et al.*[378] and the study's early focus on foreign subsidiaries.

In a similar vein as the studies in Table 3-5 and Table 3-6, *Gosselin* (1997) analyses the implementation of ABC in 161 business units of Canadian manufacturing companies. Other than the studies in section 3.2.2.3, however, *Gosselin* finds that the application of ABC in business units is more likely, the more decisions for the business unit are made at higher hierarchical levels (centralisation). According to the author, this suggests that ABC implementation in business units depends on the associated legal entities' organisational structure. *Gosselin* strives for an alignment of his results with the continuum of mechanistic and organic organisational structures. This attempt is somewhat linked to the contingency approach since organisations' control systems are stressed to be rationally contingent on its organisational structures. Therefore, the study is neither purely theoretical nor purely descriptive in nature. *Gosselin*'s finding underlines the deficiencies criticised to characterise the studies by *Ittner et al.*, *Baired et al.* and *Drury/Tayles*. Even in business units, it is necessary to account for organisational hierarchies when studying cost accounting. Nevertheless, his results do not comprise unambiguous information on the uniformity or non-uniformity of cost accounting systems. The applied scale for centralisation reflects whether decision actions are rather taken by line supervisors in the business unit or head office managers. As such, the identified higher likelihood of ABC in more centralised

377 These studies are *Howell et al.* (1987), p. 35ff., for US and *Scarbrough et al.* (1991), for Japanese cost accounting and cost management systems. The matching criterion focusses superficially on an advanced manufacturing environment only.

378 *Tani et al.* (1994), p. 79, finds 24 % of the listed Japanese companies to have transferred target costing into their foreign subsidiaries, while additional 27.3 % intend to do so. Moreover, they find target costing to be used both in a whole MNC and in some units or projects only (cf. *Tani/Kato* (1994), p. 197). Thus, in line with *Al Chen et al.* (1998), *Tani et al.* (1994) and *Tani/Kato* (1994) find mixed evidence for the uniformity of cost accounting in Japanese MNCs.

companies is equally indicative of ABC implementation being facilitated by a business units' top management as well as an associated parents' management. Yet, his study is essential for this review since *Gosselin* provides rather generalisable evidence on the relevance of organisational hierarchies for cost accounting in affiliates.

Krumwiede (2005) explores the GPK systems of 11 German companies. Most of these have cross-border operations. He provides anecdotal evidence that most researched companies experienced difficulties diffusing their cost accounting systems into US affiliates, especially if their systems have GPK characteristics. Based on Daimler's involvement with Chrysler, he reveals insecurity about the systems' benefits, lower emphasis on management accounting, fewer difficulties in reducing fixed costs through headcount reduction, less involvement with SAP consultants and a lack of costing knowledge as anecdotal reasons for such difficulties. Peculiarly, companies with *non-GPK systems* are reported to have unified cost accounting systems. These findings underline *Kellermans/Islam*'s conceptual considerations, which indicate that German-owned affiliates in the US may be less reluctant to apply rather simple cost accounting systems as compared to refined German cost accounting procedures. *Krumwiede* does not attempt to align his results on the identified explicative factors with any theoretical positions, and as such remains rather descriptive. Nevertheless, the author provides fruitful mezzo-level evidence for this review. Apparently, a strong reliance on German cost accounting traditions can affect the acceptance of parent company involvement into cost system design in Anglophone affiliates of German MNCs. The same could be true for Anglophone affiliates in Germany.

Hoffjan/Weide (2006)[379] interviewed management accountants in eight German multinationals. They explicitly highlight a certain degree of uniformity among these companies' cost type accounting (the existence of the general ledger concept and the exclusion of imputed costs). Management accounting instruments (e.g. cost accounting), however, are not found to be unified. Following the authors, instruments are rather subsidiary specific. These findings reflect a certain tension. Whereas on an aggregated macro level (the instruments) unification is not identified, it prevails on a mezzo level for cost type accounting.[380] Though the authors explicitly stress 'standardisation' to be very apparent in their sample, their findings for cost accounting are rather diverse. Including their study into this review has one particular reason. Exploratively, the authors attempt to explicate their findings. They complement previously derived explicatory variables by a MNC's internationalisation strategy, the size of a subsidiary, the value chain activities pursued by a subsidiary and the time that passed since a subsidiary became part of a MNC. All of these variables are regularly mentioned in their interviews. Nevertheless, *Hoffjan/Weide*'s study remains descriptive. The authors merely align their findings with the contingency approach but do not attempt to underpin their findings with a theoretical perspective. Still, *Hoffjan/Weide* are among the only authors aligning cost accounting in subsidiaries explicitly with the interaction of a subsidiary with its parent company. Thereby, their explorative research report becomes relevant for this study.

---

379 Available in English as *Hoffjan/Weide* (2009).

380 Peculiarly, neither the application of the general ledger concept nor the discharge of imputed costs reflects the German cost accounting traditions. As such, the study rather indicates a geocentric design.

Author/s	Contribution to the study	Countries	Theoretical basis	Level of analysis	Research method	Sample size
Anderson et al. (1995, 1999, 2001, 2002)	Provide examples of two US multinationals' application of ABC. Though both strive for a company-wide implementation, this is achieved to differing degrees. Differences in the implementation processes and the acknowledgement of affiliates' contextual factors are linked to these differences.	USA, Canada	Contingency theory (implicit)	Descriptive/ theoretical, '95: macro, '99: micro, '01 and 02: mezzo	Case study	Production plants of 2 MNCs
Mouritsen (1995)	Provides two examples that the level of unification of cost accounting in subsidiaries is a function of a parent company's holding structure.	USA, Denmark	Contingency theory (implicit)	Descriptive/ theoretical, mezzo	Case study/ anecdotal evidence	2 MNCs and their subsidiaries
Al Chen et al.(1997)	The US affiliates of Japanese companies are reflecting cost accounting traditions also characterising Japanese companies. Simultaneously, however, the researched affiliates also involve into the application of US informed cost accounting techniques.	Japan/USA	None made explicit	Descriptive mezzo	Survey	47 subsidiaries. [RR: 20 %]
Gosselin (1997)	The implementation of ABC in business units is statistically linked to a level of centralisation. Because centralisation involves hierarchical levels in- and outside the business unit, this finding, however, cannot be assessed conclusively.	Canada	Contingency theory (implicit)	Descriptive/ theoretical, macro	Survey/ questionnaire	161 business units [RR: 39 %]
Krumwiede (2005)	By regarding US affiliates, German MNCs are reasoned to strive for a unification of their cost accounting systems. The success of such a striving appears to depend on the level to which the systems reflect complex German cost accounting traditions.	Germany	None made explicit	Descriptive, mezzo	Anecdotal evidence	11 German MNC
Hoffjan/ Weide (2006)	Provide explorative evidence that the three components of cost accounting in affiliates can be unified to different extents. Contingency factor to *explain* affiliates' management accounting systems are introduced.	Germany	(Cultural) contingency theory	Descriptive/ theoretical mezzo	Expert interviews	8 MNC
Dickmann (2010)	The cost accounting systems of newly acquired subsidiaries of German MNCs are as regularly unified post transactional as they are non-unified. Moreover, the study underlines a tendency for ethnocentric cost accounting systems in German MNCs.	Germany[381]	Especially contingency theory	Descriptive/ theoretical macro	Survey/ questionnaire	97 M&A transactions [RR: 18.90 %]

Table 3-7: Studies revealing evidence for both uniform and non-uniform cost accounting systems

Dickmann (2010) studies to what extend the management accounting functions in newly merged/acquired companies are unified after the transaction. Based on 97 responses from acquiring German companies, the author highlights the post-merger cost type, cost centre and cost object accounting to be rather unified in 49 %, 48 % and 42 % of the regarded transactions. This bisection of uniform and non-uniform cost accounting systems corresponds to the evidence by *Wolfsgruber* (2011). But, in contrast to the latter, *Dickmann* does not provide any evidence on planned unifications. Thereby, he indicates ethno- and polycentric tendencies in German MNCs to be equally common. Delving into the application of imputed costs, *Dickmann* underlines that Germans favour ethnocentric cost type

[381] Only, the acquiring firms are all German. The acquired firms are both German and international.

accounting systems. Since he also finds cost accounting to be less unified after international transactions than after domestic transactions, *Dickmann*'s results indicate that cross-national differences are indeed important for the design of cost accounting systems in affiliates.[382] Moreover, *Dickmann* finds that in rather autonomous subsidiaries, cost accounting is significantly less unified, while a strong involvement of the parent (expressed by the level of cross-funcional integration) increases the uniformity of cost accounting. As such, *Dickmann*'s findings can explicate that the level of parent company engagement as well as a subsidiary's local decision rights are important precessors of the uniformity of cost accounting systems. Nevertheless, *Dickmann*'s macro level findings remain rather descriptive since the author does not derive these explicative variables from theoretical perspectives. He merely expresses that above contextual variables are '*explicable*' through the contingency approach and reflect an agency relationship.

Table 3-7 provides a summary of the above mixed evidence studies.

3.2.3 Summary

Both normative and empirical research provides a considerably diverse picture of the cost accounting systems in subsidiaries. On the one hand, there are normative calls that cost accounting systems of subsidiaries should reflect a parent company's cost accounting system (section 3.2.1). Section 3.2.2.2 finds numerous empirical studies which reveal such ethno- or geocentrically designed cost accounting systems in multinationals. On the other hand, the normative calls for affiliate specific cost accounting systems (section 3.2.1) are equally well reflected by numerous empirical studies on poly- and regiocentric cost accounting systems in MNCs (section 3.2.2.3). This level of diversity in normative and empirical research is also manifested in various empirical studies which highlight uniform and non-uniform cost accounting systems simultaneously and a corresponding normative study by *Kellermans/Islam* (2004). Finding such ambiguous results is a result of the fact the literature on cost accounting in affiliates cannot conclusively *explain* what determines cost accounting in affiliates from a theoretical perspective. A closer look at the uniformity, non-uniformity and mixed empirical literature reveals additional **deficiencies of the previous research**.

Evidence on the **uniformity of cost accounting systems** prevails in studies which focus particularly on legal organisational structures. Also, this evidence can be found in studies with a subsidiary focus as well as studies which take a parent company's perspective. Interestingly, uniformity studies are rather indicative of ethnocentric cost accounting systems. Though some impact of best practice/local adoption can be found (i.e. geocentrism), there is little indication that uniform cost accounting systems reflect other than a parent company's home-country traditions. Puzzlingly, only the studies by *Brewer* (1998), *Smith* (2005) and *Yazdifar et al.* (2008) include considerations on the performance of a uniform

[382] Since no comparison of the cost accounting systems before the mergers is reported, however, it is well possible that German companies unify cost accounting systems after international transactions more extensively. The results by *Dickmann* (2010) might merely reflect an unability to achieve the uniformity levels of national transactions in international transactions due to greater pre-merger differences.

cost accounting system.[383] Furthermore, there are considerable issues with respect to the generalisability of the findings on uniformity. Somewhat generalisable survey results are scarce and rather characterised by a macro level on the application of ABC or GPK. In contrast, more detailed mezzo level evidence can be found dominantly in company examples. Yet, these examples are especially field reports (business anecdotes) rather than refined research projects (case studies). Also, the majority of the studies on uniformity are descriptive in nature or 'explain' their finding through the contingency approach only. Evidence on the **non-uniformity of cost accounting systems** is less focussed on legal organisational sub-units but rather provides evidence for economic sub-units. In contrast to the ethno- and polycentric studies, however, most of these studies have a special focus on the affiliate rather than providing evidence for a MNC or a parent company. Also, the non-uniformity evidence does not allow for a conclusive analysis, whether the findings are rather reflective of minor adoptions or reveal foreign countries' cost accounting traditions. As such, it could not be conclusively assessed whether the studies reflect regio- or polycentric cost accounting systems. Yet, in contrast to the evidence on uniformity, the majority of the studies on non-uniformity consider the performance of cost accounting systems explicitly and find non-uniform cost accounting systems to be performing rather well.[384] Nevertheless, the generalisability of the studies in section 3.2.2.3 is equally questionable as the results from section 3.2.2.2. Generalisable large sample results are limited to macro level findings on the application of ABC. They, however, tend to disregard the effect of organisational hierarchies on affiliates' cost accounting systems. The detailed mezzo level evidence is rather based on small sample anecdotes only. Regrettably, little insights can be derived from the evidence on non-uniformity from an explicative perspective. Most of the studies remain rather broadly focused on contingency theory only. With respect to all these characteristics, the **mixed evidence studies** are comparable to the considerations on uniformity.

As such, there are several methodological and conceptual deficiencies in previous research on cost accounting in subsidiaries which highlight a multidimensional **research opportunity** regarding cost accounting in subsidiaries.

First and foremost, an opportunity arises from the **countries** covered in the previous research projects. Various studies look at companies that are headquartered in German speaking countries. Similarly, various studies regard Anglophone MNCs. For both regions, there are more studies stressing uniformity than non-uniformity. Yet, for neither of these regions, a strong dominance of uniformity or non-uniformity evidence prevails. This assertion holds also true if research on ABC is neglected. Regarding the host countries in these studies uncovers that there is considerably more evidence on German cost accounting in the Anglophone countries than on Anglophone cost accounting in Germany. With respect to the latter, *Meyer* (1988) describes the application of a German cost accounting system in the researched Anglophone company. Finding the only example of cost ac-

[383] Additional evidence with respect to the performance of cost accounting is included into the mixed evidence study by *Anderson/Young* (1999).

[384] Cf. *Meyer* (1988); *Bhimani/Pigott* (1992); *Ziegler* (1994); *Abernethy* (2001); *Ittner et al.* (2002); *Bhimani* (2003); *Bhimani et al.* (2007). Additional evidence with respect to the performance of cost accounting is included into the mixed evidence study by *Anderson/Young* (1999).

counting in an Anglophone company in Germany to be one of non-uniformity, despite a slight overall dominance of the uniformity evidence, emphasises the validity of this study's research question. Cost accounting in Anglophone companies in Germany is largely unexplored.

Also, the existing evidence on cost accounting systems in affiliates is little reliable. A large proportion of the reviewed studies are business anecdotes rather than scientific works. Also, various scientific research projects are rather exemplary and regard a limited number of cases. The majority of the **generalisable scientific surveys** on the design of cost accounting in affiliates in turn stems from research on ABC. Though there is evidence both for and against the uniform application of ABC in multinationals, the ABC focus flaws the conclusiveness of previous research. Rather than revealing any reliable evidence on subsidiaries' cost accounting systems, the evidence may rather express the specific applicability of ABC.[385] Out of the five survey studies which do not focus on ABC[386] all but *Drury/Tayles* (2005) find evidence for ethnocentric cost accounting systems. Yet, only *Drury/Tayles* (2005) have an exclusive focus on cost accounting. Hence, there is no reliable large sample evidence on the matter of cost accounting in subsidiaries.

Moreover, the current state on **how to explain cost accounting in subsidiaries** is in a deplorable condition. During the analysis in section 3.2.2.2, the importance of corporate directives, sister affiliates and subsidiaries' positive perceptions about a parent company's involvement prevail as explanatory variables. The studies in Table 3-4 from section 3.2.2.3 underline these findings. Accordingly, the absence of corporate involvements leads to subsidiaries' ability to design their systems in accordance with their information needs. Similarly, the studies to be reviewed in section 3.3 will reemphasise the importance to consider the relationship between a subsidiary and its parent to understand subsidiaries' cost accounting systems. However, the research emphasising the non-uniform design of cost accounting systems also points at the necessity to study cost accounting in affiliates with respect to these companies' production and competitive environment. Also, in both uniformity and non-uniformity research, information technologies explicate cost accounting in subsidiaries. Despite identifying such factors, however, neither the studies on the uniformity nor the research on the non-uniformity of affiliates' cost accounting systems highlight conclusively, why the identified factors are theoretically relevant. The authors especially base their derivation of such 'explanatory variables' on the contingency approach. Contingency studies, however, generally assume economic decisions to underlie the adaptation of cost accounting systems to an environmental context. Yet, designing cost accounting systems in accordance with corporate directives does not necessarily lead to economically efficient systems.[387] *Malmi* (1999), *Yazdifar et al.* (2008) and *Yazdifar/Askarany* (2010b) explicate that institutional theory which questions the dominance of efficient choices[388] is particularly applicable in this context. Such suggestions can

---

[385] Cf. *Scapens* (1996), p. 32; *Bhimani et al.* (2007), p. 14.

[386] Cf. *Firth* (1996); *Al Chen et al.* (1997); *Drury/Tayles* (2005); *Dickmann* (2010); *Wolfsgruber* (2011).

[387] *Chenhall* (2003), p. 135, points out that sub-units may be forced to implement and use certain systems.

[388] Cf. *Modell* (2002), p. 654; *Yazdifar/Askarany* (2010b), p. 7.

also be found in more general literature on MNCs.[389] Hence, recognising new institutional sociology (NIS) during the analysis of cost accounting in subsidiaries may considerably improve the rather broad understanding of the determinants of cost accounting systems in subsidiaries. Thereby, the above publications on NIS as well as the studies by *Hoffjan/Weide* (2006), *Gerlach* (2009), or *Wolfsgruber* (2011) reveal a necessity to acknowledge subsidiaries' responses to corporately induced systems (i.e. the relationship of a subsidiary and its parent company). Such a necessity is equally derivable from the management control literature.[390]

While overcoming these deficiencies, this study has to acknowledge an additional finding from section 3.2. Considerations on the uniformity of cost accounting stem from studies regarding legal entities and non-uniformity evidence stems from studies on economic subunits. This situation discloses the necessity to account for potential effects of **various organisational structures** during the analysis of cost accounting in subsidiaries. According to a recent research project, the focus on medium-sized companies can account for such effects because these are more regularly characterised by single-business units.[391]

Regarding the identified preliminary evidence, it becomes obvious that there is no large sample, mezzo level study that exclusively describes the design of cost accounting systems in medium sized German subsidiaries of Anglophone MNCs. Furthermore, few attempts were made to explain the design of cost accounting systems under the impression of both contingency factors and institutional theory while explicitly recognising the subsidiary-parent company relationship. By following the first and second research objective (cf. section 1.1), this study offsets these deficiencies. Through research questions 3a and 3b, the study makes up the insufficiency that only a minority of the reviewed studies considers the performance of cost accounting systems in affiliates.[392]

3.3 Use of cost information in affiliates

3.3.1 Normative conceptual research

Normative considerations on the use of cost information in affiliates are **virtually absent**. For this part of the literature review, only the considerations by *Kellermanns/Islam* (2004) provide some revealing insights. Their recommendation to implement an American ABC system in German and US based multinationals is based on an analysis of the actual use of cost information in affiliates.

In line with the 'technology acceptance model', a model usually applied to analyse the applicability of information technologies, *Kellermans/Islam* stress that the actual use of cost information depends on the perceived ease of use and the perceived usefulness of a cost

[389] Cf. e.g. *Kostova/Roth* (2002), p. 215, or *Cruz et al.* (2009), p. 97f.

[390] Cf. e.g. *Harzing* (1999), p. 94ff., or section 4.1.3.

[391] Cf. *Schoute* (2011), p. 124.

[392] These studies are especially focussed on ABC only (cf. *Bhimani/Pigott* (1992); *Anderson/Young* (1999); *Abernethy* (2001); *Ittner et al.* (2002) and *Bhimani et al.* (2007)). Also, they rarely align their findings with the research focus on affiliates (cf. *Meyer* (1988); *Bhimani* (2003); *Smith* (2005), and *Yazdifar et al.* (2008) for exceptions). As such, little is known on the performance of cost accounting in affiliates.

accounting system. Moreover, they explicate the relevance of users' attitude towards the use of a cost information and the behavioural intention to use a particular information system. Including *Kellermans/Islam's* considerations at this point is motivated by the fact that similar determinants of the use of cost information prevail in empirical research on different types of cost information use (section 3.3.2.3). Even though the authors do not involve into a discussion of different usage types, their work thus ensures the relevance of the results for the due discussion, which largely relies on evidence from a non-affiliate context.

3.3.2 Empirical research

3.3.2.1 Introduction

Two important strands of research on the use of cost information contribute to an understanding of different usage types in subsidiaries.

On the one hand, there are examples of the **ceremonial use** of cost information in subsidiaries. As will be seen in section 3.3.2.2, however, these studies tend to be non-generalisable, neglect the effect of cross-national differences in cost accounting and rather consider the abandonment of cost accounting systems. Also, these studies do not differentiate alternative usage types to explicate the **non-ceremonial use** of cost information.

Such a differentiation, on the other hand, is detailedly discussed in a number of German research projects regarding the typologies of *Pelz* (i.e. instrumental, conceptual and symbolic use). Even though some projects regarded affiliate companies, these studies tend to disregard the effect of organisational hierarchies. They are summarised in section 3.3.2.3. No study on *Simons*' interactive and diagnostic use of *cost information* could be identified in international research.[393] Therefore, these types of use cannot be found in this section.

Peculiarly, these two strands are bridged by the empirical study of *Ansari/Euske* (1987) which will be discussed section 3.3.2.3 due to their analysis of disaggregated usage types.

3.3.2.2 Research on the ceremonial use of cost information

There are four research projects which address the ceremonial use of cost information in subsidiaries.

Scapens/Roberts (1993) analyse the engineering division of a British multinational. Their theoretical study is informed by structuration theory.[394] Following the authors, there were serious inconsistencies in the cost accounting systems of the division's legal entities (unit companies). These inconsistencies motivate both the division's managers and the unit companies' managers to initiate a project to unify the (cost) accounting systems of all unit

---

[393] *Davila* (2000), p. 396f., regards these usage types in his study of new product development processes of 11 firms. Because the author does not report explicitly to what extent cost information is used diagnostically or interactively, his study is excluded from this review.

[394] Though *Scherm/Pietsch* (2004), p. 10, stress this theories' sociological roots, according to *Scapens* (2006), p. 7, or *Burns/Scapens* (2000), p. 4, structuration theory is an economic theory.

companies. *Scapens/Roberts* report that a favourable attitude of the unit level managers towards the projects fades away after the cost accounting project evolves into a redesign of the division's production planning systems. The unit level managers disagree with the need for a cost-based system to control the production processes and feel the new system to be imposed on them irrespectively their local perspective. Moreover, *Scapens/Roberts* link this negative perception with unit level accountants' discomfort with the new system. Accordingly, the system constrains the discretion of these employees since it could lead to their job-loss. Despite overcoming the resistance at a pilot site, the change project is eventually abandoned due to, among others, further unit-level resistance to use the new system for decision-making. *Scapens/Roberts*' case is very revealing for this review since it comprises early evidence on a lacking application of cost information for decision-making (i.e. ceremonial use) of a corporately imposed cost accounting system. Also, the explanatory variables which the authors provide are well reflective of the findings derived in section 3.2. Yet, their focus on the abandonment of the cost accounting system rather than on the prolonged provision of cost information irrespectively their local usefulness dilutes the study's conclusiveness for an analysis of the ceremonial use of cost information.

Reflecting *Scapens/Roberts* (1993), *Waeytens/Bruggeman* (1994) analyse the case of Belgian manufacturing company which imposes an ABC system on its various departments. The authors highlight that the ABC systems' initial purpose is accurate overhead allocation. They find an early replacement of this initial purpose. Accordingly, the ABC project changes into a cost management initiative. The authors show that department managers do not make use of the ABC system for such efficiency improvement decisions, however. As such, *Waeytens/Bruggeman* provide evidence for a rather ceremonially used ABC system. The authors highlight various explanatory factors for their finding. Among these are the non-attended information needs of the local managers and the departments' ability to oppose the ABC initiative (i.e. the relationship of the parent and the subsidiary). Yet, these aspects are not aligned with any explanatory theory but emerge from the study's grounded theory perspective. Nevertheless, the article by *Waeytens/Bruggeman* (1994) is of remarkable relevance for this study as they are among the first researchers to indicate that affiliate managers may respond to a coercively imposed cost accounting system for which there is no local need by using the systems in a ceremonial manner only.

In line with *Waeytens/Bruggeman*, *Malmi* (1997) uses a case study to explicate the perceived success of ABC by corporate and unit managers of a Finnish company. The study consists of evidence stressing the implementation of ABC in one production plant which is initiated by corporate managers. Though the ABC system does not yield different cost information than the previous system did, corporate managers apply it for decision-making due to its uncertainty reducing, information confirming character. The production plant managers, however, perceive no additional value but additional workload of the new overhead allocation method only. As such, *Malmi*'s research emphasises different information requirements of the corporate and the unit-level in his case company. These are potential reasons why the information derived from ABC is used non-ceremonially at the corporate level only. Also, *Malmi* argues that the ABC system visualises the unit costs of the case company more detailedly. This constrains the managerial discretions of the plant's management. Following *Malmi*, all these aspects lead to the abandonment of the

ABC system two years after its implementation. *Malmi*'s rather theoretical study stresses that unfulfilled objectives and overruled managerial discretions can lead to a ceremonial use of coercively induced cost accounting systems in affiliates. As such, *Malmi* underlines that local management's information needs as well as the relationship between a subsidiary and its parent company are important antecedents of cost information use in affiliates. Thereby, *Malmi* reassures the validity of findings by the former two research projects.

Similarly to the former, *Major/Hopper* (2005) and *Hopper/Major* (2007) conduct a case study to describe the implementation and use of ABC in a domestic affiliate in Portugal (Marconi). The implementation occurred after Marconi's parent company recommended doing so. During the implementation at Marconi, the authors find local commercial managers' information needs to be more extensively incorporated into the systems' design than local engineers' requirements. The descriptive analysis by *Major/Hopper* (2005) highlights that this led to a subsequent use of ABC by commercial managers only. In *Hopper/Major* (2007), the authors explicate these observations through, among others, NIS. Accordingly, ABC is used non-ceremonially by commercial managers but ceremonially by the engineers. This finding is due to the simultaneous occurrence of institutional pressures, an uncertain market environment and engineers' fears to lobby against the powerful commercial managers. The authors' major contribution for this study is the underlined importance of NIS for the analysis of the use of cost information. Moreover, it is revealing to find that non-ceremonial and ceremonial use of cost information is not mutually exclusive in affiliates.

In contrast to the above studies, various studies from section 3.2 include empirical evidence on the non-ceremonial use of cost information.

Yazdifar et al. (2008) report on a new (cost) accounting system which a UK firm (Parent2) imposes on a domestic subsidiary (Sub). Yet, the system is applied for actual decision-making in *Sub*. The authors link this non-ceremonial use to the favourable attitude of the subsidiary's management towards the information usefulness of the imposed system. *Yazdifar et al.* contrast their findings to the previously reviewed studies as they find evidence for the local application of *Parent2*'s system at *Sub*, despite the systems' coercively induced implementation. The authors explain their finding with the disempowerment of key local opponents and substantial trainings on the system's usefulness. Also, they report that *Sub* mimics *Parent2*'s application of the new system. Such voluntary adoption[395] can facilitate the actual application of cost information systems for decision-making.[396] Overall, the authors provide an example that favourable local assessments of an imposed system, voluntary aspects of implementation and the implementation process can ensure a non-ceremonial use of an imposed cost accounting system in subsidiaries.

Similarly, *Smith* (2005) provides evidence on a non-ceremonial use of an imposed GPK system at STIHL's US manufacturing plant. His anecdote allows for an alignment of this finding with a favourable attitude towards the imposed system by the management of the subsidiary. As such, *Smith* underlines the importance of local manager's positive percep-

395 Cf. *Modell* (2002), p. 655.

396 Cf. *Brewer* (1998), p. 247; *Schoute* (2009), p. 209.

tion of an imposed system for a non-ceremonial use of these systems. The studies by *Meyer* (1988) and *Bhimani* (2003) consist of similar evidence. Both align the implementation and use of affiliate specific cost accounting systems with an affiliate's ability to fulfil their local information needs.

All these results are well in line with the findings from the studies by *Scapens/Roberts* (1993), *Waeytens/Bruggeman* (1994), *Malmi* (1997), *Major/Hopper* (2005), and *Hopper/Major* (2007). Whereas the ceremonial use of an imposed cost accounting system is associated to a lack of local information needs and a discretion constraining character of the imposed system, the non-ceremonial use of cost information in subsidiaries is affected by affiliates' ability to fulfil their local information needs, the freedom of the affiliates to design or adapt their cost accounting systems to their local contexts and the voluntary application of a cost accounting system.

In addition to these explicitly reviewed studies (Table 3-8), various empirical management accounting studies from the public sector[397] and on hospitals[398] underline that the (non-) ceremonial use of management information is associated to an imposed (voluntary) design of cost accounting systems and a lack (existence) of local information needs. Moreover, several studies on the relevance of institutional theory for an explanation of management accounting in affiliates underline the above results.[399] Despite focussing more on the ceremonial use of information rather than on the abandonment of corporately induced systems, none of these studies provides incremental insights for this review, however. As such, they are not reviewed conclusively at this point.

Author/s	Contribution to the study	Countries	Theoretical basis	Level of analysis	Research method	Sample size
Scapens/ Roberts (1993)	The discretion constraining character of an imposed cost accounting system and local information needs determine whether or not corporately induced cost accounting systems are used ceremonially.	UK	Power relationships, structuration theory	Theoretical, micro	Case study	1 sub-unit of a MNC
Waeytens/ Bruggeman (1994)	Example that the relationship of a parent and its subsidiary and local information needs are associated with the non-ceremonial and ceremonial use.	Belgium	Grounded theory (implicit)	Descriptive/ theoretical, micro	Case study	1 company, several departments
Malmi (1997)	The ceremonial use of cost information is employee group specific. It is associated with the discretion constraining character of an imposed cost accounting system.	Finland	NIS, power relationships	Theoretical, micro	Case study	1 production plant
Hopper/ Major (2005 and 2007)	An imposed cost accounting system can be used ceremonially and non-ceremonially simultaneously. Affiliates' information needs are linked to this result.	Portugal	NIS, OIE, labour process and actor network theory	Theoretical, micro	Case study	1 subsidiary
Studies reviewed in section 3.2.1	Voluntary application of cost accounting systems and a perceived local relevance of cost information are associated with the non-ceremonial application of information.			*See section 3.2*		

Table 3-8: Studies on the ceremonial use of cost information in affiliates

[397] Cf. *Geiger/Ittner* (1996), p. 550; *Euske/Riccaboni* (1999), p. 466; *Ho/Kidwell* (2000), p. 50; *Modell* (2006), p. 219.

[398] Cf. *Lapsley* (2001), p. 91; *Kurunmaki* (2003), p. 112; *Järvinen* (2006), p. 26.

[399] Cf. *Van der Stede* (2003); *Siti-Nabiha/Scapens* (2005); *Lukka* (2007); *Cruz* (2007); *Cruz et al.* (2009), and *Cruz et al.* (2011).

As revealed in section 3.3.2.1, a number of research projects complement these findings by analysing the non-ceremonial use of cost information in a more disaggregated manner.

3.3.2.3 Research on the non-ceremonial use of cost information

Ansari/Euske (1987) combines the consideration of a ceremonial use of cost information with a disaggregated analysis of alternative ways to use cost information in a non-ceremonial manner (instrumental/conceptual and symbolic use).[400] *Ansari/Euske* regard a situation, in which 12 US military depots are forced by the Secretary of Defence to implement a common cost accounting system. They find the depots to use their systems more symbolically than instrumentally/conceptually. Both these types, however, are dominated by the ceremonial application of the new cost accounting system. As such, *Ansari/Euske* mirror the findings from the previous section. Imposing cost accounting systems on affiliates can lead to their ceremonial use. Nevertheless, the study by *Ansari/Euske* (1987) is important for this review because it is the only research project which considers the usage types of *Pelz* and *Burchell et al.* as well as the ceremonial usage type. Moreover, the study is very insightful for explicative purposes. The authors link their findings argumentatively to a perceived lack of local information usefulness of the new systems as well as the systems' imposed character. They derive these variables theoretically through NIS. Thereby, the authors underline that this theoretical perspective is not only relevant for the analysis of a cost accounting system's design in affiliates but for its use as well.

In addition to *Ansari/Euske*, three German research projects regard the instrumental, conceptual and symbolic use of *cost* information.[401] *Homburg et al.* (1998), *Aust* (1999) and *Karlshaus* (2000) centre on the use of cost information for marketing purposes, *Frank* (2000) and *Reitmeyer* (2000) focus on board members' use of cost information and *Hunhold* (2003) applies the analysis of usage types to a sample from the public sector. All these research projects are questionnaire investigations of large German samples which are especially informed by economic theories.[402] Peculiarly, the project by *Homburg et al.* (1998), *Aust* (1999) and *Karlshaus* (2000) samples German *business units* to ensure the quality of their dataset.[403] The authors, however, report that smaller research objects in their sample are legal entities rather than economic sub-units. Moreover, they disregard any issues of organisational hierarchies during data analysis. As such, despite the initial focus on affiliates, the results remain rather blurred in this respect.

---

400 For the comparability reasons, the usage types covered in *Ansari/Euske* are not labelled in accordance with the authors but by the names applied in this study (cf. section 1.2.1.2.2 for a conversion).

401 *van der Veeken/Wouters* (2002), p. 366, provide Dutch case study evidence for the use of cost information for preplanning and learning purposes. These usage types are linked to this study's instrumental and conceptual use (cf. *van der Veeken/Wouters* (2002), p. 349). Yet, *van der Veeken/Wouters* (2002) provide non-incremenal insights only. Their main finding that the environmental uncertainty has an explicatory value for the prevalence of these two usage types can be drawn from the German research projects as well. Hence, *van der Veeken/Wouters* (2002)'s non-incremental findings are excluded from this review.

402 Cf. Table 3-10 for a profound review of these studies' research methods.

403 For this and the following, cf. e.g. *Aust* (1999), p. 35.

Table 3-9 illustrates that the use of cost information tends to be analysed for decision-making managers rather than management accountants. It prevails that these information users tend to use information more for direct decision-making (i.e. instrumentally) than to gain experiences (i.e. conceptually). Though cost information is applied symbolically as well, this usage type tends to lack behind. Regrettably, the cited authors do not differentiate the symbolic use according to the suggestions by *Burchell et al.* (1980). Remarkably, these results violate the results from research on the use of management accounting information in general (section 2.3.3). In such studies, a dominance of the symbolic usage type is typically found.[404] Apparently, the use of cost information is rather specific in this regard. Because the authors from Table 3-9 do not compare the presence of the alternative usage types statistically, however, the conclusiveness of the above assertions remains unclear.

Author/s	Respondent/s	Instrumental use	Conceptual use	Symbolic use	Comment
Homburg et al. (1998)	Board members & Marketing managers	74 %	62 %	62 %	Joint dataset 1
Aust (1999)	Board members & Marketing managers	not reported	not reported	not reported	Joint dataset 1
Karlshaus (2000)	Marketing managers	15 % remaining to 100 % reported more than one type	43 %	22 %	Joint dataset 1
Frank (2000)	Board members	not reported	disregarded	disregarded	Joint dataset 2
Reitmeyer (2000)	Board members	not reported	disregarded	disregarded	Joint dataset 2
Hunold (2003)	Public treasurers	77 %	73 %	62 %	Dataset 3

Table 3-9: Presence of various types of cost information use in German organisations

All studies in Table 3-9 neglect whether organisational hierarchies affect the use of cost information. Thus, no conclusion for the use of cost information in (foreign) affiliates of MNCs can be drawn. Preliminary evidence on the use of an unspecified bundle of management accounting information in various international branches of an US multinational suggests that management accounting information are used similarly in groups.[405] Yet, no such analysis was previously performed for the use of cost information. Since general management accounting information tends to be used differently than cost information, it remains unclear, whether the findings by *Jais* (2004) indicate that the different non-ceremonial usage types are independent of corporate effects on the design of information systems.

The studies in Table 3-9 analyse a number of variables which could affect the regarded usage types. Remarkably, the surveys cannot unambiguously link a cost accounting systems' conceptual design to the different types of use.[406] *Karlshaus* (2000) cannot find a significant association between the perceived complexity of a cost accounting system and the use of cost information. In contrast, *Frank* (2000) finds the perceived quality of cost information to decrease the more complex information users perceive a cost accounting

[404] Cf. section 2.3.3 for an introducing summary of these studies' findings.

[405] Cf. *Jais* (2007), p. 159.

[406] Cf. for this and the following *Frank* (2000), p. 175ff.; *Karlshaus* (2000), p. 160; *Hunold* (2003), p. 208. *Homburg* (1998); *Aust* (1999), and *Reitmeyer* (2000), do not report applicable results in this respect.

system to be. As such, it may be argued that *Frank*'s simultaneous finding of a positive association between the instrumental use and the perceived quality[407] hints at a negative association between perceived complexity and the instrumental use. *Hunold* (2003) can confirm such a relationship. He finds a significant negative effect of the subjectively perceived complexity of a cost accounting system on the instrumental and the conceptual use. Yet, it remains empirically blurred whether the relationship between the design of a cost accounting system and its non-ceremonial use as depicted by *Kellermans/Islam* (2004) or *Ansari/Euske* (1987) can be established for an objectively measured level of cost accounting complexity.

In addition to a cost accounting system's design, above research projects find a variety of factors affecting one or another of the usage types. Besides an effect of economic uncertainties, it is most peculiar to find the characteristics of the decision makers, their interaction with cost accountants, their involvement into the design of cost accounting systems and their perceptions on cost information quality to underlie the various usage types. These findings especially amplify the necessity to consider information user's characteristics as well as the relationship of preparers and users of cost information during a study of differing types of cost information use. Neither section 3.2 nor *Ansari/Euske*'s work explicated the relevance of these effects. Even though the studies from Table 3-9 reveal little insights on the reasons, why these effects are relevant from a theoretical view-point, these results highlight that an analysis of cost information use cannot be thoroughly performed on the grounds of NIS only. Since the normative conceptual work by *Kellermanns/Islam (2004)* explicates similar effects, section 4.1.4 discusses these findings from the theoretical perspective of the dynamic theory of economic actors.[408]

Besides the explicative analysis of the usage types, most of the researchers from Table 3-9 consider performance effects of the various usage types. From a general perspective, no type of use is per se more or less adequate than another one.[409] Yet, the studies on the use of cost information stress the usage types to be influential for various measures of organisational performance (e.g. financial performance or the rationality of the decision-making processes).[410] Regardless these differing performance measures, some trends prevail. The results indicate a rather negative effect of instrumental use of cost information and a rather positive one of the conceptual usage type. No prevailing direction is reported for the symbolic use of cost information. As for the descriptive evidence on the usage types, these results can be contrasted to the results from studies that focus on the use of other information. Disregarding the variety of the applied performance measures, these studies, in tendency, find positive rather than negative effects for the majority of the usage types.

---

[407] Cf. *Frank* (2000), p. 153 and 177.

[408] For the relevance of the theoretical position, cf. *Jais* (2007), p. 7f.

[409] Cf. *March* (1987), p. 161.

[410] For this and the following, cf. *Aust* (1999), p. 117f.; *Reitmeyer* (2000), p. 129; *Frank* (2000), p. 227ff.; *Karlshaus* (2000), p. 169ff. All these assessments are either based on information users' perceptions only or conjointly on responses by preparers and users of information.

Author/s	Contribution to this study	Countries	Theoretical basis	Level of analysis	Research method	Sample size
Ansari/Euske (1987)	The study introduce the use of cost information into international literature. Their focus on affiliates reveals the relevance of a ceremonial use of information to be a considerable usage type in such a setting.	USA	NIS	Theoretical, micro	Case study	12 US military depots
Homburg et al. (1998)	The authors introduce the use of cost information into the German management accounting literature. They provide factors to explicate the different types of use as well as their effect on managerial performance.	Germany	Contingency theory	Rather descriptive, micro	Survey/ questionnaire	104 triads of German companies[411] [RR: 12.30 %]
Aust (1999)	The author provides evidence on (*Pelz*'s and) *Burchell et al.*'s types of cost information use. He provides factors to explicate the different types of use.	Germany	Contingency theory	Rather descriptive, micro	Survey/ questionnaire	114 triads of German companies[412] [RR: 12.30 %]
Karlshaus (2000)	The author provides evidence on *Pelz*'s (and *Burchell et al.*'s) types of cost information use. He provides factors to explicate the different types of use as well as their impact on managerial performance.	Germany	System and contingency theory, resource-based view	Descriptive/ theoretical, micro	Survey/ questionnaire	112 dyads of German companies[413] [RR: 12.30 %]
Frank (2000)	The author provides evidence on *Pelz*'s (and *Burchell et al.*'s) types of cost information use. He provides factors to explicate the different types of use as well as their impact on managerial performance.	Germany	Contingency theory	Rather descriptive, micro	Survey/ questionnaire	493 German companies[414] [RR: 17 %]
Reitmeyer (2000)	Provides evidence on *Pelz*'s (and *Burchell et al.*'s) types of cost information use. Provides factors to explicate the different types of use as well as their impact on managerial performance.	Germany	Especially contingency theory	Rather descriptive, micro	Survey/ questionnaire	See *Frank* (2000)
Hunold (2003)	The author analyses the use of cost information in a public sector setting. He discusses factors to explicate the different types of use as well as their effect on managerial performance.	Germany	System and contingency theory, decision theory	Descriptive/ theoretical, micro	Survey/ questionnaire	229 dyads from German town councils [RR: 13.22 %]

Table 3-10: Studies disaggregating the non-ceremonial use of cost information

Remarkably, for two usage types which are not covered in cost accounting research (rationalising and diagnostic use) negative performance effects are as common as positive ones.[415] These considerations show that the different types which disaggregate the non-

[411] Included questionnaires stem from accountants, marketing managers and board members.

[412] Included questionnaires stem from accountants, marketing managers and board members.

[413] Included questionnaires stem from accountants and marketing managers.

[414] Included questionnaires stem from board members.

[415] For the use of management information with respect to the typologies by *Pelz* and *Burchell et al.*, cf. *Vandenbosch/Huff* (1997), p. 94ff.; *Diamantopoulos/Souchon* (1998), p. 128; *Vandenbosch* (1999), p. 87ff.; *Sandt* (2004), p. 189ff.; *Schäffer/Steiners* (2005a), p. 217f.; *Jais* (2007), p. 162ff. For *Simons*' usage types in a management control setting, cf. *Abernethy/Brownell* (1999), p. 197ff.; *Bisbe/Otley* (2004),

ceremonial use indeed affect the organisational and managerial performance in a company. As the pursuit of the individual usage types, however, their performance effects in subsidiaries remain to be explored.

Table 3-10 summarises these seven research projects which analyse the use of cost information by disaggregating the non-ceremonial usage type.

3.3.3 Summary

There are two overreaching communalities in the two strands of research on the use of cost information. Both strands reveal the necessity to consider thoroughly for which persons in a company the use of cost information is regarded. The working position can affect heavily, how cost information is used. Section 5.2 elaborates on the consequences of this finding for this study. Moreover, both strands essentially demonstrate that a cost accounting system which is performing well in a subsidiary is one that can provide cost information which is relevant for an affiliate's process of management. Other than that, the findings on different usage types in affiliates are remarkably diverse. The two identified strands vary with respect to their research objects as well as the applied research methods and research objectives.

The studies on the **ceremonial use** of cost information, on the one hand, are characterised by a focus on cost accounting systems in subsidiaries. The evidence, however, is only case study based and relies on analyses of the process of institutionalisation or abandonment of cost accounting systems rather than the use of existing systems. As such, there is no reliable survey evidence on the ceremonial use of cost accounting systems in affiliates. Peculiarly, the studies' reliance on institutional theory (esp. NIS) allows for a thorough theoretical derivation of variables which can explain a ceremonial use of cost information. They highlight the interplay of corporate involvements, the fit of imposed systems to the local context (i.e. the conformity of an imposed system with local information needs) and the relationships between subsidiary and parent companies to be particularly relevant for such an analysis. Similar aspects already prevailed in the analysis of the design of cost accounting systems in subsidiaries. Therefore, the relevance of NIS for the research of cost accounting systems in subsidiaries can be reemphasised by section 3.3.2.2. Yet, the reviewed studies widely neglect cross-national differences in cost accounting. Hence, the studies in section 3.3.2.2 do not explicate whether the necessity to adapt Anglophone cost accounting in a subsidiary in Germany may be associated with a greater level of ceremonial use due to, e.g. a decreased level of locally perceived information usefulness.

The studies which regard the **non-ceremonial use** of cost information in a disaggregated manner, on the other hand, are especially survey based. As such, their results are characterised by a certain level of statistical generalisability. Unfortunately, the projects neither comprise *Burchell et al.*'s rationalising use nor do they regard Simons' diagnostic and interactive usage types. Also, the reviewed studies remain rather descriptive in nature. Despite providing thorough evidence on the antecedents of different usage types, little is

p. 722ff.; *Henri* (2006a), p. 95; *Henri* (2006b), p. 543ff.; *Naranjo-Gil/Hartmann* (2006), p. 37; *Widener* (2007), p. 778; *Bisbe/Malagueño* (2009), p. 390f.; *Hofmann et al.* (2012), p. 170.

learned how to explain such effects from a theoretical point of view. Nevertheless, the studies identify several contingencies of the use of cost information. These are not only reflecting the ones from the normative study by *Kellermanns/Islam* (2004) but also deviate substantially from the variables discussed in sections 3.2 and 3.3.2.2. Exemplarily, the inclusion of information users' personal attitudes towards (cost) information is not covered in studies on cost accounting systems in affiliates. This exemplifies a necessity for theoretical triangulation in this regard. Section 4 takes on this discussion. Regrettably, the studies in section 3.3.2.3 can neither contribute to the question whether or not cross-national differences in cost accounting affect the non-ceremonial use of cost information nor do they explicate whether the non-ceremonial usage types are affected by corporate involvements in subsidiaries.

In a nutshell, it becomes evident that no survey study assessed this far how cost information is used in affiliates by differentiating various non-ceremonial as well as a ceremonial type of cost information use. This holds particularly true for Anglophone subsidiaries in Germany, i.e. under the consideration of cross-national differences in cost accounting. By overcoming these deficiencies, this study analyses whether the case evidence aligning subsidiaries' cost information use with corporate directives is empirically generalisable. Also, it assesses whether the results for the instrumental, conceptual and symbolic use (i.e. rationalising, diagnostic and interactive) are applicable in a setting of affiliate companies.

The review in this section enlarges the **multidimensional research opportunity** derived in section 3.2. First, the need for theoretical triangulation becomes evident. Besides NIS, this study must embrace considerations of the 'dynamic theory of economic actors' as this position can explain the findings from section 3.3.2.3 from a theoretical point of view. Second, the review emphasises that usage types are generally studied for specific decision makers rather than management accountants. As such, this study has to follow a dyadic design if it was to acknowledge that subsidiaries might respond to corporately induced cost accounting systems by not using these systems during the local management process.

3.4 Implications for this study

Above all, the provided literature review underlines the necessity to describe and explain the design of cost accounting systems and the use of cost information in Anglophone subsidiary companies (research questions) by the means of an empirical research strategy (research method). It could also establish a need to consider the performance of cost accounting systems during such an analysis to derive practically relevant recommendations.

Research questions

The literature review on the **design of cost accounting systems** highlights that there is virtually no conclusive evidence about the consequences of cross-national differences in cost accounting for the design of foreign affiliates' cost accounting systems.

From a descriptive perspective, there is as much evidence for subsidiaries' cost accounting systems to be in line with a parent company's home country traditions as there is evidence for a non-uniform design. Though the review could somewhat conclusively explain these findings, it remains unclear whether the identified interrelations hold empirically true. As such, sections 3.2.1 and 3.2.2 reveal the necessity for further research on cost accounting systems in subsidiaries for descriptive and explicative reasons. Since especially the cost accounting systems in Anglophone companies in Germany remain unexplored, the preliminary derived research questions (1a) and (2a) can be enforced:

RQ (1a)	Are there differences with respect to the design of cost accounting systems in Anglophone and domestic subsidiaries in Germany?
RQ (2a)	What determines the design of cost accounting systems in Anglophone and domestic subsidiaries in Germany?

In line with conceptual suggestions,[416] the design of cost accounting systems will be measured as a single variable reflecting the complexity of the three components of a cost accounting system. As explicated in Figure 2-2 the variable will be formed by a number of 15 characteristics. The measure is labelled *complexity of cost accounting*.[417] It is chosen because of its capabilities to provide fruitful insight into the mezzo level conceptual design of foreign subsidiaries' cost accounting systems. Thereby, the measure can highlight the impact of cross-national differences in cost accounting systems.

According to section 3.2.2, the ceremonial **use of cost information** is a common response of affiliates to a coercively induced cost accounting system. Previous studies on this matter are rather case study based. Moreover, they focus especially on the process of institutionalisation or the abandonment of cost accounting initiatives rather than the use of an existing cost accounting system. As such, these findings await refinement and statistical generalisation. Moreover, it has not yet been explored, whether the non-ceremonial usage types are affected by a parent company's involvement in subsidiaries cost accounting systems as well. Remarkably, section 3.2.2 finds institutional, economical and personal influences to explain the ceremonial as well as the multiple non-ceremonial types of cost information use. Yet, to date these effects have not been regarded conjointly in a survey on Anglophone subsidiaries in Germany. Therefore, it is equally valid to pose the research questions (1b) and (2b) as introduced in section 1.

RQ (1b)	How do Anglophone and domestic subsidiaries in Germany use their cost information for managerial decision-making?
RQ (2b)	What determines the use of cost information for managerial decision-making in Anglophone and domestic subsidiaries in Germany?

Due to the ability to contribute to the preliminary state of knowledge regarding the use of cost information and the identified relevance of the ceremonial usage type for research on

---

[416] It is recommended to select measures based on their prima facie relevance. Moreover, the existance of pre-developed measures and their significant support in literature should be taken into account (cf. *Brown et al.* (2004), p. 335).

[417] Cf. *Moeschler* (2012), p. 146ff. Similarly, *Anderson et al.* (2002), p. 204, and *Drury/Tayles* (2005), p. 70f., form indeces that reflect companies' activity (cost) pools and activity (cost) drivers. *Abernethy* (2001), and *Schoute* (2009), p. 214, extent such measures by including the nature of the cost allocation bases. Similarly, *Al-Omiri/Drury* (2007), p. 403, includes the different rationales beyond overhead allocation. *Aust* (1999), p. 166; *Frank* (2000), p. 116; *Hunold* (2003), p. 151ff.; *Krumwiede et al.* (2007), p. 48, did conceptualise their complexity (or GPK) measures based on qualitative rather than quantitative assessments of the three components of a cost accounting system.

subsidiaries, cost information use will be regarded in terms of the following six usage types: instrumental, conceptual, rationalising, diagnostic and interactive use of cost information.[418]

Previous research on the **performance of cost accounting systems** in subsidiaries is remarkably diverse. Whereas the research projects on the use of cost information regularly consider the performance of cost accounting systems, the studies on the design of cost accounting in affiliates rather disregard such considerations. In addition to the introduced necessity to study the performance of cost accounting systems to pursue the pragmatic research objective, the literature review thus reveals that studying the performance of cost accounting in subsidiaries can considerably improve the knowledge on this matter. Because previous research cannot provide a conclusive answer to research questions (3a) and (3b), their validity is reassured.

RQ (3a)	How can Anglophone and domestic subsidiaries in Germany improve the design of their cost accounting systems?
RQ (3b)	How can Anglophone and domestic subsidiaries in Germany improve the use of cost information in managerial decision-making?

Given the intended dyadic design of this research project, cost accounting system's performance can be included as cost accountants' and managers' subjective satisfaction with their cost accounting systems in this study. Moreover, the performance of cost accounting systems will also be measured as a system's ability to provide cost information which is useful to fulfil a number of cost accounting objectives (goal attainment). The inclusion of two assessment-based measures of a system's performance follows the prevalence of such measures in previous research, their potential to provide insights into cross-national differences (see section 2.1.2.3) and recent calls for the application of such variables.[419]

Research Method

Finding answers to research questions (1a) and (2a) links this study with the provision of statistically reliable assertions about the design of cost accounting systems and the use of cost information in the population of Anglophone companies in Germany. Deriving reliable information on this population of companies can best be achieved by **survey**ing a sample of it[420] through a mail- and web-based questionnaire.[421] Thereby, finding thorough answers to research questions (1a) and (2a) requires a comparison of the Anglophone companies to a German control sample. Also, a restriction of the populations to small and medium sized subsidiaries is essential to account for the joint presence of economic and legal structures in subsidiaries. In addition, section 3.3.3 explicates that the simultaneous focus on both the complexity of cost accounting systems and the use of cost information by decision makers requires this research project to take a **dyadic** design.

---

418 It is recommended to select measures based on their prima facie relevance. Moreover, the existance of pre-developed measures and their significant support in literature should be taken into account (cf. *Brown et al.* (2004), p. 335).

419 Cf. *Drury/Tayles* (2005), p. 77.

420 Cf. *Birnberg et al.* (1990), p. 35; *Real/Parker* (2005), p. 4; *Riesenhuber* (2009), p. 7.

421 Cf. *Kubicek* (1975), p. 67ff.; *Birnberg et al.* (1990), p. 35; *Real/Parker* (2005), p. 11; *Van der Stede et al.* (2005), p. 657.

Above all, in addition to the revealed lack of survey research on the above matters, this research method suits the descriptive research objective best.

Epistemologically, this study roots on *Popper*'s critical rationalism. Hence, research questions (1b) and (2b) will be answered by falsifying a number of theoretically derived hypotheses. Since survey research is closely linked to theory-testing and the intention to falsify hypotheses, the chosen research strategy suits the theoretical research objective mirrored in research questions (1b) and (2b) as well.[422] For the purpose of hypotheses development, sections 3.2.3 and 3.3.3, identify '**contingency theory**', '**new institutional sociology**' and the '**dynamic theory of economic actors**' to be particularly relevant.[423] These theories can account for the importance of organisational structures, economic effects and information users' attitudes during an analysis of the design of cost accounting systems and the use of cost information in affiliates.

Describing and explaining the design and use of cost accounting in Anglophone subsidiaries in Germany through a survey will also facilitate accomplishing the **pragmatic research objective.**[424] Thereby, the dyadic design will ensure that meaningful answers can be found for research questions (3a) and (3b) through the chosen research method. It accounts for a potential 'perception gap' between the preparers and users of cost information.[425]

---

[422] Cf. *Merchant/Otley* (2006), p. 790, or similarly *Riesenhuber* (2009), p. 1ff.

[423] Section 4 reveals that these theories are particularly in line with the philosophical position of this study.

[424] Cf. *Kosiol* (1964), p. 745; *Wild* (1966), p. 22ff.; *Grochla* (1976), p. 633; *Schweitzer* (1978), p. 3ff.; *Chmielewicz* (1994), p. 17f.

[425] Cf. *Malmi* (1997), p. 495ff.; *Major/Hopper* (2005), p. 223; *McGowan/Klammer* (1997), p. 234; *Bhimani* (2003), p. 539ff.; *Pierce/O'Dea* (2003), p. 258ff.; *Dietz/Snyder* (2011), p. 38, and *Walker et al.* (2012), p. 15ff., for recent studies on differing perceptions about the performance of management accounting by users and preparers of management accounting information.

4 Theoretical foundation and hypotheses development

4.1 Theoretical foundation and basic hypotheses

4.1.1 Introduction

The conceptual considerations in sections 2 and 3 guide the description of the *complexity of cost accounting system* and the exploration of the *types of cost information use* in subsidiaries (**descriptive research objective**). Nevertheless, at this point, some expectations on research questions (1a) and (1b) are stated. With respect to the design of cost accounting in subsidiaries, section 2.2 highlights that Anglophone cost accounting traditions are less complex than German cost accounting. Also, section 3.2.3 reveals that it is slightly more common to find unified cost accounting systems in multinationals than non-unified systems. Hence, it can be expected that Anglophone subsidiaries have less complex cost accounting systems than domestic German companies (research question (1a)). Regarding the use of cost information, section 2.3.3 finds no convincing evidence on a potential difference how extensive Anglophone and German MNCs use cost information with respect to the usage types covered in this study. Also, section 3.2.2 does not show parent companies' involvement to be particular to Anglophone or German multinationals which could form an expectation of a stronger prevalence of the ceremonial usage type in Anglophone companies. Similarly, section 3.3.2.2 cannot show that subsidiaries are per se more likely to oppose corporate directives if these directives were informed by foreign cost accounting traditions. Hence, with respect to research question (1b), it must be expected that there are similar usage types present in Anglophone and domestic German companies. These two **expectations** are summarised as this study's basic hypotheses number 1 and 2:

H1:	*The complexity of cost accounting systems in Anglophone subsidiaries is lower than in domestic German subsidiaries.*
H2:	*The same types of cost information use prevail in Anglophone and domestic German subsidiaries.*

Potential **explanations** for the *complexity of cost accounting* (research questions (2a)) and the *types of cost information use* (research questions (2b)) in subsidiaries remain fragmentary this far. Section 3.2.3 highlights that previous research on the complexity of cost accounting in affiliates is essentially illustrating various contingencies only. Very few attempts are made to embrace theoretical positions such as NIS to explain the design of cost accounting in subsidiaries more conclusively. This theoretical deficiency will be overcome in this chapter by bridging the contingency approach and NIS. Section 3.3.3 highlights that NIS is relevant for the analysis of the ceremonial use of cost information as well. Yet, previous research on the non-ceremonial usage types typically embrace other explanatory factors as well. As such, it is preclosed in section 3.4 that explaining the use of cost information in subsidiaries makes it essential to embrace the dynamic theory of economic actors. Hence, this chapter also discusses this theoretical position.

To facilitate accomplishing the theoretical research objective,[426] this chapter integrates the introduced business theories into a conjoint research framework. This framework will include the expected explanations for the design of cost accounting systems and the use of cost information in subsidiaries which are empirically tested in this study. The framework reflects this study's theoretical research objective and its empirical research strategy.[427] Also, the included business theories are in line with the chosen philosophy of science as will be discussed throughout the following sections.

In addition to the complexity and use of cost accounting systems, which are explained theoretically by this study, the **performance of cost accounting systems** is included into this study for pragmatic reasons. The variable is essential to derive recommendations on how to design and use a well performing cost accounting system. Hence, other than the complexity and use of cost accounting, no attempt is made to '*explain*' a cost accounting system's performance from a theoretical point of view. Rather, several propositions are derived for the interrelation of the complexity of cost accounting systems, the use of cost information and the performance of a cost accounting system. For brevity, these propositions are also labelled hypotheses. They will be derived in section 4.2.3, i.e. detached from the theoretical positions to be discussed in section 4.1. This procedure reflects the association of the performance of cost accounting with this study's pragmatic rather than its theoretical research objective. Nevertheless, the performance of cost accounting systems is included into the figures of this section since even these propositions must be seen in the light of the explanations of a system's design and use. The theoretical antecedents of the design of cost accounting systems and the use of cost information are indirect levers for the performance of cost accounting systems.[428]

4.1.2 Contingency theory

Contingency theory assumes "that there is no single organizational structure that is highly effective for all organizations."[429] In order to work efficiently, companies (have to) adapt their structure in accordance with the context they operate in.[430] Context is assumed to persist of several factors stemming from the in- and outside of organisations.[431]

In the context of management accounting, researchers assume that there is no „universally ‚best' design for a management accounting information system"[432]. As revealed in section 3.2, contingency theory serves as the primary basis for previous research projects regarding the design of cost accounting in affiliates.

---

[426] Cf. *Kubicek* (1977), p. 17, and *Stoi* (1999), p. 87f., or *Kajüter* (2000), p. 23f. for summaries on the relevance of conceptual research frameworks.

[427] For this and the following, cf. *Kubicek* (1977), p. 22.

[428] *Pizzini* (2006), p. 192ff., and *Schoute* (2009), p. 212, provide similar arguments. Both authors analyse effects of the complexity of cost accounting on performance assessments. Other environmental and technical factors, they reason, can be included into the statistical analysis for control purposes.

[429] *Donaldson* (1996), p. 57.

[430] Cf. *Kieser* (2006), p. 215.

[431] Cf. *Gordon/Miller* (1976), p. 59; *Waterhouse/Tiessen* (1978), p. 66; *Otley* (1980), p. 413ff.

[432] *Otley* (1980), p. 416. For a review of contingency theory studies in the context of management accounting, cf. *Chenhall* (2003).

Despite its widespread presence, the *theory* is criticised for its conceptually unlimited number of factors that qualify for explanatory purposes[433] and an inadequacy to actually *explain* the design of cost accounting systems and the use of cost information in organisations.[434] This criticism reflects the **lack of theoretical grounding** which characterises the unreflected revelation of context as an influential factor in contingency theory.[435] The criticism is based on a stricter understanding of 'theory'.[436] It is sustained here. Despite attributing according factors to argumentations of economic fit (i.e. efficiency and effectiveness), the contingency *approach* cannot provide explanations for the origin of contingency factors. Hence, contingency factors await explanations on the grounds of other theories.

This attenuates the contingency approach into a **meta-concept**, which merely stresses the importance of context.[437] Thus, for the purpose of this study contingency theory implies the necessity to consider contextual factors[438] for the study of cost accounting systems and cost information use in subsidiaries.[439] Figure 4-1 illustrates the relevance of the contingency approach for this study's research framework.

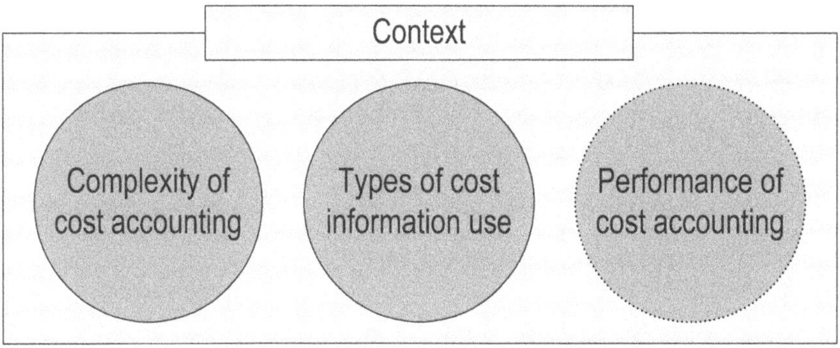

Figure 4-1: Contribution of the contingency approach for this research project

4.1.3 New institutional sociology

New Institutional Sociology (subsequently NIS) is a sociologically informed institutional theory which stems from a stream of various social sciences' (e.g. economics, political sci-

433 Cf. *Granlund* (2001), p. 145.

434 Cf. e.g. *Jones* (1985), p. 321; *Bhimani* (2004), p. 581; *Major/Hopper* (2005), p. 225.

435 Cf. e.g. *Picot* (1991), p. 157; *Kieser* (1993), p. 75; *Donaldson* (1996), p. 65; *Homburg* (1998), p. 67.

436 Theory cannot be regarded as a clearly defined phrase (cf. *Chmielewicz* (1994), p. 162). It varies e.g. under the differing philosophical positions identified in section 1.3 (cf. *Scherm/Pietsch* (2004), p. 6). For a review of alternative 'theory' definitions, cf. *Rusch* (2001), p. 91ff., or *Wolf* (2013), p. 3ff.

437 Cf. *Kieser* (1993), p. 75.

438 The differentiation of the contingency approach in accordance with the deterministic effect of context or possible organisational choices, i.e. a differentiation of structural and neo-contingency theory, will not be comprehensively discussed here. Neither perspective overcomes the lack of theoretical grounding. A discussion of the perspectives can be found in *Donaldson* (2001), p. 147ff. and 245ff.

439 For a similar argumentation, cf. *Homburg* (1998), p. 67, or *Aust* (1999), p. 35.

ence, sociology) rising interest in institutional theory.[440] NIS is built on the assumption that "(...) organizations are driven to incorporate the practices and procedures defined by prevailing rationalised concepts of organizational work and institutionalized in society"[441] for the purpose of social legitimacy.[442] As such, NIS stresses that organisations do not merely adopt organisational structures because of **technical and market driven** choices motivated by efficiency or rationality concerns,[443] but also due to coercive, normative and mimetic institutional pressures.[444] These institutional pressures may not be distinguishable empirically.[445] This holds especially true for mimetic and normative pressures as these essentially reflect organisations voluntarily chosen, though institutionally induced structure.[446] Above all, NIS stresses that there is a continuum of legitimacy and efficiency which explains organisational structures.

Despite its initial concern with organisational structures, NIS proves to be applicable for cost accounting research[447] and especially for studies on MNCs[448] as well. Accordingly, economic and institutional pressures influence the design and use of cost accounting to become isomorphic, i.e. similar, in certain organisation fields (institutional environment surrounding an organisation).[449] Such an institutional environment consists of a variety of **institutions**. According to NIS theorists, these institutions are linked to the formation and sustainment of social order.[450] They are understood to be a "standardized interaction sequence (...) that has attained a certain state of property"[451] and as such reflect universal aspects such as an academic discipline, a parent corporation, a country's legislation (e.g.

---

440 Cf. *DiMaggio/Powell* (1991), p. 1; *Scott* (2001), p. 1-18 and 37ff.; *Ahmed/Scapens* (2000), p. 165. For this study, NIS rather than general institutional theories is of interest. Hence, the framework by *Scott* (2001) which bridges various institutional perspectives is neglected.

441 *Meyer/Rowan* (1977), p. 340.

442 Cf. *Meyer/Rowan* (1977), p. 340.

443 In accordance with *Granlund/Lukka* (1998), p. 156, these may also be referred to as economic influences.

444 Cf. *DiMaggio/Powell* (1983), p. 150; *Scott* (1987), p. 508.

445 Cf. *DiMaggio/Powell* (1983), p. 150.

446 Cf. *Oliver* (1991), p. 167f.; *Modell* (2002), p. 658f.

447 Cf. section 3.

448 *Westney* (1993), p. 53ff., and *Robinson* (1996), p. 30f., express NIS to be especially applicable for the tension of uniformity (or integration in the authors' words) in multinationals and associated local responsiveness of subsidiaries. According to them, NIS enables "comparing subsidiaries both to its parent and to other organizations in the environment" (*Robinson* (1996), p. 31). Similarly, *Chung et al.* (2002), p. 125, call for such research projects. Yet, there are some shortcomings of NIS for the analysis of MNCs. Exemplarily, *Kostova et al.* (2008), p. 997ff., and *Westney* (1993), p. 67, stress a possible dificiency for the application of NIS to MNC because of an unclear definition of organisational fields. The comparison of foreign and domestic companies in one particular national setting mitigates this critique for this study. Still, this critique reveals that there might be difficulties to explain the design of cost accounting systems and the use of cost information in subsidiaries thoroughly through NIS. Consequently, the call for a critical assessment of the applicability of NIS in the context of MNC by *Kostova et al.* (2008), p. 997ff., is discussed in the limitations of this study.

449 Cf. *DiMaggio/Powell* (1983), p. 149.

450 Cf. *Meyer* (2004), p. 51.

451 Cf. *Jepperson* (1991), p. 145.

external accounting rules) or a consultancy firm.[452] Despite its initial focus on the explanations of similarities or convergence (i.e. isomorphism) in organisational fields, NIS provides a powerful tool for the explanation of organisational differences and differing organisational performance as well.[453] Accordingly, the conjoint analysis of **economic and institutional effects** facilitates the understanding of organisational structures. Figure 4-2 adapts NIS to this study's research questions by refining the relevance of contextual factors established through the contingency approach.

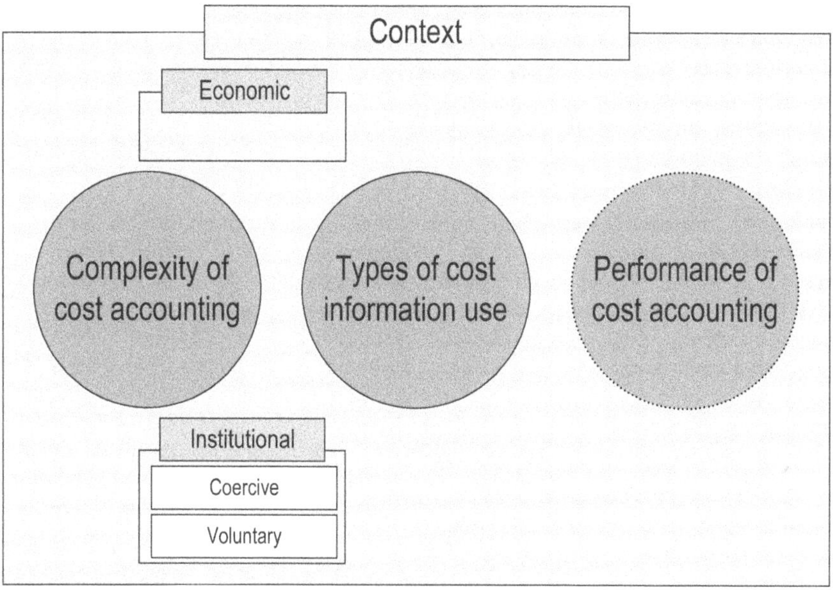

Figure 4-2: Preliminary contribution of NIS for this research project

NIS theorists initially regarded economic and institutional forces as alternative reasons for organisational structure[454] or for the design of cost accounting systems and the use of cost information. The theoretical scholars, however, soon revised this continuum. Initially, researchers substituted the continuum for the simultaneous or interacting existence of both dimensions.[455] Then, studies converted the continuum into the acknowledgement that economic choices actually reflect an institutionalised understanding of rationality (i.e.

452 Cf. *DiMaggio/Powell* (1983), p. 150ff.; *DiMaggio/Powell* (1991), p. 8f.; *Jepperson* (1991), p. 144f.

453 Cf. *Oliver* (1996), p. 163ff.; *Lounsbury* (2008), p. 353ff. Applying institutional theory to study converging as well as diverging organisational structures rather than isomorphism is in line with current trends in strategic management research (cf. *Walgenbach* (2002), p. 190ff.).

454 Cf. *DiMaggio/Powell* (1983), p. 149.

455 Cf. e.g. *Powel* (1991), p. 183; *Oliver* (1992), p. 563ff.; *Geiger/Ittner* (1996); *Granlund/Lukka* (1998), p. 156ff.; *Modell* (2002), p. 659; *Hopper/Major* (2007), p. 63.

a **social construct**[456]).[457] Because early NIS theorists had initially expressed a similar understanding of rationality[458], this development is also labelled an 'overdue recovery'.[459] For analytical purposes, however, the distinction of economic factors as those reflected by the (institutionalised) position of economic theories is generally maintained.[460] Thus, NIS stresses three determinants for the design of cost accounting systems and the use of cost information: economic ones, institutional coercive ones and institutional voluntary ones (Figure 4-2).[461]

Coercive pressures are understood to be "both formal and informal pressures exerted on organizations by other organizations upon which they are dependent (...)"[462]. In the context of subsidiaries, coercive pressures dominantly include a parent company's directives, expatriates or direct involvements of a parent company's managers.[463] In addition, coercive pressures involve the effect of national legislation (especially home and host countries' external reporting rules or tax regulations). Since the involvement of national legislation will be covered in the economic variables,[464] it is excluded at this point.

Voluntary pressures comprise both mimetic and normative pressures. The former describe influences which result from an organisation's attempt to "model themselves on other organizations [to cope with environmental uncertainty]"[465]. These pressures reason that there is an association between cost accounting systems and the state of cost accounting in a company's surroundings (especially its industry and sister affiliates).[466] Normative pressures stem from the professionalisation of a company's employees.[467] From this point

---

456 As such, NIS does not oppose a rationalistic approach towards observing a socially constructed reality. Thus, the taken philosophical compromise of a rationalistic epistemological base and a constuctivistic ontological understanding based on social constructivism ensures the combinability of NIS's ontological and *Popper*'s epistemological assumptions.

457 Cf. *Walgenbach* (2002), p. 159; *Yazdifar/Tsamenyi* (2005), p. 183; *Walgenbach* (2006), p. 360ff.; *Lounsbury* (2008), p. 350f. This discussion reflects the social-constuctivistic position that characterises NIS (cf. *Scott* (1987), p. 495ff.; *Neu* (1992), p. 229; *Carruthers* (1995), p. 315; *Mizruchi/Fein* (1999), p. 656).

458 Cf. *Meyer/Rowan* (1977), p. 354.

459 Cf. *Lounsbury* (2008), p. 351.

460 Cf. *Walgenbach* (2006), p. 363f.

461 Though NIS is typically applied for case-based research (section 3), *Modell* (2002), p. 672, claims its applicability in survey research as well and e.g. *Gupta et al.* (1994), *Malmi* (1999) or *Liang et al.* (2007) reveal this to be feasible.

462 *DiMaggio/Powell* (1983), p. 150.

463 For this and the following cf. *DiMaggio/Powell* (1983), p. 150; *Westney* (1993), p. 66 and 72ff.; *Robinson* (1996), p. 45ff.; *Granlund/Lukka* (1998), p. 157; *Kostova* (1999), p. 308ff.; *Malmi* (1999), p. 649ff.; *Yazdifar/Askarany* (2010b), p. 1ff.; *Chang et al.* (2009), p. 80; *Cheng/Yu* (2012), p. 85. The distinction reflects the management control literature which differentiates supervision vs. bureaucratic controls (cf. e.g. *O'Donnell* (2000), p. 252ff.) or personal vs. bureaucratic controls (cf. e.g. *Baliga/Jaeger* (1984), p. 26ff.; *Harzing* (1999), p. 25ff.).

464 For a discussion of external cost accounting objectives, cf. pages 89 and 101.

465 *DiMaggio/Powell* (1983), p. 151.

466 Cf. *Westney* (1993), p. 70f.; *Granlund/Lukka* (1998), p. 157; *Yazdifar/Askarany* (2010b), p. 13f, esp. table 5 or *Chung et al.* (2002), p. 114.

467 Cf. *DiMaggio/Powell* (1983), p. 152.

of view, it can be reasoned that professional institutes (such as CIMA, IMA or the ICV) or the educational background of employees influence a company's cost accounting system.[468]

Despite arguing for the relevance of **economic influences** for the design of cost accounting systems, NIS does not provide a conclusive summary of relevant economic factors which determine the cost accounting systems in subsidiaries. Given the variety of alternative factors researched,[469] neoclassical economic considerations are introduced at this point to facilitate the identification of relevant variables.

Neoclassical theory ascribes companies the responsibility to find the most economical way how to transform input factors with internal technologies and production processes into intended outputs.[470] Surrounded by the assumption of perfect competition and efficient markets, rational actors and profit-maximising (organisational) behaviour,[471] this theory informs a scholar that focus on companies' internal factor-combination processes (e.g. *Gutenberg*'s and *Heinen*'s production theory).[472] In this context, cost accounting's provision of a picture of the value creating processes and the corresponding identification of cost drivers is a means to the end of economic efficiency.[473] As such, neoclassical theory serves as an informing base for the necessity to regard a company's products and production technologies[474] when studying cost accounting systems. *Krieger* labels such aspects the **archetype of cost accounting.**[475] Moreover, this perspective provides a solid ground to argue for a contextual influence of the technological and human resources committed to cost accounting. These technical and personnel resources determine how precisely a cost accounting system can picture the archetype of cost accounting.[476]

It is necessary to mention that several authors stress the inability of neoclassical theory to provide a solid ground for an explanation of the existence of cost accounting (i.e. the need for cost information as well as its use) due to the assumptions of perfect markets.[477] By relaxing this assumption of perfect markets, academics stress the ability of neoclassical ideas to be able to explain a need for a cost accounting system.[478] Thus, the inclusion of economic considerations into the analysis of cost accounting systems makes it necessary to

---

468 For professional bodies, cf. e.g. *Westney* (1993), p. 68; *Granlund/Lukka* (1998), p. 157. For the importance of education for management accounting, cf. *Ahrens* (1999), p. 138f.; *Portz/Lere* (2010), p. 49; *Moeschler* (2012), p. 270f.

469 Cf. section 3.2.2.3.

470 Cf. *Debreu* (1976), p. 40ff.; *Christensen/Demski* (1995), p. 14ff.

471 Cf. *Möller* (2002), p. 100; *Hirsch* (2007), p. 82f.

472 Cf. *Weber* (1993a), p. 31; *Neugebauer* (1995), p. 118; *Weber* (2005), p. 75ff.

473 Cf. e.g. *Kilger* (1958), p. 558ff.; *Heinen* (1968), p. 168ff.; *Dellmann* (1979), p. 321; *Küpper* (1992), p. 40ff.; *Weber* (1993a), p. 31ff.; *Bungenstock* (1995), p. 74ff.; *Christensen/Demski* (1995), p. 14ff.; *Krieger* (1995), p. 97; *Schildbach* (1997), p. 265.

474 These two aspects can be summarised as 'product diversity' (cf. *Drury/Tayles* (2005), p. 60f.).

475 Cf. *Krieger* (1995), p. 119ff.

476 Cf. e.g. *Laßmann* (1992), p. 300, who stressed cost effectiveness as a reason to represent the archetypes in a simplified manner. Besides, section 3.2.3 reveals that various previous research project find the information technology to affect cost accounting.

477 Cf. *Pfaff* (1993), p. 18.

478 For a discussion, cf. *Schweitzer* (2006), p. 52ff.

regard environmental uncertainties which establish a **need for cost information** and the objectives of cost accounting, which are manifestations of this need.

Following these arguments, three **basic hypotheses** on the determinants of cost accounting systems in subsidiaries can be derived from this section. Apparently, **economic** as well as **coercive and voluntary institutional** factors determine the complexity of subsidiaries' cost accounting systems. These impacts will be included as *H3a*, *H3b1* and *H3b2* in this study.

H3a:	*The complexity of cost accounting systems is associated with economic variables.*
H3b1:	*The complexity of cost accounting systems is associated with coercive institutional influences.*
H3b2:	*The complexity of cost accounting systems is associated with voluntary institutional influences.*

Similarly, the provided arguments can be embodied to derive two basic hypotheses for the use of cost information. The application of cost information for decision-making evolves from the existence of environmental uncertainty (i.e. market imperfection) and the associated cost accounting objectives. In line, *Burchell et al.* (1980) explicitly highlight that the environmental uncertainty may explain why information is used differently. Hence, the variables summarised as the **need for cost information** is assumed to influence how managers make use of cost information *(H4c)*. Also, the literature review reveals that the ceremonial use of cost information is associated with the prevalence of **coercive institutional influences**. This effect is incorporated as *H4d* into this study. As such, NIS serves as a basis for the following basic hypotheses:

H4c:	*Types of cost information use are associated with the need for cost information.*
H4d:	*Types of cost information use are associated with the coercive institutional effects which determine the complexity of a cost accounting system.*

To this point, it could be derived theoretically that the design of cost accounting systems and the use of cost information in subsidiaries are subject to economic and institutional influences. In addition, the literature review emphasises the necessity to consider the relationship between a subsidiary and its parent since this **relational context** comprises a subsidiary's reaction to institutional influences. Such influences are not a focal aspect of provide macro level perspective of NIS[479] since it disregards a company's internal perceptions[480] by neglecting organisational response to institutional pressures.[481]

Despite not being of focal interest in macro level NIS, including **internal responses** to institutional pressures is argued to be possible.[482] Early NIS theorists used the initially assumed continuum of legitimacy and efficiency to highlight organisational responses to institutional pressures such as delinking imposed organisational structure from internal practice (decoupling).[483] These early considerations reflect an active involvement of organ-

479 Cf. *Walgenbach* (2006), p. 357. For a summary of the micro institutional perspective of NIS, which is proclaimed by *Zucker*, cf. *Walgenbach* (2006), p. 382ff.

480 Cf. *Scapens* (2006), p. 13.

481 Cf. *Oliver* (1991), p. 145; *Powel* (1991), p. 183; *Hirsch/Lounsbury* (1997), p. 410; *Lounsbury* (2008), p. 351.

482 Cf. *Oliver* (1991), p. 149.

483 Cf. *Meyer/Rowan* (1977), p. 356.

isational actors.[484] Nevertheless, interests, strategic actions and power are generally disregarded in purely NIS informed projects.[485] To include such elements, either theoretical triangulation[486] or expanding NIS by allowing for "resistance, awareness, pro-activeness, influence and self-interest of organizations"[487] is essential. The latter alternative is followed here because it corresponds to expansions provided by NIS theorists.[488] It has to be kept in mind, however, that such a rather pragmatic approach is partially limited in its explicatory power due to theoretical inconsistencies. These stem from (macro) NIS's focus on organisations rather than individual actors,[489] i.e. an inability to actually explain the origin of organisational (actors') interest.[490]

Addressing *Meyer/Rowan's* idea of decoupling, *Oliver* (implicitly) extends NIS conceptually. She explains that organisations 'acquiesce', 'compromise', 'avoid' or 'defy' institutional pressures.[491] On the one hand, *Oliver*'s descriptions align the design and use of cost information theoretically. Her considerations reveal that there are organisations which implement and use cost accounting systems as demanded by an institutional environment. Alternatively, organisations could implement but not use cost accounting systems as demanded by the institutional environment, or neither implement nor use cost accounting systems induced by an institutional environment. As such, subsidiaries may react to coercive institutional pressures on how to design a cost accounting system by not following a corporate directive[492] or following the directive but not applying the resulting cost accounting system for decision-making. Even though previous empirical research cannot unambiguously establish a link between the complexity of cost accounting systems and the use of cost information (section 3.3.2.3), the following basic hypothesis can thus be derived from a theoretical point of view:

---

484 Cf. *Müller-Jentsch* (2002), p. 204.

485 Cf. *Hirsch/Lounsbury* (1997), p. 410; *Walgenbach* (2006), p. 391.

486 Triangulation in this context refers to the adoption of multiple business theories (cf. *Walgenbach* (2002), p. 182ff.). Section 3.2 as well as 3.3 finds multiple theoretical perspectives (i.e. triangulation) to be common for the explanatory purposes in cost accounting research.

487 *Oliver* (1991), p. 151.

488 Cf. *Powel* (1991), p. 198f.

489 Cf. *Walgenbach* (2002), p. 182.

490 NIS can explain neither how cost accounting is institutionalised nor how the accounting systems feed back into affecting institutions (cf. *Ahmed/Scapens* (2000), p. 166). The contradicting arguments by *Bhimani* (1999), p. 425ff., and *Moeschler* (2012), p. 45f., appear due to their reliance on a micro level interpretation of NIS. Considerations of institutionalisation or feedback are regarded in studies on old institutional economics (cf. *Ahmed/Scapens* (2000), p. 166f.; *Burns/Scapens* (2000), p. 5ff.; *Siti-Nabiha/Scapens* (2005), p. 46ff.; *Scapens* (2006), p. 14–19), negotiated order (cf. *Modell* (2006), p. 220), actor-network theory or structuration theory (cf. *Briers/Chua* (2001), p. 238ff.; *Jones/Dugdale* (2002), p. 122–124) or practice theory (cf. *Ahrens/Chapman* (2007), p. 1ff.). Such explanations, however, are beyond the scope of the proposed research questions. Yet, disregarding such a discussion hides how precisely the relational context becomes important for the design of cost accounting systems and the use of cost information.

491 Cf. *Oliver* (1991), p. 151ff. The author describes 'manipulation of institutional pressures' as a fifth response to institutional impacts. Since such feedback is not covered in this study, it is disregarded.

492 *Oliver* (1991) does not restrict her arguments to coercive institutional factors but also regards voluntary institutional influences. In this study, however, only the mitigation of coercive institutional influences is included.

H4a:	*Types of cost information use are associated with the complexity of a cost accounting system.*

On the other hand, *Oliver* emphasises precisely what determines a company's positive (i.e. non-opposing) response to institutional influences. Among others, she reasons for an effect of (a) the agreement with the intentions of the impacting institution, i.e. the perceived social legitimacy, (b) the dependence on the impacting institution, (c) the conformity of institutional pressures and internal goals and (d) the non-discretion constraining character of the influence.[493]

The perception of **social legitimacy** resulting from the application of a parent company's directive appears more plausible in times when a subsidiary identifies strongly with its parent company (variable (1))[494]. The *dependence of a subsidiary*, in terms of management accounting, will manifest itself in a low autonomy with respect to the design of the management accounting function (variable (2)).[495] The *conformity of institutional pressures with internal goals* and the *discretion constraining character* are interlinked. The more comparable a subsidiary's and its parent's information needs are, the more conform are their goals and the less constraining a subsidiary perceives directives on how to design its cost accounting system (variable (3)).[496] Similarly, the more intensively a subsidiary can participate in the development of management accounting directives, the less constraining is a directive's character and the more consistent is a directive with the subsidiary's objectives (variable (4)).[497] Finally, discretion constraining institutional influences from a parent company are likely to manifest themselves in conflicts between a subsidiary and its parent (variable (5)).[498]

In a nutshell, these variables describe three aspects. The variables (1) and (2) explicate what characterises the distribution of responsibilities between a subsidiary and its parent. The variables (3) and (4) comprise a subsidiary's attitude towards its parent. Variable (5) expresses the comparability of a subsidiary and its parent with respect to their information needs. Section 3 explicates similar aspects to be important to explain how a subsidiary reacts to a corporate directive on cost accounting. Also, these variables are remarkably similar to a number of contingencies the management control literature stresses to affect MCS in multinationals.[499] Hence, *Oliver's* extension of NIS provides a thorough theoreti-

---

[493] Cf. *Oliver* (1991), p. 169ff.

[494] Accordingly, *Anderson/Young* (1999), p. 548, find that in a parent company-imposed ABC implementation, business unit managers overlook certain drawbacks of ABC if they identify with the parent company. Similar arguments reveal *Chung et al.* (2000), p. 649, and *Kostova/Roth* (2002), p. 119f., in more general settings of MNCs.

[495] For a similar argument in a non-MCS specific setting, cf. *Kostova/Roth* (2002), p. 118f.

[496] This follows directly from the consideration by *Oliver* (1991). No previous study is found on this issue.

[497] According arguments prevail in budgeting research (cf. e.g. *Chenhall* (2003), p. 129) and the analysis of performance measurement systems in subsidiaries (cf. e.g. *Dossi/Patelli* (2008), p. 132ff.). Moreover, research on control practices in joint ventures find involvement including control systems to be perceived less negatively than involvement excluding ones (cf. e.g. *Johnson et al.* (2001), p. 46).

[498] *Chenhall* (2004), p. 24, argues that managers may perceive a (coercive) introduction of ABC as personal criticism, which fosters affective conflicts. According to *Chenhall* (2004), p. 23, affective conflicts inhibit individuals' ability to cooperate. Since affective conflicts, in contrast to cognitive conflict, can be dysfunctional for decision-making (cf. ibid), these are referred to at this point.

[499] Cf. *Schmid/Kretschmer* (2009), p. 229.

cal explanation for the alignment of the design of cost accounting systems and the use of cost information in subsidiaries with the responses of these subsidiaries to their parent company's involvements.

<table>
<tr><th></th><th></th><th>Comparability</th><th>Distribution of responsibilities</th><th>Subsidiaries' attitudes</th></tr>
<tr><td>(a)</td><td>Agreement with the intentions of impacting institution</td><td></td><td></td><td>(4)
Subsidiary's identification with a parent company</td></tr>
<tr><td>(b)</td><td>Dependence on an impacting institution</td><td></td><td>(1)
Subsidiary's influence on its management accounting</td><td></td></tr>
<tr><td>(c)</td><td>Conformity of institutional pressures and internal goals</td><td rowspan="2">(5)
Perceived comparability of subsidiary and parent companies' (cost) information needs</td><td rowspan="2">(2)
Subsidiary's influence on corporate guidelines</td><td></td></tr>
<tr><td>(d)</td><td>Discretion constraining character of an influence</td><td>(3)
Number of affective conflicts in a group</td></tr>
</table>

Table 4-1: Dimensions of the relational context

Conjointly, these five factors define the **relational context** of a subsidiary with its parent.[500] Following *Oliver's* considerations, this relational context will decrease (i.e. moderate[501]) the effect of coercive institutional factors on the design of cost accounting systems and the use of cost information in subsidiaries. The more *unfavourable* the relational context, the less intensively will coercive institutional factors influence a subsidiary.[502] *Oliver's* considerations are equally relevant for the design and use[503] of cost accounting systems. As such, the following two working hypotheses can be defined:

H3c:	*The relational context between a subsidiary and its parent company moderates the association of coercive institutional influences and the complexity of subsidiaries' cost accounting systems.*
H4e:	*The relational context of the subsidiary and its parent company moderates the association between coercive institutional influences and types of cost information use.*

Figure 4-3 expands Figure 4-2 by the various individual variables which can be theoretically derived from NIS to explain the design of cost accounting systems and the use of cost information.

---

500 The importance of a 'relational context' is derived analytically by *Kostova* (1999), p. 312f.

501 Conceptually, *Modell* (2002), p. 659, stresses such a moderating effect on institutionally induced overhead cost allocation procedures. In contrast to this study, however, *Modell* regards a moderating effect of economic variables on institutional ones, too. Empirically, *Kostova/Roth* (2002), p. 226, confirm the relevance of a relational context for the adoption of an organisational practice in a subsidiary of a MNC. They find that ceremonial adoption is associated with an unfavourable relational context. The authors do not attempt to analyse a moderating effect on coercive institutional influences but focus on a direct effect of the relational context only.

502 For an according argument, cf. *Kostova* (1999), p. 317.

503 Similarly, *Menon/Varadarajan* (1992), p. 63, stress organisational structure as an important determinant of the use of information.

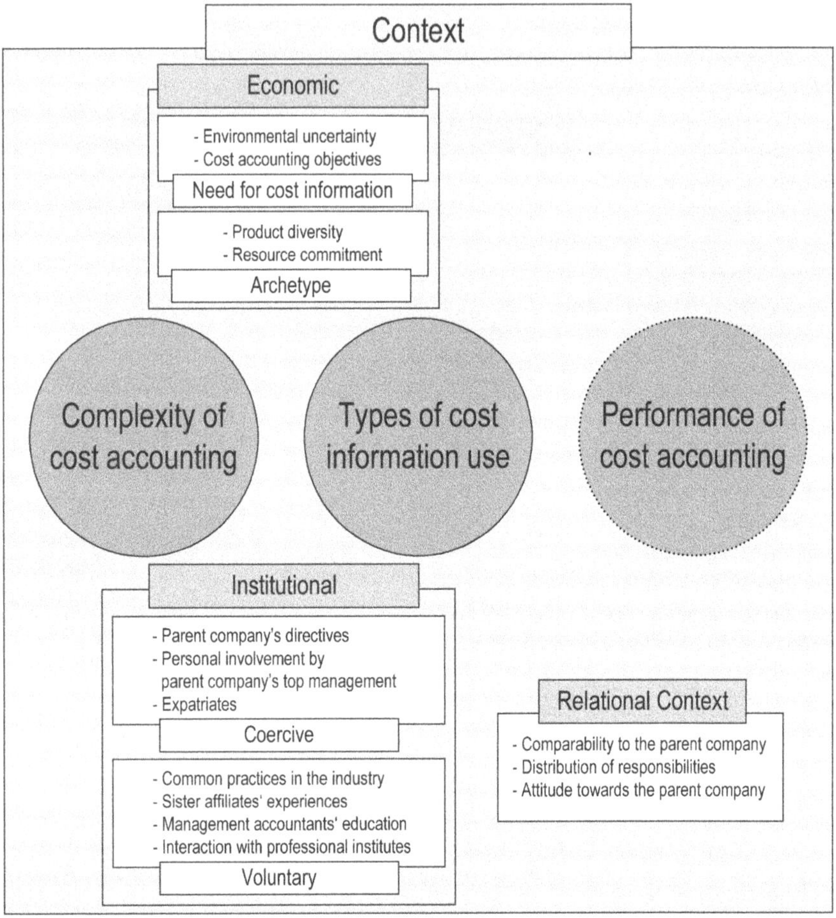

Figure 4-3: Final contribution of NIS for this research project

Despite the variety of these variables, the antecedents of non-ceremonial types of cost information use discussed in previous research remain theoretically unclear so far. The individual characteristics of information users which the literature review (section 3.3.2.3) identifies as very important to explain the non-ceremonial usage types do not prevail. Again, this shortcoming is associable to the general focus of (macro) NIS on an organisational level. Despite acknowledging organisational responses to institutional pressures, the provided pragmatic extension of NIS cannot explicate the **perspective of individual actors**. By including the dynamic theory of economic actors, section 4.1.4 overcomes this deficiency.

4.1.4 Dynamic theory of economic actors

The dynamic theory of economic actors (subsequently TEA) seeks for an explanation of behavioural issues of and between individual and collective actors.[504] It argues, that individual actors (human beings) act in order to maximise their utility and cooperate (they form collective actors) if this is expected to augment individuals' utility.[505] Such utility-maximising behaviour is determined by actors' "distinctive *abilities* ("Können") and *intentions* ("Wollen")"[506]. The abilities comprise an actor's potential to anticipate (i.e. perceive, predict and assess) their scope of action and the potential to realise certain actions.[507] These potentials are restricted by actors' cognitive abilities and knowledge. Intentions, on the other hand, express actors' individual preferences. Both, **restricted abilities and individual preferences** form individual (and collective) actors' internal or mental models. These complexity-reducing models guide and facilitate actors' decision-making and behaviours. Furthermore, actors' decision-making and behaviour are linked to so-called external models.[508] These are fully explicated rules which are, despite possible involvements of actors in the creation of these models, rather delinked from an individual actor's existence. Management accounting instruments as well as organisational structure are among the examples that the theorists provide for an external model. Additional influences are identified as actors' biophysical and emotional conditions as well as stimuli stemming from a specific decision.[509] Moreover, it is argued that individual actors' decision-making and behaviour are influenced by collective actors' internal models and that the build-up of experience feeds back into their internal models.[510]

From the above logic of TEA, it can be argued that the use of cost information for decision-making reflects decision makers' intention to maximise their utility.[511] From such a perspective, managers' use of cost information can be linked to their general **knowledge** with respect to cost accounting (potential to perceive information relevance) and their perception of cost **information quality** (potential to assess information relevance).[512] In

---

[504] Cf. *Bach et al.* (2001), p. 95 and 101f.

[505] Cf. *Bach et al.* (2001), p. 99; *Schäffer et al.* (2005), p. 5.

[506] *Jais* (2007), p. 8, accentuation in original.

[507] For this and the following, cf. *Bach et al.* (2001), p. 96f., and *Schäffer et al.* (2005), p. 8f.

[508] For this and the following, cf. *Schäffer et al.* (2005), p. 11f.

[509] Cf. *Schäffer et al.* (2005), p. 13f.

[510] Cf. *Bach et al.* (2001), p. 100; *Schäffer et al.* (2005), p. 8.

[511] Utility can be regarded as a social construct, which can be maximised through economic as well as institutional considerations (e.g. social legitimacy). Cf. *Neu* (1992), p. 228f., for a brief discussion on *utility* in a socially constructive sense. As such, this perspective appears well in line with this study's philosophical position as well as NIS.

[512] According to information systems literature, the quality of information systems, such as cost accounting, is measurable by its accuracy, relevance, representation and accessibility (cf. e.g. *Wang/Strong* (1996), p. 16). Similar quality assessments of cost accounting systems' can be identified in previous research (cf. e.g. *Hunold* (2003), p. 176). Besides, the ability to assess information relevance is regularly linked to information users' *'trust'* in cost accounting and cost accountants (cf. e.g. *Karlshaus* (2000), p. 138; *Hunold* (2003), p. 164 or *Steiners* (2005), p. 152f.). Trust, however, cannot be disjunctively delinked from perceptions of an information systems' quality as becomes evident by constructs in *Hunold* (2003), p. 164 and 176, and *Frank* (2000), p. 106f. Therefore, trust will be taken into account implicitly through the assessment of the cost accountants' quality in this study (cf. section 5.2.3.4).

addition, the effect of preferences for decision-making explicates the necessity to consider actors' **preference** for cost information for decision-making. The relevance of external models for actor's decision-making and behaviour underlines the relationship between the design of cost accounting systems (an external model) and the use of cost information as identified in H4a. Despite not explicitly stressing whether external models are of varying importance for actors if the latter had participated in the creation of an external model, TEA enables to argue for a potential effect of decision makers' **involvement** in the design of cost accounting systems on the way how they use cost information. Another important issue arises from the importance of collective actors' mental models for individuals' decision-making. Following TEA, it can be argued that the cooperation of providers and users of cost information (the frequency of **contacts**) will be relevant for cost information user's behaviour. By altering an individual's internal models, such contacts may, e.g. simplify the abilities to assess cost information. These explanatory variables reflect the empirical and normative considerations on how to explain the use of cost information (sections 3.3.1 and 3.3.2.1). As such, TEA is especially applicable for this research project.

Besides reflecting the findings from the literature review, TEA also serves as the explicit theoretical position of previous research on the usage types in a management accounting setting.[513] Moreover, the theoretical position can be linked to the taken position of social-constructivism[514] and the institutional business theories[515] which are argued to extend rather than oppose NIS.[516] Therefore, TEA complements this study's reliance on NIS by explaining why individual **decision makers' attitude** towards cost information is relevant for the way in which cost information is used. As such, TEA allows to derive the following basic hypothesis:

H4b:	*Types of cost information use are associated with managers' attitude towards cost information.*

Figure 4-4 complements Figure 4-3 by the explanatory factors derived from TEA. Conjointly, these explanatory variables allow for a thorough analysis of the antecedents of the design of cost accounting systems and the use of cost information in subsidiaries.

513 Cf. *Jais* (2007), p. 7f.

514 Cf. *Bach et al.* (2001), p. 98, and *Schäffer et al.* (2005), p. 12, for an implicit link of TEA and social-constructivism.

515 Cf. *Schäffer et al.* (2005), p. 3f.

516 Cf. e.g. *Moll et al.* (2006), p. 188; *Scapens* (2006), p. 7 and 14, for these perspectives.

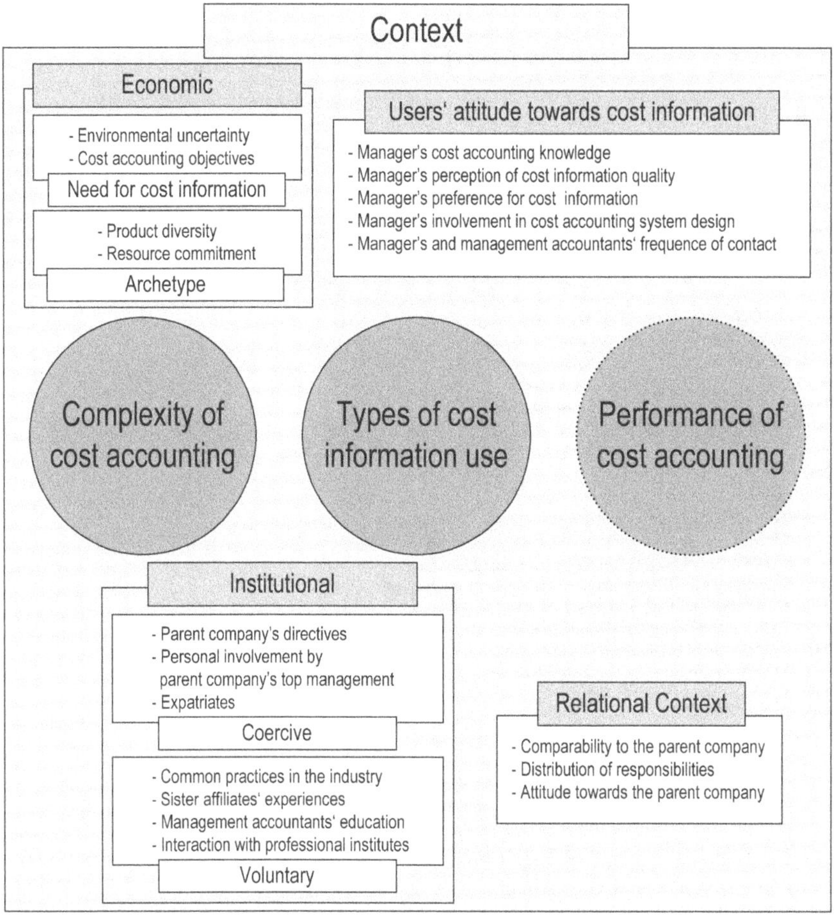

Figure 4-4: Theoretically derived explicatory variables for the design and use of cost accounting

4.1.5 Summary and integration

Throughout this chapter, four basic hypotheses on the complexity of cost accounting and five basic hypotheses on the use of cost information could be derived. Figure 4-5 summarises these hypotheses into this study's research framework. The figure comprises the theoretically most relevant explanatory variables to study the design of cost accounting systems and the use of cost information in subsidiaries. Yet, the figure does not comprise all variables which chapter 3 reveals as analysable during the exploration of cost accounting in subsidiaries. Two important **restrictions of the applied framework** have to be stressed at this point.

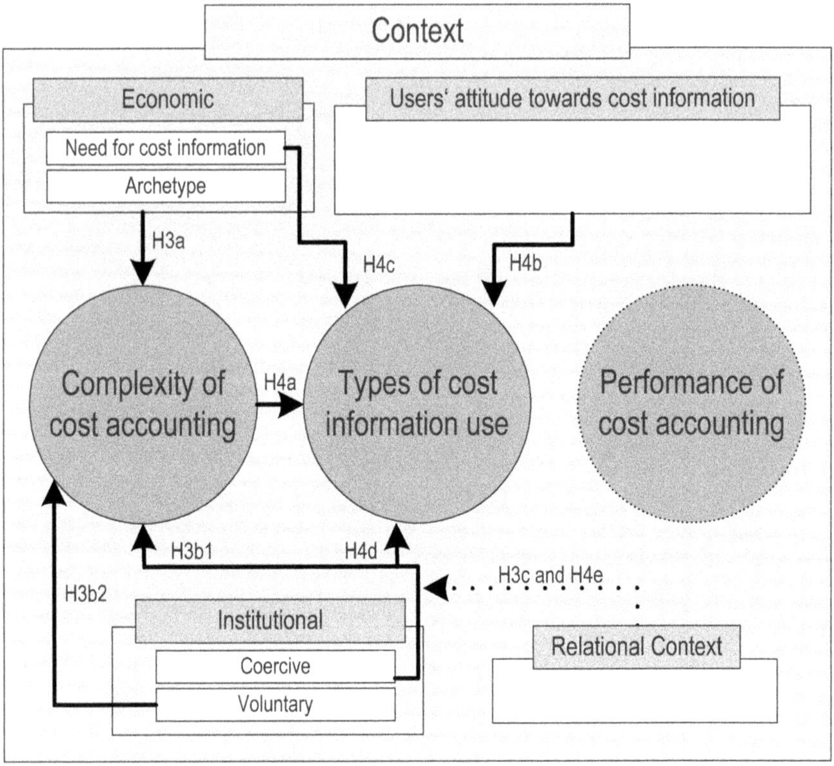

Figure 4-5: Summary of basic hypotheses on the design of cost accounting systems and the use of cost information in subsidiaries

On the one hand, general **organisational factors and industrial effects** prevailing in previous research cannot be found in above theoretical framework. Yet, the findings from the literature review reveal that organisational effects such as a subsidiary's length of affiliation[517] and size[518] as well as a parent company's form of market entry (the historical background of a subsidiary) and its size can be of (multiple) moderating or amplifying effect for cost accounting in subsidiaries as well as for the explanatory variables from Figure 4-4. Since it is out of the scope of this research to study the bases beyond parent company directives or to identify the influences beyond the relational context, these aspects are in-

---

[517] Since the length of affiliation may influence how long a parent company already affects its subsidiary's cost accounting system, this dimension of age is more relevant than the mere age of a subsidiary.

[518] According to *Krieger* (1995), p. 128ff., a company's size is linked to two aspects. On the one hand, large companies are likely to have more complex internal structures which increase the complexity of cost accounting systems. On the other hand, large companies can commit more resources to the development of cost accounting systems. The latter aspect is reflected in the explanatory variables (product diversity). Thus, the former is controlled for through a control variable on the size of a subsidiary.

cluded as control variables in the analysis.[519] Thereby, it will be considered for additional organisational characteristics such as a subsidiary's major value chain activities or a parent company's internationality as well. No industry variable can be found in Figure 4-4 because this study focusses on manufacturing companies only. Potential differences in cost accounting attributable to sub-industrial effects[520] will be covered through the voluntary institutional effects ('common practices in the industry') as well as the control variable 'size' and the variables on the 'archetype of cost accounting'.[521]

On the other hand, researchers tend to regard **culture** as an explanation for cost and management accounting in MNCs. Such considerations especially prevail for the explanation of cross-national differences.[522] Researchers stress that "(u)ltimately factor like national culture (...) affect MCS design because they affect the perceived costs and benefits of alternate designs."[523] Nevertheless, in this study, no intention is made to extract an effect of "the modal personality structure or (...) the play of (...) sets of core values"[524]. Such an attempt through the application of, e.g. the *Hofstede* or the *GLOBE* taxonomy would be diluted by difficulties with respect to the conceptualisation of culture.[525] Also, research projects on the effect of national culture are regularly criticised for their inability to explain "firm within national ownership effects"[526] or intra-national and intra-firm cultural differences.[527] Thus, in line with previous comparative cost accounting research, diverse impacts of national distinctiveness, which culture intends to display, are regarded through the explanatory variables from Figure 4-4 rather than ideationistically.[528] This procedure does not assume the absence of cultural effects. However, cultural aspects are assumed to be incorporated in explanatory factors of subsidiaries' cost accounting systems (e.g. parent company's directives, educational background, perceptions about uncertainty and usefulness of cost information, number of expatriates, distribution of responsibilities or managers' individual information needs). Depending on a parent company's origin or an em-

---

519 A similar research approach with respect to size and age can be found in *Liang et al.* (2007), p. 66ff., who research the IT-assimilation in Chinese companies, *Kostova/Roth* (2002), p. 221ff., who look at the diffusion of quality management techniques from a US MNC into its international affiliates and *Cheng/Yu* (2012), p. 93, who focus on the diffusion of Taiwanese MNCs' home country management and production practices.

520 Cf. e.g. *Moeschler* (2012), p. 264.

521 Details on the operationalisation of these variables can be found in section 5.1.

522 For a review, cf. *Bhimani* (1999), p. 417ff.

523 *Chow et al.* (1999), p. 457. *Bhimani* (1999), p. 417, reports a summary of similar arguments of culture being a filter for those factors which are actually shaping the design and use of management accounting systems.

524 Cf. *Bhimani* (1999), p. 417.

525 Cf. *Tayeb* (1994), p. 433ff.; *Ahrens* (1999), p. 11ff.; *Bhimani* (1999), p. 418ff.; *Harrison/McKinnon* (1999), p. 497. For a similar discussion, cf. *Kutschker/Schmid* (2011), p. 775ff.

526 Cf. *Brewer* (1998), p. 253ff. or *Chow et al.* (1999), p. 456.

527 Cf. e.g. *Tayeb* (1994), p. 432 or *Baird et al.* (2004), p. 389.

528 Cf. *Bhimani* (1999), p. 421ff., and *Moeschler* (2012), p. 67, for an identification of studies applying national distinctiveness accordingly ('societal effect approach'). Since it "paves the way for institutional, explanations of socially shaped control structures" (*Bhimani* (1999), p. 424) this study's approach is combinable with above theoretical (and philosophical) positions.

ployee's nationality, these variables can be of varying relevance for subsidiaries' cost accounting systems.[529]

The derived basic hypotheses can be refined hereafter with respect to the individual context variables identified in Figure 4-4. For brevity, this refinement will be done separately for the complexity of cost accounting systems and the use of cost information. Also, the following section comprises the announced derivation of propositions on the association of the performance of cost accounting systems and the system's complexity as well as the use of cost information.

These refinements were preceded by **expert interviews** in two foreign and one domestic subsidiary in Germany. Thereby, six management accountants and three commercial managers contributed to the development of this project. The interviews served pretesting purposes, i.e. the intended operationalisation of the research objects and the introduced basic hypotheses were subject to a critical assessment by these practitioners.[530] Besides helpful adjustments to the intended operationalisation, the experts widely assured the applicability of the basic hypotheses. Especially H1 and H2 proved well applicable. As such, they are excluded from the refinement in the following section.

4.2 Refinement of the basic hypotheses

4.2.1 Complexity of cost accounting systems

The complexity of subsidiaries' cost accounting systems can be theoretically aligned with economic and institutional factors as well as the relational context of a subsidiary and its parent company. At this point, the hypotheses H3a to H3c are refined with respect to the individual factors identified to form the three broad categories of influential factors. If required, hypotheses are differentiated for foreign and domestic subsidiaries.

Economic factors

Hypothesis H3a regards the influence of economic factors on the complexity of cost accounting systems in foreign and domestic subsidiaries. Thereby, two sets of economic factors are integrated. On the one hand, the need for cost information is argued to be important. On the other hand, the archetype of cost accounting influences a system's complexity.

With respect to the need for cost information, two variables prevail from a theoretical point of view. On the one hand, the need for cost information is argued to be established through market imperfections. Consequently, this study regards the extent of **perceived environmental uncertainty** as an antecedent of the complexity of cost accounting systems. In a complex environment, there are various decisions to be made. All these decisions require different pieces of cost information.[531] Therefore, a more complex cost accounting system is required. Following this argument, it can be said that a more uncertain

[529] Cf. *Ahrens* (1999), p. 15, for according arguments.

[530] Cf. *Schnell* (2012), p. 135ff., or *DeVellis* (2012), p. 104.

[531] Cf. e.g. *Bungenstock* (1995), p. 65f.

environment establishes a need for more detailed cost information.[532] This leads to the following hypothesis:

H3a1_1:	*The more uncertain the environment of a subsidiary, the more complex is its cost accounting system.*

On the other hand, the need for cost information is expressed through the objectives, for which a company applies its cost accounting system. As discussed in section 2.3.1, the **objectives of cost accounting** are measurable on different levels. In this study, the influence of using cost information for the internal purposes 'decision facilitating' and 'decision influencing', and the external purpose 'inventory valuation' as well as the use of cost information for strategic and operational activities is regarded.[533]

Different cost information is required for different decisions.[534] To be able to facilitate a company's diverse decision-making processes profoundly, complex cost accounting systems are essential[535] since these can provide detailed cost information for various tasks. In contrast, it is argued that less detailed cost information provides valuable insights for decision influencing purposes because it is more comprehensive and transparent.[536] Hence, this purpose can be associated with less complex cost accounting systems. Similar to the latter, a strong focus on externally oriented inventory valuation is expected to be linked to a less complex cost accounting system. Inventory valuation can be achieved with rather simplistic costing systems.[537] Therefore, the following hypotheses are derived:

H3a1_2:	*The more a subsidiary employs its cost accounting system for decision facilitating, the more complex is its cost accounting system.*
H3a1_3:	*The more a subsidiary employs its cost accounting system for decision influencing, the less complex is its cost accounting system.*
H3a1_4:	*The more a subsidiary employs its cost accounting system for inventory valuation, the less complex is its cost accounting system.*

A similar distinction prevails for the application of cost accounting systems for strategic and operational tasks. Based on normative assertions, previous research stresses that if cost information is strongly employed for strategic purposes, less complex cost accounting systems are more adequate.[538] In contrast, a strong emphasis on operational tasks makes rather refined cost accounting systems necessary. Therefore, the following hypotheses are derived:

532 For similar arguments, cf. e.g. *Anderson* (1995), p. 42; *Abdel-Kader/Luther* (2008), p. 7, or *Moeschler* (2012), p. 165.

533 For the connection between the complexity of a cost accounting system and the objectives, for which it is used, cf. e.g. *Merchant/Shields* (1993), p. 76ff.

534 Cf. e.g. *Bungenstock* (1995), p. 65f.

535 Cf. e.g. *Johnson/Kaplan* (1987), p. 1ff; *Sharman/Vikas* (2004), p. 29f., or *Vikas* (2006), p. 33.

536 Cf. e.g. *Merchant/Shields* (1993), p. 78; *Weber* (2007), p. 430.

537 Cf. e.g. *Drury/Tayles* (1997), p. 272.

538 For this and the following, cf. *Schoute* (2009), p. 210.

H3a1_5:	*The more a subsidiary employs its cost accounting system for operational tasks, the more complex is its cost accounting system.*
H3a1_6:	*The more a subsidiary employs its cost accounting system for strategic tasks, the less complex is its cost accounting system.*

Essentially, the analysability of H3a_2 to H3a_6 requires a disjunctive application of, e.g. either operational or strategic tasks. Since Anglophone and German companies are known to apply cost information for various tasks,[539] it is possible, however, that no disjunctive effect of the various objectives is derivable. Section 6.1.2.1.2 elaborates this potential difficulty in the ability to test H3a_2 to H3a_6.

Regarding the archetype of cost accounting, a company's products and production processes (i.e. **product diversity**)[540] are derived to determine the complexity of a cost accounting system. Additionally, it stresses that a company's ability to provide an accurate picture of the resource consumption processes, evoked by product diversity, also affects the complexity of cost accounting systems. Thus, a company's information technology as well as the prevalence of personnel resources and personnel support for cost accounting is essential for cost accounting systems in subsidiaries. Companies with diverse products and production facilities require more complex cost accounting systems to provide an adequate picture of the resource consumption which takes place in the company.[541] Hence, the following hypothesis is derived:

H3a2_1:	*The more diverse a subsidiary's products are, the more complex is its cost accounting system.*

Complementary, companies will not be able to derive the detailed picture of the diverse resource consumption evoked by their diverse products, if the applied **information technology** does not allow doing so.[542] Poor information technology may change the cost benefit consideration of providing accurate cost information because of high processing efforts. To account for this interrelation, the following hypothesis is provided:

H3a2_2:	*The better the information technology in a subsidiary, the more complex is its cost accounting system.*

Despite the need for adequate technical resources, it is equally essential to have sufficient **personnel resources** available for cost accounting. In this regard, previous research reveals the necessity for sufficient and well trained employees to establish a detailed and accurate

539 Cf. e.g. *Küpper* (1983), p. 173; *Weber* (1993b), p. 257ff.; *Innes/Mitchell* (1995), p. 144; *Shields* (1995), p. 156; *Geiger/Ittner* (1996), p. 556; *Lange/Schauer* (1996), p. 204; *Foster/Swenson* (1997), p. 114; *Groot* (1997), p. 30; *Nguyen/Brooks* (1997), p. 9; *Homburg* (1998), p. 34f.; *Währisch* (1998), p. 81; *Clarke et al.* (1999), p. 455; *Drury/Tayles* (2000), p. 45ff.; *Frank* (2000), p. 99; *Hoque* (2000), p. 147; *Innes et al.* (2000), p. 355; *Karlshaus* (2000), p. 110; *Cagwin/Bouwman* (2002), p. 19; *Cotton et al.* (2003), p. 70; *Garg et al.* (2003), p. 31; *Hunold* (2003), p. 146; *Krump* (2003), p. 231; *Chenhall* (2004), p. 31ff.; *Krumwiede/Suessmair* (2007a), p. 5; *Friedl et al.* (2009), p. 112; *Schoute* (2009), p. 215; *Stratton et al.* (2009), p. 34; *Wolfsgruber* (2011), p. 248; *Moeschler* (2012), p. 237.

540 Cf. *Drury/Tayles* (2005), p. 60.

541 Cf. *Krumwiede* (1998), p. 250f.; *Malmi* (1999), p. 659; *Drury/Tayles* (2005), p. 61; *Schoute* (2011), p. 123.

542 For this and the following, cf. e.g. *Krieger* (1995), p. 124ff.; *Krumwiede* (1998), p. 240; *Weber* (2005), p. 31f.; *Vikas* (2006), p. 36.

cost accounting system.[543] These two dimensions are summarised in this study as the 'adequacy of cost accountants'. Such internal resources are generally studied along with the implementation of ABC.[544] Recently, however, claims have been made to consider such factors more thoroughly in general studies on the design of cost accounting systems.[545] In addition, an adequate support from the company's top management is another important personnel resource during the implementation of cost accounting systems.[546] This importance, however, is equally valid for the design of cost accounting more generally. If there were little to any attention given to cost information by a company's top management team, cost accounting systems would become stunted. Consequently, it is not surprising to find calls for the inclusion of an according variable in general cost accounting studies.[547] Though this variable is more commonly employed in studies on the adoption of ABC,[548] there is preliminary evidence on a complexity increasing influence of top management support.[549] Hence, the existence of this effect is tested for in this study, as well. It is important to stress, however, that such a complexity increasing association is especially valid for the local (German) top management which is rather likely to centre on German cost accounting traditions.[550]

H3a2_3:	*The more adequate the cost accountants of a subsidiary are, the more complex is its cost accounting system.*
H3a2_4:	*The higher the support of local top managers of a subsidiary, the more complex is its cost accounting system.*

Coercive institutional factors

According to the derivation of H3b_1, three constructs can capture the coercive institutional influences which a parent company issues on its subsidiaries' cost accounting. On the one hand, parents can issue formalised **directives** on how to design a cost accounting system. On the other hand, parents are able to engage more informally through personal contacts. This latter involvement can occur through both personal involvement of the **corporate top management** as well as through **expatriate managers**. It is assumed that in Anglophone subsidiaries, an intense involvement of the parent company through any of the three variables will transfer the parent company's home country traditions of cost accounting into the subsidiary. The fact that Anglophone cost accounting traditions are less complex than German customs (cf. section 2.2) leads to the following hypotheses:

---

543 For according normative arguments, cf. e.g. *Weber* (2005), p. 32; *Krieger* (1995), p. 128.

544 Cf. e.g. *Shields* (1995), p. 150; *Anderson/Young* (1999), p. 540.

545 Cf. *Drury/Tayles* (2005), p. 78.

546 Cf. e.g. *Shields* (1995), p. 152; *Brewer* (1998), p. 244 and 247; *Krumwiede* (1998), p. 251; *Anderson/Young* (1999), p. 544.

547 Cf. *Drury/Tayles* (2005), p. 78.

548 Cf. e.g. *Shields* (1995), p. 152; *Brewer* (1998), p. 244 and 247; *Krumwiede* (1998), p. 251; *Anderson/Young* (1999), p. 544.

549 Cf. e.g. *Moeschler* (2012), p. 268.

550 For a discussion of the management support which is provided by the parent company see the discussion of institutional influences below (H3b1_1a).

H3b1_1a:	*The more an Anglophone parent engages into the design of a German subsidiary's cost accounting system through corporate directives, the less complex is the subsidiary's cost accounting system.*
H3b1_2a:	*The more an Anglophone parent's top management engages into the design of a German subsidiary's cost accounting system, the less complex is the subsidiary's cost accounting system.*
H3b1_3a:	*The more an Anglophone parent engages into the design of a German subsidiary's cost accounting system through expatriate managers, the less complex is the subsidiary's cost accounting system.*

Given the novelty of this study with respect to the analysis of the complexity of cost accounting systems in subsidiaries, no previous research can back these hypotheses. Their theoretical derivation in section 4.1 emphasises their validity, however. Also, section 3.2 shows that previous research is rather affirmative that parent companies transfer their home country cost accounting traditions into their subsidiaries.

For domestic subsidiaries, it is equally valid to expect that a strong involvement of a parent company in the design of a subsidiary's cost accounting system will affect this system's design. Yet, no assertion on the direction of this effect is feasible. Since both the parent and the subsidiary are German, they are both subject to the complex German cost accounting traditions. Hence, it depends on the current status quo of the parent's and the subsidiary's cost accounting systems whether a parent company urges its subsidiaries to increase or to decrease their systems' complexity.

H3b1_1b:	*An engagement of a domestic parent into the design of a German subsidiary's cost accounting system through corporate directives influences the subsidiary's cost accounting system.*
H3b1_2b:	*An engagement of the domestic parent's top management into the design of a German subsidiary's cost accounting system influences the subsidiary's cost accounting system.*
H3b1_3b:	*An engagement of a domestic parent into the design of a German subsidiary's cost accounting system through expatriate managers influences the subsidiary's cost accounting system.*

Voluntary institutional factors

In H3b_2, subsidiaries' cost accounting systems are associated with voluntary institutional factors. The hypothesis comprises that subsidiaries are likely to mimic the cost accounting systems in comparable companies. Such comparable companies can stem from both inside and outside a subsidiary's group. In the literature review, the effect of costing experiences made by **sister affiliates** on subsidiaries' cost accounting prevails as particularly important. Yet, previous research also considers outside opinions to be relevant. In line with the theoretical reasoning for the relevance of **industry comparisons**, previous research finds a company's industry to be relevant for the design of its cost accounting system.[551] The direction of such influences on the complexity of cost accounting systems, however, is subject to a variety of additional characteristics. For instance, the national background of the sister affiliates might mitigate this effect. Normative research on this issue rather argues for a general convergence of international management accounting practices due to mimetic pressures.[552] This underlines that mimetic factors can either increase or decrease a cost accounting system's complexity. Thus, the following hypotheses are derived:

[551] Cf. *Shields* (1998), p. 1998; *Moeschler* (2012), p. 264.
[552] Cf. *Granlund/Lukka* (1998), p. 157.

H3b2_1:	*The extent to which a subsidiary engages into the discussion of cost accounting practices with other companies from outside its group affects the complexity of its cost accounting system.*
H3b2_2:	*The extent to which a subsidiary engages into the discussion of cost accounting practices with other companies from inside its group affects the complexity of its cost accounting system.*

In addition to mimetic pressures, voluntary institutional variables also comprise a normative perspective. Following section 4.1.3, it is important to consider management accountants' educational background and their interaction with professional institutes. In line with this theoretical argument, the **educational background of management accountants** regularly prevails as an important antecedent for the design of management and cost accounting systems.[553] In Germany, the education of management and cost accountants particularly occurs through university courses in business administration.[554] This educational background can be linked to the complex cost centre accounting which characterises German cost accounting systems.[555] German cost accountants are well aware of academic and textbook considerations on how to design cost accounting systems (from a German point of view). Nevertheless, previous research cannot show a significant effect of a profound educational background provided by universities on the complexity of cost accounting systems in a German context.[556] Irrespectively if trained at a university or by practical experience, cost accountants learn about the complex design of cost accounting in Germany. As such, accountants' reliance on university education or practical experience (learning by doing) cannot be expected to affect the cost accounting system in domestic German companies. It remains unclear, however, whether this link cannot be established for Anglophone subsidiaries in Germany, either. If these companies' cost accountants rely on their conceptual management accounting education from German universities rather than being somewhat experienced in their company's Anglophone management accounting practices, they should bring German cost accounting traditions into their companies. This leads to the following hypotheses:

H3b2_3a:	*The prevalence of German university-trained cost accountants increases the complexity of cost accounting systems in subsidiaries of Anglophone subsidiaries in Germany.*
H3b2_3b:	*The prevalence of German university-trained cost accountants has no impact on the complexity of cost accounting systems in subsidiaries of domestic German subsidiaries.*

Besides these educational backgrounds, the discussion of voluntary institutional effects in section 4.1.3 highlights an effect of **professional institutes of management accountants** on the design of a company's cost accounting system.

German professional institutes such as the ICV contribute only marginally to the primary education of management accountants in Germany.[557] Yet, a strong cooperation with these institutes can be expected to increase the complexity of a cost accounting system in Anglophone companies in Germany. If a management accountant in an Anglophone firm

[553] Cf. e.g. *Granlund/Lukka* (1998), p. 165; *Ahrens/Chapman* (2000), p. 480ff.; *Portz/Lere* (2010), p. 49; *Moeschler* (2012), p. 99ff, 111ff.

[554] Cf. e.g. *Ahrens/Chapman* (2000), p. 482; *Weber et al.* (2010a), p. 28.

[555] Cf. *Portz/Lere* (2010), p. 49f.

[556] Cf. *Moeschler* (2012), p. 270.

[557] Cf. *Ahrens/Chapman* (2000), p. 482f.

used a skill learned in a course of, e.g. the ICV to adjust the companies' cost accounting system, this can tighten German cost accounting traditions in this company. Similarly, management accountants' ability to improve their education through, for example, the ICV can be expected to affect the complexity of a domestic subsidiary's cost accounting system as well. The direction of this effect, however, remains unclear due to these companies' roots in the German cost accounting traditions. Depending on the current level of complexity, it is equally possible that an insight from, e.g. the ICV leads to an increase or a decrease of the complexity of a cost accounting system.

In contrast to German institutes, Anglophone professional institutes such as CIMA or IMA are known to have an important share in the development of management accountants' capabilities in Anglophone companies.[558] Yet, the effect of Anglophone professional institutes on subsidiaries' cost accounting systems is likely to be diverse. IMA has developed a strong interest in the particularities of German cost accounting which they perceive beneficial for Anglophone companies as well.[559] This interest is likely to be put through to these institutes' member in their courses or other materials. As such, Anglophone institutes might offer insights into both their home country cost accounting traditions as well as for example, German cost accounting. Hence, it remains unclear whether a management accountant, who furthers an educational background through Anglophone professional institutes, learns about Anglophone or other cost accounting traditions. Therefore, an undirected effect of the cooperation with professional institutes of management accountants from Anglophone countries on both Anglophone and domestic German companies are proclaimed at this point. The above reasoning leads to the following hypotheses:

H3b2_4a:	*The more intensive an Anglophone subsidiary cooperates with professional institutes of management accountants from Germany, the higher is the complexity of its cost accounting system.*
H3b2_4b:	*The cooperation of a domestic German subsidiary with professional institutes of management accountants from Germany affects this company's cost accounting system.*
H2b2_5:	*The cooperation of a subsidiary in Germany with Anglophone professional institutes of management accountants affects this company's cost accounting system.*

Relational context

H3c posits that the effect, coercive institutional factors have on the cost accounting system in a subsidiary depends on the relationship between the subsidiary and its parent company. These theoretical considerations cannot be furthered at this point because they prevail equally in previous empirical studies as well.[560] Hence, based on the theoretical discussion of *Oliver* (1991), it is maintained that a more unfavourable **relational context** will reduce the impact of coercive institutional pressures in subsidiaries. This expectation

[558] For the importance of CIMA in the UK, cf. *Ahrens/Chapman* (2000), p. 480f. A similar importance of CIMA for the professionals in New Zealand and Australia is indicated by *Yazdifar/Askarany* (2010a), p. 1ff., who could mail their survey to 1,500 registered CIMA members in these countries. Similarly, the importance of IMA for the US profession is reflected in *Clinton/White* (2012), p. 40ff.

[559] Cf. *White* (2004), p. 6f.

[560] For a similar argument in the context of the transfer of a parent company's management practices into a subsidiary, cf. *Kostova* (1999), p. 317.

holds equally true for Anglophone and domestic German subsidiaries. In Anglophone subsidiaries, a more unfavourable relational context can be expected to reduce the prevalence of Anglophone cost accounting traditions at the presence of coercive influences. The moderation is expected to offset the complexity increasing effect of coercive institutional influences. In domestic subsidiaries, an unfavourable relational context can also be expected to reduce the effect of the coercive institutional factors. Since no direction can be derived for the effect of coercive institutional influences in these companies, however, this merely implies the expectation of a reversed effect of the moderation if compared to the effect of the coercive institutional influences. To reflect this moderation more thoroughly, hypothesis H3c is refined as follows:

H3c:	*The more unfavourable the relational context between a subsidiary and its parent company, the lower is the effect of coercive institutional influences on the complexity of the subsidiary's cost accounting system.*

4.2.2 Types of cost information use

From a theoretical point of view, five categories of factors determine the use of cost information in subsidiaries (complexity of cost accounting, users' attitudes towards cost information, cost information needs, coercive institutional factors and the relational context). At this point, hypotheses H4a to H4e will be refined with respect to the individual variables which form these categories of influential factors. Thereby, influential variables will only be differentiated with respect to their effect on the six different usage types if there are theoretical or empirical reasons for such a disaggregation. Similarly, the following hypotheses will only be differentiated for the Anglophone and domestic German companies, if necessary.

Complexity of cost accounting systems

Hypothesis H4a asserts that there is an association between the use of cost information by decision makers and the **complexity of the cost accounting system** the derived information stems from. Previous research on this issue has difficulties in establishing this relationship.[561] These studies, however, tend to focus on managers' perceptions about the complexity of cost accounting rather than on a more objective measure of complexity. According to these researchers' conceptual considerations,[562] a more complex cost accounting system should enable management accountants to provide decision makers with cost information that is useful for decision-making.[563] In line, it is assumed that the more complex a cost accounting system is, the more it is used (a) instrumentally, (b) conceptually, (d) diagnostically and (e) interactively.[564] For the (c) rationalising use, the same posi-

[561] Cf. section 3.3.2.1.

[562] Cf. *Hunold* (2003), p. 188f.

[563] Similarly, *Davila* (2000), p. 397, reports a positive correlation between the interactive use of cost information and the detail of a cost accounting system in his study of European and US companies.

[564] Based on a similar assumption, *Sandt* finds that the more financial/non-financial, hart/soft and qualitative/quantitative information is included in a system of key performance indicators, the more it is used instrumentally, conceptually, symbolically, diagnostically and interactively (cf. *Sandt* (2004), p. 137 and 183ff.).

tive relationship can be expected. A complex cost accounting system can prevent the derivation of thorough cost information for very timely decision-problems. This makes an ex-post rationalisation of decisions more likely. In contrast, a non-directed hypothesis is derived for (f) the ceremonial use of cost information. On the one hand, a more complex system may contain certain information which is of little decision relevance and as such excluded from the process of management. On the other hand, a more complex system does not per se reveal that the included information is perceived as irrelevant for decision-making and as such implies a ceremonial use. Hence, the undirected hypothesis best reflects the unclear effect of a complex cost accounting system on the ceremonial usage type. Therefore, H4a is refined as follows:

H4a_1a:	*The more complex a cost accounting system, the more extensively an information user applies cost information in an (a) instrumental, (b) conceptual, (c) rationalising, (d) diagnostic and (e) interactive manner.*
H4a_1b:	*There is an association between the complexity of a cost accounting system and the (f) ceremonial use of cost information.*

Users' attitudes towards cost information

Hypothesis H4b is derived on the grounds of the dynamic theory of economic actors. Following TEA, five attitudes of an information user are particularly relevant for his[565] application of cost information for decision-making.

The more an information user knows about cost information, the easier it will be for him to demand and assess cost information for a decision-problem and the easier he can apply cost information for decision facilitating or influencing.[566] Thus, the more a user knows about cost accounting, the more he will use cost information (a) instrumentally, (b) conceptually, (d) diagnostically and (e) interactively. For the (c) rationalising as well as for (f) ceremonial use of information, undirected hypotheses are derived. Whereas decision makers, who know about the relevance of cost information may be less likely to regard cost information only after a decision was made, it is also likely that knowledgeable decision makers know precisely for which decisions an ex-post rationalisation does not impinge the adequacy of a decision taken. On the one hand, a **knowledgeable information user** may be less likely to oppose a cost accounting system due to its coercively induced character, because he understands the intentions of the inducing parent company. On the other hand, a knowledgeable decision maker may find it easier to challenge the information usefulness of an induced system and as such, adopt the system more ceremonially than a less knowledgeable one would. Hence, the following hypotheses are derived:

---

565 Non- chauvinistically but for simplicity, information users are treated as masculine in the following.

566 Similar arguments can be found in *Karlshaus* (2000), p. 149; *Hunold* (2003), p. 193; *Sandt* (2004), p. 177, or *Steiners* (2005), p. 80. Remarkably, *Karlshaus* (2000), p. 149, and *Hunold* (2003), p. 193, argue for a negative effect of knowledge on the instrumental use of information. Accordingly, knowledgeable managers would rather trust their experience than new information for decision-making. Only *Hunold,* whose study has a public sector setting, can '*confirm*' this expectation, however. Thus, this suggestion is opposed at this point.

H4b_1a:	*The more knowledgeable an information user, the more extensively cost information is used (a) instrumentally, (b) conceptually, (d) diagnostically and (e) interactively.*
H4b_1b:	*There is an association between an information user's cost accounting knowledge and the (c) rationalising as well as the (f) ceremonial use of cost information.*

In a similar vein, the extent to which an information user employs cost information for decision-making theoretically depends on his **preference for cost information.**[567] Thus, cost information can be expected to be used more (a) instrumentally, (b) conceptually, (d) diagnostically and (e) interactively by a decision maker whose focus is on cost-based decision-making. Moreover, these decision makers can be expected to be more reluctant to oppose an imposed cost accounting system, i.e. to use cost information (f) ceremonially only because they want to use cost information. For the (c) rationalising use of cost information, no directed hypothesis can be derived. On the one hand, decision makers preferring cost-based decision-making may oppose to take decisions, which they would need to legitimate ex-post, without considering ex-ante cost information. On the other hand, it cannot be ruled out that these decision makers will strive for an ex-post rationalisation of any decision that could not have been taken based on cost information in the first place. Therefore, the following hypotheses are derived:

H4b_2a:	*The higher an information user's preference for cost information, the more extensively he applies cost information in an (a) instrumental, (b) conceptual, (d) diagnostic and (e) interactive manner.*
H4b_2b:	*There is an association between an information user's preference for cost information and the (c) rationalising use of cost information.*
H4b_2c:	*The higher an information user's preference for cost information, the less extensively he applies cost information in a (f) ceremonial manner.*

TEA also proves to be a solid ground for the interrelation of information users' perception of cost information and the way, in which they incorporate the information into their decision-making. Empirically, there is evidence for a positive association between a **user's perception of information quality** and the (a) instrumental, (b) conceptual and ((d) and (e)) symbolic usage types in the context of cost information[568] as well as general management accounting information.[569] Similar to users' preference for cost information, a positive evaluation of cost information should be aligned with a less extensive application of cost information in a (f) ceremonial way. The perceived relevance and reliability of information should overcome potential reservations, decision makers may have against a coercively induced system. Given an equivalent applicability of the argument provided for the preference for cost information, no directed hypothesis for (c) the rationalising use can be established. Hence, the following hypotheses are derived:

[567] For a similar and '*confirmed*' hypothesis in the context of the types of cost information use by *Burchell/Pelz*, cf. *Hunold* (2003), p. 196 and 208. Similarly, *Hofmann et al.* (2012), p. 161 and 168, posit and '*affirm*' this relationship for *Simons*' types of use in a budgeting setting.

[568] Cf. *Karlshaus* (2000), p. 124 and 165, or *Hunold* (2003), p. 195 and 208.

[569] Cf. e.g. *Steiners* (2005), p. 78ff. and 193.

H4b_3a:	*The better an information user perceives the quality of cost information, the more extensively he applies cost information in an (a) instrumental, (b) conceptual, (d) diagnostic and (e) interactive manner.*
H4b_3b:	*There is an association between an information user's perception of the quality of cost information and the (c) rationalising use of cost information.*
H4b_3c:	*The better an information user perceives the quality of cost information, the less extensively he applies cost information in a (f) ceremonial manner.*

From the theoretical considerations, it also prevails that the **involvement of information users** into the design of a cost accounting system as well as the intensity of contacts between these users and a company's management accountants determines how cost information is used. Similarly, previous research on *Pelz/Burchell*'s types of use regards such associations in a cost accounting setting. Thereby, a positive association of contacts with most types of use is supported.[570] For the involvement, however, a significant association prevails especially for the instrumental use.[571] Previous research on *Simons*' usage types particularly aligns the interactive use of information with information user's interaction with the information system as well as the personnel responsible for these systems.[572] Therefore, both the information users' involvement and their contact with management accountants is expected to affect the (a) instrumental, (b) conceptual, (d) diagnostic and (e) interactive use of cost information positively. As for the preference for cost information and the perceptions about cost information quality, information users can be expected to use their cost accounting system less (f) ceremonially if they engaged strongly into the system design and interacted extensively with the information provider. Moreover, reflecting the discussion for the preference for cost information, the effect of information users' involvement and their **contact with management accountants** for the (c) ceremonial use of information remains rather unclear. Consequently, the following hypotheses are derived:

H4b_4a:	*The more extensively an information user engages into the design of a cost accounting system, the more extensively he applies cost information in an (a) instrumental, (b) conceptual, (d) diagnostic and (e) interactive manner.*
H4b_4b:	*There is an association between an information user's involvement into cost system design and the (c) rationalising use of cost information.*
H4b_4c:	*The more extensively an information user engages into the design of a cost accounting system, the less extensively he applies cost information in a (f) ceremonial manner.*

[570] Cf. *Karlshaus* (2000), p. 142 and 165; *Hunold* (2003), p. 191f. and 208.

[571] Cf. *Frank* (2000), p. 177, who labels a similarly operationalised variable '*management attention*', or *Hunold* (2003), p. 194 and 208.

[572] *Widener* (2007), p. 766 and 778, reveals an interactive application of controls to *consume* management attention. Thus, she emphasises that an interactive use of controls requires substantial personal involvement of the information user. Similarly, *Abernethy et al.* (2010), p. 11, highlights an interactive use of planning and control systems to depend positively on the information users' leadership styles. Both researched styles are operationalised in a way that reflects personal involvement of the information user with the information providers (p. 14). *Hofmann et al.* (2012), p. 162 and 168, posits and '*affirms*' that the leadership behaviour, i.e., among others, the communication between subordinates and decision makers affects the interactive use of budgets positively.

H4b_5a:	*The more extensively an information user interacts with management accountants, the more extensively he applies cost information in an (a) instrumental, (b) conceptual, (d) diagnostic and (e) interactive manner.*
H4b_5b:	*There is an association between the extent to which information users interact with management accountants and the (c) rationalising use of cost information.*
H4b_5c:	*The more extensively an information user interacts with management accountants, the less extensively he applies cost information in a (f) ceremonial manner.*

Despite the complexity of a cost accounting system and the variables derived from the dynamic theory of economic actors, the use of cost information is aligned with three aspects from NIS.

Economic variables

From a theoretical point of view, the existence and use of cost information depends on a need for cost information for decision-making. This need is established only if there is **environmental uncertainty**. Therefore, it is little surprising to find this variable to be widely present in the analysis of different types of cost and management accounting information use. In both cost and management accounting contexts, however, studies on the (a) instrumental and (b) conceptual use rather disapprove the suggested positive dependence of these usage types on the level of (perceived) environmental uncertainty.[573] Equally, the evidence for the effect of environmental uncertainty on the (d) diagnostic and (e) interactive use of management accounting information is rather diverse. Whereas there is some evidence indicating a use increasing effect of environmental uncertainty,[574] other studies provide non-affirmative evidence.[575] Similarly, the expert interviews held for hypothesis refinement revealed that during uncertain environments, certain decisions have to be made timely and cost information is only used for (c) ex-post rationalisation use of information. Yet, uncertain environments also lead to the use of other information than costs during the management process.[576] Little insights on the dependence of the (f) ceremonial usage type on environmental uncertainty prevail in previous research. Given this diverse picture, no refinement of H4c regarding effect of environmental uncertainty on the different usage types can be justified. Hence, the undirected hypothesis is sustained.

H4c_1:	*There is an association between the level of environmental uncertainty and the extensiveness to which an information user applies cost information in an (a) instrumental, (b) conceptual, (c) rationalising, (d) diagnostic, (e) interactive and (f) ceremonial manner.*

In addition to the establishment of a need for cost information through environmental uncertainties, **cost accounting objectives** are a manifestation of this information need.

---

[573] Cf. *Frank* (2000), p. 177; *Karlshaus* (2000), p. 122 and 159; *Steiners* (2005), p. 80 and 186. For two studies which '*affirm*' an interrelation between environmental uncertainty and these usage types, cf. *Aust* (1999), p. 66 and 116ff., and *van der Veeken/Wouters* (2002), p. 366f.

[574] For both usage types, cf. *Widener* (2007), p. 765 and 778. For the interactive use of budgets, cf. *Hofmann et al.* (2012), p. 159f and 168.

[575] For both usage types, cf. *Henri* (2006a), p. 83 and 95. For the diagnostic use of budgets, cf. *Hofmann et al.* (2012), p. 159f and 168.

[576] Cf. *Hoque* (2005), p. 379. A similar discussion can be found in *Davila* (2000), p. 393 and 400, or *Steiners* (2005), p. 186f.

Hence, the way in which information users apply cost information can be expected to be a function of the fulfilled cost accounting objectives. Previous research reports the instrumental and/or conceptual usage types to be less and the diagnostic usage type to be more present in companies with a strong focus on control.[577] Similarly, *Bauer* (2002) finds *Burchell/Pelz*'s usage types to depend on a company's reliance on planning and control activities since these usage types vary during different stages of the management process.[578] *Abernethy/Brownell* (1999) align *Simons*' usage types with the fulfilment of strategic objectives. They find the interactive (diagnostic) usage type to be more prevalent in companies which experience an extensive (weak) change in their strategic position.[579] For this study, however, one particular relationship prevails with respect to the influence of cost accounting objectives. Section 2.3 conclusively aligns the different types of cost information use with the primary purposes of cost accounting. Whereas the (a) instrumental and the (b) conceptual usage type are aligned with the decision facilitating purpose, a (d) diagnostic and (e) interactive application of cost information is linked to the decision influencing purpose. Consequently, an association between the usage types and the primary purposes for which information users apply cost information can be expected.

H4c_2a:	*The more extensively an information user applies cost information for decision facilitating purposes, the more extensively he applies cost information in an (a) instrumental and (b) conceptual manner.*
H4c_2b:	*The more extensively an information user applies cost information for decision influencing purposes, the more extensively he applies cost information in a (d) diagnostic and (e) interactive manner.*

The (c) rationalising use cannot be disjunctively attributed to either of these two objectives in section 2.3. Similarly, (f) the ceremonial usage type is argued to reflect that cost information is not used during the management process. Hence, no association between the objectives and these two types are regarded in this study.

Coercive institutional factors

Besides the need for cost information, NIS reveals that the use of cost information is affected by coercive institutional influences. In line with the findings in section 3.3.2.2 and the considerations by *Oliver* (1991), it is argued that decision makers in a subsidiary are more likely to use cost information ceremonially, the more a parent company influences the cost accounting system in the subsidiary. Thus, it can be expected that the engagement of a parent company into the design of a subsidiary's cost accounting system through **directives**, **corporate top managers** and **expatriates** increases the (f) ceremonial application of cost information.

H4d_1a:	*If a parent company influences the design of a subsidiary's cost accounting system strongly through (i) corporate directives, (ii) personal involvement of the corporate top management team or (iii) expatriates, information users in the subsidiary will use cost information more extensively in (f) a ceremonial manner.*

[577] Cf. *Henri* (2006a), p. 84f. and 95.
[578] Cf. *Bauer* (2002), p. 139.
[579] Cf. *Abernethy/Brownell* (1999), p. 198.

The discussion of the ceremonial usage type in the literature review and the ceremonial use increasing effect of institutional coercive influences must be seen to indicate that institutional coercive pressures decrease the non-ceremonial use of cost information. This directed interaction, however, is hypothetical. Previous research on this issue is virtually non-existent. Some studies regard centralisation of decision rights to be a potential determinant of cost and management accounting information use. *Steiners* (2005) considers more centralised decision processes in one company to make an instrumental application of cost information more likely because top-level decision makers have to deal with more decision-problems themselves.[580] Following this argumentation, a parent company which wishes to unify cost accounting globally may also centralise associated decision rights, thus reducing a subsidiary's non-ceremonial use of information. Because *Steiners* could not find any significant results in this respect, however, his argumentation remains hypothetical. In contrast, *Hofmann et al.* (2012) find a negative association between centralised decision rights and an interactive control type.[581] Because both cited studies focus on single companies, however, the validity of their results for a subsidiary context remains limited. Also, there is some research which indicates that the ceremonial and non-ceremonial use of cost information is not mutually exclusive.[582] None of these studies found these results for a single decision maker, however. Above all, it remains explorable whether coercive institutional influences are indeed suppressing the non-ceremonial usage types in subsidiaries. Hence, H4d_1b is stated as follows:

H4d_1b:	*If a parent company affects the design of a subsidiary's cost accounting system strongly through (i) corporate directives, (ii) personal involvement of the corporate top management team or (iii) expatriates, information users in the subsidiary will use cost information less extensively in an (a) instrumental, (b) conceptual, (c) rationalising, (d) diagnostic and (e) interactive manner*

Relational context

The existence of coercive institutional influences does not necessarily foster the ceremonial and suppress the non-ceremonial use of cost information. As presented in the literature review and the theoretical foundation, this effect is likely to be moderated by the relational context of a subsidiary and its parent. For instance, if a parent company's involvement was little discretion constraining or if information users in a subsidiary identified strongly with their parent company, the ceremonial use increasing and the non-ceremonial use decreasing effect of coercive institutional influences is likely to be less apparent. As suggested in the basic hypothesis H4e, it can be expected that there is a moderating effect of the **relational context** on the different usage types. Given the lack of previous research on this interrelation, no additional underpinning of this expectation is feasible. The expected moderation is summarised by refining H4e as follows:

H4e:	*The association between coercive institutional factors and the extent to which an information user applies cost information in an (a) instrumental, (b) conceptual, (c) rationalising, (d) diagnostic (e) interactive and (f) ceremonial manner is moderated by the information user's perception of the relational context.*

580 For this and the following, cf. *Steiners* (2005), p. 56ff. and 189.

581 For this and the following, cf. *Hofmann et al.* (2012), p. 160f. and 168.

582 Cf. *Malmi* (1997); *Major/Hopper* (2005); *Hopper/Major* (2007).

4.2.3 Performance of cost accounting systems

Having clarified the hypotheses for the complexity of cost accounting systems and the use of cost information in subsidiaries, the derivation of propositions on the performance of cost accounting systems are centred hereafter. The association between the design of cost accounting systems and the use of cost information and the systems' performance is a manifestation of the contingency approach and NIS which essentially postulate that organisations adapt their internal structures to the environmental context to work rationally and legitimately. Yet, the following section will rely on a more pragmatic establishment of these interdependencies since the inclusion of the performance of cost accounting systems is not associated to this study's theoretical research objective.

In this context, it is essential to recapitulate that preparers and users of cost information can have significantly different perceptions of their cost accounting systems (see section 2.4). Hence, this section derives **propositions** for both these two group of employees. Essentially, these '*hypotheses*' shall lead to recommendations on how to design cost accounting systems and how to use cost information more effectively (research question 3).

Complexity of cost accounting

A more complex cost accounting system can be expected to enable management accountants to derive information for various decision-problems. Thereby, the system should become more relevant for decision makers and, as such, more valuable for a company. In international literature, such a direct relationship between the performance of a cost accounting system and the overall systems' design is regularly expected[583] and/or prevails[584] for the different groups of employees. In a German context, the evaluations of cost accounting were found to be improvable through the presence of contribution margin accounting as well as planned and target cost information (the time reference of cost accounting).[585] Also, the performance of cost accounting systems is found to be hampered by, e.g. mere full cost information in Germany.[586] In addition, multiple international researchers link a well performing cost accounting system with the implementation of ABC.[587] Despite these selective analyses of the performance effects of a **cost accounting system's elements**, there is no conclusive analysis that examins which of the 15 elements

[583] Cf. e.g. *Aust* (1999), p. 156, and *Schoute* (2009), p. 210f. Also, *Hunold* (2003), p. 188, provides similar expectations including both preparers and users of information. Remarkably, *Frank* (2000), p. 225 and 226, argues that the perceived complexity of cost accounting reduced the economic performance in firms due to its tangling character but has to reject this expectation.

[584] For evidence including both preparers and users of information, cf. e.g. *Pizzini* (2006), p. 196; *Moeschler* (2012), p. 310, or the applicable studies reviewed in chapter 3 (*Meyer* (1988); *Ziegler* (1994); *Bhimani* (2003); *Smith* (2005); *Yazdifar et al.* (2008)). Remarkably, there is some evidence that managers' subjective assessments of the complexity of cost accounting impinge company's market performance (cf. *Aust* (1999), p. 181).

[585] Cf. *Frank/Reitmeyer* (1999), p. 24; *Weber* (2010), p. 92, or similarly *Moeschler* (2012), p. 306.

[586] Cf. *Weber* (2010), p. 92; *Moeschler* (2012), p. 306. Also, *Frank* (2000), p. 226, finds a similar result for companies' market performance.

[587] For evidence including both preparers and users of information, cf. exemplarily *Foster/Swenson* (1997), p. 109ff., or the applicable studies reviewed in chapter 3 (*Bhimani/Pigott* (1992); *Anderson/Young* (1999), p. 525ff.; *Ittner et al.* (2002), p. 718; *Bhimani et al.* (2007)).

covered in this study affects the performance of a cost accounting system (as perceived by managers and management accountants) positively. Because no evidence on differences with respect to the performance effects of a cost accounting system prevail for Anglophone and domestic German subsidiaries, the following propositions are derived:

H5a_1a:	*The more complex a subsidiary's cost type, cost centre and cost object accounting, the higher is the performance of a cost accounting system as perceived by management accountants.*
H5a_1b:	*The more complex a subsidiary's cost type, cost centre and cost object accounting, the higher is the performance of a cost accounting system as perceived by managers.*
H5a_2:	*The positive effect of a subsidiary's cost accounting system on the system's performance varies for different elements of its cost accounting system.*

Types of cost information use

Previous research on information users' perceptions of their cost accounting system generally expects a positive association between (a) **the instrumental use** of cost information and various performance measures.[588] Yet, only *Reitmeyer* (2000) can confirm this expectation. *Frank* (2000) and *Karlshaus* (2000) find the opposite to be true.[589] Neither of these studies, however, focusses on decision makers' evaluation of their ability to fulfil their cost accounting objectives and their overall satisfaction with the system. Hence, in this study, such expectations are maintained. The more managers (can) use cost information for direct decision-making (i.e. instrumentally), the better they assess their cost accounting system. Corresponding to a previously confirmed argument for economic performance,[590] (b) **the conceptual use** of cost information can also be expected to affect managers' perceptions about a cost accounting system positively. Note that this proposition contradicts the expected and confirmed inability to align this usage type with the rationality of decision-processes explicated by *Hunold* (2003). According to him, the independence of this usage type from a clearly defined decision-problem does prohibit a rationality-assessment.[591] This study applies another measure for the performance of a cost accounting system. The satisfaction with a cost accounting system and the achievement of cost accounting objectives can rather be improved if managers acknowledge that their build-up of experiences about cost information facilitates their decision-making or their influences on others' decisions. Hence, the assumed positive association is justified.

The **rationalising usage type** (c) is poorly covered in previous cost accounting research. As such, a proposition on this usage type's performance effect cannot be conclusively derived from previous research. One previous study bases its argument for a negative association of the symbolic use of cost information and the performance of cost accounting systems on the rationalising use. Accordingly, this usage type alleviates irrational decision-making.[592] Yet, it can also be argued that an ex-post rationalisation of decisions may not affect the objective fulfilment of cost accounting at all, since ex-ante decision-making is

[588] Cf. *Karlshaus* (2000), p. 174ff.; *Frank* (2000), p. 224; *Reitmeyer* (2000), p. 51 or *Hunold* (2003), p. 223.

[589] Cf. section 3.3.2.3.

[590] Cf. *Karlshaus* (2000), p. 174ff.

[591] Cf. *Hunold* (2003), p. 222ff.

[592] Cf. *Karlshaus* (2000), p. 175f.

apparently possible irrespectively of cost information. Moreover, the ex-post rationalisation of decisions through cost information can be seen as a verification of the reasonableness of a decision (i.e. control). This understanding aligns the rationalising use of cost information with the achievement of a control objective.[593] If the rationalising use contributed to the cost accounting objectives, however, a positive association of the rationalising usage type and the performance of cost accounting as perceived by managers could be expected. Given this diversity, no expectation about an association between this usage type and managers' perceptions of the cost accounting system is derived. Hence, the due analysis will be rather explorative in this regard.

As revealed in the literature review, there is no previous cost accounting research on *Simons'* **diagnostic and interactive usage types**. For the purpose of this study, the diagnostic and the interactive usage types are both applied to describe a more decision influencing use of cost information. Thus, managers who apply cost information (d) diagnostically or (e) interactively can be expected to achieve their cost accounting objectives more extensively and be more satisfied with their cost information. This proposition is well in line with previous research. In the light of more general management accounting information, section 3.3.2.3 shows that both usage types tend to be rather positively associated with a company's managerial or financial performance.

A different picture prevails for the (f) **ceremonial use** of cost information. The studies summarised in the literature review on this usage type (Table 3-8 on p. 73) vastly indicate that a ceremonial use of cost information is rather associated with (managers') negative evaluations of their cost accounting system. Given that all these studies are case-based, however, it remains open for exploration whether such an association can be established more conclusively for a larger number of companies.

The above propositions are summarised as H5b_1 and H5b_2:

H5b_1:	*The performance of a cost accounting system as perceived by managers increases, the more they use cost information in an (a) instrumental, (b) conceptual, (d) diagnostic and (e) interactive manner.*
H5b_2:	*The performance of a cost accounting system as perceived by managers decreases, the more they use cost information in a (f) ceremonial manner.*

The application of cost information by decision makers should be important for **information providers'** assessment of a cost accounting system's performance.[594] However, it remains unclear whether the actual use of cost information by managers finds its way into management accountants' evaluation of their cost accounting systems. *Homburg et al.* (1998) report management accountants to perceive their cost information considerably better than marketing managers and board members.[595] They interpret this finding to argue that management accountants tend to disregard information users' needs. Nevertheless, the detailed analyses of the data by *Aust* (1999) and *Karlshaus* (2000) neglect this finding by regarding information users' perceptions of the cost accounting systems' com-

[593] Such an understanding was put forward during the expert interviews which preceded this hypothesis development.

[594] Cf. *Homburg et al.* (1998), p. 23ff.

[595] Cf. *Homburg et al.* (1998), p. 25.

plexity and the effect of information use on market performance.[596] The focus on information users by *Frank* (2000) and *Karlshaus* (2000)[597] could not shed light on this issue, either. *Hunold* (2003) analyses information users' assessments of the rationality of their decision-making.[598] Because information users and preparers do not assess the economic situation of the regarded municipalities differently, however, *Hunold* (2003) does not explicitly analyse whether information users' application of cost information feeds back into cost accountants' evaluation of their system.[599] As such, it remains to be explored whether information users' application of cost information affects information preparers' evaluation of their cost accounting system.

H5b_3:	*The performance of a cost accounting system as perceived by management accountants is associated with information users' application of the system.*

Hypothesis H4a posits that the complexity of a cost accounting system affects the use of cost information. Hence, it remains to be discovered, whether the interaction between the use of cost information and the complexity of a cost accounting system also influences the performance effects of the individual types of use. There is little previous research on such a potential mediation. This far, only *Frank* (2000) regards the design of cost accounting systems and the use of cost information in a conjoint model to explain the financial performance of a firm.[600] The author, however, does not consider whether the use of cost information is potentially **mediating** an **effect** stemming from the design characteristics. In this study, this aspect is taken into account by formulating the following proposition:

H5b_4:	*The use of cost information mediates the effects the design of a cost accounting system has on managers' and management accountants' assessments of the system.*

Focussing exclusively on these seven propositions corresponds to this study's pragmatic research objective.[601] Yet, doing so neglects the diversity of additional variables previously considered to '*explain*' the performance of cost accounting systems.

Contextual fit of a cost accounting system's complexity

There are two variables from Figure 4-4 which consistently prevail in international research on the performance of cost accounting. Studies interested in the successful implementation of ABC regularly regard *top management support* as a success factor for the implementation.[602] In addition, other ABC implementation studies[603] as well as more general

596 Cf. *Aust* (1999), p. 161, and *Karlshaus* (2000), p. 131ff and 177f.

597 Cf. *Frank* (2000), p. 76f., and *Reitmeyer* (2000), p. 89.

598 Cf. *Hunold* (2003), p. 218f.

599 Cf. *Hunold* (2003), p. 220.

600 Cf. *Frank* (2000), p. 226.

601 *Ittner et al.* (2002), p. 714ff., design their study to analyse the performance effects of ABC accordingly. While focusing on the direct effect of ABC on product quality, cycle time and manufacturing costs, the researchers *control* for additional factors such as the manufacturing technology.

602 For a summary, cf. *McGowan/Klammer* (1997), p. 220, or *Anderson/Young* (1999), p. 528. A similar link is stressed in more general German research projects on management accounting (for a summary, cf. *Weber et al.* (2010b), p. 325ff.).

603 Cf. e.g. *Krumwiede* (1998), p. 264; *Anderson/Young* (1999), p. 545; *Cagwin/Bouwman* (2002), p. 24.

studies on the design of cost accounting systems,[604] stress that a powerful *information technology* directly facilitates the good performance of a cost accounting system. Similarly, research on the performance effects of different usage types regard the interaction of management accountants and managers[605] or variables including the information technology applied for cost accounting[606] into their analysis.[607] Moreover, the research on the ceremonial usage types consistently aligns poor perceptions about a coercively induced cost accounting system with the involvement of the inducing parent company.[608] Other than that, the variables which are analysed for their effect on a cost accounting system's performance are rather diverse. In the context of studies on the design of cost accounting, previous research regularly regards numerous additional variables during the analysis of a system's performance.[609] These reflect the majority of the factors derived in above research framework. In more general studies on the use of management accounting information, there is a more selective focus on additional variables. Given the diverse research questions, these studies included, e.g. the characteristics of a top management team,[610] environmental uncertainties,[611] firms' innovativeness,[612] strategic change[613] or national culture[614] into their models linking various usage types to a measure of performance. Other researchers obliterate additional variables in their models by evaluating the regarded usage types or regarding performance in structural models also containing various antecedents of the information use.[615]

Despite these research efforts, the analysis of various contextual contingencies of a well performing cost accounting system is not at the core of this study. Performance is rather incorporated as a yardstick to assess the cost accounting systems in subsidiaries and to provide recommendations on potential performance improvements only. To avoid the negligence of the consideration of a **contextual contingency** of a cost accounting system's

---

604 Cf. e.g. *Krumwiede et al.* (2007), p. 26, 31f. and 40; *Friedl et al.* (2009), p. 113; *Moeschler* (2012), p. 310.

605 Cf. *Aust* (1999), p. 148 and 181, for an explicit inclusion and *Hunold* (2003), p. 223, for an implicit one.

606 Cf. *Hunold* (2003), p. 176, 218 and 225, who labels this variable 'service quality'. Similarly, Frank argues the representation of data to be reflected in his 'quality' measure as well (cf. *Frank* (2000), p. 146, 149 and 226).

607 The other two studies reviewed in section 3.3 do not include any additional variables (cf. *Karlshaus* (2000), p. 187) or focus on various other aspects characterising the decision-making process such as the use of non-financial information (*Reitmeyer* (2000), p. 122).

608 Cf. section 3.3.

609 Cf. e.g. *McGowan/Klammer* (1997), p. 220, or *Anderson/Young* (1999), p. 528, for a summary of the variables included in the analysis of the successful implementation of ABC. *Schoute* (2009), p. 215ff., discusses a variety of control variables he perceives relevant during the analysis of cost accounting performance. Similarly, *Moeschler* (2012), p. 310, regards the performance of cost information on the ground of the same variables, he regards as influential for the design of cost accounting systems.

610 Cf. *Naranjo-Gil/Hartmann* (2006), p. 37.

611 Cf. *Widener* (2007), p. 778; similarly *Steiners* (2005), p. 207.

612 Cf. *Bisbe/Otley* (2004), p. 724; *Henri* (2006b), p. 544.

613 Cf. *Abernethy et al.* (2010), p. 198.

614 Cf. *Jais* (2007), p. 177.

615 Cf. *Sandt* (2004), p. 201 and 204; *Hofmann et al.* (2012), p. 157 and 170.

performance, hypotheses H5a and H5b are complemented by an expectation brought forward by *Drury/Tayles* (2005). These authors believe that a cost accounting system which reflects its contextual factors is performing better than one that does not.[616] In an ABC setting, *Ittner et al.* (2002) provide weak evidence for the validity of such an assumption.[617] Similarly, *Moeschler* (2012) reports that cost accounting systems in German and Japanese companies are performing better, if these systems were reflecting their contextual factors.[618]

Nevertheless, it remains explorable whether *Drury/Tayles* (2005) expectation does necessarily uphold for Anglophone and domestic German subsidiaries. These companies cannot be expected to design their cost accounting systems in accordance with rational choices only since they are likely to be subject to coercive institutional influences as well. Especially if such coercive affects involve a foreign cost accounting tradition, as it is the case in the Anglophone firms, deviations from *Drury/Tayles'* expectations appear very likely. An Anglophone company which is characterised by a more complex cost accounting system than allowed by its Anglophone parent or necessary for the local environment cannot per se be expected to have a poorly performing cost accounting system. In such a case, the system would potentially be more like an average domestic German system. Hence, the local workforce might indeed feel more satisfied with the system.[619] Following these arguments, the following **proposition** is derived for both managers and management accountants.

H5c_1a:	*In domestic subsidiaries in Germany, the performance of a cost accounting system is higher, if the system is in line with the subsidiary's economic, institutional and relational context.*
H5c_1b:	*In Anglophone subsidiaries in Germany, the performance of a cost accounting system varies with the level to which the system is in line with the subsidiary's economic, institutional and relational context.*

Having clarified this study's expectations for research questions 1 and 3 as well as the theoretical underlying of research question 2, the the research design can be introduced hereafter.

616 Cf. *Drury/Tayles* (2005), p. 77.
617 Cf. *Ittner et al.* (2002), p. 724.
618 Cf. *Moeschler* (2012), p. 320f.
619 Cf. e.g. *Meyer* (1988), for according evidence. Moreover, such a proposition can be derived from the Anglophone interest in domestic German cost accounting systems and RCA which motives this study. Also, *Pizzini* (2006), p. 201f., finds cost accounting systems which are more complex than their context would suggest to be performing better than systems which are less complex than expected in a setting of US hospitals.

5 Research design

5.1 Research method

5.1.1 Survey research

The literature review in section 3 revealed that this study can achieve its research objectives best through a survey based comparison of Anglophone firms in Germany with a German control group.

Survey research is a standardised approach for the collection of information from a population through the analysis of sampling units. Thereby, interference about the wider population can be found through considerations of the sampling units.[620] Due to its quantitative character and according simplified data analysability, survey research facilitates large sample research.[621] To account for restricted resources, such large samples generally cannot be researched through field visits. As such, surveys are often carried-out by the means of mail-based questionnaires.[622] Apart from that, information collection in survey research can also be web-based, by phone or by personal interviews.[623] For the purpose of this study, a mail- and web-based[624] questionnaire can best achieve the descriptive research objective. The provision of representative questionnaire results will overcome the lack of knowledge regarding the complexity of cost accounting systems and the use of cost information in Anglophone and domestic German affiliates. Besides, survey research is linked to testing, refining and explaining existing theories.[625] As such, the data obtained with a questionnaire can be used to falsify hypotheses on the explanans of the complexity of cost accounting systems and the use of cost information. This corresponds to the issued theoretical research objective. Since the former two research objectives can facilitate the pragmatic research objective, a survey approach is most applicable for the purpose of this study.

The applicability of survey research for this research project can be underlined through a comparison of this method with two alternative research methods: experimental research and case study research.[626]

Laboratory and field experiments involve the determination of the effect which an explanatory variable has on a dependent variable through a conscious manipulation of the

---

620 Cf. e.g. *Birnberg et al.* (1990), p. 35; *Real/Parker* (2005), p. 4; *Riesenhuber* (2009), p. 7.

621 Cf. *Riesenhuber* (2009), p. 7.

622 Cf. *Kubicek* (1975), p. 67ff.; *Birnberg et al.* (1990), p. 35; *Van der Stede et al.* (2005), p. 657.

623 Cf. *Real/Parker* (2005), p. 8, and similarly *Van der Stede et al.* (2005), p. 657 or *Merchant/Otley* (2006), p. 790.

624 *Real/Parker* (2005), p. 11, stresses web-based surveys to be an alternative to the classical questionnaire distribution by mail.

625 Cf. *Merchant/Otley* (2006), p. 790, or similarly *Riesenhuber* (2009), p. 1ff.

626 Cf. *Birnberg et al.* (1990), p. 34f.; *Kubicek* (1975), p. 57f. *Merchant/Otley* (2006), p. 790, add archival research to the above enumeration. This is neglected at this point.

explanatory factor.[627] Through experimental research such effects can be isolated because of the ability to control for all other possible influences. The method's apparent link to theoretical (and pragmatic) research objectives[628] highlights its potential relevance for this study's explicative research objective. Because it is rather unfeasible to vary the identified independent variables (e.g. extent of corporate directives or product diversity), however, experiments disqualify for this study.

Case study research involves the analysis of phenomena which are indistinguishable from their context in a real-life setting.[629] Case study research is regularly based on small samples. It lacks the ability to provide evidence for the significance of its findings in statistical terms.[630] Hence, there are difficulties to argue for the relevance of a case study for a wider population (i.e. statistical generalisation).[631] Nevertheless, case studies can provide detailed insights into unique phenomena and help to generalise theories analytically rather than statistically.[632] To find an answer to research questions 1 to 3, however, the case study approach is not appropriate. The striving for a statistical representative description, explanation and evaluation of the complexity of cost accounting systems and the use of cost information cannot be fulfilled by the case study approach. Generally, this research method is appreciated for its explorative purposes.[633] From such a perspective, case study research can illustrate, motivate and inspire a subsequent large-scale analysis.[634] In this study, these purposes were achieved through the expert interviews which guided the hypotheses development. As such, case study research cannot contribute to the accomplishment of this study's objectives.

Having clarified the necessity to focus on a survey research method by collecting data through a questionnaire, a more detailed definition of the Anglophone subsidiaries to be researched in this study can be provided.

5.1.2 Definition of the sample

This study investigates the cost accounting systems in Anglophone[635] subsidiaries in Germany. Therefore, the population of legal entities which are currently owned by Anglo-

---

[627] For this and the following, cf. *Kubicek* (1975), p. 67ff.; *Birnberg et al.* (1990), p. 35; *Rack/Christophersen* (2009), p. 18f.

[628] Similarly, cf. *Yin* (2009), p. 6.

[629] Cf. *Yin* (2003), p. 4; *Yin* (2009), p. 18.

[630] This drawback of case study research is associates to an interpretation of them as qualitative research. This reflects a sample size based understanding of quality (cf. *Mayring* (2010), p. 17ff.) or corresponds to the "usually applied method of data analysis" (*Lillis/Mundy* (2005), p. 130). Yet, *Eisenhardt* (1989), p. 538, *Siggelkow* (2007), p. 20, or *Yin* (2009), p. 132f., stress that evidence in case study research can be sampled qualitatively as well as quantitatively.

[631] Cf. *Adams et al.* (2006), p. 365; *Yin* (2009), p. 15.

[632] Cf. *Lukka/Kasanen* (1995), p. 85; *Schäffer/Brettel* (2005), p. 44; *Adams et al.* (2006), p. 365; *Eisenhardt/Graebner* (2007), p. 25; *Siggelkow* (2007), p. 20; *Pratt* (2009), p. 856; *Yin* (2009), p. 15.

[633] Cf. e.g. *Lukka/Kasanen* (1995), p. 71; *Yin* (2009), p. 6.

[634] Cf. *Lamnek* (1989), p. 11ff.; *Siggelkow* (2007), p. 21.

[635] As explicated in the introduction, Anglophone firms originate from the USA and five Commonwealth countries (Great Britain, Australia, New Zealand, Canada and South Africa).

phone ultimate owners[636] was drawn from the *amadeus* database. To ensure comparability of the results with the findings from previous research,[637] the population was limited to **manufacturing companies.**[638] Moreover, companies with less than 150 or more than 2,000 employees were excluded from the population. Smaller companies were not addressed as they are likely to have rather simple cost accounting systems.[639] Larger companies were not addressed for two reasons. A recent research project shows that the focus on **medium-sized** companies for the study of cost accounting is most appealing since large companies generally consist of several organisational units which would complicate the analysis of cost accounting systems.[640] Thus, this procedure reduced potential effects of economic organisational sub-units in the sample companies. Furthermore, larger companies are likely to be more exposed to globalisation and as such to alternative cost accounting traditions.[641] Such an exposure would dilute the ability to analyse the cost accounting systems in the sample companies with respect to German and Anglophone cost accounting traditions. Hence, larger companies were excluded. The selection criteria yield 493 Anglophone companies (net of duplicates).[642]

To be able to compare the Anglophone subsidiaries with domestic German companies, the same selection criteria were applied to derive a population of domestic German subsidiaries. The *amadeus* database identified a population of almost 3,000 companies. Since the German firms are particularly needed to be able to evaluate the findings in the Anglophone sample, a **stratified random sample** was drawn from this population.[643] To ensure that the cross-sectional character of this study does not impinge the intended comparisons to an unreasonable extent, the reduction of the German population accounted for the individual manufacturing sub-industries (Nace Rec. 2 No. 10 – No. 33). In each sub-industry, the German population is reduced by randomly selecting companies from five partitions with a defined number of employees. The size categories to split the German companies of a sub-industry into five partitions were derived by splitting the according sub-industry in the Anglophone sample into five equally large groups (quintiles).

The procedure, which is illustrated in Figure 5-1, yielded a **control group** of 493 German subsidiaries. These reflected the industry and size structure of the Anglophone population almost perfectly. Minor deviations occurred due to the absence of certain size quintiles or too few companies in a sub-industry of the German population.

After determining these samples, minor adjustments were necessary due to liquidation, mergers and acquisitions or multiple legal entities at one location. The final number of subsidiaries is 470 for the Anglophone, and 487 for the German sample.

---

636 An ultimate owner is defined as a legal entity which owns a company in majority (i.e. >50 %).

637 Most research projects in the literature review (section 3) regard manufacturing companies.

638 Manufacturing companies are those firms with a Nace Rev. 2 code between 10 (manufacture of food products) and 33 (repair and installation of machinery and equipment).

639 *Flacke* (2007), p. 136ff., identified particularly small companies (less than 150 employees) to implement cost accounting systems to a minor extent.

640 Cf. *Schoute* (2011), p. 124.

641 For an according discussion, cf. e.g. *Moeschler* (2012), p. 183.

642 In the population, there are 74 % US-owned companies and 26 % Commonwealth-owned firms.

643 For details, cf. *Berekoven et al.* (2009), p. 47f.

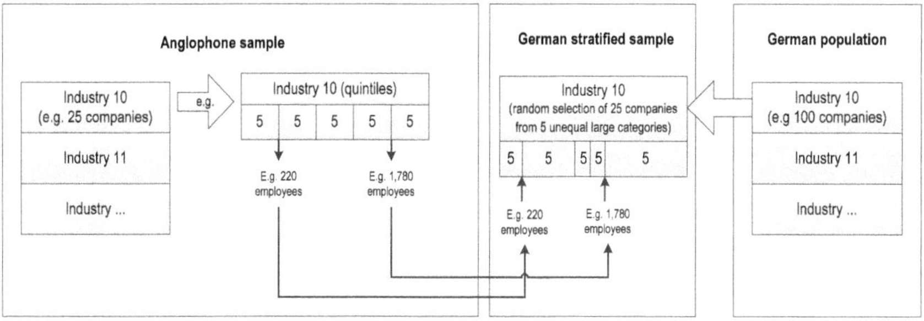

Figure 5-1: Procedure to determine the German control group

5.1.3 Introduction of the survey instrument

Besides deriving the necessity for a survey research method, the implications of the literature review also reveal that this study has to follow a **dyadic design**. As such, two questionnaires were developed to investigate the Anglophone and domestic German sample companies. Both questionnaires comprised questions on the performance of the cost accounting system. Besides, the first questionnaire consisted of one section on the complexity of cost accounting systems and two sections on the explanatory variables for this complexity (questionnaire A). Questionnaire A has 39 mostly closed-ended[644] questions on six pages (cf. Appendix 1). Moreover, the questionnaire acknowledges general **recommendations on questionnaire design**.[645] Hence both the design (e.g. on the order of the questions or the layout of the questionnaire) and the wording of the questionnaire[646] were chosen carefully. Also, questionnaire A has an appealing front- and back-cover.[647]

The second questionnaire has one section on the different types of cost information use and a second section on the associated explanatory variables (questionnaire B). On four pages, this questionnaire comprised 18 mostly closed-ended questions (Appendix 2). Also, questionnaire B had the same front and a similar back-cover as questionnaire A and equally reflected various recommendations on the design of questionnaires. Table 5-1 summarises the structure and length of the two questionnaires of this study.

	Topics	Number of questions	Number of pages (offline version)	Available languages
Questionnaire on the complexity of cost accounting (*questionnaire A*)	Your company's profile	9	8, including front- and back-cover	German and English
	Cost accounting system	24		
	Your group's profile	6		
Questionnaire on the types of cost information use (*questionnaire B*)	Cost accounting system	12	6, including front- and back-cover	German and English
	General information	6		

Table 5-1: Characteristics of the two questionnaires applied in this study

644 For a discussion of alternative question designs, cf. *Dillman et al.* (2009), p. 107ff.

645 Cf. *Dillman et al.* (2009), p. 182ff.

646 The operationalisations of the constructs in the questionnaires and the acknowledged recommendations for construct development are discussed detailed in the next section.

647 Cf. *Dillman et al.* (2009), p. 192f.

Alongside these topic related concerns, the questionnaire development considered four additional issues. Two concerns emerged from the focus on Anglophone subsidiaries in Germany. First, the questionnaire development had to account for the cross-national differences in German and Anglophone cost accounting which motivate this study. Ultimately, this study is informed by a German understanding of cost accounting. Hence, close attention had to be directed to the issue of a common perception of the questionnaire items, i.e. **conceptual, functional and measure equivalence.**[648] This was achieved by explicating the meaning of several German cost accounting traditions such as cost centres, imputed depreciation or multiple stage contribution margin accounting. The second issue concerns the **language of the questionnaires.** Given this research's focus on Anglophone subsidiaries, an English version of the questionnaire was most appealing. Yet, the complementing focus on a German control sample made a German questionnaire equally essential. Therefore, the initially developed English questionnaires were translated into German. To ensure the accuracy of the translation and maintain the previously mentioned issues of equivalence, back-translating activities were performed.[649] The back-translating researchers did not dominantly affect the design of the German questionnaire version but were familiar with the national particularities of Anglophone and German cost accounting.

A third concern referred to the intention to include both dependent and independent variables in the same questionnaire. It is commonly stressed that such a procedure can lead to biased results (**common method bias**).[650] A comprehensive scale development (see section 5.2) reduced the exposure to this risk.[651] Also, respondents were encouraged personally to provide honest answers. Nevertheless, the questionnaire could not be designed to exclude the risk of attaining results which are influenced by a common-method bias. On the one hand, the dependent and independent variables could not be derived by two distinct questionnaires or at different points in time due to resource constraints.[652] On the other hand, respondents could not be granted complete anonymity as this would have hindered an alignment of the two questionnaires. To offer the greatest extent of anonymity, respondents were ensured on the first page of the questionnaire that all provided data would be analysed anonymously. Also, a non-disclosure agreement was explicitly offered. The exposure of this study to the common method bias is investigated statistically in section 5.3.1.

The fourth concern evolved from the fact that it was decided to offer both a **mail-based and a web-based** questionnaire to account for potentially differing preferences of the respondents and to increase the response rates.[653] Besides the offline paper (or pdf) versions of the questionnaires, an online *Unipark* version of each questionnaire was developed. The online versions were designed in accordance to applicable recommendations on the design of online questionnaires.[654] Hence, the online version included a welcome screen

[648] Cf. *Holzmüller* (1995), p. 96ff and 195ff.
[649] For this and the following, cf. the recommendations by *Brislin* (1970), p. 214f.
[650] Cf. *Podsakoff et al.* (2003), p. 879ff.
[651] For this suggestion and the following recommendation, cf. *Podsakoff et al.* (2003), p. 888.
[652] For this and the following, cf. *Podsakoff et al.* (2003), p. 888.
[653] Cf. *Dillman et al.* (2009), p. 309.
[654] For the following, cf. *Dillman/Bowker* (2001), p. 66f.; *Dillman et al.* (2009), p. 195ff.

motivating the research, involved personalised links, started with the same easy introductory question as the offline questionnaire, presented the questions similarly to the offline version, was optimised for rather small screens, avoided drop-down boxes, and included a status bar to inform respondents about their progress in the questionnaire.

Having clarified these general concerns on the design of the research method, the operationalisation of the complexity of cost accounting systems, the use of cost information, the performance of cost accounting systems and the various explanatory and control variables can be introduced.

5.2 Construct measurement

5.2.1 Introduction to construct measurement

The operationalisation of the variables is directed by *DeVellis'* suggestions for scale development.[655] As an initiating step, the scope of all *constructs* (i.e. the dependent and independent variables) in the questionnaires was defined. For the design, use and performance of cost accounting systems, these explications are included in the fundamentals (section 2). For the independent variables, the definitions were explicated during the hypotheses development. Also, they will be complemented through the following operationalisations. Thereafter, the thorough definitions of all dependent and independent variables were operationalised. Thereby, all variables were transformed into questionnaire *items*. This step took different formats, depending on the characteristics of the underlying *measurement models*. Hence, the different measurement models require a brief introduction before clarifying the development procedures for the items in detail.

For a variable which cannot be observed directly (latent construct), two types of measurement models are commonly distinguished in literature.[656] In **formative measurement models**, all chosen items '*determine*'[657] the conceptual domain of a construct. Thus, no assumptions are required regarding the interrelation of the items that measure one construct. In contrast, in **reflective measurement models**, individual items are exchangeable. They are alternatives which measure the underlying construct similarly well. Thus, all items measuring one construct are expected to covary. Besides, *Diamantopoulos/Riefler* (2008) differentiate a **formatively 'defined' construct** from formative and reflective measurement models.[658] These definitions are relevant for this study, because they appear

---

[655] For this and the following, cf. *DeVellis* (2012), p. 73ff.

[656] For this and the following, cf. *Jarvis et al.* (2003), p. 200f.; *MacKenzie et al.* (2005), p. 711ff.

[657] Cf. *Diamantopoulos/Riefler* (2008), p. 1187ff.

[658] Cf. *Diamantopoulos/Riefler* (2008), p. 1187ff. Such summaries of items, however, should not be labelled a measurement *model* since it is a mathematical identity. Such identities cannot be tested for their validity since they are valid by definition. According to *Diamantopoulos/Riefler* (2008), p. 1187ff., such definitions do not capture what is meant by a *formative measurement model*. Only if a group of items *determines* an underlying latent construct, the interrelation of the items and the construct is a theoretical idea. The literature that argues against the possibility to test formative measurement models (cf. *Albers/Hildebrandt* (2006); *Homburg/Klarmann* (2006); *Schoute* (2009)) is argued to assume the former understanding of a formative measurement approach, because there are ways of testing formative measurement models (e.g. *Diamantopoulos/Winklhofer* (2001)).

similar to manifest variables (i.e. non-latent) which cannot be measured by one item only. *Widener* (2007) argues that averaging the items of a multiple item scale treats the underlying construct to be manifest.[659] As such, formatively defined constructs appear to be similar to manifest variables because they are (implicitly) argued to be measurable by average scores of their items.[660] This similarity, however, cannot be derived unambiguously from previous research.[661]

Typically, in management and cost accounting research, constructs are implicitly assumed to be reflective.[662] Yet, management accounting scholars recently called for a more explicit acknowledgment of the applied measurement models.[663] Hence, this study distinguishes reflectively measured constructs based on *Jarvis et al.*'s suggestions[664] and formatively '*defined*' measures as discussed by *Diamantopoulos/Riefler*.[665] Formative definitions are preferred over formative measurement models to express that most of the constructs in this study can be easily observed in a company and as such are rather manifest than latent. Brief definitions of the measurement '*model*' for each construct can be found throughout the following sections.

Having clarified these measurement issues, it can be explained which procedure was followed to **develop the items** for each construct. For reflective measurement models, *DeVellis* (2012) suggests developing a large number of alternative items.[666] These should then be evaluated in order to assess which items reflect the construct best. This procedure was followed.[667] In addition, the individual item design was aligned with general recommendations to keep a simple but precise wording which prevents suggestions and hypothetical issues.[668] Also, suggestions to select measures based on their prima facie relevance, significant support in previous literature and the existence of pre-developed measures were acknowledged.[669] *DeVellis* (2012) does not provide any special procedures for the operationalisation of formatively defined constructs. Since no special treatment for the development of these items could be identified elsewhere, these were developed in accordance with the above introduced recommendations on questionnaire design (e.g., a precise wording) and previous research only.

---

[659] Cf. *Widener* (2007), p. 775.
[660] Cf. *Schoute* (2009), p. 214; *Homburg/Klarmann* (2006), p. 731.
[661] *DeVellis* (2012), p. 17f., and *Backhaus et al.* (2011), p. 18, argue that the necessity for a formative or reflective measurement of latent constructs is essential because the construct cannot be observed directly and depends on the opinion of an individual under research. In contrast, *MacKenzie et al.* (2005), p. 711, find a stricter reason for the necessity of these measurement models. They align formative and reflective measurements of (latent) variables with the existence of more than two items for a construct. When to regard a construct as latent or manifest (i.e. non-latent), however, could not be determined unambiguously from conceptual consideration.
[662] Cf. *Bisbe et al.* (2007), p. 800; *Schoute* (2009), p. 214.
[663] Cf. *Bisbe et al.* (2007), p. 806.
[664] Cf. *Jarvis et al.* (2003), p. 203.
[665] Cf. *Diamantopoulos/Riefler* (2008), p. 1187ff.
[666] For this and the following, cf. *DeVellis* (2012), p. 76ff.
[667] Cf. section 5.2.2.2 and 5.2.3.4 for details.
[668] Cf. *Schnell* (2012), p. 79f.
[669] Cf. *Brown et al.* (2004), p. 335, or similarly *Dillman et al.* (2009), p. 68.

Even though the applied scales for each construct will be introduced thoroughly in the next sections, it is essential to reveal at this point that for several constructs respondents were given the opportunity to provide *no answer* (N/A) for **non-applicable items**. This was done to reflect suggestions on how to design questionnaires.[670] Following *Hair* (2010), 'missing' values due to an N/A option are negligible during data analysis.[671] Although such a procedure is somewhat problematic for manifest and reflective measures as well, it gains in severity in the light of formatively measured or defined constructs. In such situations, all items determine (or define) the conceptual domain of a construct.[672] Thus, accounting for companies in which one of the items does not apply is in apparent conflict with conventional assertions that dropping items in a formative measure alters the definition of the measure.[673] However, ensuring that all items always apply to all sample companies is a very high yardstick. Therefore, in this study, all items of a formatively defined construct are only assumed to be particularly relevant for the construct if they apply.[674] The limitations of this procedure are discussed in section 7.2.

To increase the applicability of the questionnaires, the constructs went through various **pre-testing** procedures after their initial development.[675] First, the expert interviews introduced in section 4.1.5 facilitated the testing of the questionnaire items. The experts filled in a draft version of both questionnaires and improved the items considerably. Second, the reflective measurement models for the usage types were subject to a q-sorting activity.[676] This will be described in the light of the operationalisation of the usage types (section 5.2.2.2). Third, two management accounting practitioners filled in the final draft of questionnaire A to evaluate its applicability. An additional two management accounting professionals provided insights into the applicability of questionnaire B. None of the four individuals expressed major difficulties to answer the questionnaires.

5.2.2 Operationalisation of the constructs under research

5.2.2.1 Complexity of cost accounting systems

5.2.2.1.1 Cost type accounting

Following section 2.2.2, three aspects of companies' cost type accounting can identify the prevalence of country specific cost accounting systems in Anglophone and domestic German subsidiaries.

---

[670] Cf. *Dillman et al.* (2009), p. 147f. and 210.
[671] Cf. *Hair* (2010), p. 45f.
[672] Cf. *Jarvis et al.* (2003), p. 203.
[673] Cf. *Bisbe et al.* (2007), p. 803.
[674] The treatment of the N/A option during the derivation of each construct's score will be explicitly covered throughout this section.
[675] Cf. *Schnell* (2012), p. 135ff.; *DeVellis* (2012), p. 104.
[676] Cf. *Stier* (1999), p. 80f., for a brief introduction of the q-sorting technique and *Fayard et al.* (2012), p. 176, for an application in management accounting research.

The **number of cost types** is operationalised in this study by asking respondents for the number of primary cost types in their company. Since previous findings of differing numbers of cost types might be due to a diverging understanding of the terminology 'cost type', a common understanding of this terminology is ensured by including their definition[677] in the questionnaire (conceptual and functional equivalence). The single item for this manifest variable is derived from *Moeschler* (2012) (B.2 of questionnaire A).[678]

Similarly, the **existence of imputed costs** is included in this study by providing respondents with a brief introduction of imputed costs to ensure conceptual and functional equivalence.[679] After this introduction, respondents are asked whether imputed interests and imputed depreciation are used *in separate calculations, as part of regular cost accounting* or *not at all.* This measure is also based on *Moeschler* (2012).[680] The items can be found in question B.3 of questionnaire A. It measures the manifest existence of imputed costs in a formative manner.[681]

To analyse the distinction between financial accounting and management accounting, B.1 of questionnaire A asks whether there are **two different datasets for financial accounting and for cost accounting**. To avoid misunderstandings which prevailed for a previous version of this construct in *Moeschler* (2012),[682] the question includes the terminologies '*two-book system*' and '*dual accounting system*'. In addition to the mere application of separated datasets, it appears essential to account for the extent to which these two databases differ from one another. Therefore, respondents are asked to assess the extent to which they adjust financial information of the financial accounting system to derive the information included in the cost accounting database. This aspect is measured on a seven point rating scale ranging from *no adjustments are being made* to *multiple adjustments are being made.* Since this measure implicitly assumes that there are interlinked datasets for financial and cost accounting, the rating scale is extended by an option to provide *no answer.*[683]

5.2.2.1.2 Cost centre accounting

Following the section on differences between Anglophone and German cost accounting, there are remarkable differences with respect to the understanding of *cost centres* in German and Anglophone cost accounting. To ensure a common understanding of the concept and the function of a cost centre, the questionnaire includes a brief definition in question B.4 of questionnaire A. After this introduction, the seven aspects of companies' cost centre accounting which enable this project to identify the prevalence of German or

---

677 The definition originates from *Horngren et al.* (2012), p. 49, and *Moeschler* (2012), p. 370.

678 Cf. *Moeschler* (2012), p. 157 and 370.

679 The provided definition originates from *Moeschler* (2012), p. 370.

680 Cf. *Moeschler* (2012), p. 157 and 370.

681 The complexity of a cost accounting system is measured through formative definitions because these appear similarity to manifest variables. Because the design of a cost accounting system is arguably a manifest variable, this procedure appeared most appealing.

682 Cf. *Moeschler* (2012), p. 370.

683 For the complexity subs-scores, N/A items are accepted if the average complexity score for the company can be computed. The decision rule whether the average complexity score can be determined or nor is explicated in section 5.2.2.1.4.

Anglophone cost accounting traditions in subsidiaries in Germany are included in the questionnaire.

There are explicit **rules for the formation of cost centres** in German literature. To analyse whether these rules determine the formation of cost centres in Anglophone and domestic subsidiaries in Germany, respondents are asked to assess on a seven point rating scale ranging from *not at all* to *completely* whether cost centres are formed in accordance with these rules. Question B.5 of questionnaire A illustrates the seven items applied (e.g. whether cost centres are formed to define areas of responsibility, and to aggregate homogeneous overhead costs).[684] Also, respondents are offered the possibility to provide *no answer*. The manifest construct *application of rules for the formation of cost centres* is measured by a formative definition in this study.

The **number of cost centres** is obtained by a single question asking explicitly for this figure (B.6 of questionnaire A). The item is adapted from *Moeschler* (2012).[685] In addition to the mere number of cost centres, the classification of cost centres as support and primary cost centres is a source of cross-national differences in cost accounting. With respect to this distinction, however, it remained unclear whether the low importance of support cost centres in Anglophone companies is due to the actual absence of these centres or a tendency to disregard different types of cost centres. Also, it remained likewise unclear whether German companies merely have more support cost centres whereas the number of primary cost centres does not affect the higher number of cost centres in Germany. This study explores why there are more cost centres in German firms through refined questionnaire items. Respondents are asked to indicate the percentage of the total number of cost centres that handle the company's products directly (i.e. primary cost centres) and of those that support the manufacturing process only (i.e. support cost centres).[686] Asking merely for the terminologies is avoided since these might not be present, especially in Anglophone subsidiaries (measure equivalence). Such a presence is also obtained explicitly by asking whether there is a literal differentiation of these two cost centre types. Conjointly, these three aspects define the construct on the number of cost centres in a formative manner.

The **classification of costs in cost centres** is another particularity in German and Anglophone companies. Therefore, respondents are asked in question B.12 (questionnaire A) to reveal for how many primary cost centres they differentiate costs in accordance with five characteristics. For instance, companies are asked for how many cost centres costs are split into manufacturing and non-manufacturing costs. The individual items are chosen to correspond to the cross-national differences identified in section 2.2.3. The applied seven point rating scale ranged from *in no cost centre* to *in all cost centres*. To account for the possibility of encountering companies without manufacturing facilities, respondents are offered the opportunity to provide *no answer*.

684 The individual reasons for cost centre formation are derived from *Kilger* (1979), p. 71ff., and *Keys/van der Merwe* (1999), p. 4. Moreover, the empirical investigation by *Becker* (1984), p. 111, informed the operationalisation of this measure.

685 Cf. *Moeschler* (2012), p. 157 and 370.

686 This wording is aligned with *Horngren et al.* (2012), p. 565.

In this study, the allocation of overhead costs from support to primary cost centres is called **first stage allocation.**[687] In contrast, the allocation of overhead costs from primary cost centres to products is called **second stage allocation**. Allocations were found in previous research to differ between German and Anglophone firms. To allow for a thorough analysis, the allocation bases in both stages are analysed. For comparability reasons, the operationalisation of both of these constructs is analogous. On the one hand, the nature of different allocation bases applied for overhead allocation is analysed by asking for the presence of eight different types of allocation bases (e.g. volume bases, physical measures as well as activities).[688] The question is included as B.8 (first stage allocation) and B.10 (second stage allocation) in questionnaire A.[689] On the other hand, respondents are asked for the number of individual measures applied for overhead cost allocation.[690] This question is included as B.9 (first stage allocation) and B.11 (second stage allocation) in questionnaire A. Conjointly, both the allocation bases and the number of individual measures define the constructs 'first stage allocation' and 'second stage allocation' in a formative manner.

Besides these aspects, cross-national differences between Anglophone and German cost accounting also prevail for the analysis of cost centre variances. Therefore, question B.18 includes an item asking for the intensity of **variance analysis** on the cost centre level.[691] This single item is measured by a seven point rating scale ranging from *not at all* to *very intensively.* To account for a potential absence of a detailed cost centre or cost object accounting,[692] respondents are provided with the opportunity to provide *no answer* to this question as well.

5.2.2.1.3 Cost object accounting

Six aspects of a company's cost object accounting allow for the analysis of national cost accounting traditions in Anglophone and domestic subsidiaries in Germany.

The operationalisation of the **types of cost objects** follows the introduction of the associated differences and similarities in Anglophone and German cost accounting traditions. Respondents are asked to indicate for how many of the following four types of cost objects (final products, product lines, customers, and spoilage) unit costs are derived.[693] The

---

[687] Since Anglophone literature tends to disregard non-manufacturing costs during the discussion of overhead allocation (cf. e.g. *Langfield-Smith et al.* (2006), p. 300; *Blocher et al.* (2010), p. 234f.; *Horngren et al.* (2012), p. 565) it was perceived that some companies may not allocate the costs of support *activities* to primary cost centres and products. Thus, a filter question on this issue is included as B.7 in questionnaire A.

[688] The individual bases included in this question are derived from *Schweitzer/Küpper* (2010), p. 132, and *Moeschler* (2012), p. 158.

[689] To assess whether the importance of allocation bases differs, companies are also asked to rank the applied bases by the proportion of overhead costs allocated on their grounds.

[690] This question is based on a similar operationalisation by *Drury/Tayles* (2005), p. 80.

[691] The item is designed in accordance with *Moeschler* (2012), p. 158 and 371.

[692] The question also comprises a similar item on the analysis of variances on the cost object level.

[693] Deviating from previous scales asking for a total number of cost objects is due to problems previous research encountered with such an operationalisation (cf. *Moeschler* (2012), p. 158).

applied seven point rating scale ranged from *for none* to *for all.* To account for a potential absence of, e.g. product lines, the scale includes the possibility to provide *no answer.* The question (B.14) is seen as a formative definition of the different types of cost objects, which are manifest in a company for costing purposes.

The cross-national difference with respect to the costs allocated to cost objects summarises whether a company relies on full or variable **product costing.** In line with the operationalisation in *Moeschler* (2012), respondents are asked whether unit costs are computed on a variable or full cost basis.[694] In addition, the option both bases is provided. Encouraged by additional cross-national differences, question B.15 is complemented by two items asking for additional dimensions of product costs. First, respondents are asked to indicate whether they derive manufacturing costs only, do not disaggregate manufacturing and non-manufacturing costs or apply both bases. Second, it is investigated whether product costs are determined as inventoriable costs only, comprise inventoriable and non- inventoriable costs or disaggregate the product costs according to their inventoriability. The variable 'product costing' is interpreted here as a formatively defined manifest construct of these three characteristics.

Multiple stage **contribution margin accounting** (CM accounting) is another particularity of German cost accounting. Given that the multiple stage procedure is rather less common in Anglophone firms, the question comprises a brief introduction to ensure a common understanding by all respondents (conceptual equivalence). To analyse whether the reliance on a single layer of CM accounting known from Anglophone companies prevails in their German subsidiaries, a question by *Moeschler* (2012) is adopted.[695] B.17 of questionnaire A comprises a filter question on the presence of CM accounting and a selectively applied one on the number of CM layers (e.g. CM I – CM III). Both aspects are seen to define a company's CM accounting.

The three different time horizons of cost data (actual, normal and standard costs) can be summarised as the **time reference of cost accounting.** Moreover, target costing can be seen as an additional forward-looking time horizon. Therefore, question B.16 of questionnaire A comprises a question asking respondents for how many products (i.e. cost objects) these four time horizons are determined.[696] The provided seven point rating scale ranges from *for no product* to *for all products.* Despite providing brief definitions of all time horizons and anchoring the scale at 'for no products', respondents are offered the opportunity to provide *no answer* to account for misunderstandings of any of the researched items. Conjointly, all four items define a company's time reference of cost accounting.

As for cost centre accounting, the **analysis of variances** for different cost objects comprises another difference between German and Anglophone cost accounting. As preclosed during the introduction of the item for variance analysis on cost centres, question B.18 of questionnaire A includes an item on the intensity of variance analysis on costs objects. The item is designed in accordance with the one for the cost centre level.

694 Cf. *Moeschler* (2012), p. 158.
695 Cf. *Moeschler* (2012), p. 371.
696 The question was adopted from *Moeschler* (2012), p. 371.

Besides these operationalisations, the section on the cross-national differences in cost accounting highlights that German companies are well known to prepare an **operating income statement** that differs structurally from their profit and loss account. To analyse whether such a practice deviates from the one in subsidiaries of Anglophone MNCs in Germany, a related question was adopted from *Moeschler* (2012).[697] In line with the questions on CM accounting, question B.19 comprises a filter question on the presence of an operating income statement and a selectively applied one on the extent to which the operating income statement differs structurally from the company's profit and loss account. The applied seven point rating scale ranges from *not at all* to *completely*. Moreover, respondents are offered the opportunity to provide *no answer*.

5.2.2.1.4 Formation of the complexity score

Overall, this study comprises 15 characteristics to describe the complexity of cost accounting systems. The aggregated complexity measure applied in this study is formed by these individual characteristics. In contrast to various previous studies,[698] this study thus measures the complexity of a cost accounting system through an intersubjective score.[699] Thereby the effect of individuals' diverging perceptions on the complexity measure is minimised. To derive the individual complexity scores (**complexity sub-scores**) for each of the 15 characteristics, the operationalisations revealed in the previous sections are converted into a score ranging from zero to one. A score of zero indicates a particularly simple cost accounting system, whereas a score of one indicates the most complex design of the characteristic.[700] Table 5-2 summarises the transformation of each characteristic's operationalisation into its complexity sub-score.[701] Thereby the acronym x_i describes a participant's answer to a particular item.

To derive the **aggregated complexity score**, all complexity sub-scores are averaged.[702] Four average scores are derived. One aggregated score for the cost accounting system as a

---

697 Cf. *Moeschler* (2012), p. 371.

698 *Aust* (1999), p. 166; *Frank* (2000), p. 116; *Hunold* (2003), p. 151ff.; *Krumwiede et al.* (2007), p. 48, did conceptualise their complexity (or GPK) measures based on subjective perceptions rather than in an intersubjective verifiable manner based on the three components of a cost accounting system.

699 Similar, yet less disaggregated measures can be found in *Abernethy* (2001); *Anderson et al.* (2002), p. 204; *Drury/Tayles* (2005), p. 70f.; *Schoute* (2009), p. 214; *Al-Omiri/Drury* (2007), p. 403, and *Moeschler* (2012), p. 146ff.

700 For a similar procedure, cf. *Moeschler* (2012), p. 159f.

701 According to *Hair* (2010), p. 45f., data marked as N/A is ignorable missing data. Hence, a complexity sub-score is computed as long as at least one item of a construct is marked as non *N/A*.

702 Despite being derived from (non-)linear transformations of metrically interpreted rating scales (cf. e.g. *Backhaus et al.* (2011), p. 11, for such a procedure in the light of a seven point Likert scale) and non-metric scales (e.g. for imputed costs), the aggregated complexity measure is treated as a metric variable. Given the discussion by *Backhaus et al.* (2011), p. 11, on the inability to increase the quality of a scale from non-metric to metric, this formation of the score can be criticised. The definition, however, is in line with previous research on the complexity of cost accounting systems (cf. e.g. the second measure by *Schoute* (2009), p. 214, or *Moeschler* (2012), p. 159ff., and, disputably, the second measure in *Drury/Tayles* (2005), p. 68, and *Al-Omiri/Drury* (2007), p. 411).

whole and three additional ones for cost type, cost centre and cost object accounting. As the complexity sub-scores, these mean complexity scores also rang from zero to one.

			Cost type accounting
B.2	Number of cost types[703]	$f(x_i)$ =	ln(number of cost $type_i$) / ln(max. no. of cost types)
B.3	Prevalence of imputed costs *(exemplarily for one imputed cost only)*	$f(x_i)$ =	0.00 if imputed interest is not applied at all, 0.25 if imputed interest is applied in a separate calculation, 0.50 if imputed interest is applied regularly
B.1	Separation of financial and management accounting	$f(x_i)$ =	0.0 if there is only one dataset for FA and MA 0.4 if there are two datasets + $0.1*(x_i-1)$ for the extent to which adjustments are made.
			Cost centre accounting
B.5	Rarionales for the formation of cost centres		For each item in B.5 the following function is applied: $f(x_i) = 1/(\textit{Number of items} * 6) * (x_i - 1)$ The sum of the individual item scores yields this characteristic's complexity score.
B.6	Number of cost centres[704]	$f(x_i)$ =	1/6 * {ln(number of primary cost centres) / max [ln(no. of primary cost centres)]} + 1/6 * {ln(no. of support cost centres) / max [ln(no. of support cost centres)]} + 1/3 * {0 if support and primary cost centres are not separated by name, 1 if support and primary cost centres are separated by name}
B.12	Classification of costs in cost centres		For each item in B.12 the following function is applied: $f(x_i) = 1/(\textit{Number of items} * 6) * (x_i - 1)$ The sum of the individual item scores yields this characteristic's complexity score.
B.7 to B.10	First stage allocation[705]	$f(x_i)$ =	0 if costs are not allocated among cost centres (B.7), else: ½ * [ln(number of applied $bases_i$) / ln(8)] + ½ * {ln(no. of applied $measures_i$ / max[ln(no. of applied measures)]}
B.11 to B.12	Second stage allocation[705]	$f(x_i)$ =	½ * [ln(number of applied $bases_i$) / ln(8)] + ½ * {ln(no. of applied $measures_i$ / max[ln(no. of applied measures)]}

Continued...

[703] Basing this measure on the logarithm is due to the fact that a company's number of cost types is assumed to increase the complexity of that company's cost accounting in a converging rather than a linear manner. Cf. *Moeschler* (2012), p. 160, for a similar argument.

[704] Basing this measure on the logarithm is due to the fact that a company's number of cost centres is assumed to increase the complexity of that company's cost accounting in a converging rather than a linear manner. Cf. *Schoute* (2009), p. 214, for an according definition.

[705] Basing this measure on the logarithm is due to the fact that a company's type and number of allocation bases are assumed to increase the complexity of that company's cost accounting in a converging rather than a linear manner. Cf. *Schoute* (2009), p. 214, for an according definition.

B.18	Variance analysis on a cost centre level	$f(x_i) = 1/6 * (x_i - 1)$
		Cost object accounting
B.14	Types of cost objects	For each item in B.14 the following function is applied: $f(x_i) = 1/(\textit{Number of items} * 6) * (x_i - 1)$ The sum of the individual item scores yields this characteristic's complexity score.
B.15	Product costing	For each item in B.15 the following function is applied: *f(xi) = 0 if only "full costs" are applied,* *1/6 if only variable/manufacturing/inventoriable costs are applied,* *1/3 if both bases are applied* The sum of the individual item scores yields this characteristic's complexity score.
B.17	Contribution margin accounting	$f(x_i) =$ 0.0 if CM accounting is not applied, 0.5 if CM accounting is applied + 0.1 * no. of CMs for [1< no. of CMs < 7] If more than six CMs are computed, a score of one is attributed.
B.16	Time reference of cost accounting	For each item in B.16 the following function is applied: $f(x_i) = 1/(\textit{Number of items} * 6) * (x_i - 1)$ The sum of the individual item scores yields this characteristic's complexity score.
B.18	Variance analysis on a cost object level	$f(x_i) = 1/6 * (x_i - 1)$
B.19	Operating income statement	$f(x_i) =$ 0.0 if there is only one data set for FA and MA 0.4 if there are two datasets + $0.1*(x_i - 1)$ for the extent to which there are structural differences.

Table 5-2: Computation of the complexity sub-scores

Given the possibility to provide no answer to several questions, a decision rule is established when to exclude a company from the data analysis due to an incomprehensive complexity score. No average complexity score for the cost type, cost centre and cost object accounting is determined if more than one third of the questions on the companies' cost type (i.e. one question), cost centre (i.e. two questions) and cost object accounting (i.e. two questions) are marked completely as *N/A*. If any of these three scores cannot be computed, no aggregated complexity score is determined either. Companies for which any of these four scores cannot be computed are fully excluded from the analysis. Thereby, a strong bias from not applicable questionnaire elements (i.e. N/A answers) can be avoided.

5.2.2.2 Types of cost information use

The different types of cost information use are regarded as latent constructs in this study.[706] Therefore, the suggestions provided by *DeVellis* (2012) for latent measurement

[706] Note that some researchers favour a formative design of such constructs (e.g. *Bisbe et al.* (2007), p. 807, for the interactive usage type). This study does not aim to transform the formal elements of an interactive control system into a scale to define the interactive use of cost information. Rather, it intends to

models are followed. As an initiating step, previous research on the different usage types was reviewed critically to derive item sets which potentially summarise the usage types. Table 5-3 provides insights into the sources applied for the development of these alternative items.

	Instrumental usage type	Conceptual usage type	Rationalising usage type	Diagnostic usage type	Interactive usage type	Ceremonial usage type
Vandenbosch/Huff (1997)	X					Given little survey research on this matter, this usage type was derived from definitions in *Ansari/Euske* (1987) and NIS. Furthermore, the discussions of *Diamantopoulos/Souchon* (1998); *Aust* (1999); *Hunold* (2003); *Sandt* (2004) and *Steiners* (2005) were incorporated to form the initial item set.
Aust (1999)	X	X	X	X		
Diamantopoulos/Souchon (1999)	X		X			
Davila (2000)				X	X	
Frank (2000)	X					
Marginson (2002)					X	
Hunold (2003)	X	X	X			
Sandt (2004)	X	X	X	X		
Steiners (2005)	X	X	X	X		
Henri (2006a)	X	X	X		x	
Bisbe et al. (2007)					x	
Jais (2007)			X	x	x	

Table 5-3: Sources for the operationalisation of the usage types

In addition to the application of readily developed items, several items which reflect the theoretical positioning of this study complemented these sets. Corresponding to *DeVellis* (2012) suggestions, the items were subject to a critical assessment through the expert interviews that preceded the hypotheses development and then went through a q-sorting activity.[707] For the latter, six researchers were provided with this study's definition of the usage types as well as a summary of the items that were maintained after the expert interviews. All researchers were asked to order the individual items by their ability to capture the provided definition. The results helped choosing the four[708] most applicable items for each usage type. All six types of use are measured on a seven point Likert scale, asking respondents to indicate the extent to which they agree to the individual items of each construct. The scales range from *not at all* to *completely.* The final operationalisation of the items is presented in Table 5-4 (questions A.1-A.6 of questionnaire B).

All usage types are preceded by their definition in the questionnaire. Thereby, the ability to distinguish the usage types empirically should be improved.[709] Moreover, the procedure should reduce a potential bias in the ceremonial and the rationalising usage types due to their potential social undesirability. This approach, however, has the drawback of a potentially increased response bias due to the rather suggestive character of the questions. The aggregation of the individual usage types into measureable scores is subject to the quality criteria for reflective scales that will be introduced in section 5.4.1. Hence, their meas-

find items that reflect the application of an accordingly determined latent construct. Hence, their suggestion is not followed.

707 Cf. *Stier* (1999), p. 80f., for a brief introduction of the q-sorting technique and *Fayard et al.* (2012), p. 176, for an application in management accounting research.

708 Four items are argued to be the minimum number of items to be chosen for construct measurement (cf. *Backhaus et al.* (2013), p. 133).

709 *Diamantopoulos/Souchon* (1998), p. 116f., raises concerns with respect to the empirical distinguishability of the usage types.

urement models are explicated in section 6.2.1 only. The derived scores will be regarded as quasi-metric due to the applied Likert scale.[710]

Usage type	Final operationalisation
Instrumental usage type	Cost information frequently alters my focus when resolving a particular decision-making problem.
	I actively seek cost information for decision-making.
	I regularly draw on cost information when it is difficult to differentiate among plausible solutions to a problem.
	I regularly use cost information to make a final decision on an issue of major importance.
Conceptual usage type	I regularly regard cost information to further my understanding of our business situation.
	I regularly regard cost information irrespectively of a particular decision to be made.
	I use cost information to better understand interrelations within my area of responsibility.
	I use cost information to be able to better predict future developments within my area of responsibility.
Rationalising usage type	I use cost information to justify my previously taken decisions.
	I use cost information to signal legitimacy of my previously taken decisions.
	I use cost information to seek support for my previously taken decisions.
	I use cost information to validate my point of view of a given situation.
Diagnostic usage type	I use cost information to align my subordinates' actions with the company's goals.
	I use cost information to monitor my subordinates' performance.
	I use cost information to provide feedback to my subordinates.
	I use cost information to control the activities within my area of responsibility.
Interactive usage type	I use cost information to ensure a common understanding for due decisions.
	I use cost information to provide a common view of the organisation.
	I use cost information to focus my subordinates' decisions upon the company's key success factors.
	I use cost information to involve myself inspiringly into my subordinates' decision-making.
Ceremonial usage type	I do not use our cost accounting system because it fulfils our parent company's information needs more extensively than it fulfils our local information needs.
	I use cost information to maintain a good relationship with our parent company - the information itself is of little decision relevance to me.
	I think our cost accounting system is maintained as a façade for the world to see - the information itself is of little decision relevance to me.
	I am provided with cost information because our parent company issued a resp. directive - the information itself is of little decision relevance to me.

Table 5-4: Individual items operationalising the usage types

5.2.2.3 Performance of the cost accounting system

The sections on cost accounting in Anglophone and German firms show that the performance of cost accounting systems can be measured in various ways. In this study, the two measures 'goal attainment' and 'satisfaction' are used. The construct **goal attainment** captures the performance of cost accounting systems based on an assessment of the systems' decision usefulness. The construct's operationalisation corresponds to two previous studies.[711] Respondents are first asked to indicate the extent to which they pursue a number of cost accounting objectives.[712] Thereafter, respondents are asked to assess on a seven point rating scale ranging from *not at all* to *completely*, to what extent these objectives were achieved over the last three years.[713] Similar to *Moeschler* (2012), this study defines the construct 'goal attainment' in a formative manner. Figure 5-2 illustrates the definition of the construct which ranges from zero to six (B.22-B.23 of questionnaire A and A.9–A.10

[710] According to e.g. *Backhaus et al.* (2011), p. 11, this is a common procedure.

[711] Cf. *Pizzini* (2006), p. 192, or *Moeschler* (2012), p. 173, for similar measures.

[712] The individual items are discussed in detail during the operationalisation of the cost accounting objectives (page 138).

[713] The item 'Facilitating environmental protection' is excluded from the performance measure.

of questionnaire B). Thereby values close to zero indicate a poor and values close to six a good performance.

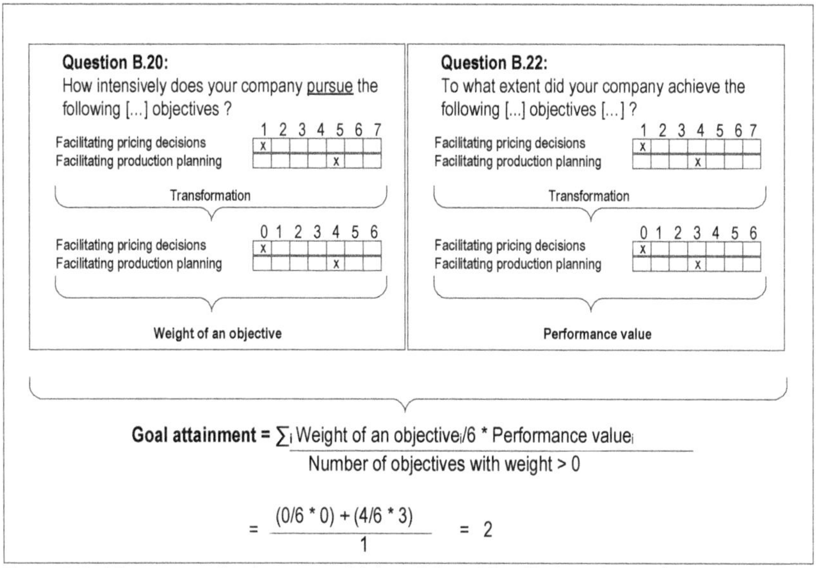

Figure 5-2: The construct 'goal attainment' (adapted from *Moeschler* (2012), p. 174)

The second measure of a cost accounting system's performance is a single item question asking respondents for their satisfaction with the information provided by the cost accounting system (B.24 of questionnaire A and A.11 of questionnaire B). The questions are adapted from *Moeschler* (2012), but were similarly applied in other studies as well.[714] The **satisfaction with the cost accounting system** is measured on a seven point rating scale ranging from *very unsatisfied* to *very satisfied.* The variable varies between zero and six.

5.2.3 Operationalisation of the explanatory factors

5.2.3.1 Economic factors

5.2.3.1.1 Need for cost information

During the development of the hypotheses summarising how the need for cost information affects the complexity of cost accounting systems and the use of cost information, two variables are highlighted to be important - the perceived environmental uncertainty and the objectives pursued with a cost accounting system.

---

[714] Cf. e.g. *Howell et al.* (1987), p. 41ff.; *Schoute* (2009), p. 215; *McGowan/Klammer* (1997), p. 230; *Moeschler* (2012), p. 174. *Widener* (2007), p. 775, expresses that such a procedure treats the underlying construct as manifest.

Cost information becomes necessary in times of high levels of **perceived environmental uncertainty** due to imperfect market information. The variable for perceived environmental uncertainty is measured by a single item question, asking respondents how predictable they perceive their environment to be. A seven point rating scale ranging from *very unpredictable* to *very predictable* is used.[715] To ensure a common understanding (conceptual equivalence) of the question, eight examples for potential sources of uncertainty are provided (e.g. production technologies or labour union actions). The question (A.3 of questionnaire A and B.3 of questionnaire B) builds upon studies which examine the eight examples separately because environmental uncertainty is a more central element of their research projects.[716] Despite being in a more compact format in this study, similar measures were previously applied in cost accounting research as well.[717]

The **objectives associated with cost accounting** are operationalised through two questions. First, it is asked how intensively cost accounting is applied for strategic (i.e. long-term) and operational (i.e. short-term) planning and control on a seven point rating scale ranging from *not at all* to *very intensively* (B.20 of questionnaire A and A.9 of questionnaire B). In addition, the same scale is employed to ask how intensively the tasks, which are typically researched in a cost accounting context, are pursued (B.21 of questionnaire A and A.10 of questionnaire B). To operationalise the application of cost accounting for performance measurement and incentive system design, the three items 'act according to business strategy', 'make cost savings' and 'trace inefficiencies to persons in charge' are adapted from *Moeschler* (2012).[718] The same holds true for the application of cost accounting to 'facilitate pricing decisions' and for 'inventory valuation'. To aggregate a company's striving for internal improvements, it is surveyed how intensively respondents wish to 'facilitate process improvements' through cost accounting.[719] A final item summarises the various decisions that a cost accounting system may facilitate during 'production planning'.[720]

The pairs of constructs (internal tasks vs. external tasks and operational objectives vs. strategic objectives) as pictured in Table 5-5 are regarded as a formative definition of their items. Table 5-5 also exemplifies which individual objectives are aggregated to form these pairs. Acknowledging the formative *definition* of the pairs, aggregation is achieved through equally weighted averages of the items.[721] By aggregating all variables in Table 5-5, a measure for the overall *extent of use* can be determined.[722]

[715] Thus, this measure is reversely coded.

[716] Cf. *Miles et al.* (1978), p. 195; *Gordon/Narayanan* (1984), p. 33ff.; *Govindarajan* (1984), p. 125ff.

[717] Cf. e.g. *Schoute* (2009), p. 208ff.

[718] For this and the following, cf. *Moeschler* (2012), p. 143 and 370.

[719] For similar items, cf. e.g. *Garg et al.* (2003), p. 31, or *Krumwiede/Suessmair* (2007a), p. 5.

[720] In adjusting the item 'capacity planning' from *Moeschler* (2012), p. 143 and 370, this study allows respondents to respond whether cost information facilitates a larger set of decision on production planning.

[721] A similar procedure is applied by *Schoute* (2009), p. 214, or *Homburg et al.* (2008), p. 141, for formative measurement models.

[722] In addition to the seven items above, B.21 and A.10 include an item asking how intensively the cost accounting system is applied for environmental protection. This item is included to account for a re-

Objective		Items
Operational		• Operational planning • Operational control
Strategic		• Strategic planning • Strategic control
Internal tasks	Decision facilitating	• Facilitating pricing decisions • Facilitating production planning • Facilitating process improvement decisions
Internal tasks	Decision influencing	• Motivating employees to act in accordance with the company's strategy • Motivating employees to make cost savings • Holding employees responsible for their actions
External tasks		• Determining the value of assets for financial reporting purposes

Table 5-5: Operationalisation of the objectives of cost accounting

5.2.3.1.2 Archetype of cost accounting systems

The hypotheses development reveals that the design of a cost accounting system depends on the complexity of a company's products and production processes (i.e. product diversity) as well as a company's ability to provide an accurate picture of the resource consumption evoked by product diversity.

The measure for **product diversity** summarises differences in the processes needed to design, manufacture and distribute the products, different production volumes and lot sizes as well as differing support given to products by non-manufacturing departments. These three aspects were described as the three complementing dimensions of product diversity.[723] For each of these three aspects of diversity,[724] respondents are asked for their agreement to a statement (A.4 of questionnaire A).[725] The applied seven point rating scale ranges from *not at all* to *completely*.[726] It also includes the possibility to provide *no answer* since some companies, for instance, may not have production facilities. Product diversity is included as a formatively defined manifest construct into this study because of its three complementing components. To reflect the formative definition, aggregation is achieved through equally weighted averages of the non-N/A[727] items.[728]

---

cently evolving application of cost accounting in Japan (cf. e.g. *Nakajima* (2004), p. 2; *Kokubu et al.* (2009), p. 15ff.; *Crönertz* (2010), p. 213; *Wagner et al.* (2010), p. 200ff.; *Nakajima* (2010)). This consideration is excluded from this thesis.

723 Cf. *Drury/Tayles* (2005), p. 60.

724 The measure is also assumed to be able to attenuate potential effects stemming from the focus upon differing manufacturing companies (e.g. food and beverage or mechanical engineering firms). For such industrial effects, cf. e.g. *Moeschler* (2012), p. 262.

725 For a similar item, cf. *Krumwiede* (1998), p. 271; *Cagwin/Bouwman* (2002), p. 30; *Drury/Tayles* (2005), p. 68, and *Moeschler* (2012), p. 127ff.

726 The items one (needed processes) and three (support departments) are reversely coded.

727 Given that there is no aggregation of all independent variables into one overall score, each independent variable is of arguably greater importance than the individual questions forming the score of a cost accounting systems' complexity. Therefore, the questionnaire items for independent variables are only

A company devoting more resources both in terms of labour and information technology can provide a more accurate picture of the resource consumption evoked by product diversity. Both these aspects are included in this study.

To account for the provision of personnel resources, two variables are taken into account. First, there is the **adequacy of cost accountants**. To derive this variable, companies are asked to assess whether the number of cost accountants[729] and the qualification of cost accountants[730] are adequate to run and enhance the cost accounting system (A.7 of questionnaire A). Thus, these two items form this study's understanding of the 'adequacy of cost accountants'. Aggregation is achieved through equally weighted averages of the non-N/A[731] items.[732] To incorporate the complementary necessity for a sufficient local **top management support**, respondents are asked to assess whether cost accountants perceive sufficient support by the subsidiary's top management team. Top management support is measured by a single item.[733] The three items on the personal resources are formulated as statements to which respondents are asked to indicate their level of agreement on a seven point rating scale ranging from *not at all* to *completely.*

Besides these two measures of the personnel resources committed to cost accounting, two additional measures are included in this study to account for the information technology applied for cost accounting (A.5 of questionnaire A). It is surveyed whether management accounting is especially supported by an **enterprise resource planning** (ERP) system or by spreadsheet calculations.[734] Previous research regularly regards different ERP solutions to account for varying processing capabilities.[735] This aspect is also covered in this study by asking whether the applied information technology can provide an accurate picture of the resource consumption which is taking place in the company. This measure corresponds to the argument that "a good cost system mirrors the manufacturing process and related support activities and quantifies them product by product"[736]. The applied information technology is measured by asking directly whether an ERP system or spreadsheet solutions are mostly applied for management accounting purposes. The construct is operationalised as a dummy variable. This dummy is coded one if an ERP system is applied and zero if a spreadsheet application is applied. Accordingly, the variable on information technology is labelled ERP. The **accuracy of the information technology** is measured on a seven point rating scale ranging from *very imprecise* to *very precise.*

---

transformed into an analysable measure if a minority of the individual items (i.e. 1 or less items for A.4) is marked as N/A. Companies which marked more N/A answers are excluded from the analysis.

728 A similar procedure is applied by *Schoute* (2009), p. 214; *Homburg et al.* (2008), p. 141, for formative measurement models.

729 For a similar item, cf. *Anderson/Young* (1999), p. 540.

730 The item is derived from *Moeschler* (2012), p. 370.

731 To include a respondent in the analysis, one of the two items of A.7 can be marked as N/A.

732 A similar procedure is applied by *Schoute* (2009), p. 214, or *Homburg et al.* (2008), p. 141, for formative measurement models.

733 For a respectively designed item, cf. *Krumwiede/Suessmair* (2007a), p. 3.

734 This operationalisation reflects the assertion of *Krumwiede* (2005), p. 31, that German companies employ more *comprehensive* IT technology than their US counterparts.

735 Cf. e.g. *Krumwiede/Suessmair* (2007a), p. 4; *Moeschler* (2012), p. 372.

736 *Jones* (1991), p. 35.

5.2.3.2 Institutional factors

5.2.3.2.1 Coercive institutional influences

The literature review and the hypotheses development exemplified that parent companies might diffuse their cost accounting traditions into subsidiaries. Such coercive institutional pressures can be either personal or through formal directives. Thereby, the personal involvement can be studied with respect to the involvement of the parent company's top management as well as expatriate managers. Thus, three measures are included in this study to investigate the extent to which a parent company engages into the design of a subsidiary's cost accounting system.

The number of **expatriate managers** is a manifest variable which is measured through a single item asking for this number (question A.6 of questionnaire A).[737] During hypotheses testing, this number of expatriates is included as the logarithmised answer to this question.[738] Using this transformation of the data reflects that the level of influence through expatriates is expected to converge, i.e. having more expatriates than a certain upper limit will not result in an additional transfer of parent company induced practices. The personal involvement of a parent company through its employees was measured by the agreement of the respondents to a single item ('*The employees responsible for cost accounting receive strong support from our parent company's top management.*'). The variable is also labelled **corporate managers** hereafter. This item shares structural similarities with the item applied to capture the subsidiary's local top management support. Therefore, it is included into A.7 of questionnaire A. Yet, these two items must be separated. The involvement of the parent's top-management transfers a parent company's cost accounting traditions rather than being an indicator for a sufficient provision of resources.[739] The **formal involvement of the parent company** is measured by asking respondents for the extent to which the parent company imposes the applicable cost types, the overhead allocation procedures and the different cost objects through corporate directives.[740] The items are measured in C.2 of questionnaire A on a seven point rating scale ranging from *not at all* to *completely*.[741] This manifest construct is *defined* formatively by an average (i.e. equally weighted) score of the items which are not marked as *N/A*.[742]

---

[737] This measure is informed by *Jaussaud/Schaaper* (2006), p. 32; *Ziener* (1985), p. 126; *Chang et al.* (2009), p. 5; *Chow et al.* (1999), p. 449f.

[738] More precisely, the following formula is applied: A value of zero is attributed if there are no expatriates. For all others, the formula: *logarithm (no. of expats) +1* is applied. Adding 1 allows differentiating companies with one expatriate from companies that do not have any expatriates.

[739] This item is based on *Chang et al.* (2009), p. 5, and *Cheng/Yu* (2012), p. 85, who stress the importance of the engagement of parents' local employees. Similarly, *Anderson/Young* (2001), p. 127, find these corporate managers to be more important than local ones for the implementation of ABC in subsidiaries.

[740] This measure is inspired by *Jaussaud/Schaaper* (2006), p. 32, and *Ferner* (2000), p. 525ff., who demonstrate the importance of formal rules empirically.

[741] A similar procedure is applied by *Schoute* (2009), p. 214, and *Homburg et al.* (2008), p. 141, for formative measurement models.

[742] To include a respondent in the analysis, one of the three items of C.2 can be marked as N/A.

5.2.3.2.2 Voluntary institutional influences

In addition to coercive institutional influences, this study investigates hypotheses on the effect of voluntary institutional factors for the complexity of subsidiaries' cost accounting systems.

The cost accounting systems in subsidiaries are likely to be in line with design opportunities which were previously approved by **sister affiliates**. Moreover, subsidiaries can mimic cost accounting systems of **companies from outside their group**. Consequently, two single items ask for the extent to which a company's cost accounting system is inspired by other companies from inside and outside its group (C.3 of questionnaire A). They are measured on a seven point rating scale ranging from *not at all* to *completely*. Also, respondents are offered the opportunity to provide *no answer* to this question.[743]

Moreover, the complexity of subsidiaries' cost accounting systems can be expected to vary according to the main source of cost accountants' knowledge (**educational background**). Therefore, respondents are asked for the main source of knowledge that enables the employees responsible for cost accounting to fulfil their tasks. Given the dominance in a previous study,[744] respondents are asked to choose whether *university/college education* or *learning by doing* constitutes the main source of knowledge for cost accountants (A.8 of questionnaire A). This study is interested in cross-national differences of cost accounting systems. Hence, asking for the mere source of such knowledge might provide a distorted picture. German universities are likely to provide a different educational background on cost accounting than Anglophone colleges do.[745] Thus, the question on the educational background also includes the necessity to choose the country of education. Three opportunities are regarded: *German-speaking countries*, *Anglophone countries* and *another country* (including Japan). For the reason of insufficient variation, however, the construct on the educational background of cost accountants will neglect this country of education. To test the hypothesis on the educational background (H3b2_3), a dummy variable is created. This variable (labelled Uni) is scaled one if cost accountants were trained in a German university and zero elsewise.

Besides these two measures, the **professionalisation of management accountants** is particularly relevant for the design of management accounting systems, such as cost accounting.[746] Thereby, professional institutes of management accountants from different geographical areas might provide their members with different management and cost accounting traditions. Consequently, two single-item constructs are included into this study to capture professionalisation (A.9 into questionnaire A). Respondents are asked, how intensively the employees responsible for cost accounting further their qualification through (e.g. courses of) professional institutes of management accountants from *German-speaking countries* and *Anglophone countries*. The applied seven point rating scale ranges from *not at all* to *very intensively*.

---

743 Both single item constructs on the mimetic pressures are excluded from data analyses due to poor data quality. Hence, no further information on these constructs' measurement models is provided.

744 Cf. *Moeschler* (2012), p. 221.

745 Cf. *Ahrens/Chapman* (1999), p. 42f.

746 Cf. *Granlund/Lukka* (1998), p. 163; *Ahrens/Chapman* (1999), p. 42f.; *Moeschler* (2012), p. 221.

5.2.3.3 The relational context

The **relational context** describes the alternative reactions of subsidiaries to coercive institutional pressures of their parent company. Given the alternative prevalence of these directions, the relational context is regarded as a formatively defined construct. In this study, five items measure the relational context (C.1 of questionnaire A and B.4 of questionnaire B.).

First, respondents are asked whether their company's cost information needs deviate from those of other companies in their group. Second, the existence of non-constructive conflicts is analysed by asking whether there are personal frictions, clashes and tensions between a subsidiary's management accountants and their counterparts in the parent company.[747] Third, the level of commitment to the parent company is measured by asking for the pride and loyalty, the employees of the subsidiary feel for being part of their parent company.[748] Fourth, it is asked whether companies can participate in the development of the accounting and finance directives issued by the parent company.[749] A final item asks the respondents whether changes in the company's management accounting function require previous consultation of the parent company.[750] All five items introduced are formulated as statements to which respondents are asked to indicate their agreement on a seven point Likert scale ranging from *not at all* to *completely*. Also, respondents are offered the opportunity to provide *no answer*.[751]

Due to the formative definition of the relational context, it is measured as an equally weighted average of its components.[752] A high value for this score shall indicate an unfavourable *relational context*. Such an unfavourable relational context mitigates the effect of coercive institutional influences on a subsidiary's cost accounting system. From a theoretical point of view, such mitigating effects are more likely if (1) the comparability of a subsidiary with its parent is low, if (2) there are multiple affective conflicts between a subsidiary and its parent, if (3) there is little identification of a subsidiary with its parent, if (4) a subsidiary cannot participate in the development of management accounting directives and, if (5) the subsidiary can change its management accounting function without consulting the parent company. As questions C.1 (questionnaire A) and B.4 (questionnaire B) are placed the end of the questionnaire, the items (3), (4) and (5) are reversely coded to ensure that respondents carefully consider this important question.

---

747 The operationalisation reflects the definition of affective conflicts by *Chenhall* (2004), p. 23ff.

748 This item was derived from a similar operationalisation in *Anderson/Young* (1999), p. 541.

749 A similar item was previously applied by *Dossi/Patelli* (2010), p. 507.

750 This measure is adopted from a similar wording in *Birkinshaw et al.* (2000), p. 335.

751 One of the five items of the relational context is excluded from the analyses due to poor data quality. To include a respondent in the analysis, two of the remaining items can be marked as N/A.

752 A similar procedure is applied by *Schoute* (2009), p. 214, and *Homburg et al.* (2008), p. 141, for formative measurement models. Aggregating the various dimensions of the relational context can be contrasted to *Kostova/Roth* (2002), p. 226, who focus on the individual dimensions of the relational context. As this study regards the relational context as the overreaching construct of interest, the chosen procedure is more adequate, however.

5.2.3.4 Users' attitude towards cost information

Besides the introduced explanatory variables, the theoretical foundation established the necessity to investigate five constructs on decision makers' personal attitudes to explain the use of cost information in subsidiaries. Except managers' perceptions of the quality of cost information, which comprises four complementing quality perspectives, all of these are measured by reflective measurement models. The items of these reflective measurement models are aggregated on the grounds of applicable quality assessments (cf. section 5.4.1). The scoring will be discussed in the empirical results and cannot be found in this section.

Managers' knowledge with respect to cost accounting (hereafter also referred to as 'knowledge') is operationalised in line with previous research. Four items are used to measure the construct.[753] The following items are applied in four previous research projects on the use of cost information:[754]

- The usefulness of cost information is easy to assess.
- I know precisely which problems to solve with cost information.

The additional two items are derived from a study on the use of cost information in the public sector as well as a study on the use of key performance indicators:

- I can distinguish different cost accounting systems.[755]
- I am aware of the strengths and weaknesses of alternative ways to design a cost accounting system.[756]

All four items are measured on a seven point Likert scale ranging from *not at all* to *completely* (B.5 of questionnaire B). Moreover, the question includes the option to provide *no answer*.[757]

The operationalisation of **managers' perceptions of the cost accounting system's quality** (hereafter also referred to as 'quality') is challenging. According to information systems literature, the quality of an information system, such as a cost accounting system, is measurable by its accuracy, relevance, accessibility and representation.[758] Furthermore, the possibility to assess information relevance is regularly linked to information users' trust in cost accounting and cost accountants.[759] Such measures of trust, however, cannot be disjunctively delinked from the chosen measures of the cost accounting systems' performance as becomes evident by constructs in *Hunold* (2003) or *Frank* (2000).[760] Hence, this study measures managers' perceptions of the quality of their cost accounting system based on

[753] Four items are argued to be the minimum number of items to be chosen for construct measurement (cf. *Backhaus et al.* (2013), p. 133).

[754] Cf. *Karlshaus* (2000), p. 148; *Frank* (2000), p. 116; *Hunold* (2003), p. 167; *Steiners* (2005), p. 109.

[755] Cf. *Sandt* (2004), p. 142.

[756] Cf. *Hunold* (2003), p. 167.

[757] For this variable, no more than one N/A item is accepted to include a respondent into the analysis.

[758] Cf. *Wang/Strong* (1996), p. 16, or similarly *Karlshaus* (2000), p. 131; *Hunold* (2003), p. 176; *Steiners* (2005), p. 110.

[759] Cf. *Karlshaus* (2000), p. 138; *Hunold* (2003), p. 164; *Steiners* (2005), p. 152f.

[760] Cf. *Hunold* (2003), p. 164 and 176; *Frank* (2000), p. 106f.

their assessment of the system's accuracy, relevance, accessibility and data presentation.[761] The resulting question is included as A.12 in questionnaire B. It includes a seven point rating scale ranging from *very poor* to *very good.* The four items of this construct are regarded as formative definitions of managers' perceptions because of their potential complementary rather than subsitutional character. Therefore, they are included as an equally weighted average in the analysis.[762]

Four items are used to operationalise **managers' preferences for cost information** (hereafter also referred to as 'preference'). In line with *Hunold* (2003), respondents are asked to assess how extensively they agree to the following items:[763]

- Cost information allows for a different perspective on problems and decisions.
- Cost information can facilitate the management of a company.
- Cost accounting is a fad and will lose in importance in the upcoming years.

Additionally, the expert interviews held before hypotheses development revealed an item, which was previously used to measure the instrumental usage type, to be rather reflective of users' preferences for cost information. Therefore, respondents are also asked for their agreement to the following statement:[764]

- I particularly use other information than cost information for decision-making (e.g. physical measures or market information).

All four items on managers' preferences for cost information are included in question B.5 of questionnaire B.[765] They are measured on the same scale as the items of the construct 'managers' knowledge with respect to cost accounting'. Also, respondents can provide *no answer*.[766] The score varies between one and seven. Thereby, one indicates a little and seven a strong preference for cost information.

The construct **managers' involvement in the design of a cost accounting system** (hereafter also referred to as 'involvement') is also measured by four items that prevail in previous research. Respondents are asked to indicate their level of agreement to the following statements (B.6 of questionnaire B):[767]

- I keep myself up to date with respect to changes and adjustments of our cost accounting system.

---

761 Cf. *Wang/Strong* (1996), p. 16 and 32, for a deduction of these four perspectives. According applications can be found in cost accounting literature to measure the quality of information technology (e.g. *Krumwiede* (1998), p. 271; *Al-Omiri/Drury* (2007), p. 407; *Moeschler* (2012), p. 396). Yet, none of these studies found the hypothesised positive effect on cost accounting systems' complexity. In contrast, the measure proved applicable in a previous study on usage types (cf. e.g. *Karlshaus* (2000), p. 131 and 165; *Hunold* (2003), p. 176 and 225, or the analysis of service quality by *Steiners* (2005), p. 110 and 193). Thus, it is integrated in this way here whereas the information technology per se regarded separately.

762 A similar procedure is applied by *Schoute* (2009), p. 214, and *Homburg et al.* (2008), p. 141, for formative measurement models.

763 For the following, cf. *Hunold* (2003), p. 165.

764 Cf. *Aust* (1999), p. 103; *Hunold* (2003), p. 183.

765 Items 3 and 4 are reversely coded.

766 For this variable, no more than one N/A item is accepted to include a respondent into the analysis.

767 Cf. for the following *Frank* (2000), p. 130; *Hunold* (2003), p. 170.

- I am interested in the design of our cost accounting system.
- I engage myself into the development of our cost accounting system.
- I promote the use of cost information in our company.

The items are measures on a seven point Likert scale ranging from *not at all* to *completely*. Also, respondents can provide *no answer*.[768]

As the above constructs, the **frequency of contacts between management accountants and managers** (hereafter also referred to as 'contact') is measured by four items (B.6 of questionnaire B). Three of these are deduced from the strand of research that also informed the other constructs in this section:[769]

- I get in touch with cost information very frequently.
- I get in touch with employees responsible for cost accounting very frequently.
- I take my time for detailed discussions with employees responsible for cost accounting.

The fourth item is aligned with these three, but acknowledges the operationalisation of an item used for managers' cost accounting knowledge:

- I get in touch with different possibilities to design a cost accounting system very frequently.

These items are measured on the same scale as manager's involvements in the design of cost accounting systems. Thus, all information on that scale applies to this construct as well.

5.2.4 Operationalisation of the control variables

Four control variables are included in the analysis of the complexity of cost accounting systems in subsidiaries. The controls are also applied to analyse management accountants' assessments of their cost accounting systems. All four control variables are manifest and measured by a single item question.

The discussion of the theoretical foundation reveals that a subsidiary's historical background can be relevant for the dependent and independent variables. A previous affiliation to, e.g. a German group might result in a comparably complex cost accounting system in a subsidiary of an Anglophone company. Also, a subsidiary which has been affiliated to its current parent for a rather short time might not yet have experienced considerable influence of the parent. Consequently, both the entry mode of the parent company as well as the length of affiliation are considered as control variables (C.5 of questionnaire A). For the former, it is asked if companies were originally set up as greenfields, brownfields or joint ventures by the current parent. This distinction corresponds to *Birskinshaw/Hood* (1998).[770] To ensure a common understanding, a brief definition of each term is added. The **form of market entry** is included in the explicative analysis as a dummy variable which takes the value 1 if the parent company acquired the subsidiary and zero if the parent company set up the business solely or conjointly with a venture partner. **The length of affiliation** is operationalised by asking for the year, in which a

[768] For this variable, no more than one N/A item is accepted to include a respondent into the analysis.
[769] For the following, cf. *Aust* (1999), p. 162; *Karlshaus* (2000), p. 137; *Hunold* (2003), p. 168.
[770] Cf. *Birkinshaw/Hood* (1998), p. 773.

company became part of its current parent company. By subtracting this figure from 2013, the length of affiliation is determined. This length of affiliation is included as a logarithmised variable into the explicative analysis. This accounts for the fact that a subsidiary which was affiliated to its current parent only recently will perceive stronger influences from that company in one additional year of affiliation than a company that is already part of its current parent for a long time.

Moreover, a **company's size** is generally controlled for in international research projects since the size can affect companies' cost accounting systems indirectly through the complexity of internal structures.[771] Therefore, respondents are asked to provide the number of full time equivalents (FTEs) employed by their company in the last financial year (A.2 of questionnaire A,). Focussing on FTEs as a measure of a company's size as opposed to sales turnover is common in German research.[772] Since international research which includes both sales and the number of employees as proxies for a company's size regularly find similar results for both measures,[773] this focus on one measure does not bias this project's results. Moreover, the number of FTEs provides an opportunity to control for industrial effects related to this study's cross-sectional character. *Groot* (1997) highlights this measures' ability to capture potentially differing labour-intensities among companies from different manufacturing sub-industries (e.g. food and beverage as well as engineering companies).[774] Thus, employing FTEs as a control for company size also complements this study's attempt to address its cross-sectional character during the explicative analysis. To account for potential size effects stemming from a large parent company, C.6 also includes a similar question for the **number of FTEs of the parent company**, (i.e. the ultimate owner). The size of the subsidiaries and their parent companies are included into the explicative analysis as logarithmised values. As for the length of affiliation, size effects are expected to be more prevalent for companies that vary between, e.g. 150 and 200 employees than for companies that vary between 1.950 and 2.000 FTEs.

All four control variables introduced above are included in the analysis of the different types of use as well. Given the focus on information users, i.e. an individual rather than a company level, the analysis of the usage types requires an additional control variable. Information users' way to use cost information and their personal attitudes towards cost information depends on their individual work experience.[775] Hence, information users' **years of work experience** complement the four other control variables during the anal-

---

[771] For a comprehensive review, cf. *Moeschler* (2012), p. 124f.

[772] Cf. e.g. *Homburg et al.* (1998), p. 14, and associated research projects by *Frank/Reitmeyer* (1999); *Aust* (1999); *Karlshaus* (2000); *Frank* (2000). A similar application prevails in *Kosmider* (1992), p. 25ff.; *Lange/Schauer* (1996), p. 204ff.; *Schiller/Rossier* (2008), p. 15; *Friedl et al.* (2009), p. 112f. The measure is not uncommon internationally either (cf. e.g. *Chenhall/Langfield-Smith* (1998), p. 3; *Schoute* (2009), p. 216).

[773] Cf. e.g. *Nguyen/Brooks* (1997), p. 14f.; *Brierley* (2008a), p. 63ff.

[774] Cf. *Groot* (1997), p. 12.

[775] This procedure reflects *Naranjo-Gil/Hartmann* (2006), p. 37 and 46, and *Karlshaus* (2000), p. 147ff., who find such personal characteristics of information users to be important antecedents of some types of information use. Since *Karlshaus* argues that work experience is also levelling, e.g. user's knowledge with respect to cost information, however, this variable is controlled for in this study rather than including it as an explanatory variable only.

yses of the usage types. As the effect of the control variable 'size', the effect of work experience on, e.g. different types of use or user's attitudes towards cost information is expected to converge. A one-year increase in work experience of a rather unexperienced manager will be more influential for his use of and attitudes towards cost information than an increase for an experienced manager. Hence, the years of work experience are logarithmised before including them in any explicative analysis.

Besides these control variables which prevail from a conceptual point of view, the analysis of the sample company's characteristics (see section 5.3.3) will discuss whether additional control variables are relevant from an empirical point of view.

5.3 Data collection, response rates and characteristics of the samples

5.3.1 Data collection and response rates

Data collection occurred between **January and May 2013**. Given the relatively small samples, the head of management accounting in all 957 companies was contacted by phone to encompass his personal commitment. If the head of **management accounting** was unavailable, a person in charge of cost accounting was contacted. A personal introduction of questionnaire B to the **board members** proved infeasible during the data collection process. Therefore, the questionnaire on the use of cost information was introduced to the companies' management accountants as well. These were then asked to pass questionnaire B on to a member of the board or the commercial manager of the company. During the introduction of the questionnaire, the firms were urged to provide truthful information to reduce the likelihood of a common method bias.[776]

		Sample size	Sent-out questionnaires (% of the sample size)	Received responses (response rate)
Anglophone sample	Questionnaire A	470	327 (68 %)	119 (36 %)
	Questionnaire B		313 (67 %)	56 (18 %)
	Dyads		313 (67 %)	50 (16 %)
German control sample	Questionnaire A	487	301 (62 %)	108 (36 %)
	Questionnaire B		282 (60 %)	54 (19 %)
	Dyads		282 (60 %)	52 (18 %)

Table 5-6: Conveyed questionnaires and received responses

The number of companies that initially agreed to participate in the study varied between 60 % and 68 % for the two samples and the two questionnaires (Table 5-6). The reasons for opposing the participation during the introducing calls are widespread, ranging from a lack of time, over a lack of an adequate cost accounting system, and a lack of interest to the general policy to not participate in questionnaire research. All firms that agreed to participate were provided with a link to the online questionnaires as well as the PDF version of the questionnaires. They could also choose from the two available languages. The information was sent via E-mail. After the initial introduction of the questionnaire, **follow-**

[776] Cf. *Podsakoff et al.* (2003), p. 888. A formal analysis of this study's exposure to a common method bias can be found at the end of the next section (cf. section 5.3.2, p. 153).

up activities were performed to ensure a good response rate. Companies were re-contacted alternately by phone and mail. Depending on the date of the first contact, companies were re-contacted up to seven times.

The data collection procedure yielded 227 responses for questionnaire A and 110 responses for questionnaire B. Both questionnaires could be collected from 102 companies. Table 5-6 presents the distribution of responses by sample.

Some responses had to be excluded due to poor **data quality**. For *questionnaire A*, there were two Anglophone companies with a mismatch in the size criterion. Furthermore, there were three Anglophone and three German companies who did not reply one or multiple questions.[777] All these companies were excluded. Moreover, the provision of an N/A category in a number of questions led to the exclusion of multiple questionnaires. Although it is argued that respectively answered items can be ignored,[778] a too extensive use of this scale option was perceived to indicate issues with respect to the comprehensiveness of the affected items. These could have reduced the overall validity of the study.

Question	Item
B.5	- aggregate heterogeneous overhead costs
B.12	- costs' variability with respect to final outputs - costs' relatedness to idle capacity / used capacity
B.14	- customers - scrap/spoilage
C.1	- our company can take a share in the development of the management accounting directives, which are imposed by our parent company.
C.3	- the cost accounting system of another company inside your group - the cost accounting system of another company outside your group

Table 5-7: Items excluded from the analyses due to data quality

Therefore, all questions including an **N/A option** were subject to a validity assessment. In five questions, there are items which are marked as N/A by at least 10 % of the replying companies. Table 5-7 provides an overview of these items. They are excluded from the forthcoming analyses. Since both items of C.3 are involved, the hypotheses on mimetic pressures (H3b2_1 and H3b2_2) cannot be tested. For the other questions, the operationalisations of the affected constructs will disregard the excluded items.

Moreover, in section 5.2 it is explained that the procedures for the aggregation of constructs including the N/A option is contingent on the number of items marked accordingly. Questionnaires in which more than five sub-scores of the overall complexity measure are completely answered using the N/A option are excluded from the analysis. Similarly, questionnaires in which a majority of items of the explicative constructs (questions A.4,

777 Questions C.4 to C.6 of questionnaire A were subject to additional assessments. These involve publicly available information. Before excluding questionnaires with missing data on these questions, an attempt was made to derive this information from public sources. A similar procedure was applied to ensure that subsidiaries from the same parent company provided equivalent information for questions C.4 and C.6 of questionnaire A.

778 Cf. *Hair* (2010), p. 45f.

A.7, C.1 and C.2) are marked as N/A are disregarded. Hence, the number of analysable questionnaires declines to 199. Table 5-8 summarises the **reconciliation of the usable responses.**

	Anglophone sample (327)	German sample (301)
Returned questionnaires	**119**	**108**
Excluded due to size criterion	2	/
Excluded due to missing values	1	2
Excluded due to complexity scores	2	1
Excluded due to complexity scores *and* independent variables	2	1
Available questionnaires for descriptive analysis *(response rate)*	***112*** *(34 %)*	***104*** *(35 %)*
Excluded due to independent variables	2	15
Usable questionnaires	**110**[779]	**89**
Usable response rate	**34 %**	**29 %**

Table 5-8: Reconciliation of the usable response rate (questionnaire A)

The high number of German companies (15) which had to be left out due to missing independent variables is particularly due to questions regarding the parent company. This indicates that in the German control group, there are a number of companies which satisfied the selection criteria but in which the subsidiary structure is merely due to legal and administrative purposes. The sample characteristics underline this indication (see section 5.3.3). The exclusion of these 15 companies does not change the validity of the comparison of cost accounting systems in Anglophone and domestic German companies.

The **data quality** in *Questionnaire B* was analysed equivalently. No questionnaires had to be excluded due to missing values or a mismatch in the size criterion. Moreover, there were no questionnaire items which are marked as N/A by more than 10 % of the respondents. The item which is marked most regularly as N/A in questionnaire B is one that had to be excluded from questionnaire A.[780] For equivalence reasons, it is excluded from the investigation of the usage types as well. Moreover, the aggregation criteria for the independent variables in the analysis of questionnaire B led to the exclusion of seven questionnaires due to the prevalence of N/As in a majority of the items of questions B.4, B.5 and B.6. Since the analysis of the hypotheses on the determinant of the usage types requires some information from questionnaire A, several responses to questionnaire B had to be excluded because of missing or uncompleted dyads. The **reconciliation** of the 92 analysable responses to questionnaire B is presented in Table 5-9.

779 Similar to the distribution in the population, 82 % of the responses stem from US-owned subsidiaries and 28 % from Commonwealth-owned subsidiaries.

780 This item is 'Our company can take a share in the development of the management accounting directives, which are imposed by our parent company' (7 % of the questionnaires).

	Anglophone sample (313)	German sample (282)
Returned questionnaires	**56**	**54**
Excluded due to size criterion	/	/
Excluded due to missing values	/	/
Available questionnaires for descriptive analysis *(response rate)*	***56*** *(18 %)*	***54*** *(19 %)*
Excluded due to independent variables	2	5
Excluded due to uncompleted dyads	7	4
Usable questionnaires	**47**[781]	**45**
Usable response rate	**15 %**	**16 %**

Table 5-9: Reconciliation of the usable response rate (questionnaire B)

5.3.2 Data sets and data quality

The preceding section emphasises that the numbers of questionnaires available for descriptive and explicative analyses differ for both the investigation of the complexity of cost accounting systems and the use of cost information. To avoid misunderstandings, both the descriptive investigation (research questions (1a) and (1b)) and the **explicative analysis** (research questions (2a) and (2b)) will be based on the questionnaires that comprise information for both analyses (datasets 1 for the complexity of cost accounting and dataset 3 for the use of cost information). For analytical purposes, and to underline the **robustness of the findings**, descriptive findings will also be provided for the questionnaires which are available for the descriptive analysis only (datasets 2 and 4 respectively). Table 5-10 defines the four datasets available for analysis.[782]

	Dataset 1		Dataset 2	
Sample	Anglophone	German	Anglophone	German
No. of questionnaires	110	89	112	104
Purpose	Descriptive and explicative analysis of questionnaire A		Validate the robustness of the descriptive analysis of questionnaire A	
	Dataset 3 (dyads)		**Dataset 4**	
Sample	Anglophone	German	Anglophone	German
No. of questionnaires	47	45	56	54
Purpose	Descriptive and explicative analysis of questionnaire B		Validate the robustness of the descriptive analysis of questionnaire B	

Table 5-10: Datasets analysed in this study

Having clarified these general aspects with respect to the analysable questionnaires, it can be turned to a thorough assessment of the data quality. Despite the necessity to disregard some investigated items during data analysis and the need to exclude some respondents due to incomprehensively answered questionnaires, the questionnaires seem to stem from rather **reliable sources**.

781 Similar to the distribution in the population, 80 % of the responses stem from US-owned and 20 % from Commonwealth-owned subsidiaries.

782 In addition, the companies from dataset 1 which did not hand in questionnaire B form a fith dataset. This dataset 5 is especially relevant for the analysis of the performance of cost accounting systems.

Two findings can underline this assertion. Firstly, the years of work experience of the respondents serve as an assessment of the likelihood that the respondents report unreliable information due to little knowledge on the researched issues. The rationale for this analysis is that the more experienced a respondent is, the greater his ability to provide substantial insights into the research objects. Table 5-11 summarises the findings for the questionnaires available for explicative analyses (datasets 1 and 3). Given the rather high **work experience** of around 20 years, the respondents' insights are unlikely to be flawed by a poor knowledge.

Mean (standard deviation)	Dataset 1		Dataset 3	
	Anglophone	German	Anglophone	German
Years of work experience	17 (9)	18 (9)	20 (9)	20 (8)

Table 5-11: Work experience of the respondents

Secondly, the **job titles** of the respondents of questionnaire B must be taken into consideration. Whereas questionnaire A could have been answered by an information provider (i.e. the head of management accounting or a personal responsible for cost accounting), questionnaire B should have been answered by an information user. As such, it was addressed to the companies' board members or commercial managers. Table 5-12 presents the working positions of the respondents of questionnaire B.[783]

	Dataset 3	
	Anglophone	German
Board members or commercial managers	68 %	69 %
Head of the (management) accounting or finance department	13 %	13 %
Member of the (management) accounting or finance department	19 %	18 %

Table 5-12: Working positions of the respondents of questionnaire B

Table 5-12 reveals that in some cases, questionnaire B has not been forwarded to a board member or was back-delegated to the management accounting department.[784] To avoid a further reduction of the analysable responses, this issue is taken into account during the analyses of the usage types by an additional control variable which reflects whether questionnaire B was answered by a user or a preparer of cost information.[785]

To assess the quality of the responses with respect to their validity for the population of Anglophone companies and the stratified German (control) sample more thoroughly, a **non-response bias** analysis is performed. Therefore, early and late respondents are compared with respect to the complexity of and satisfaction with the cost accounting systems as well as the companies' size.[786] Early (late) respondents were defined as those 15 % of the respondents that took the least (most) time to finalise questionnaire after having re-

[783] The analysis for dataset 4 shows similar results.

[784] A similar experience was recently made by *Hofmann et al.* (2012), p. 167.

[785] To do so, the dummy variable 'Board member' complements the conceptually relevant control variables (see section 5.2.4). It will take the value of one if a questionnaire was filled in by a responding company's board member or commercial manager and zero otherwise.

[786] Cf. *Armstrong/Overton* (1977), p. 397, for this suggestion.

ceived it. These two groups are compared based on a Wilcoxon rank sum test because of the small sample size.[787] Table 5-13 summarises the findings for dataset 1.[788]

	Complexity	Satisfaction	Company size
Anglophone sample (n=34)	p = 0.10 (Wilcoxon rank sum test, two-tailed)	p = 0.37 (Wilcoxon rank sum test, two-tailed)	p = 0.62 (Wilcoxon rank sum test, two-tailed)
German sample (n=27)	p = 0.81 (Wilcoxon rank sum test, two-tailed)	p = 0.20 (Wilcoxon rank sum test, two-tailed)	p = 0.66 (Wilcoxon rank sum test, two-tailed)

Table 5-13: Non-response bias analysis (questionnaire A)

As can be seen by the p-values above 0.1, none of the analysed variables is different in any of the two samples. Moreover, the achieved response rates for the questionnaire B do neither fall behind nor exceed the response rates in previous associated research. This finding emphasises the data to be valid for the Anglophone population as well as the German stratified sample.

Similarly, the responses to questionnaire B are tested for a non-response bias. Thereby, the ceremonial usage type, the satisfaction with the cost accounting system and the company size are compared for early and late respondents.[789] Table 5-14 presents the results for dataset 3.[790]

	Ceremonial use	Satisfaction	Company size
Anglophone sample (n=16)	p > 0.1 (Fligner-Policello test, U = -0.373)	p > 0.1 (Fligner-Policello test, U = -0.264)	p > 0.1[791] (Fligner-Policello test, U = -0.763)
German sample (n=13)	p = 0.60 (Wilcoxon rank sum test, two-tailed)	p = 0.02 (Wilcoxon rank sum test, two-tailed)	p = 0.67 (Wilcoxon rank sum test, two-tailed)

Table 5-14: Non-response bias analysis (questionnaire B)

The p-value of 0.02 for the level of satisfaction indicates a non-response bias in the German control group. The analyses in the following chapter will reveal that this finding can be linked to a *selection bias* which especially prevails for the domestic German firms which did hand in analysable dyads. The findings for the use of cost information appear to be somewhat stemming from companies in which there are less issues with respect to the information-usefulness of cost information or in which cost information is rather more important for decision-making.[792] The analysis of the performance of cost accounting (section 6.3.2.3) discusses this selection bias in detail.

---

787 In total, 27 German and 34 Anglophone companies are compared. Given that there are less than 30 early and late respondents, the threshold of 30, which is often argued to allow for an application of the central limit theorem, is not met. Therefore, non-parametric tests are applied.

788 The findings are stable for dataset 2.

789 Due to the small number of analysable companies, non-parametric tests are applied. Since heteroscedasticity is found for the Anglophone sample, the Fligner-Policello test is applied.

790 The findings are stable for dataset 4.

791 For comparisons of groups with less than 12 observations *Fligner/Policello* (1981), p. 165, provide a table of critical values. The reported p-values reflect these figures. The p-values in *Fligner/Policello* (1981), p. 165, are for one-tailed hypotheses (cf. *Siegel/Castellan* (1988), p. 140).

792 The analysable dyads stem from companies that have more complex cost accounting systems, evaluate the performance of their cost accounting system positively and show high levels of interaction between

The previous paragraph essentially explicates that the findings for dataset 3 are of restricted validity for the overall population of the researched subsidiaries. This holds true for both samples since the German control sample is regarded to compare the Anglophone sample with domestic German practices. However, the severity of this finding remains unclear since previous research on board members might be implicitly characterised by a similar deficiency. This is especially true because this study's response rates, despite being well below the ones of questionnaire A, are not unusual for use-studies addressed to a company's board.[793] Nevertheless, the overall representativeness of the analysis of the usage types of the populations of domestic German and Anglophone subsidiaries must be assessed rather cautiously.

As a final assessment of the data quality, the issue of a **common method bias** was taken into account. The study at hand is partially subject to this bias because dependent and independent variables for questionnaire A are derived from a single source. Moreover, the majority of variables for the explicative analysis of the use of cost information also stems from one questionnaire. To diagnose "the extent to which a common method variance may be a problem[,]"[794] a *Harman* single factor test is applied. For the Anglophone (domestic German) companies, the test yielded 19 (22) factors for questionnaire A (dataset 1) and 17 (18) factors for questionnaire B (dataset 3),[795] that have eigenvalues greater than one. Thus, there is weak evidence in favour of the absence of a common method bias.

5.3.3 Characteristics of the sample

Before engaging in a detailed analysis of the complexity of cost accounting systems and the use of cost information, the following paragraphs reveal some characteristics of the companies researched. Thereby, special attention is directed to the conceptually derived control variables. Moreover, additional characteristics of the responding companies are analysed and assessed with respect to their relevance for the forthcoming analyses.

With respect to the **size of the companies**, the sample selection criterion ensures that both the Anglophone and the German samples consist of companies with comparable size (see Table 5-15). Consequently, there is little indication that a potentially prevailing difference in the cost accounting systems (hypothesis 1) is merely due to different firm size. Nevertheless, the standard deviation reported in Table 5-15 as well as the implicitly cov-

managers and management accountants. Except for the performance in the domestic German companies, however, none of these findings is statistically significant. Because these companies are insignificantly smaller than the companies that returned questionnaire A only, this effect cannot be merely attributed to the firms' size.

793 *Henri* (2006b), p. 39f., reports a response rate of 24 %, *Widener* (2007), p. 767, one of 12.5 %. Note, however, that the German research projects on the use of cost information report a respectively computed usable response rate which is considerably higher (cf. exemplarily *Homburg et al.* (1998), p. 12f.).

794 *Podsakoff et al.* (2003), p. 889.

795 For the application of this test, cf. e.g. *Widener* (2007), p. 768, or *Hofmann et al.* (2012), p. 165.

ered industrial effects[796] underline the necessity to consider the subsidiary's size as a control factor.

	Number of employees (FTEs)							
	Dataset 1		Dataset 2		Dataset 3		Dataset 4	
	Angl.	Ger.	Angl.	Ger.	Angl.	Ger.	Angl.	Ger.
25 % quartile	242	240	246	240	240	212	241	216
50 % quartile	360	350	360	350	321	329	334	325
75 % quartile	600	563	600	553	550	500	510	500
Mean (standard deviation)	483 (365)	486 (372)	489 (371)	469 (401)	456 (347)	445 (329)	446 (359)	444 (346)
p-value (test)	0.94 (two-tailed t-test)		0.69 (two-tailed t-test)		0.88 (two-tailed t-test)		0.98 (two-tailed t-test)	

Table 5-15: Number of employees (FTEs)

Table 5-15 also reveals that in all four datasets only a minority of the researched companies has more than 500 employees. As such, there is a limited number of companies stemming from the wide ranged quartile of companies with around 500–2,000 employees. Since a similar distribution prevails in the population of the 493 Anglophone subsidiaries as well as the stratified sample of domestic German companies,[797] this finding does not impinge the due analysis but actually emphasises that the results are representative for the researched populations.

Despite this study's focus on companies of the manufacturing industry, it appears possible that some of the companies researched do not pursue any manufacturing activities but focus on other **value chain activities** (e.g. procurement or sales). To assess a potential bias stemming from the fact that questionnaire A makes multiple references to manufacturing related tasks (e.g. for the measure of product diversity), the value chain activities performed by the responding companies are analysed (see Table 5-16).

	Proportion of companies which perform a value chain activity							
	Dataset 1		Dataset 2		Dataset 3		Dataset 4	
	Angl.	Ger.	Angl.	Ger.	Angl.	Ger.	Angl.	Ger.
R&D	69 %	64 %	70 %	63 %	64 %	62 %	57 %	61 %
Procurement	81 %	69 %	81 %	67 %	79 %	64 %	70 %	63 %
Production	95 %	96 %	96 %	96 %	96 %	93 %	88 %	91 %
Sales	80 %	67 %	80 %	69 %	74 %	62 %	68 %	63 %
Others	15 %	12 %	15 %	12 %	15 %	13 %	24 %	11 %

Table 5-16: Performed value chain activities

Table 5-16 illustrates that only very few companies are not engaged in manufacturing activities (line: Production). As such, no bias can be expected from the alignment of the questionnaire with the prevalence of manufacturing activities. This assertion is reassured by the fact that there are very few companies with a special purpose character (i.e. with only one value chain activity) which do not focus on production activities (Table 5-17).[798]

[796] Appendix 3 reveals that the distribution of the regarded 23 manufacturing sub-industries varies insignificantly between the Anglophone and the domestic German companies. Hence, no bias can be expected from this broad focus on various manufacturing sub-industries.

[797] The quartiles in terms of number of employees are 215, 350 and 563 for the Anglophone subsidiaries and 200, 321 and 556 for the domestic German subsidiaries.

[798] Figures might not add up to 100 % due to rounding.

	Subsidiaries with a special purpose character							
	Dataset 1		Dataset 2		Dataset 3		Dataset 4	
	Angl.	Ger.	Angl.	Ger.	Angl.	Ger.	Angl.	Ger.
Companies with only one value chain activity	16 %	24 %	16 %	23 %	19 %	24 %	17 %	24 %
Thereof: production activities	78 %	90 %	78 %	92 %	78 %	82 %	80 %	83 %
Thereof: sales activities	11 %	0 %	11 %	0 %	11 %	0 %	10 %	0 %
Thereof: other activities	11 %	10 %	11 %	8 %	11 %	18 %	10 %	17 %

Table 5-17: Subsidiaries with a special purpose character

The few special purpose or non-producing entities are unlikely to impinge the analysis of hypotheses 3 to 5.[799] On exception prevails for this assertion. The number of performed activities is significantly different for Anglophone and domestic German companies in datasets 1 and 2 (Table 5-18). Apparently, the Anglophone subsidiaries are more heavily engaged in the entire value chain than the companies of the stratified German sample are. As such, the former companies might need to picture more (diverse) activities in their cost accounting systems. Hence, during an analysis of the differences in the cost accounting systems of the Anglophone and the domestic German firms, this aspect has to be controlled for. Being able to associate such *differences* to a parent company's involvement might be prevented otherwise.

Mean (standard deviation)	Dataset 1		Dataset 2		Dataset 3		Dataset 4	
	Angl.	Ger.	Angl.	Ger.	Angl.	Ger.	Angl.	Ger.
Number of performed value chain activities	3.4 (1.2)	3.1 (1.4)	3.4 (1.2)	3.1 (1.3)	3.3 (1.3)	3.0 (1.3)	3.3 (1.3)	3.0 (1.3)
p-value (test)	0.08 (two-tailed Welch-test)		0.05 (two-tailed Welch-test)		0.24 (two-tailed t-test)		0.33 (two-tailed t-test)	

Table 5-18: Number of performed value chain activities

To assess the **historical background** of the sample companies, their parent company's form of market entry is investigated. Most companies are brownfield investments, i.e. they were acquired by their current parent company (Table 5-19).[800] There is only a minority of companies which was set up by their current parent as wholly owned subsidiary (i.e. greenfield investment) or as a joint venture. As such, it would not be surprising to find Anglophone subsidiaries to reflect some German cost accounting traditions because of the companies' historical background. Despite the little variation, this aspect is controlled for to ensure that it is not merely the companies' history that underlies the design of cost accounting systems and the use of cost information in subsidiaries as well as the potential presence/absence of a cross-national difference.

	Form of market entry							
	Dataset 1		Dataset 2		Dataset 3		Dataset 4	
	Angl.	Ger.	Angl.	Ger.	Angl.	Ger.	Angl.	Ger.
Brownfields	86 %	63 %	87 %	60 %	85 %	73 %	84 %	70 %
Greenfields	11 %	35 %	11 %	38 %	15 %	24 %	16 %	28 %
Joint Ventures	3 %	2 %	3 %	2 %	/	2 %	/	2 %
p-value (test)	0.00 (Fisher's exact test)		0.00 (Fisher's exact test)		0.24 (Fisher's exact test)		0.14 (Fisher's exact test)	

Table 5-19: Form of market entry

799 Robustness checks underlining this assertion can be found in the sections on the explicative analyses.

800 Numbers might not add up to 100 % due to rounding.

Besides the form of market entry, the **length of affiliation** can influence the dominance of a parent company's coercive pressures. The results on the length of affiliation vary with respect to the findings for the form of market entry (Table 5-20). On average, the Anglophone companies have been part of their group for around 16 years. For the domestic German firms, the mean is 22 years. Since these values vary considerably among Anglophone and domestic German subsidiaries and differ significantly between these groups, the relevance of this figure as a control variable can be underlined.

Mean (standard deviation)	Length of affiliation (in years)							
	Dataset 1		Dataset 2		Dataset 3		Dataset 4	
	Angl.	Ger.	Angl.	Ger.	Angl.	Ger.	Angl.	Ger.
Brownfields	13 (10)	17 (16)	13 (9)	17 (16)	13 (8)	15 (12)	14 (11)	17 (15)
Greenfields	33 (14)	33 (24)	38 (34)	34 (26)	48 (41)	34 (29)	44 (37)	46 (38)
Joint Ventures	18 (15)	18 (1)	18 (15)	18 (1)	/	17 (/)	/	17 (/)
Average	16 (16)	22 (20)	16 (16)	23 (22)	18 (21)	20 (19)	19 (21)	25 (27)
p-value (test)	0.02 (two-tailed Welch-test)		0.00 (two-tailed Welch-test)		0.69 (two-tailed t-test)		0.20 (two-tailed Welch-test)	

Table 5-20: Length of affiliation

In addition to the analysis of the sample companies' characteristics, it is essential to introduce some particularities of their **parent companies**. First, it must be stressed that some of the returned questionnaires are from subsidiaries with a common parent. Table 5-21 presents the number of parent companies in each dataset. In all datasets, the number of parent companies roughly reflects the number of returned questionnaires. Moreover, there are no subsidiaries which share a common parent with more than two other companies. Hence, no substantial bias can be expected from this fact.

	Number of parent companies							
	Dataset 1		Dataset 2		Dataset 3		Dataset 4	
	Angl.	Ger.	Angl.	Ger.	Angl.	Ger.	Angl.	Ger.
Number of parent companies with one subsidiary	93	80	95	95	43	41	52	49
Number of parent companies with two subsidiaries	7	3	7	3	2	2	2	1
Number of parent companies with three subsidiaries	1	1	1	1	/	/	/	1
Total number of parent companies in the dataset	101	84	103	99	45	43	54	51
Total number of subsidiaries in the dataset	110	89	112	104	47	45	56	54

Table 5-21: Number of parent companies in the datasets

Also, the limited number of sister affiliates prevents a detailed descriptive analysis of interfirm effects. Therefore, the issue of subsidiaries with a common parent company will not be considered during the descriptive analyses. In the explicative analyses, however, the prevalence of potentially similar subsidiaries of a common parent (i.e. autocorrelation) is accounted for through the application of robust cluster estimators.

Having clarified this general finding, it can be turned to the characteristics of the parents. Table 5-22[801] shows that only very few of the researched subsidiaries are held for investing purposes only (financial holding).[802] Instead, the parent companies engage thoroughly in

[801] Numbers might not add up to 100 % due to rounding.

[802] For an introduction of holding structures, cf. *Kreikebaum* (2002), p. 135ff.; *Schreyögg* (2008), p. 113f., and *Kutschker/Schmid* (2011), p. 602ff.

the strategic and financial activities of the subsidiaries (strategic holding) or additionally perform operating activities as well (operational holding).[803]

	Holding structure							
	Dataset 1		Dataset 2		Dataset 3		Dataset 4	
	Angl.	Ger.	Angl.	Ger.	Angl.	Ger.	Angl.	Ger.
Financial holding	5 %	12 %	6 %	13 %	6 %	13 %	5 %	15 %
Strategic holding	37 %	43 %	37 %	45 %	26 %	36 %	27 %	41 %
Operational holding	57 %	45 %	57 %	42 %	68 %	51 %	68 %	44 %
p-value (test)	0.10 (Chi² test)		0.06 (Chi² test)		0.24 (Fisher's exact test)		0.03 (Fisher's exact test)	

Table 5-22: Parent company's holding structure

Mirroring the fact that in the Anglophone sample there are significantly more operational holdings (Table 5-22), Table 5-23 reveals that the Anglophone companies have significantly larger parent companies (18.839 FTEs) than the domestic German companies (8.165 FTEs). A strikingly similar structure can be found for the number of foreign countries, the parent companies are operating in (i.e. their internationality). The parents of the Anglophone subsidiaries own subsidiaries in significantly more foreign countries (34 in dataset 1) than the parents of the domestic German firms (24 in dataset 1).

Mean (standard deviation)	Number of employees of the parent company							
	Dataset 1		Dataset 2		Dataset 3		Dataset 4	
	Angl.	Ger.	Angl.	Ger.	Angl.	Ger.	Angl.	Ger.
Financial holding	793 (1,116)	1,550 (2,829)	722 (1,036)	1,425 (2,608)	1,232 (1,560)	603 (936)	1,232 (1,560)	486 (823)
Strategic holding	14,204 (32,599)	2,165 (5,209)	14,204 (23,206)	1,767 (4,745)	2,189 (3,328)	2,682 (6,745)	1,844 (3,041)	6,873 (23,016)
Operational holding	23,573 (42,149)	15,684 (27,527)	23,205 (41,917)	14,291 (26,592)	24,101 (47,572)	15,714 (31,124)	21,150 (44,311)	15,076 (30,600)
Average	18,839 (37,941)	8,165 (19,871)	18,506 (37,917)	7,022 (18,579)	17,047 (40,452)	9,065 (23,402)	14,912 (37,509)	9,276 (25,407)
p-value (test)	0.01 (two-tailed Welch-test)		0.00 (two-tailed Welch-test)		0.25 (two-tailed t-test)		0.39 (two-tailed t-test)	

Table 5-23: Parent companies' number of employees (FTEs)

The parents' holding structures, their internationality as well as their size can affect the availability of resources in a subsidiary as well as the existence of corporate directives or the favourability of the relational context. Given the similarity of these three variables, it is reasonable to focus on the parent company's size as a control variable. Future research engaging in an explanation of parent company influences on subsidiaries may wish to account for differences in a parent company's structure more thoroughly. Since this study regards whether a parent company affects its subsidiaries' cost accounting but disregards why there is such an influence, the applied procedure is justified.[804]

[803] Table 5-23 uncovers a potential reason for the large difference between the number of domestic German companies in dataset 1 and 2. It prevails that those 15 companies that had to be excluded due to uncompleted questions on their parent companies increase the percentage of operational holdings (42 % to 45 %). In contrast, the percentages of both strategic and financial holdings decrease (13 % to 12 %, and 45 % to 43 %). Hence, in these 15 companies the legal entity status of the subsidiaries might merely serve legal and administrative purposes for these companies' business operations.

[804] Robustness checks underlining this assertion can be found in the sections on the explicative analyses.

5.4 Methods of data analysis

5.4.1 Quality criteria for construct measurement

This study applies differing measurement models for the operationalisation of its constructs. These models generally contain a measurement error. To assess whether a measurement model measures what it is supposed to measure (i.e. validity) without an extensive measurement error (i.e. reliability)[805], a number of different analyses are applied. Due to the different rationales of formative and reflective measurement models as well as formatively defined measures, these analyses vary in accordance with the applied measurement model.[806]

In **reflective measurement models**, individual items are a reflection of the underlying latent construct. Their reliability and validity analyses are deeply interwoven with factor analytical considerations as well as classical test theory.[807] Following previous research,[808] this study applies a variety of measures suggested to serve reliability and validity assessments.[809] Assessments of the *reliability* of the reflective measurement models are based on four measures. From classical test theory, the measure Cronbach's alpha is applied. From confirmatory factor analytical considerations,[810] this study employs a factor's composite reliability, the measure average variance extracted as well as the items' factor loadings.[811]

Cronbach's alpha measures the unidimensionality of a reflective scale based on the positive correlation of the scale's individual items.[812] It assesses the reliability of a construct by evaluating an unweighted sum of the individual items.[813] The measure does so by comparing the proportion of the total variance of the summed construct that is explained by the summed correlation of the individual items against the same ratio if all items were perfectly positively correlated.[814] Thus, the value of coefficient alpha can vary between zero and one.[815] An alpha value of one indicates that all individual items of a measure are perfectly

---

805 Cf. *Stier* (1999), p. 51 and 56; *Hair* (2010), p. 45f.

806 Cf. *Bisbe et al.* (2007), p. 803.

807 For this and the following, cf. *Homburg/Giering* (1996), p. 8; *Lee/Hooley* (2005), p. 367ff.; *Bisbe et al.* (2007), p. 802f.; *Backhaus et al.* (2013), p. 127ff.

808 Cf. *Engelen* (2007), p. 185ff.

809 Cf. *Homburg/Baumgartner* (1995), p. 169ff., or *Homburg/Giering* (1996), p. 8ff., for a summary.

810 For an overview of the procedures applied for confirmatory factor analysis, cf. *Backhaus et al.* (2013), p. 127ff.

811 To assess the adequacy of any factor analytical procedures, the Kaiser-Meyer-Olkin criterion (KMO value ≥ 0.5) will be reviewed (cf. *Backhaus et al.* (2011), p. 342f.). Additionally, the analysis will consider the unidimensionality of a construct as suggested by *Bisbe/Malagueño* (2009), p. 383, based on the number of factors with eigenvalues greater than one (Kaiser criterion) (cf. *Backhaus et al.* (2011), p. 359, for details). Both preceding analyses are based on the principal factor model of explorative factor analysis in this study. This method appears appropriate since it forms constructs based on the cause of the correlation between summarised items (cf. *Backhaus et al.* (2011), p. 356f., for a discussion of alternative models available for factor analysis).

812 Cf. *Cronbach* (1951), p. 297ff., or *Tenenhaus et al.* (2005), p. 163f., for a summary.

813 Cf. *Bortz/Schuster* (2010), p. 429.

814 Cf. *Tenenhaus et al.* (2005), p. 163f.

815 Cf. *Homburg/Giering* (1996), p. 8.

positively correlated.[816] In contrast, a low alpha value indicates an unreliable measurement model. It is generally argued that an alpha value below 0.7 indicates an unreliable measurement model.[817] A factor's **composite reliability**[818] comprises a similar idea as Cronbach's alpha.[819] Rather than assessing an unweighted sum of the individual items, however, it evaluates the consistency of a measurement model based on the factor loadings of a construct's items. As such, the measure evaluates how well the individual items measure the underlying construct.[820] Like coefficient alpha, this measure can also vary between zero and one, whereby higher values indicate a higher level of reliability. Previous research suggested a composite reliability above 0.6 or 0.7 to indicate an adequate level of reliability.[821] Also based on factor analytical considerations, the **average variance extracted (AVE)** provides an additional possibility to measure the reliability of a reflective measurement model.[822] It describes the amount of a construct's variance that is explained by its items.[823] The measure varies between zero and one, and a value closer to one indicates high reliability.[824] The AVE's threshold value is generally argued to be 0.5 because an AVE < 0.5 signals that a construct's variance that is explicable by the measurement error exceeds the variance which is linked to the measures' items.[825] If coefficient alpha, the composite reliability or the AVE indicate a rather poor reliability of a construct, it is recommended to eliminate some items to improve the quality of the construct.[826] Accordingly, this choice should centre on items that show little correlation with the aggregated measure. In a similar vein, it is argued that an individual item is reliable if it shares more than 50 % of its variance with the underlying construct.[827] This implies that a reliable item should load with no less than 0.7[828] (**standardised factor loadings**) on an underlying factor. Underachieving this threshold might thus provide further insights into the items that should be excluded from the measurement of a construct.

The *validity* of a reflective measurement model is examined in this study by considering their content and discriminant validity.[829] The content validity is established through the

---

816 Cf. *Tenenhaus et al.* (2005), p. 163f.

817 Cf. *Homburg/Giering* (1996), p. 8.

818 In accordance with a respective summary in *Götz/Liehr-Gobbers* (2004), p. 734, this measure is labelled 'composite reliability' rather than 'internal consistency measure' as done by *Moeschler* (2012), p. 210.

819 For this and the following, cf. *Götz/Liehr-Gobbers* (2004), p. 727 and 734.

820 For this and the following, cf. *Homburg/Giering* (1996), p. 10f.

821 For a summary, cf. *Götz/Liehr-Gobbers* (2004), p. 728 and 734.

822 Cf. *Homburg/Giering* (1996), p. 11.

823 Cf. *Engelen* (2007), p. 201.

824 Cf. *Homburg/Giering* (1996), p. 11.

825 Cf. *Fornell/Larcker* (1981), p. 46; *Chin* (1998), p. 321.

826 Cf. exemplarily *Homburg/Giering* (1996), p. 8; *Götz/Liehr-Gobbers* (2004), p. 728.

827 For this and the following, cf. *Hulland* (1999), p. 198, and the summaries by *Götz/Liehr-Gobbers* (2004), p. 727, and *Engelen* (2007), p. 200.

828 In PLS research, it is argued that this value could be particularly hard to be achieved. It is thus argued that items which load with less than 0.4 or 0.5 onto a factor should be dropped (cf. *Hulland* (1999), p. 198.

829 The content validity involves a clear definition of each construct and its items. The discriminant validity assesses whether different constructs can be empirically distinguished (cf. *Homburg/Giering* (1996), p. 7, or *Stier* (1999), p. 57ff.). Authors stress the discriminant validity to be complementable by the

provided descriptions of the measures' operationalisations. The discriminant validity is tested through the **Fornell-Larcker criterion.** *Fornell/Larcker* (1981) argue that a reflectively measured construct can be assessed to be valid if the measure's AVE is greater than the squared correlation between the regarded construct and other constructs.[830] This criterion will be applied in this study to analyse discriminant validity among the different usage types as well as among the factors identified to describe user's attitudes towards cost information.

Table 5-24 summarises the information to be provided for the quality assessment of reflective constructs as well as their thresholds. Two statistical computer programs are used to perform these quality assessments. Cronbach's alpha and the adequacy of factor analysis are computed in *Stata12.* The remaining four confirmatory factor analysis related measures are computed in *AMOS.*

Adequacy of factor analysis		Reliability analysis				Validity analysis
KMO	No. of eigen-values > 1	Cronbach's alpha	Composite reliability	Standardised factor loadings	AVE	Fulfilment of the Fornell-Larcker criterion
≥ 0.5	< 2	≥ 0.7	≥ 0.6	≥ 0.7; or 0.4	≥ 0.5	Yes

Table 5-24: Quality criteria for reflective measurement models

In this study, reflective measurement models are especially present during the analysis of different types of cost information use. Due to their reliance on structural equation modelling, previous studies on the use of cost information from Germany aggregated reflectively measured constructs based on factor analysis into 'factor scores'.[831] International research on this matter, however, tends to rely on composite (i.e. mean) scores.[832] In these studies, confirmatory factor analysis is applied for reliability and validity checks only. The latter procedure is followed in this study.

The analysis of **formative measurement models** is rarely discussed internationally, especially with respect to management accounting. Prominently, *Diamantopoulos/Winkelhofer* (2001) stressed the content validity of such constructs and their items to be of virtual importance for quality assessment.[833] Detailed descriptions of each construct under research can be found in this study's fundamentals (section 2) and the section on the applied operationalisations (section 5.2). Hence, the content validity of these measures is reasonably addressed. Some researchers argue that quantitative or formal assessments of formative measurement models' validity and reliability are rather inexistent.[834] However, there are some suggestions for applicable procedures. Because formative measurement models tend to be aggregated in structural equation models (such as PLS) based on linear regressions, it is suggested to analyse a potential measurement error (i.e. reliability) based on measures of

convergent validity (cf. *Stier* (1999), p. 57), which can be measured by Cronbach's alpha and a factor's composite reliability (cf. *Hulland* (1999), p. 199).

830 Cf. *Fornell/Larcker* (1981), p. 46.

831 Examples include *Frank/Reitmeyer* (1999); *Aust* (1999); *Karlshaus* (2000), or *Frank* (2000).

832 Cf. *Abernethy/Brownell* (1999), p. 196; *Widener* (2007), p. 769; *Henri* (2006a), p. 90; *Bisbe/Malagueño* (2009), p. 383.

833 Cf. *Diamantopoulos/Winklhofer* (2001), p. 271.

834 Cf. *Homburg/Klarmann* (2006), p. 731f.; *Albers/Hildebrandt* (2006), p. 13.

multicollinearity.[835] Similarly, it is argued that the validity of individual items in formative constructs can be measured based on the "strength of the path from the indicator to the composite latent construct"[836] in a (multiple indicators multiple causes) structural equation model.[837] Additionally, it is suggested that the items of a formative model could be correlated with an additional variable summarising "the essence of the constructs".[838] Finally, it is reasoned that the nomological validity, i.e. the prevalence of theoretically derived interrelations with other constructs,[839] can be analysed.[840]

It remains unclear whether these suggestions apply equally for **formatively defined measures**, which are dominantly applied in this study. The defined character of these variables suspends any measurement error.[841] Therefore, a numerical assessment of their reliability appears disputably impractical. Validity assessments, however, appear achievable. The measures' content validity is established through the definition and operationalisation of these measures in the previous chapters. The nomological validity of the respectively measured constructs can be assessed during the due explicative analysis. In this sense, an inability to '*accept*' hypotheses 1 to 5 could be due to rather poor construct validity. The analysis of individual items' multicollinearity is perceived to be of little validity assessing character in this study because formatively defined constructs are not aggregated based on regression analysis. For a similar reason, validity is not being assessed based on the *paths* in a structural equation model. The unavailability of alternative variables for each formatively measured construct prevents such a validity assessment.[842] Remarkably, the focus on the content and the nomological validity is well in line with the only previous cost accounting study which considers issues of different measurement models thoroughly despite not applying structural equation modelling.[843]

Having clarified these considerations on the constructs' reliability and validity, the statistical methods applied in this study can be introduced.

5.4.2 Descriptive analyses

Descriptive analyses are applied to characterise the available data of all participants by a limited number of parameters.[844] To describe the data's **central tendency**, the arithmetic mean or the more robust median are computed. To analyse the **dispersion** of the data, the standard deviation is regarded. Such analyses allow for a description of a single variable (e.g. the number of cost types in domestic German subsidiaries). These parameters can

835 Cf. *Diamantopoulos/Winklhofer* (2001), p. 272; *Götz/Liehr-Gobbers* (2004), p. 729.
836 Cf. *MacKenzie et al.* (2005), p. 727.
837 For these arguments, cf. *Diamantopoulos/Winklhofer* (2001), p. 272f.; *Diamantopoulos/Riefler* (2008), p. 1189.
838 *Diamantopoulos/Winklhofer* (2001), p. 272. For an application in marketing research, cf. *Homburg et al.* (2008), p. 141.
839 Cf. *Homburg/Giering* (1996), p. 7.
840 Cf. *Diamantopoulos/Winklhofer* (2001), p. 273.
841 Cf. *Diamantopoulos/Riefler* (2008), p. 1188.
842 Future cost accounting research may wish to consider according variables more thoroughly.
843 Cf. *Schoute* (2009), p. 213ff.
844 For this and the following, cf. *Auer/Rottmann* (2012), p. 34f and 49f.; *Schira* (2012), p. 43f and 53f.

be applied to summarise the complexity, use and performance of cost accounting systems as well as the explanatory factors and control variables. They, however, cannot be used for hypotheses testing per se. Hypotheses 1 and 2 expect the presence or absence of differences in the complexity and use of cost accounting systems in Anglophone and domestic German subsidiaries. It essentially strives for a comparison of the central tendencies in these two populations. Measures of the central tendency and dispersion of the data, however, can only be used to compare, e.g. the number of cost types in the two samples. To analyse whether such a comparison is likely to prevail in the researched population of subsidiaries, statistical inferences have to be applied.[845]

Statistical inferences will be applied in this study to test whether the differences and commonalities in the complexity and use of cost accounting in the sample of Anglophone and domestic German subsidiaries is likely to prevail for the underlying populations.[846] For this matter, different tests are available.

Parametric tests examine hypotheses based on parameters of central tendency or dispersion by (non)-falsifying an alternative hypothesis.[847] These tests (e.g. unpaired and paired t-tests or ANOVA) generally require the analysed variable to be normally distributed in the population.[848] It is argued that for a sample size >30, the normal distribution of a variable can be assumed to hold due to the central limit theorem.[849] Moreover, if two independent groups are compared, these tests generally require the populations to have homogeneous variances with respect to the analysed variable (homoscedasticity).[850] Besides, parametric tests are available for metrically scaled constructs only.[851] To compare metric homoscedastic figures of Anglophone and domestic German subsidiaries, this study applies parametric unpaired[852] t-tests. If a Levene test[853] detects heteroscedasticity, the t-tests will

845 Cf. *Auer/Rottmann* (2012), p. 307.

846 These tests will be relevant during the explicative analysis as well.

847 Cf. *Auer/Rottmann* (2012), p. 352.

848 Cf. *Bortz/Schuster* (2010), p. 122; *Leonhart* (2013), p. 203.

849 Cf. *Genschel/Becker* (2005), p. 223; *Bortz/Schuster* (2010), p. 86f. and 114; *Auer/Rottmann* (2012), p. 364 and 372.

850 Cf. *Bender et al.* (2007), p. e25; *Leonhart* (2013), p. 211ff. This assumption does not necessarily need to be met since there are alternatives such as the Welch test to handle this issue (cf. e.g. *Skovlund/Fenstad* (2001), p. 92; *Bortz/Schuster* (2010), p. 122; *Auer/Rottmann* (2012), p. 372, or *Leonhart* (2013), p. 181f.).

851 Cf. *Bender et al.* (2007), p. e25; *Leonhart* (2013), p. 199.

852 The German sample companies are derived as a stratified random sample from a population of German companies by taking into account certain characteristics of the Anglophone population. Nevertheless, unpaired tests are performed here because it was unfeasible to match each responding Anglophone company perfectly to one of the German responses. Thus, it proved unfeasible to compute tests based on of differences in the signs or ranks of a variable of two matched companies.

853 For details on this test, which is rather robust in the times of non-normally distributed variables, cf. *Levene* (1960), p. 278ff. In addition to the Levene test, two variants of the test as proposed by *Brown/Forsythe* (1974), p. 364ff., are taken into account. Only if more than one of the three tests signals heteroscedasticity, the t-test is substituted by the Welch test.

be transformed into a respectively more robust parametric Welch test.[854] The normality of the tested variables will not be tested separately if the number of observations available for the test exceeds 30 observations. To test whether, e.g. the different usage types prevail to a different extent among the Anglophone or the domestic German companies, one-sample t-tests are applied.

Other than above, the measures of central tendency or dispersion are less relevant in **non-parametric tests**. Rather, these tests base their inference statistics on ranked variables or the direction with which a variable varies from a certain value.[855] Non-parametric tests do not rely on an assumption about the distribution of the tested variable in the population under consideration.[856] Furthermore, these tests do not require metrically scaled variables, but can be used for ordinal scales too.[857] For the comparison of (independent) groups, however, there are arguments that non-parametric tests depend on the assumption of homoscedasticity,[858] among others.[859] The non-parametric Wilcoxon Mann-Whitney U-Test[860] is applied for variables that are measured on ordinal scale.[861] It is replaced by the robust Fligner-Policello rank order test if a Levene test[862] detects heteroscedasticity.[863]

For both parametric and non-parametric tests, the symbols *, ** and *** are applied to indicate whether an alternative hypothesis can be falsified at a **significance level** of 10 % (marginally significant), 5 % (significant) and 1 % (highly significant).

In contrast to the propositions and expectations for the descriptive findings on the complexity of cost accounting systems and the use of cost information (hypotheses 1 and 2), hypotheses 3–5 conjecture on theoretical underlyings of the complexity, use and performance of cost accounting in subsidiaries. They are analysed through linear regression models. These are introduced in the next section.

---

854 This procedure is well in line with some authors, who explicitly debate the issue of heteroscedasticity during the choice parametric and non-parametric tests (cf. e.g. *Ruxton* (2006), p. 690). It also reflects suggestions to prefer parametric tests because of their greater power (cf. *Leonhart* (2013), p. 229).

855 Cf. *Genschel/Becker* (2005), p. 314.

856 Cf. *Leonhart* (2013), p. 229.

857 Cf. *Bender et al.* (2007), p. e24.

858 Cf. *Kasuya* (2001), p. 1247; *Skovlund/Fenstad* (2001), p. 86f.; *Bender et al.* (2007), p. e25. Note that some non-parametric tests such as the 'robust rank test' do not depend on this assumption (cf. *Kasuya* (2001), p. 1248, for details).

859 Cf. *Skovlund/Fenstad* (2001), p. 86f.; *Bortz et al.* (2008), p. 81, for the assumption that these tests also require the compared variables to have equally shaped distributions. As this threshold is somewhat hard to attain and is generally disregarded in research, it is neglected in this study.

860 This test is also labelled Wilcoxon rank sum test.

861 For nominally scaled variables, group comparisons of the Anglophone and the German sample are based on a Chi^2 distribution test, or, if less than five observations are present for each category, on the Fisher's exact test (cf. *Siegel/Castellan* (1988), p. 123, for this suggestion).

862 Cf. *Levene* (1960), p. 278ff., for details on this test, which is rather robust in the times of non-normally distributed variables. In addition to the Levene test, two variants of the test as proposed by *Brown/Forsythe* (1974), p. 364ff., are taken into account. Only if more than one of the three tests signals heteroscedasticty, the U-test is substituted by the Fligner Policello test.

863 For a suggestion on the robust rank order test (also labelled Fligner-Policello test), cf. *Kasuya* (2001), p. 1248; *Siegel/Castellan* (1988), p. 137ff.

To assess the applicability of these explicative analyses, **bivariate correlations** between the independent and the dependent variable are investigated. Correlations measure the strength and the direction between any two constructs.[864] There are two alternatives to express the correlation between two variables.[865] *Pearson's* correlation coefficient reveals linear interdependencies. In comparison, *Spearman*'s rank correlation coefficient shows a monotonic interdependency only. Both coefficients vary between minus one (negative association) and one (positive interdependency). The higher the absolute value of the coefficients, the stronger is the correlation. In addition, interference statistics can assess whether a correlation coefficient is statistically significant. Since the correlation analysis prepares the application of linear regression models, the coefficients by *Pearson* will be applied in this study. However, references will be made to the coefficients by *Spearman* if these revealed different results for the non-metric measures (e.g. the dummy variable on university education).

5.4.3 Explicative analyses

5.4.3.1 Multivariate regression analysis

This study employs multivariate linear regression analysis (hereafter also OLS regression) to test the set of hypotheses 3 to 5.[866] This analysis regards causal-relationships between a dependent (e.g. the complexity of cost accounting systems) and a number of independent (i.e. the theoretically derived) variables.[867] Thereby, the association between the independent variables and the dependent one is expressed through regression coefficients which reflect expectable marginal changes in the dependent variable if the independent variable increases by one unit.[868] Because no hypothesis regards the differing magnitudes of, for instance, institutional and economic factors, **non-standardised regression coefficients** are applied.

The analysis requires both dependent and independent variables to be metrically scaled.[869] It is flexible enough, however, to allow for binary coded non-metric independent variables (dummy-variables), as well. In the case of a nominal independent variable, logistic regressions are available. These will be discussed thoroughly in section 5.4.3.2. In addition to this scale-based service condition, the applicability and the interpretability of the multivar-

---

864 Cf. *Hair* (2010), p. 156; *Auer/Rottmann* (2012), p. 92ff.

865 For this and the following, cf. *Auer/Rottmann* (2012), p. 92ff.; *Schira* (2012), p. 96ff.

866 Given that all these sets have single independent variables (complexity of cost accounting, types of cost information use or the performance of cost accounting), this analysis is justified (cf. *Backhaus et al.* (2011), p. 14f and 18). Moreover, the mere number of formatively defined variables places additional emphasis on the choice of this technique as compared to, for example, structural equation models (cf. *Albers/Hildebrandt* (2006), p. 25).

867 Cf. *Backhaus et al.* (2011), p. 14.

868 For this and the following, cf. *Backhaus et al.* (2011), p. 70.

869 For this and the following, cf. *Backhaus et al.* (2011), p. 14f. For a detailed discussion on the interpretation of this study's measure of cost accounting complexity as a metrically scaled construct, see footnote 702.

iate linear regression technique depend on a number of additional conditions.[870] Due to the central limit theorem and sample sizes (see section 5.3.3), it can be assumed that the error terms are asymptotically normal.[871] As such, the analysis of the significance levels of the regressions estimator based on t-tests is arguably unbiased.[872] Furthermore, this study focuses on an analysis of potential issues stemming from **heteroscedasticity, autocorrelation** and **multicollinearity** to account for potential imprecision and inefficiency of the estimator of the linear regression model.[873] Moreover, the existence of **endogeneity** (e.g. reversed causalities) can hinder the ability to derive meaningful results through OLS regressions.[874] A discussion of this study's potential exposure to endogeneity can be found throughout section 6 and section 7.3.

Non-constant variances (heteroscedasticity) and correlation of the error term (autocorrelation) make ordinary least square estimators imprecise.[875] To account for potential heteroscedasticity and a potential autocorrelation stemming from the fact that some subsidiaries from the same parent company are analysed, this study applies **adjusted sandwich estimators.**[876] These estimators are consistent at the presence of heteroscedasticity and especially account for effects stemming from similarities among subsidiaries of the same parent (autocorrelation).[877] Multicollinearity describes the issue that independent variables are linear functions of one-another. High levels of multicollinearity bias the estimations of linear regressions due to redundant information.[878] To account for multicollinearity, the regression analysis is validated by variance inflation factors (VIF).[879] A VIF of one indicates that there is no multicollinearity between a considered variable and all other independent variables in the multivariate regression model.[880] As a threshold for a harmful level of multicollinearity, it is often reasoned that no variables' VIF should be greater than ten.[881]

One particular issue in the light of multicollinearity is the analysis of **moderating effects**, which are important for this study to test hypotheses 3c and 4c. These regard the effect of the relational context on the interrelation between coercive institutional influences and the design of cost accounting systems and the use of cost information. In multiple regression analyses, moderations are included as interaction terms between the moderated and

---

870 For details, cf. *Backhaus et al.* (2011), p. 85f.; *v. Auer* (2011), p. 145ff.

871 Cf. *Backhaus et al.* (2011), p. 96; *Auer/Rottmann* (2012), p. 476.

872 Cf. *Backhaus et al.* (2011), p. 97.

873 Cf. *Backhaus et al.* (2011), p. 92ff.; *v. Auer* (2011), p. 146ff.

874 Cf. *v. Auer* (2011), p. 149.

875 Cf. *Backhaus et al.* (2011), p. 97; *v. Auer* (2011), p. 391 and 427.

876 According to *Rogers* (1993), p. 19, these estimators can be traced back to *Huber* (1967), p. 221ff., and *White* (1980), p. 817ff. The ones provided by *Stata12* are rather in line with *Huber* (cf. *StataCorp* (2011), p. 296). For a discussion of these estimators in statistical textbooks, cf. e.g. *Wooldridge* (2007), p. 864ff., or *Gould et al.* (2010), p. 12.

877 Cf. *Wooldridge* (2007), p. 869; *Cameron/Trivedi* (2010), p. 85.

878 Cf. *Backhaus et al.* (2011), p. 93f.; *v. Auer* (2011), p. 148f and 520ff.

879 Cf. *Backhaus et al.* (2011), p. 95.

880 Cf. *Chatterjee/Hadi* (2012), p. 248ff.

881 Cf. *Diamantopoulos/Winklhofer* (2001), p. 272; *Hair* (2010), p. 204.

the moderating variable.[882] This introduces additional multicollinearity into a regression model.[883] To mitigate higher levels of multicollinearity, it is disputably recommended[884] to use mean-centred or standardised (i.e. z-scores) of the variables applied in the analysis of moderating effects.[885] More prevalently, such procedures are recommended to be able to interpret the regression coefficients of the moderated and the moderating variables.[886] If a moderating effect (i.e. an interaction term of two variables) is included into a regression analysis, the regression coefficients of the interacted variables represent conditional effects.[887] More precisely, they represent the effect which an independent variable has on the dependent variable, if the other variable in the moderation has a value of zero.[888] Centring or standardising the underlying non-categorical variables allows interpreting such zero-points as the variable's means.[889] The regression coefficient of the interaction term then represents the changes in the impact of the moderated variable on the dependent variable if the moderating variable was increased by one unit.[890] Moreover, if the actual values of regression coefficients, measured on different scales are to be compared[891] or if moderating effects are computed for two values of different non-categorical scales,[892] it is suggested to standardise the variables of the regression model (i.e. deduct the mean and divide by the standard deviation).[893] In such cases, however, the regression coefficients express what happens to the dependent variable if a dependent variable changes by one unit of standard deviation.[894] To identify a moderating effect, a stepwise procedure is recommended, i.e. a regression model containing the moderation must be compared with the same model net

882 Cf. *Aguinis* (2004), p. 12.

883 Cf. *Hair* (2010), p. 181.

884 For the argumentation that this striving does not change the precision of parameter derivation in a regression model, cf. *Echambadi/Hess* (2007), p. 443.

885 Cf. *Aguinis* (1995), p. 1149; *Hartmann/Moers* (1999), p. 302; *Frazier et al.* (2004), p. 120; *Robinson/Schumacker* (2009), p. 6f.

886 Cf. *Hartmann/Moers* (1999), p. 301; *Reis/Judd* (2000), p. 374; *Aguinis* (2004), p. 37 and 39; *Frazier et al.* (2004), p. 120; *Echambadi/Hess* (2007), p. 443; *Leonhart* (2013), p. 351ff.

887 For this and the following, cf. *Cohen* (2003), p. 260; *Aguinis* (2004), p. 36; *Frazier et al.* (2004), p. 121.

888 Note that the interpretability of these 'lower-order coefficients' of centralised variables is not universally agreed on. Some management accounting scholars (cf. *Hartmann/Moers* (1999), p. 301 and *Dunk* (2003), p. 797) question such interpretability.

889 Given that the variables included in the moderation analysis are especially measured on seven point rating scales which have a 'zero value' indicated by the scale level one, centring procedures are followed for the variables of the interaction. This is well in line with suggestions by *Cohen* (2003), p. 296. Note that *Cohen* (2003), p. 266 and 267, stresses that it is not necessary to centre the dependent and independent variables which are not included in the moderation.

890 Cf. *Dunk* (2003), p. 799f.; *Reis/Judd* (2000), p. 374.

891 Cf. *Aguinis* (2004), p. 38f.

892 Cf. *Leonhart* (2013), p. 351ff., along with *Frazier et al.* (2004), p. 120.

893 Cf. *Friedrich* (1982), p. 824 or *Cohen* (2003), p. 282ff., for a suggested procedure. The authors express that their procedure is preferable over the use of standardised regression coefficients.

894 Cf. *Frazier et al.* (2004), p. 120; *Aguinis* (2004), p. 39. This latter procedure, however, will not be considered because no comparison of the strength, with which the various independent variables affect the dependent variable is intended.

off the moderation.[895] The comparison of the two models will be performed based on an F-test.[896]

Despite analysing moderating effects, a potential **mediating effect** of the use of cost information was introduced during the hypotheses development. Following hypothesis H5a_4, the way managers' make use of cost information is potentially a better proxy to express the effect of a cost accounting systems' design on the systems' performance. To analyse mediating effects in regression models, *Baron/Kenny* suggest a three-stage procedure.[897] First, a linear regression must show that the mediator (use of cost information) is significantly influenced by the mediated variable (complexity of cost accounting systems). Second, a significant influence of the mediated variable on the independent variable (performance) is to be tested through a linear regression. Third, it must be tested whether a statistically significant effect of a mediated variable is weakened or disappears if the independent variable is regressed on both the mediator and the mediated variable.

As a final remark it is necessary to stress that the **fit of the regression models** (i.e. its explanatory power) will be assessed based on the adjusted R^2 and the (significance of the) F-statistic. The adjusted R^2 expresses how much of the variation of a dependent variable can be explained by the independent variables, while, in contrast to R^2, accounting for the number of independent variables.[898] The F-statistic encompasses the analysis that all derived regression coefficients are actually different from zero in the underlying population.[899]

5.4.3.2 Logistic regression analysis

The multivariate regression analysis applied to test the set of hypotheses H3 cannot explain the origin of a *potential difference* in the design of cost accounting systems in Anglophone and domestic subsidiaries in Germany. In order to find preliminary evidence on factors that make the presence or absence of a cross-national difference in subsidiaries of Anglophone MNCs more likely, a logistic regression will be applied.[900] This regression technique takes a **binary variable,** which mirrors whether there is a cost accounting system in the Anglophone subsidiaries that is less complex than in domestic German subsidiaries, as its dependent variable. It sustains the independent variables from the OLS regression.

The results of a logistic regression can be presented in a twofold manner.[901] On the one hand, **odds ratios** can be determined. They represent the factor by which the probability of finding a cross-national difference changes if an independent variable increases by one measurement unit. An odds ratio which is greater (smaller) than one reflects the factor by

[895] Cf. *Aguinis* (2004), p. 10ff.; *Hair* (2010), p. 181.
[896] For this suggestion, cf. *Aguinis* (2004), p. 14f.
[897] For this and the following, cf. *Baron/Kenny* (1986), p. 1177. According to *Voets* (2013), p. 137, the suggestions by *Baron/Kenny* are commonly applied for mediation analyses.
[898] Cf. *Backhaus et al.* (2011), p. 74ff.
[899] Cf. *Backhaus et al.* (2011), p. 76ff.
[900] For this regression technique, cf. *Cohen* (2003), p. 482ff.; *Backhaus et al.* (2011), p. 250ff.
[901] For this and the following, cf. *Cohen* (2003), p. 492ff.; *Backhaus et al.* (2011), p. 265f.

which an increase in the analysed independent variable increases (decreases) the likelihood of the existence/absence of a cross-national difference. An odds ratio of one indicates the absence of any association. On the other hand, the direction of impact is expressible in terms of *logits*. These would express the direction of the relationship between an independent variable and the existence/absence of the cross-national difference. A positive logit value means that there is a positive association, whereas a negative logit value indicates a negative association. This study applies the odds ratios only. Similar to the t-tests applied for the linear multivariate regression, the analysis whether the derived regression coefficients (here odds ratios) prevail for the population (statistical significance) is assessed by a Wald statistic.[902]

The logistic regression analysis will also include a discussion of the interaction between coercive institutional influences and the relational context. As in an OLS regression, moderations can be included in logistic regressions by including **interaction terms** between the moderator (relational context) and the moderated variable (coercive institutional influences).[903] In a logistic regression model, however, this effect is interpreted differently than in an OLS regression. According to *Jaccard* (2001), the odds ratio of the interaction effect "is the multiplicative factor by which the multiplicative factor of X [i.e. the moderated factor] changes given a 1-unit increase in Z [i.e. the moderating factor]."[904] Hence, an interaction effect with an odds ratio greater than one indicates that the moderator increases the conditional probability of the moderated variable[905], whereas an odds ratio smaller than one decreases the conditional effect of the moderated variable. The interaction can be argued to be statistically significant if the logistic coefficient/the odds ratio is statistically significant.[906] As for the linear multivariate regression, the prevalence of the interaction has to be evaluated. Rather than using the F-test, however, this has to be done on the grounds of a Wald test for a logistic regression.[907] Thereby, the interaction between the relational context and the three coercive institutional influences is tested *as a chunk*, i.e. it is tested whether any of the three interactions is different from zero.[908]

Similar to the ordinary OLS regressions, the overall **fit of the logistic regression** model has to be evaluated. For logistic regression, there are measures which provide similar information as the adjusted R^2 in OLS regressions. In this study, a measure expressing the number of correctly classified cases (count R^2) is incorporated.[909] In addition, McFaddens's pseudo R^2 is determined.[910] The overall fit of the model, which is assessed by the F

[902] For details, cf. *Backhaus et al.* (2011), p. 280.
[903] Cf. *Jaccard* (2001), p. 17.
[904] *Jaccard* (2001), p. 44.
[905] As in OLS regressions, the odds ratio of the moderated variable reflects a conditional effect of the variable if the moderator has a value of zero (cf. *Jaccard* (2001), p. 42f.).
[906] Cf. *Jaccard* (2001), p. 16.
[907] For details, cf. *Cohen* (2003), p. 507f. The Likelihood ratio test appears difficult to apply due to the robust cluster estimates.
[908] Cf. *Jaccard* (2001), p. 63f.
[909] For details, cf. *Backhaus et al.* (2011), p. 271ff.
[910] For details, cf. *Backhaus et al.* (2011), p. 270. This measure is related to the likelihood ratio test. As this test is arguably difficult to implement in this study, the conclusiveness of McFaddens's pseudo R^2 might be reduced in this study.

statistic in the ordinary OLS regression, is analysed for this study's logistic regressions by the Wald tests.[911] The alternative or complementary application of the likelihood ratio test is inhibited in this study by the necessity to use robust cluster estimators to account for the existence of subsidiaries with a common parent company.[912]

Structure of the following chapter

Having clarified this study's statistical methods, it can be turned to the empirical results on the complexity of cost accounting systems and the use of cost information. By analysing the returned questionnaires, the following chapter provides answers to this study's research questions. Thereby, the chapter proceeds as follows

First, section 6.1.1 reports the descriptive findings for the complexity of cost accounting systems in Anglophone and domestic German subsidiaries. Thereby, an answer to research questions (1a) is provided by testing hypothesis 1. Thereafter, section 6.1.2 tests the hypotheses on theoretical determinants of cost accounting systems in Anglophone and domestic German subsidiaries (explicative analysis). It includes a discussion of research question (2a).

Subsequently, section 6.2.1 investigates how the sample companies' managers apply cost information. Thereby, an answer to research questions (1b) is discussed by testing hypothesis 2. These descriptions are succeeded by an investigation of research question (2b) and the associated hypotheses tests to explicate the determinants of the six usage types covered in this study.

Finally, the chapter investigates whether the complexity of cost accounting systems and the use of cost information can lever the performance of cost accounting systems. To do so, section 6.3.1 presents the descriptive findings on the performance of cost accounting systems. Thereafter section 6.3.2 tests the propositions on the performance effects of the complexity (section 6.3.2.1) and use (section 6.3.2.2) of subsidiaries' cost accounting systems. Also, it is tested whether the performance of a cost accounting system depends on its adaptation to an organisation's economic and institutional context (section 6.3.2.3). Conjointly, these analyses provide answers to research questions (3a) and (3b).

[911] For details, cf. *Cohen* (2003), p. 507f.

[912] Cf. *Hosmer/Lemeshow* (2000), p. 212f. and 221; *Magnussen/Köhl* (2006), p. 124.

6 Empirical results

6.1 Complexity of cost accounting systems

6.1.1 Descriptive evidence

6.1.1.1 Cost type accounting

6.1.1.1.1 Number of cost types

In question B.2 of questionnaire A, respondents were asked for the **number of primary cost types** which they distinguish in their cost accounting systems. The number of cost types ranges from 4 to 1,000 in the Anglophone subsidiaries and from 10 to 2,000 in the domestic German sample (datasets 1 and 2). On average, there are significantly less primary cost types in the Anglophone subsidiaries (176) than in the domestic German ones (235). As revealed in Table 6-1, this finding holds similarly true for datasets 1 and 2. The associated complexity sub-score takes the maximum number of cost types (2,000) into account. It shows that this characteristic is significantly more complex in the domestic German companies.

	How many primary cost types does your company have?			
	dataset 1		dataset 2	
	Anglophone	German	Anglophone	German
min. (max.)	4 (1,000)	10 (2,000)	4 (1,000)	10 (2,000)
Mean (median)	176 (100)	235 (150)	174 (100)	220 (138)
p-value (test)	0.08 (two-tailed t-test)		0.14 (two-tailed t-test)	
Complexity sub-score	**0.60**	**0.66**	**0.60**	**0.65**
p-value (test)	0.00 (two-tailed Welch test)		0.01 (two-tailed Welch test)	

Table 6-1: Number of primary cost types

Despite only analysing subsidiaries operating in Germany, this finding reflects the differences between German and Anglophone cost accounting traditions identified in section 2.[913] Moreover, the findings for the German companies are in line with a previous investigation, which finds between 227 and 294 cost types in German manufacturing companies of similar size.[914] Regrettably, it cannot be evaluated whether the Anglophone subsidiaries are more comparable with Anglophone or German traditions. There is no previous research on the exact number of cost types in Anglophone subsidiaries.

913 Cf. section 2.2.2, p. 12.

914 Cf. *Moeschler* (2012), p. 245. Other studies on this issue find an average of 112 cost types in rather small German firms of 50-1,000 employees (cf. *Frank/Reitmeyer* (1999), p. 22) and an average of 786 cost types in a sample of the 250 largest German companies (cf. *Friedl et al.* (2009), p. 112). Finding figures which lie in between these latter two for a sample of small to medium sized companies emphasises the plausibility of this finding.

6.1.1.1.2 Recognition of imputed costs

In question B.3 of questionnaire A, respondents revealed to what extent imputed costs are recognised in their cost accounting systems. The results show that a large proportion of the Anglophone subsidiaries does not consider imputed costs at all (40.9 % and 51.8 %). In contrast, **imputed depreciation** (74.2 %) and **imputed interest** (71.9 %) are applied in the majority of the domestic German companies, especially as part of regular cost accounting (Table 6-2). A Chi^2 test identifies these differences as statistically significant. The transformation of these findings into a complexity sub-score retains the significant difference. No deviation can be found between dataset 1 and 2.

	To what extent do you apply the following imputed costs?			
	dataset 1		dataset 2	
	Anglophone	German	Anglophone	German
Imputed depreciation				
Not at all	40.9 %	25.8 %	40.2 %	24.0 %
In separate calculations only	35.5 %	23.6 %	34.8 %	26.0 %
As part of regular cost accounting	23.6 %	50.6 %	25.0 %	50.0 %
p-value (test)	0.00 (Chi^2 distribution test)		0.00 (Chi^2 distribution test)	
Imputed interest				
Not at all	51.8 %	28.1 %	51.8 %	27.9 %
In separate calculations only	31.8 %	27.0 %	32.1 %	27.9 %
As part of regular cost accounting	16.4 %	44.9 %	16.1 %	44.3 %
p-value (test)	0.00 (Chi^2 distribution test)		0.00 (Chi^2 distribution test)	
Complexity sub-score	**0.37**	**0.60**	**0.37**	**0.61**
p-value (test)	0.00 (two-tailed t-test)		0.00 (two-tailed t-test)	

Table 6-2: Recognition of imputed costs

As for the number of cost types, this finding reflects the differences of Anglophone and German cost accounting traditions quite well.[915] The tendency to neglect imputed costs in the Anglophone subsidiaries rather deviates from the common German practice. As such, there is additional evidence for the prevalence of Anglophone cost type accounting traditions in the Anglophone subsidiaries. Similarly, the findings for the domestic German sample mirror previous evidence from the mechanical engineering and food and beverage industries.[916]

6.1.1.1.3 Separation of financial and management accounting

In question B.1 of questionnaire A, respondents clarified whether they have two separated datasets for financial and management accounting. Both Anglophone (65.5 %) and domestic German (55.1 %) subsidiaries tend to apply only **one dataset for financial and management accounting** (Table 6-3). Though there are more domestic German companies with two sets of accounts, a Chi^2 test reveals that the differences in the distribution are insignificant. These results are stable for both dataset 1 and 2.

---

915 For this and the following, cf. 2.2.2, p. 12.

916 Cf. *Moeschler* (2012), p. 248.

	Does your company have two separated datasets for financial reporting and for cost accounting (so-called two-book system or dual accounting system)?			
	dataset 1		dataset 2	
	Anglophone	German	Anglophone	German
Yes	34.6 %	44.9 %	35.7 %	43.3 %
No	65.5 %	55.1 %	64.39 %	56.7 %
p-value (test)	0.14 (Chi2 distribution test)		0.26 (Chi2 distribution test)	

Table 6-3: Availability of alternative datasets for financial and management accounting

For the Anglophone subsidiaries, this finding reflects the reliance on the general ledger concept known from Anglophone companies (section 2).[917] In contrast to the prevailing opinion, however, many domestic German companies also use one set of accounts for financial and management accounting.

There are two potential explanations for this result. On the one hand, the finding mirrors recent evidence that German companies tend to strive for an alignment of financial and management accounting information.[918] On the other hand, applying the same dataset for both financial and management accounting does not necessarily imply that the same information is used for these two business functions. Multiple domestic German companies report to apply imputed costs on a regularly basis. These, however, are excluded from financial accounting, by law. Having only one dataset might thus merely reflect the applied information technology. Spreadsheets (present in 37 % of the domestic German companies in dataset 1 that report a single dataset)[919] could be used to adjust financial accounting information to derive cost information. ERP systems (present in 63 % of the domestic German companies in dataset 1 that report a single dataset) might be powerful enough to include both financial and management accounting information in one dataset only but analyse them separately.

Additionally, the respondents who apply two datasets were asked for the extent, to which they **alter their financial accounting information to derive the dataset for management accounting.** To this question, both the Anglophone and the domestic German subsidiaries tend to provide mean ratings (Table 6-4). In line with the above argument, this finding also deviates from the common findings on cost accounting traditions of German and Anglophone companies. Despite difficulties with respect to the understandability of the question, this similarity might reflect the large proportion of brownfield investments (86 %) among the 37 Anglophone subsidiaries which have two separated datasets.

	To what extent is the financial reporting information adjusted to derive the dataset for cost accounting? (Scale: 1 = no adjustments are being made, 7 = multiple adjustments are being made)			
	dataset 1		dataset 2	
	Anglophone (n = 37)	German (n = 40)	Anglophone (n = 39)	German (n = 45)
mean (median)	3.9 (4)	3.7 (4)	3.82 (4)	3.58 (4)
p-value (test)	0.44 (two-tailed t-test)		0.56 (two-tailed t-test)	

Table 6-4: Structural differences in the datasets for financial and management accounting

[917] For this and the following, cf. section 2.2.2, p.12.

[918] Cf. *Jones/Luther* (2005), p. 188f.; *Friedl et al.* (2009), p. 114; *Heimel et al.* (2012), p. 59.

[919] Section 6.1.2.1.1.1 presents the empirical evidence for subsidiaries' information technologies.

Aggregating these two outcomes into the **complexity sub-score** sustains the identified similarities for the Anglophone and the domestic German subsidiaries for dataset 2 (Table 6-5). In dataset 1, however, there is statistical evidence that domestic German companies are slightly more complex at a 10 % level.[920] This is due to the larger difference in the proportions of Anglophone and domestic German subsidiaries with separated accounts in dataset 1 (Table 6-4). As such, this finding is especially linked to the fact that 10 of the 15 domestic subsidiaries that differentiate datasets 1 and 2 do not have different databases for financial and management accounting. Potentially, this must be seen as indication that the application of different databases is less associated to the subsidiaries' origin but more reflective of, e.g. the subsidiaries' cost accounting objectives. In line with this argument, the 15 excluded companies apply cost accounting less extensively than the remaining domestic companies from dataset 1.[921] Because the number of cost types and the recognition of imputed costs reveal that the Anglophone companies do indeed have less complex cost type accounting procedures, however, this difference between dataset 1 and 2 does not overstress this section's results too extensively.

	dataset 1		dataset 2	
	Anglophone	German	Anglophone	German
Complexity sub-score	**0.24**	**0.30**	**0.24**	**0.29**
p-value (test)	0.17 (two-tailed t-test)		0.35 (two-tailed t-test)	

Table 6-5: Complexity sub-score for the separation of financial and management accounting

6.1.1.1.4 Complexity of cost type accounting

Aggregating these three complexity sub-scores into a single measure for the complexity of cost type accounting leads to the following results.

	dataset 1		dataset 2	
	Anglophone	German	Anglophone	German
Complexity score	**0.40**	**0.52**	**0.40**	**0.51**
p-value (test)	0.00 (two-tailed t-test)		0.00 (two-tailed t-test)	

Table 6-6: Complexity of cost type accounting

Table 6-6 highlights that cost type accounting in Anglophone subsidiaries (0.40) is significantly less complex than cost type accounting in domestic German companies (0.52). There are only minor differences between dataset 1 and 2 in this regard. As such, there is substantial evidence to support hypothesis 1 with respect to cost type accounting. Domestic German companies have more complex cost type accounting systems than Anglophone subsidiaries.

---

920 This can be seen by bisecting the reported two-tailed test results.

921 Overall, cost information appears less relevant for these 15 companies since the extent of use in these companies is considerably lower (mean = 4.30) than in dataset 1 (4.63).

6.1.1.2 Cost centre accounting

6.1.1.2.1 Number of cost centres

Question B.6 of questionnaire A referred to the **number cost centres**. In line with previous research,[922] the domestic German subsidiaries have significantly more cost centres (152)[923] than the Anglophone subsidiaries (117) (Table 6-7).[924] In contrast to a previous comparison of Germany and the US which identifies considerably more cost centres in German manufacturing companies (175) than in US firms (17),[925] the difference is smaller in this study. This hints at the presence of Anglophone and German traditions in the Anglophone subsidiaries in this regard.

	Please indicate the following for your company: number of cost centres.			
	dataset 1		dataset 2	
	Anglophone	German	Anglophone	German
min. (max.)	9 (900)	31 (1,200)	9 (900)	30 (1,200)
Mean (median)	117 (90)	152 (98)	120 (90)	145 (100)
p-value (test)	0.08 (two-tailed t-test)		0.17 (two-tailed t-test)	

Table 6-7: Number of cost centres

During the discussion of the differences in Anglophone and German cost accounting, it was suggested that such a variation could be due to the higher number of support cost centres in Germany.[926] This study's findings can underpin this suggestion. Whereas the number of **primary cost centres** differs insignificantly between the domestic and the Anglophone subsidiaries (Table 6-8), the number of **support cost centres** is significantly larger in the domestic German companies in both datasets (Table 6-9).[927] This result clarifies that the higher number of cost centres in domestic German companies can actually be attributed to the number of support cost centres.

	Number of primary cost centres			
	dataset 1		dataset 2	
	Anglophone	German	Anglophone	German
min. (max.)	1 (900)	1.2 (720)	1 (900)	1.2 (720)
Mean (median)	62 (30)	76 (43)	61 (30)	72 (46)
p-value (test)	0.37 (two-tailed t-test)		0.40 (two-tailed t-test)	

Table 6-8: Number of primary cost centres

---

922 Cf. section 2.2.3, p. 14f.

923 In a comparable study, *Moeschler* (2012), p. 250, finds on average 129 cost centres in mechanical engineering and 267 cost centres in food and beverage firms. In a cross-sectional study of rather small firms (50 – 1.000 employees), *Frank/Reitmeyer* (1999), p. 22, find an average of 85 cost centres. In their study of the 250 largest German firms, *Friedl et al.* (2009), p. 112, find an average of more than 4,000 cost centres. The differences could be due to sample-induced differences and size related effects.

924 For dataset 2, a one-tailed t-test reveals domestic German subsidiaries to have significantly *more* cost centres at a 10 % significance level.

925 Cf. *Krumwiede/Suessmair* (2007a), p. 6.

926 Cf. 2.2.3, p. 14f.

927 This can be seen by bisecting the reported two-tailed test results.

	Number of support cost centres			
	dataset 1		dataset 2	
	Anglophone	German	Anglophone	German
min. (max.)	0 (353)	0 (532)	0 (439)	0 (532)
Mean (median)	55 (40)	76 (50)	58 (40)	72 (48)
p-value (test)	0.04 (two-tailed t-test)		0.17 (two-tailed t-test)	

Table 6-9: Number of support cost centres

Moreover, these findings can clarify the discussion from section 2 on the existence of support cost centres in Anglophone firms.[928] For their German subsidiaries, the low number of support cost centres in Anglophone firms can be associated with a reduced 'importance' attributed to the establishment of support cost centres. This interpretation anchors on the finding that 95 % of the Anglophone firms have support cost centres, but only a minority (35 %) distinguishes them literally from primary cost centres. In contrast, this literal discrimination is found for a majority of the domestic German firms (57 %). These statistically significant differences in distribution mirror the cross-national difference with respect to the focus on support cost centres (Table 6-10).

	Does your company namely distinguish between primary and support cost centres?			
	dataset 1		dataset 2	
	Anglophone	German	Anglophone	German
Yes	34.6 %	57.3 %	33.9 %	56.7 %
No	65.4 %	42.7 %	66.1 %	43.3 %
p-value (test)	0.00 (Chi² distribution test)		0.00 (Chi² distribution test)	

Table 6-10: Literal separation of primary and support cost centres

Aggregating these findings into the **complexity sub-score** maintains the previously identified differences for the Anglophone and the domestic German subsidiaries. The domestic German subsidiaries are significantly more complex in this respect than the Anglophone subsidiaries (Table 6-11). There are no differences for datasets 1 and 2.

	dataset 1		**dataset 2**	
	Anglophone	German	Anglophone	German
Complexity sub-score	**0.47**	**0.58**	**0.47**	**0.58**
p-value (test)	0.00 (two-tailed Welch test)		0.00 (two-tailed Welch test)	

Table 6-11: Complexity sub-score for the number of cost centres

6.1.1.2.2 Rationales for cost centre formation

Linked to the high number of cost centres in Germany, German academic literature provides detailed suggestions how and when to form a cost centre. The prevalence of according rationales was investigated by question B.5 of questionnaire A. All rationales for cost centre formation are equally present in the Anglophone and the domestic German subsidiaries (Table 6-12). This finding holds true for both datasets.

For the Anglophone subsidiaries, the extensive presence of multiple rationales for cost centre formation (complexity sub-score = 0.75) is surprising. From the discussion in sec-

928 For this and the following, cf. section 2.2.3, p. 14.

tion 2, a rather simple reliance on the various rationales for cost centre formation would have been expected.[929] Yet, the findings should not be seen to oppose Anglophone cost accounting traditions. Anglophone companies are known to form cost centres more extensively for **responsibility accounting purposes** (items (1)-(3) from Table 6-12) than for **overhead cost allocation** ((4)-(6)). In line, each of the elements ((1)-(3)) scores significantly higher on the applied scale than each of the items ((4)-(6)).[930] Above all, the formation of cost centres in line with all six items from Table 6-12 suggests that there are both German and Anglophone cost accounting traditions present in the Anglophone subsidiaries.

	To what extent are cost centres within your company formed to... (Scale: 1 = not at all, 7 = completely)			
	dataset 1		dataset 2	
	Anglophone	German	Anglophone	German
(1) define areas of responsibility?	6.11	6.19	6.13	6.09
(2) identify localities of cost incurrence?	6.25	6.29	6.27	6.31
(3) plan and control costs?	6.13	6.17	6.13	6.06
(4) aggregate homogeneous overhead costs?	4.58	4.33	4.61	4.36
(5) assign overhead costs to the company's products?	4.88	5.20	4.92	5.24
(6) establish causal relations between cost incurrence and the company's products?	4.88	4.59	4.92	4.62
p-value (test)	For all individual rationales, the comparisons of the Angl. and Ger. subsidiaries are statistically insignificant (two-tailed parametric tests).			
Complexity sub-score	**0.75**	**0.75**	**0.75**	**0.75**
p-value (test)	0.94 (two-tailed t-test)		0.78 (two-tailed t-test)	

Table 6-12: Rationales for cost centre formation

For the domestic German subsidiaries, the high complexity with respect to the applied formation rules (complexity sub-score = 0.75) mirrors the high number of cost centres (Table 6-7). Nevertheless, the results in Table 6-12 provide a diverse picture regarding the presence of German cost accounting traditions. On the one hand, the items ((1)-(3)) are rated significantly higher than the items ((4)-(6)) in the domestic German subsidiaries as well. This apparently violates the discussion in section 2,[931] which suggests that cost centre formation in German firms is as reflective of responsibility accounting as it is concerned with a purposeful allocation of overhead costs. Because items (4) to (6) still score above the mid-point of the applied scale, however, the result does not oppose these German cost accounting traditions with respect to cost centre formation. Apparently, the aims of responsibility accounting and a refined overhead allocation are perceived by practitioners to have conflicting objectives. These findings might indicate a research-practice gap. The conceptual discussions on overhead allocation and cost centre design in German academia might not be fully reflected in German companies due to, for example, cost-benefit considerations.

---

929 For the following, cf. section 2.2.3, p. 13f.

930 Multiple one-sample t-tests were performed to compare the individual rationales for Anglophone subsidiaries in each dataset. Neither (1), (2) and (3) nor (4), (5) and (6) differ from one-another.

931 For the following, cf. section 2.2.3, p. 13f.

Peculiarly, the formation of cost centres for (5) the assignment of overhead costs differs significantly from (4) the formation for the aggregation of homogeneous costs and (6) for the establishment of causal relations during overhead cost allocation in the domestic German subsidiaries. Apparently, overhead allocation per se is more important for these companies than the refined allocation of indirect costs with a common cause according to the levels of evoked resource consumption. No such difference can be found for the former three rationales ((1)-(3)). In line with this outcome, sections 6.1.1.2.4 and 6.1.1.2.5 show first and second stage overhead allocation procedures to be rather simple in the regarded domestic German subsidiaries.

6.1.1.2.3 Categorisation of costs on cost centres

Question B.12 of questionnaire A surveyed a number of different cost categories according to which costs can be classified on cost centres. Table 6-13 summarises the results on this question. In terms of their **inventoriability** (i.e. period vs. product costs), costs are categorised on significantly more cost centres in the Anglophone subsidiaries (43.5 %) than in domestic German subsidiaries (35.7 %). In contrast, the distinction of **primary and secondary costs** is significantly more common in the domestic German subsidiaries (74.8 % vs. 67.0 %). Both results reflect the cost accounting tradition of German and Anglophone companies.[932]

	In how many primary cost centres are costs categorised with respect to the following characteristics?			
	dataset 1		dataset 2	
	Anglophone	German	Anglophone	German
(1) Costs' inventoriability	43.5 % *	35.7 %	43.0 %	36.0 %
(2) Costs' relatedness to manufacturing [i.e. (non-) manufacturing costs]	72.8 %	71.3 %	72.2 %	70.0 %
(3) Costs' original occurrence in the cost centre [i.e. primary and secondary costs]	67.0 %	74.8 % *	66.7 %	74.2 *
p-value (test)	For most characteristics, the comparisons of the Angl. and Ger. subsidiaries are statistically significant.[933] If significant, this is indicated by the significance levels *, ** or ***.			
Complexity sub-score	**0.64**	**0.64**	**0.64**	**0.63**
p-value (test)	0.90 (two-tailed Welch test)		0.85 (two-tailed Welch test)	

Table 6-13: Classifications of costs on cost centres

Remarkably, no difference prevails for the separation of **manufacturing and non-manufacturing costs**. The suggested cross-national difference on the allocation of manufacturing costs (Anglophone firms) and both manufacturing and non-manufacturing costs (German firms) to products[934] is not mirrored by a remarkable difference in the categorisation of costs on primary cost centres in Anglophone and domestic German subsidiar-

[932] Cf. section 2.2.3, p. 15, and section 2.2.4, p. 20f.

[933] One-tailed parametric tests are performed for items (1) and (3) because section 2 suggests that costs inventoriability is of greater importance in Anglophone companies, whereas primary and secondary costs are more common in German companies. For the distinction of manufacturing and non-manufacturing costs, the results do not vary significantly in both one-tailed and two-tailed tests.

[934] Cf. section 2.2.4, p. 23.

ies.[935] It remains open for exploration whether there is indeed a difference with respect to the relevance of manufacturing and non-manufacturing costs for management accounting purposes in Anglophone and German companies. In this study, no such difference can be found.[936]

The complexity sub-score for the classification of costs on primary cost centres varies insignificantly between Anglophone (0.64) and domestic German (0.64) subsidiaries. It does not reflect the identified cross-national differences due to their offsetting nature.[937]

6.1.1.2.4 First stage overhead allocation

Questions B.7, B.8 and B.9 of questionnaire A regarded the first stage overhead cost allocation procedures. The results show that there are significantly more domestic German than Anglophone subsidiaries that apply first stage overhead allocation procedures (79.8 % vs. 69.1 %). Table 6-14 illustrates that this finding is stable for datasets 1 and 2.

	Are costs that are accumulated within support cost centres allocated to primary cost centres?			
	dataset 1		dataset 2	
	Anglophone	German	Anglophone	German
Yes	69.1 %	79.8 %	69.6 %	79.8 %
No	30.9 %	20.2 %	30.4 %	20.2 %
p-value (test)	0.09 (Chi² distribution test)		0.09 (Chi² distribution test)	

Table 6-14: Adoption rates for first stage overhead allocation

Although the cross-national differences on overhead allocation procedures were derived for the design rather than the **presence of overhead allocation procedures**,[938] this finding rather reflects the more detailed overhead allocation procedures known from German firms. It actually mirrors the results of a previous study on this matter.[939] Moreover, aligning this finding with the cross-national differences in German and Anglophone overhead allocation can be underlined by the fact that this finding reflects the reduced number of support cost centres in the Anglophone subsidiaries.

Little differences prevail for the type and number of **different allocation bases** applied for first stage overhead allocation (Table 6-15). Only the allocation bases '*direct labour cost*' and the '*execution of activities*' are applied significantly more often in Anglophone subsidiaries than in the domestic German companies. During the introduction of the cross-national differences in overhead allocation, a strong presence of these two allocation bases in Anglophone companies prevailed.[940] Hence, the result is well reflecting Anglophone cost accounting traditions. In line with the focus on cost centre formation for responsibility accounting purposes, this study's findings, thus, underline an apparent presence of

[935] The results are stable for datasets 1 and 2.

[936] The finding on the segregation of manufacturing and non-manufacturing costs for product costing purposes (cf. section 6.1.1.2.3, p. 188.) reveals likewise results.

[937] The difficulty to mirror the identified cross-national difference through the complexity of these companies' cost accounting systems limits the conclusiveness of this complexity sub-score.

[938] Cf. section 2.2.3, p. 16f.

[939] *Krumwiede/Suessmair* (2007a), p. 6, report similar figures for the allocation of costs from support to primary cost centres for German and US companies.

[940] For this and the following, cf. section 2.2.3, p. 16f.

Anglophone cost accounting traditions in this regard in the Anglophone companies. Other than in the introduction of Anglophone and German cost accounting traditions, however, no difference in the variety of applied bases can be identified.[941]

	Are the following bases used to allocate costs from support cost centres to primary cost centres?			
	dataset 1		dataset 2	
	Anglophone (n = 76)	German (n = 71)	Anglophone (n = 78)	German (n = 83)
(1) Direct material costs	39.5 %	39.4 %	41.0 %	39.7 %
(2) Direct labour costs	59.2 % *	43.7 %	60.3 % *	47.0 %
(3) Space based measures	86.8 %	90.1 %	84.6 %	91.6 %
(4) Weight based measures	22.4 %	18.3 %	23.1 %	18.1 %
(5) Time based measures	68.4 %	74.7 %	69.2 %	75.9 %
(6) Other physical unit based measures	47.4 %	54.9 %	47.4 %	55.4 %
(7) The execution of a specific activity	39.5 % **	22.5 %	38.5 % **	22.9 %
(8) The duration of a specific activity	35.5 %	25.4 %	35.9 %	27.7 %
p-value (test)	Most comparisons of Angl. and Ger. subsidiaries for each individual characteristic are statistically insignificant in two-tailed Chi^2 tests. If significant, this is indicated by the significance levels *, ** or ***.			
Number of applied allocation bases				
min. (max.)	0 (8)	0 (8)	0 (8)	0 (8)
Mean (median)	4.0 (4)	3.7 (3)	4.0 (4)	3.8 (4)
p-value (test)	0.60 (two-tailed Welch test)		0.49 (two-tailed Welch test)	

Table 6-15: Allocation bases applied for first stage overhead allocation (dataset 1)

Reflecting the above evidence, there is no significant variation in the distribution of the **most extensively applied bases** in Anglophone and domestic German subsidiaries (Table 6-16[942]). For dataset 1, Table 6-16 illustrates that in both Anglophone and domestic German subsidiaries, time based measures are used to allocate the largest proportions of overhead costs from support to primary cost centres. The second most extensively applied basis tends to be space (e.g. m^2 or m^3). For the third most extensively applied basis, other physical units (e.g. kWh or joules) and space-based measures are most frequently marked. Regardless these similarities, it is revealing to find that direct material and direct labour costs are not generally used to allocate large proportions of overhead costs during first stage overhead allocation. Measures of time, space and other physical units are of greater relevance. Since these latter measures are likely to reflect the extent to which a primary cost centre consumes the resources of a support cost centre, this finding is very reasonable.

[941] This result may be due to an unclear definition of overhead allocation procedures in previous research. Whether the identified traditions describe first or second stage allocation remained rather disguised in section 2.2.3, p. 16f.

[942] The percentages are based on all companies that engage into a first stage overhead allocation. Therefore, the figures per column do not add up to 100 %. Some companies do not use any of the provided bases or use less than three bases and, therefore, could not report a complete answer to this question.

	Please rank the top three of all applied allocation bases in accordance with the proportion of the total indirect costs allocated to primary cost centres.					
	Most heavily applied basis		2nd most heavily applied basis		3rd most heavily applied basis	
	Anglophone (n = 76)	German (n = 71)	Anglophone (n = 76)	German (n = 71)	Anglophone (n = 76)	German (n = 71)
(1) Direct material costs	18.4 %	14.5 %	6.6 %	7.0 %	4.0 %	5.6 %
(2) Direct labour costs	11.8 %	11.3 %	23.7 %	14.1 %	7.9 %	8.5 %
(3) Space based measures	17.1 %	14.1 %	**25.0 %**	**36.6 %** **	**18.4 %**	**29.6 %** **
(4) Weight based measures	4.0 %	5.6 %	4.0 %	0.0 %	4.0 %	1.4 %
(5) Time based measures	**35.5 %**	**40.9 %**	15.8 %	16.9 %	9.2 %	7.0 %
(6) Other physical unit based measures	5.3 %	5.6 %	7.9 %	7.0 %	**15.8 %**	**15.5 %**
(7) The execution of a specific activity	1.3 %	1.4 %	5.3 %	5.6 %	7.9 %	1.4 %
(8) The duration of a specific activity	4.0 %	4.2 %	4.0 %	5.6 %	6.7 %	5.6 %
p-value (test)[943]	0.99 (Fisher's exact test)		0.52 (Fisher's exact test)		0.50 (Fisher's exact test)	

Table 6-16: Most important allocation bases for first stage overhead allocation (dataset 1)

Given that these allocation bases comprise a variety of different measures, respondents were also asked for the **number of individual measures** applied to allocate overhead costs. In contrast to the similarity with respect to the applied overhead cost allocation bases, the number of applied measures differs significantly between the Anglophone and the domestic German subsidiaries (Table 6-17).

	How many different measures are applied in your company to allocate costs from support cost centres to primary cost centres?			
	dataset 1		dataset 2	
	Anglophone (n = 76)	German (n = 71)	Anglophone (n = 78)	German (n = 83)
min. (max.)	1 (15)	1 (70)	1 (15)	1 (70)
Mean (median)	4.5 (4)	6.5 (4)	4.5 (4)	6.6 (4)
p-value (test)	0.01 (two-tailed Welch test)		0.05 (two-tailed Welch test)	

Table 6-17: Number of individual measures used for first stage overhead allocation

Domestic German subsidiaries apply on average significantly more individual measures (6.5) than Anglophone subsidiaries (4.5). As such, the national cost accounting traditions with respect to the diversity of applied individual measures[944] prevails in this study. In contrast to Anglophone practice, however, there is little evidence for a plant-wide overhead allocation bases in the Anglophone subsidiaries. Accordingly, in datasets 1 and 2 there are merely six companies applying only one measure for the purpose of first stage overhead allocation. This finding might reflect a spilover effect of German cost accounting traditions which is linked to the large number of brownfield investments among the Anglophone subsidiaries.[945] At the same time, this finding could also be linked to the un-

[943] Besides testing whether in any dataset there are differences with respect to the distribution of the most important overhead allocation bases, the percentages of each individual basis are compared for the Anglophone and the domestic German subsidiaries. If a Chi^2 or a Fisher's exact test identfy the distribution to be different, this is shown by the significance levels *, ** or ***.

[944] Cf. section 2.2.3, p. 16f.

[945] Cf. section 5.3.3, p. 156.

clear description of overhead allocation procedures in previous research.[946] Whether the introduced cost accounting traditions describe first or second stage allocation procedures, remained rather unclear.

Aggregating the number of different allocation bases and the number of individual measures into a **complexity sub-score**[947] maintains the identified similarities and differences (Table 6-18). The two-tailed p-values below 0.2 in both datasets indicate that the domestic German subsidiaries have a significantly higher complexity sub-score than the Anglophone subsidiaries. Yet, the results are significant at a 10 % level only.

	dataset 1		dataset 2	
	Anglophone	German	Anglophone	German
Complexity sub-score	**0.32**	**0.37**	**0.33**	**0.38**
p-value (test)	0.17 (two-tailed Welch test)		0.12 (two-tailed t-test)	

Table 6-18: Complexity sub-score for first stage overhead allocation

Above all, the low complexity sub-scores indicate that first stage overhead cost allocation procedures in both the Anglophone and the domestic German subsidiaries are relatively simple.

6.1.1.2.5 Second stage overhead allocation

In question B.10 and B.11 of questionnaire A, respondents disclosed the detail of their second stage overhead cost allocation procedures. As Table 6-19 illustrates, the **number of applied allocation bases** varies significantly between Anglophone and domestic German companies. Whereas Anglophone firms in dataset 1 and 2 use, on average, more than three bases, the domestic German subsidiaries apply less than three bases. This difference appears particularly due to the greater reliance on activity-based allocation procedures in Anglophone subsidiaries. Only for these bases, the level of application differs significantly between the two groups. This reliance on activity-based allocation procedures reflects previous research on adoptions rates of ABC in Anglophone companies as compared to German companies.[948] Nevertheless, finding Anglophone companies to rely on a greater variety of different bases for overhead allocation appears to contradict previous research on overhead allocation practices known from German and Anglophone companies. Yet, this contradiction remains inconclusive because section 2 cannot clearly differentiate previous research with respect to first and second stage allocation.

It is remarkable to find a number of similarities and difference with respect to the **allocation bases** which are applied for first stage (Table 6-15) and second stage (Table 6-19) overhead allocation. For both stages, time based measures and direct labour costs are widely applied. Hence, for each allocation, the consideration of labour is very important. In contrast, space based measures are more common for first stage allocation, whereas the opposite holds true for direct material costs. Both findings are well explicable. The alloca-

946 For this and the following, cf. section 2.2.3, p. 16f.

947 For comparability reasons, the score is derived based on the maximum number of allocation bases and individual measures of dataset 2. These maximum values do not differ from the ones in dataset 1, however. Hence, the results would not have changed if dataset 1 served as a basis for determining the score.

948 Cf. section 2.2.3, p. 17.

tion of indirect cost to products as a proportion of direct cost is internationally a well-known practice.[949] Also, whereas support cost centres can be easily allocated based on m^2 (e.g. rents), it appears difficult to think of resources despite water or gas that can be aligned easily with a product in terms of a space-based measure.

	Are the following bases used to allocate costs from primary cost centres to products?					
	dataset 1			dataset 2		
	Anglophone		German	Anglophone		German
(1) Direct material costs	60.0 %		57.3 %	60.7 %		58.7 %
(2) Direct labour costs	58.2 %		47.2 %	58.9 %		50.0 %
(3) Space based measures	33.6 %		31.5 %	33.9 %		31.7 %
(4) Weight based measures	26.4 %		21.4 %	26.8 %		22.1 %
(5) Time based measures	72.7 %		65.2 %	73.2 %		66.4 %
(6) Other physical unit based measures	26.4 %		19.1 %	27.7 %		20.2 %
(7) The execution of a specific activity	26.4 %	**	13.5 %	25.9 %	**	12.5 %
(8) The duration of a specific activity	33.6 %	***	11.2 %	33.9 %	***	12.5 %
p-value (test)	Most comparisons of Angl. and Ger. subsidiaries for each individual characteristic are statistically significant in two-tailed Chi² tests. If significant, this is indicated by the significance levels *, ** or ***.					
Number of applied allocation bases						
min. (max.)	0 (8)		0 (8)	0 (8)		0 (8)
Mean (median)	3.4 (3)		2.7 (2)	3.4 (3)		2.7 (2)
p-value (test)	0.01 (two-tailed Welch test)			0.01 (two-tailed Welch test)		

Table 6-19: Allocation bases applied for second stage overhead allocation

Other than that, it is remarkable to find the measures which are associated with ABC ((7) – ((8)) to be more common for first than second stage allocation in the domestic German companies. German ABC is rather more relevant for the allocation of non-manufacturing costs in Germany.[950] In the studied manufacturing companies, these costs are likely to occur in cost centres that support the manufacturing process only (i.e. support cost centres). Hence above results are linked to German cost accounting traditions in this regard. In contrast, ABC in Anglophone companies refines the allocation of both manufacturing and non-manufacturing costs.[951] Therefore, the finding that ABC associated measures are less specific to first and second stage allocation in Anglophone companies is in line with Anglophone traditions as well.

Regarding the **most extensively applied bases** for second stage allocation, Table 6-20 exemplifies that indirect (i.e. averaging) allocation bases[952] such as direct material and direct labour cost assign the largest proportions of overhead costs in the Anglophone subsidiaries. This finding reflects the broad overhead allocation procedures known from Anglophone cost accounting traditions.[953]

---

[949] Cf. section 2.2.3, p. 16f.

[950] Cf. *Horváth/Mayer* (1995), p. 59f.

[951] Cf. section 2.2.3, p. 17.

[952] Cf. section 2.2.3, p. 15.

[953] Cf. section 2.2.3, p. 15f.

Despite finding time-based measures to be the most extensively applied, domestic German subsidiaries also rely strongly on direct material and direct labour costs for overhead allocation (Table 6-20[954]). Even though there is some evidence for such rather simple overhead allocation measures in German companies,[955] this finding is rather surprising. German companies are generally known for their refined overhead cost allocation based on direct allocation bases. Thus, for the German companies, a prominence of measures (3) – (8) would have reflected such traditions. Though deviating from common whispers about German cost accounting, these findings mirror the results for the 'rationales for cost centre formation'.[956] The discussion around Table 6-12 reveals that the domestic German subsidiaries form cost centres less extensively to allocate overhead costs according to the internal consumption of resources. The mere allocation of overhead costs is argued to be more extensively considered for cost centre formation. As such, it is not inconsistent to find overhead allocation bases in these companies which rather reflect an average-based allocation.

	Please rank the top three of all applied allocation bases in accordance to the proportion of the total indirect costs allocated to products.					
	Most heavily applied basis		2nd most heavily applied basis		3rd most heavily applied basis	
	Anglophone	German	Anglophone	German	Anglophone	German
(1) Direct material costs	**36.4 %**	32.6 %	13.6 %	15.7 %	3.6 %	4.5 %
(2) Direct labour costs	10.9 %	6.7 %	**32.7 %**	**25.8 %**	4.6 %	6.7 %
(3) Space based measures	1.8 %	4.5 %	3.6 %	2.3 %	10.0 %	**12.4 %**
(4) Weight based measures	5.5 %	5.6 %	5.5 %	2.3 %	7.3 %	5.6 %
(5) Time based measures	31.8 %	**33.7 %**	15.5 %	18.0 %	**11.8 %**	5.6 %
(6) Other physical unit based measures	0.9 %	2.3 %	2.7 %	4.5 %	6.4 %	5.6 %
(7) The execution of a specific activity	0.0 %	1.2 %	1.8 %	5.6 %	9.1 %	2.3 % **
(8) The duration of a specific activity	3.6 %	1.2 %	5.5 %	0.0 % **	9.1 %	3.4 % *
p-value (test) 957	0.66 (Fisher's exact test)		0.20 (Fisher's exact test)		0.38 (Fisher's exact test)	

Table 6-20: Most important allocation bases for second stage overhead allocation

In contrast to first stage allocation, the number of **individual measures applied for second stage allocation** does not vary significantly between Anglophone and domestic German subsidiaries (Table 6-21). Despite allocating overhead costs especially based on indirect allocation bases (direct material and direct labour costs), the subsidiaries apply on average about three allocation bases. Hence, second stage allocation procedures are not too simplistically performed by the means of direct costs only. These results are stable for both datasets.

954 The percentages are based on all companies that engage into a second stage overhead allocation. Therefore, the figures per column do not add up to 100 %. Some companies do not use any of the provided bases or use less than three bases and, therefore, could not report a complete answer to this question.

955 Cf. section 2.2.3, p. 16.

956 Cf. section 6.1.1.2.2.

957 Besides testing whether in any dataset there are differences with respect to the distribution of the most important overhead allocation bases, the percentages of each individual basis are compared for the Anglophone and the domestic German subsidiaries. If a Chi^2 or a Fisher's exact test find different distributions, this is shown by the significance levels *, ** or ***.

	How many different measures are applied in your company to allocate costs from primary cost centres to products?			
	dataset 1		dataset 2	
	Anglophone	German	Anglophone	German
min. (max.)	0 (15)	0 (28)	0 (15)	0 (32)
Mean (median)	3.2 (3)	3.1 (3)	3.2 (3)	3.4 (3)
p-value (test)	0.78 (two-tailed t-test)		0.75 (two-tailed t-test)	

Table 6-21: Number of individual measures used for second stage overhead allocation

The aggregation of the number of different allocation bases and the number of individual measures into an **complexity sub-score**[958] maintains the identified similarities and differences of the second stage overhead cost allocation in Anglophone and domestic German subsidiaries (Table 6-22). Thus, finding the Anglophone subsidiaries to be more complex with respect to the second stage overhead allocation is especially attributable to the application of activity based costing.

	dataset 1		**dataset 2**	
	Anglophone	German	Anglophone	German
Complexity sub-score	**0.39**	**0.33**	**0.39**	**0.35**
p-value (test)	0.07 (two-tailed t-test)		0.12 (two-tailed t-test)	

Table 6-22: Complexity sub-score for second stage overhead allocation

As for the first stage allocation procedures, the comparably low complexity sub-scores (0.39 and 0.33) emphasise that second stage overhead allocation in Anglophone and domestic German subsidiaries is rather simple. This assertion can be underlined by the result that almost one fourth of the companies[959] applies only a single measure for second stage overhead allocation. Remarkably, the Anglophone subsidiaries have significantly more complex second stage allocation procedures than the domestic German firms. This results, however, is especially reflecting the reliance of Anglophone firms on ABC. As such, this finding is well in line with Anglophone cost accounting traditions. It does not dilute the plausibility of the above findings.

One very peculiar finding prevails from the previous pages. Stereotype Anglophone overhead allocation procedures pictured in previous research[960] might rather reveal the second stage allocation practices in Anglophone firms. In contrast, the tendency to describe German overhead allocation as rather more diverse appears to hold especially true for the first stage overhead allocation procedures. Future comparative research on this matter would be fruitful.

958 For comparability reasons, the score is derived based on the maximum number of allocation bases and individual measures found in dataset 2 in both datasets. These maximum values, however, do not differ substantially from the ones in dataset 1. Thus, this procedure does not bias the results considerably.

959 In dataset 1, there are 23.6 % of the Anglophone subsidiaries and 27.7 % of the domestic German subsidiaries with a single allocation measure. In dataset 2, the proportions are 23.2 % (Anglophone) and 24.0 % (German).

960 For this and the following, cf. section 2.2.3, p. 15f.

6.1.1.2.6 Cost variance analysis

In question B.18 of questionnaire A, respondents assessed the intensity of **cost variance analysis on the cost centre level**. Both Anglophone (mean = 5.5) and domestic German subsidiaries (mean = 5.5) rely on such analyses rather intensively (Table 6-23).[961] The intensive analysis of cost centre variances is in line with previous research on the particularities of German and Anglophone cost accounting.[962] Peculiarly, this study does not find the domestic German subsidiaries to focus more intensively on variance analysis though a previous finding revealed this interrelation to hold for a comparison of Anglophone and German firms. Yet, it remains unclear whether this finding aligns the Anglophone subsidiaries with German cost accounting traditions in this regard. For an according assertion, the picture of previous research on the issue of variance analysis on different levels (cost centre and cost object) is rather too obscure.

	How intensively do you analyse cost variances on the cost centre level? (Scale: 1 = not at all, 7 = very intensively)			
	dataset 1		dataset 2	
	Anglophone	German	Anglophone	German
Mean (median)	5.50 (6)	5.50 (6)	5.52 (6)	5.37 (6)
p-value (test)	1.0 (two-tailed t-test)		0.48 (two-tailed t-test)	
Complexity sub-score	**0.75**	**0.75**	**0.75**	**0.73**
p-value (test)	1.0 (two-tailed t-test)		0.48 (two-tailed t-test)	

Table 6-23: Cost variance analysis on the cost centre level

6.1.1.2.7 Complexity of cost centre accounting

Aggregating the six complexity sub-scores in a measure of the complexity of cost centre accounting reveals the following results (Table 6-24).

	dataset 1		**dataset 2**	
	Anglophone	German	Anglophone	German
Complexity score	**0.55**	**0.57**	**0.55**	**0.57**
p-value (test)	0.30 (two-tailed t-test)		0.49 (two-tailed t-test)	

Table 6-24: Complexity of cost centre accounting

In contrast to cost type accounting, there are insignificant differences for the design of cost centre accounting in Anglophone (0.55) and domestic German subsidiaries (0.57) in dataset 1. A similar result prevails for dataset 2.

Nevertheless, the discussion in section 6.1.1.2 reveals that Anglophone subsidiaries share multiple similarities with cliché cost accounting traditions known from Anglophone companies. For instance, they have a comparably low number of cost centres, categorise cost centre costs with respect to period and product costs, focus on direct material and direct labour costs to allocate overhead costs to products (second stage allocation) or apply ABC more intensively.

Thus, the design of cost centre accounting, despite not reemphasising the validity of hypothesis 1 in significant terms for the aggregated complexity score, underlines the preva-

[961] These findings are stable for dataset 2.

[962] For this and the following, cf. section 2.2.4, p. 24f.

lence of different cost accounting traditions in Anglophone and domestic German subsidiaries.

6.1.1.3 Cost object accounting

6.1.1.3.1 Different types of cost objects

In question B.14 of questionnaire A, respondents were asked for the different types of cost objects they assign costs to. As presented in Table 6-25, there are little differences in dataset 1 with respect to the percentage of cost objects for which Anglophone and domestic German subsidiaries determine product costs. Both tend to assign costs to the majority of their **products** (85.2 % vs. 79.6 %) and **product lines** (60.6 % vs. 57.9 %). No difference prevails for dataset 2.

	For how many of the following objects are unit costs computed as part of regular cost accounting?			
	dataset 1		dataset 2	
	Anglophone	German	Anglophone	German
Final products (per unit)	85.2 %	79.6 %	85.5 %	79.5 %
Product lines	60.6 %	57.9 %	60.5 %	57.0 %
p-value (test)	For both cost objects the comparisons of Anglophone and domestic German subsidiaries are statistically significant in two-tailed parametric tests (both datasets).			
Complexity sub-score	**0.74**	**0.70**	**0.74**	**0.67**
p-value (test)	0.37 (two-tailed t-test)		0.26 (two-tailed t-test)	

Table 6-25: Existence of alternative cost objects

Potential cross-national differences with respect to the applied cost objects were expected for customers (i.e. **customer profitability analysis**) and **idle capacity**.[963] The items on these two cost objects, however, had to be excluded from this analysis due to poor data quality.[964] For the two remaining items, section 2 could not find any differences between Anglophone and German cost accounting. As such, the insignificant differences with respect to these characteristics are little surprising, yet also little revealing.

6.1.1.3.2 The design of product costing

In question B.15 of questionnaire A, respondents explicated the dimensions of their companies' product cost information.

The majority of Anglophone (61.8 %) and domestic German companies (51.7 %) determines both **variable and full costs** during the analysis of unit costs (Table 6-26).[965] For both groups, this finding is rather in line with commonly stressed German cost accounting traditions.[966] Peculiarly, however, the domestic German subsidiaries (34.8 %) rely

963 The section stressed that the costs of idle capacity are more commonly determined in German companies. Besides, the stronger reliance on ABC in Anglophone companies could be accompanied by a stronger reliance on customers as a cost object (cf. section 2.2.4, p. 19).

964 Cf. section 5.3.1, p. 149.

965 Since there are little differences between dataset 1 and 2, this paragraph discusses dataset 1 only.

966 For this and the following, cf. section 2.2.4, p. 20f.

more heavily on mere full costing than the Anglophone subsidiaries (24.6 %). Though the distribution of these answers is statistically insignificant, this result does not correspond to regularly accentuated differences of Anglophone and German cost accounting traditions. These findings cannot be clarified by a stronger focus on strategic (i.e. long-term) decisions in the German subsidiaries since there are no statistically significant differences in this respect.[967] As such, it can merely be concluded that application of variable and full costing differs insignificantly between the Anglophone and the domestic German subsidiaries. It remains concealed which cost accounting traditions are reflected in the subsidiaries. Since section 2 also reveals evidence as the one reported here for both Anglophone and German companies, the result suggests that the common whisper on cross-national differences for variable and full costing in Anglophone and German firms awaits further refinement. Potentially, future considerations of the decisions supported by variable and full costs in business practice can help to understand the above results. Thereby, it could also be analysed whether the difficulty in interpreting the above results is associable to a potential gap between conceptual considerations on the design of product costing and the common product costing practices of Anglophone and German firms.

	How are product costs (per unit) determined as part of regular cost accounting? Please consider the following characteristics:			
	dataset 1		dataset 2	
	Anglophone	German	Anglophone	German
Variability				
Only on a variable cost basis	13.6 %	13.5 %	13.4 %	12.5 %
Only on a full cost basis	24.6 %	34.8 %	24.1 %	33.7 %
On both bases	**61.8 %**	**51.7 %**	**62.5 %**	**53.9 %**
p-value (test)	0.26 (Chi² distribution test)		0.30 (Chi² distribution test)	
Reference to manufacturing processes				
Only on a manufacturing cost basis	**48.2 %**	**51.7 %**	**48.2 %**	**48.1 %**
Only on a manufacturing and non-manufacturing cost basis	10.0 %	7.9 %	9.8 %	6.7 %
On both bases	41.8 %	40.5 %	42.0 %	45.2 %
p-value (test)	0.82 (Chi² distribution test)		0.69 (Chi² distribution test)	
Inventoriability				
Only on an inventoriable cost basis	**53.6 %**	**42.7 %**	**52.7 %**	37.5 % **
Only on an inventoriable and non-inventoriable cost basis	16.4 %	21.4 %	16.1 %	19.2 %
On both bases	30.0 %	36.0 %	31.3 %	**43.3 %** *
p-value (test)	0.30 (Chi² distribution test)		0.08 (Chi² distribution test) Please also see footnote 968	
Complexity sub-score	**0.64**	**0.61**	**0.64**	**0.64**
p-value (test)	0.43 (two-tailed t-test)		0.90 (two-tailed t-test)	

Table 6-26: Product costing

967 Cf. section 6.1.2.1.1.1, p. 199f.

968 Besides testing whether in any dataset there are differences with respect to the prevalence of more complex product costing procedures, the individual values for each characteristic are compared for the Anglophone and domestic German subsidiaries. If the distribution differs a Chi^2 or a Fisher's exact test, this is shown by the significance levels *, ** or ***.

Similar diverse results prevail for the differentiation of product costs into **manufacturing and non-manufacturing** costs. The most common dimension of product costs in both Anglophone (48.2 %) and domestic German (51.7 %) subsidiaries are manufacturing costs only (dataset 1 in Table 6-26). For the Anglophone subsidiaries, this is in line with the preliminary stressed focus on manufacturing costs for product costing purposes in Anglophone companies.[969] Yet, this finding can be equally linked to the interception of terminology 'manufacturing costs' and the Anglophone focus on non-manufacturing costs as period costs (i.e. non-inventoriable).[970] If manufacturing costs were essential for financial accounting purposes, this would explicate why many companies interested in manufacturing and non-manufacturing costs keep them separated (41.8 %). Peculiarly, only a minority of the domestic German companies (40.5 %) are in-line with the suggested traditions of German companies to determine both the manufacturing and the non-manufacturing costs of their products.[971] Given the limited number of studies which reveal this procedure in German firms, this finding urges for the necessity of future research to determine whether German firms actually assign both manufacturing and non-manufacturing costs to their products on a regular basis. Because this study's results are stable for both datasets and hold similarly true for the cost centre level, the results suggest that there are no such communalities.

As a final characteristic, question B.15 also analysed how the ability to capitalise a cost figure affects the design of the subsidiaries' cost object accounting system. Anglophone management accounting is often argued to be more closely linked to financial accounting than German management accounting.[972] With respect to the analysis of **inventoriable costs** for product costing purposes, financial accounting appears to be more relevant for the design of cost object accounting in the Anglophone subsidiaries as well. Table 6-26 illustrates that most Anglophone subsidiaries disregard period costs for product costing purposes, i.e. they derive product costs as inventoriable costs only (53.6 %). As such, this result is well in line with according Anglophone traditions. Financial accounting requirements affect the design of product costing in the Anglophone subsidiaries.[973] These results are stable for dataset 2. In contrast to the Anglophone companies, domestic German subsidiaries rely less extensively on the derivation of inventoriable costs only (42.7 %). Also, they tend to neglect costs' inventoriability for product costing purposes more extensively (21.4 % vs. 16.4%) and focus more intensively on the separation of inventory and non-inventory costs (36.0 % vs. 30.0 %) if they were to derive product costs with respect to these dimensions. This finding holds true for both datasets.

Because 13 of the 15 excluded domestic German companies separate inventoriable and non-inventoriable costs for product costing purposes, these differences are significant in dataset 2 only, however. Despite this distortion in dataset 1, both datasets reveal the same tendency – whereas Anglophone subsidiaries centre on inventoriable costs for product costing (around 53 % in both datasets), domestic German ones rather neglect this distinc-

---

969 Cf. section 2.2.4, p. 23.

970 Cf. *Garrison et al.* (2006), p. 36ff.; *Kajüter* (2011), p. 104.

971 Cf. section 2.2.4, p. 23.

972 Cf. section 2.2.2, p. 12; section 2.2.3, p. 15, and section 2.2.4, p. 23.

973 Similar results prevail for the differentiation of period and product costs on the cost centre level as well.

tion or differentiate inventoriable and non-inventoriable product costs (57.3 % in dataset 1 and 62.5 % in dataset 2). Thus, the finding underlines that there are differences with respect to the importance of financial accounting for cost accounting design in Anglophone and domestic German subsidiaries.[974]

The high **complexity sub-scores** determined for the design of product costing procedures mirror the small proportion of companies which regard product costs irrespectively of their level of variability, reference to the manufacturing processes or inventoriability. Given that Anglophone and domestic German subsidiaries cannot be differentiated statistically for these characteristics, the scores do not vary significantly between these two groups either. Nevertheless, there is some evidence for Anglophone cost accounting traditions with respect to the differentiation of product costs in accordance with their reference to the manufacturing process and their inventoriability in Anglophone subsidiaries.

6.1.1.3.3 Contribution margin accounting

In question B.17 of questionnaire A respondents provided information on their company's contribution margin accounting. Table 6-27 illustrates that Anglophone subsidiaries (74.6 %) apply contribution margin accounting significantly less often than domestic German subsidiaries (89.9 %).[975] This result reflects the stronger reliance on refined contribution margin accounting systems known from German companies if compared to Anglophone firms.[976] Also, the **adoption rates for CM accounting** in the Anglophone subsidiaries are higher than commonly known for their home-countries.[977] Hence, the Anglophone subsidiaries rather reflect a mixture of Anglophone as well as German cost accounting traditions in this regard.

	Do you compute (a) contribution margin(s)?			
	dataset 1		dataset 2	
	Anglophone	German	Anglophone	German
Yes	74.6 %	89.9 %	75.0 %	87.5 %
No	25.4 %	10.1 %	25.0 %	12.5 %
p-value (test)	0.01 (Chi² distribution test)		0.02 (Chi² distribution test)	

Table 6-27: Application of contribution margin accounting

In contrast to commonly stressed cross-national differences,[978] however, the domestic German companies are not found to differentiate significantly more contribution margin layers than the Anglophone companies. Table 6-28 reveals an insignificant difference for the average number of the differentiated **CM layers**. Yet, the most commonly distin-

974 The finding reflects the (insignificantly) higher application of cost information for inventory valuation in the Anglophone subsidiaries (cf. section 6.1.2.1.1.1, p. 199).

975 These results are stable for dataset 2.

976 Cf. section 2.2.4, p. 22f.

977 *Krumwiede/Suessmair* (2007a), p. 6, find 47 % of the researched US manufacturing companies to rely on CM accounting. *Dugdale et al.* (2006), p. 71, identifies contribution margin concepts in 68 % of their sample of UK companies. Similarly, *Drury/Tayles* (2006), p. 413, report that 57 % of the researched UK companies attribute importance to CM accounting. Finally, *Kim/Song* (1990), p. 30, argue that 59 % of the researched US companies apply CM for goal setting purposes.

978 Cf. section 2.2.4, p. 22f.

guished number of CM layers in the Anglophone companies (48 % in dataset 1 reported two CMs), falls behind the most common figure in the domestic German companies (33 % report three CM layers). Hence, there is some evidence for the prevalence of Anglophone cost accounting traditions in the Anglophone companies. Nevertheless, the regular reliance on more than one CM layer for contribution margin accounting in the Anglophone companies is distinguishable from the direct costing practices known from domestic Anglophone companies.[979] Yet, the results for the Anglophone subsidiaries are not necessarily a reflection of German cost accounting traditions. This assertion holds especially true because the 71 brownfield investments among the 82 Anglophone companies, which apply CM accounting, report less layers (mean = 2.5) than the 11 greenfield investments (mean = 3.1). As such, the result could reflect that multiple stage CM accounting procedure is also known and applied in Anglophone companies.

	Number of contribution margin layers in CM accounting			
	dataset 1		dataset 2	
	Anglophone (n = 82)	German (n = 80)	Anglophone (n = 84)	German (n = 91)
min. (max.)	1 (6)	1 (8)	1 (6)	1 (8)
Mean (median)	2.5 (2)	2.6 (3)	2.5 (2)	2.7 (3)
p-value (test)	0.61 (two-tailed Welch test)		0.55 (two-tailed Welch test)	

Table 6-28: Number of CM layers in contribution margin accounting

On an aggregated basis, domestic German subsidiaries have a significantly more complex CM accounting than Anglophone subsidiaries (Table 6-29). Since the **complexity sub-score** recognises both the application of CM accounting as well as the number of CM layers, this result is decent. It especially reflects the higher adoption rate of CM accounting in the domestic German subsidiaries. Moreover, the score also mirrors the distribution of the CM layers. 60 % of the Anglophone subsidiaries but only 49 % of the domestic German subsidiaries do have less than three CM layers. The results are stable for datasets 1 and 2.

	dataset 1		dataset 2	
	Anglophone	German	Anglophone	German
Complexity sub-score	**0.49**	**0.59**	**0.49**	**0.58**
p-value (test)	0.01 (two-tailed Welch test)		0.02 (two-tailed Welch test)	

Table 6-29: Complexity sub-score for contribution margin accounting

6.1.1.3.4 Time reference of cost accounting

In question B.16 of questionnaire A respondents reported the time horizons of their product cost information. The majority of the subsidiaries derive actual, normal and standard costs for at least one product. In contrast, target costs are determined in a minority of the firms only (Table 6-30).[980] These findings are consistent for both Anglophone and domestic German subsidiaries.

---

[979] For this and the following, cf. section 2.2.4, p. 22f.

[980] Multiple Wilcoxon signed rank sum tests reveal that target cost information are determined in a significantly different proportion of the companies than actual, normal and standard costs. In both datasets the differences are significant at a 1 % level for both Anglophone and domestic German firms.

	Proportion of companies that determine a time horizon for at least one of their products			
	dataset 1		dataset 2	
	Anglophone	German	Anglophone	German
Actual costs (occurred costs)	93 %	91 %	93 %	91 %
Normal costs (averaged costs)	64 %	66 %	64 %	67 %
Standard costs (planned costs)	87 %	86 %	87 %	86 %
Target costs (allowable costs derived from market prices)	43 %	43 %	43 %	46 %
p-value (test)	The application of all time horizons varies insignificantly in individual comparisons of the Angl. and Ger. subsidiaries in both datasets (chi² tests).			

Table 6-30: Time references of costs on the cost object level (adoption rates)

Interestingly, the adoption of **target costing** practices in the Anglophone subsidiaries lies in between recently explored adoption rates from domestic Anglophone companies[981] and domestic German firms.[982] Moreover, given that the existing German evidence stems from rather large organisations, it is not surprising that the adoption rates in the domestic German subsidiaries fall behind the ones found in previous research. Furthermore, target costing is applied significantly less intensively than standard costing (Table 6-31[983]). Hence, this study's results cannot underline previous arguments for the obsolescence of standard costing in today's manufacturing environment.[984]

	For how many products are the following costs determined? (Interpretation of the scale: 0% = for no product, 100% = for all products)			
	dataset 1		dataset 2	
	Anglophone	German	Anglophone	German
Actual costs (occurred costs)	81.0 %	79.0 %	81.2 %	77.9 %
Normal costs (averaged costs)	51.9 %	52.9 %	52.3 %	52.7 %
Standard costs (planned costs)	76.7 %	76.1 %	77.1 %	74.8 %
Target costs (allowable costs derived from market prices)	26.3 %	23.5 %	25.8 %	25.1 %
p-value (test)	All time horizons vary insignificantly in individual comparisons of the Angl. and Ger. subsidiaries in both datasets (two-tailed parametric tests).			

Table 6-31: Time references of costs on the cost object level (proportion of costed products)

Besides these assertions, the percentages of products for which **actual, normal, standard** and **target costs** are computed reveal further details. Overall, the percentages do not vary significantly between Anglophone and domestic German subsidiaries. Thus, this study cannot find the stronger prevalence of standard costs in the Anglophone subsidiaries (Table 6-31) that prevails in the research project by *Krumwiede/Suessmair*.[985] Whether this

---

981 *Yazdifar/Askarany* (2012), p. 388, report that 23 % of UK/NZ/AU manufacturing firms adopt target costing practices at least as a trial. *Kim et al.* (2002), p. 608, find target costing to be present in 40 % of US manufacturing firms.

982 Cf. *Kajüter* (2005), p. 91, who reports that 55 % of German manufacturing and non-manufacturing companies apply target costing. Similarly high adoption rates (68 %) are presented for Germany by *Schäffer/Steiners* (2005b), p. 322f.

983 One-tailed t-tests among the Anglophone and domestic German subsidiaries show that target costs are computed for significantly less products than standard costs in each data set.

984 For a discussion of the potential obsolecence of standard costing for today's manufacturing environment cf. e.g. *Guilding et al.* (1998), p. 569, or *Sulaiman et al.* (2005), p. 109ff.

985 Cf. *Krumwiede/Suessmair* (2007a), p. 6.

result is linked to the inconclusiveness of *Krumwiede/Suessmair* or reflects that the Anglophone subsidiaries are adapted to the German context in this respect remains unclear, however. This is especially true because, *Krumwiede/Suessmair* focus on the application of standard costing for decision-making rather than their mere determination. It remains possible that, despite finding standard costs to be determined for similar proportions of products, standard costs are used for a greater variety of decisions in the Anglophone companies. Section 6.1.1.3.5 further elaborates on this issue.

Overall, Table 6-30 and Table 6-31 reveal that there is no difference with respect to the different time horizons of cost information in the Anglophone and domestic German subsidiaries. This finding reflects that there are little distinctive patterns of German and Anglophone cost accounting with respect to application of actual, normal, standard and target costing.[986] The derived **complexity sub-score** maintains this finding for both datasets (Table 6-32).

	dataset 1		dataset 2	
	Anglophone	German	Anglophone	German
Complexity sub-score	**0.59**	**0.59**	**0.59**	**0.59**
p-value (test)	0.94 (two-tailed t-test)		0.89 (two-tailed t-test)	

Table 6-32: Complexity sub-score for the time references of cost accounting

The high complexity sub-scores in both Anglophone and domestic German subsidiaries result from the high adoption rates for actual, normal and standard costing as well as the large proportion of products for which these three time horizons are computed.

6.1.1.3.5 Product cost variance analysis

The intensity of cost variance analysis on the cost object level was obtained in question B.18 of questionnaire A. Both groups determine **cost variances for** their **cost objects** rather intensively (Table 6-33).

	How intensively do you analyse cost variances on the cost object level (Scale: 1 = not at all, 7 = very intensively)			
	dataset 1		dataset 2	
	Anglophone	German	Anglophone	German
Mean (median)	4.73 (5)	5.08 (6)	4.75 (5)	5.03 (6)
p-value (test)	0.19 (two-tailed t-test)		0.26 (two-tailed t-test)	
Complexity sub-score	**0.62**	**0.68**	**0.62**	**0.67**
p-value (test)	0.19 (two-tailed t-test)		0.26 (two-tailed t-test)	

Table 6-33: Cost variance analysis on the cost object level

Nevertheless, the intensity of variance analysis in dataset 1 is significantly less intensive in the Anglophone subsidiaries (4.73) than the domestic German subsidiaries (5.08).[987] Because the results can be approved at a 10 % significance level only and disappear for dataset 2, the conclusiveness of this difference remains subject to further analyses. Little insights on the plausibility of this finding can be derived from the commonly discussed An-

---

[986] Cf. section 2.2.4, p. 24.

[987] For dataset 1, bisecting the reported p-value highlights that the domestic German subsidiaries pursue variance analysis on the cost centre level more intensively at a 10 % significance level.

glophone and German cost accounting traditions.[988] This far, researchers could especially reveal differences for variance analysis on the cost centre level between domestic German and Anglophone companies.

An alternative interpretation of the above findings provides a potential pathway to explicate why there are differences with respect to variance analysis on the cost centre level, despite being significant for dataset 1 only. In the previous section, the determination of, e.g. actual or standard costs does not vary between Anglophone and domestic German subsidiaries. Hence, the significantly more intensive variance analysis in domestic German firms of dataset 1 might suggest that **actual and standard product costs are applied for different purposes** in the Anglophone and the domestic German subsidiaries. In the domestic German subsidiaries, the intensive analysis of variances reflects the strong German tradition of engaging cost information for control purposes.[989] For the Anglophone subsidiaries, the less intensive analysis of variances on the cost object level, regardless the availability of standard and actual costs, might be linked to the relevance of standard costing for inventory valuation in Anglophone firms.[990] In addition, the finding could reflect that standard costs are applied more extensively for an unspecified portfolio of managerial purposes[991] other than variance analysis.

The ability to find a significant difference for dataset 1 only can be seen as additional evidence for the validity of these assertions. In the 15 domestic German companies excluded from dataset 1 cost information is applied less intensively for control purposes (mean = 4.0 out of 7) than in the remaining companies (mean = 5.1). As such, the decreased and insignificant difference in the intensity of variance analysis between Anglophone and domestic German subsidiaries in dataset 2 appears explicable.

6.1.1.3.6 Structure of operating income statements

Question B.19 of questionnaire A investigated the **existence** and structure **of an operating income statement** for managerial purposes. Operating income statements are found in a vast majority of the domestic German subsidiaries (69.7 %). Also, Table 6-34 reveals these statements to be equally common in Anglophone subsidiaries (64.6 %). These findings are stable for datasets 1 and 2.

	In addition to your P/L statement, do you have a separate operating income statement for managerial purposes?			
	dataset 1		dataset 2	
	Anglophone	German	Anglophone	German
Yes	64.6 %	69.7 %	64.3 %	71.2 %
No	35.4 %	30.3 %	35.7 %	28.8 %
p-value (test)	0.45 (Chi² distribution test)		0.28 (Chi² distribution test)	

Table 6-34: Operating income statement for managerial purposes

988 For this and the following, cf. section 2.2.4, p. 24f.

989 Cf. section 2.3.2, p. 29. Also, this finding is in line with previous research on variance analysis in Germany (cf. section 2.2.4, p. 24f.).

990 Cf. *Drury et al.* (1993), p. 35.

991 Cf. *Krumwiede/Suessmair* (2007a), p. 6.

In line with this interpretation, Anglophone subsidiaries report their income statements to deviate more strongly from their P/L format (4.10) than the domestic German companies (3.79). Finding this difference (Table 6-35) to be significant in a one-tailed test for dataset 2 might also be explicable by the P/L formats. The 15 domestic German companies excluded from dataset 1 are affiliated to rather domestic parent companies, i.e. the parent companies operate in a limited number of foreign countries (mean = 5 countries). In contrast, the companies from dataset 1 are affiliated to somewhat more internationally oriented parents (mean = 21 countries). As such, the latter may rely more commonly on the internationally recognised function of expense format. If the internal income statements still had a nature of expense format, this would explain why the difference of the P/L and the operating income statement are larger in dataset 1 than in dataset 2. Moreover, the results might reflect that cost information is applied less extensively for decision-making and -influencing in the 15 German companies excluded from dataset 2.[992] Hence, it is potentially less crucial for these companies to have a **structurally** very **different internal income statement.** As such, these subsidiaries increase the variation of the structural differences between the Anglophone and the domestic German subsidiaries. Both provided explanations clarify why the domestic German firms deviate more extensively from the Anglophone companies in dataset 2 which in turn might facilitate the identification of the difference as statistically significant.

	To what extent does your operating income statement for managerial purposes differ structurally from your P/L statement? (Scale: 1 = not at all, 7 = completely)			
	dataset 1		dataset 2	
	Anglophone (n = 70)	German (n = 62)	Anglophone (n = 71)	German (n = 74)
Mean (median)	4.10 (4)	3.79 (4)	4.13 (4)	3.68 (3)
p-value (test)	0.31 (two-tailed t-test)		0.12 (two-tailed t-test)	

Table 6-35: Structural differences between the operating income statement and the P/L

In both the Anglophone and the domestic German subsidiaries, the results reported in Table 6-35 are mean-ratings. It remains rather unclear, however, whether these ratings signal difficulties with respect to the applied scale or indicate moderate differences between the subsidiaries' operating income statements and their P/L statement. For the Anglophone companies, no previous study could be identified to assess the plausibility of the above findings. Since the previous study which regarded a similar question for domestic German companies also finds mean-ratings,[993] it cannot shed any light on this issue either.

	dataset 1		**dataset 2**	
	Anglophone	German	Anglophone	German
Complexity sub-score	**0.46**	**0.47**	**0.46**	**0.48**
p-value (test)	0.73 (two-tailed t-test)		0.68 (two-tailed Welch test)	

Table 6-36: Complexity sub-score for the operating income statement

Aggregating the previous two findings into a **complexity sub-score** yields insignificantly higher values for the domestic German companies (Table 6-36). Hence, the marginally

[992] Cost information is applied considerably less extensively in these 15 companies (mean = 4.3 out of 7) than in dataset 1 (4.6). For a detailed analysis of the cost accounting objectives, cf. section 6.1.2.1.1.1.

[993] Cf. *Moeschler* (2012), p. 257.

higher adoption rates in the domestic German subsidiaries (Table 6-34) offsets the lower deviation from the P/L (Table 6-35) in these companies.

6.1.1.3.7 Complexity of cost object accounting

Aggregating these six complexity sub-scores into a measure of the complexity of cost object accounting reveals the following results (Table 6-37).

	dataset 1		dataset 2	
	Anglophone	German	Anglophone	German
Complexity score	**0.59**	**0.61**	**0.59**	**0.61**
p-value (test)	0.40 (two-tailed t-test)		0.42 (two-tailed t-test)	

Table 6-37: Complexity of cost object accounting

As for the analysis of cost centre accounting, the overall complexity scores vary statistically insignificantly between Anglophone (0.59) and domestic German subsidiaries (0.61). These results are stable for datasets 1 and 2.

Nevertheless, the preceding sections align the cost object accounting practices in both groups with the cost accounting traditions from their home-countries. Despite not being reflected significantly in the complexity scores, the discussion of cost object accounting thus provides evidence for the validity of hypothesis 1 for cost object accounting as well.

6.1.1.4 Complexity of the cost accounting system

Table 6-38 summarises the 15 individual complexity sub-scores that are derived throughout sections 6.1.1. In dataset 1, the cost accounting systems of domestic German subsidiaries are more complex than those in Anglophone subsidiaries in Germany for 11 of the 15 complexity sub-scores. For seven of these 11 sub-scores, the results are statistically significant.[994] Four individual complexity sub-scores are higher in the Anglophone subsidiaries (marked by square brackets). Only one of these (the second stage overhead allocation procedures) is statistically significant, however. As discussed in section 6.1.1.2.5, this finding is especially due to the application of activity-based costing in the Anglophone subsidiaries.

Interestingly, Table 6-38 indicates that Anglophone subsidiaries in Germany especially differ from their domestic German counterparts in terms of cost type accounting ((1) – (3)). This finding reflects the discussion on groups' cost accounting which emphasises the necessity for a common chart of accounts/cost type accounting in MNCs.[995] Also, the result can be linked to the fact that the Anglophone parent companies influence their sub-

[994] Significance levels in Table 6-38 are based on one-tailed parametric tests to test whether domestic German companies have more complex cost accounting systems than Anglophone ones. The diamonds (#) provided for second stage allocation reflects that the test actually rejects hypothesis 1 rather than the associated null hypothesis. In contrast to the expectation in hypothesis 1, it is tested whether the higher complexity in the Anglophone subsidiaries is statistically significant.

[995] Cf. section 3.3.1, p. 43. MNCs' reliance on uniform cost type accounting also prevails in two of the business anecdotes on German MNCs that were discussed in the literature review (cf. *Noack* (2000); *Hoffjan/Weide* (2006)).

sidiaries' cost type accounting significantly more extensively, if compared to cost centre or cost object accounting.[996] Hence, it is little surprising to find cost type accounting in Anglophone subsidiaries to be rather more in line with their parent companies' cost accounting traditions than cost centre and cost object accounting.

Mean values	Dataset 1				Dataset 2			
	Anglophone		German		Anglophone		German	
(1) Number of cost types	**0.60**		**0.66**	***	**0.60**		**0.65**	***
(2) Recognition of imputed costs	**0.37**		**0.60**	***	**0.38**		**0.61**	***
(3) Separation of financial and management accounting	**0.24**		**0.30**	*	0.24		0.29	
(4) Number of cost centres	**0.47**		**0.58**	***	**0.47**		**0.58**	***
(5) Rationales for cost centre formation	0.75		0.75		[0.75]		[0.75]	
(6) Classification of costs on cost centres	0.64		0.64		[0.64]		[0.63]	
(7) First stage allocation	**0.32**		**0.37**	*	**0.33**		**0.38**	*
(8) Second stage allocation	[0.39]	##	[0.33]		[0.39]	#	[0.35]	
(9) Variance analysis on cost centres	0.75		0.75		[0.75]		[0.73]	
(10) Types of cost objects	[0.74]		[0.70]		[0.74]		[0.70]	
(11) Product costing	[0.64]		[0.61]		[0.64]		[0.64]	
(12) Contribution margin accounting	**0.49**		**0.59**	***	**0.49**		**0.58**	***
(13) Time reference of cost accounting	[0.59]		[0.59]		[0.59]		[0.59]	
(14) Variance analysis on cost objects	**0.62**		**0.68**	*	0.62		0.67	
(15) Operating Income statement	0.46		0.47		0.45		0.48	
Complexity score	**0.54**		**0.57**		**0.54**		**0.57**	
p-value (test)	0.01 (two-tailed t-test)				0.02 (two-tailed t-test)			

Table 6-38: Summary of the complexity of cost accountings systems

For these latter two components, only 1/3 of the researched characteristics are significantly more complex in the domestic German companies. Remarkably, both statistically significant characteristics for cost centre accounting (number of cost centres and first stage allocation procedure) as well as the CM accounting practices are found by a previous comparison of German and Anglophone cost accounting to be more complex in domestic German companies as well.[997] Finding significant results for these characteristics in Anglophone subsidiaries in Germany indicates that Anglophone MNCs actually transfer their cost accounting practices into their foreign subsidiaries.

The statistically significant findings for dataset 1 widely persist for dataset 2. Only the significant difference for scores *(3) Separation of financial and management accounting* and *(14) variance analysis on cost objects* do not prevail. As discussed, this inability to find a significant difference for these sub-scores might reflect that cost accounting is applied less extensively for decision-making in the 15 domestic companies excluded from dataset 1. None of the previously insignificant differences becomes significant for dataset 2. There are multiple scores that were larger for the domestic German companies in dataset 1 which become larger for the Anglophone companies in dataset 2. Yet, none of these scores

[996] Cf. section 6.1.2.1.1.2, p. 202.

[997] Cf. *Krumwiede/Suessmair* (2007a), p. 6.

is significant. Overall, the analysis does not reveal that the exclusion of the 15 domestic German and two Anglophone subsidiaries that distinguish dataset 1 and 2 causes any substantial bias for the due explicative analysis.

Hypothesis test for the expectations summarised as H1

Aggregating all 15 complexity sub-scores into a mean score representing the complexity of the entire cost accounting system reveals strong support for the expectations summarised as hypothesis 1. The cost accounting systems of Anglophone subsidiaries[998] in Germany (0.54) are significantly less complex than the systems in comparable domestic German subsidiaries (0.57) at a 1% significance level (one-tailed). This result is stable for dataset 2. Due to this 'confirmative' hypothesis test, there is affirmative evidence for research question 1. Anglophone subsidiaries in Germany share various similarities with Anglophone cost accounting traditions. Similarly, the cost accounting practices in the domestic German subsidiaries are linked to previously identified German cost accounting traditions.

These results correspond well with *Harzing/Sorge* (2003), who argue that "Multinationals appear to follow tracks of coordination and control in which they have become embedded in their country of origin."[999] Section 6.1.2.2 reveals that this assertion is especially attributable to the level of corporate top management support.

6.1.2 Explicative evidence

6.1.2.1 Determinants of cost accounting systems in subsidiaries

6.1.2.1.1 Evidence on the independent variables

This study tests 24 hypotheses to explain the complexity of cost accounting systems in both Anglophone and domestic German subsidiaries. These 24 hypotheses comprise 19 explanatory variables. Two voluntary institutional influences (common costing practice in the subsidiaries' institutional context and costing experiences from sister affiliates) are excluded due to implausible responses (see section 5.3.1). The following sections will briefly introduce the remaining 17 variables. Due to data availability, results are provided for dataset 1 only.

6.1.2.1.1.1 Economic determinants

The **perceived environmental uncertainty** was surveyed through question A.3 of questionnaire A. It is perceived insignificantly different by Anglophone and domestic German subsidiaries. Moreover, both groups provide rather moderate levels of uncertainty, i.e. the average rating is close to the mid-point of the scale (Table 6-39).

---

[998] Among the Anglophone subsidiaries, a two-tailed test does not identify any significant differences between the complexity of cost accounting systems in greenfield and brownfield investments.

[999] *Harzing/Sorge* (2003), p. 206.

Mean value	How predictable are the developments in your company's environment? (Scale: 1 = very predictable 7 = very unpredictable)	
	Anglophone	German
Perceived environmental uncertainty (management accountants)	3.96	4.15
p-value (test)	0.25 (two-tailed t-test)	

Table 6-39: Perceived environmental uncertainty (dataset 1)

Besides the perceived environmental uncertainty, there are hypotheses for five cost accounting objectives. Despite the internal purposes 'decision facilitating' and 'decision influencing', and the external task 'inventory valuation', the hypotheses regard the application of cost information for 'operational' and 'strategic objectives'. The application of the **cost accounting objectives** was researched by questions B.20 and B.21 of questionnaire A. The empirical results show that the Anglophone and the domestic German subsidiaries apply these objectives equally intensively (Table 6-40). In addition, in both groups the objective (3) inventory valuation (5.89 and 5.84) is pursued significantly more intensively than the (1) decision facilitating (4.75 and 4.52) and the (2) decision influencing purposes (4.03 and 4.13). Also, the (1) decision influencing purpose significantly exceeds the (2) decision facilitating one. With respect to the differentiation of operational and strategic tasks, the (4) former is applied significantly more intensively (5.77 and 5.78) than (5) the latter (4.34 and 4.41).

Mean values	Pursuit of cost accounting objectives (Scale: 1 = not at all, 7 = very intensively)	
	Anglophone	German
(1) Decision facilitating	4.75	4.52
(2) Decision influencing	4.03	4.13
(3) Inventory valuation	5.89	5.84
(4) Operational	5.77	5.78
(5) Strategic	4.34	4.41
p-value (test)	For each objective, individual comparisons are performed based on two-tailed parametric tests. If significant, this is indicated by the significance levels *, ** or ***.	
	Individual comparisons of (1) – (3) and (4) – (5) reveal the identified differences to be significant at a 10 % level (two-tailed tests)	Individual comparisons of (1) – (3) and (4) – (5) reveal the identified differences to be significant at a 10 % level (two-tailed tests)

Table 6-40: Cost accounting objectives reported by management accountants (dataset 1)

For the German domestic subsidiaries, the relation between operational and strategic objectives as well as decision facilitating and decision influencing reflects German cost accounting traditions.[1000] Given the similarity of the statistical results, these traditions are also reflected in the Anglophone subsidiaries. Thereby, these findings rather contradict the similarly strong emphasis on decision facilitating and decision influencing in Anglophone literature. The result might reflect that the longer traditions of responsibility accounting in Anglophone countries are of academical rather than practical nature. Peculiarly, cost accounting is most heavily applied for external purposes, i.e. financial accounting oriented inventory valuation in both groups. Commonly, the dominance of external tasks is associated to Anglophone cost accounting traditions only.[1001] Thus, finding inventory valuation

[1000] For this and the following, cf. section 2.3.2, p. 29.

[1001] Cf. section 2.2.2, p. 12, section 2.2.3, p. 15, and section 2.2.4, p. 23.

to dominate the pursued cost accounting objectives in the domestic German companies somehow contradicts previous research on this matter. This assertion, however, is rather rigid. On the one hand, the task (3) 'inventory valuation' is as extensively pursued as an (unspecified) number of (4) 'operational objectives'.[1002] On the other hand, the variety of internal tasks is very broad. Out of the six regarded internal tasks, the Anglophone companies report 91 % and the domestic German companies 92 % to be pursued by their cost accounting system.[1003] Hence, above result rather suggests that cost accounting is as important for multiple internal decisions as it is for inventory valuation. Moreover, the interrelation of (3) inventory valuation and (4) operational decision-making suggests that the individual tasks chosen to survey the internal cost accounting objectives are complemented by additional ones in the subsidiaries.

Aggregating the five objectives from Table 6-40 into a measure of the 'extent of use' maintains the results from Table 6-40. The cost accounting systems are applied equally intensively in Anglophone (4.62) and domestic German subsidiaries (4.63). Since, the scores are larger than the mid-point of the applied seven point scale (Table 6-41), the cost accounting systems can be seen to be used rather intensively.

Mean values	**Pursuit of cost accounting objectives** (Scale: 1 = not at all, 7 = very intensively)	
	Anglophone	German
Extent of use	4.62	4.63
p-value (test)	0.93 (two-tailed t-test)	

Table 6-41: Cost accounting objectives - extent of use (dataset 1)

Product diversity was surveyed in this study by question A.4 of questionnaire A. Table 6-42 summarises the average product diversity discovered in dataset 1. Finding mean rating for the construct 'product diversity' hints that the products, production processes and non-manufacturing activities are moderately diverse in both Anglophone and domestic German subsidiaries. The scores do not differ significantly between the Anglophone (4.04) and domestic German subsidiaries (4.16).

Mean values	**Product diversity** (Interpretation of the scale: 1 = no diversity, 7 = highest level of diversity)	
	Anglophone subsidiaries	Domestic German subsidiaries
Product diversity	4.04	4.16
p-value (test)	0.47 (two-tailed t-test)	

Table 6-42: Product diversity (dataset 1)

The information technology applied for management accounting was explored by question A.5 of questionnaire A. In the Anglophone and the domestic German subsidiaries, enterprise resource planning software (**ERP**) is significantly more common than spreadsheet applications.[1004] Though the results are particularly similar to a previous study, which reveals ERP systems in 81 % of German and 65 % of US companies, there is no

[1002] The applied two-tailed t-tests show p-values of 0.40 (Anglophone subsidiaries) and 0.70 (domestic German subsidiaries).

[1003] The presence of tasks is determined by counting all companies that reported an objective to be somehow pursued (i.e. the scale (1 = not at all, 7 = very intensively) is marked (2) – (7)).

[1004] Chi^2 tests disapprove the hypothesis that there is an equal split between ERP software and spreadsheet solutions in both the Anglophone and the domestic German firms.

statistically significant difference between the applications of ERP software or spreadsheet applications between these two groups in this study.[1005] Table 6-43 summarises these results.

	Which information technology does your company mostly apply for management accounting purposes?	
	Anglophone	German
ERP	70.0 %	64.0 %
Spreadsheets	30.0 %	36.0 %
p-value (test)	0.37 (Chi² distribution test)	

Table 6-43: Applied information technologies (dataset 1)

To investigate different processing capabilities of alternative information technologies, respondents were asked how precisely their IT systems can picture the resource consumption in their companies (**IT processing capabilities**). Table 6-44 presents the results according to the applied information technologies.[1006] Overall, the precision of the information technology is quite high in both Anglophone (5.11) and domestic German subsidiaries (5.39).

Mean values	How precisely does the information technology, which your company mostly applies for management accounting purposes, picture the resource consumption that actually takes place in your company? (Scale: 1 = very imprecisely, 7 = very precisely)	
	Anglophone	German
ERP	5.20 *	5.61
Spreadsheets	4.87	5.00
Average	5.11	5.39
p-value (test)	For both information technologies, the precision is compared based on two-tailed parametric tests. If significant, this is indicated by the significance levels *, ** or ***.	

Table 6-44: Processing capabilities of the applied information technology (dataset 1)

On average, as well as for the application of spreadsheets, no statistically significant difference prevails with respect to the processing capabilities of the information technology between Anglophone and domestic German subsidiaries. Interestingly, however, there is such a difference for the ERP systems. In addition to potentially different ERP systems in place, this higher processing capability of ERP systems in domestic German subsidiaries appears to be linked to previous findings that Anglophone companies do not exploit the full potential of their information technologies.[1007]

The two variables regarding the provision of personnel resources were both investigated by question A.7 of questionnaire A. The respondents evaluate both the **adequacy of cost accountants** and the extent of **local top management support** rather positively. The variables score above the mid-point of the applied seven point rating scale (Table 6-45). Nevertheless, neither the adequacy of cost accountants, nor the local top management support varies significantly between Anglophone and domestic German subsidiaries.

[1005] Cf. *Krumwiede/Suessmair* (2007b), p. 51.

[1006] Finding ERP systems to have better processing capabilities than spreadsheets underlines the validity of the applied measurement models.

[1007] Cf. *Krumwiede/Suessmair* (2007a), p. 2. Accordingly, *Al-Sayed et al.* (2012), p. 144f., and *Clinton/White* (2012), p. 63, report that management accounting tools are only gradually implemented into ERP systems in Anglophone companies.

Mean values	Personnel resources for cost accounting (Interpretation of the scale: 1 = very poor/no support, 7 = not improvable/very strong support)	
	Anglophone	German
Adequacy of cost accountants	5.11	5.11
p-value (test)	0.99 (two-tailed t-test)	
Local top management support	4.86	5.01
p-value (test)	0.49 (two-tailed t-test)	

Table 6-45: Personnel resources for cost accounting (dataset 1)

For none of the introduced economic variables, there are statistically significant differences between the Anglophone and the domestic German subsidiaries. As such, both of these groups arguably operate in similar economic settings. Consequently, the differences of these companies' cost accounting systems should be rather attributable to the prevalence of institutional influences. This suggestion is analysed during hypothesis testing.

6.1.2.1.1.2 Institutional determinants

The coercive institutional influences of a parent company on its subsidiaries' cost accounting systems are argued to prevail through directives, personal involvement of the parent's top managers and the employment of expatriates.

The **prevalence of directives** was researched by question C.2 of questionnaire A. There is at least one directive in the majority of the researched companies (Table 6-46).[1008] Yet, there are more Anglophone subsidiaries experiencing the influence of at least one directive than domestic German subsidiaries (85.5 %, and 70.8 %). Furthermore, in both Anglophone and domestic German subsidiaries, the directives are most common for cost type accounting, followed by cost centre and cost object accounting.

Presence of directives	To what extent does your parent company impose the following cost accounting issues through corporate directives?	
	Anglophone	German
(1) The applicable cost types	79.1 %	69.5 %
(2) The procedures for overhead cost allocation	74.6 %	60.7 %
(3) The different cost objects	70.6 %	53.9 %
Directive for at least one of (1), (2), (3)	85.5 %	70.8 %

Table 6-46: Corporate directives on cost accounting (dataset 1)

The extent to which corporate directives explicate how to design the cost accounting systems is perceived to be rather moderate (Table 6-47) by both Anglophone (3.67) and domestic German subsidiaries (3.43). A two-tailed test reveals that these average figures do not vary significantly. Similarly, the Anglophone and German parent company's affect their subsidiaries (1) cost type, (2) cost centre and (3) cost object accounting rather moderately. Neither of these variables varies between the Anglophone and the domestic German subsidiaries.

[1008] The table provides the percentages of companies that reported that there is some extent of influence through corporate directives (i.e. the scale (1 = not at all, 7 = completely) is marked (2) – (7)).

Peculiarly, cost type accounting (1) tends to be more extensively influenced than cost centre accounting (2) and cost object accounting (3) in both groups.[1009] These differences between the effect on (1) cost type and (2) cost centre as well as (1) and (3) cost object accounting are statistically significant at a 1 % level (two-tailed). This finding is in line with the strong prevalence of Anglophone cost type accounting traditions in the Anglophone companies.

Extensiveness of directives' effects (mean values)	To what extent does your parent company impose the following cost accounting issues through corporate directives? (Scale: 1 = not at all, 7 = completely)	
	Anglophone	German
(1) The applicable cost types	4.28	4.31
p-value (test)	0.93 (two-tailed Welch test)	
(2) The procedures for overhead cost allocation	3.37	3.11
p-value (test)	0.40 (two-tailed Welch test)	
(3) The different cost objects	3.34	2.87
p-value (test)	0.14 (two-tailed t-test)	
(4) Average (variable: 'directives')	3.67	3.43
p-value (test)	0.40 (two-tailed Welch test)	

Table 6-47: Extent of influence on cost accounting through corporate directives (dataset 1)

The personal involvement of a parent company's top management into the complexity of subsidiaries' cost accounting systems was surveyed by the last item in question A.7 of questionnaire A. There is no statistically significant difference with respect to this support of **corporate managers** between the two groups (Table 6-48). Moreover, the support is rather moderate in both Anglophone (3.61) and domestic German subsidiaries (3.70).

Mean values	Personal involvement of a parent company's top management (Interpretation of the scale: 1= no support, 7 = very strong support)	
	Anglophone	German
Corporate managers	3.61	3.70
p-value (test)	0.74 (two-tailed t-test)	

Table 6-48: Corporate top management support for cost accounting (dataset 1)

Complementing the evidence on moderate influences of parent companies through directives and corporate managers, there are relatively few **expatriates** in the subsidiaries' management accounting functions. Expatriates are present in 19 Anglophone subsidiaries and 16 domestic German subsidiaries only. Thus, for the vast majority of the Anglophone (82.7 %) and the domestic German (82.2 %) subsidiaries, there are no expatriates at all. If present, there are on average three expatriates in the Anglophone subsidiaries and two in the domestic German subsidiaries. These numbers, however, do not differ significantly.

Finding statistically insignificant differences for the level of coercive institutional influences does not violate the assumption that the significantly less complex cost accounting systems in the Anglophone subsidiaries can be associated to their parent companies' influence. The extent of influence does not provide any insights about the cost accounting traditions conveyed by a parent company. Such a difference in the meaning of several ex-

[1009] A similar finding with respect to cost type accounting and overhead allocation was recently provided by *Heimel et al.* (2012), p. 59.

planatory variables is explicitly expected by this study.[1010] Given the evidence on the significant differences between the cost accounting systems, it is very likely that directives or personal involvements in Anglophone subsidiaries convey Anglophone cost accounting traditions. Section 6.1.2.2.2 will shed light on this issue in statistical terms.

Besides the coercive institutional influences, voluntary institutional influences are expected to affect cost accounting systems in subsidiary companies. Question A.8 of questionnaire A determined where the **employees responsible for cost accounting acquired most of their knowledge**. Previous literature reveals a university degree in business administration to be particularly common for management and cost accountants in Germany.[1011] In line with this communality, the cost accountants of the majority of domestic German companies are university trained (59.6 %).

	Where did the employees responsible for cost accounting in your company acquire most of the knowledge they need to fulfil their tasks?	
	Anglophone	German
Universities/Colleges located in		
a German-speaking country	52.8 %	58.7 %
an Anglophone country	/	0.9 %
another country	2.3 %	
At work "learning by doing" in companies located in		
a German-speaking country	44.9 %	42.7 %
an Anglophone country	/	1.8 %
another country	/	1.8 %
p-value (test)	0.30 (Chi² distribution test)	

Table 6-49: Primary source of knowledge for cost accounting (dataset 1)

The same holds true for the Anglophone subsidiaries (55.1 %). Since cost accountants in Anglophone companies are generally less extensively educated by university courses on business administration,[1012] it is surprising to find the overall distribution of educational backgrounds in the Anglophone and the domestic German subsidiaries to vary insignificantly. As there are very few expatriates in the Anglophone subsidiaries which might have experienced an Anglophone career path, this finding is likely to reflect the employment of German cost accountants in the Anglophone subsidiaries. As such, the results are well explicable. Hence, in both groups cost accountants were mostly educated in Germany (Table 6-49). Since hypothesis H3b2_3 conjectures on the effect of being educated at a German university, this result underlines the validity of the data to test this hypothesis. Yet, this result disables any analysis on the effect of national specific education.

Management accountants in Anglophone companies are generally educated through **professional institutes of management accountants.**[1013] Hence, question A.9 of questionnaire A surveyed how intensively the cost accountants further their education through German and Anglophone professional institutes of management accountants. In the ma-

[1010] Cf. section 4.1.5, p. 99.
[1011] Cf. section 4.2.1, p. 105f.
[1012] Cf. section 4.2.1, p. 105f.
[1013] Cf. section 4.2.1, p. 105.

jority of both Anglophone (76.6 %) and domestic German subsidiaries (78.7 %), management accountants receive some professional training by institutes from German speaking countries (Table 6-50).[1014] In contrast, only in a minority of the subsidiaries there are further trainings by Anglophone associations. The proportion, however, is substantially larger for the Anglophone subsidiaries (28.2 % vs. 14.6 %). Despite revealing that German companies may be little aware of Anglophone associations of management accountants, this finding essentially underlines the nomological validity of the constructs.

	Proportion of companies in which management accountants further their education through professional institutes of management accountants	
	Anglophone	German
German-speaking countries	76.6 %	78.7 %
Anglophone countries	28.2 %	14.6 %

Table 6-50: Existence of advanced trainings by professional institutes of management accountants (dataset 1)

Despite finding that cost accountants from both groups commonly further their education through professional institutes from Germany, the intensity of these further trainings is quite low (2.8 vs. 2.9) and insignificantly different in the two groups (Table 6-51). Also, the intensity of further trainings through Anglophone institutes is quite low for both groups (1.5 vs. 1.2). Despite being at a low level, the cost accountants in the Anglophone subsidiaries experience a significantly more intensive professional training from the Anglophone institutes than their counterparts from the domestic German subsidiaries.

These findings are quite insightful for the Anglophone subsidiaries. As exemplified, professional institutes play a very important role in the education of management accountants in their parent companies' home countries. Thus, the education of management accountants in the Anglophone subsidiaries seems contrastable to the likely educational background of their counterparts in the parent companies. Not only are these employees especially trained in Germany, but they also have experienced little professional training from Anglophone institutes of management accountants.

Mean values	How intensively do the employees responsible for cost accounting in your company further their qualification through professional institutes of management accountants from the following geographical areas? (Scale: 1 = not at all, 7 = very intensively)	
	Anglophone	German
German-speaking countries	2.8	2.9
p-value (test)	0.69 (two-tailed t-test)	
Anglophone countries	1.5	1.2
p-value (test)	0.02 (two-tailed Welch test)	

Table 6-51: Intensity of advanced trainings by professional institutes of management accountants (dataset 1)

All in all, two peculiar findings are worthwhile to be emphasised at this point. Cost accountants in the Anglophone subsidiaries are especially educated in Germany. Assuming these employees' influence on the design of their companies' cost accounting systems, it is little surprising to find cost accounting in the Anglophone subsidiaries to share multiple

[1014] The table provides the proportion of companies that reported that there is some further training by professional institutes (i.e. the scale (1 = not at all, 7 = very intensively) is marked (2) – (7)).

characteristics with German cost accounting traditions. In a similar vein, the cost accountants from the Anglophone subsidiaries commonly receive professional trainings from professional institutes of management accountants from Germany. Since these are expected to convey German cost accounting traditions,[1015] the prevalence of German cost accounting traditions is, even though the intensities of these trainings are quite low, little surprising. The due explicative analysis tests whether these voluntary institutional effects on the Anglophone subsidiaries' cost accounting systems prevail in statistical terms.

6.1.2.1.1.3 Relational context

This study predicts that the **relational context** of a subsidiary with its parent moderates the effect of a parent company's coercive influence. Subsidiaries are expected to oppose their parent company's directive if (1) the subsidiary has rather different cost information needs, (2) there are extensive affective conflicts, (3) the subsidiary does not identify itself with its parent company and (4) the subsidiary can change its management accounting function without consulting its parent company.[1016] All these items were investigated by question C.1 of questionnaire A.

Mean values	**Please characterise the relationship between your company and your parent company.** (Interpretation of the scale: 1 = not unfavourable, 7 = completely unfavourable)	
	Anglophone	German
(1) Different information needs	4.13	3.94
p-value (test)	0.47 (two-tailed t-test)	
(2) Affective conflicts	2.40	2.08
p-value (test)	0.08 (two-tailed t-test)	
(3) Lack of identification	4.10	4.01
p-value (test)	0.71 (two-tailed t-test)	
(4) Ability to change management accounting function	3.81	4.60
p-value (test)	0.07 (two-tailed t-test)	
Relational context	3.56	3.71
p-value (test)	0.27 (two-tailed t-test)	

Table 6-52: Management accountants' perceptions of the relational context (dataset 1)

The means for the individual components of the formatively defined relational context as well as the composite score are presented in Table 6-52. Only two of the researched components of the relational context ((2) and (4)) differ significantly between Anglophone and domestic German subsidiaries. Whereas there are (at a low level) more affective conflicts in Anglophone than in domestic German subsidiaries, the latter companies can change their management accounting function more extensively without consulting their parent company. Overall, however, there are moderate mean values (3.6 and 3.7) for the relational context. The relationship between Anglophone and domestic German subsidiaries and their parents is little unfavourable. Hence, the likelihood that the subsidiaries oppose their parent companies' coercive involvement is rather low. The meaning of this ra-

[1015] Cf. section 4.2.1, p. 105.

[1016] Additionally, the participation of a subsidiary in the development of management accounting directives is relevant. As explicated in section 5.3.1, this item is excluded from the analysis due to poor data quality.

ther favourable relationship for the forthcoming analysis, however, remains unclear. On the one hand, it could hinder the identification of a moderating effect on the coercive institutional influences. On the other hand, the coercive institutional influences score similarly low on the applied scale. Therefore, the moderation effect might still prevail, since a low level of corporate involvement might be offset by a low level of an unfavourable relational context.

6.1.2.1.2 Correlation analysis

Appendix 4 summarises the linear correlations between the dependent and independent variables as well as the controls.[1017] For the *Anglophone subsidiaries*, there are three peculiar findings.

First, the **relational context** and all three **coercive institutional influences** correlate rather weakly, yet highly significantly (1 % level) in a negative manner (r = -0.29; -0.26; - 0.38). Thus, the more extensive a parent company is involved in its subsidiary, the less unfavourable is the relational context. Either a subsidiary perceives the relationship with its parent to be more unfavourable if the parent engages very little into its management accounting or a parent is less likely to impose a cost accounting practice if there is a rather tense relationship with its subsidiary. These associations could be due to an implicit prevalence of the suggested moderation. If there is a rather unfavourable situation, a subsidiary may report little influence on its cost accounting system simply because they have previously opposed it. On the other hand, the result might be due to the fact that the longer the time of affiliation, the less unfavourable the relational context (r = -0.19, p = 5 %). Thus, the researched companies appear to *learn* to get along with their parent over time. If the suggested moderation between the relational context and the coercive institutional pressures cannot be identified in section 6.1.2, this correlation has to be reconsidered. The finding, however, underlines that the relational context and coercive institutional influences are indeed intertwined and as such merit in-depth analysis.

Second, the researched **cost accounting objectives** are rather strongly correlated (min. r = 0.09, max. r = 0.64) with one another in a mostly highly significant manner. Also, the objectives are correlated with several of the other variables in a significant to highly significant manner. Accordingly, the pursuit of cost accounting objectives is moderately correlated with the local top management support (min. r = 0.11; max. r = 0.40), the adequacy of cost accountants (min. r = 0.18; max. r = 0.32), the processing capability of the information technology (min. r = 0.22; max. r = 0.35) and university trained employees (min. r = 0.20; max. r = 0.36). Neither correlation is surprising. Strong top management support indicates an overall interest in cost information. Thus, it is little peculiar to find cost information extensively used for decision-making in these situations. Moreover, if there are sufficient personnel and technical resources to run and enhance the cost accounting system (i.e. a high adequacy of cost accountants and a high processing capability of the information technology), the system is likely to be designed in a way that allows generating useful and readily applicable information. In a similar vein, a university trained em-

[1017] The Spearman correlations reveal no differences with respect to the forthcoming discussions.

ployee may be better equipped to derive decision-useful information from a cost accounting system which, as a result, is used extensively. The rather strong intercorrelations of the objectives mean that a company which applies its cost accounting system rather extensively does so for all suggested objectives. Especially for Anglophone companies, which are known to focus on both decision influencing and decision facilitating, this finding is actually as expected. In sum, however, the extensive intercorrelation[1018] of the different objectives dilutes the ability to test H3al_2 to H3a_6 separately. Consequently, H3al_2 - H3al_6 are regarded conjointly by analysing the following hypothesis:

H3al_2 - H3al_6:
The more extensively a subsidiary uses cost information for decision-making, the more complex is its cost accounting system.

Third, there is a moderate and significantly positive correlation between the **adequacy of cost accountants** with both university training (r = 0.19, p = 5 %) as well as the further trainings through German professional institutes (r = 0.25, p = 1 %). Also, these latter two variables are correlated moderately and significantly with **local top management support.**[1019] As above, these associations are very reasonable. The cost accountants' ability to run and enhance a costing system is likely to depend on their educational background and professional trainings. A manager interested in cost information is likely to allocate sufficient resources to cost accounting to design the system to derive useful information. Thus, finding high levels of professional trainings and the employment of university trained cost accountants in companies, whose managers support their cost accountants strongly, is well explicable.

In the sample of domestic *German subsidiaries*, several particularly interesting correlations can be identified as well. On the one hand, there are similarly strong and significant intercorrelations between the **cost accounting objectives** as found for the Anglophone subsidiaries.[1020] This finding reinforces the necessity to analyse H3al_2 to H3al_6 conjointly. On the other hand, there are three additional particularities.

First, the rather strong and highly significant negative correlation between the **institutional coercive influences** and the **relational context** prevails (min. r = -0.49, max. r = - 0.35). In contrast to the Anglophone subsidiaries, however, the negative correlation between the length of affiliation and the relational context does not exist (r = 0.04, insignificant). This might suggest that an unfavourable relational context decreases over time in the Anglophone subsidiaries only since these learn about their parents' *foreign* management accounting traditions. Nevertheless, these interactions merit cautious consideration during the forthcoming moderation analysis.

Second, there is a significant and moderately strong correlation between the level of **perceived environmental uncertainty** and the **decision facilitating** use of information (r = - 0.35, p = 1 %). Thus, in domestic German companies cost information is used less in-

[1018] Seven out of ten intercorrelations have a significant correlation coefficient of above 0.4.

[1019] The correlation for university education has a correlation coefficient of 0.23 and a significance level of 5 %. For the German institutes of management accountants, the values are r = 0.36 and p = 1 %.

[1020] Four out of ten correlation coefficients are above 0.4. An additional two are above 0.3. All of these are highly significant.

tensively for thorough decision-making if the environmental context is very unpredictable. This finding appears to dissent from the establishment of a theoretical need for cost information though market imperfection (environmental uncertainties). However, this association does not necessarily violate that cost information needs arise from environmental uncertainty. The correlation might rather reflect that cost information is less important in the German subsidiaries if these operate in particularly unpredictable environments. Similarly, *Moeschler* (2012) identified a negative correlation between managers' overall interest in cost information and the dynamics of a company's environment.[1021] As such, the finding is linked to previous research which finds the use of non-financial information to be associated with organisational performance if the environment is highly uncertain.[1022] In a similar context, costs' outdatedness is used as an explanation for a reduced application of cost information during uncertain environmental conditions.[1023] Hence, the identified correlation might merely be due to the dominance of other information than costs in a company's decision processes in times of an unpredictable environment.

Third, **product diversity** correlates moderately yet significantly with the **cost accounting objectives** 'decision influencing' ($r = -0.27$, $p = 1$ %), 'operational objectives' ($r = -0.22$, $p = 5$ %) and 'strategic objectives' ($r = -0.22$, $p = 5$ %) in a negative manner. This finding appears rather consistent. A high level of product diversity (i.e. differing production volumes or little communalities in the utilisation of support departments) can aggravate the establishment of meaningful means-end relationships during overhead allocation. As such, costs cannot be easily associated to cost objects in a way that reflects the resource-consumption evoked by a product. Such 'inaccuracies' in a company's cost accounting system are known to impinge the decision usefulness of cost information.[1024] Also, inaccurate cost information is likely to restrict the applicability to influence others behaviour. Applying distorted cost information might be perceived unfair since the actual cost information may not reflect the responsibilities of an influenced employee. Thus, finding product diversity to impinge the application of cost information may be due to their reduced decision usefulness.

From the viewpoint of multicollinearity, this section reveals little problems with respect to the ability to test the hypotheses on the various explanatory variables separately. Only for the numerous cost accounting objectives the correlation analysis signals the necessity to look more broadly on the extent of use rather than individual objectives. Also, most correlations can be easily explained. Thereby, the results are indicative for a reasonable nomological validity of the formatively defined constructs included in this section. Nevertheless, the mere number of correlations underlines the necessity to test for issues of multicollinearity during the linear regression analyses.

[1021] Cf. *Moeschler* (2012), p. 379.

[1022] Cf. e.g. *Hoque* (2005), p. 379. A similar discussion can be found in *Davila* (2000), p. 393 and 400, or *Steiners* (2005), p. 186f.

[1023] For a similar argument, cf. *Karlshaus* (2000), p. 161.

[1024] Cf. e.g. *Bhimani/Pigott* (1992); *Bhimani* (2003).

6.1.2.1.3 Hypotheses testing

6.1.2.1.3.1 Introduction

The determinants of the complexity of cost accounting systems in Anglophone and domestic German subsidiaries are analysed through linear regression models. For both these groups, two models are computed. Model (a) consists of the 17 independent variables and the four control[1025] variables. Model (b) includes three additional interaction terms. These interaction terms are included to test for the moderating effect of the relational context (hypothesis H3c).[1026]

The hypotheses tests especially rely on an analysis of the average complexity scores (Table 6-53). Moreover, various hypotheses are discussed in the light of models which take the complexity scores for cost type, cost centre and cost object accounting as their dependent variables (Appendix 5). These will be especially regarded to discuss the absence of a hypothesized association more thoroughly. Also, these additional models complement the discussion if there were unexpected directions of the regression coefficients in Table 6-53. Some of the directed hypotheses have to be rejected due to such unexpected signs of the regression coefficients. To derive meaningful explanations for such unpredicted results, these coefficients are treated as if the identified sign was expected. If e.g. the regression results reveal that an expected positive sign is actually smaller than zero and has a p-value below 0.1 (one-tailed test), then the coefficient will be treated as 'quasi significant'. To allow for an immediate identification of such findings, the asterisk (*) usually used to tag significant findings is replaced by a diamond (#).[1027]

Given the reliance on two models (model (a) and model (b)) and the analysis of several complexity scores, it is essential to explicate when to reject or to accept the hypotheses. Results which are not present for models (a) and (b) are regarded as less robust findings. Combined with the prevalence of a finding for the four complexity scores, this will be taken into account during the rejection of the hypotheses. Suggested interrelations are accepted (i.e. not rejected)[1028] conditionally if they are of little robustness or of selective presence. Also, hypotheses are rejected conditionally if evidence to support a hypothesis does not outweigh results which require its rejection.

[1025] These controls are the subsidiary's size and its length of affiliation as well as the parent's form of market entry and its size. Additionally controlling for financial holdings which *Weißenberger* (2003), p. 206ff., describes as least influential for a subsidiary's control system would not change the results considerably. Also, the inclusion of the number of value chain activities does not substantially change the results. Neither of these additional controls would change the conclusions to be drawn in section 6.3.3.

[1026] All four variables involved in the moderation analysis ('directives', 'corporate managers', 'expatriates' and 'relational context') were centred before including them into the analyses.

[1027] This procedure will be evaluated critically in the limitations (section 7.2) since it restricts how rigorously this study follows its epistemological positioning.

[1028] Non-rejected hypotheses will be synonymously labeled as 'accepted' hereafter. This is done for terminological reasons (cf. section 1.3 for this study's epistemological position (incl. fallibism)).

Linear regression model - dataset 1 (unstandardised regression coeff.)	**Dependent variable: cost accounting complexity**					
	Anglophone subsidiaries			German subsidiaries		
	E.S.	Model (a)	Model (b)	E.S.	Model (a)	Model(b)
Perceived environmental uncertainty	+	0.0105 *	0.0114	+	-0.0131	-0.0141
Extent of use	+	0.0501 ***	0.0492 ***	+	0.0403 ***	0.0389 ***
Product diversity	+	-0.0029	-0.0005	+	0.0090	0.0089
ERP *(dummy)*	+	0.0275	0.0270	+	0.0265 *	0.0257
IT processing capabilities	+	0.0025	0.0017		0.0288 ***	0.0293 ***
Adequacy of cost accountants	+	0.0013	0.0004	+	-0.0074	-0.0080
Top management support	+	0.0177 **	0.0159 **	+	-0.0178 ##	-0.0166 #
Relational context *(centralised)*	/	-0.0071	-0.0085	/	0.0036	0.0039
Directives *(centralised)*	-	0.0026	0.0021	+/-	-0.0032	-0.0022
Directives **x** Rel. context *(centralised)*	+		-0.0031	-/+		-0.0003
Corporate managers *(centralised)*	-	-0.0247 ***	-0.0231 ***	+/-	0.0090	0.0099
Corp. managers **x** Rel. context *(central.)*	+		-0.0003	-/+		0.0036
Expatriates *(centralised)*	-	-0.0021	0.0139	+/-	0.0077	-0.0107
Expatriats **x** Rel. context *(centralised)*	+		0.0205 **	-/+		-0.0216
University training *(dummy)*	+	-0.0132	-0.0108	0	-0.0135	-0.0208
Professional institutes - German	+	0.0082	0.0087	+/-	0.0064	0.0068
Professional institutes - Anglophone	+/-	0.0140	0.0121	+/-	0.0117	0.0054
Size subsidiary	/	0.0130	0.0144	/	0.0091	0.0069
Form of market entry *(dummy)*	/	0.0091	0.0109	/	0.0186	0.0152
Length of affiliation	/	-0.0132	-0.0098	/	0.0178 *	0.0227 *
Size parent company	/	0.0033	0.0037	/	-0.0005	0.0002
Constant	/	0.0290	0.0181		0.2233 **	0.2337 **
R^2		43.41 %	44.73 %		43.76 %	45.41 %
adjusted R^2		32.20 %	31.50 %		29.30 %	28.30 %
F		3.26	3.86		6.04	5.47
Significance		0.0001	0.0000		0.0000	0.0000
VIF_{max}		2.16	2.28		2.14	2.65
F (moderation)		1.28			1.02	

Table 6-53: Multivariate regression results on determinants of the complexity of cost accounting (dataset 1)

Table 6-53 summarises the findings of the linear regression analysis for the average complexity score. The significant F-values indicate that the explanatory power of the model is acceptable. Moreover, the adjusted R^2 for model (a) and (b) for the Anglophone (32.20 %, 31.50 %) and domestic German subsidiaries (29.30 %, 28.30 %) are rather high,[1029] indicating a considerable fitness of the proposed model. Moreover, multicollinearity is not an issue in models (a) and (b). The maximum VIFs fall behind the threshold of 10. Autocorrelation and heteroscedasticity are not tested for, because the regression analysis is based on robust estimators in this respect.[1030] The significance levels in Table 6-53 are based on one-tailed tests for directed hypotheses and on two-tailed tests for undirected hypotheses and the controls.

6.1.2.1.3.2 Economic determinants

For both Anglophone and domestic German subsidiaries, hypothesis H3a1_1 suggests a positive association between the level of **perceived environmental uncertainty** and the complexity of cost accounting systems. In the *Anglophone subsidiaries*, the association is positive and marginally significant[1031] for the average complexity score (model (a)) in Table 6-53). Moreover, this result also prevails for cost type accounting and cost centre accounting (esp. model (a) in Appendix 5 – Table 1). As such, there is conditional empirical support for H3a1_1 for these companies. For the *German domestic subsidiaries*, no such influence can be identified (Table 6-53). In contrast to the hypothesis, higher levels of environmental uncertainty are actually associated 'quasi significantly' with a lower complexity of cost object accounting (cf. Appendix 5 – Table 2). Despite violating hypothesis H3a1_1, this result can be linked to the additional effect of environmental uncertainty discussed during the correlation analysis. Unpredictable economic conditions can lead to a focus on other (non-financial) information for decision-making. Overall, hypothesis H3a1_1 has to be rejected for the domestic German companies. It can be 'accepted conditionally' for the Anglophone companies, however.

Since the difference between the perceptions on environmental uncertainty in Anglophone and domestic German subsidiaries vary insignificantly,[1032] above finding suggests that these two groups react differently to environmental uncertainty. This proposal could be investigated more intensively in the future by regarding the effect of uncertainty avoiding behaviours in Anglophone and German subsidiaries. Potentially, there are within firm or within country effects of such cultural values on the design and use of cost accounting and other information systems. As such, future research on the *cultural contingency* of cost accounting such as the one by *Brewer* (1998) would improve the understanding of this study's finding.

Hypotheses H3a1_2 to H3a1_6 regard the influence of information needs on the design of cost accounting systems. If all cost accounting objectives are regarded conjointly as a

---

[1029] In a similar study, *Moeschler* (2012), p. 268, reports adj. R^2 values of 31.9 % for an analysis of domestic German companies and 15.6 % for a sample of Japanese companies. Previous research on the complexity of cost accounting rather falls behind these fit statistics (cf. *Moeschler* (2012), p. 267).

[1030] As discussed in section 5.4.3.1, the regression analysis is performed based on 'adjusted sandwich estimators'.

[1031] For brevity, the following discussion does not differentiate literally between marginally significant (10 % level), significant (5 % level) and highly significant (1 %) results. This information is presented in Table 6-53 and Appendix 5. Unexpectedly directed findings with a p-value below 0.1 (one sided test) will be literally distinguished by labelling them 'quasi significant'.

[1032] Cf. section 6.1.2.1.1.1, p. 199.

measure of the **extent of use**[1033], significant positive effects can be found in both samples (models (a) and (b) in Table 6-53). Since different costs are generally needed for different purposes, this finding is well explicable. The more purposes are followed, the more diverse cost information is needed and the more complex a cost accounting system needs to be. Thus, the rationale beyond H3a1_2 to H3a1_6 (i.e. an alignment of the complexity of cost accounting systems with the need for cost information) can be sustained. Neither for the Anglophone subsidiaries, nor for the domestic German subsidiaries the conjoint hypothesis H3a1_2-H3a1_6 can be rejected.

Hypothesis H3a2_1 predicts a positive association between **product diversity** and the design of cost accounting systems. This association prevails neither for the Anglophone subsidiaries, nor for the domestic German subsidiaries in statistically significant terms (Table 6-53). However, there is one interesting particularity in this regard. The applied measure of product diversity is significant in previous studies of overhead cost allocation practices,[1034] insignificant in a study on cost object accounting[1035] and failed in a study on all three components of a cost accounting system.[1036] Thus, the absence of an association between product diversity and the average complexity of cost accounting systems might be merely a result of this variables' restricted effect on overhead allocation procedures (i.e. cost centre accounting). Despite for the *domestic German subsidiaries* only, the significantly positive association between the complexity of the cost centre accounting system (includes overhead allocation procedures) is found in this study as well (Appendix 5). The absence of a similar result for the *Anglophone subsidiaries* might be linked to the fact that overhead allocation practices (cost centre costing) in these companies are more consistently influenced by their parents (Appendix 5). This might complicate the systems' alignment with internal structures.

Because this study's finding mirrors previous research on the importance of product diversity, hypothesis 3a2_1 is 'accepted conditionally' for the domestic German companies. Yet, H3a2_1 has to be rejected for the Anglophone subsidiaries. The expected relation between product diversity and the average complexity scores as well as the scores for cost type, cost centre and cost object accounting is insignificant.

Hypothesis H3a2_2 regards the effect of information technology for the complexity of cost accounting systems. For the *Anglophone subsidiaries*, no significant association between the average complexity score and the application of an **ERP system** can be found (Table 6-53). The same holds true for the **processing capabilities** of an information technology. Yet, there are some revealing findings for the complexity sub-scores in the Anglophone subsidiaries. The expected significantly positive effect of the mere existence of an ERP system prevails for the complexity of cost type accounting (Appendix 5). Moreover, the expected significant effect also prevails for the processing capabilities in the analysis of the complexity of cost centre accounting. The better the information technolo-

---

[1033] For the measure 'extent of use', cf. section 6.1.2.1.1.1.

[1034] Cf. e.g. *Al-Omiri/Drury* (2007), p. 403, for a review of studies on ABC and *Drury/Tayles* (2005), p. 74, for a more general example.

[1035] Cf. *Al-Omiri/Drury* (2007), p. 420.

[1036] Cf. *Moeschler* (2012), p. 235.

gy, the easier it is to reflect the consumption of resources more thoroughly for overhead allocation. However, there also is an unexpected 'quasi significantly' negative effect of the processing capabilities on the complexity of cost type accounting. This latter result contradicts the positive effect of the existence of an ERP system. It may reflect that Anglophone parent companies use information technologies with good processing capabilities to diffuse the applicable cost types into their German subsidiaries more extensively. Yet, compared to the application of spreadsheet solutions, the mere existence of an ERP technology still increases the ability to regard various cost types or to maintain two datasets for financial and management accounting.[1037] But, the better the processing capabilities of the systems get, the more an Anglophone parent may ensure the application of its common chart of accounts.[1038] This rather weak evidence for the influence of an ERP technology on the complexity of cost accounting in the Anglophone subsidiaries is well in line with previous research. Anglophone companies are known not to exploit the full potential of their ERP technologies.[1039] For the *domestic German subsidiaries*, the suggested positive effect of information technologies exists as suggested (Table 6-53). Both the mere existence of ERP software (model (a) only) and the processing capabilities of the applied information technology allow companies to maintain more complex cost accounting systems. This finding is due to an effect of the information technology on the complexity of cost object and cost centre accounting (Appendix 5). The result reflects previous research which identifies SAP[1040] to be particularly common in German companies.[1041] As such, there is strong support for H3a2_2 for the domestic German subsidiaries. For the Anglophone subsidiaries, there is similar support for the hypothesis. It is, however, less conclusive due to the apparent use of information technologies to diffuse Anglophone cost accounting traditions.

Hypothesis H3a2_3 predicts a positive effect of adequately equipped cost accountants on the complexity of cost accounting systems. Univocally, the **adequacy of cost accountants** has a non-expected 'quasi significant' negative effect on the complexity of cost type accounting (Appendix 5). The more adequate the cost accountants in the two researched groups are, the less attention appears to be given to a detailed and unique dataset for cost information (not reported). Despite violating the expected sign of H3a2_3, this finding might be reflecting a recent tendency of German management accountants. These strive for a more extensive alignment of management and financial accounting information nowadays.[1042] The finding could also be a side effect of the parent companies' directives in this regard. Local cost accountants may be unable to develop their company's cost type accounting. Remarkably, the expected positive effect of the adequacy of cost accountants prevails for the complexity of cost centre accounting in the *Anglophone subsidiaries*

[1037] In contrast to these two aspects of the complexity measure for the cost type accounting system, no association between information technology and the application of imputed costs was found.

[1038] For the dominance of the general ledger concept in Anglophone companies, cf. section 2.1.2.1.3.

[1039] Cf. *Krumwiede/Suessmair* (2007a), p. 2, and similarly *Clinton/White* (2012), p. 63.

[1040] The management accounting module of SAP is infused by the complex German GPK practices (cf. *White* (2004), p. 6; *Vikas* (2006), p. 36; *Kilger et al.* (2012), chapter 1 (footnote 137) and p. 389).

[1041] Cf. e.g. *Krumwiede/Suessmair* (2007a), p. 4.

[1042] Cf. *Friedl et al.* (2009), p. 114; *Heimel et al.* (2012), p. 59.

(Appendix 5). The better a company's cost accountants, the more they ensure that their cost accounting system reflects their companies' efforts towards responsibility accounting and overhead allocation. No statistically significant result is found for the level of cost object accounting. Given the absence of the expected association between the average complexity score and the adequacy of cost accounting and the diverse findings in Appendix 5, H3a2_3 is rejected at this point. It is essential to note, however, that the results for cost type and cost centre accounting do not contradict the rationale beyond H3a2_3. Rather, German cost accountants may strive for a simplification of cost type accounting nowadays. Also, they might be unable to contribute substantially to the design of cost centre and cost object accounting practices of their subsidiary. Moreover, in the Anglophone subsidiaries, the domestic cost accountants still rely extensively on the establishment of detailed cost centre accounting systems. As such, the hypothesis rejection is marked as a conditional rejection for both groups.

Hypothesis H4a2_4 regards if **local top management support** is associated positively with the complexity of cost accounting systems. In both Anglophone and domestic German subsidiaries, local top managers 'significantly' influence the complexity of cost accounting (Table 6-53). However, only in *Anglophone subsidiaries*, the effect has the expected positive sign. As such, hypothesis H3a2_4 cannot be rejected for these companies. Besides the suggested resource-related explanation underlying H3a2_4, this finding could indicate that German cost accounting traditions find their way into Anglophone subsidiaries through local top management support. For the *domestic German subsidiaries*, an extensive involvement of local managers is associable with less complex cost accounting systems (Table 6-53). As such, hypothesis H3a2_4 has to be rejected for the domestic German subsidiaries. There are two potential explanations for this unexpected result.[1043] On the one hand, the identified negative influence might reflect managers' attempt to keep cost information understandable. Despite for cost type accounting in particular, there is evidence that the domestic German information users prefer less complex cost accounting systems for decision-making.[1044] On the other hand, the size of the companies may underlie this result. 61 % of the domestic German subsidiaries are smaller than their parent company. Thus, the finding might reflect local top managers' striving to fit the cost accounting system transferred by a large parent to the local context (size effect). Thereby, the inability to derive the insignificant effect of top management support on cost type accounting procedures (Appendix 5) appears well in line with a finding suggesting that domestic German parent companies diffuse somewhat simple cost type accounting procedures in the first place (cf. p. 218). This latter explanation, however, lacks some conclusiveness. Domestic German subsidiaries do report only moderately different cost infor-

[1043] At this point, no concerns with respect to the measure's validity need to be raised. The measure is rather reliable if compared to answers given in questionnaire B. An according Pearson correlation analysis in dataset 3 reveals information users to report a significantly higher level of satisfaction with their cost accounting system if their management accountants reported a heavy involvement of the local top managers (i.e. the users). Thus, users appear to be more satisfied with their cost information if they engage extensively into the system's design.

[1044] This finding evolves from analysing the usage types. It will be discussed detailedly in section 6.2.

mation needs if compared to their parents.[1045] Hence, the necessity for local adjustment cannot be conclusively established.

6.1.2.1.3.3 Coercive institutional determinants and the relational context

The set of hypotheses H3b1 regards how parent companies affect the cost accounting systems in subsidiaries. H3c suggests that these coercive institutional influences are moderated by the relational context between a subsidiary and its parent company.

For the *Anglophone companies*, two expected significant effects can be identified with respect to the coercive institutional influences on the average complexity score (Table 6-53). There is a significant negative effect of **corporate managers' involvement** (H3b1_2a) in models (a) and (b). This suggests that corporate managers' involvement has a decreasing effect on the complexity of these subsidiaries' cost accounting system (if there is an average relational context). As such, there is substantial evidence for the validity of hypothesis H3b1_2a for the Anglophone subsidiaries. Parent companies are indeed influential for the design of cost accounting systems in subsidiaries. This influence, however, prevails for corporate managers' personal involvement only. Neither for **directives** (H3b1_1a), nor for the presence of **expatriates** (H3b1_3a) such direct or conditional effects can be identified in Table 6-53. Hence, there is no straight evidence to support H3b1_1a and H3b1_3a.

Finding personal effects to be influential whereas the rather bureaucratic provision of directives is not, is very insightful. Despite the presence of both directives as well as corporate managers' involvement (cf. section 6.2.2.1.3.3) and regardless a positive correlation between these two variables (cf. Appendix 4), a parent company's personal involvements appear more influential for the design of cost accounting than the mere provision of directives. Whether this finding is due to, for example, imprecise or discretionary directives or a greater acceptance of coercive pressures that are brought forward through personal discussions, cannot be ultimately explained by this study. Especially the latter argument appears reasonable. Previous research finds control mechanisms which include local involvements to ensure the application of control systems in subsidiaries.[1046] Also, such involvement reduces conflicts between affiliates and their parent companies.[1047]

Being able to support H3b1_2a (corporate managers) but unable to support H3b1_1a (directives) and H3b1_3a (expatriates) for the average complexity measure must not be revised considerably if the analyses on the **complexity sub-scores** (Appendix 5 – Table 1) are taken into account. Nevertheless, there are some particularly puzzling findings in this regard for the complexity sub-scores for cost type, cost centre and cost object accounting. One of these particularities is exemplarily discussed at this point. Corporate directives are 'quasi significantly' associated with the complexity of cost type accounting. Apparently, for this sub-score, a more intensive provision of directives increases the complexity of cost

[1045] Cf. 6.1.2.1.1.3, p. 206. A similar analysis for dataset 3 reassured this finding for the questionnaires returned from the information users.

[1046] Cf. e.g. *Dossi/Patelli* (2008), p. 132 and 139; *Schäffer et al.* (2010), p. 313.

[1047] Cf. e.g. *Johnson et al.* (2001), p. 46.

accounting (if there is an average relational context). Disaggregating this score into the individual complexity sub-scores that were discussed in section 6.1.1, reveals this finding to hold in particular for the determination of imputed costs (model (a) and (b)). Three alternative explanations for this unexpected relationship appear reasonable. First, Anglophone directives on cost type accounting may place a stronger emphasis on the application of imputed costs nowadays. Though this explanation corresponds to the increasing acknowledgement of GPK in the Anglophone world, it appears unlikely. Such an interpretation contradicts the commonly highlighted particularities of Anglophone cost accounting. Second, this finding might be due to reversed causality, i.e. endogeneity which is linked to this study's focus on brownfield investments.[1048] Subsidiaries which (still) rely on German cost accounting traditions with respect to the application of imputed costs, might be confronted with more extensive directives on how to design their cost type accounting.

Finally, there might be a **methodological explanation** for this result. This methodological issue could equally underlie the unexpected finding of a conditional positive effect of directives on the complexity of cost centre accounting. Hypothesis H3b1_1a (directives) is derived from the premise that cost accounting directives transfer Anglophone cost accounting traditions into Anglophone subsidiaries in Germany. The regression analyses in Table 6-53 and Appendix 5, however, merely show that *among* the Anglophone subsidiaries, a more extensive influence of corporate directives is associated with a higher complexity of these companies' cost centre accounting.[1049] These analyses do not include any comparison with the identified complexity scores from the domestic German subsidiaries. Thus, no assertion can be made whether a directive increases the complexity in the Anglophone subsidiaries on a level above the complexity of domestic German subsidiaries. Therefore, the counter-intuitive result for the effect of directives on the complexity of cost accounting in Table 6-53 and Appendix 5 cannot ultimately serve to test the hypothesis on coercive institutional effects (H3b1_1a to H3b1_3a). To account for this methodological difficulty, section 6.1.2.2 will apply the suggested research framework to an analysis of the presence and absence of the cross-national differences (i.e. the presence or absence of less complex cost accounting systems) in the Anglophone subsidiaries.

Regarding the **moderation effect of the relational context** (H3c), there is a significant positive interaction effect between the number of expatriates and the relational context in the Anglophone subsidiaries (Table 6-53). Thus, the effect of expatriate managers on the complexity of cost accounting is more positive if the relational context is unfavourable rather than favourable. The conclusiveness of this effect remains somewhat unclear, however. There is no significant conditional effect of expatriates. Interpreting above finding as a reduction in the complexity *de*creasing effect of expatriates would thus be too rigid. There are no moderation effects for corporate directives and corporate managers' involvement at all (Table 6-53). Hence, the moderation effect for expatriate managers provides weak support for H3c only. This is especially true because the inclusion of all three

[1048] The potential presence of simultaneity is a limitation of this study. Endogeneity impinges the interpretability of regression results.

[1049] This finding prevails for the first stage allocation procedures only.

interaction-terms is statistically insignificant in the joint F-test of the moderation variables (Table 6-53). No additional insights prevail in Appendix 5. The moderation is significant for expatriates' effect on cost type accounting level and 'quasi significant' for the effect of directives on cost centre accounting. In each case, however, the results lack conclusiveness due to unexpected conditional effects or a surprising direction of the effect. As for the analysis of H3b1_1a to H3b1_3a, however, these rather surprising findings can be associated with the introduced methodological problem in the linear multivariate regression applied in this section. Hence, the final assessment of these hypotheses is postponed to section 6.1.2.2.

For the *domestic German subsidiaries*, the parent company's influence through directives, corporate managers and expatriates does not affect the design of cost accounting systems (Table 6-53). In models (a) and (b), there are only insignificant regression coefficients for all three coercive institutional influences. Hence, in the domestic subsidiaries, corporate influences cannot be aligned with the overall complexity of subsidiaries' cost accounting systems. Moreover, the interaction terms of the coercive institutional variables and the relational context are insignificant in model (b) of Table 6-53 as well. Thus, there is no interaction effect in the domestic German subsidiaries, either.[1050] Yet, these findings do not lead to an un**conditional rejection** of H3b1_1a to H3b1_3a and H3c for the domestic German companies because there is some support for the hypothesized effects in the analyses of the **complexity scores** for **cost type**, **cost centre** and **cost object** accounting. (Appendix 5 – Table 2).

For cost type accounting, there is a positive and significant interaction term between corporate managers' involvement and the relational context. This means that the effect from corporate managers' involvement on the complexity of cost centre accounting is more positive, if the relational context is rather unfavourable. At a first glance, this finding appears counter-intuitive. Violating the expectations from section 4.2.1, it suggests that corporate managers have a higher complexity increasing effect if opposition is more likely. Rephrasing above sentence might shed some light on this issue. Accordingly, this finding means that if opposition is more likely, the complexity *de*creasing effect of corporate managers is *lower*. If corporate directives or personal involvement from the corporate level induce a less complex cost type accounting (e.g. the exclusion of imputed costs or the integration of financial and management accounting databases),[1051] this finding reflects a logical interaction.[1052] Consistent with this interpretation, there is a significant negative conditional effect of parent company directives on the complexity of cost type accounting. The more extensively a parent company influences the cost types of a subsidiary through directives, the less complex the cost type accounting is if there is an average relational context. Both these findings are in line with the above discussion how local top managers affect the complexity of the cost accounting system. Thus, there is **evidence for** both the

---

[1050] The insignificant F-value of 1.04 for the comparison of models (a) and (b) indicates that there is no interaction effect in these companies.

[1051] Large German cooperations advocate the alignment of financial and management accounting nowadays (cf. *Friedl et al.* (2009), p. 114).

[1052] The unconditional and conditional effects of corporate managers are not distinguishable from zero. This disables a conclusive interpretation of this effect.

influence of the parent company and for the moderation effect of the relational context for the complexity of **cost type accounting**.

The absent coercive and relational effects for the average complexity score in the domestic German subsidiaries can be linked to **offsetting associations** that emerge in the analysis of cost centre accounting and cost object accounting procedures (Appendix 5). In the former analysis, there is a significant negative interaction effect between corporate managers' involvement and the relational context. Thus, the effect from corporate managers on the complexity of cost centre accounting is lower, if the relational context is rather unfavourable. In other words, if opposition is more likely, the complexity increasing effect of corporate managers is lower.[1053] This indicates that the transfer of complex cost allocation requirements and cost centre formation procedures from the parent is opposed if the relational context is unfavourable. Similarly, there is a significant negative interaction effect between the relational context and expatriate managers in the analysis of cost object accounting (Appendix 5). If opposition is more likely, the extent to which expatriates affect the level of complexity is lower.[1054] Though the associated unconditional effects in model (a) as well as the conditional effects in model (b) are insignificant, both results indicate that parent companies' involvements into **cost centre and cost object accounting** affects these systems' complexity.

Hence, in the domestic German subsidiaries there is some support for the effect of corporate directives (H3b1_1b). However, given that it is present for cost type accounting only, a 'conditional acceptance' appears most appealing. For the relational context (H3c), an according approach reflects not only above discussion but also the fact that the introduction of the moderation terms improves the models' explanatory power and leads to mostly significant F-tests (Appendix 5). For H3b1_2b (corporate managers) and H3b1_3b (expatriates), there is no supportive evidence. They have to be rejected at this point. Because their moderation effects are selectively present, however, this rejection is regarded as conditional only.

Despite all difficulties with respect to the set of hypothesis H3b, one important finding emerges from above **discussion**: Anglophone parent companies indeed influence the complexity of their German subsidiaries' cost accounting systems to a significant extent. Such an association exists similarly for domestic German subsidiaries, despite selectively for the scores on cost type, cost centre and cost object accounting only. These results are particularly important considering the literature review in section 3. Similar evidence already prevailed in all studies discussed in section 3.2.2.2. But, in contrast to *Malmi* (1999), *Clarke et al.* (1999) or *Yazdifar/Askarany* (2010b), who show the importance of parent companies for the adoption of ABC in affiliates, this study complements this research by insights on the validity of such effects for cost accounting in more general terms.

1053 Despite the insignificance of the conditional effect of corporate managers, its positive sign does not violate this assertion.

1054 Because the associated conditional effect of expatriates has a negative sign, this finding remains inconclusive.

Moreover, the results can be argued to question the validity of the findings in the research projects on business unit specific cost accounting systems.[1055] Though all these projects consider affiliates (business units), neither regards the effect of superior organisational levels in that company or group. In the light of this study's results, these authors must be criticised strongly for neglecting one important factor underlying the design of cost accounting in affiliates. Emphasising that it is particularly relevant to acknowledge different hierarchical levels during the analysis of cost accounting in affiliates reclaims the idea of *Gosselin* (1997). It appears a fruitful path to improve the state of knowledge on cost accounting in affiliates by applying considerations as the one in this study to an analysis of business units as well.

6.1.2.1.3.4 Voluntary institutional determinants

The set of hypotheses H4b2 looks at the effect of voluntary institutional influences for the design of cost accounting systems in subsidiaries.

The more extensive the cost accountants in the *Anglophone subsidiaries* receive further trainings from German professional institutes of management accountants, the more complex are these companies' cost centre accounting systems (Appendix 5 – Table 1). The effect is robust for both model (a) and model (b) for the number of cost objects, first stage allocation procedures, and the classification of costs on cost centres (not reported). Recalling the discussion in section 4.2.1 and the findings in section 6.1.1, such complexity increasing effects of German professional institutes on cost centre accounting practices in Anglophone companies might indicate that these institutes diffuse German cost accounting traditions into foreign subsidiaries in Germany.[1056] Thus, the result supports hypothesis H3b2_4a (**German professional institutes**). Other than suggested by the moderate intensity of professional trainings through German institutes of management accountants, this finding mirrors the importance of professional institutes for management accounting practices known from the Anglophone world.[1057] As for the coercive institutional effects, however, it remains unclear at this point whether the professional trainings in question actually decreases a cross-national difference in the Anglophone subsidiaries. Hence, a final '*acceptance*' or rejection of H3b_2_4a will be postponed into section 6.1.2.2. Neither in Table 6-53 nor in Appendix 5, there is an association between university training and the complexity scores in the Anglophone subsidiaries. Thus, there is a strong indication for the need to reject the hypothesis on **university education** (H3b2_3a). Peculiarly, there is a marginally significant finding for a positive association between the cooperation with **Anglophone professional institutes** (H3b2_5) and the cost type accounting score (model (a)). Given the discussion on the effect of directives on cost type accounting, this finding can be due to an actual transfer of German cost accounting traditions through Anglophone institutes as expected during hypotheses development, more extensive trainings to counteract German cost accounting traditions (endogeneity) or the depicted

[1055] Cf. section 3.2.2.3, p. 61 (Table 3-6).

[1056] This result underlines *Granlund/Lukka*'s argument that the professionalisation of management accountants indeed leads to the convergence of management accounting practices (*Granlund/Lukka* (1998), p. 157).

[1057] Cf. e.g. *Ahrens/Chapman* (2000), p. 480f., for the UK.

methodological issues. The finding provides weak support for H3b2_5. As for the former discussion, however, a final rejection/acceptance is postponed. The predicted associations stem from an expectation about the diffusion of German cost accounting traditions. Hence, all these hypotheses are reconsidered in the light of the presence/absence of a cross-national difference.

For the *domestic German subsidiaries*, the insignificant results for university education and further trainings from professional institutes (Table 6-53) hold true for the results on cost type, cost centre and cost object accounting (Appendix 5) as well. Thus, hypothesis on **German professional institutes** (H3b2_4b) and **Anglophone professional institutes** (H3b2_5) must be rejected unconditionally for these companies. Because Anglophone institutes of management accountants appear to be rather unknown in the domestic German subsidiaries (cf. section 6.1.2.2), the rejection of H3b2_5 is not surprising.[1058] More remarkably, the common cooperation of researched domestic German subsidiaries with professional institutes of management accountants from Germany does affect the complexity of cost accounting systems in these companies either. In combination with economic and institutional coercive influences, these institutes appear to be rather unimportant for the design of companies' cost accounting systems. In contrast to the former two hypotheses, there is no evidence for the rejection of H3b2_3b (**university education**). In a situation where both parent and subsidiaries are located in Germany, it is indeed irrelevant for the design of the subsidiaries' cost accounting systems whether cost accountants fulfil their tasks based on university education or practical experiences. For the domestic German subsidiaries, both the rejection of H3b2_4b and H3b2_5 (professional institutes) and the support of H3b2_3b (university education) mirror previous findings by *Moeschler* (2012).[1059]

This result suggests that the analysis of the educational background of management accountants as well as further trainings through professional institutes are more important for comparisons of management accounting practices in two countries[1060] or for the analysis of difficulties during the diffusion of management control practices from one country to another[1061] than for the comparison of control systems in a single country setting.

6.1.2.2 Determinants of the cross-national differences in cost accounting

6.1.2.2.1 Evidence on the dependent and independent variables

As stressed continuously throughout the above hypotheses tests, some hypotheses tests remain incomplete this far because the cost accounting systems of the Anglophone subsidiaries were investigating irrespective of the complexity scores in the domestic German subsidiaries. This holds especially true for the set of hypotheses H3b1 (coercive institutional

---

[1058] Nevertheless, these findings contrast *Granlund/Lukka* (1998), p. 157, who argue that the professionalisation of management accountants is a potential source for international convergence of management accounting practices.

[1059] Cf. *Moeschler* (2012), p. 268.

[1060] Cf. e.g. *Ahrens/Chapman* (1999), p. 42f.

[1061] Cf. e.g. *Liedl* (1999), p. 120; *Kajüter* (2011), p. 113.

determinants), H3b2 (voluntary institutional determinants) and H3c (relational context). None of these hypotheses can be assessed conclusively by looking at the differences in the complexity scores among the Anglophone subsidiaries only. The expected negative sign for H3b1_1a for instance, arises from the fact that directives are expected to transfer Anglophone cost accounting traditions into the Anglophone subsidiaries. As such, the identified positive effect of corporate directives on the complexity of cost type accounting in these firms does not necessarily violate H3b1_1a. Without a yardstick for the complexity of domestic German cost accounting systems, the result that among the Anglophone subsidiaries such an increase prevails does not mean that a directive does not transfer Anglophone cost accounting traditions. This methodological deficiency is overcome hereafter by regressing the introduced determinants on the cross-national differences in the Anglophone subsidiaries (logistic regression).

Analysing these cross-national differences requires to substitute the **dependent variable** analysed this far (complexity scores). Instead, the presence of a cost accounting system that is less complex than the systems in the domestic German subsidiaries has to be investigated. Thus, the dummy variable '*CND*' is created. This variable has a value of one if an Anglophone company has a less complex system than the mean German company and zero elsewise.[1062] The accordingly defined cross-national differences are present in about 2/3 of the Anglophone subsidiaries (Table 6-54).[1063] This result is especially attributable to the difference in the companies' cost type accounting. For cost centre and cost type accounting, there is an almost equal split between companies, for which these differences are (not) found.[1064] Finding the cross-national differences to be more apparent for cost type than for cost centre and cost object accounting reflects the result that only for the former the complexity sub-score varies significantly between Anglophone and domestic German subsidiaries.

	Cost type accounting	Cost centre accounting	Cost object accounting	Cost accounting
Anglophone subsidiaries with a less complex cost accounting system than an average German subsidiary	70.91 %	54.55 %	51.82 %	**65.45 %**

Table 6-54: Existence of cross-national differences in the Anglophone subsidiaries (dataset 1)

The **independent variables** of the analysis are the ones investigated this far (economic determinants, coercive and voluntary institutional determinants and the relational context). It is essential to explicate, however, that the expected sign in all hypotheses tests has to be reversed at this point. The reason for the reversal can be clarified best by an example. Hypothesis H3b1_1a suggests a decreasing effect of a parent company's directives on the

[1062] More precisely, the measure is derived by attributing a value of one to those subsidiaries which have a complexity score that is lower than the mean complexity score of the domestic German companies in the same manufacturing sub-industry. This procedure is followed to account for the cross-sectional character of this study and to avoid biased results in this respect.

[1063] Similarly, *Joseph et al.* (1996), p. 85, identified group accounting rules to determine internal accounting systems in 64 % of a sample of UK firms.

[1064] Interestingly, this finding reflects the almost equal split of uniform and non-uniform cost accounting systems regularly found for German and Austrian MNCs (cf. *Mellewigt* (1995), p. 202; *Littkemann* (2001), p. 1285; *Dickmann* (2010), p. 217ff.; *Wolfsgruber* (2011), p. 248ff.).

complexity of cost accounting systems in the Anglophone subsidiaries. The decrease can be predicted because Anglophone parents are expected to transfer their traditionally less complex Anglophone cost accounting traditions. Thus, directives are likely to increase the odds for the cross-national differences. Because the due logistic regression analysis relies on odds ratios, the expected direction of this independent variable thus is >1 (increases the likelihood of '*CND*').[1065] Similar arguments can be found for each determinant.

With regard to the **control variables**, this section relies on the same variables as the OLS regression. Other than the separate analysis of the Anglophone and the domestic German subsidiaries, however, the investigation of the cross-national differences has to account for the number of value chain activities in these companies. Though this number is rather stable among the Anglophone subsidiaries as well as the domestic German subsidiaries, it varies significantly between these groups. The Anglophone subsidiaries perform more value chain activities than the domestic German firms.[1066] As such, the Anglophone subsidiaries might need to picture more (diverse) activities in their cost accounting systems. Hence, disregarding this control would hamper the ability to associate the difference in the complexity of cost accounting systems to for example, a parent company's involvement. This control variable was less crucial in the analysis of the previous section since the rather stable number of value chain activities among the Anglophone as well as the domestic German subsidiaries is unlikely to affect the analyses of differences in these groups.[1067]

6.1.2.2.2 Hypotheses testing

Similar to section 6.1.2.1, this section comprises an analysis of the independent variables in a model without (model (a)) and another one with the moderation effect of the relational context (model (b)).[1068] Also, the section does not only discuss the cross-national difference for the average complexity score (Table 6-55) but also for the sub-scores on the complexity of cost type, cost centre and cost object accounting (Appendix 6).

With respect to hypotheses testing, this section focusses on those interrelations that comprise the transfer of national cost accounting traditions. As such, the section especially looks at set of hypotheses H3b1 (coercive institutional determinants), H3b2 (voluntary institutional determinants) and H3c (relational context). These hypotheses are assessed with respect to their robustness (models (a) and (b)) and selective presence (complexity scores) to decide on their rejection.

1065 Odds ratios are higher than one if an explanatory factor increases the likelihood for the existence of the cross-national differences.

1066 Cf. section 5.3.3, p. 156.

1067 A robustness check of the analysis in Table 6-53 and Appendix 5 underlines this assertion. The inclusion of the number of value chain activities does not substantially change the results. Merely, the variable 'ERP' would lose in significance in model (b) (Table 6-53 and Appendix 5) of the domestic German subsidiaries. The control variable itself remains insignificant.

1068 All four variables involved in the moderation analysis ('directives', 'corporate managers', 'expatriates' and 'relational context') were centred before including them into the analyses.

Logistic regression model - dataset 1 (odds ratios)	E.S.	Anglophone subsidiaries Dependent variable: Variable '*CND*' Model (a)	 Model(b)
Perceived environmental uncertainty	<1	0.6328 *	0.6239 *
Extent of use	<1	0.0900 ***	0.1009 ***
Product diversity	<1	1.1994	0.9439
ERP *(dummy)*	<1	0.1919 **	0.2084 **
IT processing capabilities	<1	0.6678 *	0.6991
Adequacy of cost accountants	<1	1.0089	1.1592
Top management support	<1	0.3134 ***	0.3241 ***
Relational context	/	1.3645	1.2702
Directives *(centr.)*	>1	1.0194	1.0647
Directives **x** Rel. context *(centr.)*	<1		1.2438
Corporate managers *(centr.)*	>1	3.4025 ***	3.2021 ***
Corp. managers **x** Rel. context *(centr.)*	<1		1.1754
Expatriates *(centr.)*	>1	0.8845	0.3894 #
Expatriates **x** Rel. context *(centr.)*	<1		0.2530 ***
University training *(dummy)*	<1	3.0960 #	3.8547 #
Professional institutes - German	<1	0.8845	0.8828
Professional institutes - Anglophone	≠1	0.3979 ***	0.4688 *
Size subsidiary	/	1.7063	1.7927
Number of value chain functions	/	1.0163	1.0313
Form of market entry *(dummy)*	/	0.1665 **	0.1655 *
Length of affiliation	/	1.9905	1.5186
Size parent company	/	0.9170	0.9389
Constant	/	1.38e+09 ***	4.57e+08 ***
MacFaddens's pseudo R^2	-----	45.50 %	48.10 %
Count R^2	-----	81.80 %	82.70 %
Wald test	-----	40.73	57.32
Significance	-----	0.0026	0.0001
VIF_{max}	-----	2.16	2.29
Wald test (moderation)	-----	6.57 *	

Table 6-55: Logistic regression results for the Anglophone subsidiaries on the determinants of cross-national differences in cost accounting (dataset 1)

The levels of significance in Table 6-55 are based on one-tailed tests for the directed hypotheses and on the two-tailed tests for undirected hypotheses as well as the controls. As before, some few of the expected directed effects of determinants have a reversed sign. To derive meaningful explanations for such unpredicted results, their odds ratios are treated as if the identified sign was expected. If e.g. the regression result reveals that an expected positive effect (odds ratio > 1) is actually negative (odds ratio < 1) and has a p-value below 0.1 (one-tailed test), the coefficient will be treated as 'quasi significant'. To allow for an immediate identification of such findings, the asterisk (*) usually used to tag significant findings is replaced by a diamond (#).[1069]

The R^2 measures and the significant results for the Wald test suggest that the applied models are of considerable explanatory power. In addition, the reported variance inflation factors indicate that the models do not face any multicollinearity issues. Because the results are based on robust estimators, heteroscedasticity and autocorrelation are not an issue. On an aggregated basis, Table 6-55 widely confirms all significant findings from Table 6-53. Yet there are some notable results which have to be discussed in detail.

Economic determinants

With respect to the economic variables, it is worthwhile noting that H3a2_2 (information technology) which was weakly supported in the previous section only, is reinforced by Table 6-55. The existence of **ERP software** as well as the **IT processing capabilities** decrease the likelihood that an Anglophone subsidiary has a cost accounting system that is less complex than the average system in the domestic German subsidiaries. The same holds true for the level of **perceived environmental uncertainty**. In Anglophone subsidiaries, whose operating environment is rather unpredictable, the likelihood to find Anglophone cost accounting traditions decreases. Other than in Table 6-53, this effect can be identified for both model (a) and model (b). As such, there is strong support for hypothesis H3a1_1 (environmental uncertainty) in Anglophone companies.

Despite underlining the results for the economic variables from the previous section, the logistic regression uncovers several additional significant results with respect to the coercive and voluntary institutional pressures (H3b1 and H3b2), the relational context (H3c) as well as the control variables. These findings are discussed hereafter to finalise the analysis of these hypotheses.

Coercive institutional determinants and the relational context

During the analysis how **corporate directives** affect the complexity of cost accounting systems in Anglophone subsidiaries, section 6.1.2.1.3.3 reveals some difficulties with respect to the support for hypothesis H3b1_1a. Whereas no effect of corporate directives could be found for the average complexity score, an unexpected positive one emerged for the complexity of cost type accounting. No effects were found for cost centre and cost object accounting. The logistic regression in this section also finds no effect of corporate directives for the cross-national differences on the average complexity score (Table 6-55). This finding, however, becomes somehow more explicable by the analysis in this section due to interesting results for the scores on cost type, cost centre and cost object accounting.

The absence of any effect from corporate directives for the cross-national differences on the **cost centre level** also prevails in the logistic regression (Appendix 6). Despite still vio-

[1069] This procedure will be evaluated critically in the limitations (section 7.2) since it restricts how rigorously this study follows its epistemological positioning.

lating hypothesis H3a2_1, the lacking effect of corporate directives is somewhat linked to a potentially greater effectiveness of personal control mechanisms as discussed in the previous section. As above, there is no evidence for the validity of H3c (relational context) for the level of cost centre accounting either. The moderation effect is insignificant.

For the **cost object accounting** score, the expected effect of corporate directives can be found in the logistic regression (model (a) and model (b) in Appendix 6). The more extensively a parent company issues directives how to design the cost object accounting system, the more likely is an Anglophone-informed cost object accounting system in the Anglophone subsidiaries (if the relational context has an average value). Moreover, for cost object accounting, the moderating effect of the relational context is significant (cf. Appendix 6). Other than expected, however, the Anglophone subsidiaries are not found to oppose parent company directives but to stick to directives more extensively if the relational context is more unfavourable. Though emphasising an interaction of coercive institutional influences and the relational context, this result violates the expectations from section 4.2.1 (H3c).[1070]

The counter-intuitive finding that corporate directives increase the complexity of **cost type accounting** in Anglophone subsidiaries prevails in the performed logistic regression analysis (model (a) and model (b)). The more extensive such an influence, the less likely is the presence of a cost type accounting system that lacks behind the complexity of an average domestic German company. This finding exists for the number of cost types as well as the application of imputed costs (not reported). Nevertheless, it appears rather inconclusive to expect Anglophone companies to issue directives which do not reflect their national cost accounting traditions. Reassuring that the content of the directive may not explain this counter intuitive finding, the complexity of the cost type accounting is more likely to represent the expected cross-national differences, the longer a subsidiary is affiliated to its parent (cf. Appendix 6). Therefore, the result must be attributed to the previously discussed issue of reversed causality. The more cost type accounting is still reflecting German cost accounting traditions in an Anglophone subsidiary, the more extensively these companies are confronted with corporate directives. With respect to the moderating effect of the relational context (H3c), there is a significant effect of the interaction term 'Directives x Rel. context (centr.)'. In contrast to expectations, however, the odds ratio is higher than one. Because the effect counteracts the associated conditional effect of the corporate directives, however, this finding provides conditional support for H3c.

Above all, the discussion of corporate directives (H3a2_1) supports this hypothesis for the cross-national difference in cost object accounting. For cost centre accounting, there are no according effects. Endogeneity dilutes the analysis of the effects on the cost type level. This deficiency leads to offsetting effects on the cost object and the cost type accounting level. These, in turn, hinder an association of directives with the cross-national differences on the average complexity score. Therefore, **H3a2_1** has to be rejected at this point. This rejection, however, does not indicate that corporate directives are unimportant. The OLS and the logistic regressions reveal a significant importance of corporate directives for the

[1070] The effect of the relational context is discussed in detail after the analysis of coercive institutional effects.

design of cost accounting systems in Anglophone subsidiaries. As such, the hypothesis is '**conditionally rejected**' only. Future research on this issue is needed to shed further light on the question whether and especially how corporate directives on cost accounting find their way into foreign subsidiaries. Thereby, the issue of reversed causality must be considered thoroughly.

In contrast to corporate directives, the OLS regression finds substantial support for the effect of **corporate managers** on their subsidiaries' cost accounting systems (hypothesis H3b1_2a). The logistic regression can reassure the findings from the previous sections. In Anglophone subsidiaries in Germany, the (conditional) likelihood to find a cost accounting system that is less complex than the one of an average domestic German company increases, if corporate managers from the parent company engage extensively in the design of that cost accounting system. This finding is consistent for the three complexity scores on cost type, cost centre and cost object accounting (Appendix 6) and the average complexity score (Table 6-55). As such, hypothesis **H3b1_2a** can be **'accepted'**. With respect to the associated moderation (H3c), however, no evidence can be found. Neither in Table 6-55 nor in Appendix 6, there are significant interaction effects between the relational context and corporate managers' involvement.

Hypothesis H3b1_3a concerns the effect of **expatriate managers** for the complexity of cost accounting systems in Anglophone subsidiaries. For the average complexity score (Table 6-55), there is no unconditional influence of expatriates in the Anglophone subsidiaries (model (a)). In model (b), however, there is a significant conditional effect of expatriates. But, in contrast to the expectations, the odds ratio below 1 indicates that at an average relational context, a one-unit increase in the logarithmised number of expatriates makes it less likely to find a cost accounting system that is less complex than the one in an average domestic German company. This result is attributable to respective effects for cost type and cost centre accounting (cf. Appendix 6). For the difference in the cost centre accounting score, this finding stresses that the similar finding from the OLS regression cannot be attributed to methodological issues but could summarise another issue of reversed causality (i.e. endogeneity). The results might show that Anglophone parent company try to affect their subsidiaries' cost centre accounting systems more extensively through expatriates if these systems were still very different from the parents' home-country traditions. As such, despite the significant importance of expatriate managers for the design of cost accounting systems in Anglophone subsidiaries in Germany, **H3b1_3a** has to be **rejected**. Yet, in line with hypothesis H3b1_1a, this rejection is only **conditional**. For the level of cost object accounting for instance, the unconditional effect of expatriates prevails as expected.

Despite these unexpected findings, the significant odds ratio for the associated interaction term ('Expatriates x Rel. context (centr.)') has the expected direction in Table 6-55. If there is a more unfavourable relational context, then the odds ratio for expatriate managers is quartered.[1071] As such, there is substantial evidence for the existence of a moderating effect in this regard. Nevertheless, the effect of the moderation rather violates the expectations of H3c. The moderation enforces the effect that expatriates have at an average rela-

[1071] Following *Hosmer/Lemeshow* (2000), p. 50, the odds ratios of 0.2530 can be interpreted accordingly.

tional context rather than offsetting it. This violation, however, is especially attributable to a similar finding for the difference in cost type accounting practices (cf. Appendix 6). As such, it might be intertwined with German practitioners' striving for a simplification of cost type accounting. For cost centre accounting, the insignificant conditional effect of expatriates disables the thorough interpretation of the interaction effect which prevails as expected on this level.

By and large, the provided evidence on the **moderating effect of the relational context** (H3c) is very diverse. For the average complexity score, there is an expected significant interaction effect which improves the quality of the model.[1072] The effect, however, is present for the coercive influences stemming from expatriate managers. These in turn have an unexpected reversed conditional effect that is likely a result of endogeneity. The analyses of the complexity scores for cost type, cost centre and cost object accounting find a moderating effect for cost accounting directives concerning cost type and cost object accounting. In either case, however, the interaction has an unexpected direction. As already discussed during the correlation analysis (6.1.2.1.2), this inability to identify the presence of the expected interaction effect thoroughly might be due to its implicit presence. Accordingly, respondents might have incorporated the opposition toward the parent company's influences into their answers to the questionnaire. Also, this finding could be linked to the fact that subsidiaries respond to corporate directives by *using* the system differently rather than actually opposing the implementation and design of cost accounting systems. Section 6.2 investigates this suggestion more thoroughly by looking at the different types of cost information use. Above all, an unconditional rejection of H3c for the Anglophone companies would violate the findings for cost type and cost object accounting with respect to corporate directives as well as the suggested implicit presence of the effect. But, a conditional 'acceptance' would not reflect the unexpected results with respect to the expatriate managers. Hence, **H3c** is '**conditionally rejected**' at this point. Future research is needed to establish the interrelation between the relational context and the effect of coercive institutional influences more thoroughly.

Voluntary institutional determinants

The **university education** of the cost accountants in Anglophone subsidiaries (H3b2_3a) could not be linked to these companies' cost accounting systems through the OLS regressions. In contrast, the logistic regression finds university education to be positively associated with the likelihood for the cross-national differences (Table 6-55). As such, it cannot be argued that German university trained employees in Anglophone subsidiaries are rather ensuring that cost accounting systems in these companies are more closely aligned with German cost accounting traditions. In fact, the opposite is true, university trained employees facilitate the employment of cost accounting systems which are substantially less complex than an average German system. Even though such a result might reflect that the conceptual skills of university trained employees facilitate the understanding of non-German cost accounting traditions, this finding violates hypothesis H3b2_3a. Hence, hypothesis **H3b2_3a** has to be **rejected**. Having cost accountants, who fulfil their tasks based on the knowledge they gained in a German university, does not transfer German

[1072] This can be seen by the significant Wald statistic.

cost accounting traditions into Anglophone subsidiaries in Germany. Because the result exists for the average score only but cannot be found for the differences in cost type, cost centre and cost object accounting (Appendix 6), the meaning of this finding cannot be discussed in greater depth.

The logistic regression analyses (Table 6-55 and Appendix 6) do not suggest that cost accountants who receive extensive trainings from **German associations of management accountants** transfer German cost accounting traditions into their Anglophone subsidiaries (H3b2_4a). As such, the supportive results for H3b2_4a from the OLS regression on the complexity of cost centre accounting cannot be sustained. Even though further trainings from German institutes affect the complexity of cost (centre) accounting positively, this does not significantly counteract the complexity decreasing effect of parent companies. To reflect that professional trainings of German associations of management accountants are an important issue for the diverging complexity of cost centre accounting *among* Anglophone subsidiaries, **H3b2_4a** is '**rejected conditionally**' only.

For the extensiveness of further trainings from **Anglophone institutes of management accountants** (H3b2_5), all regression models except the one for cost centre accounting show odds ratios that are lower than 1 and significant (Table 6-55 and Appendix 6). In line with the finding for cost type accounting from the OLS regression, the analyses applied in this section thus provide substantial evidence that in Anglophone subsidiaries, whose employees receive further trainings from these institutes, cross-national differences are less likely. As explicated during the establishment of H3b2_5, this finding could be linked to the current interest of Anglophone professional institutes in German cost accounting traditions. Nevertheless, the finding raises some issues. There is an alternative explanation. In line with the argumentation provided for the effect of corporate directives, the finding might be due to reversed causalities. Cost accountants in Anglophone subsidiaries that still rely on German cost accounting traditions might be asked by their parent company to further their education through Anglophone institutes of management accountants to ensure their future understanding of the Anglophone practices. Due to this endogeneity induced issue, hypothesis **H3b2_5** is '**accepted conditionally**' only. Despite finding substantial statistical support for the hypothesis, future research should take a closer look at the reasons, why cost accountants in Anglophone subsidiaries further their education through institutes such as CIMA or IMA. Thereby attention can be directed to the national cost accounting traditions brought forward in professional trainings of these institutes.

Control variables

Despite being concerned with the control variables for which there are no formal hypotheses, some additional results are relevant at this point. The likelihood to find the cross-national differences in those Anglophone subsidiaries that were not formally set up by their current parents is less than a fifth[1073] of the one that prevails for a greenfield investment (**form of market entry**). Similarly, the cross-national differences are more likely to

[1073] Following *Hosmer/Lemeshow* (2000), p. 50, the odds ratios of 0.1665 (0.1655) (Table 6-55) can be interpreted accordingly.

prevail with respect to cost centre accounting in those Anglophone subsidiaries that are associated with a rather **large parent company**. In addition, the cross-national differences with respect to cost type accounting are more likely to prevail, the longer a subsidiary is associated with its current Anglophone parent (**length of affiliation**).

As such, the logistic regression reinforces the assertion from above: There is statistically sound evidence for an association between cost accounting in Anglophone subsidiaries in Germany and the Anglophone parent companies. Moreover, the direction of this association is intuitive. The longer a subsidiary perceives the effects of its parent or the more likely a parent company is to attribute substantial resources to cost accounting (size effect), the less complex is cost accounting in Anglophone subsidiaries in comparison to domestic German firms. Being unable to attribute these effects completely to the intended explicatory variables must be credited to the fact that cost accounting systems evolve over time. Hence, a cross-section analysis at one point in time may not be able to picture such effects perfectly. Future panel-data analysis may be very revealing in this regard.

6.1.3 Summary

Throughout section 6.1.1, substantial evidence for **differences of cost accounting in Anglophone and domestic German subsidiaries** prevails. These differences show that Anglophone subsidiaries employ significant less complex cost accounting systems than their domestic German counterparts. Moreover, the differences are especially prevalent for those characteristics of a cost accounting system which were previously attributed to the information usefulness of German cost accounting (e.g. the determination of imputed costs, numerous support cost centres, thorough first stage allocation or the extensiveness of CM accounting).

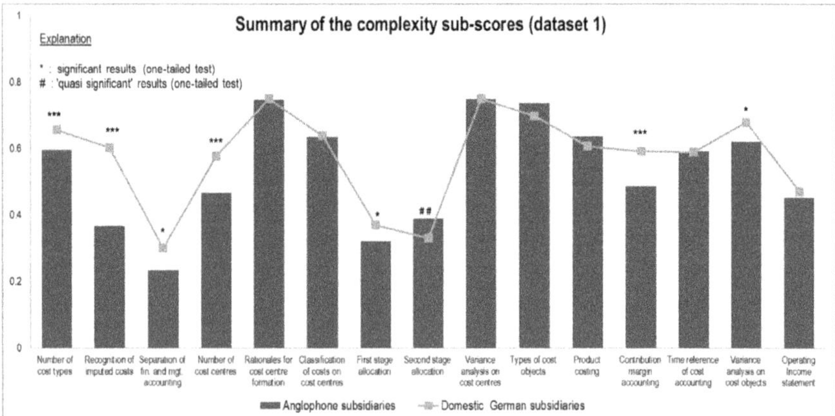

Figure 6-1: Summary of the complexity sub-scores (dataset 1)

Thus, Anglophone subsidiaries in Germany share similarities with cost accounting traditions from their parent company's country of origin. As such, there is substantial evidence to support hypothesis H1. The cost accounting systems of Anglophone subsidiaries in

Germany are significantly less complex than the systems in comparable domestic German subsidiaries. Figure 6-1 illustrates these results for dataset 1.

Section 6.1.2 **tests** various **hypotheses** to explain the cost accounting systems of the Anglophone and the domestic German subsidiaries. The section tries to align the cost accounting systems in both Anglophone and domestic German subsidiaries with economic and institutional determinants. Thereby, it is also taken into account that coercive institutional influences might be opposed by a subsidiary if there is an unfavourable relationship between the company and its parent. Aggregately, Figure 6-2 summarises the categories of influential variables for which there is (conditional) support ((✓)) for the suggested interactions.[1074]

The analysis of the **economic determinants** in the *Anglophone subsidiaries* is rather straightforward. As presented in Table 6-56, two thirds of the hypothesized associations could be supported.

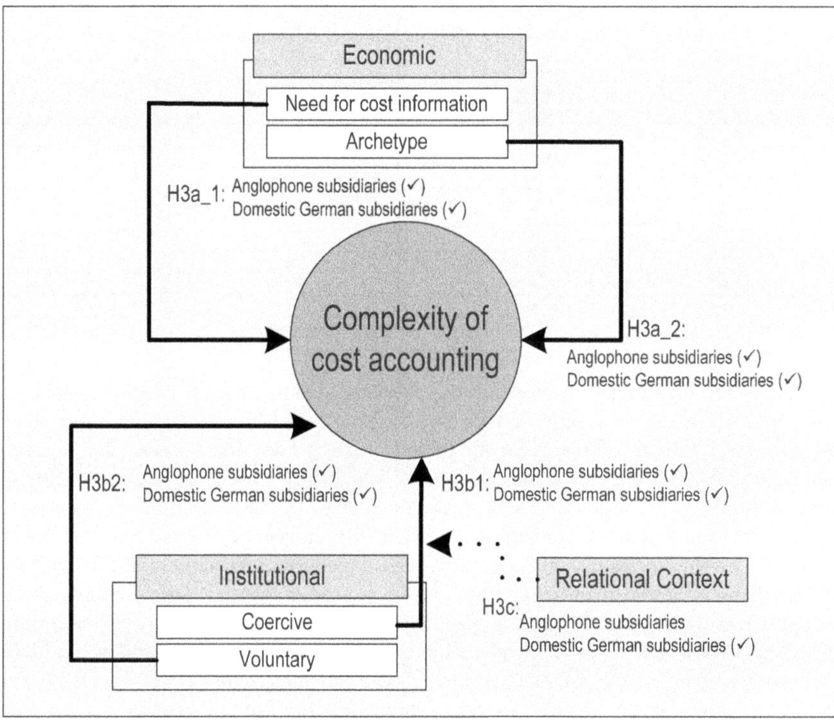

Figure 6-2: Aggregated summary of the hypotheses tests (complexity of cost accounting)

In contrast, the association of institutional determinants with the subsidiaries' cost accounting systems is more diverse than expected during the hypotheses development. The

[1074] A detailed summary of the 'accepted' and rejected hypothesis is provided in Table 6-56 (p. 232).

expected transfer of Anglophone cost accounting traditions through **coercive institutional pressures** exists for corporate managers' personal involvement only. Hence, two thirds of the hypotheses on coercive institutional determinants have to be rejected for the Anglophone subsidiaries. Despite finding corporate directives and expatriate managers to be influential for the design of subsidiaries' cost accounting systems, the transfer of Anglophone cost accounting traditions through these institutional factors could not be established thoroughly. Also, there is only restricted evidence for the **moderating effect of the relationship** between a subsidiary and its parent company on the impact of coercive influences. The relationship does not consistently counteract the effects of coercive influences. As such, the effect of the interaction can be rather contrasted to the expectations. Similarly, the diffusion of cost accounting traditions through university training and further training of professional institutes of management accounting cannot be established unconditionally (**voluntary institutional determinants**).

		Anglophone subsidiaries	German subsidiaries
H3a1_1	Perceived environmental uncertainty	(✓)	X
H3a1_2 - H3a1_6	Extent of use	✓	✓
H3a2_1	Product diversity	(X)	(✓)
H3a2_2	Information technology	✓	✓
H3a2_3	Adequacy of cost accountants	(X)	(X)
H3a2_4	Top management support	✓	X
H3b1_1a & H3b1_1b	Directives	(X)	(✓)
H3b1_2a & H3b1_2b	Corporate managers	✓	(X)
H3b1_3a & H3b1_3b	Expatriates	(X)	(X)
H3b2_1	Outside parties	Not tested due to poor data quality (cf. section 5.3.1)	
H3b2_2	Other group companies		
H3b2_3a & H3b2_3b	University training	X	✓
H3b2_4a & H3b2_4b	Professional institutes - German	(X)	X
H3b2_5	Professional institutes - Anglophone	(✓)	X
H3c	Relational context	(X)	(✓)
Explanation: ✓ = accepted hypothesis, (✓) = conditionally accepted hypothesis, X = rejected hypothesis, (X) = conditionally rejected hypothesis			

Table 6-56: Detailed summary of the hypotheses tests (complexity of cost accounting)

As discussed conclusively throughout the previous sections, several of the (conditional) rejections are based on results that do not disapprove the importance of voluntary and coercive institutional influences for the design of cost accounting systems. The rejections are rather attributable to endogeneity. The expected cause and effect relationships might not be thoroughly identifiable due to issues of reversed causality. The current design of a cost accounting system in an Anglophone subsidiary appears to be as important for the extent of parent companies' influences through directives, expatriates or the provision of Anglophone informed management accounting education, as these latter variables are for the systems' design. Hence, the (conditional) rejections reflect a necessity for future research. It is essential to establish the interaction between the current design of cost accounting systems in Anglophone subsidiaries and the antecedent or subsequent personal and bureaucratic involvements of a parent company. The same holds true for the provision of home country informed management education. Also, it remains to be explored whether the unexpected results for the moderating effect of the relational context could be due to its greater relevance for the use of cost information.

Despite these unexpected and dissatisfying issues, the discussion in section 6.1.2 shows important results. Above all, the results reassure the assertion that any investigation of cost accounting systems in affiliates (i.e. legal and economic organisation sub-units) remains inconclusive if they neglect institutional influences such as those from a parent company. As such, the assessment of previous research from section 3.2.2.3, which will be discussed more thoroughly for the domestic German subsidiaries, can be underlined by the results from the Anglophone subsidiaries. Moreover, there is one particularly notable result stemming from the analysis of the Anglophone subsidiaries. The ability to align the descriptively derived cross-national difference very consistently with the personal involvement of corporate managers from the Anglophone parents reveals that these differences are actually attributable to the diffusion of Anglophone cost accounting traditions. As summarised in section 3.2.3, there was preliminary evidence for such an association in section 3.2.2.2. However, this study is the first that documents this association conclusively for a large sample of companies.

In the *domestic German companies*, the results of the hypotheses tests are equally diverse. For the **economic determinants**, only half of the hypotheses can be supported. Similarly, only for corporate directives, the analysis identifies some statistical evidence for the effect of **coercive institutional influences**. For the other two variables, no such interrelation can be found. Nevertheless, the moderating effects of the relational context on the parents' personal involvements (corporate management support and expatriates) reveal that there is indeed an association between these coercive institutional variables and the cost accounting systems in the domestic German subsidiaries as well. As such, the findings are in line with previous evidence on the strong influence of German parent companies for subsidiaries' cost accounting systems.[1075] Hence, the results underline the raised critique of the vast contingency literature focussing on cost accounting in affiliates irrespectively of corporate effects.[1076] Simultaneously, this study's findings also suggest that the absence of corporate standards on cost accounting affects the cost accounting systems in subsidiaries significantly. Thereby, the results can generalise the according case reports on cost accounting at Siemens which are summarised in the literature review.[1077]

By and large, section 6.1.2 provides solid answers to research question (2a). Both economic and institutional influences determine the design of cost accounting systems in Anglophone and domestic German subsidiaries. Yet, the hypotheses tests in this study are remarkably multifaceted. Whereas some effects are present as expected, others are found to contradict the expectations or could not be identified at all. This level of diversity must be seen as a shortcoming of the theoretical positioning applied for hypotheses development in this study (new institutional sociology). The theory cannot explain the interaction between economic and institutional variables. This interaction, however, is influential for the joint analysis of these variables. As such, this study can complement the debate on the explanatory power of NIS for multinationals which was initiated by *Kostova et al.* (2008), p. 997ff. For the analysis of cost accounting in subsidiaries, a refinement of NIS with respect to the dominance of institutional and economic variables might be worthwile. To inaugurate such considerations, empirical research on the ability to align the dominance

[1075] Cf. section 3.2.2.2, p. 49, p. 50 and p. 54.
[1076] Cf. section 3.2.2.3, p. 61.
[1077] Cf. section 3.2.2.3, p. 57.

of coercive and institutional variables with perceptions on economic and legitimising benefits might be fruitful. Also, future researchers can take this study's result to engage more carefully into the analysis of the conceptual considerations by *Modell* (2002). The author also argues that the effect of economic influences on the design of cost accounting systems depends on the prevalence of coercive and voluntary institutional influences.[1078] Complementing *Modell*'s considerations, this study reveals that in a subsidiary context the coercive institutional factors reflecting parent companies' personal involvements are particularly relevant to be considered when studying the interaction of economic and institutional variables.

6.2 Types of cost information use

6.2.1 Descriptive evidence

Among others, the previous section raises the question whether the effects of coercive institutional variables and the relational context on the complexity of cost accounting systems are ambiguous since subsidiaries respond to these variables more extensively by using cost information differently. By presenting the usage types which were surveyed by questions A.1 to A.6 of questionnaire B, this section also elaborates on this assertion. This section first investigates the reliability and validity of the applied measurement models. Subsequently, it is discussed how cost information is used in the Anglophone and the domestic German subsidiaries to test whether there are indeed similarly usage types in both these groups (hypothesis 2). Thereafter, the section aligns its findings with previous research on the covered usage types to assess the validity of the results in this light as well.

Quality assessment of the applied measurement models

All types of cost information use are measured by reflective measurement models in this study. Thus, their validity and reliability can be assessed numerically.[1079] Table 6-57 summarises the results for all questionnaire items that were investigated to measure the usage types.[1080]

For all types of cost information use, there are no issues with respect to the applicability of the factor analytical reliability and validity assessments. Both the Kaiser criterion (i.e. no. of eigenvalues > 1) and the Kaiser-Meyer-Olkin criterion (KMO) are fulfilled. Moreover, most reliability criteria are met. Only the threshold for the factor loadings of 0.7 is not met consistently. Because of the high values for Cronbach's alpha and the composite reli-

[1078] Cf. *Modell* (2002), p. 653ff.

[1079] To avoid differences in the meaning of the latent variable *usage type X* in Anglophone and domestic German companies, this analysis is done conjointly for both groups. Otherwise, the underlying factor analysis would potentially derive differing factor scores for the same latent construct. The application of "equivalent measurement models" is also favoured by *Jais* (2007), p. 137. Nevertheless, he analyses the reliability and validity of the measurement models separately for the different nationalities in his study. Since there is no conceptual argument why a usage type's measurement model should differ for the two researched groups, the forthcomingly applied procedures appear conceptually more appealing.

[1080] To be able to derive factor loadings for each item of a latent construct, the model specification suggested by *Backhaus et al.* (2013), p. 149ff., is followed.

ability, however, this underachievement of the threshold appears acceptable.[1081] With respect to the (discriminant) validity of the six measures, the instrumental and the conceptual usage types cannot be distinguished empirically from one another. Conceptually, *Diamantopoulos/Souchon* (1998) argue that it might indeed be difficult to distinguish different types of information use empirically.[1082] Empirically, *Diamantopoulos/Souchon* (1999), *Hunholt* (2003) and *Jais* (2007) already experienced this to be true for the instrumental and the conceptual usage types as well.[1083] In line with these authors, these two types are aggregated hereafter.

	Adequacy of factor analysis		Reliability analysis				Validity analysis
	KMO	No. of eigen-values > 1	Cronbach's alpha	Composite reliability	Standardised factor loadings	AVE	Fulfilment of the Fornell-Larcker criterion
Instrumental use	min. = 0.67	1	0.82	0.83	min. = 0.62	0.54	No, indistinguishable from the conceptual usage type
Conceptual use	min. = 0.56	1	0.80	0.80	min. = 0.45	0.52	No, indistinguishable from the instrumental usage type
Rationalising use	min. = 0.66	1	0.81	0.82	min. = 0.50	0.53	Yes
Diagnostic use	min. = 0.75	1	0.87	0.87	min. = 0.75	0.63	Yes
Interactive use	min. = 0.73	1	0.84	0.84	min. = 0.72	0.57	Yes
Ceremonial use	min. = 0.69	1	0.88	0.89	min. = 0.67	0.66	Yes

Table 6-57: Reliability and validity assessments of the usage types (dataset 3)

Table 6-58 summarises the quality assessments of the usage types after this aggregation. As before, factor analytical reliability and validity assessments are fulfilled. Furthermore, there is little evidence for an unreliable measurement of the remaining five usage types. Nevertheless, there still is an issue of distinguishing all usage types empirically. Whereas the average variance extracted of the decision facilitating usage type is 0.50, the squared correlation between this usage type and the interactive use of information is 0.54. This finding seems to mirror conceptuals overlapping of *Simons*' and *Pelz/Burchell*'s usage types.[1084] In the design of the questionnaire, however, the two usage types do not share such conceptual similarities (cf. section 5.2.2.2). Since this mismatch in the quality criteria prevails for one of the two types only and given the small difference between the AVE and the squared correlation, these usage types are not aggregated. Since there are significant differences between the composite scores of these two usage types, this procedure appears rather justified.

Having clarified the reliability and validity of the applied measurement models, the focus can be shifted to the descriptive results for the usage types. Due to their reliance on structural equation modelling, previous studies on the use of cost information from Germany

1081 This is especially true since *Hulland* (1999), p. 198, argue for a threshold of 0.4 for the standardised factor loadings.

1082 Cf. *Diamantopoulos/Souchon* (1998), p. 116f.

1083 Cf. *Diamantopoulos/Souchon* (1999), p. 4; *Hunold* (2003), p. 186; *Jais* (2007), p. 153.

1084 Cf. *Hirst/Baxter* (1993), p. 191; *Abernethy/Brownell* (1999), p. 191; *Tuomela* (2005), p. 301; *Henri* (2006a), p. 80ff.; *Widener* (2007), p. 760; *Abernethy et al.* (2010), p. 5, or the discussion on p. 33.

aggregated the usage types based on factor analysis into 'factor scores'.[1085] International research on this matter, however, tends to rely on composite (i.e. mean) scores.[1086] For brevity, this latter procedure is followed in this study.

	Adequacy of factor analysis		Reliability analysis				Validity analysis
	KMO	No. of eigen-values > 1	Cronbach's alpha	Composite reliability	Standardised factor loadings	AVE	Fulfilment of the Fornell-Larcker criterion
Instr. /Conc. Use	min. = 0.74	1	0.88	0.88	min. = 0.43	0.50	No, indistinguishable from the interactive usage type
Rationalising use	min. = 0.66	1	0.81	0.82	min. = 0.50	0.53	Yes
Diagnostic use	min. = 0.75	1	0.87	0.87	min. = 0.75	0.63	Yes
Interactive use	min. = 0.73	1	0.84	0.84	min. = 0.72	0.57	Yes
Ceremonial use	min. = 0.69	1	0.88	0.89	min. = 0.67	0.66	Yes

Table 6-58: Revised reliability and validity assessments of the usage types (dataset 3)

Applied types of cost information use

Cost information is used similarly extensively in an instrumental/conceptual (5.7 and 5.67), diagnostic (4.46 and 4.66) and interactive (4.92 and 4.89) manner in the Anglophone and the domestic German subsidiaries (Figure 6-3). These similarities in the use of cost information reflect that there are no differences for the pursued cost accounting objectives in these two groups.[1087] As such, there is tremendous support for hypothesis H2. There are little differences with respect to those usage types which could be clearly attributed to the primary purposes of cost accounting.[1088] Yet, in contrast to H2, the rationalising (4.99 and 4.51) and the ceremonial usage types (1.81 and 1.51) can be found significantly more extensively in the Anglophone subsidiaries.[1089]

Taking these significant differences as an indication for a conceptual similarity of the rationalising and the ceremonial usage type permits to interpret this finding as a conceptually unforeseen manifestation of what *Oliver* (1991) describes as avoidance and defiance of institutional pressures (cf. section 4.1.3). Apparently, in the light of subsidiaries, the rationalising use of cost information is another way to respond to parent company initiatives (avoidance) which dilute an information system's local usefulness.[1090] This suggests

[1085] Examples include *Frank/Reitmeyer* (1999); *Aust* (1999); *Karlshaus* (2000), or *Frank* (2000).

[1086] Cf. *Abernethy/Brownell* (1999), p. 196; *Widener* (2007), p. 769; *Henri* (2006a), p. 90; *Bisbe/Malagueño* (2009), p. 383.

[1087] This finding from dataset 1 (cf. section 6.1.2.1.1.1, p. 199) is reflected in the analysis of the information users in dataset 3 as well (cf. section 6.2.2.1.1.3, p. 245).

[1088] Cf. section 2.3, p. 27.

[1089] For most usage types, the comparisons of Anglophone and domestic German subsidiaries are statistically insignificant (one-tailed parametric tests). If significant, this is indicated by the significance levels *, ** or ***. Despite minor changes, these findings are stable if only actual board members are regarded (cf. Appendix 7 – Figure 1). Similarly, the results are stable for dataset 4 (cf. Appendix 7 – Figure 2). For dataset 4, however, there is no significant difference between the ceremonial use in Anglophone and domestic German subsidiaries. Given these similarities, the following information is provided for dataset 3 only.

[1090] Cf. *Oliver* (1991), p. 151ff.

that there might indeed be differences regarding the use of cost information in subsidiaries as a response to corporate directives which could have hampered the analysis in the previous sections. During the explicative analyses of the usage types, this finding will be investigated in detail.

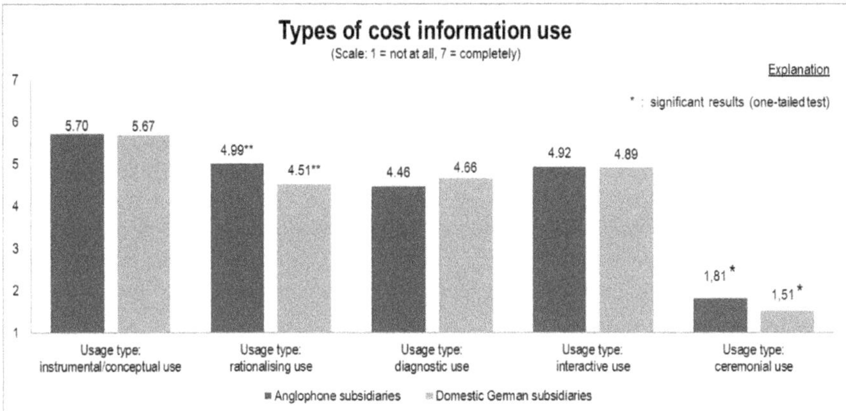

Figure 6-3: Descriptive evidence on the types of cost information use (dataset 3)

The result for the **ceremonial usage type** is very revealing. As suggested, it can be interpreted as subsidiaries' defiance of corporate directives. Previous research on this usage type either looks at domestic subsidiaries or disregards the effect of cross-national differences in management accounting (cf. section 3.3.2.2). As such, this study complements previous research. Anglophone subsidiaries, which are urged (personally) to apply Anglophone cost accounting traditions, use their cost accounting systems more extensively in a ceremonial manner than the domestic German subsidiaries. Even though the result suggests that a parent's transfer of its national cost accounting traditions into a foreign subsidiary fosters the ceremonial use, this finding does not conclusively hint at a stronger likelihood for the ceremonial use in foreign subsidiaries. This is especially due to the response bias (section 5.3.1) among the German subsidiaries. Potentially, there are companies from the domestic German population which would have reported higher levels of the ceremonial use but did not hand in questionnaire B in the first place.

The finding for the **rationalising use** is peculiar. At a first glance, the result only shows that in the Anglophone subsidiaries it is more common to take decisions irrespectively a previous consideration of cost information. This finding might merely reflect the alternative responses to environmental uncertainty that surfaced during the analysis of the complexity of cost accounting systems in section 6.1.2.1.1.1. Thereby, it could reflect alternative preferences for cost information. Since the decision maker in the Anglophone and the domestic German subsidiaries do not report significantly different preferences for cost information,[1091] however, there must be complementing reasons for this result. As pre-

[1091] The descriptive results for the explanatory variable 'preference for cost information' can be found in section 6.2.2.1.1.2, p. 244.

closed, it might uncover that there are alternative possibilities to respond to a coercively induced cost accounting system which does not (fully) meet local information needs. In addition to using such cost accounting systems ceremonially, subsidiaries can apparently avoid the induced system by using its information for the ex-post rationalisation of previously taken decisions as well. Both these strategic responses seem to be stronger in the Anglophone subsidiaries which are faced by alternative cost accounting traditions. Unfortunately, the conclusiveness of this interpretation is restricted. During the hypotheses tests (section 6.2.2), the conceptual similarities of the ceremonial and the rationalising usage type are more prevalent for the domestic German subsidiaries. As such, the identified difference with respect to the rationalising use of cost information appears to reflect the ambiguity in the empirical meaning of this usage type. Besides showing different levels of ex-post decision rationalisation, the Anglophone subsidiaries also differ from their domestic German counterparts with respect to the avoidance of parent companies' directives. Since the hypotheses tests for the set of hypotheses H4 reveal meaningful insights into this issue, the discussion of the rationalising usage types will be taken up again in section 6.2.2.

Comparison to prior research

The statistically insignificant differences for the remaining usage types prevent additional comparisons of the Anglophone and domestic German subsidiaries. In order to analyse whether this study's findings can be aligned with previous research on the usage types in the context of cost accounting (cf. section 3.3.2) and management accounting (cf. section 2.3.3), the intensity of the five usage types are compared hereafter. Individual one-tailed t-test comparisons show that the three **symbolic usage types** (i.e. the (2) rationalising, (3) diagnostic and (4) interactive usage type) are significantly less extensively present than the (1) **instrumental/conceptual** use of information (Table 6-59). The finding holds true for both Anglophone and domestic German subsidiaries.

	(1) Instr./conc. use	(2) Rationalising use	(3) Diagnostic use	(4) Interactive use
(1) Instrumental/ Conceptual use		Angl.: (1) > (2) *** Ger. : (1) > (2) ***	Angl.: (1) > (3) *** Ger. : (1) > (3) ***	Angl.: (1) > (4) *** Ger. : (1) > (4) ***
(2) Rationalising use			Angl.: (2) > (3) ** Ger. : (2) < (3)	Angl.: (2) > (4) Ger. : (2) < (4) **
(3) Diagnostic use				Angl.: (3) < (4) *** Ger. : (3) < (4)
(5) Ceremonial use	Angl.: (5) < (1) *** Ger. : (5) < (1) ***	Angl.: (5) < (2) *** Ger. : (5) < (2) ***	Angl.: (5) < (3) *** Ger. : (5) < (3) ***	Angl.: (5) < (4) *** Ger. : (5) < (4) ***

Table 6-59: One-tailed t-test comparisons of the usage types (dataset 3)

For the domestic German subsidiaries, this finding reflects previous research. In cost accounting studies, the symbolic usage type(s) are usually found to fall behind the instrumental/conceptual one (cf. section 3.3.2.1). Given the lack of previous evidence for these relations in an Anglophone cost accounting setting, no such comparison is possible at this point. The identified relationship can be contrasted to the one found in previous research focussing on the use of other information than costs in an Anglophone setting (cf. section 2.3.3). However, this difference is equally present for German companies if studies on the use of 'cost information' and 'other management accounting information' are compared (cf. section 3.3.2.3). Hence, the deviation appears to be linked to the specific applicability of cost information. Above all, the finding reveals that the usage types in the Anglophone subsidiaries in Germany also reflect the previously derived relationships in German companies (section 3.3.2.1). Because most responding decision makers from the Anglophone subsidiaries are Germans,[1092] this finding might be linked to the nationality of the decision makers rather than the origin of the subsidiaries' parents.

Table 6-59 also provides evidence on the significant differences between the individual usage types which disaggregate **the symbolic use of information** (cf. section 2.3.3). The relationship of the (2) rationalising use of cost information, (3) the diagnostic and (4) interactive use of information for the Anglophone subsidiaries can be contrasted to *Vandenbosch* (1999),[1093] *Henri* (2006)[1094] and *Jais* (2007)[1095]. They find the latter two types of use to be more prevalent in Anglophone companies.[1096] As exemplified above, their focus on the use of management accounting information in general terms impinges the conclusiveness of this difference, however. The only study (*Sandt* (2004)) found to regard both *Pelz/Burchell*'s ((1), (2) and conjointly (3) and (4)) and *Simons*' usage types ((3) and (4)) cannot be applied for a conclusive comparison, either. In a German setting, *Sandt* finds little differences with respect to the symbolic use[1097] and the diagnostic use, but remarkable ones between the symbolic use and the interactive use. Issues of construct operationalisation, however, impinge these comparisons.[1098] In contrast to the work by *Sandt* (2004), the research project by *Steiners* (2005) yields similar and rather comparable[1099] results for the findings from the domestic German companies. As this study, *Steiners* finds management accounting information to be less intensively applied in (2) a rationalising manner[1100] than in a decision influencing[1101] manner ((3) and (4)).[1102] No additional insights can be drawn from the other research projects summarised in section 3.3.2.

[1092] The majority of the respondents to questionnaire B in dataset 3 are of German nationality (91 % for the Anglophone subsidiaries and 100 % for the domestic German subsidiaries).

[1093] *Vandenbosch* regards similar usage types as the ones included here. Her constructs 'focusing attention' ('score keeping') share similarities with the interactive (diagnostic) use of information regarded in this study. The rationalising use of information is covered in her study by the construct 'legitimize decisions' (cf. *Vandenbosch* (1999), p. 87).

[1094] *Henri* reports two usage types similarly to the ones of *Simons* ('monitoring' and 'attention focusing') to be more heavily applied than one type similarly to the rationalising one ('legitimisation') (cf. *Henri* (2006a), p. 91).

[1095] The three items used to form the symbolic usage type in *Jais'* study are rather comparable to this study's operationalisation of the rationalising use (cf. *Jais* (2007), p. 150f.). Similarly, the interactive and the diagnostic usage types applied in this study are comparable to *Jais*' operationalisation.

[1096] Cf. *Jais* (2007), p. 158f.

[1097] The symbolic usage type comprises the rationalising use of information (cf. Table 2-5).

[1098] Among others, *Sandt* operationalised *Pelz*'s symbolic use through items reflecting *Burchell et al.*'s rationalising and ammunition machines. Because the latter comprises aspects reflected in *Simons*' typology (cf. Table 2-5), *Sandt*'s results are little revealing or even misleading. Note that *Sandt* (2004), p. 173, analysed the three usage types from Pelz's typology separately from *Simons*' ones because of such overlapping definitions.

[1099] As for the findings by *Jais* (2007), *Steiners*' focus on management accounting information rather than cost information weakens the conclusiveness of the identified similarity.

[1100] *Steiners* according usage type is labelled 'execution ex post' (cf. *Steiners* (2005), p. 141).

[1101] *Steiners* labels his according usage type, which informed the interactive and diagnostic types of this study, 'execution ex ante' (cf. *Steiners* (2005), p. 140).

[1102] Cf. *Steiners* (2005), p. 182.

In contrast to the comparison of *Burchell et al.*'s (3) rationalising use with *Simons*' (3) **diagnostic** and (4) **interactive use**, there are multiple reference points to assess this study's results for *Simons*' usage types. For the domestic German companies, the insignificant dominance of the interactive usage type reflects the diverse picture provided by previous findings. Whereas *Sandt* (2004) finds the interactive usage type to be dominating the use of performance measurement systems,[1103] *Hofmann et al.* (2012) report the diagnostic type to be more important in their study of the use of budgets.[1104] In contrast, the significant dominance of the interactive use of cost information in the Anglophone companies contradicts previous research stressing the diagnostic use of management accounting information to be more apparent in Anglophone companies and their subsidiaries.[1105] For both the Anglophone and the domestic German subsidiaries, non-affirmative findings might be linked to the personal attitudes of the responding managers and the context in which their firms operate. These variables determine the interactive (and diagnostic) engagement of management accounting information.[1106] Also, this study might contradict previous findings due to its focus on cost information rather than management accounting information more generally and the respondents' German nationality.

In both Anglophone and domestic German subsidiaries, cost information is used very little in a **ceremonial** manner. As such, it is little surprising to find the composite scores for this usage type to fall significantly behind the scores of the other four usage types (Table 6-59). There is one particularity in this regard. In all companies that report the ceremonial usage type to be present,[1107] cost information is used non-ceremonially as well.[1108] This indicates that it is not the cost accounting system per se which is subject to ceremonial adoption. Rather, the ceremonial use of cost information appears to be restricted to some pieces of a cost accounting system's information. Other pieces of cost information, however, remain valuable for decision-making.

Hypothesis test for the expectations summarised as H2

In summary, the German decision makers[1109] in both the Anglophone and domestic German subsidiaries use cost information similarly. Especially with respect to the instrumental/conceptual use, the diagnostic and the interactive usage type, only insignificant differences prevailed. Yet, previous assertions which argue that cross-national differences in management accounting are likely to prevail for the use rather than the design of man-

---

[1103] Cf. *Sandt* (2004), p. 173. Note that this comparison cannot be ultimately assessed because of the unique operationalisation of the interactive usage type provided by *Sandt*.

[1104] Cf. *Hofmann et al.* (2012), p. 175.

[1105] Cf. *Henri* (2006a), p. 91; *Jais* (2007), p. 158f.; *Widener* (2007), p. 768.

[1106] Cf. *Naranjo-Gil/Hartmann* (2006), p. 37; *Henri* (2006a), p. 95; *Widener* (2007), p. 776f.; *Abernethy et al.* (2010), p. 11; *Hofmann et al.* (2012), p. 168.

[1107] The ceremonial usage type is regarded present if a company reports a composite score above 1.

[1108] Because the non-ceremonial usage types ((1), (2), (3), (4)) tend to have smaller composite scores in subsidiaries that report to use some pieces of cost information in a ceremonial manner (Appendix 8), these findings do not indicate that there is an issue with respect to data quality here.

[1109] The majority of the respondents to questionnaire B in dataset 3 are of German nationality (91 % for the Anglophone subsidiaries and 100 % for the domestic German subsidiaries).

agement accounting systems cannot be regarded as obsolete.[1110] Such an assessment would build on the assumption that cost information in the Anglophone subsidiaries is used in a similar manner as it would be in domestic Anglophone companies. Because the majority of the respondents of questionnaire B are Germans, this assumption is questionable. Moreover, no information on the exact cost information used for decision-making is regarded in this study. Future research interested in potential differences in the use of cost information in different countries may wish to look at different levels of aggregation than the one chosen in this study.

Since the findings for the instrumental/conceptual, the diagnostic and the interactive usage type support hypotheses H2, whereas the significant differences for the rationalising and the ceremonial usage type do not, **H2** is '**accepted conditionally**'. Taken the significant differences of two usage types to restrict the support for H2 rather than rejecting it is most reasonable because these two usage types do not describe the thorough application of cost information for decision-making. Whereas the rationalising use describes the use of cost information to legitimise a taken decision ex post, the ceremonial use is characterised by maintaining a cost accounting system irrespectively its relevance for local decision-making.

Hence, the **answer to research question 1b** is twofold. On the one hand, both Anglophone and domestic German companies cannot be differentiated with respect to the application of cost information for decision-making. As such, there is substantial evidence that subsidiaries do actually use their cost information during the management process. On the other hand, these two groups are somewhat distinguishable with respect to potential strategic responses to their parent companies' involvements into cost accounting. Apparently, the Anglophone subsidiaries respond to their parents' involvement more extensively by avoiding and defying corporate directives. This latter assertion lacks some conclusiveness, however. Whereas the participation bias among the domestic German subsidiaries might inflate the difference for the ceremonial use, an unexpected dual meaning of the rationalising use disables its unrestricted interpretation as an attempt to avoid corporate involvements.

6.2.2 Explicative evidence

6.2.2.1 Determinants of the types of cost information use in subsidiaries

6.2.2.1.1 Evidence on the independent variables

Section 4.2.2 derives 22 hypotheses to explain the use of cost information in Anglophone and domestic German subsidiaries. These 22 hypotheses comprise 13 variables which are briefly introduced in the following sections. Since only the questionnaires from dataset 3 comprise complete information for the explicative analysis of the usage types, this section includes evidence from this dataset only.

[1110] For an according conceptual suggestion, cf. *Granlund/Lukka* (1998), p. 155. For empirical evidence, cf. *Shields* (1998), p. 507; *Kostova/Roth* (2002), p. 229f.; *Chenhall* (2003), p. 135; *Schoute* (2009), p. 209.

6.2.2.1.1.1 Complexity of the cost accounting system

As in dataset 1, the Anglophone subsidiaries in dataset 3 have significantly less complex cost accounting systems than the domestic German subsidiaries (Table 6-60). The difference, however, is significant at a 10 % level only.

Being unable to approve the 1 % significance level from dataset 1 reflects that there are fewer significant differences for the complexity sub-scores. Though the lower complexity of the Anglophone subsidiaries endures for the sub-scores on (1) the number of cost centres, (3) the separation of financial and management accounting and (7) first stage allocation, the differences lose their statistical significance.[1111] For the previously insignificant differences, there are no changes. Compared to dataset 1, some additional scores are slightly larger for the Anglophone subsidiaries in dataset 3 (square brackets mark complexity sub-scores which are larger in the Anglophone subsidiaries). The differences, however, remain statistically insignificant.

Mean values	Dataset 1				Dataset 3			
	Anglophone		German		Anglophone		German	
(1) Number of cost types	0.60		0.66	***	0.61		0.64	
(2) Recognition of imputed costs	0.37		0.60	***	**0.38**		**0.63**	***
(3) Separation of financial and management accounting	0.24		0.30	*	0.26		0.33	
(4) Number of cost centres	0.47		0.58	***	**0.47**		**0.62**	***
(5) Rationales for cost centre formation	0.75		0.75		[0.76]		[0.75]	
(6) Classification of costs on cost centres	0.64		0.64		[0.67]		[0.65]	
(7) First stage allocation	0.32		0.37	*	0.31		0.33	
(8) Second stage allocation	[0.39]	##	[0.33]		[0.42]	###	[0.31]	
(9) Variance analysis on cost centres	0.75		0.75		[0.78]		[0.73]	
(10) Types of cost objects	[0.74]		[0.70]		[0.76]		[0.71]	
(11) Product costing	[0.64]		[0.61]		[0.65]		[0.62]	
(12) Contribution margin accounting	0.49		0.59	***	**0.44**		**0.59**	***
(13) Time reference of cost accounting	[0.59]		[0.59]		[0.66]		[0.63]	
(14) Variance analysis on cost objects	0.62		0.68	*	**0.62**		**0.75**	***
(15) Operating Income statement	0.46		0.47		[0.45]		[0.45]	
Complexity score (standard deviation)	0.54 (0.13)		0.57 (0.11)		**0.55 (0.11)**		**0.58 (0.10)**	
p-value (test)	0.01 (two-tailed t-test)				0.09 (two-tailed t-test)			

Table 6-60: Complexity sub-scores (dataset 3)

The influence of cost accounting systems on the different types of use will be analysed separately for the Anglophone and domestic German subsidiaries. Because there are little differences in the means and standard deviations of the average complexity scores in da-

[1111] Significance levels in Table 6-60 are based on one-tailed parametric tests to test whether domestic German companies have more complex cost accounting systems than Anglophone ones. The diamonds (#) provided for second stage allocation reflects that the test actually rejects this expectation rather than the associated null hypothesis. It is tested whether the higher complexity in the Anglophone subsidiaries is statistically significant.

taset 1 and 3, it is not expected that the decreased significance of the results in dataset 3 impinges the comparability of the analyses with the results from section 6.1.[1112]

6.2.2.1.1.2 Users' attitudes towards cost information

From a theoretical point of view, section 4.1.4 differentiates five constructs to describe user's attitudes towards cost information (managers' **knowledge** with respect to cost accounting, managers' **preferences** for cost information, managers' **involvement** in the design of a cost accounting system, the frequency of **contacts** between management accountants and managers, and managers' perceptions of the cost accounting system's **quality**). Details on the operationalisation of these five constructs, which were surveyed through A.12, B.5 and B.6 of questionnaire B, can be found in section 5.2.3.4.

All constructs but managers' perceptions of the cost accounting system's quality are measured reflectively. Hence, these constructs are subject to a quantitative analysis of their reliability and validity (cf. section 5.4.1). Table 6-61 summarises the results of the reliability and validity analysis[1113] as well as the preceding assessment of the applicability of factor analytical considerations. All reflective constructs are of discriminant validity (Fornell-Larcker criterion). Also, the thresholds for an adequate application of such factor analytical considerations are met for all but the construct '*preference*'. This construct ('*preference*') does not pass the reliability tests either. Following the literature,[1114] the item which correlates least with the sum of the other items of the construct is excluded to increase the constructs' reliability.[1115] Given the relatively low minimal factor loading (0.36) and the AVE below 0.5 of the construct '*knowledge*', a similar procedure is followed for this variable as well.[1116]

	Adequacy of factor analysis		Reliability analysis				Validity analysis
	KMO	No. of eigen-values > 1	Alpha	Composite reliability	Standardised factor loadings	AVE	Fulfilment of the Fornell-Larcker criterion
Knowledge	min. = 0.60	1	0.76	0.77	min. = 0.36	0.49	Yes
Preference	min. = 0.40	1	0.46	0.60	min. = 0.13	0.36	Yes
Involvement	min. = 0.74	1	0.91	0.92	min. = 0.76	0.74	Yes
Contact	min. = 0.68	1	0.77	0.82	min. = 0.58	0.53	Yes
Quality	This construct is measured based on a formatively defined measurement model, which is not subject to above criteria.						

Table 6-61: Reliability and validity assessments of users' attitudes (dataset 3)

The exclusion of the two items heals the quality issues for the information user's '*knowledge*'. The AVE of the revised construct exceeds the threshold of 0.5 (Table 6-62). Also, the minimal factor loading, despite being less than 0.7, achieves the minimum value of 0.4 suggested by *Hulland* (1999).[1117] For the construct '*preference*', the applicability of

[1112] A two-tailed comparison of the mean complexity scores in the companies in dataset 1 that also returned questionnaire B (dataset 3) with those that did not (dataset 5) reveals insignificant differences.

[1113] To be able to derive factor loadings for each item of a latent construct, model specification was applied in accordance with the example in *Backhaus et al.* (2013), p. 149ff.

[1114] Cf. *Churchill* (1979), p. 68; *Homburg/Giering* (1996), p. 8f.

[1115] The excluded item is '*I particularly use other information than cost information for decision-making (e.g. physical measures or market information).*' Its factor loading is 0.13.

[1116] The excluded item is '*The usefulness of cost information is easy to assess.*' Its factor loading is 0.36.

[1117] Cf. *Hulland* (1999), p. 198.

factor analysis can be ensured. Yet, the revision of the construct[1118] cannot ensure that all reliability measures overcome the set thresholds. Nonetheless, the construct *'preference'* is not excluded from the forthcoming analysis[1119] since the identified values for Cronbach's alpha and the AVE are close to the suggested thresholds. An according procedure, however, comes at the cost of less conclusive hypotheses tests for this construct. Therefore, the associated findings are interpreted with caution.

	Adequacy of factor analysis		Reliability analysis				Validity analysis
	KMO	No. of eigen-values > 1	Alpha	Composite reliability	Standardised factor loadings	AVE	Fulfilment of the Fornell-Larcker criterion
Knowledge	min. = 0.75	1	0.77	0.82	min. = 0.50	0.61	Yes
Preference	min. = 0.53	1	0.61	0.67	min. = 0.23	0.45	Yes
Involvement	min. = 0.74	1	0.91	0.92	min. = 0.76	0.74	Yes
Contact	min. = 0.68	1	0.77	0.82	min. = 0.58	0.53	Yes
Quality	This construct is measured based on a formatively defined measurement model, which is not subject to above criteria.						

Table 6-62: Revised reliability and validity assessments of users' attitudes (dataset 3)

There are no significant differences between Anglophone and domestic German subsidiaries for any of the five composite scores measuring users' attitudes towards cost information (Figure 6-4).

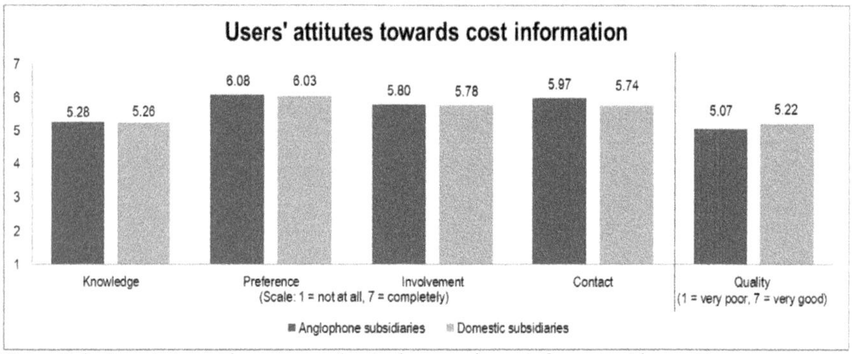

Figure 6-4: Descriptive evidence on users' attitudes towards cost information (dataset 3)

Consistently, information users in both groups report rather extensive knowledge with respect to cost accounting, extensive preference for cost information, extensive involvement into cost system design and extensive contacts with cost accountants. Merely infor-

[1118] Given that the confirmatory factor analysis is performed conjointly for two constructs with four items and two constructs with three items (i.e. 14 empirically measured items), there are 105 empirical variances and covariances to estimate the 34 parameters of the model. Thus, despite having constructs with three items only, there are sufficient degrees of freedom to assess the constructs' reliability conclusively (cf. *Backhaus et al.* (2013), p. 133f.).

[1119] Excluding an additional item could not conclusively overcome the issue of questionable reliability. Despite finding Cronbach's alpha to increase above the threshold of 0.7, the reliability of the indicators remains questionable since the maximum squared factor loading exceeds its logical upper bound of 1. According to *Backhaus*, such a finding indicates a model misspecification that would dilute the interpretability of the findings (cf. *Backhaus et al.* (2013), p. 143f.).

mation users' perceptions about the cost information's quality are slightly lower than the other four variables. Nevertheless, the construct still scores considerably above the mean point of the applied seven point scale.

6.2.2.1.1.3 Economic determinants

Two economic variables are relevant for the analysis of the different types of cost information use. First, there are users' perceptions about the **environmental uncertainty** (question B.3 of questionnaire B). Information users in the Anglophone subsidiaries perceive their environment more predictable than their counterparts from the domestic German subsidiaries (Table 6-63). This reflects the results from questionnaire A (management accountants' perceptions). For comparability, these results are included in Table 6-63. In contrast to the results from questionnaire A, however, the perceived uncertainty differs significantly between Anglophone and domestic German subsidiaries if information users are compared. Moreover, managers (i.e. information users) of both groups perceive the developments in their company's environment slightly more stable than the management accountants do. Only for the Anglophone companies, however, these differences are significant (1 % level, not reported). Because the due section focusses on the responses by managers, this finding does not impinge the intended analysis.

Mean values Information users [management accountants]	**How predictable are the developments in your company's environment?** (Scale: 1= very predictable 7 = very unpredictable)	
	Anglophone	German
Perceived environmental uncertainty	3.32 [3.91]	4.07 [4.13]
p-value (test) (analysis for users' responses)	0.04 (two-tailed t-test)	

Table 6-63: Perceived environmental uncertainty (dataset 3)

Besides the perceived environmental uncertainty, **cost accounting objectives** determine how cost information is used. The hypotheses development identifies the split into decision facilitating and decision influencing to be particular relevant for the analysis of different types of cost information use. For information users, these objectives were surveyed in question A.7 of questionnaire B. The reported mean values are presented in Table 6-64. To assess the plausibility of the results, the table includes the findings for the management accountants as well (question B.20 of questionnaire A).

Mean values users [management accountants]	**Pursuit of cost accounting objectives** (Scale: 1 = not at all, 7 = very intensively)	
	Anglophone	German
(1) Decision facilitating	5.13 [4.73]	4.98 [4.82]
(2) Decision influencing	4.50 [3.94]	4.50 [4.25]
p-value (test) (analyses for users' responses)	For each objective, individual comparisons were performed based on two-tailed parametric tests. If significant, this is indicated by the significance levels *, ** or ***.	
	Individual comparisons of (1) – (2) reveal the identified differences to be significant at a 1 % level (two-tailed t-tests)	Individual comparisons of (1) – (2) reveal the identified differences to be significant at a 10 % level (two-tailed t-tests)

Table 6-64: Cost accounting objectives reported by managers (dataset 3)

As in dataset 1,[1120] the differences for Anglophone and domestic German subsidiaries are insignificant (Table 6-64). In line with this analysis of the management accountants, information users in both Anglophone and domestic German subsidiaries report that cost information is employed more extensively for decision facilitating tasks than for decision influencing ones.[1121]

For both decision facilitating and decision influencing purposes, the mean values of information users differ from the ones of the management accountants. The former apply cost information more extensively for both decision facilitating and decision influencing. Comparisons of the pursued cost accounting objectives in the returned dyads (questionnaire A and questionnaire B of the same company) show that the differences are statistically different from zero at a 10 % level (two-tailed t-test). This result is in line with *Karlshaus* (2000) and *Garg* (2003) for individual cost accounting objectives.[1122] Nevertheless, the explanation by *Karlshaus* (2000) that there are misconceptions in management accounting departments about the importance which managers attribute to cost information appears indefensible. The analysis of the performance of cost accounting (section 6.3) finds that managers and management accountants share similar perceptions on their cost accounting systems. Moreover, this study reassures the finding by *Garg* (2003) that there is some level of agreement about the most important tasks between these employees. Accordingly, the relationship between the most highly rated objectives is similar for management accountants and managers (not reported). As such, the above results rather reveal that management accountants and managers are responsible for different tasks. Thereby, the results reflect the division of labour between information users and preparers.[1123] Through the analysis of the performance of cost accounting systems, section 6.3 investigates whether these differences in the pursuit of cost accounting objectives are accompanied by diverging assessments of the decision usefulness of cost information.

6.2.2.1.1.4 Institutional determinants and the relational context

In hypothesis H4d, cost information in subsidiaries is expected to be used more nonceremonially if there is little or an accepted level of engagement of a parent company into the design of subsidiaries' cost accounting systems.

The **coercive institutional pressures** which the management accountants of the subsidiaries in dataset 3 reported in questions A.6, A.7 and C.2 of questionnaire A are summarised in Table 6-65. For comparability, the table also includes the answers from dataset 1. The results for 'corporate directives' and 'global top management support' (i.e. variable 'corporate managers') from dataset 3 are similar to dataset 1. For the number of 'expatriate managers', however, the picture is slightly different. This number falls considerably

---

[1120] Cf. section 6.1.2.1.1.1, p. 199 (Table 6-40).

[1121] For a discussion of this finding in the light of previous research on cost accounting objectives in Anglophone and domestic German companies, cf. section 6.1.2.1.1.1, p. 199.

[1122] For this and the following, cf. *Karlshaus* (2000), p. 110; *Garg et al.* (2003), p. 31f.

[1123] This assertion holds especially true since no such differences were found for the variables '(4) Operational' and '(5) Strategic', which regard the application of cost information irrespectively of certain tasks (cf. section 6.1.2.1.1.1). Similarly, the rating of the objective '(3) External' is not found to be rated differently by management accountants and managers in the same company.

behind its value from dataset 1 in Anglophone subsidiaries of dataset 3. Moreover, there are less domestic German subsidiaries without expatriate managers in dataset 3 (77.8 %) than in dataset 1 (82.2 %). In contrast, this proportion is stable for the Anglophone subsidiaries (83.0 % and 82.7 %). Given that the differences between the coercive effects on the companies in dataset 1 and 3 are limited, these findings must not be seen to restrict the comparability of the results to be discussed with the analyses for the complexity of cost accounting.

Mean values dataset 3 [dataset 1]	**Coercive institutional influences** (Interpretation of the scale for (1) and (2): 1 = absent, 7 = very high)	
	Anglophone	German
(1) Cost accounting directives	3.82 [3.67]	3.66 [3.43]
p-value (test) - dataset 3	0.72 (two-tailed Welch test)	
(2) Corporate top management support	3.55 [3.61]	3.73 [3.70]
p-value (test) - dataset 3	0.63 (two-tailed t-test)	
(3) Average number of expatriates (if > 0)	1.50 [3.32]	2.10 [2.06]
p-value (test) - dataset 3	0.65 (Wilcoxon rank sum test)	

Table 6-65: Coercive institutional influences (dataset 3)

To investigate whether information users' perceptions of their parent company affects how they respond to coercive institutional pressures, they are asked to assess the **relational context** (B.4 of questionnaire B). To ensure comparability, the construct is aggregated just as management accountants' evaluation of the relational context. Hence, the relational context is derived as a composite score summarising to what extent information users perceive that (a) the subsidiary has cost information needs which diverge from other group companies, (b) there are extensive affective conflicts with the parent company, (c) the subsidiary does not identify with its parent company and (e) the subsidiary can change its management accounting function without consulting with its parent company. Table 6-66 summarises the responses given by the information users to theses four items. It also comprises the answers by their companies' management accountants.

As for the management accountants, Table 6-66 reveals insignificant differences with respect to information users' perceptions of the relational context. Moreover, information users also report the relational context to be only slightly unfavourable. The surveyed mean values fall behind the midpoint of the applied scale.

In contrast to the results from dataset 1 (Table 6-52), however, the individual items of the relational context are assessed differently by the respondents in dataset 3. The significant differences in dataset 1 disappear for dataset 3, whereas differences in dataset 3 do not prevail in dataset 1. These deviations between the results for dataset 1 and dataset 3 are stable for management accountants and information users in dataset 3 despite for the item (e) "*ability to change the management accounting function*". As such, this finding does not indicate a substantially different understanding of the question by respondents of dataset 1 and dataset 3. The findings can rather be attributed to the selection bias (see section 5.3.1) or the underlying characteristics of dataset 1 and 3. Exemplarily, the results might reflect that the Anglophone subsidiaries have smaller, whereas the domestic German subsidiaries have larger parent companies in dataset 3 (see section 5.3.3). As such, the identifiable differences for the individual items do not impinge the conjoint interpretation of the findings from dataset 1 and 3.

Mean values users [management accountants]	Please characterise the relationship between your company and your parent company. (Interpretation of the scale: 1 = not unfavourable, 7 = completely unfavourable)	
	Anglophone	German
(1) Different information needs	3.77 [4.00]	4.36 [4.33]
p-value (test) (analysis for users' responses)	0.14 (two-tailed t-test)	
(2) Affective conflicts	2.44 [2.38]	2.40 [2.23]
p-value (test) (analysis for users' responses)	0.87 (two-tailed t-test)	
(3) Lack of identification	3.99 [4.31]	4.51 [4.40]
p-value (test) (analysis for users' responses)	0.12 (two-tailed t-test)	
(4) Ability to change management accounting function	3.83 [3.89]	3.33 [4.20]
p-value (test) (analysis for users' responses)	0.24 (two-tailed t-test)	
Relational context	3.51 [3.65]	3.65 [3.80]
p-value (test) (analysis for users' responses)	0.49 (two-tailed t-test)	

Table 6-66: Managers' perceptions of the relational context (dataset 3)

Finding rather moderate levels of coercive institutional influences and a little unfavourable rational context in dataset 3 may explain why cost information is not too extensively used in a ceremonial manner (hypothesis H4d1_1a). The due regression analysis on the determinants of the usage types tests this assertion for its empirical support.

6.2.2.1.2 Correlation analysis

There are several notable findings from the analysis of linear correlations between the dependent and independent variables as well as the controls to be analysed in this section (see Appendix 9).[1124] Three of them are presented hereafter.

For the *Anglophone subsidiaries*, the analysis first reveals that the identified 'learning process' between a subsidiary and its parent company persists. Apparently, they learn to embark on one another Despite being insignificant, there is a weak negative association between the **length of affiliation** and information users' perceptions of the **relational context** (r = -0.11, insignificant).

Second, it is remarkable to be unable to identify the significantly negative association between **coercive institutional** pressures and the **relational context** for the information users. Rather, the correlation analysis shows that local decision makers perceive the relationship with their parent more unfavourable, the more corporate managers support the subsidiaries' management accounting functions (r = 0.30, p = 5 %). This finding suggests that Anglophone subsidiaries may not oppose coercive institutional pressures on the design of their cost accounting system but actually respond through different usage types.

[1124] Associated to the relatively small sample size of dataset 3, some of the significant levels of the linear correlations cannot be confirmed by *Spearman*'s rang correlation. This will be noted below.

There are additional correlations which can underline this interpretation. There is a significant positive (negative) correlation between the level of ceremonial (instrumental/conceptual) use and the relational context (r = 0.27, p = 10 %, and r = -0.24, p = 10 %). In line with these findings, information users apply cost information less intensively for decision influencing (r = -0.33, p= 5 %) and decision facilitating (r = -0.33, p= 5 %) if there was an unfavourable relational context. Apparently, information users in the Anglophone subsidiaries use cost information less intensively during the process of management, if they perceive the relationship with their parent company to be rather unfavourable.[1125] This can be seen as implicit evidence for the suggested moderation effect. The interrelation must be kept in mind for an interpretation of the due regression analysis.

Third, the two **cost accounting objectives** distinguished in the analysis of the different types of use (decision facilitating and decision influencing) are significantly correlated (r = 0.50, p =1 %). Nevertheless, these two types of use are not aggregated at this point. There are two particular reasons for this procedure. On the one hand, the instrumental/conceptual usage type is more strongly correlated with the decision facilitating objective (r = 0.60, p = 1 %) than the decision influencing one (r = 0.47, p = 1 %). On the other hand, the diagnostic and interactive usage types are more strongly and more significantly correlated with the decision influencing objective (r = 0.65, p = 1 % and r = 0.50, p = 1 %) than with the decision facilitating one (r = 0.29, p = 5 % and r = 0.36, p = 5 %). Both these findings are in line with the hypotheses (H4c_2a and H4c_2b). Hence, interesting findings in this regard can be anticipated.

For the *domestic German subsidiaries*, the correlation analysis first underlines a significant negative association between the decision facilitating **objective**, the decision influencing objective as well as the cost accounting system's complexity and the level of **perceived environmental uncertainty** (min. r = -0.52, max. r = -0.26). Moreover, the perceived environmental uncertainty is also moderately associated with each non-ceremonial usage type (i.e. the instrumental/conceptual, rationalising, diagnostic and interactive use) in a negative manner (min. r = -0.34, max. r = -0.19). Except for the instrumental/conceptual usage type, these associations are significant. All above findings are in line with the discussion provided during the correlation analysis for questionnaire A (section 6.1.2.1.2). As such, they underline that cost information may not be the core consideration in domestic German subsidiaries if decisions have to be made in times of a particular uncertain environment.

Second, there is a moderate negative association between information users' perceptions of the **quality of their cost accounting systems** and an unfavourable **relational context** (r = -0.35, p = 5 %). Also, corporate top management's involvement correlates positively with the ceremonial usage type (r = 0.35, p = 5 %). Information users in the domestic German subsidiaries do not only detach cost information from the management process if their system is affected by their parent company but also tend to assess the quality of their (affected) systems more negatively the more unfavourable the relation with their parent company is. These correlations mirror the similar finding for the Anglophone subsidiaries.

[1125] In an analysis of the *Spearman* correlation coefficients most of these interrelations lose statistical significance. The sign of the coefficients, however, is not affected.

Subsidiaries might actually respond to corporate pressures how to design a cost accounting system and to an unfavourable relational context more extensively through their use of the system than by adjustments to the system's design.

Finally, it is reassuring to find insignificant associations between the control variable **board member** and all five **usage types**. Apparently, the fact that some board members passed on the response to questionnaire B to their management accountants does not bias the results considerably.[1126]

6.2.2.1.3 Hypotheses testing

6.2.2.1.3.1 Introduction

This study tests hypotheses on five different types of cost information use. All five usage types have to be analysed for both Anglophone (Table 6-67) and domestic German subsidiaries (Table 6-68) in dataset 3. Moreover, for both Anglophone and domestic German subsidiaries, two models have to be computed. Model (a) consists of the 13 independent variables and the six controls.[1127] Model (b) includes three additional interaction terms. These interaction terms are included to test for the moderating effect of the relational context on the coercive institutional influences (hypothesis H5e).[1128] Thus, there are 20 linear regression models to be discussed hereafter. To restrict the due section to a manageable length, and to reflect the nature of the hypotheses (i.e. rather similar hypotheses for various types of use), it is most appropriate to group the forthcoming discussion according to the independent variables rather than the individual types of use. Chapter 6.2.3 summarises the results for each usage type.

The significance levels in Table 6-67 and Table 6-68 are based on one-tailed t-tests for directed hypotheses and on two-tailed t-tests for undirected hypotheses. Some of the directed hypotheses have to be rejected due to unexpected signs of the regression coefficients. To derive meaningful explanations for such unpredicted results, these coefficients are treated as if the identified sign was expected. If e.g. the regression result reveals that an expected positive sign is actually smaller than zero and has a p-value below 0.1 (one-tailed test), then the coefficient will be treated as 'quasi significant'. To allow for an immediate identification of such findings, the asterisk (*) usually used to tag significant findings is replaced by a diamond (#).[1129]

[1126] This finding holds true for the Anglophone subsidiaries as well (cf. Appendix 9).

[1127] The controls are the subsidiary's size, and its length of affiliation as well as the parent's form of market entry and its size. Additionally it is considered whether responding information users are board members and how many years of work experience they have. Descriptive evidence on these variables can be found in sections 5.3.2 and 5.3.3. Additional robustness checks of the results were done by including the parent company's holding structure (possible restriction of local decision rights) and the subsidiary's value chain activities (complexity of the local decision-making processes). Neither variable would have changed the conclusions drawn from the due analysis.

[1128] All four variables involved in the moderation analysis ('directives', 'corporate managers', 'expatriates' and 'relational context') were centred before including them into the analyses.

[1129] This procedure will be evaluated critically as a limitation (section 7.2) since it restricts how rigorously this study follows its epistemological positioning.

Given the reliance on two models (model (a) and model (b)), it is essential to explicate when to reject or to accept a hypothesis. Results which are not present for models (a) and (b) are regarded as less robust findings. Suggested interrelations are 'accepted conditionally' if they are of little robustness. Also, hypotheses are 'rejected conditionally' if there is some statistical support for the basic rationale beyond a hypothesis. For brevity, Table 6-67 and Table 6-68 present only the directions of the significant and 'quasi significant' regression coefficients. These findings form the basis for the forthcoming discussion. The detailed regression results can be found in Appendix 10.

The significant F-values in Table 6-67 indicate an adequate fit of the models for the **Anglophone subsidiaries.** This is confirmed by moderate to high adjusted R^2 values which vary between 9.7 % (model (a) for the interactive usage type) and 53.0 % (model (b) for the instrumental/conceptual usage type). These results are in line with previous studies on *Pelz*'s and *Burchell et al.*'s[1130] and *Simons*'[1131] usage types. The reported VIFs (max. = 8.38) fall behind the generally proposed threshold of 10. Hence, multicollinearity is not an issue. The proposed models fit the data from the **domestic German subsidiaries** adequately, as well. Merely for model (b) of the ceremonial usage type there is an insignificant F-value. This finding, however, rather disapproves the suggested interaction effect for the ceremonial use of cost information only. For the associated (a) model, there is a significant F-value. Overall, moderate to high adjusted R^2 values are found for the German data as well. They vary between 7.9 % (model (a) for the rationalising usage type) and 56.5 % (model (a) for the diagnostic usage type). Hence, there is no substantial deviation from previous research with respect to model fitness for the data obtained from the domestic German subsidiaries either. As for the Anglophone subsidiaries, multicollinearity does not impinge the provided results since the VIFs are below 10 (max. = 4.61). Autocorrelation and heteroscedasticity are not tested for separately because the regression analyses use robust standard errors.[1132]

1130 *Hunold* (2003), p. 247ff., reports R^2s between 23.1 % (symbolic use) and 26.6 % (instrumental use), *Sandt* (2004), p. 184ff., finds R^2s between 15 % (symbolic use) and 45 % (conceptual use), *Steiners* (2005), p. 186ff., finds R^2s between 0 % (construct of diagnostic use involving items and environmental factors) and 31 % (construct of diagnostic use involving items and information user's characteristics).

1131 *Widener* (2007), p. 776, finds R^2s of 11.7 % for the interactive and 21.3 % or the diagnostic use. *Naranjo-Gil/Hartmann* (2006), p. 37, report an R^2 of 25.7 % (23.3 %) for the interactive (diagnostic) use. *Hofmann et al.* (2012), p. 168, mention R^2s of 40 % for the interactive and 50 % for the diagnostic use.

1132 The standard errors are estimated by 'adjusted sandwich estimators'.

Linear regression model - dataset 3 (unstandardised regression coeff.)	Anglophone subsidiaries														
	Instrum. / concept. use			Rationalising use			Diagnostic use			Interactive use			Ceremonial use		
	E.S.	Model (a)	Model (b)	E.S.	Model (a)	Model (b)	E.S.	Model (a)	Model (b)	E.S.	Model (a)	Model (b)	E.S.	Model (a)	Model (b)
Complexity of cost accounting	+	+ **	+ **	+			+			+			+/-		
Knowledge	+			+			+			+			+/-		
Preference	+	+ **	+ **	+/-			+			+			-	- ***	- ***
Quality	+			+/-			+			+			-	- *	
Involvement	+			+/-			+			+			-	- ***	- ***
Contact	+			+/-			+			+		- #	-	+ ##	+ ##
Perceived environmental uncertainty	+/-			+/-			+/-			+/-	+ *		+/-	- ***	- **
Objective: decision facilitating	+			/			/			/			/		
Objective: decision influencing	/			/			+	+ ***	+ ***	+	+ **	+ *	/		
Relational context (centralised)	/			/	+ **	+ ***	/			/			/	+ *	+ **
Directives *(centralised)*	-	- *	- *	-	- **	- ***	-			-			+		
Directives **x** Rel. context *(centralised)*	+		- ###	+		- #	+			+		- #	-		
Corporate managers *(centralised)*	-		+ #	-	- *		-			-			+		
Corp. managers **x** Rel. context *(central.)*	+			+			+			+		+ **	-		- ***
Expatriates *(centralised)*	-	+ #		-			-			-			+	- ###	- #
Expatriates **x** Rel. context *(centralised)*	+			+		+ ***	+			+			-		- **
Size subsidiary	/			/			/			/			/		
Form of market entry *(dummy)*	/			/	- **	- ***	/	- *	- *	/			/		
Length of affiliation	/			/			/			/			/		
Size parent company	/			/			/			/			/		
Years of work experience	/			/			/			/			/		+ *
Board member *(dummy)*	/			/	- **	- *	/			/			/		- *
Constant	/			/			/			/			/	+ ***	+ ***
R^2		69.46 %	75.48 %		55.30 %	62.68 %		61.50 %	65.26 %		47.00 %	58.32 %		63.86 %	71.16 %
adjusted R^2		48.00 %	53.00 %		23.90 %	28.50 %		34.40 %	33.40 %		9.70 %	20.10 %		38.40 %	44.70 %
F		9.03	17.02		6.23	17.93		6.71	7.30		7.01	5.99		4.98	6.38
Significance		0.0000	0.0000		0.0000	0.0000		0.0000	0.0000		0.0000	0.0000		0.0000	0.0000
VIF_{max}		8.30	8.38		8.30	8.38		8.30	8.38		8.30	8.38		8.30	8.38
F (moderation)		2.48 *			2.35 *			1.38			2.05			3.17 **	

Table 6-67: Compact regression results on the determinants of the five usage types - Anglophone subsidiaries in dataset 3

Linear regression model - dataset 3 (unstandardised regression coeff.)	Domestic German subsidiaries														
	Instrum. / concept. use			Rationalising use			Diagnostic use			Interactive use			Ceremonial use		
	E.S.	Model (a)	Model (b)	E.S.	Model (a)	Model (b)	E.S.	Model (a)	Model (b)	E.S.	Model (a)	Model (b)	E.S.	Model (a)	Model (b)
Complexity of cost accounting	+	- #		+	- ##		+	- #		+			+/-		
Knowledge	+			+		+ *	+			+			+/-	- **	- **
Preference	+			+/-			+			+		+ *	-	- ***	- **
Quality	+	+ ***	+ **	+/-			+			+	+ **		-		
Involvement	+			+/-		- **	+			+			-		
Contact	+	+ **	+ *	+/-			+			+			-		
Perceived environmental uncertainty	+/-			+/-	- *	- *	+/-			+/-			+/-		
Objective: decision facilitating	+			/			/			/			/	- **	- **
Objective: decision influencing	/			/			+	+ ***	+ ***	+	+ ***	+ ***	/		
Relational context (centralised)	/			/	+ **	+ **	/			/			/		
Directives *(centralised)*	-	- *	- *	-		+ #	-			-			+	+ **	+ **
Directives **x** Rel. context *(centralised)*	+			+			+			+			-		
Corporate managers *(centralised)*	-	+ ##		-			-			-			+		
Corp. managers **x** Rel. context *(central.)*	+			+		- ##	+		- ##	+			-		
Expatriates *(centralised)*	-			-	- *	- ***	-	- ***	- ***	-			+		
Expatriates **x** Rel. context *(centralised)*	+			+		- ###	+			+		- ###	-		
Size subsidiary	/			/			/			/	- *		/	- *	
Form of market entry *(dummy)*	/			/			/			/			/		
Length of affiliation	/			/			/			/		+ *	/		
Size parent company	/			/			/	- **	- *	/			/		
Years of work experience	/			/	+ *		/	+ **	+ *	/			/		
Board member *(dummy)*	/			/			/			/			/		
Constant	/			/	+ **		/			/			/	+ ***	+ ***
R^2		59.76 %	61.41 %		45.68 %	67.50 %		75.30 %	77.37 %		66.24 %	74.03 %		68.01 %	70.04 %
adjusted R^2		29.20 %	22.80 %		7.90 %	35.00 %		56.50 %	54.70 %		40.60 %	48.10 %		43.70 %	40.10 %
F		3.06	3.97		3.47	31.12		12.98	9.47		2.11	6.91		1.91	1.4
Significance		0.0012	0.0001		0.0004	0.0000		0.0000	0.0000		0.0222	0.0000		0.0406	0.1723
VIF_{max}		4.49	4.61		4.49	4.61		4.49	4.61		4.49	4.61		4.49	4.61
F (moderation)		0.4			5.33 ***			1.1			2.71 *			0.55	

Table 6-68: Compact regression results on the determinants of the five usage types - domestic German subsidiaries in dataset 3

6.2.2.1.3.2Complexity of cost accounting systems

Managers in the *Anglophone subsidiaries* use cost information more extensively in an instrumental/conceptual manner if their companies have a rather **complex cost accounting system**. Redoing the regression analysis for the three complexity scores on cost type, cost centre and cost object accounting shows that this finding can be attributed to both cost type (model (a) and model (b)) and cost centre accounting (model (b)). Other than expected, however, no such association prevails for the rationalising, diagnostic[1133] and interactive use. Similarly, the complexity of the cost accounting system has no effect on the ceremonial use of cost information, either. As such, hypothesis H5a can be supported for the instrumental/conceptual use of information in the Anglophone subsidiaries only. This finding suggests that the German decision makers in Anglophone subsidiaries prefer their local cost accounting traditions for decision-making.[1134] Being unable to align the usage types which share structural similarities with the purpose 'decision influencing' (diagnostic and interactive use) with the complexity of cost accounting systems might be attributable to the fact that associated tasks can arguably be fulfilled based on less detailed cost information (section 4.2.1). The inability to align the rationalising and the ceremonial use with the design of cost accounting systems indicated that these usage types reflect that information systems are actually 'decoupled' from managerial decision-making. Moreover, all the above findings show that managers use cost information selectively. Hence, rather than striving for an alignment of the entire cost accounting system with managers' use of information, future research should focus on single pieces of cost information to study the use of costs in Anglophone subsidiaries.

For the domestic *German subsidiaries*, the **complexity of the cost accounting system** affects the use of cost information in an instrumental/conceptual, rationalising and diagnostic manner negatively at a 10 % to 5 % 'quasi significance' level (model (a)). Taking a look at the complexity scores for cost type, cost centre and cost object accounting reveals explicatory insights to this unexpected result.

	Model (a)		Model (b)	
	Component	Effect	Component	Effect
Instr. / concept. use	Cost type accounting	neg.##	Cost type accounting	neg.##
Rationalising use	Cost object accounting	neg.##	Cost object accounting	neg.##
Diagnostic use	Cost type accounting	neg.##	Cost type accounting	neg.#
Interactive use	Cost type accounting Cost object accounting	neg.# neg.#	Cost centre accounting	pos.*
Ceremonial use	Cost type accounting	pos.**	Cost type accounting	pos.**

Table 6-69: Complexity scores affecting the usage types in the domestic German subsidiaries

For the instrumental/conceptual use and the diagnostic use, this finding is associable to the complexity of cost type accounting (one-sided tests). Cost object accounting determines the finding for the rationalising use of information (Table 6-69). The table also

[1133] For the diagnostic use of information, a significant positive association prevails for the complexity of cost centre accounting in models (a) and (b).

[1134] A revised regression model substituting the complexity score for the dummy variable on the cross-national differences reveals a significant negative association between that variable and the instrumental/conceptual use (for the variable '*CND*', cf. section 6.1.2.2, p. 222).

reports that, among others, there is a 'quasi significant' negative association between the complexity of cost type accounting and the interactive use (model (a)) and a significant positive association between the complexity of cost type accounting and the ceremonial use of information.

It appears as if it is particularly the complexity of the **cost type accounting** which evokes the unexpected negative association of the cost accounting score and the usage types. Redoing the linear regression models for the three individual complexity sub-scores summarised as 'cost type accounting' identifies the following components to underlie the identified effects (Table 6-70):

	Model (a)		Model (b)	
	Component	Effect	Component	Effect
Instr. / concept. use	Recognition of imputed costs	neg.##	Recognition of imputed costs	neg.#
Diagnostic use	Separation of the datasets for management and financial accounting	neg.##	Separation of the datasets for management and financial accounting	neg.#
Interactive use	Separation of the datasets for management and financial accounting	neg.#	/	/
Ceremonial use	Number of cost types *and* Recognition of imputed costs	pos.** pos.*	Number of cost types *and* Recognition of imputed costs	pos.** pos.*

Table 6-70: Complexity sub-scores affecting the usage types in the domestic German subsidiaries

The evidence in Table 6-70 (one-sided tests) suggests that the existence of imputed costs (or multiple cost types) prevents a conclusive use of cost information for decision-making in the domestic German companies. Since these complexity sub-scores are strongly affected by the parent companies (section 6.1), it is little surprising to find them to affect the ceremonial application positively. Both can be seen as evidence that management accountants (or parent companies) may need to explain imputed costs more conclusively to managers to reemphasise their relevance and decision usefulness. Furthermore, Table 6-70 also reveals that the separation of financial and management accounting information impinges the decision influencing use of cost information (diagnostic and interactive use). This finding suggests that managers might have difficulties to choose which of the alternative financial measures (management accounting and financial accounting information) can influence their subordinates' behaviour best.[1135] Both these interpretations can be easily linked to previous research indicating that managers, who perceive their cost accounting system to be complex, tend to use cost information less extensively in an instrumental and conceptual manner.[1136]

Even though the unexpected negative association of the instrumental/conceptual, the rationalising and the diagnostic use of cost information with the complexity of the cost accounting system can be conclusively explained, hypothesis H5a has to be rejected for the domestic German companies. There is no support for the expected positive effect. Moreover, hypothesis H5a has to be rejected for the interactive and the ceremonial usage types as well. For neither of the latter two, a significant association with the average complexity of cost accounting can be identified. Yet, for these two types, the rejection is conditional since the analyses for the complexity of cost type, cost centre and cost object accounting

[1135] For a similar argument, cf. *Angelkort* (2010), p. 160f.

[1136] Cf. section 3.3.2.3, p. 75. Similarly, *Heimel et al.* (2012), p. 58, provide recent evidence on German executives' request for a simplified cost accounting.

point out various expected effects (Table 6-69). Above all, these results reflect the negative effect of local top management support on the complexity of cost accounting in the domestic German subsidiaries (cf. sections 6.1.2.1.3.2). The information users in these companies appear to be in favour of comprehensive, unambiguous information rather than very detailed cost information which might be open for interpretation.

6.2.2.1.3.3 Users' attitudes towards cost information

In hypothesis H4b_1, **users' knowledge** with respect to cost information is argued to increase the non-ceremonial use of cost information and to decrease the ceremonial use of cost information. In contrast to these expectations, there is no association for any of the five usage types in the sample of *Anglophone subsidiaries* (Table 6-68). Hence, hypotheses H4b_1a and H4b_1b have to be rejected for these companies.

In the sample of *domestic German subsidiaries*, knowledgeable managers tend to use cost information significantly more in a rationalising manner (model (b)) and significantly less in a ceremonial manner (model (a) and model (b)). These findings support hypothesis H4b_1b (ceremonial use) and provides evidence that H4b_1a can be 'conditionally accepted' for the rationalising use. The diverging findings for the rationalising and the ceremonial use are very insightful. They might suggest that knowledgeable managers prefer a more gently avoidance of a disliked involvement by their parent company over its strict defiance.[1137] Hence, despite finding some support for these hypotheses, the meaning of the findings is rather different than suggested in section 4.2.2. Above all, the expected importance of users' knowledge cannot be established for the majority of the five types of use in the domestic German subsidiaries either.

These results are particularly surprising. **Previous research**, though applying structural equation models for German companies, regularly established the link between managers' knowledge and their use of information.[1138] Hence, despite potential measurement issues and differences in the statistical methods, a reason for the inability to align the use of cost information with managers' knowledge might be this study's focus on subsidiaries. In this context, the use of cost information appears to depend more on the influence of and the relationship with the parent company (section 6.2.2.1.3.5) than on decision makers' personal attitudes. The results for domestic German subsidiaries underline this interpretation. As such, this finding highlights the necessity for future research comparing the use of cost information in subsidiaries and single companies. Such studies could explore whether

[1137] Such an interpretation is capable to explicate the differences found in the meaning of the rationalising usage type in the Anglophone and the domestic German subsidiaries. Potentially, the Anglophone subsidiaries do not use cost information rationalisingly to circumvent corporate directives (any more) due to their reflection of a foreign cost accounting tradition but prefer a less graceful defiance. As such, the meaning of the rationalising use in the Anglophone subsidiaries reveals greater similarities with both perspectives covered in this usage type: the mere application of cost information for ex post rationalisation as well as the unintendedly captured avoidance of corporate directives. Somewhat in line with this interpretation, there is more suggestive evidence for 'shadow systems' in the Anglophone subsidiaries (section 6.3). Also, the selection bias present in dataset 3 for the domestic German subsidiaries suggests fewer issues with respect to the usefulness of cost information in these companies (section 6.3).

[1138] Cf. section 3.3.2.3, p. 76, or *Sandt* (2004), p. 188; *Steiners* (2005), p. 191.

a more thorough inclusion of organisational characteristics during the analysis of different usage types can deepen the understanding, how and why cost information is (not) included for decision-making.

The set of hypotheses H4b_2 argues that **managers' preference** for cost information determines how they use it. As for H4b_1, the suggested association can be identified for a minority of the regarded usage types only. In the *Anglophone subsidiaries*, managers, who are in great favour of cost information, tend to use this information significantly more extensively in a decision facilitating manner (instrumental/conceptual use). Moreover, they maintain the cost accounting system significantly less extensively for ceremonial reasons. The latter influence holds true for the *domestic German subsidiaries* as well. Other than in the Anglophone subsidiaries, however, in the domestic German ones the interactive application of cost information increases significantly with information users' preference for cost information (model (b)). In neither of the two groups, the preference for cost information is significantly associated with the rationalising and the diagnostic use of cost information.

Overall, the lack of 'quasi significant' associations between the managers' preference for cost information and the usage types illustrate that the **reliability issues** raised for this variable in section 6.2.2.1.1.2 do not appear to impinge the regression analysis. Nevertheless, it is somewhat difficult to align this study's findings with the two **previous research** projects looking at different types of management accounting information use and information users' preference for information. In these projects, significant positive associations with *Burchell et al.*'s[1139] and *Simons*'[1140] types of information use prevail. The significant negative association of users' preference for cost information and the ceremonial usage type can conclusively complement these findings. Apparently, information users do not only increase their use of cost information in various ways if they like cost information, but they are also more reluctant to maintain their cost accounting system for ceremonial purposes. This study's findings cannot reassure the importance of managers' preferences for cost information for the four non-ceremonial usage types. In both the Anglophone and the domestic German subsidiaries, only for one usage type each, an according association prevails. In line with the discussion for users' knowledge, the results for users' preferences (H4b_2) might be associated with the research objects of this study. Given the lack of prior efforts to compare the use of information in subsidiaries and single companies, this matter remains subject to further research because the finding could, despite little according evidence, also be due to the quality of the applied measurement model.

The set of hypotheses H4b_3 aligns the use of cost information with users' perceptions about the **quality of cost information**. In the *Anglophone sample*, managers apply cost information significantly more extensively in a ceremonial manner if they perceive the information quality to be poor (model (a)). In the *domestic German subsidiaries*, managers apply cost information significantly more extensively in an instrumental/conceptual manner if the information quality is perceived particularly well (models (a) and (b)). Furthermore, managers apply cost information significantly more extensively to engage them-

[1139] Cf. *Hunold* (2003), p. 196 and 208.
[1140] Cf. *Hofmann et al.* (2012), p. 161 and 168.

selves interactively into their subordinates' decision-making if cost information is perceived to be of good quality (model (a)) in the domestic German companies. As such, there is support for H4b_3c (ceremonial use) for the Anglophone companies, whereas H4b_3b (rationalising use) and H4b_3a (remaining usage types) have to be rejected. In contrast, in the domestic German sample H4b_3a holds true for the instrumental/conceptual and the interactive usage types, whereas H4b_3b (rationalising use) and H4b_3c (ceremonial) have to be rejected. In either case, hypotheses rejections are due to a lack of statistical associations.

As for the former two hypotheses, this study's results with respect to the ceremonial use in the Anglophone subsidiaries complement **prior research**. Previous studies regularly approve that a positive assessment of information quality increases the instrumental conceptual and symbolic use of cost and management accounting information.[1141] Apparently, a poor quality of cost information cannot only decrease the non-ceremonial usage types in single companies but also fosters the ceremonial use in subsidiaries. Since there is only selective evidence to support the set of hypotheses H4b_3, however, the findings for managers' perceptions of information quality reemphasise that in subsidiaries, managers' information use may be deeply interwoven with requirements concerning the design of information systems posited by parent companies.

According to the set of hypotheses H4b_4, managers use cost information differently if they involve into the design of the cost accounting system. In the sample of *Anglophone subsidiaries*, managers use cost information significantly more in a ceremonial manner if they cannot or do not involve themselves into the system's design (model (a) and model (b)). Hence, there is conclusive evidence in favour of H4b_4c (ceremonial use) in these companies, whereas the hypotheses on all other usage types (H4b_4a and H4b_4b) have to be rejected. There is no association between these latter usage types and the **involvement of managers** into the system's design. In the *domestic German subsidiaries*, decision makers use cost information significantly less extensively to rationalise previously taken decisions if they are heavily involved in the system's design (model (b)). As such, H4b_4b cannot be rejected for these companies. In contrast, no evidence supports H4b_4a and H4b_4c.

These results are particularly revealing. The findings in **previous research** are rather affirmative of a positive influence of management involvement on the actual use of cost information.[1142] These findings cannot be reassured explicitly at this point. But, both the rationalising use of information as well as the ceremonial use of information do not involve the ex-ante inclusion of cost information into decision-making. Hence, above results assure the findings in former research implicitly because managers use cost information more extensively in ways that do not involve the (ex-ante) consideration of cost infor-

[1141] Cf. *Frank* (2000), p. 177; *Karlshaus* (2000), p. 160; *Steiners* (2005), p. 193. *Hunold* (2003), p. 208, reports a negative association but weakens the validity of his finding by issues of measure validity and endogeneity (p. 212).

[1142] For *Burchell et al.*'s instrumental usage type, cf. *Frank* (2000), p. 177; *Hunold* (2003), p. 208. For *Simons*' interactive use, cf. *Widener* (2007), p. 778; *Abernethy et al.* (2010), p. 11; *Hofmann et al.* (2012), p. 168.

mation for decision-making if they (i) do not or (ii) cannot participate in the development of a cost accounting system. Given the focus on subsidiaries, interpretation (ii), i.e. the inability to participate in system development, is well in line with the previously derived assertion that users' attitudes towards cost information may not be as important for the use of cost information in subsidiaries as they are in single companies. Since no differentiation is made in the questionnaire to analyse whether a low level of management involvement is reflective of (i) managers' explicit choice or (ii) their inability to do so, however, this finding must be considered as an interpretative indication for such an association only. All in all, the findings especially underline the apparent conceptual similarity of the ceremonial and the rationalising use of cost information.

Hypothesis H4b_5 aligns the use of cost information with the number of contacts between managers (i.e. information users) and management accountants (i.e. information providers). In the *Anglophone sample*, the responses only reveal two non-expected findings. Whereas managers use cost information less extensively in an interactive manner the more they are in **contact with management accountants** (model (b)), they employ the system more extensively in a ceremonial manner when there are multiple contacts with management accountants (model (a) and model (b)). Besides unlikely measurement issues, a peculiar interpretation for each finding can be found. Superficially, the finding for the interactive use of information is puzzling because managers' personal interaction with their subordinates is precisely what characterises this usage type. Yet, the finding could suggest that management accountants are not the core subordinates, whose decisions are influenced by managers in an interactive manner. The unexpected positive association between the number of contacts and the ceremonial use of cost information might be linked to another issue of endogeneity. The finding might reflect that managers, whose cost information needs cannot be met through their companies' cost accounting system, have to interact more extensively with their management accountants. Thereby, the managers may explore alternative information sources that fulfil their information needs.[1143] Determining reversed causality (i.e. endogeneity) to explain the reported findings flaws the regression results for the ceremonial use (H4b_5c). Rather than preceding the ceremonial use, contacts might become necessary because of an according application of the system. Overall, hypothesis H4b_5a, H4b_5b and H4b_5c have to be rejected for the Anglophone subsidiaries. **Previous research** on this issue regularly finds a positive effect of contacts between providers and users of information for the use of cost information.[1144] As such, this result appears particularly attributable to the focus on subsidiaries.

[1143] In line, a study of 65 Italian subsidiaries of international MNCs find 86 % of these to have both, an imposed and a locally developed performance measurement system (cf. *Dossi/Patelli* (2008), p. 140). Similarly, *Schäffer et al.* (2010), p. 312, find 25 % of the 148 Chinese subsidiaries of international MNCs researched, to have an additional performance measurement system. Thereby, the need for detailed analysis is the primary reason for the second system. Also, *Luther et al.* (2010), p. 84, provide a similar interpretation in a context of dependent organisations.

[1144] For *Burchell et al.*'s instrumental and symbolic usage types, cf. *Karlshaus* (2000), p. 161; *Hunold* (2003), p. 208. For *Simons*' interactive use, cf. *Widener* (2007), p. 778; *Abernethy et al.* (2010), p. 11; *Hofmann et al.* (2012), p. 168.

In contrast to the findings for the Anglophone sample, the results for the *domestic German subsidiaries* reassure previous results with respect to the instrumental/conceptual use of cost information. The more interaction there is between managers and management accountants, the more managers use cost information in an instrumental/conceptual manner (model (a) and model (b)). Hence, there is some evidence to support H4b_5a for the domestic German companies. The hypotheses for the rationalising and the ceremonial usage types (H4b_5b H4b_5c), however, have to be fully rejected. There is no statistically significant evidence for an effect of the number of contact between information users and providers on these usage types. As revealed above, this result could be associable to this study's focus on subsidiaries. The discussion on the institutional determinants (section 6.2.2.1.3.5) finds empirical support for this assertion. Nevertheless, future comparisons of subsidiaries and single companies in this regard would be helpful to understand the effect of information users' personal attitudes on the use of cost information in subsidiaries.

6.2.2.1.3.4 Economic determinants

From an economic perspective, the perceived environmental uncertainty and the general purposes of cost accounting (i.e. decision facilitating vs. decision influencing) are expected to influence the various usage types.

With respect to the **perceived environmental uncertainty**, hypothesis H4c_1 expects an undirected significant association with all five usage types. In line with two former studies,[1145] the managers of the *Anglophone subsidiaries* use cost information significantly more extensively in an interactive manner (model (a)) if the environment is rather uncertain. Given a finding by *Widener* (2007), this might be seen as an indication that the source of the perceived uncertainty is competitive uncertainty rather than technological or operational uncertainty.[1146] Moreover, there is a significant negative association between the environmental uncertainty and the ceremonial use of information (model (a) and model (b)) in the Anglophone subsidiaries. This finding can be linked to a theoretical consideration of NIS. Accordingly, companies are likely to mimic certain behaviours to respond to environmental uncertainties.[1147] Such reproductions reflect a voluntary institutional effect,[1148] which might heal the disapproval of a coercively induced cost accounting system.[1149] Hence, the result with respect to the ceremonial use might reflect subsidiary managers' attempts to mimic their parent company's application of cost information. In doing so, they are rather reluctant to question the information of a coercively induced cost accounting system because the induced system reduces the complexity of a decision-problem. Despite these findings, hypothesis H4c_1 is only 'accepted conditionally' for the Anglophone subsidiaries. Thereby it is acknowledged that the perceived environmental uncertainty cannot be associated with the remaining three usage types. Notably, this result reflects previous findings for the instrumental/conceptual usage type.[1150] As already dis-

[1145] Cf. *Widener* (2007), p. 778; *Hofmann et al.* (2012), p. 168.
[1146] Cf. *Widener* (2007), p. 778.
[1147] Cf. *DiMaggio/Powell* (1983), p. 151.
[1148] Cf. *Oliver* (1991), p. 167f.; *Modell* (2002), p. 658f.
[1149] For a similar finding, cf. *Yazdifar et al.* (2008) as discussed in section 3.3.2.2, p. 72.
[1150] Cf. *Frank* (2000), p. 177; *Karlshaus* (2000), p. 159; *Steiners* (2005), p. 186.

cussed during the correlation analysis in section 6.2.2.1.2, this could be linked to a substitution of cost information for other (non-financial) information at the times of high environmental uncertainty.

The findings for H4c_1 in the *domestic German subsidiaries* are peculiar. There is a significant negative association between the perceived environmental uncertainty and the rationalising use of information (model (a) and model (b)) in these companies. This result underlines the proposed conceptual similarity of the rationalising and the ceremonial use of cost information in the domestic German subsidiaries. Apparently, these companies might be more reluctant to avoid their parent companies' systems because following parent companies' orders reduces the complexity of decision processes during high levels of environmental uncertainty. Nevertheless, hypothesis H4c_1 cannot be accepted unconditionally for the domestic subsidiaries. The significant association between the perceived environmental uncertainty and the usage types is restricted to the rationalising use only.

The regression model in Table 6-67 cannot establish a significant link between the objective **decision facilitating** and the instrumental/conceptual use in *the Anglophone subsidiaries*. As such, H4c_2a has to be rejected for these companies. This is rather surprising since these two variables correlate strongly and significantly ($r = 0.60$, $p = 1\ \%$).[1151] It appears as if the identified relationship is overruled by other determinants of this type of use. Since this usage type is affected heavily by coercive institutional influences from the parent companies (see Table 6-67), this finding could be due to managers' reduced ability to let their personal attitudes and their objectives determine how to use cost information in a subsidiary context. In contrast, the expected positive association between the objective **decision influencing** and both the diagnostic and the interactive use of cost information prevails in the Anglophone subsidiaries. An extensive pursuit of the decision influencing objectives is accompanied by an extensive use of cost information in diagnostic and interactive manners in these firms (model (a) and model (b)). As such, there is strong support for hypothesis H4c_2b, which suggests an according interrelation. Besides the acceptance of H4c_2b, these results are underlining the nomological validity of the cost accounting objectives and the usage types. In section 2.3.3, *Simons*' types of cost information use are introduced because *Pelz*'s and *Burchell et al.*'s types incomprehensively summarise the use of cost information with respect to the decision influencing purpose. Being able to 'accept' H4c_2b underlines the validity of these conceptual considerations.

These arguments can be reinforced by the results from the *German domestic subsidiaries*. The suggested interaction between the decision influencing objective and both the diagnostic and the interactive use of cost information is present. As such, H4c_2b can be accepted for these firms as well. Managers in these subsidiaries use cost information more extensively in both a diagnostic and an interactive manner, the more they report their company to emphasise the application of cost information for decision influencing tasks (model (a) and model (b)). As for the Anglophone subsidiaries, however, H4c_2a has to be rejected for the domestic German subsidiaries. There is no association between the composite score for the objective 'decision facilitating' and the instrumental/conceptual use of cost information. Peculiarly, however, cost information is applied less extensively in

[1151] Cf. Appendix 9.

a ceremonial manner, the more extensively the objective 'decision facilitating' is pursued. Hence, for the domestic German subsidiaries there is evidence that the more extensively cost information facilitates, e.g. pricing or production planning decisions (see section 5.2.3.1.1), the less a cost accounting system is delinked from the management process, regardless its coercively induced character. As such, this finding emphasises that there is an association between the pursuit of decision facilitating tasks and the actual use of cost information. Other than expected in H4c_2a, however, this effect cannot be found for the instrumental/conceptual usage type.

6.2.2.1.3.5 Institutional determinants and the relational context

This far, the necessity to reject several hypotheses is attributed to this study's focus on subsidiaries. By testing the set of hypotheses H4d on the influence of coercive institutional factors (directives, corporate managers' involvement and expatriates) and the moderating effect of the relational context (H4e), the following section presents empirical evidence for this assertion. Table 6-67 and Table 6-68 show that managers' use of cost information is indeed determined by the coercive institutional influences on subsidiaries' cost accounting systems. Yet again, the identifiable interrelations are more diverse than theoretically derived in section 4.2.2.

In both the Anglophone and the domestic German subsidiaries, one important result is that bureaucratic means of parent company control (i.e. corporate directives) have to be distinguished from personal controls (i.e. corporate managers' involvement and expatriates). This necessity reflects the corresponding result that personal involvements through corporate managers are rather more influential for the design of subsidiaries' cost accounting systems than directives (in the Anglophone subsidiaries).

Parent companies' directives and the moderating effect of the relational context

As expected, cost information is used less intensively in an instrumental/conceptual manner in *Anglophone subsidiaries* whose cost accounting systems are influenced strongly by a parent company's directives. This finding prevails both unconditionally (model (a)) and conditionally on the relational context (model (b)). Other than expected, however, for this usage type there is a negative and significant interaction effect between **corporate directives** and the **relational context**. Apparently, managers who perceive a rather unfavourable relationship with their parent company, do not overcome the use-reducing effect of directives but instead react stubborn. If there are extensive directives on how to design a cost accounting system in their companies, managers do not merely tend to use cost information less but reduce their application of information even further, the more unfavourable the relational context. The same interaction effect is present for the interactive use of information. Because the conditional effect of corporate directives is insignificantly smaller than zero for this usage type, however, the finding is only indicative for a stubborn reaction. All these findings support H4d_1 for the discussed usage types. Yet, they contradict H4e in this regard. The relational context does not counteract the directives.

Peculiarly, the interrelations found for the instrumental/conceptual use hold equally true for the rationalising use in Anglophone subsidiaries. Though this result reflects H4d_1, it contradicts the proposed **conceptual similarity of the rationalising and the ceremonial**

usage type. The identified directions rather align the rationalising use with the instrumental/conceptual use as it was conceptually intended (section 2.3.3). But, if the defiance of corporate involvements (i.e. ceremonial use) was regarded as an escalation of their avoidance, which is apparently comprised in the rationalising use, the reason for this result might still reflect the conceptual similarity of these two usage types. Potentially, the Anglophone subsidiaries do not use cost information rationalisingly to circumvent corporate directives due to their reflection of a foreign cost accounting tradition (any more) but prefer a less graceful defiance. As such, the meaning of the rationalising use in the Anglophone subsidiaries reveals greater similarities with both perspectives covered in this usage type: the mere application of cost information for ex post rationalisation as well as the unintendedly captured avoidance of corporate directives. There are two additional reasons why a conceptual overlapping of the rationalising and the ceremonial usage type cannot be ruled out for the Anglophone subsidiaries. First, there are robust positive associations of these two usage types with the relational context. Despite not being expected, these signal that managers apply cost information more strongly in a rationalising and ceremonial manner if they dislike the relationship with the parent company.[1152] Second, the control variable 'Board member' is significantly negative for both these two usage types. Actual board managers appear to disapprove the decision relevance of using cost information in a rationalising and ceremonial manner.

With respect to the ceremonial use, no effect of corporate directives prevails in Anglophone subsidiaries. This reveals the necessity to reject H4d_2 (directives) and H4e (moderating effect of the relational context) in this regard. Acknowledging the direct effect of the relational context, however, this result merely signals that subsidiary managers' ceremonial use of cost information is less reliant on corporate cost accounting directives per se but rather stems from an (associated) unfavourable relational context. Because there is no statistical association between *Simons'* usage types (diagnostic and interactive use) and corporate directives, H4d_1 has to be rejected in this respect. The same holds true for H4e for the diagnostic use of information. All these insignificant results can be associated to the strong relevance of the objective 'decision influencing' for these usage types.

For the *domestic German subsidiaries*, the results reflect the expectations from section 4.2.2 more thoroughly. The more extensive a subsidiary is subject to **cost accounting directives**, the less cost information is used in an instrumental/conceptual manner but the more it is used ceremonially. These findings support H4d_1 and H4d_2. Moreover, there is an ensuring finding with respect to the provided discussion of the rationalising use of information in the domestic German subsidiaries. The managers apply cost information (at the presence of an average relational context) more extensively in a rationalising manner (model (b)). Despite contradicting hypothesis H4d_1, this reveals a similar influence of corporate directives on the rationalising use as on the ceremonial use.[1153] This finding

[1152] An according effect prevails in *Kostova/Roth* (2002), p. 226, too.

[1153] As in the Anglophone sample, additional evidence that the rationalising use of cost information and the ceremonial use of cost information may share similarities in meaning stems from the finding that for the rationalising use of information there is a significant (conditional) direct effect of the relational context. An unfavourable relationship with their parent company makes managers in domestic German

underlines the conceptual similarity of these two usage types.[1154] Other than in the Anglophone subsidiaries, there is no interaction effect of the **relational context** on the association between corporate directives and the use of cost information. Hence, in this regard there is no evidence for H4e.

Parent companies' personal involvement and the moderating effect of the relational context

Parent companies' personal involvement into the cost accounting systems of *Anglophone subsidiaries* affects the use of cost information differently than the more bureaucratic involvement through corporate directives. Parent companies' personal involvement through **corporate managers** (model (b)) and **expatriates** (model (a)) is associated positively with the instrumental/conceptual use of cost information. Despite violating the expectations of H4d_1, this finding corresponds to the results of section 6.1.2. In Anglophone subsidiaries, parents' personal involvement does not only ensure that subsidiaries' cost accounting systems are more thoroughly aligned with the corporate one, but also ensures that the systems are used in an instrumental/conceptual manner. In line, personal involvement through expatriate managers also ensures that subsidiary managers use the Anglophone informed cost accounting system less extensively in a ceremonial manner. Furthermore, there is a significant negative effect of corporate managers' involvement on the rationalising use of cost information in model (a). Given above discussion, this hypothesis-confirming finding may have a twofold meaning, however. On the one hand, it might suggest that subsidiaries actually dislike parent companies' involvement and, as such, use cost information less intensively for ex-post decision-rationalisation. On the other hand, the unexpected effect of corporate managers for the instrumental/conceptual use provides an alternative explanation. Possibly, the parent companies can ensure through their personal involvements that their subsidiaries apply cost information less intensively in a manner that avoids the institutional effects. As already mentioned, the incomprehensive meaning of the rationalising use in the Anglophone sample avoids an unambiguous interpretation of this result, however. Despite finding rather explicable results, these discoveries contradict H4d_1. The personal engagement of Anglophone firms into their subsidiaries in Germany has another effect than expected. Rather than fostering the ceremonial use and inhibiting the non-ceremonial use, personal involvements ensure a thorough application of the Anglophone informed cost accounting systems in the Anglophone subsidiaries.

With respect to the **moderating effects of the relational context**, the findings for the parent companies' personal involvement are rather peculiar. Other than for corporate di-

---

subsidiaries use cost information 'merely' for ex-post rationalisation of decisions. Thereby, unpopular interferences of the parent companies can, potentially, be avoided.

1154 Two reasons why this similarity is more apparent in the domestic German subsidiaries prevail. First, the result appears linked with the traditional importance German management accountants attribute to cost information for decision facilitating (section 2.3.2). Thereby the ex-post rationalisation of cost information may become less desirable for day-to-day decision-making. As such, rationalising and the instrumental/conceptual use of information are more dissimilar. Second, domestic German subsidiaries may (still) attempt to avoid their parent companies' interferences rather than defying them more actively. As such, the rationalising use forfeits its initially intended conceptual meaning and pictures the companies' attempt to circumvent corporate standards.

rectives, the interaction terms of the relational context and parent's personal involvement have the expected signs for managers' rationalising, interactive and ceremonial use of cost information. Hence, there is evidence that the coercive institutional determinants affect managers' application of cost information differently if they perceive the relationship with their parent company more unfavourable. These results appear to support the suggested moderating effect (H4e). Yet, the interpretation of the results remains somewhat incomprehensive. For the **ceremonial use**, the negative conditional effect of expatriates reveals that an unfavourable relational context enforces the effect of expatriates rather than offsetting it. Similarly, there is a negative interaction effect of corporate managers and the relational context. From the viewpoint of H4e, these findings remain rather unclear. Both findings would become explicable, however, if personal involvements moderated the effect of a relational context rather than vice versa. Since there are conditional and unconditional positive effects of the relational context on the ceremonial use of information, the findings would suggest that expatriates and corporate managers can decrease the positive effect of an unfavourable relational context on the ceremonial use of information.[1155] Though there is a similar effect for the rationalising use in the domestic German companies, this interpretation remains hypothetical and should be subject to future research.

The meaning of the significant positive interaction of expatriates and the relational context on the **rationalising use** remains similarly unclear. Tere is an insignificantly negative effect of the expatriates on this usage type which would be offset. But, the insignificance of the unconditional effects (Appendix 10) prevents a purposeful interpretation. Regarding this finding as an indication for the reversed direction of the moderating effect would suggest that expatriates enforce the positive effect of the relational context on this usage type. Both findings highlight a rather positive perception of the rationalising usage type by the parent companies. Since there is some evidence that subsidiaries apply this usage type to avoid Anglophone cost accounting traditions, however, the unforeseen empirical ambiguity of this usage type prevents a convincing interpretation of the result. The significant positive interaction effect of corporate managers and the relational context on the **interactive usage type** cannot be conclusively interpreted either. The insignificance of the associated conditional effect of corporate managers and the insignificant F-test prevents a meaningful investigation of the underlying rationales.

In a nutshell, the results underline that Anglophone parent companies, which involve themselves into the design of their German subsidiaries' cost accounting system, must bear the consequences of their engagement for local managers' information use in mind as well. Thereby, the parent companies must also consider local managers' perceptions on the relational context very carefully. These perceptions determine how subsidiary managers react to corporate involvements into the design of their subsidiary's cost accounting system. In this sense, the rationale behind hypothesis H4e can be sustained. Given the

[1155] These findings might suggest that inconclusive results on the relational context and the coercive institutional determinants during the investigation of the complexity of cost accounting systems are indeed aligned with a greater relevance of these variables for the usage types (cf. section 6.1.2.2.2, p. 228, and section 6.1.3, p. 232).

differing meanings of the moderating effects and the inconclusive evidence on the directions, however, the hypothesis itself must be rejected.

The results for the *domestic German subsidiaries* are similar with respect to the effect of parent companies' personal involvement on the instrumental/conceptual use of information. As above, **corporate managers**' personal involvement ensures the actual instrumental/conceptual use of cost information (model (a)). Also, an extensive reliance on **expatriates** is linked to a reduced rationalisation of previously taken decisions (model (a) and model (b))[1156] in the domestic German companies. Whereas these findings reflect the necessity to reject H4d_1 for the instrumental/conceptual use, they support this hypothesis for the rationalising use. Other than suggested during hypotheses development, however, the supportive evidence seems to be linkable to subsidiaries' apparent ability to avoid corporate cost accounting standards by using their cost information rationalisingly. If there are few expatriates, a subsidiary may find it easier to avoid corporate standards on cost accounting whereas a higher number of expatriates prevents such avoiding behaviour. Puzzlingly, expatriates are not found to ensure that local managers do indeed use cost information in a diagnostic manner. Rather, a high number of expatriates decreases the diagnostic use of cost information (model (a) and model (b)) as it was expected in H4d_1. As such, the finding does not fully correspond to the former interpretation that parent companies can ensure the non-dysfunctional use of cost information in the domestic German subsidiaries through personal involvement. This finding might reflect that the expatriates rather than the researched managers perform the control activities captured by the diagnostic usage type in these circumstances.[1157]

Above all, these findings are quite remarkable. A personal involvement of parent companies ensures the use of cost information in subsidiaries during the management process. The finding for the diagnostic usage type suggests that such involvements also ensure a focus on those tasks which the subsidiaries are supposed to fulfil.

The **moderating effect of the relational context** (H4e) on the parent companies' personal involvements can be identified for the rationalising, the diagnostic and the interactive use of cost information in the domestic German subsidiaries. Other than expected, however, all these effects are negative. For the rationalising use, the negative moderating effects between expatriates and the relational context as well as the corporate managers and the relational context might disclose the reversed direction of the moderating effect as found for the ceremonial usage type in the Anglophone subsidiaries. Parent companies' personal involvement might reduce the effect of an unfavourable relational context on the rationalising use of information. As such, the finding would suggest that the parent companies can prevent the avoidance of corporate directives during highly unfavourable relational contexts through personal involvements. This interpretation, of course, violates H4e. The other two findings are similarly peculiar. Taking the negative effect of expatri-

[1156] Alternatively, this must be seen as evidence that parent companies hamper the application of cost information for ex-post rationalisation of decisions.

[1157] Finding the control variable 'size parent company' to be similarly significant might be interpreted in both ways. Either larger parent companies prohibit the decision influencing use per se, or they rather centralise the according decision rights. Thus, the cause of this result remains concealed.

ates on the diagnostic use into account, the negative interaction of corporate managers and the relational context might be seen as evidence that local managers pay little attention to the diagnostic use of cost information if there is an unfavourable relational context. Assuming that a parent company's personal involvement into the design of cost accounting is accompanied by a transfer of diagnostic tasks into the parent company, this can be seen as evidence that the subsidiary give away the responsibilities for such control alike activities rather stubbornly the more unfavourable the relational context becomes. Since the conditional effect of corporate directives is positive and insignificant (cf. Appendix 10), and the associated F-Test is insignificant, the interpretation remains inconclusive, however. For the interactive use, the significant negative interaction between expatriates and the relational context seems to offset the positive conditional effect of expatriates (cf. Appendix 10). Yet, this finding does not necessarily reflect H4e. Since the conditional and unconditional effect of 'expatriates' are insignificant, this interpretation is ambiguous.

Above all, the presented results rather violate the rationale beyond H4e. Nevertheless, the findings are particularly enlightening. As already stated for the Anglophone subsidiaries, parent companies involving themselves into the design of their subsidiaries' cost accounting systems must consider the consequences of their engagement for managers' information use as well. Though their personal involvement can rather ensure the actual use of cost information and appears to offset dysfunctional effects of an unfavourable relational context, they have to consider managers' perceptions about the relational context very carefully.

Despite all difficulties with respect to the directions of the statistical associations, the above discussion reassures that the rather surprising findings with respect to users' attitudes towards cost information or users' cost accounting objectives are potentially due to this study's focus on subsidiaries. Subsidiary managers' use of cost information is determined by the interrelation of their personal attitudes, their information needs as well as a parent companies' bureaucratic and personal engagement and the associated relational context. Finding more miscellaneous results than expected reveals a necessity for future research. Especially conceptual explorations on the effect of a relational context and its interrelation with personal and bureaucratic means of control appear necessary. Thereby, *Olivers'* considerations on this relationship as well as NIS as an explicatory concept for management accounting in subsidiaries could be improved.[1158]

[1158] Cf. *Kostova et al.* (2008), p. 997ff.

6.2.3 Summary

Descriptive findings

The descriptive evidence in section 6.2.1 can widely support hypothesis 2. Managers in both **Anglophone and domestic German subsidiaries** do indeed **use cost information similarly** to prepare decisions (i.e. in an instrumental/conceptual manner) or to influence others' decision-making (i.e. in a diagnostic and an interactive manner). Somehow in contrast to hypothesis 2, managers in the Anglophone subsidiaries are also found to use cost information significantly more in rationalising and ceremonial manners than their domestic German counterparts. Because neither of these usage types involves the thorough inclusion of cost information for decision-making,[1159] however, this does not mean that cost information is used differently during the management process. The finding rather indicates that, for some reason, the managers in the Anglophone subsidiaries perceive their cost information to be less applicable during the process of management (ceremonial use) and simultaneously perceive the necessity to take more decisions irrespectively the ex-ante consideration of costs (rationalising use) than their counterparts in the domestic German companies. These differences could be attributed to the participation bias in questionnaire B (cf. section 5.3.1). Finding the two somehow unfavourable usage types less extensively in the domestic German subsidiaries might reflect that the responding firms have fewer problems with respect to the applicability of their cost accounting systems.

By 'accepting' hypothesis 2 conditionally, this study stands in apparent contrast with previous research projects according to which cost information is likely to be used differently by companies of different national origin.[1160] But, given that virtually all respondents of questionnaire B are of German nationality, acknowledging the missing evidence on the use of cost information in the Anglophone (and German) parent companies and considering the lack of data on the different pieces of cost information used for decision-making (e.g. variable or full costing) this assertion awaits future specification.

Explicative findings

In section 6.2.2, linear regression analyses determine whether the use of cost information is explicable by the **research model** derived in section 4.2.2. Figure 6-5 illustrates for which of the five groups of determining variables there are (conditionally) 'accepted' hypotheses (✓) in the model.

[1159] As discussed extensively throughout the previous sections, this can be seen as a conceptually unexpected manifestation of what *Oliver* (1991), p. 151ff., described as avoidance and defiance of institutional pressures.

[1160] For an according conceptual suggestion, cf. *Granlund/Lukka* (1998), p. 155. For empirical evidence, cf. e.g. *Shields* (1998), p. 507; *Kostova/Roth* (2002), p. 229f.; *Chenhall* (2003), p. 135; *Schoute* (2009), p. 209.

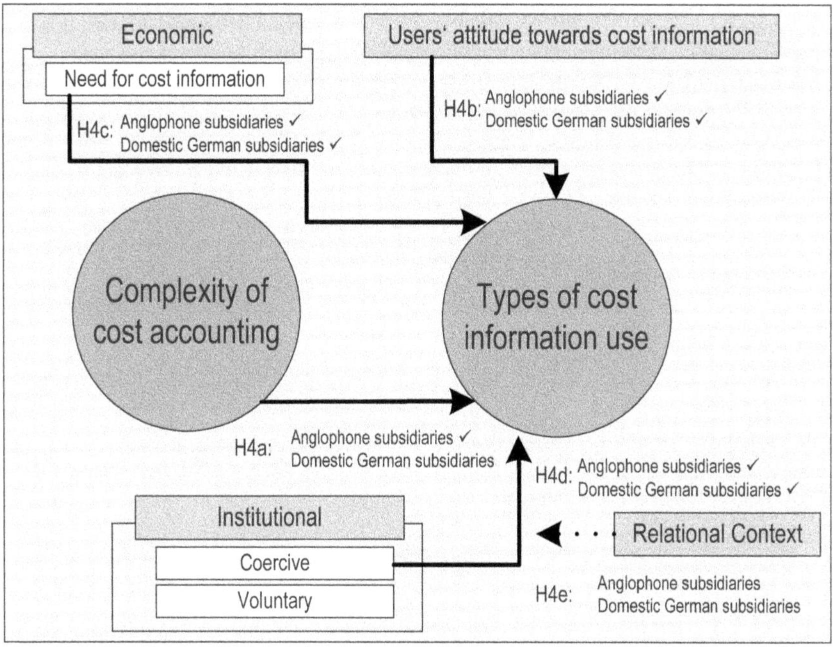

Figure 6-5: Aggregated summary of the hypotheses tests (use of cost information)

Table 6-71 refines Figure 6-5 by looking at the five individual usage types. Thereby, findings which prevail for model (a) or model (b) or for a complexity sub-score only, are marked by brackets to reveal their reduced robustness. They are seen as 'conditionally accepted' expectations.

Anglophone subsidiaries	Instrumental / conceptual	Rationalising	Diagnostic	Interactive	Ceremonial
H4a: Complexity of cost accounting	✓				
H4b: Users' attitudes	✓				✓
H4c: Need for cost information			✓	✓	✓
H4d: Coercive institutional effects	✓	✓			
H4e: Relational context					
Domestic German subsidiaries	**Instrumental / conceptual**	**Rationalising**	**Diagnostic**	**Interactive**	**Ceremonial**
H4a: Complexity of cost accounting				(✓)	(✓)
H4b: Users' attitudes	✓	(✓)		(✓)	✓
H4c: Need for cost information		✓	✓	✓	
H4d: Coercive institutional effects	✓	✓	✓		✓
H4e: Relational context					
Explanation: ✓ = accepted hypothesis, (✓) = conditionally accepted hypothesis					

Table 6-71: Determinants of the usage types (overview: non-rejected hypotheses)

For the Anglophone subsidiaries, effects from all groups of determinants but the relational context can be found. In the domestic German companies, neither the influence of the complexity of the cost accounting system, nor the interaction effect of the relational context prevails as expected. In both Anglophone and domestic German subsidiaries, this selective importance of the determinants is linked to the rejection of several hypotheses due to unexpectedly directed interactions. Acknowledging these unforeseen results illustrates that in both Anglophone and domestic German subsidiaries it is equally important to consider the five theoretically derived categories of independent variables (Table 6-72). This can be reassured through the significant F-tests for the models as reported in Table 6-67 and Table 6-68.

Anglophone subsidiaries		Instrumental / conceptual	Rationalising	Diagnostic	Interactive	Ceremonial
H4a:	Complexity of cost accounting	✓				
H4b:	Users' attitudes	✓			±	✓ | ±
H4c:	Need for cost information			✓	✓	✓
H4d:	Coercive institutional effects	✓ | ±	✓			±
H4e:	Relational context	±	±	±		±
Domestic German subsidiaries		**Instrumental / conceptual**	**Rationalising**	**Diagnostic**	**Interactive**	**Ceremonial**
H4a:	Complexity of cost accounting	±	±	±	(✓) | ±	(✓)
H4b:	Users' attitudes	✓	(✓)		(✓)	✓
H4c:	Need for cost information		✓	✓	✓	
H4d:	Coercive institutional effects	✓ | ±	✓ | ±	✓		✓
H4e:	Relational context		±	±	±	

Explanation: ✓ = accepted hypothesis, (✓) = conditionally accepted hypothesis, ± = unexpected 'quasi significant' effect

Table 6-72: Determinants of the usage types (overview: non-rejected hypotheses and unexpected results)

Despite violating the hypotheses, the detailed discussion of these findings throughout the previous sections found rather convincing explanations for the unexpected results. As such, the results especially show that the interaction of the five independent variables with the various types of cost information use is more miscellaneous than expected in section 4.2.2. This holds particularly true for influences from parent companies on subsidiary managers' use of cost information and the relational context. For all usage types but the diagnostic[1161] one in the Anglophone subsidiaries, there is a (conditional) expected or an unexpected effect stemming from the affiliation of the subsidiaries to a parent company. Strikingly, this finding reinforced the conclusion drawn in section 6.2.2.1.3.5. The use of cost information in subsidiaries cannot be studied irrespectively the influence of regarded firms' parent companies.

Table 6-73 and Table 6-74 expand Table 6-72 by taking all individual variables regarded throughout the previous sections into account. Other than for the results on the complexity of cost accounting, there is no remarkable difference between the determinants of the usage types in the Anglophone and the domestic German subsidiaries. For both, Table 6-73 and Table 6-74 reveal that only a selection of the hypotheses can be 'accepted'. These results indicate that in subsidiaries managers' application of cost information is determined by the interplay of the researched variables. Since previous research does not focus thoroughly on subsidiaries, this selective importance, especially with respect to personal attitudes towards cost information, is such a particularity of this study which re-

[1161] This finding is particularly due to the strong correlation of the diagnostic usage type with the variable objective '*decision influencing*' (Appendix 9).

mained unexpected during the introduction of the usage types (chapter 2) and the establishment of the research framework (chapter 4).

Anglophone subsidiaries		Instrumental / conceptual	Rationalising	Diagnostic	Interactive	Ceremonial
H4a:	Complexity of cost accounting					
	Complexity of cost accounting	✓				
H4b:	Users' attitudes					
H4b_1:	Knowledge					
H4b_2:	Preference	✓				✓
H4b_3:	Quality					(✓)
H4b_4:	Involvement					✓
H4b_5:	Contact				±	±
H4c:	Need for cost information					
H4c_1:	Perc. environmental uncertainty				(✓)	✓
H4c_2:	Objective: decision facilitating		*No hypothesis*	*No hypothesis*	*No hypothesis*	*No hypothesis*
H4c_3:	Objective: decision influencing	*No hypothesis*	*No hypothesis*	✓	✓	*No hypothesis*
H4d:	Coercive institutional effects					
	Directives	✓	✓			
	Corporate managers	±	(✓)			
	Expatriates	±				±
H4e:	Relational context					
	Relational context	±	±		±	±
Explanation: ✓ = accepted hypothesis, (✓) = conditionally accepted hypothesis, ± = unexpected 'quasi significant' effect						

Table 6-73: Determinants of the usage types (details: non-rejected hypotheses and unexpected results) - Anglophone subsidiaries

Anglophone subsidiaries		Instrumental / conceptual	Rationalising	Diagnostic	Interactive	Ceremonial
H4a:	Complexity of cost accounting					
	Complexity of cost accounting	±	±	±	(✓),±	(✓)
H4b:	Users' attitudes					
H4b_1:	Knowledge		(✓)			✓
H4b_2:	Preference				(✓)	✓
H4b_3:	Quality	✓			(✓)	
H4b_4:	Involvement		(✓)			
H4b_5:	Contact	✓				
H4c:	Need for cost information					
H4c_1:	Perc. environmental uncertainty		✓			
H4c_2:	Objective: decision facilitating		*No hypothesis*	*No hypothesis*	*No hypothesis*	*No hypothesis*
H4c_3:	Objective: decision influencing	*No hypothesis*	*No hypothesis*	✓	✓	*No hypothesis*
H4d:	Coercive institutional effects					
	Directives	✓	±			✓
	Corporate managers	±				
	Expatriates		✓	✓		
H4e:	Relational context					
	Relational context		±	±	±	
Explanation: ✓ = accepted hypothesis, (✓) = conditionally accepted hypothesis, ± = unexpected 'quasi significant' effect						

Table 6-74: Determinants of the usage types (details: non-rejected hypotheses and unexpected results) - domestic German subsidiaries

The information summarised in Table 6-73 and Table 6-74 and the discussions throughout section 6.2.2.1.3 reveal **four particularly illustrative results** for practitioners and management accounting researchers.

(1) Relevance of the ceremonial usage type

In both the Anglophone and the domestic German subsidiaries the ceremonial use of cost information can be explained comparatively well by the provided model. This result **complements previous research** on the ceremonial use of information considerably. The results highlight that the ceremonial use can be researched by the means of survey research as well. As such, this study helps in generalising the evidence for this usage type which prior research especially explored based on case studies.

In this context, there is another curiosity in the data. In the light of subsidiaries, the **ceremonial and the rationalising use** appear to share **conceptual similarities**. Whereas the former can be considered as a defiance of parent companies' directives, the latter may be described as their more gently avoidance.[1162] From such a perspective, it is remarkable to find the regression results for the rationalising use of information in the domestic German subsidiaries to be particularly similar of what was expected for the ceremonial use. If the German subsidiaries favoured the rationalising use of induced cost accounting systems to avoid their parent companies' costing standards over a more active defiance, it could be explained why the former could be explained easier by the regressions. In the Anglophone subsidiaries, the picture is in some way different. In these companies the ceremonial use of cost information to defy coercively induced Anglophone cost accounting traditions might (already) be a more common practice (despite at a low level).[1163] Hence, the suggested model applies rather well. In contrast, there is inconclusive evidence for the effect of the Anglophone subsidiaries' affiliation to their parent for the rationalising use. This suggests that managers do not only use this usage type to avoid corporate initiatives, but also to justify a previous decision irrespective of any effect of the parent companies. Anglophone subsidiaries appear to avoid their parent companies' systems less selectively or might favour the defiance of their parent companies' Anglophone cost accounting traditions over a discrete avoidance.

For **practitioners**, this latter finding is very important. The results sensitise parent companies for the necessity to consider their involvement into the design of their subsidiaries' cost accounting systems from other perspectives than corporate control. First, the involvement into the system's design actually affects local managers' application of the system as well. Second, the effect of the involvement is intertwined with subsidiaries' perceptions about the relationship with the parent company. Being able to align the relational context more conclusively with the ceremonial and rationalising usage types than with the complexity of cost accounting systems might suggest that subsidiaries react to negative perceptions about a parent company (relational context) more consistently by using cost information in a ceremonial or rationalising manner than by correcting the design of their

[1162] Cf. *Oliver* (1991), p. 151ff. Moreover, this finding reveals why previous authors urged that the symbolic use of information comprises a ceremonial perspective (cf. section 2.3.3, p. 34).

[1163] The significant negative effect of brownfield investments (control: form of market entry) on the rationalising usage type can be interpreted accordingly. Also, this can be reassured by the finding that the average level of ceremonial use in the domestic German subsidiaries (mean = 1.51 out of 7) falls behind the one in Anglophone subsidiaries with (mean = 1.96) and without (mean = 1.61) a cross-nationally different cost accounting system.

cost accounting systems. Hence, MNCs perceiving an unfavourable relational context or a high level of rationalising applications of cost information in their subsidiaries can take this as a hint for the reduced application of their corporate cost accounting standards for thorough decision-making in the subsidiaries.

(2) Relevance of the non-ceremonial usage types

As for the ceremonial usage type, this study complements **prior research** on the non-ceremonial usage types. It uncovers the possibility to explain non-ceremonial use in a subsidiary context through an extension of the models generally researched irrespectively of organisational hierarchies. Thereby, it finds that diverging results on the determinants of the non-ceremonial usage types in previous research might be attributed to unattended issues of organisational hierarchies.

In addition to that, there is an acknowledgeable difference between the usage type derived from *Pelz* (1978) and *Burchell et al.* (1980) and the ones derived from *Simons* (1995).

In both the Anglophone and the domestic German subsidiaries, *Simons*' types of use (**interactive and diagnostic**) are particularly linked to the **objective** 'decision influencing'. This finding corresponds well to the strong correlation between these variables (Appendix 9) and emphasises the nomological validity of the applied measurement models. Yet, the correlation between the two variables is in some way impinging the conclusiveness of the results for these two findings (autocorrelation). Computing the regression analyses for the diagnostic and the interactive usage types without the two objectives (not reported) reveals both usage-types to be more extensively associable with users' attitudes and the interaction between corporate managers and the relational context (Anglophone subsidiaries) and the perceived environmental uncertainty, managers' attitudes and corporate managers' involvement (domestic German subsidiaries).

For the **instrumental/conceptual** use of information, little particularities prevail. In both the Anglophone and the domestic German subsidiaries, managers respond to extensive **corporate directives** by rather not applying resulting cost information in this manner and even react stubborn the more unfavourable the relational context is. In contrast, there is weak evidence that a parent companies' **personal involvement** can actually ensure that local managers apply cost information for decision-making. This distinct effect of personal and bureaucratic controls is in line with the findings for the complexity of the cost accounting systems (section 6.1.2). Moreover, in both researched groups, managers' personal attitudes towards costs effect how intensively they use cost information in an instrumental/conceptual manner. Other than in prior research, however, these personal effects are less dominantly present in this study's sample of subsidiaries.

These findings **pioneer future research projects**. They show that an understanding of managers' application of cost information during the process of management depends not only on their personal characteristics and the design of their cost accounting systems, but also on the level of a parent company's involvement and managers' perception of the relationship with their parent company. Future comparisons of subsidiaries and single companies may explore whether the diverse findings on the determinants of the use of cost information in previous research (section 3.3.2.1) could be due to unattended coercive institutional effects.

(3) Relevance of the effects of cost accounting systems' complexity

The influence of the design of cost accounting systems on managers' use of cost information is multifaceted. In the *Anglophone subsidiaries*, a cost accounting system which is less aligned with the Anglophone cost accounting traditions increases the actual use of cost information in an instrumental/conceptual manner.[1164] This is especially true for the design of the cost type and cost centre accounting systems. Apparently, German managers in Anglophone subsidiaries in Germany prefer **German cost accounting traditions** for decision-making. Which individual elements of the subsidiaries' cost accounting systems are thorough levers to improve the usefulness of cost information in Anglophone subsidiaries in Germany is investigated in the next section.

In contrast, there is weak evidence that a detailed cost type accounting system impinges a thorough application of cost information by managers in the *domestic German subsidiaries*. The analysis identified the application of imputed costs and the separation of management and financial accounting information to determine this result. Management accountants in domestic German subsidiaries might need to consider the **information usefulness of their cost accounting systems** more carefully. The next section provides evidence for this assertion and illustrates how to improve the design and use of cost accounting in these companies.

(4) Relevance of the selection bias

The description and explanation of the use of cost information is affected by the selection bias which especially prevails in the domestic German subsidiaries (see section 5.3.1). Thus, above findings remain less conclusive and less generalisable than the ones on the complexity of cost accounting systems. As explained above, this matter **paves the way for future research** on the use of cost information in subsidiaries. Thereby not only future empirical work would be fruitful to assess how intensively the selection bias affected this study's results. From a theoretical or conceptual perspective, it would be helpful to explore the interplay of coercive institutional determinants, the relational context and information users' attitudes more conclusively.

6.3 Performance of cost accounting systems

6.3.1 Introduction and descriptive evidence

The performance of cost accounting systems is regarded in this study by investigating two performance metrics. A single item captures the respondents' **satisfaction** with their cost accounting system. The formatively defined measure **degree of goal attainment** summa-

[1164] Section 6.2.2.1.3.2 discussed the variable 'complexity of the cost accounting system' only. A revised regression model substituting this variable by the existence of a cross-national difference finds a significant negative association between '*CND*' and the instrumental/conceptual use in the Anglophone companies (for the variable '*CND*', cf. section 6.1.2.2).

rises the degree to which the respondents achieve 11 cost accounting objectives. Both measures are scaled zero to six.[1165] Thereby, increasing scale values indicate an increase in performance. Table 6-75 summarises the results for these two performance measures.

		Performance of cost accounting systems (Interpretation of the scales: 0 = very low, 6 = very high)					
		Cost accountants (dataset 1)		Cost accountants (dataset 3)		Managers (dataset 3)	
		Anglophone	German	Anglophone	German	Anglophone	German
Satisfaction	min.	0	0	0	1	0	1
	max.	6	6	6	6	6	6
	mean	4.04	4.15	4.15	4.33	4.27	4.33
p-value (test)		0.52 (two-tailed t-test)		0.47 (two-tailed t-test)		0.83 (two-tailed t-test)	
				Anglophone: 0.32 (two-tailed one sample t-test) German 1.00 (two-tailed one sample t-test)			
Goal attainment	min.	0	0.13	0.11	1.35	0.50	0.92
	max.	6	5.24	6	4.63	5.82	4.63
	mean	2.81	2.82	2.97	3.04	3.08	3.07
p-value (test)		0.95 (two-tailed t-test)		0.76 (two-tailed t-test)		0.98 (two-tailed t-test)	
				Anglophone: 0.40 (two-tailed one sample t-test) German: 0.72 (two-tailed one sample t-test)			
Comparison of Satisfaction & Goal attainment		0.00 (two-tailed t-test)	0.00 (two-tailed t-test)	0.00 (two-tailed t-test)	0.00 (two-tailed t-test)	0.00 (two-tailed t-test)	0.00 (two-tailed t-test)

Table 6-75: Descriptive evidence on the performance of cost accounting systems

On an aggregated basis, there are no differences in the perceptions of the cost accounting systems in Anglophone and domestic German subsidiaries. This result holds true for managers' and management accountants' answers for both performance measures. It is stable for dataset 1 and 3. In addition, there are no differences in the assessments provided by managers and cost accountants (available for dataset 3 only).[1166] Again, this is valid for both applied measures of performance. Remarkably, management accountants and managers rate their satisfaction significantly higher than their degree of goal attainment. Whereas for the variable *goal attainment* mean ratings prevail, the variable *satisfaction* is evaluated rather positively, i.e. well above the mid-point (3) of the applied scale. All these findings are regarded in detail hereafter.

Previous research consistently reports differences in the evaluations of managers and management accountants (**user-preparer-perception gap**).[1167] As such, it is surprising that management accountants' perceptions of their cost accounting systems reflect the ones of their managers in this study. Previous research does not devote considerable effort towards the explanation of such perception gaps.[1168] It remains for future research projects to ex-

---

[1165] Section 5.2.2.3 reveals how this measure is operationalised.

[1166] The *differences* in the performance evaluations provided by managers and management accountants of the same firm are insignificantly different from zero in both Anglophone and domestic German subsidiaries (cf. Appendix 11 – Table 1). This finding holds true if it is controlled for the fact that some of the questionnaires were not filled in by board members.

[1167] For recent studies on differing perceptions about the performance of management accounting by users and preparers of management accounting information, cf. *Malmi* (1997), p. 495ff.; *Major/Hopper* (2005), p. 223; *McGowan/Klammer* (1997), p. 234; *Bhimani* (2003), p. 539ff.; *Pierce/O'Dea* (2003), p. 258ff.; *Dietz/Snyder* (2011), p. 38, and *Walker et al.* (2012), p. 15ff.

[1168] For an exception, cf. *Bhimani* (2003), p. 525ff.

plore whether, e.g. the rather extensive interaction between the management accountants and the local top management[1169] or similar beliefs about cost information between managers and management accountants[1170] underlies the small perception gap identified in this study. According factors would well reflect previous suggestions by *Bhimani* (2003).[1171] For the purpose of this study, it is essential to conclude that in the researched subsidiaries, managers and management accountants agree on the usefulness (i.e. goal attainment) of their cost accounting system and are equally satisfied with the system's information.

The level of **satisfaction** is significantly **exceeding** the degree of **goal attainment**. For the German companies, this result mirrors a previous finding by *Moeschler* (2012).[1172] A similar finding in an Anglophone setting prevails in the work by *Foster/Swenson* (1997). The authors find a mere management evaluation to exceed other assessments of cost accounting systems; including two which are concerned with the application of cost information for certain objectives or decisions.[1173] In contrast, the tendency to rate the satisfaction with a cost accounting system higher than the ability to fulfil the goals pursued with the system contradicts *Schoute* (2009).[1174] He finds that the satisfaction with an ABC system scores below the application of the system for decision-making. *Schoute* (2009), however, applies two single item questions to derive this result. Above all, the different operationalisations dilute a conclusive discussion of this study's performance constructs on the grounds of previous research. Also, both measures show that the researched companies assess their cost accounting systems rather positively, but simultaneously reveal substantial room for improvements.

All in all, the identified difference in the level of satisfaction and the degree of goal attainment might merely suggest that these two constructs describe different dimensions of the performance of a cost accounting system. As such, the significant difference of these measures provides a remarkable starting point to analyse the performance effects of both the design of cost accounting systems and the use of cost information. The consequences of the identified differences for the forthcoming analysis cannot be anticipated unambiguously, however. On the one hand, both performance measures are strongly correlated for both managers and management accountants.[1175] This suggests that the different magni-

[1169] Cf. section 6.1.2.1.1.1, p. 202 (the values for 'local top management support' in dataset 3 are 4.87 (5.13) for the Anglophone (domestic German) subsidiaries), and section 6.2.2.1.1.2, p. 244 (constructs 'involvement' and 'contact').

[1170] Arguably, the identified agreement on the most important objectives as well as the agreement on the extent to which operational and strategic cost information objectives are pursued (cf. section 6.2.2.1.1.3) can be interpreted accordingly. Also, managers' strong preference for cost information (Figure 6-4) underlines this assertion.

[1171] Conceptually *Bhimani* (2003), p. 525, derives such interrelations. Yet, in his empirics (p. 539ff.), no discussion of the interaction between management accountants and managers can be found.

[1172] Cf. *Moeschler* (2012), p. 303.

[1173] Cf. *Foster/Swenson* (1997), p. 118. However, these authors provide rather negative assessments. They report mean ratings of the single item based management assessment, whereas the factors for the degree of goal attainment fall beyond the mid-point of the applied scale.

[1174] For this and the following, cf. *Schoute* (2009), p. 216.

[1175] The correlation tables can be found in Appendix 11.

tudes of the measures might not affect the analysis of the design of cost accounting systems and the use of cost information as levers of performance. On the other hand, there are differences in the distribution of the two measures (Figure 6-6 and Figure 6-7).[1176] Accordingly, there is a dominance of the categories '4' and '5' for the variable *satisfaction* in both samples. These differences in distribution may very well lead to a different effect of the cost accounting systems and use of cost information on the two performance measures. Section 6.3.2 will discuss in detail whether there are any consequences stemming from the different magnitudes attributed to the two performance measures

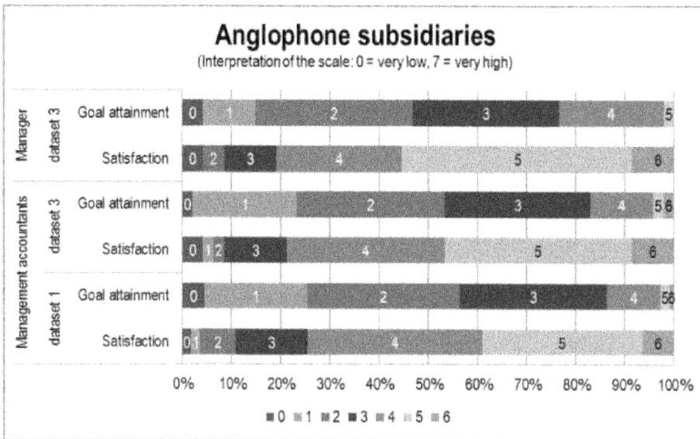

Figure 6-6: Distribution of the performance measures in the Anglophone subsidiaries

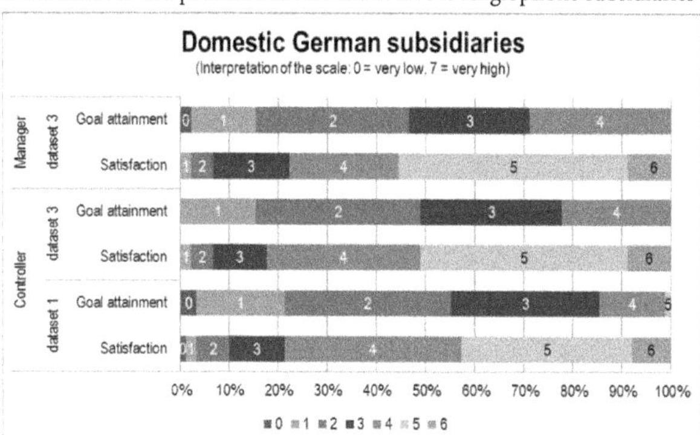

Figure 6-7: Distribution of the performance measures in the domestic German subsidiaries

For several reasons, it is peculiar to find both, **Anglophone** and **domestic German subsidiaries** to report equal levels of satisfaction and goal achievement. First, there is the prior research which finds German companies to be more satisfied with their cost accounting

[1176] Since various items form the variable 'goal attainment', it does not fall into the discrete interval [0, 1, 2, 3, 4, 5, 6] but varies continuously between zero and six. To picture both distributions in a similar manner, a summary of the goal attainment variable is provided. Exemplarily, category '2' summarises all companies that report a goal attainment that is higher or equal to '2' but lower than '3'.

systems than Anglophone firms.[1177] Moreover, the finding can be contrasted to several studies which stress Anglophone companies to be rather dissatisfied with their current cost accounting systems.[1178] Besides suggesting that such differences are a potential reflection of culturally induced response styles, the data reveals one interesting particularity in this regard. The Anglophone subsidiaries which are characterised by the cross-national differences for the average complexity score[1179] (‘*CND*’ = 1) report the performance of their cost accounting system to be significantly lower than the companies that are not characterised by such differences (‘*CND*’ = 0). Again, this finding holds true for both management accountants and managers (dataset 3). Apparently, Anglophone subsidiaries which have to apply Anglophone cost accounting traditions are less satisfied than those Anglophone subsidiaries that do not. This finding is well in line with *Meyer* (1988) who reports the preference for German cost accounting traditions in an Anglophone subsidiary in Germany.[1180] German cost accounting traditions seem to be a potential pathway to improve the performance of cost accounting systems in the Anglophone subsidiaries.

Mean values	**Performance of cost accounting systems in Anglophone subsidiaries** (Interpretation of the scale: 0 = very low, 6 = very high)					
	Cost accountants (dataset 1)		Cost accountants (dataset 3)		Managers (dataset 3)	
	'CND' = 0 n = 38	'CND' = 1 n = 72	'CND' = 0 n = 19	'CND' = 1 n = 28	'CND' = 0 n = 19	'CND' = 1 n = 28
Satisfaction	4.47	3.81	4.63	3.82	4.89	3.85
p-value (test)	0.01 (two-tailed t-test)		0.07 (two-tailed ranksum test)		0.00 (two-tailed Fligner-Policello test)	
			Anglophone (1): 0.79 (two-tailed signed rank test) Anglophone (0): 0.36 (two-tailed signed rank test)			
Goal attainment	3.39	2.50	3.65	2.50	3.70	2.65
p-value (test)	0.00 (two-tailed ranksum test)		0.01 (two-tailed ranksum test)		0.00 (two-tailed ranksum test)	
			Anglophone (1): 0.33 (two-tailed signed rank test) Anglophone (0): 0.52 (two-tailed signed rank test)			
Comparison of Satisfaction & Goal attainment	0.00 two-tailed t-test	0.00 two-tailed t-test	0.01 two-tailed signed rank test	0.00 two-tailed signed rank test	0.00 two-tailed signed rank test	0.00 two-tailed signed rank test

Table 6-76: Descriptive evidence on the effect of the cross-national differences (‘*CND*’) on the performance of cost accounting in the Anglophone subsidiaries

Yet, it remains to be explored whether these results also suggest that Anglophone MNCs could benefit from German cost accounting traditions.[1181] Finding subsidiaries of Anglophone firms in Germany to prefer their host country’s cost accounting traditions especially suggests that German management accountants and managers prefer German cost accounting traditions. Future research must explore whether German cost accounting traditions are indeed beneficial for entire Anglophone MNCs. In this study, potential corporate benefits are not subject to analysis.

[1177] Cf. *Krumwiede/Suessmair* (2007a), p. 4.

[1178] For a summary of US evidence, cf. *Sharman* (2003b), p. 44; *Clinton/Webber* (2004), p. 22. For evidence from the UK, Australia and New Zealand, cf. *Yazdifar/Askarany* (2010a), p. 4.

[1179] For the variable ‘*CND*’, cf. section 6.1.2.2, p. 222.

[1180] Cf. *Meyer* (1988), p. 53ff.

[1181] Cf. e.g. *Sharman* (2003b), p. 44; *Friedl et al.* (2005), p. 61; *Mackie* (2006), p. 33ff. For a summary, cf. *Vikas* (2006), p. 37ff.

6.3.2 Hypothesis testing

6.3.2.1 Complexity of cost accounting systems as a lever of performance

A graphical exploration can best alleviate the analysis of interdependences between management accountants' and managers' evaluation of their cost accounting systems and the systems' complexity.

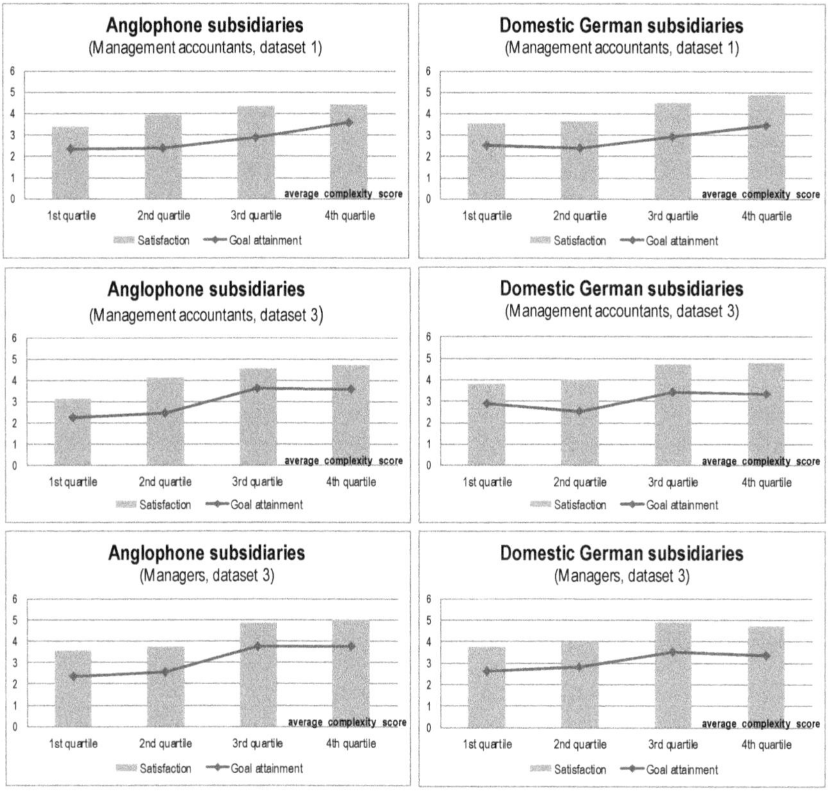

Figure 6-8: Performance assessments ordered by quartiles of the complexity scores

Figure 6-8 pictures the degree of goal attainment and satisfaction for management accountants and managers in dataset 1 and dataset 3 by the quartiles of the average complexity score. In both Anglophone and domestic German subsidiaries, the performance of a cost accounting system is evaluated higher, the more complex a company's cost accounting system is. This graphical analysis provides preliminary evidence to **support the set of hypotheses H5a**. Both managers and management accountants do indeed evaluate their cost accounting systems' performance higher, the more complex the system is. Remarkably, there is a diminishing (saturating) effect for the degree of goal attainment reported by the management accountants and managers of the domestic German (Anglophone) subsidiaries in dataset 3. Apparently, there is an upper bound for the level of complexity, beyond which an increase in the degree of goal attainment is unlikely.[1182] The value of the complexity score at the end of the third quartile appears to hide away this effect in dataset 1 (0.60 for the Anglophone subsidiaries and 0.66 for the domestic German subsidiaries). Refining this analysis by dividing the complexity score into smaller groups than quartiles uncovers a similar effect to be present for dataset 1 as well.[1183] The identification of this upper bound complements the suggestions summarised in set of hypotheses H5a. A similar finding was previously provided by *Moeschler* (2012).[1184]

Despite finding preliminary support for H5a, the above analysis **cannot test this hypothesis** conclusively. The analysis does neither control for differences in, e.g. the companies' size nor does it provide any insights whether there are certain elements of the companies' cost accounting systems, whose redesign can considerably improve the systems' performance. These deficiencies are considered hereafter through a multivariate regression analysis. The linear **regression models** summarising the performance effects of the complexity of cost accounting are pictured in Table 6-77 (Anglophone subsidiaries) and Table 6-79 (domestic German subsidiaries). The models take the level of satisfaction or the degree of goal attainment as their dependent variables. The independent variables in the models are the 15 complexity sub-scores introduced in section 6.1.1. The control variables presented in section 6.1.2 (management accountants) and 6.2.2 (managers) complete the models.

The significant F-values in Table 6-77 and Table 6-79 reveal that the regression **models fit the data** from the Anglophone and the domestic German subsidiaries adequately. This assertion is reassured by the mostly satisfying adjusted R^2 values (min. = 17.50 % and 0.50 %; max. = 41.50 % and 61.70 %). Multicollinearity is no issue in Table 6-77 and Table 6-79. The VIFs (max. = 4.68 and 4.66) fall behind the generally proposed threshold of 10. Autocorrelation and heteroscedasticity are not tested because the regression analyses rely on robust estimators.[1185] The significance levels in Table 6-77 and Table 6-79 are based on one-tailed t-tests for directed hypotheses and on two-tailed t-tests for the control variables.[1186]

[1182] In dataset 3, this level is particularly similar for Anglophone and domestic German subsidiaries. The third quartile takes a value of 0.65 (Anglophone subsidiaries) and 0.68 (domestic German subsidiaries).

[1183] In the domestic German subsidiary, the threshold for the complexity score beyond which an increase in the degree of goal attainment becomes less likely is around 0.67 and 0.68. Similarly, an increase of the complexity score beyond a value between 0.65 and 0.68 appears to impede a further increase of the performance measure in the Anglophone subsidiaries.

[1184] Cf. *Moeschler* (2012), p. 316ff.

[1185] The standard errors are estimated by 'adjusted sandwich estimators'.

[1186] The expected performance increasing effect of a complex cost accounting system does not prevail for each complexity sub-score. If the regression result show that the expected positive sign is actually significantly smaller than zero (i.e. the regression reveals not only a negative coefficient but also a p-value below 0.1 in a one-tailed t-test), this coefficient will be treated as 'quasi significant'. To allow for an immediate identification of such findings, the asterisk (*) usually used to tag significant findings is replaced by a diamond (#). This procedure will be evaluated critically in the limitations (section 7.2) since it restricts how rigorously this study follows its epistemological positioning.

Interestingly, the sub-scores explain the degree of goal attainment better than the level of satisfaction in the Anglophone subsidiaries. The opposite holds true for the domestic German subsidiaries. These findings could be due to the distribution of the performance metrics as pictured in section 6.3.1 (e.g. Figure 6-6). The clustering of certain responses (values '4' and '5') might affect the identification of linear interdependencies. However, the results rather appear to reflect the **influence of the usage types** on the performance measures. In the Anglophone subsidiaries, the effect of the usage types seems relatively weaker for the degree of goal attainment if compared to the level of satisfaction.[1187] Similarly, the exceptionally low adjusted R^2 of 0.50 % for management accountants' degree of goal attainment in the domestic German subsidiaries appears to reflect[1188] that management accountants in these firms base their degree of goal attainment not mainly on their cost accounting system's design but on the use of cost information instead.[1189]

Having clarified these general characteristics of Table 6-77 and Table 6-79, the findings for the *Anglophone subsidiaries* can be presented in detail. Even though the 15 complexity sub-scores explain the degree of goal attainment better than the level of satisfaction in these firms, the results for the sub-scores are not substantially different. Therefore, the findings from Table 6-77 are presented conjointly hereafter.

General description of the findings

Both management accountants' and managers' performance evaluations are positively associated with numerous variables describing the **cost centre accounting** system. Consistently for both measures, the *rationales for cost centre formation* and the *analysis of cost centre variances* are positively linked to managers' and management accountants' performance evaluations. For the degree of goal attainment, the *number of cost centres* is equally influential. Overall, all sub-scores used to describe the cost centre level are significantly and positively associated with one or another performance measure as assessed by management accountants or managers. Hence, cost centre accounting appears to be a powerful performance lever in the Anglophone subsidiaries. In line, the significant positive effect also prevails for the associated mean complexity score (model (b) in Table 6-81 and Table 6-83).

In contrast, only two of the three components describing the companies' **cost type accounting** are associated with the performance measures (*number of cost types* and *recognition of imputed costs*). Whereas an increase in the complexity of these sub-scores can increase the degree of goal attainment in dataset 3, a higher *number of cost types* rather hampers management accountants' satisfaction in dataset 1. These mixed effects are mirrored by merely selective significant links between the mean complexity score summarising cost type accounting and the performance metrics (model (b) in Table 6-81 and Table 6-83).

[1187] Section 6.3.2.2 provides substantial evidence for these effects.

[1188] Besides, the analysis of the performance by quartiles of the average complexity score provides another potential reason for this finding. Figure 6-8 illustrates that the degree of goal attainment in the domestic German subsidiaries cannot be increased linearly by the level of complexity. Rather, there is evidence for a diminishing or even negative marginal utility of increasing the level of complexity beyond a certain level. This result might prevent the analysis of linear effects of the complexity sub-score on this performance measure. A similar effect can be identified for the Anglophone subsidiaries.

[1189] Section 6.3.2.2 analyses such interdependences, which also hold for managers, in depth.

Linear regression model (**Anglophone subsidiaries**, unstandardised regression coefficients)		Goal attainment			Satisfaction		
		Management accountants		Managers	Management accountants		Managers
	E.S.	dataset 1	dataset 3	dataset 3	dataset 1	dataset 3	dataset 3
Number of cost types	+	0.0129	0.7203	1.8517 *	-0.9678 #	-2.0200	0.7427
Recognition of imputed costs	+	0.2765	0.9289 *	-0.3948	-0.3088	0.0029	-0.2753
Separation of fin. and man. accounting	+	-0.0647	0.3200	0.3657	-0.3957	-0.4838	-0.0362
Number of cost centres	+	0.9709 **	2.6331 ***	2.4412 ***	-0.8953	-0.5004	-0.3431
Rationales for cost centre formation	+	1.4889 ***	3.1125 **	2.4475 **	1.7334 **	1.9600	2.1735 *
Categorisation of costs on cost centres	+	0.9344 **	0.9421	0.0955	-0.0662	0.1191	-0.3835
First stage overhead allocation	+	0.4509	-0.2322	1.3620 **	-0.4141	-0.4479	0.0533
Second stage overhead allocation	+	0.3389	-0.1471	-0.4019	1.1174 **	0.6915	0.0238
Cost variance analysis on cost centres	+	1.2129 ***	1.1999 *	1.1090	1.1938 **	1.6651 *	2.5403 *
Different types of cost objects	+	-0.5557 #	-0.0070	2.3973 **	0.2940	-0.1699	1.8320 *
Design of product costing	+	0.1456	1.0993 *	0.6908	0.0945	0.8036	0.4934
Contribution margin accounting	+	0.3489	0.0345	-0.8187	-0.1101	-0.0108	-0.9789 #
Time reference of cost accounting	+	0.5993	-1.5191	-3.1621 #	1.0173 *	1.4034	-0.8198
Product cost variance analysis	+	0.2043	-0.4247	-0.3670 ##	0.8783 **	0.5005	-0.1418
Operating income statement	+	0.3074	-0.2683	0.1923	0.1572	-0.3638	-0.5272
Size subsidiary	/	-0.1583	0.0985	-0.2405	-0.0774	-0.0971	0.0616
Form of market entry	/	0.1066	0.0838	-0.1523	0.1595	0.2891	-0.5408
Length of affiliation	/	0.3029 **	0.4289	0.2266	0.1262	-0.0178	-0.5049
Size of the parent company	/	0.0252	0.0489	-0.0543	-0.0269	-0.0585	-0.0934 *
Years of work experience	/			-0.3869			-0.0139
Board members	/			-0.2881			-0.7971 **
Constant	/	-1.0887	-4.1151	0.4320	1.7498	2.4259	3.0203
R^2		45.20 %	61.67 %	70.08 %	39.05 %	53.96 %	67.70 %
Adjusted R^2		32.10 %	31.30 %	41.50 %	24.60 %	17.50 %	31.00 %
F-value		5.32	4.99	4.38	2.52	1.93	4.59
Significance		0.0000	0.0000	0.0000	0.0018	0.0394	0.0000
VIF max.		1.90	4.49	4.68	1.90	4.49	4.68

Table 6-77: Regression results for the effect of the complexity sub-scores on the performance of cost accounting - Anglophone subsidiaries

The results for the **cost object accounting** system are fairly diverse as well. Cost object accounting appears to intrude managers' degree of goal attainment (*time reference* and *variance analysis*) and satisfaction (*contribution margin accounting*).[1190] Positive effects are restricted to the *number of cost objects*. For the management accountants in dataset 3 in turn, the performance effect of cost object accounting is rather absent.[1191] Only for their degree of goal attainment, there is one positive effect (*design of product costing*). For the management accountants in dataset 1 the picture is similarly widespread. Whereas the *different cost objects* are linked negatively with their goal attainment, their satisfaction is associated positively with the *time reference* and the analysis of *product cost variances*. Reflecting these mixed results, only one significant link between the performance measures and the mean score summarising the cost object level can be found (model (b) in Table 6-83).

Above all, the findings indicate that Anglophone subsidiaries willing and able to design their cost accounting systems in a satisfying and goal attaining manner should pay particularly close attention to the design of their responsibility accounting and overhead allocation practices (i.e. cost centre accounting).

The effect of the cross-national differences

Three of the components that exhibit a cross-national difference in dataset 1 and 3, respectively, are negatively associated with a performance measure (*number of cost types*, *contribution margin accounting* and *product cost variance analysis*). In contrast, four of the variables are positively associated with one or another performance measure (*imputed costs*, *number of cost centres*, *first stage allocation and variance analysis*). Other than the negative associations, these positive associations can be identified more conclusively for management accountants than for managers.[1192] As such, it must be clarified that the Anglophone subsidiaries cannot increase the performance of their cost accounting system by default through an adoption of **German cost accounting traditions**. They need to consider carefully for which of the complexity sub-score, which are characterised by a cross-national difference, an orientation towards domestic German companies is worthwhile.

Comparison of management accountants and managers

In line with the **'lack' of a perception gap** in dataset 3, none of the significant complexity sub-scores is positively associated with managers' perceptions, whereas it is negatively associated with management accountants' performance evaluation or vice versa. As presented above, there are similar effects for the variable *number of cost centres* and *rationales for cost centre formation* with respect to the degree of goal attainment and for the variable *cost centre variance analysis* with respect to the level of satisfaction. Other than that, there are some additional findings, which are not shared by managers and management accountants.

[1190] Interestingly, all these latter variables were previously identified to be rather positively associated with a well performing cost accounting system in a German context (cf. section 4.2.3, p. 114). Since the domestic German subsidiaries are similar to the Anglophone subsidiaries in this respect (cf. the discussion around Table 6-79), this cannot be interpreted as a specificity of the Anglophone subsidiaries, however.

[1191] Differences between the results for managers and management accountants are discussed shortly.

[1192] This difference between managers and management accountants is discussed in the next paragraph.

For the sub-scores of the companies' cost type and cost centre accounting, these additional findings comprise only positive associations. For example, the results suggest that a high *number of cost types* (the regular recognition of *imputed costs*) increases managers' (management accountants') degree of goal attainment. With respect to cost object accounting, managers' performance evaluations are positively affected by the application of *different cost objects*, only. Simultaneously, a diverse number of different cost figures per cost object (i.e. the extensive reliance on *standard, normal, actual and target cost figures*) or various productivity measures (information from *variance analysis* and the complementing contribution margins in a multiple staged *CM accounting* system) impair managers' performance evaluations. These negative performance effects suggest that managers perceive different cost and profitability figures rather confusing. Since there are no such impeding effects for the management accountants in dataset 3, management accountants in the Anglophone subsidiaries should scrutinise the **usefulness** of different time horizons and/or multiple staged contribution margins **for managerial decision-making**.

Comparison of the datasets

There are four complexity sub-scores which increase (decrease) the performance assessments of management accountants in dataset 1, but decrease (increase) the evaluations provided by managers (dataset 3). Only for the *types of cost objects*, however, such a finding prevails for the same performance measure (goal attainment). For the *number of cost types*, the *time reference of cost information* and the *product cost variance analysis*, such a deviation emerges if the effects found for the degree of goal attainment and the level of satisfaction are compared. Given that these findings do not persist for management accountants in dataset 3, the implication of this finding remains somewhat unclear. It might be seen as additional indication that the **lack of a perception gap** in dataset 3 is indeed attributable to a close interaction of the managers and management accountants in this dataset.

As in section 5.3.2, there is little indication that the selection bias for the domestic German companies which provided both questionnaires persists for the Anglophone subsidiaries. The findings for management accountants in dataset 3 do not violate the ones from dataset 1.[1193] Though there are some findings that prevail for one dataset only, the overall results are consistent. This holds especially true for the variable goal attainment. For the variable satisfaction, Table 6-77 shows that the various significant results found for dataset 1 cannot be reassured for dataset 3. Given that in both datasets the variable is similarly distributed (Figure 6-6), this could be attributed to the fact that management accountants in dataset 3 also **acknowledge their managers' application** of the cost accounting system rather than the systems' design per se (section 6.3.2.2). Potentially, this is not equally true for companies that handed in questionnaire A only.

All in all, Table 6-77 and the provided discussion rather reflect the expected associations between the complexity and performance of cost accounting systems. For **management accountants' evaluations** (H5a_1a), the results are particularly supportive with respect to cost centre accounting. These sub-scores as well as their mean (model (b) in Table 6-83)

[1193] There are no complexity sub-scores which are positively associated with management accountants' performance assessments in dataset 1 but negatively with management accountants' responses in dataset 3 or vice versa.

affect both performance metrics significantly in a positive manner. In contrast, there are only a few significant findings for the cost type and cost object level. Moreover, these tend to be negative in some cases. Because the mean score for cost type (cost object) accounting affects management accountants' degree of goal attainment (level of satisfaction) positively (model (b) in Table 6-83), however, the results still provide conditional support for H5a_1a in this regard. For **managers' assessments** (H5a_1b), the results also reveal a performance increasing effect of a complex cost centre accounting. Again, the sub-scores as well as their mean (model (b) in Table 6-81) affect both performance metrics positively. Also, there is a positive association between managers' performance assessments and cost type accounting. Because the effect is restricted to one sub-score and does not persist for the associated mean score (model (b) in Table 6-81), however, this result supports H5a_1b conditionally only. With respect to cost object accounting, the number of negative performance effects outweighs the number of positive ones. As such, despite finding no significant negative influence of the associated mean score (model (b) in Table 6-81), H5a_1b must be rejected in this regard.

Table 6-78 summarises these findings. It also reveals that the mixed performance effects of the sub-scores are well in line with the diversity suggested in **H5a_2**. Little additional insights can be drawn from the few significant control variables. Most notably, the insignificant control variable 'form of market entry' suggests that the presented results apply to both greenfield and brownfield investments.

		Cost type Accounting	Cost centre accounting	Cost object accounting
H5a_1a:	Management accountants' perceptions	(✓)	✓	(✓)
H5a_1b:	Managers' perceptions	(✓)	✓	±
H5a_2:	Diversity of the effects	✓	✓	✓
Explanation: ✓ = accepted hypothesis, (✓) = conditionally accepted hypothesis, ± = unexpected 'quasi significant' effect				

Table 6-78: Summary of the hypotheses tests for H5a (performance effects of the 15 complexity sub-scores) - Anglophone companies

Having tested the set of hypotheses H5a for the Anglophone subsidiaries, it can be turned to the domestic German subsidiaries.

The test of H5a in the *domestic German subsidiaries* is based on the empirical results in Table 6-79. In contrast to the Anglophone subsidiaries, the comparison of the adjusted R^2s reveals that the various complexity sub-scores can explain the level of satisfaction better than the degree of goal attainment in the domestic German subsidiaries. This holds especially true for dataset 3. It has already been stressed that this finding seems to reflect that the degree of goal attainment is especially influenced by the use of cost information rather than the design of the cost accounting systems in the domestic German companies from dataset 3 (cf. section 6.3.2.2). Moreover, this finding might also reflect the diminishing effect of increasing the complexity of cost accounting systems beyond a certain threshold of the complexity score (cf. Figure 6-8).[1194] Nevertheless, Table 6-79 shows that the findings for both performance measures are particularly consistent. As such, the results from the domestic German companies are also presented conjointly for the two performance measures.

[1194] For the level of satisfaction, there is *merely* a saturating effect.

Linear regression model (**Domestic German subsidiaries**, unstandardised regression coefficients)	E.S.	Goal attainment			Satisfaction		
		Management accountants		Managers	Management accountants		Managers
		dataset 1	dataset 3	dataset 3	dataset 1	dataset 3	dataset 3
Number of cost types	+	0.1984	-0.8966	-1.3580	-0.7919	-2.4086 ##	-1.3250 #
Recognition of imputed costs	+	-0.1319	-0.3451	-0.0362	-0.2007	-0.4494	-0.2870
Separation of fin. and man. accounting	+	0.1504	-0.3951	-0.1723	0.1633	0.0003	-1.1317 ##
Number of cost centres	+	1.0056 **	1.3069	0.9264	0.7075	1.3882 *	2.5989 **
Rationales for cost centre formation	+	0.5679	0.9593	0.8006	0.6442	0.3271	1.5450
Categorisation of costs on cost centres	+	-0.7547 #	-0.5983	-0.8709 #	-0.1751	-1.6523 ###	-1.9059 ###
First stage overhead allocation	+	0.8467 **	0.7002	0.4313	0.8006 **	1.2702 **	0.9026
Second stage overhead allocation	+	-0.5376	-0.6320	-1.0598 #	-0.4571	-0.7452	0.6372
Cost variance analysis on cost centres	+	1.1924 ***	0.9240	2.0177 *	1.6904 ***	1.2413 **	2.3146 ***
Different types of cost objects	+	0.7645 *	1.0630	0.8415	1.6354 ***	1.7429 ***	0.0546
Design of product costing	+	0.1163	-0.0876	-1.6625 #	-0.1110	-0.7212 #	0.2160
Contribution margin accounting	+	-0.1192	-0.0623	0.5808	-0.6946 ##	-0.8019 #	-0.0708
Time reference of cost accounting	+	1.1387	0.0558	-0.0104	0.1732	0.1096	1.6306 *
Product cost variance analysis	+	0.4447 **	0.9158	0.9357	0.8052 *	0.8775 *	0.9670 *
Operating income statement	+	-0.0930	0.2875	-0.3382	0.2094	0.8872 **	0.4036
Size subsidiary	/	0.0830	-0.2504	0.0010	0.1005	0.0276	-0.3247
Form of market entry	/	-0.1536	-0.3580	0.1282	0.2524	0.4825	0.2430
Length of affiliation	/	-0.1973 *	-0.2624	-0.3206 *	-0.0032	-0.3837 ***	-0.4439 **
Size of the parent company	/	-0.0201	-0.0010	0.0389	-0.0345	-0.0689	-0.1810 ***
Years of work experience	/			0.6955			-0.3239
Board members	/			0.1362			0.6179
Constant	/	-0.5235	2.5549	-0.5010	0.3186	3.5588	3.6822
R^2		51.11 %	47.75 %	68.87 %	57.99 %	79.91 %	78.63 %
Adjusted R^2		35.40 %	0.50 %	34.50 %	44.50 %	61.70 %	55.00 %
F-value		6.18	2.71	8.48	8.69	9.06	15.49
Significance		0.0000	0.0044	0.0000	0.0000	0.0000	0.0000
VIF max.		2.43	4.31	4.66	2.43	4.31	4.66

Table 6-79: Regression results for the effect of the complexity sub-scores on the performance of cost accounting - domestic German subsidiaries

General description of the findings

The performance effects of the cost type, cost centre and cost object accounting design in the domestic German subsidiaries vary more extensively than in the Anglophone subsidiaries. Most consistently, the complexity of **cost type accounting** with respect to the *number of cost types* and the *separation of financial and management accounting information* appears to have a negative effect on the level of satisfaction with a cost accounting system. Despite some difficulties to underline such negative effects when analysing the link between the mean score for cost type accounting and managers' performance assessments (model (b) in Table 6-82), these findings suggest that domestic German subsidiaries prefer a simplified cost type accounting.[1195] This assertion especially holds because the above sub-scores also impinge managers' diagnostic use of the cost information (section 6.2.2.1.3.2), which in turn has a positive performance effect (section 6.3.2.2).

The results for **cost centre accounting** are widespread. The *number of cost centres* and the application of *cost centre variance analysis* are rather consistently associable to manager's and management accountants' performance evaluations in a positive manner. Moreover, management accountants' performance assessments increase with a more complex *first stage allocation* procedure. Equally consistent, the ability to derive cost centre costs in accordance with various cost figures such as primary and secondary costs (*categorisation of cost centre costs*) impinges the degree of goal attainment and satisfaction of managers and management accountants. For the *rationales for cost centre formation* and the *second stage allocation* procedures there are no or only one (negative) significant result(s). Despite finding the *categorisation of cost centre costs* and the *second stage allocation* procedures to be negatively associated with the regarded performance measures, the design of cost centre accounting procedures is a strong lever for a well performing cost accounting system in the domestic German companies as well. The mean score for cost centre accounting is significantly positively associated with the performance measures.[1196]

A similarly diverse picture prevails with respect to the companies' **cost object accounting**. Rather consistently, the evaluations provided by management accountants are associated positively with the *application of numerous cost objects*, but negatively with the application of *contribution margin accounting*. Moreover, the performance assessments by managers and management accountants are rather consistently affected positively by the determination of *product cost variances*, but negatively by a complex *product costing*. Hence, the existence of a variety of cost or profitability figures per cost object (i.e. *contribution margin accounting* and the design of *product costing*) impinges the performance of cost accounting systems in the domestic German companies as well. Other than in the Anglophone subsidiaries, however, this effect is more visible for management accountants. For the remaining two complexity sub-scores, there is evidence for a positive dependence of managers' (management accountants') level of satisfaction on the *time reference of cost accounting* (existence and design of an *operating income statement*). Aggregately, the design of cost object accounting provides a powerful lever of the performance of cost accounting in the domes-

[1195] This result is associated with the recently evolving tendency of German firms to align management and financial accounting (cf. section 6.1.1.1.3, p. 173f.).

[1196] Cf. Section 6.3.2.2, p. 293 and p. 298 (model (b)).

tic German subsidiaries. Analysing the mean score for cost object accounting reveals that the positive impacts of the sub-scores rather offset the negative ones.[1197]

Above all, in the domestic German subsidiaries, complex cost centre and cost object accounting systems influence managers' and management accountants' satisfaction positively. Also, there is evidence for a positive effect of a simplified cost type accounting system on the satisfaction levels. For the degree of goal attainment, in turn, the domestic German firms cannot merely take the design of their cost accounting system as a lever of performance but must especially consider how managers use cost information (cf. section 6.3.2.2). Moreover, any improvements to the design of cost accounting systems in the domestic German subsidiaries must embrace close interactions with these companies' parents. Since the length of affiliation to a parent company consistently affects the performance of cost accounting negatively, the affiliation to a parent per se seems to hamper the (perceived) usefulness of cost information in the domestic German subsidiaries.

Comparison of the datasets

The results for the management accountants in dataset 1 and dataset 3 are particularly similar for their level of satisfaction. Interestingly, the additional significant results found for dataset 3 are especially negative. This can be interpreted by acknowledging that the companies in dataset 3 have rather more complex cost accounting systems than those in dataset 1 that did not return questionnaire B (dataset 5).[1198] Potentially, the additional negative results and the threshold for performance improvements through an increased complexity score are coherent. This would suggest that the results in Figure 6-8 are particularly due to the *number of cost types*, the *categorisation of costs on cost centres* or the *design of product costing*.

The 15 complexity sub-scores cannot be associated with management accountants' degree of goal attainment in dataset 3 (Table 6-79). In sharp contrast, there are multiple significant findings for management accountants from dataset 1. Irrespectively of the number of observations, two particular explanations for this result surface from the previous and the due analyses. On the one hand, the respondents did not report three of the seven possible scale items for the degree of goal attainment (Figure 6-7). This might have hindered the identification of the interdependencies. On the other hand, management accountants' degree of goal attainment can be ascribed to their managers' use of cost information in dataset 3.[1199] Rather than looking at the design of the system per se, the systems' applicability for decision-making appears more relevant for these individuals. Hence, an extensive interaction between management accountants and managers in dataset 3, which could be a manifestation of the **selection bias** for questionnaire B, appears to differentiate the results for management accountants' degree of goal attainment in dataset 1 and 3.

Comparison of management accountants and managers

Since the complexity sub-scores can be associated to management accountants' degree of goal attainment only, the comparison of management accountants and managers in da-

[1197] Cf. Section 6.3.2.2, p. 293 and p. 298 (model (b)).
[1198] Cf. section 6.3.2.3, p. 298 (model (b)).
[1199] A consistent result is found for managers' degree of goal attainment as well.

taset 3 is restricted to the level of satisfaction. In this regard, the results for managers and management accountants in dataset 3 are similar. Five out of the seven significant findings for the managers are equally prevailing for management accountants (*number of cost types, number of cost centres, categorisation of costs on cost centres, cost centre variance analysis* and *product cost variance analysis*). Hence, there is evidence that managers and management accountants agree on the information-usefulness of the design alternatives for their cost accounting systems. Nevertheless, negative effects of the *separation of financial and management accounting* and the positive effect of the *time reference of cost accounting* are unique to the managers. Thus, management accountants in the domestic German subsidiaries **should not disobey the key characteristics** that are important to their managers. This is especially true because five additional complexity sub-scores are uniquely associated with management accountants' level of satisfaction (Table 6-79).

All in all, the evidence in Table 6-79 supports **H5a_2**. There are selective effects stemming from the 15 complexity sub-scores in the domestic German subsidiaries. The selective negative findings for the cost type accounting violate the expectations for the performance assessments by **management accountants** (H5_1a). As such, H5_1a has to be rejected. With respect to cost centre and cost object accounting, however, the positive associations between the individual sub-scores outweigh the negative ones. Hence, the hypothesis can be accepted conditionally. The same picture prevails for **managers**' assessments (H5a_1b). Whereas the evidence for the sub-scores of cost type accounting point to a rejection of the hypothesis, the evidence for cost centre and cost object accounting is as often as expected as it is contradicting the expectations. Since the average scores for cost centre and cost object accounting tend to have a significant positive effect on managers' performance evaluations,[1200] however, a conditional acceptance best reflects the results. Table 6-80 summarises these results.

		Cost type accounting	Cost centre accounting	Cost object accounting
H5a_1a:	Management accountants' perceptions	±	(✓)	(✓)
H5a_1b:	Managers' perceptions	±	(✓)	(✓)
H5a_2:	Diversity of the effects	✓	✓	✓
	Explanation: ✓ = accepted hypothesis, (✓) = conditionally accepted hypothesis, ± = unexpected 'quasi significant' effect			

Table 6-80: Summary of the hypotheses tests for H5a (performance effects of the 15 complexity sub-scores) - domestic German subsidiaries

6.3.2.2 Use of cost information as a lever of performance

This section explores the association between the usage types and the performance assessments provided by managers and management accountants (H5b). The analysis will be threefold. First, the association of managers' performance evaluations and their usage types is analysed (H5b_1 and H5b_2). Second, the effect of managers' use of cost information for management accountants' performance assessments is examined (H5b_3). Finally, it will be investigated whether the usage types mediate the relationship between the complexity of cost accounting systems and their performance (H5b_4). Thereby, the separate analyses of performance effects evoked by the design of cost accounting systems and

[1200] Cf. Section 6.3.2.2, p. 293 and p. 298 (model (b)).

the use of cost information will be joined to provide a conclusive summary of the preliminarily raised interrelations between the two performance levers.

(1) Managers' performance evaluations

Hypothesis H5b_1 (performance effects of the non-ceremonial usage types) and H5b_2 (performance effect of the ceremonial usage type) are tested through linear regression analyses. The dependent variables in the regression models are the degree of goal attainment or the level of satisfaction. The independent variables are the four non-ceremonial usage types (instrumental/conceptual, rationalising, diagnostic and interactive), the ceremonial usage type as well as the controls from sections 6.2.2. The empirical results for the hypotheses tests can be found in model (a) of Table 6-81 (Anglophone subsidiaries) and Table 6-82 (domestic German subsidiaries).[1201] All (a) models are of good fit. The adjusted R^2s are rather high and F-values are significant. Also, in all (a) models the VIFs fall behind the threshold of 10. Hence, multicollinearity is not an issue. As for all other regression models in this study, standard errors are based on 'adjusted sandwich estimators'. Hence, heteroscedasticity and autocorrelation are not tested. The significance levels in Table 6-81 and Table 6-82 are based on one-tailed tests for directed hypotheses[1202] and two-tailed tests for non-directed hypotheses and the controls.

The data underlines that the two performance metrics measure rather different aspects. Managers' degree of goal attainment is associated with all but the diagnostic usage type in the *Anglophone subsidiaries* (Table 6-81 (model (a)). In contrast, only the instrumental/conceptual type influences their level of satisfaction. Remarkably, however, the adjusted R^2 values for both performance measures are similar (45.10 %, and 42.30 %). Apparently, managers have to use cost information in various ways to fulfil their diverse cost accounting objectives. In contrast, managers' level of satisfaction is affected by their ability to use cost information for decision facilitating (i.e. in an instrumental/conceptual manner) only. Including the complexity scores maintains this dissimilar variety of performance levers (model (c)). These findings sensitise practitioners who are interested in an improvement of their cost accounting systems to consider carefully what the goals of such a development are. Without a thorough **understanding of the performance metric**, improvements might grasp at nothing. Also, such improvements must be done conjointly with the subsidiaries' parents. There are significant effects of the control 'length of affiliation'.

Looking more closely at the signs of the regression coefficients demonstrates that the positive results for the **instrumental/conceptual** (both performance measures) and the **inter-**

[1201] Due to data availability, the results are provided for dataset 3 only. Table 6-81 and Table 6-82 also comprise two (b) models and two (c) models. These will be discussed during the analysis of hypothesis H5b_4.

[1202] Some of the directed hypotheses have to be rejected due to unexpected signs of the regression coefficients. To derive meaningful explanations for such unpredicted results, these coefficients are treated as if the identified sign was expected. If e.g. the regression result show that an expected positive sign is actually smaller than zero and has a p-value below 0.1 (one-tailed test), than the coefficient will be treated as 'quasi significant'. To allow for an immediate identification of such findings, the asterisk (*) usually used to tag significant findings is replaced by a diamond (#). This procedure will be evaluated critically in the limitations (section 7.2) since it restricts how rigorously this study follows its epistemological positioning.

active use (goal attainment) are well in line with hypothesis H5b_1. In contrast to the expectations in H5b_2, however, there is no negative effect of the **ceremonial use** on the performance measures. Rather, there is a 'quasi significantly' positive effect of the ceremonial usage type on the degree of goal attainment. At a first glance, this finding appears highly suspicious. The result suggests that managers attain their goals better, the less they use cost information during the management process. But, given that previous researchers found locally developed *and* corporately imposed performance measurement systems in subsidiaries,[1203] this finding might reflect that Anglophone subsidiaries employ alternative locally developed information systems to fulfil their cost information needs if they perceive their cost accounting system to be particularly reflective of their parents' information needs (ceremonial use). As such, this finding reflects the positive association for this usage type with the number of contacts between management accountants and managers. Moreover, the result could also hint at a rather selective use of cost information. A ceremonial application of some pieces of cost information may enable the subsidiaries to focus purposefully on relevant information.

There is also a significant negative influence stemming from the **rationalising use** of information on managers' degree of goal attainment in the Anglophone subsidiaries. Given the twofold empirical meaning of this usage type in these subsidiaries (cf. section 6.2.3), there are two potential explanations for this result. The finding might reflect the rationale that cost information which is used in a rationalising manner is used less intensively for ex-ante decision-making (H5b_2). As such, the usage type may prevent the achievement of common cost accounting objectives. In addition, this result might also mirror that the rationalising usage type unintendedly captures a gently response to corporate directives. Such a more gently avoidance of corporate effects is potentially associated less extensively with the simultaneous implementation of an alternative 'shadow system'. Thus, in comparison to the defiance of corporate standards (ceremonial use), the avoidance (still) hampers the achievement of cost accounting objectives.[1204]

All in all, the results in Table 6-81 support hypothesis H5b_1 for the Anglophone subsidiaries for all but the diagnostic use of information. These findings rather contradict **previous research** on the instrumental/conceptual use of cost information but correspond to general management accounting research on *Simons*' diagnostic and interactive use.[1205] In contrast, H5b_2 has to be rejected for the Anglophone subsidiaries due to the identified positive effect of the ceremonial use on the performance metrics. Hence, the negative connotation of the ceremonial use which characterises the previous research on this usage type[1206] cannot be underpinned at this point. As discussed above, however, the existence of 'shadow systems' and the selective use of information could be valid interpretations of this finding.

[1203] Cf. *Dossi/Patelli* (2008), p. 140; *Schäffer et al.* (2010), p. 312. As such, the findings are indicative for the existence of 'shadow systems' in these companies.

[1204] Future research is needed to establish a link between the rationalising and ceremonial use and the existence of alternative information systems.

[1205] For the performance effects of these usage types in previous research, cf. section 3.3.2.3, p. 76.

[1206] All prior studies on this usage type reviewed in section 3.3.2.2 implicitly describe this usage type as a negative response to corporate involvements.

Linear regression model (**Anglophone subsidiaries**, unstandardised regression coefficients)		Managers (dataset 3)					
		Goal attainment			Satisfaction		
	E.S.	Model (a)	Model (b)	Model (c)	Model (a)	Model (b)	Model (c)
Cost type accounting	+		0.1064	-0.5662		-0.7870	-1.6231 ##
Cost centre accounting	+		6.6703 ***	4.1940 ***		3.6754 **	1.7071 *
Cost object accounting	+		-0.1761	0.1847		1.1964	0.4431
Instrumental/conceptual use	+	0.7887 ***		0.5510 ***	0.7763 ***		0.7906 ***
Rationalising use	+/-	-0.3976 **		-0.2447 **	-0.1572		-0.1054
Diagnostic use	+	0.0481		-0.0337	-0.0235		-0.0577
Interactive use	+	0.4347 ***		0.3688 **	0.0468		-0.0338
Ceremonial use	-	0.3810 ###		0.3613 ###	-0.2580		-0.2276
Size subsidiary	/	-0.6840 ***	-0.7110 **	-0.8098 ***	0.4694	0.0738	0.4453
Form of market entry	/	0.1216	0.0754	0.0578	-0.5879	-0.6390	-0.7214
Length of affiliation	/	0.1005	0.2806 *	0.1529	-0.4169 **	-0.3789	-0.4219 **
Size of the parent company	/	-0.0870	0.0068	-0.0390	-0.0668	-0.0735	-0.0390
Years of work experience	/	-0.1387	-0.2368	-0.3527	-0.1158	-0.1901	-0.3537
Board members	/	-0.2686	-0.2393	-0.2382	-0.2435	-0.5547	-0.2988
Constant	/	2.5608	3.5837 **	2.4633 *	0.8176	4.4256 *	1.1570
R^2		58.23 %	52.92 %	75.59 %	56.07 %	35.56 %	61.69 %
Adjusted R^2		45.10 %	41.50 %	60.60 %	42.30 %	19.90 %	44.90 %
F-value		9.48	10.36	20.20	5.20	2.07	5.83
Significance		0.0000	0.0000	0.0000	0.0000	0.0539	0.0000
VIF max.		2.69	2.18	3.16	2.69	2.18	3.16

Table 6-81: Regression results for the performance effects of the use of cost information (managers' perspective) - Anglophone subsidiaries

Linear regression model (Domestic German subsidiaries, unstandardised regression coefficients)	E.S.	Managers (dataset 3)					
		Goal attainment			Satisfaction		
		Model (a)	Model (b)	Model (c)	Model (a)	Model (b)	Model (c)
Cost type accounting	+		-0.5095	0.6147		-1.3496	-0.8114
Cost centre accounting	+		1.7633 *	0.5605		3.6547 **	3.3873 *
Cost object accounting	+		1.6626 *	0.5196		3.5581 ***	2.9123 **
Instrumental/conceptual use	+	-0.0532		-0.0732	0.0768		-0.0499
Rationalising use	+/-	-0.1513 *		-0.1397	0.0857		0.1588
Diagnostic use	+	0.4142 ***		0.4121 ***	0.3297 *		0.2257
Interactive use	+	0.2129		0.2337 *	-0.1481		-0.0829
Ceremonial use	-	-0.1743		-0.1713	-0.2633 **		-0.1854
Size subsidiary	/	-0.2751	-0.2472	-0.2293	-0.0816	-0.1713	-0.1404
Form of market entry	/	0.0539	0.0661	0.0741	0.3005	0.0331	0.0108
Length of affiliation	/	-0.0595	-0.1070	-0.0681	-0.1001	-0.2467	-0.1913
Size of the parent company	/	0.1144 **	0.0834 *	0.1117 **	-0.0487	-0.1038 **	-0.1033 **
Years of work experience	/	0.2659	0.4480	0.0957	-0.0706	-0.3415	-0.5847
Board members	/	0.2758	0.1067	0.1067	0.4251	0.1723	0.1412
Constant	/	1.2857	1.0379	0.6533	3.8815 **	4.0466	3.9283
R^2		64.66 %	37.28 %	66.69 %	37.87 %	42.35 %	53.64 %
Adjusted R^2		52.90 %	21.20 %	51.10 %	17.20 %	27.50 %	32.00 %
F-value		14.93	4.23	14.68	3.60	2.42	4.37
Significance		0.0000	0.0006	0.0000	0.0013	0.0260	0.0001
VIF max.		2.65	1.80	2.73	2.65	1.80	2.73

Table 6-82: Regression results for the performance effects of the use of cost information (managers' perspective) - domestic German subsidiaries

A virtually different picture prevails in the *domestic German subsidiaries* (Table 6-82 – model (a)). Underlining the complementary analysis of the performance effects resulting from the complexity of cost accounting, the five usage types explain a greater proportion of the variance of managers' degree of goal attainment (adj. R^2 = 52.9 %) than their level of satisfaction (adj. R^2 = 17.2 %). Apparently managers in the domestic German companies actually base their level of satisfaction on the characteristics of the underlying cost accounting system rather than their use of cost information.[1207] In comparison, managers' ability to attain the compendium of objectives appears rather informed by the way in which they use their cost information for decision-making. During the analysis of H5b_4, these results are discussed in depth. Ultimately, these explorations reveal that in the domestic German subsidiaries it is essential to consider the goal of potential improvements of cost accounting systems very carefully as well. Alternative **performance metrics** can be improved by different levers. Moreover, such improvements cannot be initiated without consulting the subsidiaries' parents. There is a significant effect of the control 'size of the parent company' for both performance metrics.

The individual regression coefficients reveal that the **instrumental/conceptual use** of cost information cannot be aligned with any of the two performance measures. This result reflects the mixed findings from previous German research for the performance effect of these usage types.[1208] Nevertheless, the finding leads to a rejection of H5b_1 in this respect. Interestingly, there is a consistent positive finding for the diagnostic usage type (Table 6-82 (models (a)). As expected, this usage type has a positive effect on both the degree of goal attainment and the level of satisfaction. The **diagnostic usage type** comprises traditional control based involvement of managers into their subordinates' decision-making. As such, the particular relevance of this usage type for managers' evaluation of their cost accounting system in domestic German subsidiaries might reflect that German companies are sometimes characterised to apply cost accounting more extensively for control than for planning activities.[1209] There are two particularly interesting effects with respect to the **ceremonial and the rationalising use** of cost information in the domestic German subsidiaries. In line with the Anglophone subsidiaries, the rationalising use is significantly negatively associated with managers' degree of goal attainment. The ceremonial use is significantly negatively associated with managers' level of satisfaction. These findings reinforce the suggested conceptual similarity of these two types in the domestic German subsidiaries.[1210] Though neither of these findings persists if it is accounted for the complexity of cost accounting systems (model (c)), it is revealing to find the ceremonial use to disturb the level of satisfaction whereas the rationalising use hampers the degree of goal attainment. As pre-disclosed continuously, the satisfaction is rather more affected by the design of the system in the domestic German companies whereas the degree of goal attainment reflects the usage types. Potentially, the findings for the ceremonial and the

[1207] For this and the following, cf. model (a) and model (b) in Table 6-82.

[1208] Cf. section 3.3.2.3, p. 76.

[1209] Cf. *Küpper* (1993), p. 610.

[1210] As discussed for the Anglophone subsidiaries, the finding might also suggest that cost information which is used in a rationalising manner is used less intensively for a thorough decision-making and, as such, makes the achievement of common cost accounting objectives infeasible.

rationalising usage types can thus be associated to the fact that domestic German companies appear to prefer a gently avoidance of their parent companies' cost accounting standards over a more abrasive defiance. The evidence on hypothesis H4 (determinants of the use of cost information) suggested likewise. It remains unclear, however, why the expected negative effect for the ceremonial usage types only prevails in the domestic German subsidiaries. It cannot be conclusively derived from the data whether this finding suggests that the German subsidiaries, e.g. oppose their parents' cost accounting systems fully if they decide to use the system ceremonially whereas the Anglophone subsidiaries disregard certain pieces of information during a ceremonial application of their systems only.

Overall, the presented results for the domestic German subsidiaries contradict H5b_1 with respect to the instrumental/conceptual use. Other than that, there is strong support for the hypothesis with respect to the diagnostic use of information. Concerning the interactive and the rationalising use of information, the evidence reveals H5b_1 to be 'conditionally acceptable'. Though are some expected effects, these can only be observed without (rationalising use) or in conjunction with (interactive use) an integration of the conceptual design of cost accounting in the above models. Similarly, there is conditional support for H5b_2 in the domestic German subsidiaries. Irrespective of the design of a cost accounting system, the ceremonial use hampers managers' satisfaction with their cost accounting system in these firms. Future research on the use of alternative or complementing information systems in subsidiaries could be light shedding to determine the meaning of these results more thoroughly.

(2) Management accountants' performance evaluations

Hypothesis H5b_3 expects that the way in which managers use cost information feeds back into management accountants' assessment of their cost accounting systems. This hypothesis is tested equivalently to the ones presented for the analysis of managers' performance evaluations. Hence, the analysis comprises the five types of use and the controls included to investigate the determinants of a cost accounting systems' complexity[1211] as its independent variables. The dependent variables are the degree of goal attainment or the level of satisfaction. Table 6-83 (Anglophone subsidiaries) and Table 6-84 (domestic German subsidiaries) summarise the identified results (model (a)).[1212]

All (a) models are of good fit. The adjusted R^2s are acceptable[1213] and F-values are significant. Also, in all (a) models the VIFs fall behind the threshold of 10. Hence, multicollinearity is not an issue. As for all other regression models in this study, standard errors are

[1211] Excluding the control variables reflecting managers' working position and years of work experience at this point reflects the focus on management accountants. An inclusion would not have changed the results in Table 6-81 and Table 6-82 considerably. Merely in the domestic German subsidiaries, the complexity of cost object accounting in model (c) (variable goal attainment) gains significance. The additional control variables remain insignificant.

[1212] Due to data availability, the results are provided for dataset 3 only. Table 6-83 and Table 6-84 also comprise two (b) models and two (c) models. These will be discussed during the analysis of hypothesis H5b_4.

[1213] The adjusted R^2 values from the analyses of managers and management accountants are compared during the discussion of the mediating effect of the usage types (H5b_4).

based on 'adjusted sandwich estimators'. Hence, heteroscedasticity and autocorrelation are not tested. The significance levels in Table 6-83 and Table 6-84 are based on one-tailed tests for the three directed hypotheses on the effects of the design of cost accounting and two-tailed tests for non-directed hypothesis on the use of cost information and the controls.

Taking a closer look at the usage types that feed-back into management evaluations of their systems' performance reveals interesting results. In the *Anglophone subsidiaries*, managers' use of cost information in a decision facilitating manner (**instrumental/conceptual use**) is mirrored by management accountants' assessments of their cost accounting system (Table 6-83). Moreover, the **ceremonial use** affects management accountants' degree of goal attainment positively. Similar to the comparable finding for the managers, this exploration might point at the existence of an alternative cost accounting system or indicates that only certain pieces of cost information are used ceremonially in the Anglophone subsidiaries. These findings suggest that management accountants in the Anglophone subsidiaries consider their managers' application of cost information to evaluate the system's performance. The results are robust if the cost accounting system's conceptual design is taken into account (model (c)). Thus, the empirics support H5b_3 for two usage types. During the upcoming discussion of the mediating effect of the usage types (H5b_4), it will be analysed whether managers' use of information or the design of a cost accounting system is more influential for management accountants' assessment of their cost accounting system.

For the *domestic German subsidiaries*, there is conditional support for H5b_3 as well. The **diagnostic use** of cost information is positively and significantly associated with management accountants' degree of goal attainment and their level of satisfaction. The finding mirrors the result for the managers. Hence, it could reflect the importance which managers in the domestic German subsidiaries attribute to this usage type during the evaluation of their cost accounting systems. Moreover, managers' **ceremonial use** of information inhibits management accountants' level of satisfaction. This finding also reflects the results from the managers. Apparently, management accountants acknowledge if their managers (can) use cost information during the process of management (diagnostic use) and consider whether managers regard their cost accounting system to be more useful for a parent company's information needs than for decision-making in the subsidiary (ceremonial use). As such, H5b_3 cannot be rejected for the domestic German companies either. The management accountants in these companies consider their managers' use of cost information to assess a cost accounting system.

Linear regression model (**Anglophone subsidiaries**, unstandardised regression coefficients)	E.S.	**Management accountants (dataset 3)**					
		Goal attainment			Satisfaction		
		Model (a)	Model (b)	Model (c)	Model (a)	Model (b)	Model (c)
Cost type accounting	+		1.4115 *	0.8683		-1.0440	-1.8781 ##
Cost centre accounting	+		6.1651 ***	4.7357 ***		2.9827 *	2.5306 *
Cost object accounting	+		-0.6148	-0.4585		1.9971 *	1.1835
Instrumental/conceptual use	+	0.7681 ***		0.3932 *	0.7393 ***		0.6378 **
Rationalising use	+/-	-0.1908		-0.0297	0.0022		0.1011
Diagnostic use	+	0.0891		0.0234	-0.0462		-0.0992
Interactive use	+	0.1073		0.0785	-0.2841		-0.3839
Ceremonial use	-	0.3658 **		0.2974 *	-0.2905		-0.2733
Size subsidiary	/	-0.1254	-0.2672	-0.2891	0.4266	-0.0582	0.3961
Form of market entry	/	-0.1288	-0.1249	-0.1044	-0.2534	-0.1435	-0.3729
Length of affiliation	/	0.0906	0.2281	0.1744	0.0251	0.0013	-0.0029
Size of the parent company	/	-0.0356	0.0366	0.0051	-0.0878	-0.0934	-0.0436
Years of work experience	/						
Board members	/						
Constant	/	-1.1095	0.0507	-1.6066	0.4476	2.9922	-0.1586
R^2		35.64 %	40.95 %	49.93 %	34.02 %	30.21 %	47.69 %
Adjusted R^2		20.00 %	30.30 %	32.30 %	18.00 %	17.70 %	29.20 %
F-value		3.41	5.68	4.72	2.43	2.68	3.58
Significance		0.0030	0.0001	0.0001	0.0246	0.0213	0.0009
VIF max.		2.67	2.15	3.05	2.67	2.15	3.05

Table 6-83: Regression results for the performance effects of the use of cost information (management accountants' perspective) – Anglophone subsidiaries

Linear regression model (Domestic German subsidiaries, unstandardised regression coefficients)	E.S.	Management accountants (dataset 3)					
		Goal attainment			Satisfaction		
		Model (a)	Model (b)	Model (c)	Model (a)	Model (b)	Model (c)
Cost type accounting	+		-1.2494 ##	-0.3901		-1.5340 ##	-0.9450
Cost centre accounting	+		2.3838 **	0.9994		2.8705 **	1.6827
Cost object accounting	+		2.5188 **	1.5413		3.5349 ***	2.5023 ***
Instrumental/conceptual use	+	0.2194		0.1772	0.3729		0.3053
Rationalising use	+/-	-0.0751		-0.0276	-0.0051		0.0700
Diagnostic use	+	0.3860 ***		0.3006 *	0.2595 *		0.1191
Interactive use	+	0.0189		0.0662	-0.2395		-0.1719
Ceremonial use	-	-0.0315		0.0419	-0.3087 **		-0.1907
Size subsidiary	/	-0.2258	-0.2936	-0.2807	0.0567	-0.0475	-0.0488
Form of market entry	/	-0.2837	-0.3171	-0.4588	0.2033	-0.1695	-0.1087
Length of affiliation	/	-0.0529	-0.1339	-0.0961	-0.0787	-0.1987	-0.1532
Size of the parent company	/	0.0803	0.0342	0.0571	0.0028	-0.0496	-0.0379
Years of work experience	/						
Board members	/						
Constant	/	1.3804	2.8643 **	0.8829	2.3682	2.6226 *	1.9027
R^2		45.48 %	30.56 %	50.98 %	42.87 %	41.82 %	54.47 %
Adjusted R^2		31.50 %	17.40 %	32.60 %	28.20 %	30.80 %	37.40 %
F-value		5.93	3.47	5.65	6.51	3.48	5.69
Significance		0.0000	0.0050	0.0000	0.0000	0.0050	0.0000
VIF max.		2.49	1.41	2.53	2.49	1.41	2.53

Table 6-84: Regression results for the performance effects of the use of cost information (management accountants' perspective) - domestic German subsidiaries

In contrast to the Anglophone subsidiaries, however, the findings for the level of satisfaction disappear if the design of cost accounting systems is included into the analyses (model (c)). Apparently, the management accountants in the domestic German subsidiaries consider their managers' use of cost information more relevant for the degree of goal attainment but base their level of satisfaction on the design of their cost accounting system. Yet, this does not necessarily mean that management accountants ignore their managers' opinions. The findings actually mirror a similar result for the managers in the domestic German subsidiaries.[1214] Hence, the findings for the level of satisfaction are similar for both managers and management accountants. But, rather than finding the use of cost information to determine the satisfaction of both these groups, the design of the cost accounting system per se drives this performance metric. Nevertheless, management accountants should bear in mind not to lose sight of their management accountants' perceptions. Finding some differences for the complexity sub-scores which affect managers' and management accountants' level of satisfaction underlines this assertion.[1215]

(3) The mediating effect of the usage types

As explicated in section 6.2.2.1.3.2, the complexity of cost accounting has some effect on the use of cost information. As such, the association of both the design of cost accounting systems and the use of cost information with managers' and management accountants' performance evaluations raises the question whether the complexity of cost accounting systems might affect the systems' performance through the usage types as well. This interaction is taken on by regarding the mediating effect of the use of cost information suggested in H5b_4. During this investigation, it can also be clarified whether the design of cost accounting systems or the use of cost information is more influential for managers' and management accountants' assessments of their cost accounting systems.

According to *Baron/Kenny* (1986),[1216] there are several **preconditions** to identify a mediating effect in a regression model (cf. section 5.4.3.1). First, the mediator (use of cost information) must be significantly influenced by the mediated variable (complexity of cost accounting systems). In the domestic German subsidiaries, this premise is arguably weakly fulfilled since one or another complexity score affects each of the usage types (section 6.2.2.1.3.2). In the Anglophone subsidiaries, however, this first requirement is met for the effect of cost type and cost centre accounting on the instrumental/conceptual use and the effect of cost centre accounting on the diagnostic use only. Hence, section 6.2.2.1.3.2 shows that neither the average complexity score nor the complexity scores for cost type, cost centre and cost object accounting have a significant effect on all types of cost information use. These results prevent the ability to identify a potential moderating effect of the use of cost information conclusively. The data in this study does not meet *Baron/Kenny*'s first requirement.

To avoid a dismissal of any analysis on H5b_4, Table 6-81 to Table 6-84 still comprise an analysis that is informed by the suggestions of *Baron/Kenny* (1986). Whereas model (b) reflects their second step (i.e. the regression of the mediated variables on the dependent

---

[1214] Cf. Table 6-82 (model (c)).

[1215] Cf. section 6.3.2.1, p. 288f.

[1216] Cf. *Baron/Kenny* (1986), p. 1177.

variable),[1217] model (c) takes on the third step recommended by *Baron/Kenny* (1986) (i.e. the regression of the dependent variable on the mediated and mediating variable). If a significant effect found in model (b) decreases or disappears in model (c), this would indicate a mediating effect. The forthcoming discussion discloses interesting results for the dominance of the conceptual design of cost accounting systems and the use of information for managers' and management accountants' performance evaluations. Yet, because the first criterion of *Baron/Kenny* (1986) is not comprehensively met, the discussion provides rather **explorative evidence** for or against the suggested mediating effect.

In the *Anglophone companies* both the complexity scores and the usage types are significantly associated with the performance metrics of managers and management accountants.[1218] The adjusted R^2 values of the models which comprise the complexity scores and the usage types (model (c)) are higher than the ones for the separate models on the usage types (model (a)) and complexity scores (models (b)). These findings (Table 6-85) can be interpreted as evidence that in the Anglophone subsidiaries, managers and management accountants evaluate their cost accounting system based on the system's design and its application during the management process. Despite this similarity, management accountants and managers seem to attach **different weights** to the design of the cost accounting systems and its application during the management process. The adjusted R^2 values from Table 6-81 and Table 6-83 indicate that the main bases for managers' assessments of their cost accounting systems are the usage types. Accordingly, managers' use of information explains their performance evaluations better than the complexity scores do (Table 6-85). In contrast, management accountants' evaluations rest more consistently on the characteristics of the system's design rather than managers' usage types. The variation in management accountants' degree of goal attainment can be described better by the design of the cost accounting system. For the level of satisfaction both, the design and the use are equally relevant. This finding must not be mistaken for largely different opinions of managers and management accountants, however. Though these findings underline that management accountants in the Anglophone subsidiaries must consider their managers' opinions on cost accounting very carefully,[1219] there is a common theme for both managers and management accountants' performance metrics. Consistently, the complexity scores seem to affect the degree of goal attainment of both managers and management accountants more extensively than they influence the level of satisfaction (Table 6-85). This finding mirrors that the 15 complexity sub-scores explain a larger proportion of variance of the degree of goal attainment than of the level of satisfaction (section 6.3.2.1). Above all, these nuanced findings reveal that managers and management accountants in the Anglophone subsidiaries consider both the **design of a cost accounting system and the use of cost information** to assess their system. Whether this conjoint

[1217] Note that the results for model (b) in Table 6-81 to Table 6-84 reflect the ones in Table 6-77 and Table 6-79. The relationships between the adjusted R^2 are equal. If the performance assessments of managers, for example, can be explained better than the one of management accountants in Table 6-77 (e.g. 31.0 % vs. 17.5 % for the level of satisfaction), then the same holds true in Table 6-81 to Table 6-84 (e.g. 19.9 % vs. 17.7 %).

[1218] This can be seen in Table 6-81 (model (c)) and Table 6-83 (model (c)).

[1219] Cf. section 6.3.2.1, p. 275f.

consideration can be associated to Anglophone subsidiaries' exposure to alternative cost accounting traditions appears an interesting field for future research.

Given these results, it is not surprising to find little support for a widespread **mediating effect** of the usage types (H5b_4) in the Anglophone subsidiaries. Table 6-83 reveals disappearing significance levels for the effect of cost type accounting (cost object accounting) on management accountants' degree of goal attainment (level of satisfaction) only. Since in neither case the effect of all complexity scores disappears or loses in significance, however, this provides conditional support for H5b_4 only.

Comparison of adjusted R^2 (Table 6-81 to Table 6-84)		Dataset 3					
		Anglophone subsidiaries			Domestic German subsidiaries		
		Usage types (model (a))		Complexity scores (model (b))	Usage types (model (a))		Complexity scores (model (b))
Managers	Goal attainment	45.1 %	>	41.5 %	**52.9 %**	>	21.2 %
		Conjoint effect (model (c)): **60.6 %**			Conjoint effect (model (c)): 51.1 %		
	Satisfaction	42.3 %	>	19.9 %	17.2 %	<	27.5 %
		Conjoint effect (model (c)): **44.9 %**			Conjoint effect (model (c)): **32.0 %**		
Management accountants	Goal attainment	20.0 %	<	30.3 %	**31.5 %**	>	17.4 %
		Conjoint effect (model (c)): **32.3 %**			Conjoint effect (model (c)): **32.6 %**		
	Satisfaction	18.0 %	≥	17.7 %	28.2 %	<	30.8 %
		Conjoint effect (model (c)): **29.2 %**			Conjoint effect (model (c)): **37.4 %**		

Table 6-85: Mediating effect of the usage types (adjusted R^2 values of the regression models)

The results for the *domestic German subsidiaries* are quite peculiar. The adjusted R^2 values of the models regarding the effect of the usage types (model (a)) and the complexity scores (model (b)) in Table 6-82 and Table 6-84 show that both management accountants' and managers' degree of **goal attainment** can be explained better by the **types of information** use than the complexity of the cost accounting systems (Table 6-85). In contrast, the **complexity of the cost accounting** system explicates a greater proportion of the variance from the **level of satisfaction** than the usage types do. These conclusions are not violated by the conjoint analysis of usage types and complexity scores (model (c)).

Nevertheless, these conjoint analyses complement the findings from Table 6-85. The identified effects from the usage types in model (a) persist for management accountants' and managers' degree of goal attainment in model (c). Moreover, the introduction of the usage types actually supresses the significant results for the complexity scores (model (b)) for this performance measure. This result supports H5b_4 with respect to the **degree of goal attainment**. The design of the subsidiaries' cost accounting systems are, if at all,[1220] acknowledged in managers' and management accountants' degree of goal attainment through the (diagnostic) usage types (**mediating effect**).

In contrast, the significant effects of the usage types on managers' and management accountants' **level of satisfaction** (model (a)) disappear if the **complexity scores** are introduced in the analysis (model (c)). Simultaneously, the significant effects of the complexity scores for the level of satisfaction (model (b)) are rather persistent in model (c). This finding can be seen to reassure the results from the comparison of the adjusted R^2 values of models (a) and (b). The level of satisfaction in the domestic German subsidiaries is

[1220] Since the adjusted R^2 values of the (c) models do not consistently outweigh the ones from the (a) models (Table 6-85), it remains undeterminable whether there actually is an indirect effect of the complexity scores.

formed by considerations of the systems' complexities rather than the usage types.[1221] Since there are identical findings in this respect for managers and management accountants, however, this does not suggest that management accountants and managers lose track of one another. As such, the rationale beyond analysing the mediating analysis of the usage types (H5b_4) cannot be rejected by these results either.

Above all, managers and management accountants in the domestic German subsidiaries appear to share a common view on the basis for their assessments of the cost accounting systems as well. But, other than in the Anglophone subsidiaries, in the domestic German subsidiaries the level of satisfaction and goal attainment cannot be attributed to both the design of the system and the use of its information. Rather, the use of information drives the degree of goal attainment, whereas the systems' complexity affects the level of satisfaction.[1222]

Summary and recommendations

A summary of this section's findings is presented in Table 6-86. For H5b_1 and H5b_2, the table summarises whether there is significant support for a hypothesis. If this support is restricted to one performance measure only, it is regarded as conditional. Also, the table reveals if there were any unexpectedly directed findings. Marking H5b_3 as conditionally acceptable reflects the restriction of the findings to few usage types in both the Anglophone and the domestic German subsidiaries. In the light of H5b_4, the restricted acceptance reflects that the mediation is limited to one performance measure (domestic German subsidiaries) or prevails for a selection of the complexity scores only (Anglophone subsidiaries).

Summary of the hypotheses tests			Instrumental/ conceptual use	Rationalising use	Diagnostic use	Interactive use	Ceremonial use
(1)	H5b_1	Managers' performance evaluation	Anglophone: ✓ German: X	Anglophone: (✓) German: (✓)	Anglophone: (X) German: ✓	Anglophone: (✓) German: X	*No hypothesis*
	H5b_2	Managers' performance evaluation	*No hypothesis*	*No hypothesis*	*No hypothesis*	*No hypothesis*	Anglophone: ± German: (✓)
(2)	H5b_3	Management accountants' performance evaluation	Anglophone subsidiaries: (✓) Domestic German subsidiaries: (✓)				
(3)	H5b_4	Mediating effect of the usage types	Anglophone subsidiaries: (✓) Domestic German subsidiaries: (✓)				
Explanation: ✓ = accepted hypothesis, (✓) = conditionally accepted hypothesis, X = rejected hypothesis, ± = unexpected 'quasi significant' effect (rejection)							

Table 6-86: Summary of the hypotheses tests for H5b (performance effects of the use of cost information)

Translating this section's results into **practical recommendations** for practitioners is challenging due to the restricted support for various hypotheses. In the Anglophone subsidiar-

[1221] The adjusted R^2 of the model (c) for the level of satisfaction are slightly higher than the ones in the (b) models. This indicates that the usage types are not disregarded for this performance measure either.

[1222] This latter result is particularly revealing. Management accountants' degree of goal attainment, which is especially influenced by the use of cost information, is significantly higher in the companies from dataset 3 if compared to the companies from dataset 1 that did not return questionnaire B (dataset 5). As such, this finding corresponds to the selection bias in dataset 3. In the companies from dataset 1 that did not return questionnaire B, cost information may be less conclusively incorporated for managerial decision-making. The following section analyses this assertion empirically.

ies, a very consistent influence of the instrumental/conceptual usage types prevails. Similarly, in the domestic German subsidiaries, there is multiple evidence for a performance increasing effect of the diagnostic use of information. Yet, recommending Anglophone and domestic German subsidiaries to focus on these usage types would mistake these types as unconditional on these companies' characteristics. Since section 6.2.3 finds the former type to depend on managers' preference for cost information and the latter to depend on the pursuit of decision influencing objectives, these usage types appear particularly fruitful under these circumstances only. There are two additional findings, which appear rather peculiar and relevant for practitioners.

The section reveals that a rationalising use of cost information is associated with a reduction in managers' ability to achieve their cost accounting objectives. Hence, for subsidiaries it is crucial to ensure that cost information can actually be applied for managerial decision-making *before* a decision action is taken. This information becomes even more relevant because the rationalising usage type appears conceptually similar to the ceremonial one. MNCs which find their subsidiaries to use cost information especially for rationalising purposes may need to reconsider the information usefulness of their cost accounting systems for the management processes in subsidiaries.

Moreover, the section highlights that managers and management accountants have similar perceptions on relevant design characteristics and usage types. These results suggest that the comparable performance assessments by managers and management accountants are indeed linked to similar belief systems about cost information or close interactions between managers and management accountants (section 6.3.1). As such, the finding amplifies an assertion of previous researchers that a strong interaction between managers and management accountants is one way to ensure a well performing cost accounting system (section 4.2.3 and 6.3.1). Complementary, the varying relevance of the complexity sub-scores and the usage types suggest that management accountants' retrieval of their managers' information needs during personal interactions must occur continuously and concisely. This suggestion reflects the recommendations determined on the grounds of the performance effects of the 15 complexity sub-scores, which urged management accountants not to lose sight of their managers' perspectives on cost accounting.

6.3.2.3 The contextual fit of cost accounting systems as a lever of performance

The following investigation is devoted to the call by *Drury/Tayles* (2005) to analyse whether cost accounting systems that reflect their context perform better than systems that do not (Hypothesis H5c).

In order to analyse the assumption by *Drury/Tayles* (2005), the regression results used to test H3 (determinants of the average complexity score)[1223] are applied to predict an expected, context reflecting complexity score for each company. By subtracting this prediction from the actual complexity score, a value is determined which expresses whether a company applies a system which is more (> zero) or less (< zero) complex than predicted

[1223] For the predictions, the models including the moderating effect of the relational context are applied (cf. Table 6-53 (model (b)), p. 211).

by the contextual variables. Those companies, whose cost accounting systems do not exceed or fall behind a predicted value by more than half a standard deviation,[1224] are **defined to have a system that reflects the contextual factors**. Companies, whose cost accounting system deviates by more than half a standard deviation from its predicted value, are defined to have a more or less complex system (Figure 6-9).[1225] This procedure is applied separately for Anglophone and domestic German subsidiaries.[1226]

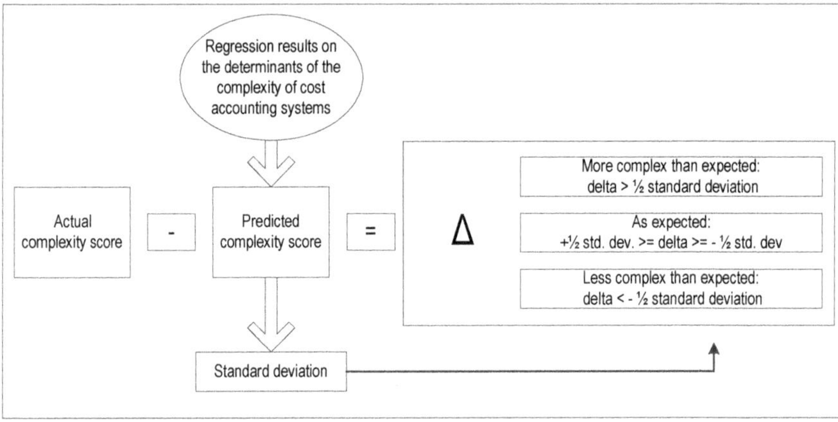

Figure 6-9: Definition of a cost accounting system which reflects its context

To evaluate whether there are better performing cost accounting systems in subsidiaries whose systems reflect these firms' contextual variables, a graphical analysis suggested by *Moeschler* (2012)[1227] is applied. Thereby, the deviation from a mean performance rating is pictured by the context contingent design of a cost accounting system. If the expectation by *Drury/Tayles* (2005) was to hold, there should be a positive deviation from the mean performance rating for those companies whose cost accounting systems reflect their context. Simultaneously, the deviation from the mean rating should be less positive or even negative in those companies that have cost accounting systems which are not reflecting the company' context. Figure 6-10 presents two **examples** which graphical results would support the expectations by *Drury/Tayles* (2005).

1224 This threshold is chosen to have a similar number of subsidiaries in each of the three resulting groups. Because the forthcoming figures picture a deviation from a mean performance rating, this facilitates the comparability of the bars in each figure.

1225 Similar approaches were previously applied by *Ittner et al.* (2002), p. 720ff.; *Pizzini* (2006), p. 201 and *Moeschler* (2012), p. 316ff.

1226 In this section, the context reflection of a cost accounting system is derived based on the regression results provided in section 6.1.2.1.3 (i.e. dataset 1). Thereby it is ensured that the context adequacy is assessed through all companies which provided analysable information. The mean ratings of the performance measures, however, are provided for dataset 1 and dataset 3 respectively. This is done to avoid misinterpretation of the performance figures. If deviance in dataset 3 would be compared against the mean rating in dataset 1, this would lead to uninterpretable results because the mean performance rating in dataset 3 exceeds the one in dataset 1.

1227 Cf. *Moeschler* (2012), p. 316ff.

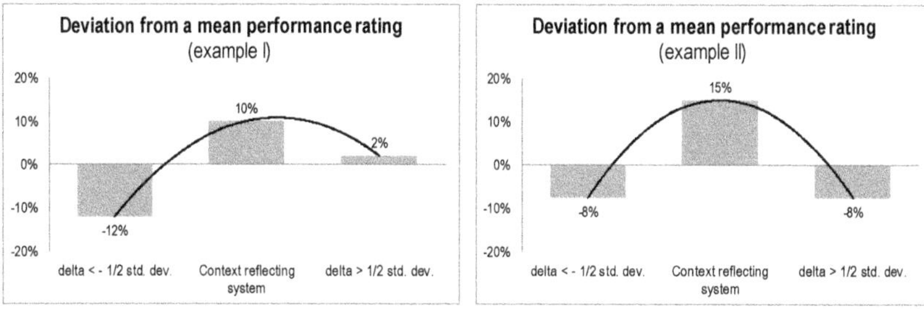

Figure 6-10: Graphical illustration of hypothesis H5c_1a

Since the **Anglophone subsidiaries** may prefer German cost accounting traditions to the Anglophone cost accounting traditions in their group, H5c_1b argues that the suggestion by *Drury/Tayles* (2005) does not necessarily hold in these subsidiaries. Hence, it is not too surprising to find Figure 6-11 to reveal a picture that is reversed if compared to the examples pictured in Figure 6-10. In contrast to the suggestions by *Drury/Tayles* (2005), the Anglophone subsidiaries that align their cost accounting system with their economic context, voluntary and coercive institutional pressures and the relational context assess their systems' performance to lack behind. Rather than favouring a context reflecting system, these companies **prefer to disentangle their systems** from what would best reflect their economic and voluntary institutional surroundings as well as their parents' bureaucratic and personal involvements and the relational context.

The cost accounting systems in the Anglophone subsidiaries are rather in line with Anglophone cost accounting traditions. It could be revealed that this circumstance is determined by Anglophone parents' impact on these subsidiaries. Hence, the finding in Figure 6-11 indicates that the Anglophone subsidiaries in Germany rather prefer to deviate from their parent companies' cost accounting traditions.[1228] A similar result prevails if the Anglophone companies with and without cross-national differences are compared (cf. Table 6-76 in section 6.3.1). Puzzling, however, more complex cost accounting systems than contextually expectable from the economic and voluntary institutional determinants as well as contextually allowed by the parent companies and the relational context perform better for the degree of goal attainment only.[1229] For the level of satisfaction, a less complex cost accounting system than predictable by the contextual variables is performing best for management accountants in dataset 1 and managers in dataset 3. For management accountants in dataset 3, a deviation in either direction is evaluated equally.

[1228] The limited number of greenfield investments (15 in dataset 1, and seven in dataset 3), prevents a sound refinement of this analysis according to green- and brownfields. Potentially, however, the expectation by *Drury/Tayles* (2005) might hold in greenfield subsidiaries. In the two (one) greenfield investments in dataset 1 (dataset 3) which have a context reflecting system, managers' and management accountants' degree of goal attainment exceeds the one of the companies with a more or less complex system. There is no such result for the level of satisfaction.

[1229] Expecting a more complex cost accounting to be preferable stems from the assumption that these systems would be more in line with German cost accounting traditions.

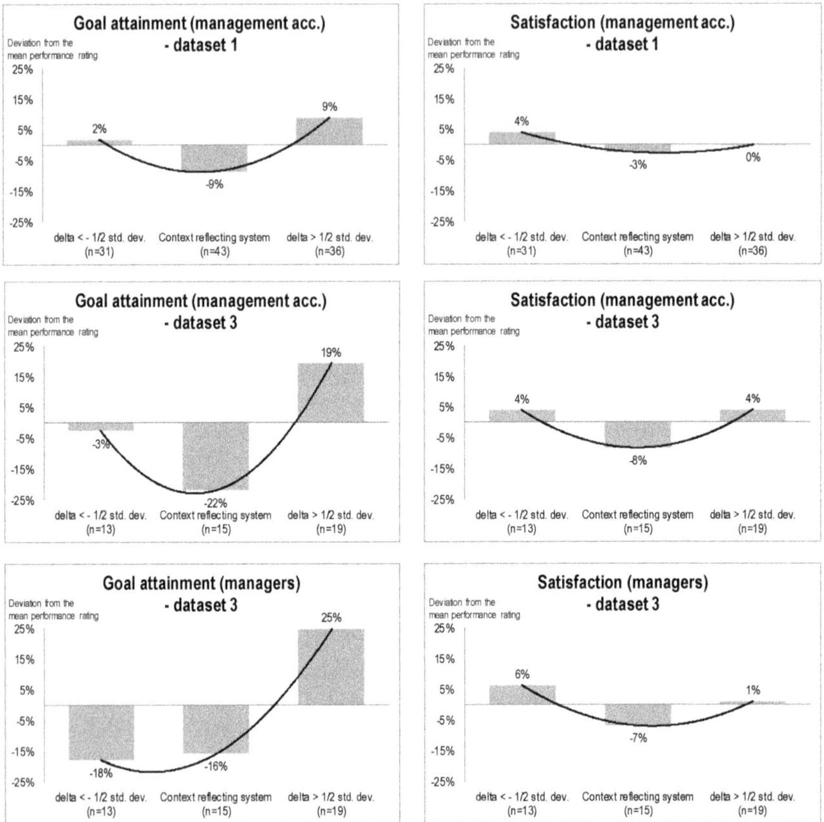

Figure 6-11: Performance effects of a context contingent cost accounting system Anglophone subsidiaries (datasets 1 and 3)

These mixed results seem to be linked to the findings on the determinants of the two performance metrics. For both performance measures, the design of cost accounting systems and the use of cost information are complements for both the managers and management accountants in the Anglophone subsidiaries. Yet, section 6.3.2.2 also finds the degree of goal attainment to be more reliant on the complexity of cost accounting than the level of satisfaction is. This difference suggests that the finding on a higher degree of goal attainment in subsidiaries with more complex cost accounting systems than contextually predicted reflects that this performance metric is actually affected extensively by the design of a cost accounting system in the Anglophone subsidiaries. In a similar vein, finding less complex cost accounting systems than predicted by the contextual variables to increase the satisfaction with the cost accounting systems might mirror the effect of the usage types. Several findings suggest so. First, management accountants' satisfaction in dataset 3 is equally explicable by the usage types and the complexity scores (Table 6-85). These findings could be mirrored by the equal effects of more and less complex cost accounting systems than predicted by the context for these management accountants' satisfaction. Likewise, the satisfaction increasing effect of a cost accounting system which is less complex than predicted by the contextual variables for the managers in dataset 3 might reflect that the variation in their level of satisfaction can be explained better by the usage types than the complexity scores (Table 6-85). It remains undeterminable whether the suggested interpretation can also explain the findings for the management accountants from dataset 1. There is no data on the usage types in that dataset. Arguably, the 'lack' of a selection bias for the Anglophone subsidiaries in dataset 3 and the similar distributions of the performance metrics in datasets 1 and 3[1230] suggests so.

Overall, these results underline that practitioners have to act very conscientiously if they were to improve their cost accounting systems. As explicated before, without a thorough **understanding of the performance metric** to be enhanced, improvements might grasp at nothing. Also, the results link the performance of cost accounting systems in the Anglophone subsidiaries to the extent in which these systems are designed in accordance to economic, institutional and relational variables. Hence, the evidence in Figure 6-11 supports H5c_1b.

In addition to these findings, two peculiar results can be determined from Figure 6-11. First, **managers** and **management accountants** perceive the impeding (increasing) effect of a considerably simple (refined) cost accounting system differently in the Anglophone subsidiaries from dataset 3. Sustaining a less complex cost accounting system than predicted by the contextual variables is associated with a stronger negative effect for managers' than management accountants' degree of goal attainment. Similarly, the positive effect of having a more complex cost accounting system than predicted by the contextual variables is higher for managers' degree of goal attainment as well. These findings can complement the discussion that management accountants in the Anglophone subsidiaries should consider carefully which individual components of their companies' cost accounting systems are most relevant for managers. Such a consideration and the subsequent refinement of the relevant complexity scores might improve managers' degree of goal attainment to a greater extent than management accountants' one.

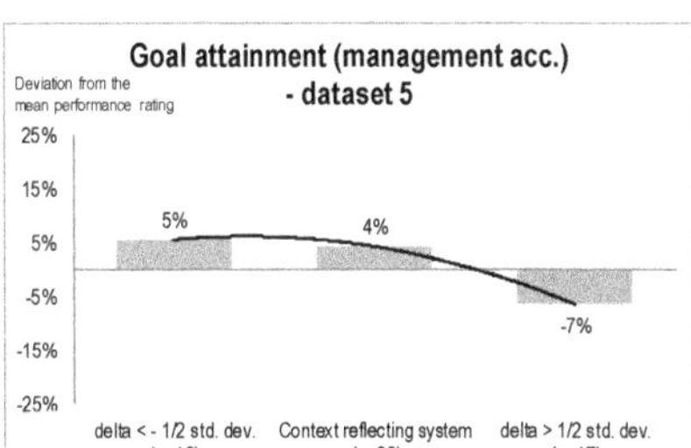

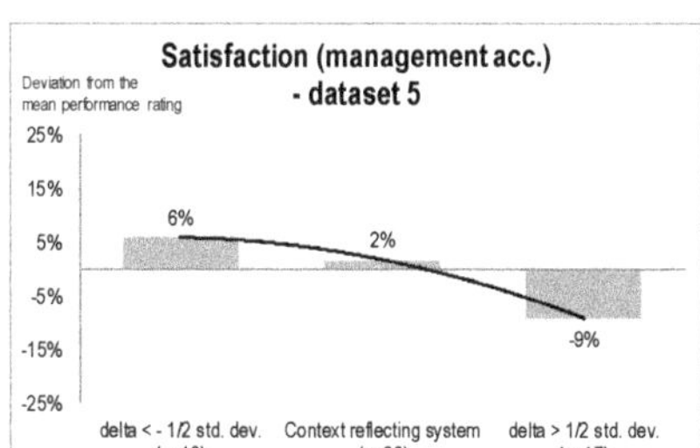

Figure 6-12: Performance effects of a context contingent cost accounting system Anglophone subsidiaries (dataset 5)

[1230] Cf. section 6.3.1, p. 277.

Second, the results in Figure 6-11 show higher amplitudes of the effects for the management accountants' performance evaluations in dataset 3 if compared to dataset 1. This effect can be attributed to those companies from dataset 1 that did hand in questionnaire A only (dataset 5). Analysing these companies uncovers a potential reason for their **incomplete participation.** In dataset 5, an increase in the complexity of the subsidiaries' cost accounting systems beyond the contextually predicted level is rather decreasing the performance of the cost accounting systems (Figure 6-12). In contrast, a decrease in the complexity, which suggests a greater alignment with Anglophone cost accounting traditions, augments the performance.[1231] As such, it can be argued that these companies may not have participated due to little expected benefits from comparing themselves more thoroughly with their domestic German counterparts.

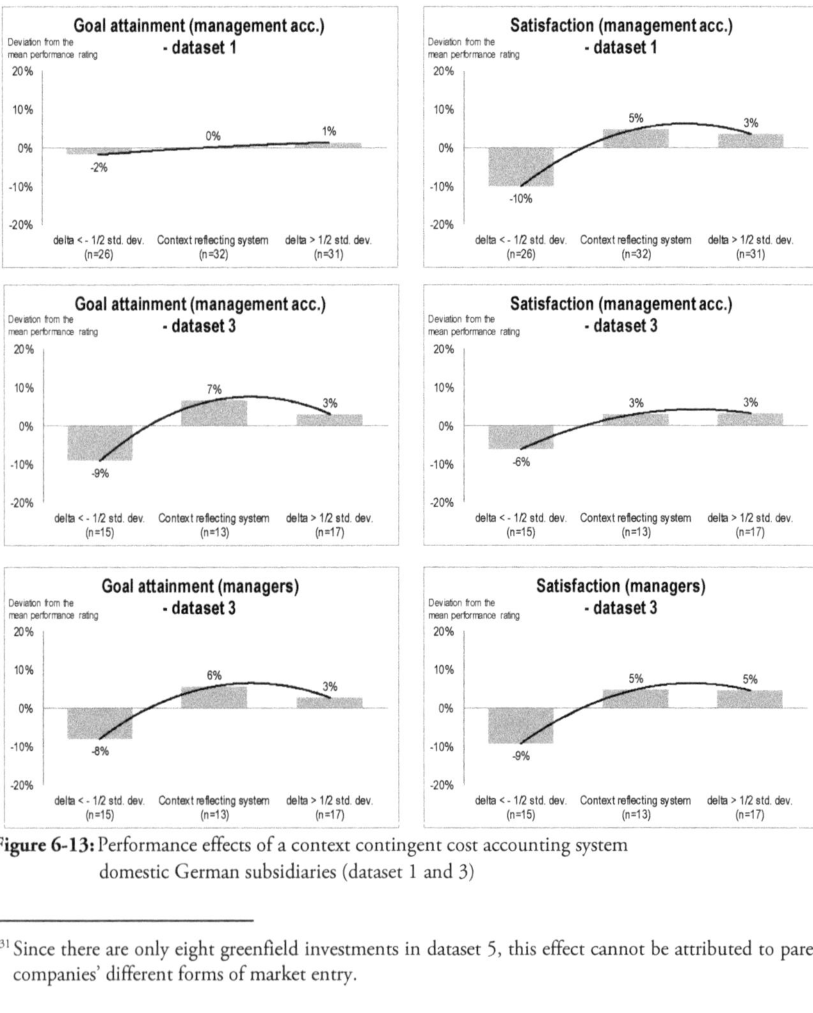

Figure 6-13: Performance effects of a context contingent cost accounting system domestic German subsidiaries (dataset 1 and 3)

[1231] Since there are only eight greenfield investments in dataset 5, this effect cannot be attributed to parent companies' different forms of market entry.

For the **domestic German subsidiaries**, the expectations of *Drury/Tayles* (2005) are well reflected by the data (Figure 6-13). A less complex cost accounting system than predicted by the contextual variables is consistently perceived to be negative. Moreover, a more complex cost accounting system than contextually explicable is, in tendency, performing worse than the cost accounting systems that are reflecting the economic and institutional environment. These results are rather stable for both performance measures as well as managers and management accountants. Hence, there is substantial support for H5c_1a.

Similar to the Anglophone subsidiaries, the findings in Figure 6-13 can explain why several companies from dataset 1 did not hand in questionnaire B (dataset 5). Thereby, the identified **participation bias** in the domestic German subsidiaries (dataset 3) can be clarified. Other than for the Anglophone subsidiaries, an application of above analysis for dataset 5 reveals no particularity for the level of satisfaction (Figure 6-14). The pictures in Figure 6-13 and Figure 6-14 cannot be differentiated extensively. However, a virtually different picture than for dataset 3 prevails for the degree of goal attainment in dataset 5. In these subsidiaries, pursuing less complex cost accounting systems than predicted by the context is preferred over contextually adequate systems as well as systems that are more complex than projected. Since these results counteract the ones from dataset 3, it becomes explicable why there is no association between the extent to which a subsidiary's cost accounting system reflects its context and the degree of goal attainment for the management accountants in dataset 1 (Figure 6-13).

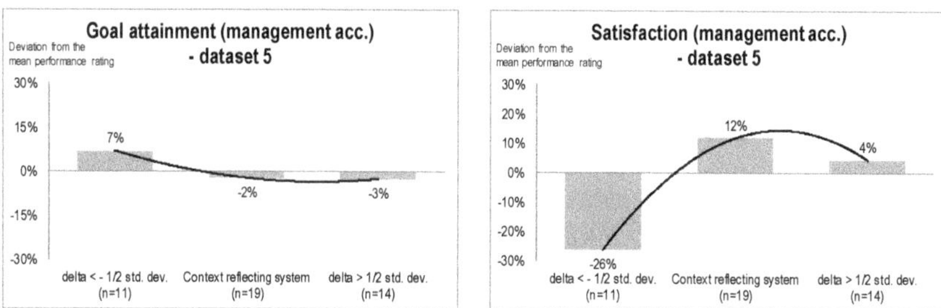

Figure 6-14: Performance effects of a context contingent cost accounting system domestic German subsidiaries (datasets 5)

On the one hand, this suggests a similar effect as in the Anglophone subsidiaries. Companies might not have responded to questionnaire B because of a perceived lack to benefit from this research project in terms of potential improvements to the design of their cost accounting systems. On the other hand, there is no difference between datasets 3 and 5 with respect to the level of satisfaction.[1232] Yet, this level of satisfaction is more exclusively associated with the complexity of cost accounting in the domestic German subsidiaries.[1233] In comparison, the degree of goal attainment is particularly linked to the use of cost in-

[1232] This result mirrors the findings for the complexity sub-scores. Similar complexity sub-scores are associated with the level of satisfaction reported by management accountants in dataset 1 and managers in dataset 3 (cf. Table 6-79 on p. 286).

[1233] For this and the following, cf. section 6.3.2.2, p. 301f.

formation in dataset 3. The complexity of cost accounting systems is merely indirectly associated with the degree of goal attainment in these firms (mediating effect). Hence, the finding for the degree of goal attainment in dataset 5 signals that it is not the design of the cost accounting system but another source which leads to the participation bias in the domestic German sample.

In the analysis of dataset 1, the individual complexity sub-scores affect management accountants' degree of goal attainment, whereas in dataset 3 they do not.[1234] These results suggest that in the domestic German subsidiaries of dataset 5, the design of cost accounting systems rather than their application for managerial decision-making drives the degree of goal attainment. This hints at an **issue with respect to the use of cost information** in dataset 5. Whether this result is linked to a less intensive use of cost information during the process of management (usage types) and difficulties in the cooperation of managers and management accountants,[1235] however, remains concealed. The findings might equally reveal a greater focus on other information than costs for decision-making. In line with this latter suggestion, management accountants from dataset 5 pursue the cost accounting objectives significantly less intensive than the management accountants from dataset 3.[1236] Despite these unclear explanations, the results show that the domestic German subsidiaries from dataset 5 appear to have handed-in questionnaire A only because there are issues with respect to the use of cost information for decision-making.

In a nutshell, the results in this section support H5c_1a and H5c_1b (Table 6-87). The ability to confirm the expectations by *Drury/Tayles* (2005) for the domestic German subsidiaries mirrors previous results from one-country settings.[1237] In addition, the results for the Anglophone subsidiaries can complement previous studies considerably. Since the results from these firms are contrary to the beliefs of *Drury/Tayles* (2005), their expectation might especially hold for companies in a one-country setting. In foreign subsidiaries, the validity of the expectation appears strongly associated with the comparability of the cost accounting traditions from the involved home and host countries.

	Anglophone subsidiaries	Domestic German subsidiaries
H5c_1a: Context reflecting system	*No hypothesis*	✓
H5c_1b: Context reflecting system	✓	*No hypothesis*
Explanation: ✓ = accepted hypothesis		

Table 6-87: Summary of the hypotheses tests for H5a (performance effects of a context contingent cost accounting system)

By and large, this section presents empirical evidence for the generally hold assumption that differences in cost accounting traditions are important to be acknowledged by MNCs. If a MNC was to transfer its home-country cost accounting traditions into its

[1234] Cf. section 6.3.2.1, p. 286.

[1235] In comparison to dataset 3, there is a considerable, though insignificantly lower level of top management support in dataset 5.

[1236] Disaggregating the goal attainment variable into the extent to which cost objectives are pursued and the extent to which they are fulfilled reveals both to be significantly higher in the companies that did return questionnaire B in comparison to those that did not (one-tailed significance level of 5 %). Neither of these differences is present in the Anglophone subsidiaries.

[1237] Cf. section 4.2.3, p. 119.

subsidiaries, the information usefulness of cost accounting systems in a foreign subsidiary can fade. From an academic perspective, this finding is very insightful. It questions the explanatory power of contingency theory for the analysis of cost accounting as well as other management control systems[1238] in *foreign* subsidiaries. Since the performance of cost accounting systems which reflect their economic and institutional context is inferior to the one of the systems that do not, it cannot be justified to argue that subsidiaries adjust their internal structures to their contextual factors for the reason of (economic) efficiency. On similar grounds, the contingency approach was included as a meta-concept into this study. Yet, at this point these conceptual considerations from section 4.1.2 can be refined. They seem particularly true for the analysis of cost accounting systems in subsidiaries if these are confronted by cross-national differences in management accounting. Future research may take on this finding by assessing the explanatory power of the contingency approach for other management control systems in subsidiaries. Also, these assertions should be validated during the analysis of other affiliates such as business units as well.

6.3.3 Summary

The descriptive evidence in section 6.3.1 finds no differences in the performance assessments provided by the Anglophone and the domestic German subsidiaries. Remarkably, however, the section reveals that Anglophone subsidiaries which are characterised by cross-national differences in cost accounting are significantly less satisfied and achieve their goals significantly less than those Anglophone subsidiaries which rather apply German cost accounting traditions. Moreover, the **descriptive evidence** in section 6.3.1 finds no gap in the perceptions management accountants and managers hold about the performance of their companies' cost accounting systems. For the Anglophone subsidiaries, this finding seems interrelated with the fact that managers and management accountants interact and base their performance assessments on both the design of cost accounting systems and the use of cost information. In the German companies, this finding might reflect the response bias. Dataset 3 seems to comprise those domestic German subsidiaries with cost information that is useful for managerial decision-making (section 6.3.2.3).

Despite these findings, it prevails that managers and management accountants assess the performance of their cost accounting systems better if asked for a level of satisfaction than for a degree of goal attainment. Throughout section 6.3.2.3, this difference in magnitude between the two performance measures can be aligned with the different considerations which form the basis of two performance metrics. The degree of goal attainment is dominantly influenced by the use of cost information in the domestic German subsidiaries. In contrast, the level of satisfaction is especially affected by the design of the cost accounting system in these subsidiaries. In the Anglophone subsidiaries both the design of the cost accounting systems and the use of cost information are relevant for the performance measures. Their weights vary for management accountants and managers, however. Remarkably, an increase in the complexity of cost accounting systems can improve managers' degree of goal attainment more intensively than management accountants' degree of goal attainment even though the usage types dominate the former measure.

[1238] Following *Chenhall* (2003), p. 129, cost accounting can be seen as a management control system.

These latter findings facilitate the derivation of **practical recommendations**. The results reveal that Anglophone and domestic German subsidiaries willing to improve the information usefulness of their cost accounting systems (degree of goal attainment) may wish to consider managers' information needs very carefully before adjusting a cost accounting system. Rather than merely adapting the design of the cost accounting system, it seems crucial to ensure that cost information is applicable for managerial decision-making. Thereby, management accountants need to warrant that managers perceive the ability to **apply cost information into ex-ante decision-making** rather than ex-post decision-rationalisation. Since section 6.2 shows that the rationalising use of information is particularly aligned with the researched companies' parents, however, this suggestion requires considerable interaction between the management accountants and the managers in subsidiaries with the corporate employees.

With respect to the design of the cost accounting system, the *Anglophone subsidiaries* tend to prefer more complex cost accounting systems than allowed by the parent company and suggested by other contextual factors. Accordingly, adjustments to these companies' **cost centre accounting** systems are good levers to increase the performance of cost accounting. Since the design of cost accounting is contingent on the parent companies, however, these findings merely mean that Anglophone subsidiaries may wish to engage into a discussion whether a redesign of their cost centre accounting system is perceived feasible by the corporate level. Moreover, it is interesting to find that only for managers' performance assessments, there are negative effects of complexity sub-scores (in dataset 3). Hence, in these companies, **management accountants should particularly interact with their managers** during a potential redesign of their cost accounting system. In this light, it becomes important that the extent of potential performance improvements through a more complex cost accounting system is relatively higher for managers' degree of goal attainment. If only management accountants' performance assessment triggered a decision whether to alter a cost accounting system, the favourability of such a choice would be less appealing.

For the *domestic German subsidiaries*, complex cost centre and cost object accounting systems are good performance levers. Moreover, the results show rather consistently that managers and management accountants prefer less complex **cost type accounting** systems. This finding especially holds for the level of satisfaction. Nevertheless, a recommendation to decrease the complexity of cost type accounting is of value for the degree of goal attainment as well. A complex cost type accounting impinges the diagnostic use of cost information (section 6.2.2). This usage type in turn, increases the degree of goal attainment and mediates the effect of the complexity scores (section 6.3.2.2). Moreover, the fact that management accountants' level of satisfaction can be associated to a greater variety of complexity sub-scores suggests that a close **interaction between managers and management accountants** during a potential redesign of a cost accounting system is important for these companies as well. This assertion can be reinforced by the discovery that the selection bias in the domestic German subsidiaries (dataset 3) is associated with apparent issues regarding the decision usefulness of cost information in the companies that handed in questionnaire A only (dataset 5). Despite a focus on other information than costs, this suggests that the decision relevance of cost information in the firms of dataset 5 has to be ensured through thorough interactions of the management accountants and the managers. Other than that, the domestic German subsidiaries assess the performance of their cost accounting systems comparably high if the system reflects the companies' economic *and* institutional environment (section 6.3.2.3). Hence, the domestic German subsidiaries can be urged to compromise their economic context (e.g. level of product diversity or available cost accounting resources) *and* their parents' directives to determine the optimal level of complexity for their cost accounting systems.

7 Conclusions and outlook

7.1 Main findings and implications

This study investigated cost accounting systems in the population of approximately 500 small- to medium-sized Anglophone subsidiaries in the German manufacturing industry. Moreover, an equally large control group of domestic German subsidiaries from the same industry was regarded. In all these subsidiaries, the head of management accounting was invited to respond to a questionnaire on the design of cost accounting systems. In addition, a board member in the subsidiaries was asked to respond to a questionnaire on the use of cost information during the management process. This research design was motivated by differences of Anglophone and German cost accounting traditions and a superficial understanding of cost accounting in subsidiaries. Based on these premises, six research questions were analysed. The main findings for these questions and their implications for practitioners and researchers are presented in this section.

RQ (1a)	**Are there differences with respect to the design of cost accounting systems in Anglophone and domestic subsidiaries in Germany?**

For a sample of 110 Anglophone and 89 domestic German subsidiaries (dataset 1), sections 6.1.1 and 6.1.2.2 show that the **Anglophone subsidiaries have significantly less complex cost accounting systems** than their domestic German counterparts. Thus, there is affirmative evidence for research question (1a). There are differences in the design of cost accounting systems in about two thirds of the Anglophone subsidiaries in Germany if compared to domestic German firms. This result can be attributed to the transfer of Anglophone cost accounting traditions. These traditions especially prevail for the companies' number of cost types, the recognition of imputed costs, the separation of financial and management accounting information, the number of cost centres, the allocation of overhead costs from support to primary cost centres, the detail of contribution margin accounting and the analysis of cost variances on the cost object level.

These descriptive findings are the first to show reliably that Anglophone subsidiaries in Germany are characterised by Anglophone cost accounting traditions. As such, the common assertion that cross-national differences in management accounting are relevant for business practitioners in MNCs can be approved statistically by this thesis. The results are particularly relevant for **academics**. They underline the necessity for and relevance of comparative management accounting research and explorations of management accounting practices in foreign subsidiaries. Furthermore, these results sensitise **practitioners** in Anglophone multinationals which are interested in taking over or setting up business operations in Germany for the need to consider cross-national differences in cost accounting. Also, the results reveal that Anglophone companies interested in German cost accounting traditions can learn about such traditions through their subsidiaries in Germany. Several German cost accounting traditions can (still) be found in the Anglophone subsidiaries.

RQ (1b)	How do Anglophone and domestic subsidiaries in Germany use their cost information for managerial decision-making?

The use of cost information is analysed for a sample of 47 Anglophone and 45 domestic German subsidiaries (dataset 3) in section 6.2.1. In line with the rationale beyond research question 1b, it is found that cost accounting systems are sometimes only maintained to fulfil a parent company's directive irrespectively of any local information usefulness. Remarkably, this ceremonial usage type can be identified more extensively in the Anglophone subsidiaries. Besides this defiance of corporate involvements, an additional, unexpected result emerged from the data. Accordingly, the subsidiaries also respond to their parent companies' involvements by using cost information for the rationalisation of previously taken decisions only. Thereby, they seem to avoid their parent companies' cost accounting standards. As for the ceremonial use of information, the Anglophone subsidiaries are also found to use cost information more intensively in this rationalising manner than their domestic German counterparts. The latter two findings are peculiar. They indicate that **subsidiaries might avoid and defy a parent company's involvement** more extensively, if an implemented cost accounting system reflects traditions that are dissimilar from the national cost accounting traditions of the subsidiary's host country. Deplorably, the conclusiveness of these results is restricted. On the one hand, the conceptual similarity of the rationalising and the ceremonial use is more consistent for the domestic German subsidiaries. On the other hand, a participation bias can be identified for the 45 domestic German subsidiaries. Questionnaire B was returned especially by those domestic German firms that are rather satisfied with their systems and for which there appear to be fewer issues regarding the usefulness of cost information for managerial decision-making. Hence, those German subsidiaries in which cost information is used more extensively to avoid and to defy corporate involvements might not have responded in the first place. Moreover, the results from section 6.2.1 do not suggest that the two discussed usage types dominate the use of cost information in the researched subsidiaries. There is substantial evidence that the subsidiaries do indeed use cost information during the management process even though these are affected by their parent companies. This 'non-ceremonial use' of cost information cannot be differentiated for the Anglophone and the domestic German subsidiaries. Both use cost information most extensively to prepare an immediately due decision or to make experiences which aid future decision-making. As such, the findings reveal a twofold answer to research question (1b). Whereas subsidiaries do respond to corporate cost accounting initiatives by using cost information differently, the usage types which help to avoid or to defy these involvements of parent companies are not dominant. Both Anglophone and domestic German subsidiaries use cost information during the process of management in a decision facilitating and decision influencing manner.

The provided discussion is very relevant for **academics**. It highlights that it is possible to study strategic reactions of subsidiaries to parent company initiatives through large-scale survey research. Thus, previous case based evidence in this regard can be substantially improved by evidence that is more generalisable. Yet, the study is somewhat opposing previous assertions that cost information might be used differently in companies of different national origin. No such difference can be identified if different usage types are studied for German decision makers in Anglophone and domestic German subsidiaries. For **prac-**

titioners, the results uncover the ability of multinationals to assess the decision relevance of their global cost accounting systems by an investigation of the manners in which local managers use cost information. An extensive application for ex-post rationalisation suggests a reduced usefulness of cost information for subsidiaries' decision-problems.

RQ (2a)	**What determines the design of cost accounting systems in Anglophone and domestic subsidiaries in Germany?**

Section 6.1.2 reveals that finding an answer to research question (2a) is not direct and straightforward. The data from dataset 1 confirms that the studied categories of influential variables (economic determinants, institutional coercive determinants, institutional voluntary determinants and the relationship of a subsidiary and its parent company) are all important for explicative purposes. Yet, the results also show that the precise hypotheses on the determinants of cost accounting in Anglophone and domestic German subsidiaries which chapter 4 derives based on **NIS merit considerable refinement**. The identified relationships between the design of cost accounting systems and the above variables are more miscellaneous than expected from existent theoretical and empirical investigations on cost accounting in subsidiaries and business units. Furthermore, issues of reversed causality challenge the hypotheses tests.

Most conclusively, the less complex cost accounting systems in *Anglophone subsidiaries* can be aligned with the personal involvement of corporate managers. Also, further trainings for cost accountants by Anglophone institutes of management accountants such as IMA or CIMA affect the cost accounting systems in these companies. For the *domestic German companies* an unexpected finding is most remarkable. Local top managers appear to strive for a simplification of cost accounting systems these days. Also, corporate directives are found to lead to a simplification of the cost type accounting practices in these subsidiaries. Hence, the domestic German subsidiaries seem to aim at a simplification of their cost accounting systems. Beyond that, the identified interrelations are remarkably diverse. In both groups, the relationship of subsidiaries with their parent companies is influential for their cost accounting systems. It levels the influence of the parents. Yet, the effect does not consistently offset coercive institutional effects as it was expected but also tends to enforce coercive institutional effects. With respect to the economic determinants, only the extent with which management accountants apply cost information for decision-making and the information technology consistently increase the complexity of cost accounting in Anglophone and domestic German subsidiaries. Voluntary institutional determinants only prevail for the Anglophone subsidiaries. In the domestic German subsidiaries, the expected association between, e.g. university education and the design of cost accounting systems cannot be found.

Despite all deficiencies, the above answer of research question (2a) is very pertinent to **academics**. It highlights that any explication of cost accounting in subsidiaries remains inconclusive if corporate effects are not accounted for. Also, the results point up the necessity to attribute substantial efforts towards the development of theoretical positions which can explicate the interrelation of economic and institutional determinants. Thereby, this study raises several questions for future research (see section 7.3). The relevance of these findings for **practitioners** can be seen in the possibility to provide them with a prediction of the complexity that would reflect their economic and institutional surroundings. The comparison of such a predicted design with the current status quo of their cost accounting system can help practitioner to assess whether they can substantially improve their cost accounting system (see research question 3a).

RQ (2b)	**What determines the use of cost information for managerial decision-making in Anglophone and domestic subsidiaries in Germany?**

Just as the analyses of research question (2a), the attempts to explain the use of cost information in dataset 3 point out **difficulties of current organisational and business theories** to explain the use of cost information in subsidiaries. Even though all four categories of influential variables (information needs, coercive institutional determinants, the relational context and users' personal attitudes) facilitate the explanation of the usage types, the regression analyses in section 6.2.2 reject several of the derived hypotheses. As for research question (2a) this result is especially due to an underwhelming conceptualisation of the interplay between the various determinants of the use of cost information in previous research. Also, issues of reversed causality impinge the respective analyses.

Most consistently, *Anglophone companies* can ensure the application of cost information in their subsidiaries through their personal engagement whereas bureaucratic directives are rather not serving this purpose. Nevertheless, the existence of cross-national differences in cost accounting still impinges the local applicability of cost information in a decision facilitating manner. Also, a more unfavourable relational context fosters the use of cost information to avoid and to defy an imposed cost accounting system in these companies. In the *domestic German subsidiaries*, it is most notable to find the complexity of cost accounting systems to obstruct the use of cost information. As above, this finding suggests a potential development towards more simplified cost accounting procedures, especially with respect to cost type accounting in German companies. In addition, corporate cost accounting directives in these companies also prevent the thorough use of cost information in a decision facilitating manner but promote their ceremonial application. Moreover, the personal attitudes of the information users and their information needs are equally important for the use of cost information in these subsidiaries.

The implications of these results for **academics** mirror the ones discussed for research question (1b) and (2a). First, the ceremonial use is emphasised to be analysable as well as explicable through survey research. Since this usage type was merely analysed case based in prior research, these findings considerably complement the current scientific knowledge. Second, the analyses illustrate the necessity for future research to increase the theoretical explicability of the use of cost information in subsidiaries (see section 7.3). Additionally, there are two important results from research question (2b) for **practitioners**. MNCs willing to ensure the application of their cost accounting systems in subsidiaries should rely on personal rather than bureaucratic involvements. Furthermore, local managers' perceptions about the relationship of a subsidiary and its parent have to be considered by management accountants in both parent and subsidiaries to avoid an incomprehensive application of cost information for decision-making. In this regard, little distinctive pattern for Anglophone and German companies prevail.

RQ (3a)	How can Anglophone and domestic subsidiaries in Germany improve the design of their cost accounting systems?

To answer research question (3a), both management accountants (datasets 1 and 3) and managers (dataset 3) provided two assessments of their cost accounting systems. First, they revealed how satisfied they are with their systems and second, they reported how extensively they can achieve a number of cost accounting objectives (e.g. pricing, process improvements or holding employees responsible for their actions).

From a descriptive perspective, it is remarkable to find **management accountants and managers** to have similar perceptions of their cost accounting systems' performance in both groups of companies. It is equally remarkable to find that in the Anglophone companies, whose cost accounting systems are less complex than an average domestic German system, the performance of cost accounting lacks significantly behind the one of Anglophone subsidiaries which are not characterised by such cross-national differences. Above all, however, there are no differences in Anglophone and domestic German subsidiaries with respect to the performance of cost accounting. Peculiarly, this similarity holds also true for an upper bound in the level of complexity of a cost accounting system, beyond which a further refinement in the design of a cost accounting system cannot increase the system's performance. According to the data, no improvements can be realised beyond a complexity score of approximately 0.65-0.68, i.e. if around 65 %-68 % of the maximum level of complexity as defined in this study is achieved.

Interestingly, the elements of a cost accounting system, for which there are remarkable cross-national differences (see RQ (2a)), cannot be identified as the strongest levers of performance in the *Anglophone subsidiaries*. Rather, **refined cost centre accounting procedures** (i.e. the number of cost centres, the rationales for cost centre formation and the variance analysis on the cost centre level) can help to augment the performance of cost accounting systems as perceived by managers and management accountants in these subsidiaries. Moreover, it is remarkable to find that the diversity of information on cost objects (i.e. contribution margin accounting, time references in cost accounting and variance analysis on the cost object level) impinges managers' assessments of their cost accounting systems. Apparently, management accountants must reconsider the decision usefulness of having various information on the economic situation of cost objects or need to engage into a discussion with their managers to establish the decision relevance of according figures. Despite sensitising management accountants for this particularity, however, managers and management accountants seem to agree on the characteristics of their cost accounting systems which affect these systems' performance. These findings hold similarly true for both performance measures.

In the *domestic German subsidiaries*, the findings from research questions (2a) and (2b) on the preference for a **simplified cost type accounting** can be reassured through the performance analyses. In contrast, the refinement of cost centre and cost object accounting fosters managers' and management accountants' performance evaluations. Yet, one remarkable finding prevails in this regard. The performance decreasing effect of a having diverse information on the economic situation of cost objects (i.e. different categories of cost centre costs, product costing and contribution margin accounting) also prevails for the domestic German subsidiaries. Other than for the Anglophone subsidiaries, however, this finding persists for both managers and management accountants in the domestic German subsidiaries. Despite this similarity, management accountants in the domestic German subsidiaries should not disobey the key characteristics which are important to their managers. This is especially true because some of the characteristics of a cost accounting system are associated to managers' or management accountants' perceptions of the systems' performance only. Notably, the performance effects of the design of cost accounting systems in the domestic German subsidiaries can be conclusively derived for the level of satisfaction only. If these companies were to improve managers' and management accountants' degree of goal attainment, it is more important to take managers' application of cost information into account (see (3b)).

In addition, the cost accounting systems in the domestic German subsidiaries work best, if they reflect the companies' economic and institutional context. Hence, these subsidiaries should compromise their economic context and their parent company's engagement in order to derive a well performing cost accounting system. In contrast, in the Anglophone subsidiaries, cost accounting systems that are more complex than the context would predict are more suitable to achieve cost accounting objectives. These companies seem to **prefer German to Anglophone cost accounting traditions**. Hence, they may wish to discuss the information usefulness of their cost accounting systems with their parent companies.

Since the answer to research question (3a) identifies characteristics of a cost accounting system which can serve as levers to improve the systems' performance, these results are very relevant for **practitioners**. Yet, it is essential to reveal that following such suggestions in both the Anglophone and the domestic German subsidiaries requires a thorough engagement of the corresponding parent companies since these are influential for the cost accounting systems (see RQ (2a)). Though the discussion on research question (3a) is addressing practitioners, the findings are very relevant for **academics** as well. Especially the results on the performance of cost accounting systems which do or do not deviate from a contextual prediction are very meaningful. Apparently, the contingency approach, which argues that contextual variables are reflected in a company's internal structures for the means of (economic) efficiency, has difficulties in explaining cost accounting systems in subsidiaries if these are confronted by alternative cost accounting traditions.

RQ (3b)	How can Anglophone and domestic subsidiaries in Germany improve the use of cost information in managerial decision-making?

To find an answer to research question (3b), the performance metrics (level of satisfaction and degree of goal attainment) are associated with the individual types of cost information use included in this study.

In the *Anglophone subsidiaries*, these usage types indeed affect management accountants' and managers' performance evaluations. Consistently, both acknowledge that the instrumental/conceptual use of cost information can increase a system's performance. Moreover, both perceive a performance increasing effect of the **ceremonial use** of cost information. For this latter result, there are two potential explanations. On the one hand, it might indicate that a necessity to apply cost accounting systems in a ceremonial manner leads to the use of alternative information systems in subsidiaries. On the other hand, it could reveal that the Anglophone subsidiaries do not use their entire cost accounting system in a ceremonial manner but defy only certain pieces of cost information in order to be able to focus on the most relevant ones. In the *domestic German subsidiaries*, the results show that both management accountants and managers consider the use of cost information for their degree of goal attainment only. Thereby, the use of cost information to influence and control subordinates' decision-making (**diagnostic use**) is found to be a strong lever of performance. The satisfaction with cost accounting systems in domestic German subsidiaries relies more heavily on the complexity of the systems. Moreover, there is some evidence in both groups of companies that the application of cost information for ex-post decision **rationalisation** decreases managers' evaluation of their cost accounting system.

There is one very remarkable finding with respect to the use of cost information for the domestic German subsidiaries. As introduced, for the degree of goal attainment both management accountants and managers in dataset 3 perceive the use of cost information more relevant than the design of their cost accounting systems. In this context, the companies from dataset 1 that did not return questionnaire B are found to have a lower degree of goal attainment than their counterparts from dataset 3. Also, management accountants' degree of goal attainment can be associated to the design of cost accounting systems in dataset 1, whereas this is not the case for dataset 3. This suggests that there are issues with respect to the use of cost information for decision-making in the domestic German companies that did not hand in questionnaire B. Thus, the management accountants in these companies should **reconsider the information usefulness of their cost accounting systems**, have to comprehend their managers' information needs more thoroughly or need to explain the decision relevance of cost information to their managers more conclusively.

In addition to these recommendations for **practitioners** in domestic German subsidiaries, the above findings highlight that management accountants in both groups of companies should comprehend how their managers use cost information and explore the corresponding information needs to increase the performance of their cost accounting systems. Hence, the above suggestion according to which management accountants should not lose sight of managers' perspectives during the improvement of cost accounting systems can be reassured at this point. This argument can be further enforced by the result that in the Anglophone subsidiaries changes of the cost accounting systems can improve the performance assessments of managers more extensively than the one of management accountants. Despite these general assertions, recommending specific usage types would be of little practical relevance. The specific dependence of individual usage types on managers' preferences, information needs and especially the involvement of the parent company would prevent the unconditional applicability of such recommendations. This study responds to the various calls for more research on the use of management accounting information. As such, the findings are important for **academics** as well. Not only does this study contribute thoroughly to the pragmatic research objective but it also paves the way for future research projects which are illustrated in section 7.3.

7.2 Limitations

This study is subject to several limitations. These arise from the chosen research design, the quality of the obtained data and the applied methods of data analysis.

Limitations of the research design

The empirical results uncover a limitation of this study which can be attributed to the applied **theoretical basis**. Despite ensuring the relevance of the compendium of explicatory variables determined from the applied positions (NIS and TEA), the results in chapter 6 show that existent theoretical considerations on cost accounting systems in subsidiaries and business units cannot explain the interaction of the various influential factors. This theoretical deficiency limits this study's hypotheses development and the rigour of the statistical analysis. Being able to identify this deficiency, however, arises from conducting this research. Hence, the revelation of a theoretical limitation can be equally seen as a particular strength of this project. The findings contribute to the refinement of the explanatory power of NIS for the analysis of MNC as called for by *Kostova et al.* (2008).

Another limitation originates in the empirical **survey strategy**. In contrast to an experimental study, the survey method cannot isolate the effect that a determinant has on a research object. Only experimental research can ensure that the identified interactions between an explanans and its explanandum are thoroughly isolated.[1239] As such, the study's ability to extract explanations for the design and use of cost information is restricted. Yet, the various robustness checks performed throughout this study reveal a sufficient reliability of explanatory analyses.

Moreover, the **sample selection** limits this study's results. The identification of the German control group could have been improved through the application of statistical methods (propensity scoring[1240]). Because the stratified sample is formed through a similarly multi-criterial, yet manual procedure, however, such scoring models might have merely improved the intersubjective documentation of the sample selection procedure. More critical are the applied sample selection criteria. Essentially, the results are only valid for Anglophone subsidiaries from the manufacturing industry in Germany with 150-2,000 employees and the respectively determined domestic German stratified sample. The results can neither be generalised to a wider population of larger Anglophone subsidiaries (from other industries or in other countries), nor do they represent the population of domestic German subsidiaries or apply to foreign subsidiaries of German companies. Assuming that there might be similar results for Anglophone multinationals operating in for instance, Japan or for subsidiaries of German groups in the USA or the UK remains hypothetical and open for exploration.

Also linked to the *sample selection*, the conjoint analysis of various manufacturing sub-industries and foreign subsidiaries from the USA as well as five Commonwealth countries can be argued to limit the conclusiveness of the results. Potentially, unattended effects stemming from industrial sub-categories or the different nations conceal certain interrelations in the data. Nevertheless, this broad focus was essential to ensure a reasonably large

---

[1239] Cf. *Kubicek* (1975), p. 67ff.; *Birnberg et al.* (1990), p. 35; *Rack/Christophersen* (2009), p. 18f.
[1240] Cf. e.g. *Rosenbaum/Rubin* (1985), p. 33ff.

population of Anglophone subsidiaries in Germany. Several robustness checks reveal unimportant effects of the conjoint analysis of various Anglophone companies for the validity of the findings on the complexity of cost accounting systems[1241] and the use of cost information.[1242] Also, industrial effects seem rather unlikely since the distribution of subindustries does not vary between the Anglophone and the domestic German sample[1243] and because such effects were partially covered through the control variables on the subsidiaries' size.[1244] Hence, the severity of this limitation is restricted.

Limitations due to data quality

The constructs for the dependent and independent variables were mostly surveyed through multiple items in this study. During the discussion of the according **measurement models**, the question is raised, what differentiates a manifest from a latent construct. Though many of the constructs included in this study are regarded as rather manifest (e.g. the cost accounting system in a company or the diversity in products and the production processes), they cannot be measured by a single item. Considering a respective discussion by *Diamantopoulos/Riefler* (2008), these 'measurement models' are thus seen as formative definitions of these constructs. Thereby, numerical assessments of a potential measurement error are excluded due to their inappropriateness and a lack of verifying alternative measures. This procedure can be criticised for the waived application of quantitative reliability assessments. In line with the conceived development of the questionnaires, however, the correlation analyses showed that the according 'measurement models' are of reasonable nomological validity. Also, the discussion on appropriate tests for different measurement models is only recently evolving in management accounting research.[1245] As such, the extent to which the applied procedure restricts this study's results remains limited.

In addition to these measurement issues, there are additional sources that potentially limit the reliability of this study's results. Even though the applied Harman-test (section 5.3.1) finds no indication for the presence of a **common method bias**, the design of the questionnaires (section 5.2) cannot exclude the risk that the identified determinants of the complexity of cost accounting systems are associated to the single source of the dependent and independent variables. Yet, such an effect appears rather unlikely. The analyses of the

---

1241 Analysing the robustness of the results in Table 6-38 (section 6.1.1) reveals US subsidiaries to have insignificantly less complex systems than Commonwealth firms (one-tailed t-test, p-value = 0.11). Analysing the robustness of Table 6-53 and Table 6-55 (section 6.1.2) by controlling for the US subsidiaries uncovers little differences in the explicatory factors. Most remarkably, the perceived environmental uncertainty loses its significance.

1242 Considering the sample distribution does not affect the results in section 6.2.1. Though the Commonwealth countries use cost information more extensively, the differences are insignificant, except for the diagnostic use. Analysing the robustness of Table 6-55 (section 6.2.2) by controlling for the US subsidiaries points out only one difference in the reported significances. For the rationalising use, managers' preferences gain a significant effect.

1243 Cf. Appendix 3.

1244 Cf. section 5.2.4, p. 147.

1245 For the implicit coverage of measurement models in management accounting research, cf. e.g. *Bisbe et al.* (2007), p. 800, or *Schoute* (2009), p. 214.

usage types and the performance metrics are particularly in line with the findings for the complexity scores. Since the usage types and the performance measures are analysed based on information from different sources (questionnaire A and questionnaire B), a bias in the results for the complexity scores is improbable, too. In contrast, the results of questionnaire B (usage types) are indeed subject to a **participation bias** in the domestic German sample. This reduces the generalisability of the respective results. This bias, however, led to the revelation of interesting insights on the meaning of the rationalising usage type and emphasises potential issues with respect to the information usefulness in domestic German companies. As such, despite restricting the conclusiveness of the findings, the bias facilitates the determination of various implications. These merit future validation, of course.

Limitations due to data analysis

To test its hypotheses, this study largely applies linear regression models. Though this technique could be reasonably justified, it limits the analysis to **linear interrelations** between the dependent and independent variables. One deficiency of this procedure becomes very apparent for the analyses of the performance effects. Identifying the performance of cost accounting systems to stagnate if these systems reach a certain level of complexity (upper bound), cannot be included conclusively in the subsequent regression analyses. As such, it remains to be explored whether the recommendations given in section 7.1 on how to improve the researched companies' cost accounting systems need clarification because they might be valid for a certain range of the identified complexity sub-scores only. Potentially, the negative effect of, for example, contribution margin accounting on the performance measures in the domestic German companies is relevant only after a certain level of refinement has been reached in this regard. Another limitation, which is associated to regression models, is the problem of reversed causalities (i.e. endogeneity). This problem especially conceals the effects of institutional coercive effects on the design of cost accounting systems and the use of cost information in the Anglophone subsidiaries.

The limitation of the this study's theoretical basis required a discussion of various determinants in sections 6.1.2, 6.2.2 and 6.3.2 for which substantial evidence exists for a hypothesis rejection due to a reversed sign of the regression coefficient. In order to do so, the diamond (#) is introduced to tag that an applied t-test actually rejects the posed hypotheses rather than its Null-hypothesis. This procedure limits the rigour in the application of the **epistemological positions of critical rationalism**. Nevertheless, the conclusions drawn from the respective findings are well in line with *Popper*'s suggestion to falsify a current state of knowledge. By following the applied procedure, the study merely takes a further step and reveals a refined understanding of cost accounting in subsidiaries, which merits future falsification.

7.3 Perspectives on future research

This study reveals the necessity of future research on a variety of issues regarding cost accounting in subsidiaries, or more generally, in groups. Moreover, two of this study's limitations detect the importance of future research on theoretical positions in and the methodological rigour of management accounting research.

Theoretical positions and the methodological rigour of management accounting research

For the organisation and business theories applied, there are two peculiar findings in this study. First, the results on performance effects of contextually adapted cost accounting systems question the relevance of the contingency approach for the investigation of foreign subsidiaries' exposure to diverging cost accounting traditions. This finding accentuates the theoretical shortcomings of the contingency approach.[1246] It sensitises future management accounting researchers who wish to rely on this business '*theory*' for explanatory purposes for essential adjustments to its viewpoint: During the analysis of subsidiaries or business units, the explanation of contextually adequate structures require to broaden the understanding of economic '*rationality*' in the contingency approach. Accordingly, the fulfilment of corporate directives would need to be '*rational*'. Such an understanding, however, aligns this approach with the discussion on the social constructivistic understanding of rationality that is debated in the light of NIS (section 4.1.3). Hence, this finding sensitises future researchers on a potentially **low explanatory power of the contingency approach** in comparison to other business theories. This assertion merits future research.

Second, the discussion throughout sections 6.1.2 and 6.2.2 reveal a lack of theoretical understanding regarding the determinants of the design of cost accounting systems and the use of cost information in subsidiaries. This result can be seen in the light of *Kostova et al.* (2008) who invite researchers to engage in assessments of the applicability of NIS for the analysis of MNCs. Accordingly, the extended version of **NIS** applied in this study can indeed explicate which categories of variables determine the design of cost accounting systems and the use of cost information in Anglophone and domestic subsidiaries in Germany. Yet, the applied theoretical positions **need considerable refinement**. Most relevantly, future conceptual and empirical research should establish the interaction of institutional, economic and relational variables. According calls are long known in the context of human resource management (cf. *Gooderham et al.* (1999), p. 526ff.).[1247] As such, this discipline might provide a potential starting point for management accounting researchers. Also, the normative considerations by *Modell* (2002), p. 659, on the interrelation of institutional and economic variables may guide such a refinement. Thereby, special attention should be directed to the differentiation of coercive institutional variables into personal and bureaucratic controls.

From a methodological perspective, section 7.2 reveals a limitation of this study regarding the quantitative reliability assessments of its constructs. The section attributed this limitation to a difficulty in identifying thorough considerations of management accounting scholars on the differences of **latent and manifest management accounting constructs**. Hence, future research on measurement models in management accounting research such as *Bisbe et al.* (2007), p. 800, or *Schoute* (2009), p. 214, would be fruitful. Such considerations could transfer the refined debate on measurement models known from marketing

---

[1246] Cf. *Jones* (1985), p. 321; *Granlund* (2001), p. 145; *Bhimani* (2004), p. 581; *Major/Hopper* (2005), p. 225.

[1247] Similarly, cf. *Tempel/Walgenbach* (2012), p. 230ff.

scholars (sections 5.1 and 5.4.1) to a management accounting context. Thereby, it should be clarified what constitutes a latent construct in management accounting research. According studies could explicate whether readily observable management accounting systems such as cost accounting systems, which cannot be measured by a single item scale, must be subject to numerical reliability assessments from, e.g. classical test theory.

Research on cost accounting in groups

This study indicates that Anglophone subsidiaries in Germany prefer to deviate from their parent companies' directives on cost accounting to improve the usefulness of their cost information for decision-making. This subsidiary standpoint has to be associated to the corresponding **perspective of** Anglophone **parent companies**. From the viewpoint of an Anglophone multinational, it might be acceptable that local cost accounting systems remain of little information usefulness as long as the information's practicability on the corporate level offsets such deficiencies. Hence, future research on cost accounting in multinationals should engage into a comparison of the performance of cost accounting systems as perceived by both subsidiary and corporate managers. Moreover, according research projects can strive for an explanation of the level of corporate involvement into subsidiaries' cost accounting systems. The extent to which a parent company is involved in its subsidiaries serves merely as an explicatory variable in this study. Future research should engage into an explanation of this level to understand better why parent companies influence their subsidiaries. This latter assertion holds true for German companies with and without cross-border operations, as well. Also, it would be fruitful to uncover whether German-owned subsidiaries in, e.g. the US or the UK are characterised by German cost accounting traditions and whether the local workforce is in favour of these traditions.

Moreover, this study urges future empirical researchers on cost accounting to consider organisational characteristics more thoroughly. This study's results uncover two deficiencies of the current tendency to regard business units for cost accounting research. The assumption that cost accounting in business units can be analysed better than in entire firms can be questioned due to the unifying efforts of corporate levels. Also, the tendency to look at business units without acknowledging the effect of corporate levels has to be criticised. Hence, two pathways for future research arise. First, there is a need to uncover the effect of **functionally or geographically oriented economic structures** for cost accounting in organisations. Second, corporate influences should be included in the analysis of cost accounting in a sample of business units to improve the early evidence by *Gosselin* (1997) that in business units the corporate level is of acknowledgeable importance for cost accounting as well.

By conducting the research projects called for in the above two paragraphs, future scholars can improve the alignment of the conflicting findings on cost accounting systems in subsidiaries (uniformity) and in economic organisational structures (non-uniformity) as revealed in section 3.2.2. Thereby it appears essential to focus not only on cross-sectional but also **panel-data analysis** to discover how, e.g. the effect of a parent company on its affiliates evolves over time. Such foci could also overcome the raise issue of reversed causality that limits this study.

In addition to these perspectives on future research, the discoveries on the design of cost accounting systems in this study's samples as well as the corresponding conceptual descriptions of cross-national differences in cost accounting reveal a potential for future comparative research on **cost accounting in domestic German and domestic Anglophone companies**. Accordingly, it would be revealing to discover the similarities and differences in, for example, the first and second stage overhead allocation procedures, the level of variance analysis or the types of different cost objects that characterise cost accounting in these geographical areas more conclusively.

The results on the **use of cost information** uncover three important pathways for future research. First, there is a need for future studies comparing the application of cost information in **subsidiaries and single companies**. In these studies, special attention should be directed to information users' personal attitudes. It remains to be explored whether the extent to which information users' personality affects their use of cost information for decision-making actually depends on coercive effects of, for example, a parent company as it is suggested in this study. Second, the investigation of different usage types could centre on the analysis of alternative manners in which managers in subsidiaries respond to corporately induced information systems. In this study, the **rationalising and the ceremonial usage types** prevail as most relevant for such an analysis since they are apparently capable to capture the strategic responses with which managers can 'tackle' institutional involvements. During such considerations, it would be very interesting to reveal the existence and the effect of alternative information systems ('shadow systems') in subsidiaries. Thereby, this study's findings on the diverging performance effects of the ceremonial and the rationalising usage in the Anglophone subsidiaries could potentially be clarified. Also, such a focus may be light shedding for the effect of the relational context. As revealed in section 6.1.3, the diversity of the findings on the determinants of the complexity of cost accounting might reflect that subsidiaries adjust their use of cost information in response to an unfavourable relational context more extensively than the design of their cost accounting systems. Third, this study's results question the validity of the assumption that cost information is **used differently in organisations of different national background**. Yet, because there is little evidence on the use of cost information in domestic Anglophone companies, this result remains far from being conclusive. Hence, it would be interesting to discover the different manners in which domestic Anglophone companies use cost information. Alternatively, future research on the cross-national differences in the use of cost information could take a closer look on the actual pieces of information used for certain decisions because the analysis of usage types might be too broad to discover according differences.

In addition to future research on the design of cost accounting systems and the use of cost information, sections 4.2.3 and 6.3.1 reveal that there are multiple research opportunities regarding the **performance of cost accounting**. Future scholars could investigate which of the variables that determine the design of cost accounting systems and the use of cost information are also levers to improve the performance of cost accounting systems. Exemplarily, they could analyse whether the performance of cost accounting in Anglophone subsidiaries can be improved by the application of better information technologies. On the other hand, it appears essential to consider in more detail how to explain a perception gap between the users and preparers of management accounting information. In this study, corresponding explications by *Bhimani* (2003) such as the interaction of management accountants and managers could be underlined as being plausible. Yet, future research is needed to analyse these relationships in statistical terms.

By and large, this study contributes considerably to the current state of knowledge on the consequences of cross-national differences in cost accounting for multinationals as well as the issue of management accounting in subsidiaries. The findings further the understanding of cost accounting in subsidiaries on a mezzo and micro level. They also illustrate remarkable insights into the performance of cost accounting systems. Simultaneously, the study paves the way for future research on cross-national differences in cost accounting, the use of cost information and the interaction of cost accounting and organisational hierarchies. Much is yet to be explored on this matter.

Appendix

Appendix 1: Questionnaire A

WESTFÄLISCHE
WILHELMS-UNIVERSITÄT
MÜNSTER

IUR
Chair of International
Accounting
Prof. Dr. Peter Kajüter

Cost Accounting in German Subsidiaries of Anglophone Firms

Motivation

This questionnaire is part of a research project conducted by the Chair of International Accounting at the University of Münster (Germany). The project's objective is to compare cost accounting systems in German subsidiaries of Anglophone companies with cost accounting systems in domestic German companies. More specifically, it shall be explored whether an alignment of cost accounting systems with the traditions known from a parent company's home or a subsidiary's host country has implications for the success of subsidiaries' cost accounting systems. In order to facilitate this analysis, it will also be explored how cost information serves for managerial decision-making.

Contents:

Please note:

This research is completely confidential. All data from the questionnaire will be aggregated and then used for statistical purposes only. Any data, which would allow the identification of your business, will thus be eliminated before being published. A non-disclosure agreement will be signed upon request.

Please mark the appropriate response alternative(s) with an "x" or write in the designated boxes.

In this questionnaire, several questions are concerned with your company's parent company. Please answer these questions with respect to the organisation that is the head of the group, which your company is associated to (i.e. your company's ultimate owner).

Fax number for return of survey: +49 / 251 / 83 22848

If you have any questions, please do not hesitate to contact:

Moritz Schröder

e-mail: moritz.schroeder@wiwi.uni-muenster.de

phone: +49/ 251/ 83 22677

Section A – Your company's profile

A.1 **Which of the following corporate functions does your company perform?** (Multiple answers are possible)

☐ Research & Development ☐ Procurement ☐ Production ☐ Sales ☐ Other (please specify): ________________

A.2 **Please indicate the following figures for the last financial year of your company:**

Average number of employees [full-time equivalents (FTEs)]: ___________ (FTEs)

Number of subsidiary companies directly owned by your company: ___________ (subsidiaries)

A.3 **How predictable are the developments in your company's environment?**
(Consider e.g. manufacturing technology, competitors' actions, market demand, product attributes/design, raw material availability, raw material prices, government regulation and labour union actions.)

1 = very unpredictable,..............................., very predictable = 7

1	2	3	4	5	6	7
☐	☐	☐	☐	☐	☐	☐

A.4 **To what extent do the following statements describe your company's products?**

1 = not at all, ..., completely =7

	1	2	3	4	5	6	7	N/A
Most products require about the same processes to be designed, manufactured and distributed.	☐	☐	☐	☐	☐	☐	☐	☐
There are major differences in product volumes and lot sizes.	☐	☐	☐	☐	☐	☐	☐	☐
Utilisation of support departments (e.g. inventory management or in-house logistics) is about the same for each product.	☐	☐	☐	☐	☐	☐	☐	☐

A.5 **Which information technology does your company mostly apply for management accounting purposes?**

Most information is handled through the application of: (Please tick <u>one</u> check-box only.)

☐ an enterprise resource planning system (e.g. SAP) ☐ spread sheets (e.g. Microsoft Excel).

How precisely does the information technology, which your company mostly applies for management accounting purposes, picture the resource consumption that actually takes place in your company?

1 = very imprecisely,..............................., very precisely = 7

1	2	3	4	5	6	7
☐	☐	☐	☐	☐	☐	☐

A.6 **How many expatriate managers worked for your company's management accounting function during the last financial year?**

____ (FTEs) [Expatriate managers are employees who were delegated by your parent company to work for your company]

A.7 **To what extent do the following statements describe your company?**

1 = not at all,........................, completely = 7

	1	2	3	4	5	6	7	N/A
The number of employees responsible for cost accounting is appropriate to run and enhance the company's cost accounting system.	☐	☐	☐	☐	☐	☐	☐	☐
The employees responsible for cost accounting are particularly qualified to run and enhance the company's cost accounting system.	☐	☐	☐	☐	☐	☐	☐	☐
The employees responsible for cost accounting receive strong support from <u>our company's</u> top management.	☐	☐	☐	☐	☐	☐	☐	☐
The employees responsible for cost accounting receive strong support from <u>our parent company's</u> top management.	☐	☐	☐	☐	☐	☐	☐	☐

A.8 **Where did the employees responsible for cost accounting in your company acquire <u>most of the knowledge</u> they need to fulfill their tasks?** (Please tick <u>one</u> check-box only.)

Universities/Colleges located in:

☐ German-speaking countries (GER, A, CH)
☐ Anglophone countries (USA, CAN, UK, NZ, AUS, ZA)
☐ Japan
☐ Another country

At work "learning by doing" in companies located in:

☐ German-speaking countries (GER, A, CH)
☐ Anglophone countries (USA, CAN, UK, NZ, AUS, ZA)
☐ Japan
☐ Another country

A.9 **How intensively do the employees responsible for cost accounting in your company further their qualification through professional institutes of management accountants from the following geographical areas?**

1 = not at all,..........................., very intensively = 7

	1	2	3	4	5	6	7
German-speaking countries (e.g. Internationaler Controller Verein)	☐	☐	☐	☐	☐	☐	☐
Anglophone countries (e.g. Chartered Institute of Management Accountants)	☐	☐	☐	☐	☐	☐	☐
Japan (e.g. Japanese Association of Management Accounting)	☐	☐	☐	☐	☐	☐	☐

Section B.1 – Conceptual design of the cost accounting system

B.1 **Does your company have two separated datasets for financial reporting and for cost accounting (so-called two-book system or dual accounting system)?**

☐ Yes ☐ No ➔ **If no, please continue with B.2.**

To what extent is the financial reporting information adjusted to derive the dataset for cost accounting?

1 = no adjustments are being made,..........................., multiple adjustments are being made = 7

1	2	3	4	5	6	7	N/A
☐	☐	☐	☐	☐	☐	☐	☐

B.2 **How many primary cost types does your company have?**

________(primary cost types)

(Each of these cost items represents the consumption of an externally obtained resource that is accounted for separately in the cost accounting system, e.g. cost of steal or lease costs.)

B.3 **Imputed costs** are costs that are neither conform to actual cash flows nor to financial reporting requirements. They are recognised specifically for cost accounting purposes. Thereby the actual consumption of resources can be captured more precisely. There are two main types of imputed costs:

- Imputed depreciation is calculated on replacement costs instead of historical costs. It shall ensure a maintenance of assets.
- Imputed interest comprises the cost of capital required by investors (opportunity cost).

To what extent do you apply the following imputed costs?

Imputed depreciation	☐ Not at all	☐ In separate calculations only	☐ As part of regular cost accounting
Imputed interest	☐ Not at all	☐ In separate calculations only	☐ As part of regular cost accounting

B.4 The **assignment of costs** to cost objects depends on the characteristics of the assigned cost types. The following figure illustrates the assignment of costs. **Direct costs** (e.g. direct material or direct labour costs) can be traced unambiguously to cost objects. **Indirect costs** (e.g. depreciation or overhead costs) have to be allocated by an allocation rule. This rule-based allocation of indirect costs can be facilitated by identifying areas of cost incurrence (known as cost centres or cost pools in English and *Kostenstelle* in German).

Areas of cost incurrence that facilitate the allocation of indirect costs shall be referred to as **cost centres** hereafter. If these constructs are known by a different label in your company, please answer the following questions accordingly.

The following questions will be answered with respect to constructs known as:

☐ Cost centres ☐ Cost pools ☐ Kostenstelle ☐ Other (please specify): ________________

B.5 **To what extent are cost centres within your company formed to:**

1 = not at all,............................., completely = 7

	1	2	3	4	5	6	7	N/A
define areas of responsibility?	☐	☐	☐	☐	☐	☐	☐	☐
identify localities of cost incurrence?	☐	☐	☐	☐	☐	☐	☐	☐
plan and control costs?	☐	☐	☐	☐	☐	☐	☐	☐
aggregate homogeneous overhead costs?	☐	☐	☐	☐	☐	☐	☐	☐
aggregate heterogeneous overhead costs?	☐	☐	☐	☐	☐	☐	☐	☐
assign overhead costs to the company's products?	☐	☐	☐	☐	☐	☐	☐	☐
establish causal relations between cost incurrence and the company's products?	☐	☐	☐	☐	☐	☐	☐	☐

B.6 **Please indicate the following for your company:**

Number of cost centres:____________

_______% thereof are <u>primary cost centres</u>. These centres summarise costs of organisational areas that **do handle** the company's products **directly**.

\+ _______% thereof are <u>support cost centres</u>. These centres summarise costs of organisational areas that support the manufacturing process but **do *not* handle** the company's products **directly**.

= 100 %

Does your company namely distinguish between primary and support cost centres?

☐ Yes ☐ No

B.7 **Are costs that are accumulated within support cost centres allocated to primary cost centres?**

☐ Yes ☐ No ➔ **If not, please continue with B.10.**

B.8 **Are the following bases used to allocate costs from support cost centres to primary cost centres?**

Please rank the top three of all applied allocation bases in accordance to the proportion of the total indirect costs allocated to primary cost centres. (1 = most heavily applied basis, 2 = second most heavily applied basis, 3 = third most heavily applied basis)

		Yes	No	Rank
Direct material <u>costs</u>		☐	☐	
Direct labour <u>costs</u>		☐	☐	
Space based measures	(e.g. m^2 of space leased or m^3 of water consumed)	☐	☐	
Weight based measures	(e.g. kg of resources or products handled)	☐	☐	
Time based measures	(e.g. labour or machine hours)	☐	☐	
Other physical unit based measures	(e.g. kWh, joules)	☐	☐	
The execution of a specific activity	(e.g. number of setups or inspections)	☐	☐	
The duration of a specific activity	(e.g. number of setup or inspection *minutes*)	☐	☐	

B.9 **How many different measures are applied in your company to allocate costs from support cost centres to primary cost centres?**

1 measure	2	3	4	5	More than 5 measures (please indicate):
☐	☐	☐	☐	☐	

B.10 **Are the following bases used to allocate costs from primary cost centres to products?**

Please rank the top three of all applied allocation bases in accordance to the proportion of the total indirect costs allocated to products. (1 = most heavily applied basis, 2 = second most heavily applied basis, 3 = third most heavily applied basis)

		Yes	No	Rank
Direct material <u>costs</u>		☐	☐	
Direct labour <u>costs</u>		☐	☐	
Space based measures	(e.g. m^2 of space leased or m^3 of water consumed)	☐	☐	
Weight based measures	(e.g. kg of resources or products handled)	☐	☐	
Time based measures	(e.g. labour or machine hours)	☐	☐	
Other physical unit based measures	(e.g. kWh, joules)	☐	☐	
The execution of a specific activity	(e.g. number of setups or inspections)	☐	☐	
The duration of a specific activity	(e.g. number of setup or inspection *minutes*)	☐	☐	

B.11 **How many different measures are applied in your company to allocate costs from primary cost centres to products?**

1 measure	2	3	4	5	More than 5 measures (please indicate):
☐	☐	☐	☐	☐	

B.12 **In how many primary cost centres are costs categorised with respect to the following characteristics?**

	1 = in no cost centre,..., in all cost centres =7							
	1	2	3	4	5	6	7	N/A
Costs' variability with respect to final outputs	☐	☐	☐	☐	☐	☐	☐	☐
Costs' inventoriability	☐	☐	☐	☐	☐	☐	☐	☐
Costs' relatedness to manufacturing [i.e. (non-)manufacturing costs]	☐	☐	☐	☐	☐	☐	☐	☐
Costs' original occurrence in the cost centre [i.e. primary and secondary costs]	☐	☐	☐	☐	☐	☐	☐	☐
Costs' relatedness to idle capacity / used capacity	☐	☐	☐	☐	☐	☐	☐	☐

B.13	**How intensively does your company apply activity based costing in the following departments to allocate overhead costs?**	1 = not at all........., very intensively =7							
		1	2	3	4	5	6	7	N/A
	Manufacturing departments	☐	☐	☐	☐	☐	☐	☐	☐
	Non-manufacturing departments	☐	☐	☐	☐	☐	☐	☐	☐

B.14	**For how many of the following objects are unit costs computed as part of regular cost accounting?**	1 = for none of these,..., for all of these = 7							
		1	2	3	4	5	6	7	N/A
	Final products (per unit)	☐	☐	☐	☐	☐	☐	☐	☐
	Product lines	☐	☐	☐	☐	☐	☐	☐	☐
	Customers	☐	☐	☐	☐	☐	☐	☐	☐
	Scrap/spoilage	☐	☐	☐	☐	☐	☐	☐	☐

B.15 **How are <u>product costs</u> (per unit) determined as part of regular cost accounting? Please consider the following characteristics:**

Variability (with respect to final output)	☐ Only on a variable cost basis	☐ Only on a full cost basis	☐ On both bases
Reference to manufacturing processes	☐ Only on a manufacturing cost basis	☐ Only on a manufacturing and non-manufacturing cost basis	☐ On both bases
Inventoriability	☐ Only on an inventoriable cost basis	☐ Only on an inventoriable and non-inventoriable cost basis	☐ On both bases

B.16	**For how many <u>products</u> are the following costs determined?**	1 = for no product,..., for all products = 7							
		1	2	3	4	5	6	7	N/A
	Actual costs (occurred costs)	☐	☐	☐	☐	☐	☐	☐	☐
	Normal costs (averaged costs)	☐	☐	☐	☐	☐	☐	☐	☐
	Standard costs (planned costs)	☐	☐	☐	☐	☐	☐	☐	☐
	Target costs (allowable costs derived from market prices)	☐	☐	☐	☐	☐	☐	☐	☐

B.17 **Contribution margin accounting** can facilitate the analysis of products' profitability. In traditional direct costing, contribution margins for cost objects are determined as sales less variable costs. Fixed costs are subtracted as a lump sum thereafter. Hence, only one contribution margin (**CM I**) is calculated (see left example below). If fixed costs are broken down in accordance to a least assignable level (e.g. product or plant level), additional contribution margins (**CM II, CM III, CM IV**, etc.) can be distinguished (see right example below).

Example of CM accounting under traditional direct costing

	Product A	Product B	Total
Sales	120,000 €	100,000 €	220,000 €
- Variable costs	80,000 €	50,000 €	130,000 €
= CM I	**40,000 €**	**50,000 €**	**90,000 €**
- Fixed costs	-	-	70,000 €
= Net operating income	-	-	20,000 €

Example of refined CM accounting

	Product A	Product B	Total
Sales	120,000 €	100,000 €	220,000 €
- Variable costs	80,000 €	50,000 €	130,000 €
= CM I	**40,000 €**	**50,000 €**	**90,000 €**
- Fixed costs (product level)	10,000 €	20,000 €	30,000 €
= CM II	**30,000 €**	**30,000 €**	**60,000 €**
- Fixed costs (plant level)	-	-	40,000 €
= Net operating income	-	-	20,000 €

Do you compute (a) contribution margin(s)? ☐ Yes ☐ No ➔ **If not, please continue with B.18.**

<u>If yes:</u>

Please indicate the highest contribution margin (CM) you determine (CM I, CM II, CM III, etc.): ________

B.18	**How intensively do you analyse cost variances on the...**	1 = not at all,........., very intensively =7							
		1	2	3	4	5	6	7	N/A
	cost centre level?	☐	☐	☐	☐	☐	☐	☐	☐
	cost object level?	☐	☐	☐	☐	☐	☐	☐	☐

B.19 **In addition to your P/L statement, do you have a separate operating income statement for managerial purposes?**

☐ Yes ☐ No ➔ **If no, please continue with B.20**

To what extent does your operating income statement for managerial purposes differ structurally from your P/L statement?

1 = not at all ,..., completely = 7

1	2	3	4	5	6	7	N/A
☐	☐	☐	☐	☐	☐	☐	☐

Section B.2 – Objectives of the cost accounting system

B.20	**How intensively does your company <u>pursue</u> the following cost accounting objectives?**	1 = not at all,.................., very intensively = 7						
		1	2	3	4	5	6	7
	Facilitating pricing decisions	☐	☐	☐	☐	☐	☐	☐
	Facilitating production planning	☐	☐	☐	☐	☐	☐	☐
	Facilitating process improvement decisions	☐	☐	☐	☐	☐	☐	☐
	Facilitating environmental protection	☐	☐	☐	☐	☐	☐	☐
	Motivating employees to act in accordance with the company's strategy	☐	☐	☐	☐	☐	☐	☐
	Motivating employees to make cost savings	☐	☐	☐	☐	☐	☐	☐
	Holding employees responsible for their actions	☐	☐	☐	☐	☐	☐	☐
	Determining the value of assets for financial reporting purposes	☐	☐	☐	☐	☐	☐	☐
B.21	**How intensively does your company <u>apply</u> its cost accounting system for the following tasks?**	1 = not at all,.................., very intensively = 7						
		1	2	3	4	5	6	7
	operational planning	☐	☐	☐	☐	☐	☐	☐
	operational control	☐	☐	☐	☐	☐	☐	☐
	strategic planning	☐	☐	☐	☐	☐	☐	☐
	strategic control	☐	☐	☐	☐	☐	☐	☐

Section B.3 – Performance of the cost accounting system

B.22	**To what extent did your company <u>achieve</u> the following cost accounting objectives over the last three years?**	1 = not at all,......................., completely = 7						
		1	2	3	4	5	6	7
	Facilitating pricing decisions	☐	☐	☐	☐	☐	☐	☐
	Facilitating production planning	☐	☐	☐	☐	☐	☐	☐
	Facilitating process improvement decisions	☐	☐	☐	☐	☐	☐	☐
	Facilitating environmental protection	☐	☐	☐	☐	☐	☐	☐
	Motivating employees to act in accordance with the company's strategy	☐	☐	☐	☐	☐	☐	☐
	Motivating employees to make cost savings	☐	☐	☐	☐	☐	☐	☐
	Holding employees responsible for their actions	☐	☐	☐	☐	☐	☐	☐
	Determining the value of assets for financial reporting purposes	☐	☐	☐	☐	☐	☐	☐
B.23	**To what extent did your cost accounting system ensure <u>the fulfillment</u> of the following tasks over the last three years?**	1 = not at all,......................., completely = 7						
		1	2	3	4	5	6	7
	operational planning	☐	☐	☐	☐	☐	☐	☐
	operational control	☐	☐	☐	☐	☐	☐	☐
	strategic planning	☐	☐	☐	☐	☐	☐	☐
	strategic control	☐	☐	☐	☐	☐	☐	☐

B.24 **How satisfied are you overall with the information provided by your cost accounting system?**

1 = very unsatisfied,..., very satisfied = 7

1	2	3	4	5	6	7
☐	☐	☐	☐	☐	☐	☐

Section C – Your group's profile

		1 = not at all,................, completely = 7							
C.1	**Please characterise the relationship between your company and your parent company. To what extent do you agree to the following statements?**	1	2	3	4	5	6	7	N/A
	There are a lot of personal frictions, clashes and tensions between management accountants of our company and those of our parent company.	☐	☐	☐	☐	☐	☐	☐	☐
	Employees of our company feel very much pride and loyalty to work for our parent company.	☐	☐	☐	☐	☐	☐	☐	☐
	Our company can take a share in the development of the management accounting directives, which are imposed by our parent company.	☐	☐	☐	☐	☐	☐	☐	☐
	Our company cannot change our management accounting without consulting our parent company.	☐	☐	☐	☐	☐	☐	☐	☐
	To perform their tasks effectively, other companies in our group do not depend heavily on our company.	☐	☐	☐	☐	☐	☐	☐	☐
	Our company is important for other companies in our group with respect to product and production development.	☐	☐	☐	☐	☐	☐	☐	☐
	Our company differs significantly from other companies in our group with respect to cost information needs.	☐	☐	☐	☐	☐	☐	☐	☐

		1 = not at all,................, completely = 7							
C.2	**To what extent does your parent company impose the following cost accounting issues through corporate directives?**	1	2	3	4	5	6	7	N/A
	The applicable cost types	☐	☐	☐	☐	☐	☐	☐	☐
	The procedures for overhead cost allocation	☐	☐	☐	☐	☐	☐	☐	☐
	The different cost objects	☐	☐	☐	☐	☐	☐	☐	☐

		1 = not at all,................, completely = 7							
C.3	**To what extent have the following issues inspired your company to further develop its own cost accounting system?**	1	2	3	4	5	6	7	N/A
	The cost accounting system of another company <u>inside</u> your group	☐	☐	☐	☐	☐	☐	☐	☐
	The cost accounting system of another company <u>outside</u> your group	☐	☐	☐	☐	☐	☐	☐	☐

C.4 **Which description best describes your parent company's involvement into your company's activities?**

☐ Our parent company engages into our company's financial activities only. It does not pursue any operating activities and manages us and other subsidiaries as a collection of assets (Financial Holding).

☐ Our parent company engages into our company's financial and strategic activities. It does not pursue any operational activities itself (Strategic Holding).

☐ Our parent company engages into our company's strategic, financial and operating activities. It pursues operational activities on its own (Operational Holding).

C.5 **Please indicate the following with respect to your company's association with your parent company:**

Year of affiliation (i.e. the year your company became part of your current parent company):____________________

Parent company's form of market entrance
- ☐ The parent company set up our company (Greenfield).
- ☐ The parent company acquired our company (Brownfield).
- ☐ The parent company and additional corporate partners set up our company as a joint venture.

C.6 **Please indicate the following figures for the last financial year of <u>your parent company</u>:**

Average number of employees (full-time equivalents): __________ (FTEs)

Percentage of sales from non-domestic sources : ☐ 0-15% ☐ 16-30% ☐ 31-45% ☐ 46-60% ☐ 61-75% ☐ more than 75%

Number of <u>foreign countries</u>, in which there are subsidiaries of your parent company: ____________ (foreign countries)

➔[Foreign countries are all countries but your parent company's home country.]

Thank you for your help!

We would like to express our sincere thanks for spending some of your valuable time to participate in our survey. Your answers are of high importance to the success of this study. We will therefore gladly provide you with the results of our survey presumably in the first quarter of 2014 after having completed the investigation.

☐ If you are interested in the results of our study and would like to benchmark your company with others matched by industry and size, please tick this box.

☐ We may wish to contact you to further discuss some of the responses you have given and to obtain more information about the specifics of your company's cost accounting system. Please tick this box if you are willing to further discuss relevant issues.

Your name: ______________________________

Years of work experience: ______________________________

Company: ______________________________

Address: ______________________________

____

E-mail-address: ______________________________

Phone number: ______________________________

Further comments on this project:

If you have any questions regarding this study, please contact

Moritz Schröder

e-mail: moritz.schroeder@wiwi.uni-muenster.de

phone: +49/ 251/ 83 22677

Appendix 2: Questionnaire B

WESTFÄLISCHE
WILHELMS-UNIVERSITÄT
MÜNSTER

IUR
Chair of International
Accounting
Prof. Dr. Peter Kajüter

Cost Accounting in German Subsidiaries of Anglophone Firms

Motivation

This questionnaire is part of a research project conducted by the Chair of International Accounting at the University of Münster (Germany). The project's objective is to compare cost accounting systems in German subsidiaries of Anglophone companies with cost accounting systems in domestic German companies. More specifically, it shall be explored whether an alignment of cost accounting systems with the traditions known from a parent company's home or a subsidiary's host country has implications for the success of subsidiaries' cost accounting systems. In order to facilitate the latter analysis, it will also be explored how cost information serves for managerial decision-making.

Contents:

Please note:

This research is completely confidential. All data from the questionnaire will be aggregated and then used for statistical purposes only. Any data, which would allow the identification of your business, will thus be eliminated before being published. A non-disclosure agreement will be signed upon request.

Please mark the appropriate response alternative(s) with an "x" or write in the designated boxes.

In this questionnaire, several questions are concerned with your company's parent company. Please answer these questions with respect to the organisation that is the head of the group, which your company is associated to (i.e. your company's ultimate owner).

Fax number for return of survey:

+49 / 251 / 83 22848

If you have any questions, please do not hesitate to contact:

Moritz Schröder

e-mail: moritz.schroeder@wiwi.uni-muenster.de

phone: +49/ 251/ 83 22677

Section A.1 – Types of cost information use

A.1 Cost information can be used to build-up background knowledge for future decisions to be made.
To what extent do you agree to the following statements?

	1 = not at all,..................., completely = 7						
	1	2	3	4	5	6	7
I regularly regard cost information to further my understanding of our business situation.	☐	☐	☐	☐	☐	☐	☐
I regularly regard cost information irrespectively of a particular decision to be made.	☐	☐	☐	☐	☐	☐	☐
I use cost information to better understand interrelations within my area of responsibility.	☐	☐	☐	☐	☐	☐	☐
I use cost information to be able to better predict future developments within my area of responsibility.	☐	☐	☐	☐	☐	☐	☐

A.2 Cost information can be used to make a particular decision.
To what extent do you agree to the following statements?

	1 = not at all,..................., completely = 7						
	1	2	3	4	5	6	7
Cost information frequently alters my focus when resolving a particular decision-making problem.	☐	☐	☐	☐	☐	☐	☐
I actively seek cost information for decision-making.	☐	☐	☐	☐	☐	☐	☐
I regularly draw on cost information when it is difficult to differentiate among plausible solutions to a problem.	☐	☐	☐	☐	☐	☐	☐
I regularly use cost information to make a final decision on an issue of major importance.	☐	☐	☐	☐	☐	☐	☐

A.3 Cost information can be used to justify, legitimise and rationalise a previously taken decision.
To what extent do you agree to the following statements?

	1 = not at all,..................., completely = 7						
	1	2	3	4	5	6	7
I use cost information to justify my previously taken decisions.	☐	☐	☐	☐	☐	☐	☐
I use cost information to signal legitimacy of my previously taken decisions.	☐	☐	☐	☐	☐	☐	☐
I use cost information to seek support for my previously taken decisions.	☐	☐	☐	☐	☐	☐	☐
I use cost information to validate my point of view of a given situation.	☐	☐	☐	☐	☐	☐	☐

A.4 Cost information can be used to track subordinates' performance.
To what extent do you agree to the following statements?

	1 = not at all,..................., completely = 7						
	1	2	3	4	5	6	7
I use cost information to align my subordinates' actions with the company's goals.	☐	☐	☐	☐	☐	☐	☐
I use cost information to monitor my subordinates' performance.	☐	☐	☐	☐	☐	☐	☐
I use cost information to provide feedback to my subordinates.	☐	☐	☐	☐	☐	☐	☐
I use cost information to control the activities within my area of responsibility.	☐	☐	☐	☐	☐	☐	☐

A.5 Cost information can be used to get actively involved into subordinates' decision-making.
To what extent do you agree to the following statements?

	1 = not at all,..................., completely = 7						
	1	2	3	4	5	6	7
I use cost information to ensure a common understanding for due decisions.	☐	☐	☐	☐	☐	☐	☐
I use cost information to provide a common view of the organisation.	☐	☐	☐	☐	☐	☐	☐
I use cost information to focus my subordinates' decisions upon the company's key success factors.	☐	☐	☐	☐	☐	☐	☐
I use cost information to involve myself inspiringly into my subordinates' decision-making.	☐	☐	☐	☐	☐	☐	☐

A.6 Cost information is sometimes determined irrespectively of local information needs due to parent company directives, for instance. To what extent do you agree to the following statements?

	1 = not at all,..................., completely = 7						
	1	2	3	4	5	6	7
I do not use our cost accounting system because it fulfills our parent company's information needs more extensively than it fulfills our local information needs.	☐	☐	☐	☐	☐	☐	☐
I use cost information to maintain a good relationship with our parent company - the information itself is of little decision relevance to me.	☐	☐	☐	☐	☐	☐	☐
I think our cost accounting system is maintained as a façade for the world to see - the information itself is of little decision relevance to me.	☐	☐	☐	☐	☐	☐	☐
I am provided with cost information because our parent company issued a respective directive - the information itself is of little decision relevance to me.	☐	☐	☐	☐	☐	☐	☐

Section A.2 – Objectives of the cost accounting system

		1	2	3	4	5	6	7
A.7	**How intensively does your company <u>pursue</u> the following cost accounting objectives?**	1 = not at all,..............., very intensively = 7						
		1	2	3	4	5	6	7
	Facilitating pricing decisions	☐	☐	☐	☐	☐	☐	☐
	Facilitating production planning	☐	☐	☐	☐	☐	☐	☐
	Facilitating process improvement decisions	☐	☐	☐	☐	☐	☐	☐
	Facilitating environmental protection	☐	☐	☐	☐	☐	☐	☐
	Motivating employees to act in accordance with the company's strategy	☐	☐	☐	☐	☐	☐	☐
	Motivating employees to make cost savings	☐	☐	☐	☐	☐	☐	☐
	Holding employees responsible for their actions	☐	☐	☐	☐	☐	☐	☐
	Determining the value of assets for financial reporting purposes	☐	☐	☐	☐	☐	☐	☐
A.8	**How intensively does your company <u>apply</u> its cost accounting system for the following tasks?**	1 = not at all,..............., very intensively = 7						
		1	2	3	4	5	6	7
	operational planning	☐	☐	☐	☐	☐	☐	☐
	operational control	☐	☐	☐	☐	☐	☐	☐
	strategic planning	☐	☐	☐	☐	☐	☐	☐
	strategic control	☐	☐	☐	☐	☐	☐	☐

Section A.3 – Performance of the cost accounting system

		1	2	3	4	5	6	7
A.9	**To what extent did your company <u>achieve</u> the following cost accounting objectives over the last three years?**	1 = not at all,...................., completely = 7						
		1	2	3	4	5	6	7
	Facilitating pricing decisions	☐	☐	☐	☐	☐	☐	☐
	Facilitating production planning	☐	☐	☐	☐	☐	☐	☐
	Facilitating process improvement decisions	☐	☐	☐	☐	☐	☐	☐
	Facilitating environmental protection	☐	☐	☐	☐	☐	☐	☐
	Motivating employees to act in accordance with the company's strategy	☐	☐	☐	☐	☐	☐	☐
	Motivating employees to make cost savings	☐	☐	☐	☐	☐	☐	☐
	Holding employees responsible for their actions	☐	☐	☐	☐	☐	☐	☐
	Determining the value of assets for financial reporting purposes	☐	☐	☐	☐	☐	☐	☐
A.10	**To what extent did your cost accounting system ensure <u>the fulfillment</u> of the following tasks over the last three years?**	1 = not at all,...................., completely = 7						
		1	2	3	4	5	6	7
	operational planning	☐	☐	☐	☐	☐	☐	☐
	operational control	☐	☐	☐	☐	☐	☐	☐
	strategic planning	☐	☐	☐	☐	☐	☐	☐
	strategic control	☐	☐	☐	☐	☐	☐	☐

A.11 How satisfied are you overall with the information provided by your cost accounting system?

1 = very unsatisfied,..., very satisfied = 7

1	2	3	4	5	6	7
☐	☐	☐	☐	☐	☐	☐

		1	2	3	4	5	6	7
A.12	**Please assess the following characteristics of the information provided by your company's cost accounting system.**	1 = very poor,.................., very good = 7						
		1	2	3	4	5	6	7
	<u>Accuracy</u> *(The system provides credible, reliable, unbiased and trustworthy information.)*	☐	☐	☐	☐	☐	☐	☐
	<u>Relevance</u> *(The system provides a complete set of applicable and timely information that is beneficial for decision-making. The amount of provided data is appropriate.)*	☐	☐	☐	☐	☐	☐	☐
	<u>Accessibility</u> *(The system can be accessed easily and quickly and is reasonably secured.)*	☐	☐	☐	☐	☐	☐	☐
	<u>Presentation of data</u> *(The system provides information that is clearly defined and easy to understand. The data is presented compactly and data formats do not change continuously.)*	☐	☐	☐	☐	☐	☐	☐

Section B – General information

B.1 Please indicate the following concerning your position in your company:

Job title (e.g. CEO, CFO, etc.): ______________________

Years of work experience: ______________________ (Years)

Years of work experience in your current company: ______________________ (Years)

B.2 Please indicate the following concerning your demographics:

Nationality: ______________________

Gender: ☐ male ☐ female

B.3 How predictable are the developments in your company's environment?

(Consider e.g. manufacturing technology, competitors' actions, market demand, product attributes/design, raw material availability, raw material prices, government regulation and labour union actions.)

1 = very unpredictable,..., very predictable = 7

1	2	3	4	5	6	7
☐	☐	☐	☐	☐	☐	☐

B.4 Please characterise the relationship between your company and your parent company.

To what extent do you agree to the following statements?

1 = not at all,..........., completely = 7

	1	2	3	4	5	6	7	N/A
There are a lot of personal frictions, clashes and tensions between management accountants of our company and those of our parent company.	☐	☐	☐	☐	☐	☐	☐	☐
Employees of our company feel very much pride and loyalty to work for our parent company.	☐	☐	☐	☐	☐	☐	☐	☐
Our company can take a share in the development of the management accounting directives, which are imposed by our parent company.	☐	☐	☐	☐	☐	☐	☐	☐
Our company cannot change our management accounting without consulting our parent company.	☐	☐	☐	☐	☐	☐	☐	☐
To perform their tasks effectively, other companies in our group do not depend heavily on our company.	☐	☐	☐	☐	☐	☐	☐	☐
Our company is important for other companies in our group with respect to product and production development.	☐	☐	☐	☐	☐	☐	☐	☐
Our company differs significantly from other companies in our group with respect to cost information needs.	☐	☐	☐	☐	☐	☐	☐	☐

B.5 Information users' perceptions of cost accounting influences the way how they use cost information.

To what extent do you agree to the following statements?

1 = not at all,......., completely = 7

	1	2	3	4	5	6	7	N/A
Cost information allows for a different perspective on problems and decisions.	☐	☐	☐	☐	☐	☐	☐	☐
Cost information can facilitate the management of a company.	☐	☐	☐	☐	☐	☐	☐	☐
I particularly use other information than cost information for decision-making (e.g. physical measures or market information).	☐	☐	☐	☐	☐	☐	☐	☐
Cost accounting is a fad and will lose in importance in the upcoming years.	☐	☐	☐	☐	☐	☐	☐	☐

	1	2	3	4	5	6	7	N/A
The usefulness of cost information is easy to assess.	☐	☐	☐	☐	☐	☐	☐	☐
I know precisely which problems to solve with cost information.	☐	☐	☐	☐	☐	☐	☐	☐
I can distinguish different cost accounting systems.	☐	☐	☐	☐	☐	☐	☐	☐
I am aware of the strengths and weaknesses of alternative ways to design a cost accounting system.	☐	☐	☐	☐	☐	☐	☐	☐

B.6 **Information users' involvement into the design and operation of a cost accounting system influences the way how they use cost information. To what extent do you agree to the following statements?**

	1 = not at all,........, completely = 7							
	1	2	3	4	5	6	7	N/A
I get in touch with cost information very frequently.	☐	☐	☐	☐	☐	☐	☐	☐
I get in touch with employees responsible for cost accounting very frequently.	☐	☐	☐	☐	☐	☐	☐	☐
I take my time for detailed discussions with employees responsible for cost accounting.	☐	☐	☐	☐	☐	☐	☐	☐
I get in touch with different possibilities to design a cost accounting system very frequently.	☐	☐	☐	☐	☐	☐	☐	☐

	1	2	3	4	5	6	7	N/A
I keep myself up to date with respect to changes and adjustments of our cost accounting system.	☐	☐	☐	☐	☐	☐	☐	☐
I am interested in the design of our cost accounting system.	☐	☐	☐	☐	☐	☐	☐	☐
I engage myself into the development of our cost accounting system.	☐	☐	☐	☐	☐	☐	☐	☐
I promote the use of cost information in our company.	☐	☐	☐	☐	☐	☐	☐	☐

Thank you for your help!

We would like to express our sincere thanks for spending some of your valuable time to participate in our survey. Your answers are of high importance to the success of this study. We will therefore gladly provide you with the results of our survey presumably in the first quarter of 2014 after having completed the investigation.

☐ If you are interested in the results of our study and would like to benchmark your company with others matched by industry and size, please tick this box.

☐ We may wish to contact you to further discuss some of the responses you have given and to obtain more information about the specifics of your company's cost accounting system. Please tick this box if you are willing to further discuss relevant issues.

Your name: ______________________________

Company: ______________________________

Address: ______________________________

____

E-mail-address: ______________________________

Phone number: ______________________________

Further comments on this project:

If you have any questions regarding this study, please contact

Moritz Schröder

e-mail: moritz.schroeder@wiwi.uni-muenster.de

phone: +49/251/8322677

Appendix 3: Questionnaires per manufacturing sub-industry

Questionnaires per manufacturing sub-industry	Dataset 1		Dataset 2		Dataset 3		Dataset 4	
	Angl.	Ger.	Angl.	Ger.	Angl.	Ger.	Angl.	Ger.
Manufacture of food products	1	4	1	4	0	0	0	0
Manufacture of beverages	1	0	1	0	0	1	0	1
Manufacture of tobacco products	0	1	0	1	1	0	1	0
Manufacture of textiles	0	2	0	2	1	0	1	0
Manufacture of wearing apparel	0	0	1	0	0	0	0	0
Manufacture of leather and related products	0	0	0	0	0	0	0	0
Manufacture of wood and of products of wood and cork, except furniture; manufacture of articles of straw and plaiting materials	1	1	1	1	1	0	1	0
Manufacture of paper and paper products	4	4	5	4	1	3	1	3
Printing and reproduction of recorded media	0	0	0	0	0	0	0	0
Manufacture of coke and refined petroleum products	2	0	2	0	0	2	0	2
Manufacture of chemicals and chemical prod-ucts	10	12	11	12	6	3	6	3
Manufacture of basic pharmaceutical products and pharmaceutical preparations	3	3	3	3	2	3	3	3
Manufacture of rubber and plastics products:	9	11	10	12	5	3	6	6
Manufacture of other non-metallic mineral Products	3	1	4	1	1	3	1	4
Manufacture of basic metals	5	4	5	4	2	0	2	1
Manufacture of fabricated metal products, except machinery and equipment	7	7	10	7	3	5	3	6
Manufacture of computer, electronic and optical products	14	12	16	12	8	5	9	6
Manufacture of electrical equipment	8	10	8	10	3	7	5	7
Manufacture of machinery and equipment n.e.c.	12	19	15	20	7	5	9	7
Manufacture of motor vehicles, trailers and semi-trailers	5	9	7	9	2	2	2	2
Manufacture of other transport equipment	0	1	0	1	0	0	1	0
Manufacture of furniture	1	0	1	0	0	1	0	1
Other manufacturing	4	5	4	5	2	2	3	2
Repair and installation of machinery and Equipment	0	3	0	3	2	0	2	0
Fisher's exact test	p = 0.86		p = 0.76		p = 0.57		p = 0.75	

Appendix 4: Correlation analysis (questionnaire A)

Anglophone subsidiaries (Pearson correlation - dataset 1)	**Complexity of cost accounting**	Size of the parent company	Length of affiliation	Form of market entry	Size of the subsidiary	Management Accounting Institutions (Angl.)	Management Accounting Institutions (Ger.)	University training	Expatriates	Corporate managers' involvement	Parent company directives	Relational Context	Local top management support	Adequacy of cost accountants	IT processing capabilities	ERP	Product diversity	Objective: operational decision-making	Objective: strategic decision-making	Objective: inventory valuation	Objective: decision influencing	Objective: decision facilitating
Perceived environmental uncertainty	0.06	-0.24**	0.03	-0.01	0.13	0.19*	0.16*	-0.10	0.07	-0.06	-0.12											
Objective: decision facilitating	0.52***	-0.08	0.22**	-0.15	0.05	0.02	0.19**	0.36***	0.16*	0.04	0.05											
Objective: decision influencing	0.42***	0.05	0.19**	-0.23**	0.14	-0.15	0.09	0.23**	0.20**	0.20**	0.25***											
Objective: inventory valuation	0.26***	0.01	0.17*	-0.07	-0.03	-0.15	0.08	0.20**	0.02	0.00	0.05											
Objective: strategic decision-making	0.30***	-0.14	0.12	-0.23**	0.03	0.18*	0.33***	0.25***	0.09	0.40***	-0.01											
Objective: operational decision-making	0.42***	-0.08	0.02	-0.02	0.09	0.01	0.21**	0.33***	0.09	0.19**	-0.01											
Product diversity	0.01	0.02	0.01	-0.02	0.10	0.04	0.05	0.04	-0.18*	-0.16*	-0.06											
ERP	0.17*	0.11	0.06	-0.14	0.06	-0.03	-0.04	0.29***	0.10	-0.01	0.01											
IT processing capabilities	0.20**	0.12	0.16*	-0.01	0.13	-0.08	0.02	0.17*	0.13	0.16*	0.17*											
Adequacy of cost accountants	0.17*	-0.03	0.01	-0.10	-0.24**	-0.01	0.25***	0.19**	0.01	0.30***	-0.09											
Local top management support	0.27***	0.01	0.06	-0.15	-0.06	-0.02	0.36***	0.23**	0.10	0.49***	-0.01											
Relational Context	-0.06	-0.09	-0.19**	0.13	0.01	-0.04	0.10	-0.03	-0.29***	-0.26***	-0.38***											
Parent company directives	0.04	0.23**	0.17*	-0.11	0.19**	0.07	-0.22**	-0.04	0.11	0.21**												
Corporate managers' involvement	-0.09	-0.14	-0.08	-0.04	-0.12	0.15	0.25***	0.11	0.08													
Expatriates	0.13	-0.08	-0.06	-0.07	0.12	0.12	-0.07	0.13														
University training	0.19*	0.02	0.07	-0.16*	-0.10	0.13	0.20**															
Management Accounting Institutions (Ger.)	0.17*	-0.27***	0.07	-0.22**	-0.19**	0.15																
Management Accounting Institutions (Angl.)	0.06	-0.15	0.07	-0.07	0.06																	
Size of the subsidiary	0.18*	0.20**	0.11	-0.04																		
Form of market entry	-0.13	0.01	-0.33***																			
Length of affiliation	0.11	0.22**																				
Size of the parent company	0.06																					

Explanation:

Bold type: significant at a 1 % level
Italic type: significant at a 5 % and 10 % level

Grey marked boxes above the diagonal are correlations between variables of a common theoretic source

Continued...

Anglophone subsidiaries (Pearson correlation - dataset 1)	Complexity of cost accounting	Size of the parent company	Length of affiliation	Form of market entry	Size of the subsidiary	Management Accounting Institutions (Angl.)	Management Accounting Institutions (Ger.)	University training	Expatriates	Corporate managers' involvement	Parent company directives	Relational Context	Local top management support	Adequacy of cost accountants	IT processing capabilities	ERP	Product diversity	Objective: operational decision-making	Objective: strategic decision-making	Objective: inventory valuation	Objective: decision influencing	Objective: decision facilitating
Perceived environmental uncertainty												0.17*	-0.15	-0.13	-0.27***	0.00	0.10	-0.03	-0.05	0.03	-0.13	0.03
Objective: decision facilitating												-0.20**	0.16	0.17*	0.35***	0.18*	0.01	0.64***	0.45***	0.37***	0.46***	
Objective: decision influencing												-0.20**	0.36***	0.22**	0.22**	0.14	-0.11	0.47***	0.42***	0.26***		
Objective: inventory valuation												-0.10	0.11	0.18*	0.28***	0.03	-0.09	0.41***	0.09			
Objective: strategic decision-making												-0.21**	0.40***	0.31***	0.23**	0.03	0.06	0.44***				
Objective: operational decision-making												-0.16	0.26***	0.32***	0.33***	0.14	0.02					
Product diversity												0.25***	-0.11	0.07	-0.06	0.13						
ERP												0.19**	0.01	0.03	0.12							
IT processing capabilities												-0.16*	0.26***	0.30***								
Adequacy of cost accountants												-0.02	0.56***									
Local top management support												-0.08										
Relational Context																						
Parent company directives																						
Corporate managers' involvement																						
Expatriates																						
University training																						
Management Accounting Institutions (Ger.)																						
Management Accounting Institutions (Angl.)																						
Size of the subsidiary																						
Form of market entry																						
Length of affiliation																						
Size of the parent company																						

Explanation:

Bold type: significant at a 1 % level
Italic type: significant at a 5 % and 10 % level

Grey marked boxes above the diagonal are correlations between variables of a common theoretic source

Appendix 4 – Table 1: Anglophone subsidiaries

Domestic German subsidiaries (Pearson correlation - dataset 1)	Complexity of cost accounting	Size of the parent company	Length of affiliation	Form of market entry	Size of the subsidiary	Management Accounting Institutions (Angl.)	Management Accounting Institutions (Ger.)	University training	Expatriates	Corporate managers' involvement	Parent company directives	Relational Context	Local top management support	Adequacy of cost accountants	IT processing capabilities	ERP	Product diversity	Objective: operational decision-making	Objective: strategic decision-making	Objective: inventory valuation	Objective: decision influencing	Objective: decision facilitating
Perceived environmental uncertainty	-0.28***	-0.34***	0.20*	-0.09	-0.07	0.00	-0.16	-0.08	-0.11	-0.27***	-0.21**											
Objective: decision facilitating	0.47***	0.13	-0.05	0.06	0.07	0.04	0.07	-0.08	0.02	0.32***	0.24**											
Objective: decision influencing	0.26**	0.16	0.02	-0.08	0.27**	0.09	-0.02	-0.17	0.03	0.23**	0.13											
Objective: inventory valuation	0.38***	0.07	-0.12	0.17	0.00	0.04	0.13	-0.06	-0.16	0.12	0.12											
Objective: strategic decision-making	0.29***	0.06	-0.20*	0.10	-0.07	-0.18*	-0.06	-0.22**	0.09	0.18*	0.05											
Objective: operational decision-making	0.39***	0.11	-0.19*	0.12	0.07	0.10	-0.01	-0.07	-0.05	0.16	0.11											
Product diversity	-0.07	-0.10	-0.03	0.10	0.03	-0.14	-0.16	-0.02	0.01	-0.15	-0.13											
ERP	0.26**	0.05	-0.12	0.20*	0.07	-0.15	-0.14	-0.05	-0.07	0.10	0.08											
IT processing capabilities	0.43***	0.16	-0.01	-0.08	0.16	0.06	0.08	0.03	-0.10	0.22**	0.07											
Adequacy of cost accountants	0.21**	0.02	-0.02	0.05	0.15	0.09	-0.02	0.09	0.07	0.34***	-0.05											
Local top management support	0.04	-0.03	-0.08	0.17	0.03	-0.07	0.05	0.08	0.11	0.45***	-0.17											
Relational Context	0.03	0.08	0.04	0.08	0.03	-0.18*	-0.08	0.02	-0.37***	-0.35***	-0.49***											
Parent company directives	0.16	0.22**	-0.07	0.01	-0.01	0.21*	0.06	-0.07	0.23**	0.27***												
Corporate managers' involvement	0.21**	-0.07	-0.04	-0.06	0.01	-0.02	-0.01	0.26**	0.31***													
Expatriates	-0.02	-0.11	-0.09	-0.17	-0.04	0.13	-0.05	0.13														
University training	-0.06	-0.05	0.18*	-0.21**	0.06	0.05	0.26**															
Management Accounting Institutions (Ger.)	0.07	-0.03	-0.09	-0.01	-0.06	0.25**																
Management Accounting Institutions (Angl.)	0.1	0.18*	0.18*	-0.25**	0.18*																	
Size of the subsidiary	0.19*	0.22**	0.18*	-0.18*																		
Form of market entry	-0.01	0.13	-0.36***																			
Length of affiliation	0.06	-0.18																				
Size of the parent company	0.13																					

Explanation:

Bold type: significant at a 1 % level
Italic type: significant at a 5 % and 10 % level

Grey marked boxes above the diagonal are correlations between variables of a common theoretic source

Continued…

Domestic German subsidiaries (Pearson correlation - dataset 1)	Complexity of cost accounting	Size of the parent company	Length of affiliation	Form of market entry	Size of the subsidiary	Management Accounting Institutions (Angl.)	Management Accounting Institutions (Ger.)	University training	Expatriates	Corporate managers' involvement	Parent company directives	Relational Context	Local top management support	Adequacy of cost accountants	IT processing capabilities	ERP	Product diversity	Objective: operational decision-making	Objective: strategic decision-making	Objective: inventory valuation	Objective: decision influencing	Objective: decision facilitating
Perceived environmental uncertainty												-0.04	-0.16	-0.20*	-0.25**	-0.03	0.15	-0.13	-0.18*	-0.20*	-0.14	-0.35***
Objective: decision facilitating												0.03	0.12	0.27***	0.25**	0.32***	-0.27***	0.46***	0.20*	0.48***	0.28***	
Objective: decision influencing												0.04	0.28***	0.25**	0.26**	0.13	-0.13	0.34***	0.34***	0.16		
Objective: inventory valuation												0.10	0.00	0.16	0.15	0.20*	-0.09	0.41***	0.16			
Objective: strategic decision-making												-0.07	0.21**	0.18*	0.18*	0.03	-0.22**	0.45***				
Objective: operational decision-making												0.04	0.17	0.53***	0.33***	0.13	-0.22**					
Product diversity												0.02	-0.10	-0.16	-0.20*	0.09						
ERP												-0.01	0.12	0.07	0.25**							
IT processing capabilities												0.06	0.35***	0.53***								
Adequacy of cost accountants												0.06	0.53***									
Local top management support												-0.07										
Relational Context																						
Parent company directives																						
Corporate managers' involvement																						
Expatriates																						
University training																						
Management Accounting Institutions (Ger.)																						
Management Accounting Institutions (Angl.)																						
Size of the subsidiary																						
Form of market entry																						
Length of affiliation																						
Size of the parent company																						

Explanation:

Bold type: significant at a 1 % level
Italic type: significant at a 5 % and 10 % level

Grey marked boxes above the diagonal are correlations between variables of a common theoretic source

Appendix 4– Table 2: Domestic German subsidiaries

Appendix 5: Multivariate regression results on the determinants of the complexity of cost type, cost centre and cost object accounting (dataset 1)

Linear regression model - dataset 1 (unstandardised regression coeff.)	E.S.	**Anglophone subsidiaries**			
		Cost type accounting		Cost centre accounting	
		Model (a)	Model (b)	Model (a)	Model(b)
Perceived environmental uncertainty	+	0.0211 *	0.0253 *	-0.0011	0.0012
Extent of use	+	0.0436 ***	0.0412 **	0.0447 ***	0.0457 ***
Product diversity	+	0.0031	0.0107	0.0012	0.0014
ERP *(dummy)*	+	0.0614 *	0.0606 *	0.0212	0.0221
IT processing capabilities	+	-0.0265 ##	-0.0297 ###	0.0158 **	0.0133 *
Adequacy of cost accountants	+	-0.0376 ##	-0.0406 ###	0.0150 *	0.0143 *
Top management support	+	0.0396 ***	0.0348 ***	0.0094	0.0092
Relational context	/	0.0057	0.0016	0.0018	0.0024
Directives[1248] *(centralised)*	-	0.0190 ###	0.0197 ###	0.0047	0.0059
Directives **x** Rel. context *(centralised)*	+		-0.0067		0.0046
Corporate managers *(centralised)*	-	-0.0144 *	-0.0103	-0.0228 ***	-0.0230 ***
Corp. managers **x** Rel. context *(centr.)*	+		-0.0039		-0.0008
Expatriates *(centralised)*	-	0.0027	0.0498 #	0.0128	0.0194 #
Expatriates **x** Rel. context *(centralised)*	+		0.0589 **		0.0068
University training *(dummy)*	+	-0.0138	-0.0046	-0.0131	-0.0098
Professional institutes - German	+	-0.0093	-0.0088	0.0130 *	0.0126 *
Professional institutes - Anglophone	+/-	0.0307 *	0.0244	0.0024	0.0011
Size subsidiary	/	-0.0388	-0.0371	0.0146	0.0145
Form of market entry *(dummy)*	/	0.0070	0.0131	0.0669 ***	0.0692 ***
Length of affiliation	/	-0.0159	-0.0062	-0.0048	-0.0037
Size parent company	/	0.0008	0.0015	-0.0016	-0.0017
Constant	/	0.4377 **	0.4208 **	-0.0258	-0.0232
R^2		27.36 %	32.31 %	47.29 %	47.86 %
adjusted R^2		13.00 %	16.20 %	36.90 %	35.40 %
F		2.44	3.04	3.85	3.77
Significance		0.0027	0.0001	0.0000	0.0000
VIF_{max}		2.16	2.30	2.17	2.29
F (moderation)		2.62 *		0.49	

Continued...

[1248] In contrast to the analysis of the average complexity score, the directives for cost type, cost centre and cost object accounting are included disaggregatedly at this point. Thereby, it is ensured that the complexity score for cost type accounting can be associated with the directives on cost type accounting rather than with directives on e.g. cost centre accounting.

Linear regression model - dataset 1 (unstandardised regression coeff.)	E.S.	**Anglophone subsidiaries**			
		Cost object accounting			
		Model (a)		Model(b)	
Perceived environmental uncertainty	+	0.0195	*	0.0144	
Extent of use	+	0.0629	***	0.0588	***
Product diversity	+	-0.0107		-0.0075	
ERP *(dummy)*	+	0.0072		0.0082	
IT processing capabilities	+	0.0037		0.0080	
Adequacy of cost accountants	+	0.0088		0.0061	
Top management support	+	0.0164	*	0.0129	
Relational context	/	-0.0228		-0.0273	
Directives[1249] *(centralised)*	-	-0.0045		-0.0074	
Directives **x** Rel. context *(centralised)*	+			-0.0143	#
Corporate managers *(centralised)*	-	-0.0302	***	-0.0276	***
Corp. managers **x** Rel. context *(centr.)*	+			-0.0018	
Expatriates *(centralised)*	-	-0.0215		-0.0100	
Expatriates **x** Rel. context *(centralised)*	+			0.0189	
University training *(dummy)*	+	-0.0186		-0.0226	
Professional institutes - German	+	0.0109		0.0140	
Professional institutes - Anglophone	+/-	0.0140		0.0137	
Size subsidiary	/	0.0419		0.0471	
Form of market entry *(dummy)*	/	-0.0529		-0.0469	
Length of affiliation	/	-0.0308	*	-0.0228	
Size parent company	/	0.0095		0.0094	
Constant	/	-0.1380		-0.1703	
R^2	-----	34.91 %		36.86 %	
adjusted R^2	-----	21.90 %		21.60 %	
F	-----	3.88		3.77	
Significance	-----	0.0000		0.0000	
VIF_{max}	-----	2.14		2.31	
F (moderation)		1.20			

Appendix 5 - Table 1: Anglophone subsidiaries

[1249] In contrast to the analysis of the average complexity score, the directives for cost type, cost centre and cost object accounting are included disaggregatedly at this point. Thereby, it is ensured that the complexity score for cost type accounting can be associated with the directives on cost type accounting rather than with directives on e.g. cost centre accounting.

Linear regression model - dataset 1 (unstandardised regression coeff.)	E.S.	**German subsidiaries**			
		Cost type accounting		Cost centre accounting	
		Model (a)	Model (b)	Model (a)	Model(b)
Perceived environmental uncertainty	+	0.0068	-0.0021	-0.0075	-0.0059
Extent of use	+	0.0461 **	0.0577 ***	0.0289 **	0.0258 **
Product diversity	+	0.0014	-0.0057	0.0236 ***	0.0275 ***
ERP *(dummy)*	+	0.0140	0.0393	-0.0147	-0.0243
IT processing capabilities	+	0.0086	0.0064	0.0310 ***	0.0307 ***
Adequacy of cost accountants	+	-0.0416 ##	-0.0443 ##	0.0069	0.0076
Top management support	+	-0.0177	-0.0151	-0.0156 #	-0.0150 #
Relational context	/	0.0001	-0.0244	-0.0127	-0.0053
Directives[1250] *(centralised)*	+/-	-0.0124	-0.0162 **	-0.0037	-0.0025
Directives **x** Rel. context *(centralised)*	-/+		0.0039		-0.0065
Corporate managers *(centralised)*	+/-	0.0145	0.0115	0.0097	0.0106
Corp. managers **x** Rel. context *(centr.)*	-/+		0.0448 ***		-0.0161 ***
Expatriates *(centralised)*	+/-	-0.0045	-0.0170	0.0079	0.0048
Expatriates **x** Rel. context *(centralised)*	-/+		-0.0373		0.0043
University training *(dummy)*	0	0.0326	0.0252	-0.0237	-0.0213
Professional institutes - German	+/-	0.0105	0.0209	0.0104	0.0064
Professional institutes - Anglophone	+/-	0.0219	0.0189	-0.0064	-0.0155
Size subsidiary	/	-0.0015	0.0028	0.0185	0.0138
Form of market entry *(dummy)*	/	-0.0160	-0.0319	0.0263	0.0254
Length of affiliation	/	0.0091	0.0228	0.0157	0.0122
Size parent company	/	-0.0087	-0.0069	0.0037	0.0041
Constant		0.5032 *	0.4478 *	0.0464	0.0813
R^2		15.70 %	27.99 %	37.84 %	42.77 %
adjusted R^2		- 5.90 %	5.40 %	21.90 %	24.80 %
F		2.00	2.91	3.80 %	4.07
Significance		0.0185	0.0003	0.0000	0.0000
VIF_{max}		2.12	2.63	2.10	2.59
F (moderation)		4.19 ***		3.18 **	

Continued...

[1250] In contrast to the analysis of the average complexity score, the directives for cost type, cost centre and cost object accounting are included disaggregatedly at this point. Thereby, it is ensured that the complexity score for cost type accounting can be associated with the directives on cost type accounting rather than with directives on e.g. cost centre accounting.

Linear regression model - dataset 1 (unstandardised regression coeff.)	E.S.	**German subsidiaries** Cost object accounting Model (a)		Model(b)	
Perceived environmental uncertainty	+	-0.0306	##	-0.0303	##
Extent of use	+	0.0507	***	0.0447	***
Product diversity	+	-0.0019		-0.0008	
ERP *(dummy)*	+	0.0742	***	0.0684	**
IT processing capabilities	+	0.0398	***	0.0427	***
Adequacy of cost accountants	+	-0.0062		-0.0054	
Top management support	+	-0.0263	##	-0.0253	#
Relational context	/	0.0136		0.0194	
Directives[1251] *(centralised)*	+/-	-0.0070		-0.0016	
Directives **x** Rel. context *(centralised)*	-/+			0.0048	
Corporate managers *(centralised)*	+/-	0.0090		0.0118	
Corp. managers **x** Rel. context *(centr.)*	-/+			0.0019	
Expatriates *(centralised)*	+/-	0.0166		-0.0248	
Expatriates **x** Rel. context *(centralised)*	-/+			-0.0443	*
University training *(dummy)*	0	-0.0300		-0.0456	
Professional institutes - German	+/-	0.0006		0.0003	
Professional institutes - Anglophone	+/-	0.0285		0.0207	
Size subsidiary	/	0.0049		-0.0009	
Form of market entry *(dummy)*	/	0.0339		0.0302	
Length of affiliation	/	0.0248		0.0325	*
Size parent company	/	0.0006		0.0017	
Constant		0.2641		0.2900	
R^2	-----	46.57 %		48.94 %	
adjusted R^2	-----	32.80 %		32.90 %	
F	-----	4.91		5.31	
Significance	-----	0.0000		0.0000	
VIF_{max}	-----	2.13		2.87	
F (moderation)		1.61			

Appendix 5 - Table 2: Domestic German subsidiaries

[1251] In contrast to the analysis of the average complexity score, the directives for cost type, cost centre and cost object accounting are included disaggregatedly at this point. Thereby, it is ensured that the complexity score for cost type accounting can be associated with the directives on cost type accounting rather than with directives on e.g. cost centre accounting.

Appendix 6: Logistic regression results on the determinants of cross-national differences in cost type, cost centre and cost object accounting (Anglophone subsidiaries in dataset 1)

Logistic regression model - dataset 1 (odds ratios)	E.S.	Anglophone subsidiaries			
		Cost type accounting		Cost centre accounting	
		Model (a)	Model (b)	Model (a)	Model(b)
Perceived environmental uncertainty	<1	0.9089	0.8955	0.8960	0.8535
Extent of use	<1	0.8048	0.8497	0.4697 **	0.4500 **
Product diversity	<1	1.1792	1.0767	0.9602	0.9944
ERP *(dummy)*	<1	0.1269 ***	0.0995 **	0.3830 *	0.3622 **
IT processing capabilities	<1	1.1450	1.1633	0.6501 *	0.6779 *
Adequacy of cost accountants	<1	1.4681 #	1.5041 #	1.0048	0.9808
Top management support	<1	0.5710 **	0.6332 **	0.5745 **	0.5759 **
Relational context	/	1.9029 **	2.0865 **	0.9126	0.8818
Directives[1252] *(centr.)*	>1	0.6989 ###	0.7079 ###	0.9124	0.8721
Directives **x** Rel. context *(centr.)*	<1		1.2191 #		0.8645
Corporate managers *(centr.)*	>1	1.3892 **	1.2993 *	1.6563 **	1.6861 **
Corp. managers **x** Rel. context *(centr.)*	<1		1.0092		0.9825
Expatriates *(centr.)*	>1	0.9250	0.5404 #	0.6836 #	0.7286
Expatriates **x** Rel. context *(centr.)*	<1		0.5265 **		1.0838
University training *(dummy)*	<1	0.8651	0.8407	1.7653	1.6069
Professional institutes - German	<1	0.9829	0.9597	0.8669	0.8813
Professional institutes - Anglophone	≠1	0.6103 *	0.6760	0.6223	0.6336
Size subsidiary	/	1.9864	1.9205	0.8743	0.8611
Number of value chain functions	/	1.3747	1.3180	1.5417 **	1.5346 **
Form of market entry *(dummy)*	/	0.8953	0.7654	0.1302 **	0.1237 **
Length of affiliation	/	1.7639 *	1.6224	0.9727	0.9804
Size parent company	/	1.1507	1.1489	1.2516 **	1.2612 **
Constant	/	0.0389	0.0517	20.032 **	23.595 **
MacFaddens's pseudo R^2		25.70 %	28.80 %	25.50 %	26.10 %
Count R^2		72.70 %	75.50 %	77.30 %	78.20 %
Wald test		28.52	31.61	17.10	18.35
Significance		0.0738	0.0843	0.5834	0.6852
VIF_{max}		2.16	2.33	2.17	2.31
Wald test		4.52		0.84	

Continued…

[1252] In contrast to the analysis of the average complexity score, the directives for cost type, cost centre and cost object accounting are included disaggregatedly at this point. Thereby, it is ensured that the complexity score for cost type accounting can be associated with the directives on cost type accounting rather than with directives on e.g. cost centre accounting.

Logistic regression model - dataset 1 (odds ratios)	E.S.	Anglophone subsidiaries	
		Cost object accounting	
		Model (a)	Model(b)
Perceived environmental uncertainty	<1	0.6456 **	0.6756 *
Extent of use	<1	0.2424 ***	0.2615 ***
Product diversity	<1	1.2486	1.0869
ERP *(dummy)*	<1	1.5488	1.3580
IT processing capabilities	<1	1.1216	1.0276
Adequacy of cost accountants	<1	0.6559 *	0.7498
Top management support	<1	0.6701 **	0.7038 *
Relational context	/	1.1829	1.0561
Directives[1253] *(centr.)*	>1	1.1901 *	1.3415 **
Directives **x** Rel. context *(centr.)*	<1		1.5633 ###
Corporate managers *(centr.)*	>1	1.6753 ***	1.5707 **
Corp. managers **x** Rel. context *(centr.)*	<1		0.9892
Expatriates *(centr.)*	>1	1.8750 **	0.5016
Expatriates **x** Rel. context *(centr.)*	<1		0.2043 ***
University training *(dummy)*	<1	1.0326	1.1278
Professional institutes - German	<1	1.2371	1.1451
Professional institutes - Anglophone	≠1	0.5163 **	0.5500 *
Size subsidiary	/	0.5338	0.4645
Number of value chain functions	/	0.8141	0.7728
Form of market entry *(dummy)*	/	1.6043	1.2484
Length of affiliation	/	1.5911	1.1954
Size parent company	/	0.8648	0.8721
Constant	/	4,521,254 ***	18,680,673 ***
MacFaddens's pseudo R^2		28.20 %	34.20 %
Count R^2		77.10 %	77.10 %
Wald test		23.32	34.65
Significance		0.2236	0.0421
VIF_{max}		2.15	2.34
Wald test		8.67 **	

Appendix 6: Anglophone subsidiaries

[1253] In contrast to the analysis of the average complexity score, the directives for cost type, cost centre and cost object accounting are included disaggregatedly at this point. Thereby, it is ensured that the complexity score for cost type accounting can be associated with the directives on cost type accounting rather than with directives on e.g. cost centre accounting.

Appendix 7: Robustness checks of the usage types

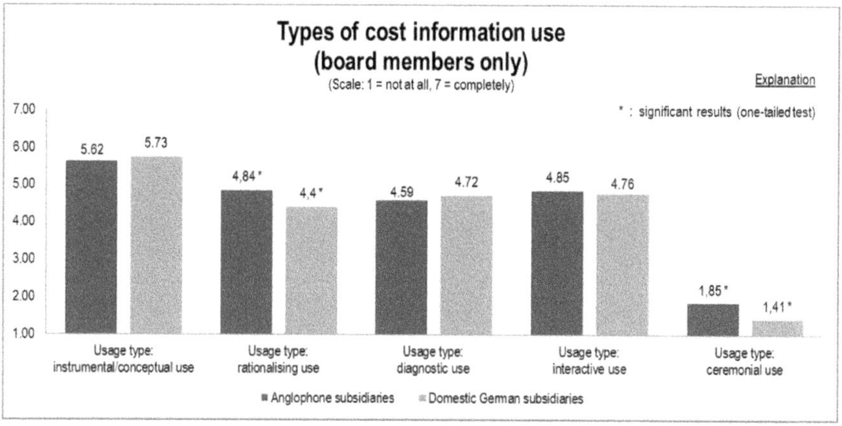

Appendix 7 – Figure 1: Types of use as reported by board members only

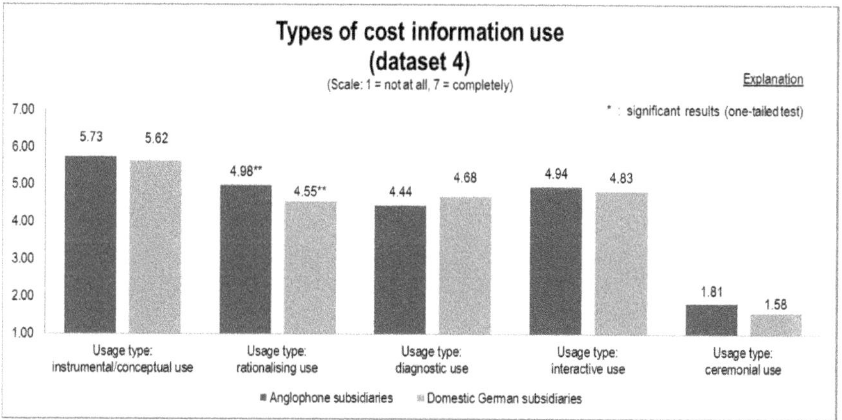

Appendix 7 – Figure 2: Types of use for dataset 4

Appendix 8: Mean values for the non-ceremonial usage types for different levels of the ceremonial use of cost information

Mean values (scale: 1 = not at all, 7 = completely)		(1) Instrumental/ conceptual use	(2) Rationalising use	(3) Diagnostic use	(4) Interactive use
Anglophone subsidiaries	(5) Ceremonial use = 1	**5.75**	**5.12**	4.30	**5.16**
	(5) Ceremonial use ≠ 1	5.71	4.89	**4.55**	4.78
German subsidiaries	(5) Ceremonial use = 1	**5.86**	**4.47**	**5.12**	**4.95**
	(5) Ceremonial use ≠ 1	5.38	4.62	4.24	4.7

Appendix 9: Correlation analysis (questionnaire B)

Anglophone subsidiaries (Pearson correlation - dataset 3)	**Usage type: instrumental/conceptual**	**Usage type: rationalising use**	**Usage type: diagnostic use**	**Usage type: interactive use**	**Usage type: ceremonial use**	Complexity of cost accounting	Attitude: Knowledge	Attitude: Preference	Attitude: Quality	Attitude: Involvement	Attitude: Contact	Perceived environmental uncertainty	Objective: Decision facilitating	Objective: Decision influencing	Relational Context	Corporate managers' involvement	Expatriates	Parent company directives	Size of the subsidiary	Form of market entry	Length of affiliation	Size of the parent company	Work experience
Board Member	-0.12	-0.18	0.13	-0.08	0.04	-0.04	-0.05	0.18	-0.26*	-0.34**	-0.23												
Working experience	0.13	0.13	-0.06	0.10	-0.01	-0.04	-0.08	0.16	0.05	-0.02	-0.03												
Size of the parent company	-0.09	-0.17	0.04	0.00	0.31**	-0.05	-0.39***	0.04	-0.23	-0.24	-0.04												
Length of affiliation	0.06	-0.01	0.11	0.16	0.07	0.13	-0.12	0.11	-0.14	-0.06	0.07												
Form of market entry	-0.13	-0.21	-0.32**	-0.23	0.09	-0.22	-0.02	-0.01	0.06	-0.22	-0.13												
Size of the subsidiary	-0.10	-0.23	0.15	0.06	0.29**	0.21	-0.17	-0.16	-0.09	-0.20	-0.17												
Parent company directives	0.10	0.22	0.12	-0.01	-0.09	0.04	-0.14	-0.15	-0.07	-0.17	-0.04												
Expatriates	0.26*	0.06	0.12	0.15	-0.19	0.00	0.11	0.16	0.27*	0.18	0.31**												
Corporate managers' involvement	-0.32**	-0.37***	0.03	-0.08	0.20	-0.03	-0.08	-0.11	-0.15	-0.18	-0.20												
Relational Context	-0.24*	0.05	-0.11	-0.17	0.27*	-0.22	-0.10	-0.22	-0.23	-0.33**	-0.28*												
Objective: Decision influencing	0.47***	0.24*	0.65***	0.50***	-0.29**	0.42***	0.48***	0.36**	0.40***	0.23	0.31**												
Objective: Decision facilitating	0.60***	0.27*	0.29**	0.36**	-0.34**	0.49***	0.44***	0.23	0.48***	0.44***	0.31**												
Perceived environmental uncertainty	-0.21	0.11	-0.28*	-0.06	-0.04	-0.31**	-0.18	-0.26*	-0.11	-0.21	-0.22												
Attitude: Contact	0.33**	0.24*	0.24	0.11	-0.25*	0.07	0.37***	0.08	0.37***	0.69***													
Attitude: Involvement	0.43***	0.23	0.12	0.18	-0.46***	0.23	0.61***	-0.05	0.59***														
Attitude: Quality	0.44***	0.24*	0.13	0.37**	-0.49***	0.17	0.45***	0.10															
Attitude: Preference	0.44***	0.26*	0.36**	0.39***	-0.35**	0.10	0.33**																
Attitude: Knowledge	0.50***	0.29**	0.38***	0.33**	-0.47***	0.27*																	
Complexity of cost accounting	0.49***	0.09	0.39***	0.24	-0.13																		
Usage type: ceremonial use	-0.43***	-0.22	-0.10	-0.40***																			
Usage type: interactive use	0.63***	0.57***	0.57***																				
Usage type: diagnostic use	0.44***	0.36**																					
Usage type: rationalising use	0.58***																						

Explanation:

Bold type: significant at a 1 % level
Italic type: significant at a 5 % and 10 % level

Grey marked boxes above the diagonal are correlations between variables of a common theoretic source or represent intercorrelations of the usage types

Continued…

Anglophone subsidiaries (Pearson correlation - dataset 3)	Usage type: instrumental/conceptual	Usage type: rationalising use	Usage type: diagnostic use	Usage type: interactive use	Usage type: ceremonial use	Complexity of cost accounting	Attitude: Knowledge	Attitude: Preference	Attitude: Quality	Attitude: Involvement	Attitude: Contact	Perceived environmental uncertainty	Objective: Decision facilitating	Objective: Decision influencing	Relational Context	Corporate managers' involvement	Expatriates	Parent company directives	Size of the subsidiary	Form of market entry	Length of affiliation	Size of the parent company	Work experience
Board Member												-0.16	-0.11	-0.02	0.10	-0.04	-0.22	0.21	-0.10	0.10	-0.17	-0.12	_0.24*_
Working experience												-0.10	0.07	-0.12	0.05	_-0.25*_	-0.06	0.18	-0.13	0.01	0.06	0.00	
Size of the parent company												-0.22	-0.19	-0.15	0.05	_0.31**_	-0.09	-0.13	0.23	-0.05	_0.32**_		
Length of affiliation												-0.08	0.18	0.04	-0.11	_0.30**_	-0.06	_-0.34**_	0.17	__-0.50***__			
Form of market entry												0.01	-0.16	-0.17	0.22	-0.21	-0.07	-0.02	-0.02				
Size of the subsidiary												-0.18	-0.04	0.13	0.02	_0.26*_	-0.16	0.02					
Parent company directives												0.01	-0.11	0.00	0.15	_-0.29**_	0.06						
Expatriates												0.02	0.13	0.23	-0.03	0.01							
Corporate managers' involvement												0.08	-0.18	-0.06	_0.30**_								
Relational Context												__0.43***__	_-0.33**_	_-0.33**_									
Objective: Decision influencing												_-0.31**_	__0.50***__										
Objective: Decision facilitating												-0.17											
Perceived environmental uncertainty																							
Attitude: Contact																							
Attitude: Involvement																							
Attitude: Quality																							
Attitude: Preference																							
Attitude: Knowledge																							
Complexity of cost accounting																							
Usage type: ceremonial use																							
Usage type: interactive use																							
Usage type: diagnostic use																							
Usage type: rationalising use																							

Explanation:

Bold type: significant at a 1 % level
Italic type: significant at a 5 % and 10 % level

Grey marked boxes above the diagonal are correlations between variables of a common theoretic source or represent intercorrelations of the usage types

Appendix 9 – Table 1: Anglophone subsidiaries

Domestic German subsidiaries (Pearson correlation - dataset 3)	Usage type: instrumental/conceptual	Usage type: rationalising use	Usage type: diagnostic use	Usage type: interactive use	Usage type: ceremonial use	Complexity of cost accounting	Attitude: Knowledge	Attitude: Preference	Attitude: Quality	Attitude: Involvement	Attitude: Contact	Perceived environmental uncertainty	Objective: Decision facilitating	Objective: Decision influencing	Relational Context	Corporate managers' involvement	Expatriates	Parent company directives	Size of the subsidiary	Form of market entry	Length of affiliation	Size of the parent company	Work experience
Board Member	0.10	-0.13	0.06	-0.17	-0.16	0.47***	0.02	-0.04	-0.04	-0.17	0.23												
Working experience	0.19	0.07	0.38**	0.15	-0.34**	0.52***	0.10	0.03	0.19	0.02	0.04												
Size of the parent company	0.15	0.28*	0.06	0.22	-0.09	0.08	-0.07	-0.18	-0.03	-0.21	-0.02												
Length of affiliation	0.04	-0.06	-0.19	0.13	-0.04	-0.04	0.04	-0.01	-0.12	0.19	-0.14												
Form of market entry	0.16	0.32**	0.25*	0.21	0.15	0.04	-0.03	-0.10	0.28*	-0.13	-0.03												
Size of the subsidiary	0.10	-0.06	0.10	0.03	-0.19	0.12	-0.16	0.02	0.02	-0.03	0.05												
Parent company directives	-0.25*	-0.21	-0.18	-0.24	0.01	-0.02	-0.22	-0.29*	-0.19	-0.39***	-0.28*												
Expatriates	0.13	0.13	0.29*	-0.16	-0.14	0.12	0.02	0.01	0.19	-0.18	-0.11												
Corporate managers' involvement	-0.23	0.22	0.01	-0.13	0.35**	-0.06	-0.08	-0.20	-0.20	-0.01	0.22												
Relational Context	-0.04	0.09	-0.20	-0.20	0.06	0.00	-0.13	-0.03	-0.35**	-0.15	0.07												
Objective: Decision influencing	0.44***	0.26*	0.68***	0.57***	-0.28*	0.28*	0.10	0.16	0.37**	0.10	0.06												
Objective: Decision facilitating	0.21	0.26*	0.39***	0.06	-0.34**	0.38**	0.16	-0.02	0.23	-0.18	0.13												
Perceived environmental uncertainty	-0.19	-0.33**	-0.34**	-0.27*	0.00	-0.26*	0.06	0.11	-0.22	0.19	0.06												
Attitude: Contact	0.25*	0.02	0.17	0.13	-0.13	0.27*	0.37**	0.29*	0.28*	0.61***													
Attitude: Involvement	0.13	0.03	0.08	0.32**	-0.04	0.00	0.44***	0.54***	0.18														
Attitude: Quality	0.60***	0.23	0.55***	0.48***	-0.38***	0.24	0.31**	0.37**															
Attitude: Preference	0.33**	0.09	0.24	0.32**	-0.42***	-0.02	0.32**																
Attitude: Knowledge	0.19	0.21	0.14	0.22	-0.37**	0.23																	
Complexity of cost accounting	0.24	-0.05	0.27*	0.00	-0.31**																		
Usage type: ceremonial use	-0.51***	-0.11	-0.32**	-0.19																			
Usage type: interactive use	0.62***	0.35**	0.42***																				
Usage type: diagnostic use	0.53***	0.36**																					
Usage type: rationalising use	0.23																						

Explanation:

Bold type: significant at a 1 % level
Italic type: significant at a 5 % and 10 % level

Grey marked boxes above the diagonal are correlations between variables of a common theoretic source or represent intercorrelations of the usage types

Continued…

Domestic German subsidiaries (Pearson correlation - dataset 3)	Usage type: instrumental/conceptual	Usage type: rationalising use	Usage type: diagnostic use	Usage type: interactive use	Usage type: ceremonial use	Complexity of cost accounting	Attitude: Knowledge	Attitude: Preference	Attitude: Quality	Attitude: Involvement	Attitude: Contact	Perceived environmental uncertainty	Objective: Decision facilitating	Objective: Decision influencing	Relational Context	Corporate managers' involvement	Expatriates	Parent company directives	Size of the subsidiary	Form of market entry	Length of affiliation	Size of the parent company	Work experience
Board Member												-0.04	0.18	0.04	0.16	0.03	-0.05	0.02	0.14	-0.08	-0.05	-0.03	0.14
Working experience												-0.13	0.13	__0.44***__	-0.22	-0.04	0.01	0.18	0.23	0.09	-0.12	0.09	
Size of the parent company												__-0.42***__	_0.25*_	_0.31**_	0.20	0.25	-0.16	-0.04	0.23	0.23	-0.17		
Length of affiliation												0.24	-0.20	-0.09	-0.04	-0.12	-0.07	-0.06	0.05	_-0.33**_			
Form of market entry												_-0.31**_	0.10	0.16	-0.01	0.13	-0.06	_-0.28*_	-0.11				
Size of the subsidiary												-0.08	-0.22	0.24	0.12	-0.04	-0.18	-0.03					
Parent company directives												-0.11	0.12	0.05	-0.02	0.22	_0.27*_						
Expatriates												-0.14	_0.37**_	0.12	-0.18	0.22							
Corporate managers' involvement												_-0.33**_	0.23	-0.06	0.11								
Relational Context												0.18	0.08	-0.19									
Objective: Decision influencing												_-0.32**_	0.21										
Objective: Decision facilitating												__-0.52***__											
Perceived environmental uncertainty																							
Attitude: Contact																							
Attitude: Involvement																							
Attitude: Quality																							
Attitude: Preference																							
Attitude: Knowledge																							
Complexity of cost accounting																							
Usage type: ceremonial use																							
Usage type: interactive use																							
Usage type: diagnostic use																							
Usage type: rationalising use																							

Explanation:

Bold type: significant at a 1 % level
Italic type: significant at a 5 % and 10 % level

Grey marked boxes above the diagonal are correlations between variables of a common theoretic source or represent intercorrelations of the usage types

Appendix 9 – Table 2: Domestic German subsidiaries

Appendix 10: Detailed regression results on the determinants of the five usage types

Linear regression model - dataset 3 (unstandardised regression coeff.)	Dependent variable: instrumental/conceptual use					
	Anglophone subsidiaries			German subsidiaries		
	E.S.	Model (a)	Model (b)	E.S.	Model (a)	Model (b)
Complexity of cost accounting	+	2.0085 **	1.8883 **	+	-1.9640 #	-1.1122
Knowledge	+/-	0.1530	0.1493	+/-	-0.0263	-0.0489
Preference	+	0.4478 **	0.4520 **	+	0.1540	0.2549
Quality	+	0.0462	-0.0531	+	0.2985 ***	0.2411 **
Involvement	+	0.2993	0.3499	+	-0.1586	-0.1826
Contact	+	-0.1738	-0.2366	+	0.3604 **	0.3762 *
Perceived environmental uncertainty	+/-	0.1178	0.0886	+/-	-0.2189	-0.1915
Objective: decision facilitating	+	0.1565	0.1672	+	-0.0895	-0.0803
Objective: decision influencing	/	0.0421	0.0444	/	0.1175	0.1088
Relational context (centralised)	/	0.0357	0.0974	/	0.2292	0.2033
Directives *(centralised)*	-	-0.1379 *	-0.1751 *	-	-0.1302 *	-0.1195 *
Directives **x** Rel. context *(centralised)*	+		-0.1248 ###	+		0.0083
Corporate managers *(centralised)*	-	0.0776	0.1055 #	-	0.1306 ##	0.1286
Corp. managers **x** Rel. context *(central.)*	+		0.0513	+		0.0631
Expatriates *(centralised)*	-	0.4507 #	0.3899	-	-0.2198	-0.1482
Expatriates **x** Rel. context *(centralised)*	+		0.1687	+		-0.2106
Size subsidiary	/	0.0058	-0.0034	/	-0.1767	-0.1127
Form of market entry *(dummy)*	/	0.2018	0.1187	/	-0.0027	0.0512
Length of affiliation	/	0.1806	0.0766	/	0.2622	0.2573
Size parent company	/	0.0863	0.0895	/	0.0458	0.0407
Years of working experience	/	-0.0043	-0.0017	/	0.4363	0.3239
Board member	/	0.0111	0.0417	/	0.1936	0.0988
Constant	/	-2.6514	-1.5931	/	2.7501	2.0349
R^2		69.46 %	75.48 %		59.76 %	61.41 %
adjusted R^2		48.00 %	53.00 %		29.20 %	22.80 %
F		9.03	17.02		3.06	3.97
Significance		0.0000	0.0000		0.0012	0.0001
VIF_{max}		8.30	8.38		4.49	4.61
F (moderation)		2.48 *			0.40	

Appendix 10 –Table 1: Instrumental/Conceptual use

Linear regression model - dataset 3 (unstandardised regression coeff.)	Dependent variable: rationalising use					
	Anglophone subsidiaries			German subsidiaries		
	E.S.	Model (a)	Model (b)	E.S.	Model (a)	Model (b)
Complexity of cost accounting	+	-0.3997	-0.3237	+	-5.2204 ##	-3.2703
Knowledge	+/-	0.0977	0.1638	+/-	0.3401	0.4161 *
Preference	+/-	0.5064	0.4644	+/-	-0.1152	0.0802
Quality	+/-	0.1438	-0.0399	+/-	0.2077	0.1764
Involvement	+/-	-0.0994	-0.0769	+/-	-0.0704	-0.4771 **
Contact	+/-	0.1578	0.0874	+/-	-0.0705	0.0918
Perceived environmental uncertainty	+/-	0.0669	-0.0293	+/-	-0.4099 *	-0.3711 *
Objective: decision facilitating	/	0.1010	0.1339	/	-0.0486	0.0969
Objective: decision influencing	/	0.0889	0.0933	/	0.1287	0.1363
Relational context (centralised)	/	0.4396 **	0.5633 ***	/	0.4996 **	0.5323 **
Directives *(centralised)*	-	-0.2858 **	-0.4314 ***	-	0.0788	0.1478 #
Directives **x** Rel. context *(centralised)*	+		-0.1214 ##	+		0.1242
Corporate managers *(centralised)*	-	-0.1364 *	-0.1336	-	0.1279	-0.1071
Corp. managers **x** Rel. context *(central.)*	+		0.0190	+		-0.1996 ##
Expatriates *(centralised)*	-	0.3729	-0.0881	-	-0.6224 *	-0.6775 ***
Expatriates **x** Rel. context *(centralised)*	+		0.7040 ***	+		-0.5811 ###
Size subsidiary	/	-0.2422	-0.3048	/	-0.3186	-0.1110
Form of market entry *(dummy)*	/	-1.2976 **	-1.9067 ***	/	0.0415	0.4326
Length of affiliation	/	-0.0887	-0.4022	/	0.1616	0.2275
Size parent company	/	0.0082	0.0272	/	0.0208	-0.0363
Years of working experience	/	0.0060	-0.0260	/	0.8820 *	0.5092
Board member	/	-0.7672 **	-0.8281 *	/	0.0093	-0.3295
Constant	/	2.5812	5.4412	/	6.2090 **	4.1225
R^2		55.30 %	62.68 %		45.68 %	67.50 %
adjusted R^2		23.90 %	28.50 %		7.90 %	35.00 %
F		6.23	17.93		3.47	31.12
Significance		0.0000	0.0000		0.0004	0.0000
VIF_{max}		8.30	8.38		4.49	4.61
F (moderation)		2.35 *			5.33 ***	

Appendix 10 – Table 2: Rationalising use

Linear regression model - dataset 3 (unstandardised regression coeff.)	**Dependent variable: diagnostic use**					
	Anglophone subsidiaries			German subsidiaries		
	E.S.	Model (a)	Model (b)	E.S.	Model (a)	Model (b)
Complexity of cost accounting	+	1.4603	1.1976	+	-2.5663 #	-2.2206
Knowledge	+	0.3382	0.3132	+	-0.0669	-0.0619
Preference	+	0.2494	0.2548	+	-0.0029	-0.0492
Quality	+	-0.0115	-0.0673	+	0.2616	0.3084
Involvement	+	-0.1500	-0.0944	+	-0.1862	-0.1610
Contact	+	0.2362	0.1758	+	0.1232	0.0072
Perceived environmental uncertainty	+/-	-0.0109	-0.0219	+/-	-0.1463	-0.1153
Objective: decision facilitating	/	-0.0664	-0.0611	/	0.2009	0.2251
Objective: decision influencing	+	0.4604 ***	0.4471 ***	+	0.5508 ***	0.6066 ***
Relational context (centralised)	/	0.2194	0.2044	/	0.1043	0.1272
Directives *(centralised)*	-	-0.0707	-0.0598	-	0.0541	0.0564
Directives **x** Rel. context *(centralised)*	+		-0.0964	+		-0.0872
Corporate managers *(centralised)*	-	-0.0055	0.0485	-	0.0926	0.0168
Corp. managers **x** Rel. context *(central.)*	+		0.1144	+		-0.1468 ##
Expatriates *(centralised)*	-	0.1901	0.2572	-	-0.7319 ***	-0.8283 ***
Expatriates **x** Rel. context *(centralised)*	+		-0.1014	+		0.1901
Size subsidiary	/	0.2568	0.2932	/	0.0161	-0.2223
Form of market entry *(dummy)*	/	-1.2511 *	-1.1035 *	/	-0.1660	-0.3220
Length of affiliation	/	-0.0958	-0.1199	/	-0.0558	-0.0620
Size parent company	/	0.1164	0.1152	/	-0.1372 **	-0.1105 *
Years of working experience	/	-0.1365	-0.1627	/	0.7088 **	0.7489 *
Board member	/	0.4758	0.6192	/	0.0113	0.0513
Constant	/	-2.9868	-2.5829	/	1.7333	2.7404
R^2		61.50 %	65.26 %		75.30 %	77.37 %
adjusted R^2		34.40 %	33.40 %		56.50 %	54.70 %
F		6.71	7.30		12.98	9.47
Significance		0.0000	0.0000		0.0000	0.000
VIF_{max}		8.30	8.38		4.49	4.61
F (moderation)		1.38			1.10	

Appendix 10 – Table 3: Diagnostic use

Linear regression model - dataset 3 (unstandardised regression coeff.)	Dependent variable: interactive use					
	Anglophone subsidiaries			German subsidiaries		
	E.S.	Model (a)	Model (b)	E.S.	Model (a)	Model (b)
Complexity of cost accounting	+	-0.1349	-0.4905	+	-2.8261	0.0316
Knowledge	+	0.1360	0.1477	+	0.0576	-0.0171
Preference	+	0.4494	0.4112	+	0.1037	0.4041 *
Quality	+	0.2400	0.1038	+	0.3078 **	0.1429
Involvement	+	0.2262	0.2913	+	0.0705	0.0207
Contact	+	-0.3880	-0.4911 #	+	0.0608	0.0531
Perceived environmental uncertainty	+/-	0.2597 *	0.1895	+/-	-0.2871	-0.1849
Objective: decision facilitating	/	-0.0407	-0.0143	/	-0.0794	-0.0446
Objective: decision influencing	+	0.3291 **	0.2948 *	+	0.3871 ***	0.3837 ***
Relational context (centralised)	/	0.0029	-0.0303	/	0.1103	0.0347
Directives *(centralised)*	-	-0.1080	-0.1572	-	-0.0329	0.0003
Directives **x** Rel. context *(centralised)*	+		-0.1248 #	+		-0.0176
Corporate managers *(centralised)*	-	0.0284	0.1143	-	-0.1180	-0.1487
Corp. managers **x** Rel. context *(central.)*	+		0.2114 **	+		0.1480
Expatriates *(centralised)*	-	0.2237	0.0375	-	-0.1553	0.0371
Expatriates **x** Rel. context *(centralised)*	+		0.1349	+		-0.5775 ###
Size subsidiary	/	0.2185	0.2656	/	-0.3663 *	-0.2741
Form of market entry *(dummy)*	/	-0.3993	-0.4882	/	-0.0252	0.0636
Length of affiliation	/	0.2300	0.0493	/	0.2981	0.2763 *
Size parent company	/	0.1135	0.1238	/	0.0327	0.0305
Years of working experience	/	0.1316	0.0258	/	0.2291	-0.1044
Board member	/	0.0947	0.3390	/	-0.0882	-0.3657
Constant	/	-3.7648	-1.8631	/	3.6272	1.8354
R^2		47.00 %	58.32 %		66.24 %	74.03 %
adjusted R^2		9.70 %	20.10 %		40.60 %	48.10 %
F		7.01	5.99		2.11	6.91
Significance		0.0000	0.0000		0.0222	0.0000
VIF_{max}		8.30	8.38		4.49	4.61
F (moderation)		2.05			2.71 *	

Appendix 10 – Table 4: Interactive use

Linear regression model - dataset 3 (unstandardised regression coeff.)	**Dependent variable: ceremonial use**					
	Anglophone subsidiaries			German subsidiaries		
	E.S.	Model (a)	Model (b)	E.S.	Model (a)	Model (b)
Complexity of cost accounting	+/-	0.1764	0.3257	+/-	0.8109	1.8443
Knowledge	+/-	0.0430	-0.0251	+/-	-0.2437 **	-0.3051 **
Preference	-	-0.7470 ***	-0.6638 ***	-	-0.5843 ***	-0.5073 **
Quality	-	-0.1680 *	-0.0530	-	-0.0104	-0.0677
Involvement	-	-0.8701 ***	-0.8724 ***	-	0.2481	0.3614
Contact	-	0.5327 ##	0.5926 ##	-	-0.2147	-0.3190
Perceived environmental uncertainty	+/-	-0.3889 ***	-0.2888 **	+/-	-0.1071	-0.0525
Objective: decision facilitating	/	0.1037	0.0679	/	-0.2614 **	-0.2789 **
Objective: decision influencing	/	-0.0999	-0.0582	/	0.0487	0.0679
Relational context (centralised)	/	0.2716 *	0.3329 **	/	0.0851	0.0445
Directives *(centralised)*	+	-0.0544	0.0420	+	0.1621 **	0.1587 **
Directives **x** Rel. context *(centralised)*	-		0.0104	-		-0.0853
Corporate managers *(centralised)*	+	-0.0221	-0.0757	+	-0.0634	-0.0370
Corp. managers **x** Rel. context *(central.)*	-		-0.1715 ***	-		0.0794
Expatriates *(centralised)*	+	-0.9929 ###	-0.5491 #	+	-0.1463	-0.0681
Expatriates **x** Rel. context *(centralised)*	-		-0.3640 **	-		-0.0402
Size subsidiary	/	0.2048	0.1777	/	-0.3490 *	-0.4665
Form of market entry *(dummy)*	/	-0.8542	-0.4588	/	0.0526	-0.0901
Length of affiliation	/	-0.4257	-0.1727	/	-0.1753	-0.2103
Size parent company	/	0.0049	-0.0155	/	-0.0702	-0.0421
Years of working experience	/	0.2438	0.3967 *	/	-0.4632	-0.5040
Board member	/	-0.4432	-0.6333 *	/	-0.0571	-0.0792
Constant	/	10.1084 ***	7.6984 ***	/	11.5838 ***	11.7246 ***
R^2		63.86 %	71.16 %		68.01 %	70.04 %
adjusted R^2		38.40 %	44.70 %		43.70 %	40.10 %
F		4.98	6.38		1.91	1.40
Significance		0.0000	0.0000		0.0406	0.1723
VIF_{max}		8.30	8.38		4.49	4.61
F (moderation)		3.17 **			0.55	

Appendix 10 – Table 5: Ceremonial use

Appendix 11: Comparison of performance evaluations by management accountants and managers (dataset 3)

Dataset 3	Difference in management accountants' (1) and managers' (2) performance assessments [(1) - (2)]	
	Satisfaction	Goal attainment
Anglophone subsidiaries	mean = - 0.13 p-value = 1.00 (for H_1: mean = 0; two-tailed one sample t-test)	mean = - 0.11 p-value = 0.7213 (for H_1: mean = 0; two-tailed one sample t-test)
German subsidiaries	mean = 0.00 p-value = 0.3225 (for H_1: mean = 0; two-tailed one sample t-test)	mean = - 0.03 p-value = 0.4049 (for H_1: mean = 0; two-tailed one sample t-test)

Appendix 11 – Table 1: Differences in performance evaluation of management accountants and managers of the same company

Pearson correlations	Anglophone subsidiaries – dataset 3			
	Satisfaction (Cost accountants)	Goal attainment (Cost accountants)	Satisfaction (Manager)	Goal attainment (Manager)
Satisfaction (Cost accountants)		0.3302 **	0.7846 ***	0.3614 ***
Goal attainment (Cost accountants)			0.4799 ***	0.7326 ***
Satisfaction (Manager)				0.4037 ***

Appendix 11 – Table 2: Pearson correlations between management accountants' and managers' performance assessments (Anglophone subsidiaries)

Pearson correlations	Domestic German subsidiaries – dataset 3			
	Satisfaction (Cost accountants)	Goal attainment (Cost accountants)	Satisfaction (Manager)	Goal attainment (Manager)
Satisfaction (Cost accountants)		0.5885 ***	0.8524 ***	0.5824 **
Goal attainment (Cost accountants)			0.5373 ***	0.8171 ***
Satisfaction (Manager)				0.5187 ***

Appendix 11 – Table 3: Pearson correlations between management accountants' and managers' performance assessments (domestic German subsidiaries)

References

Abdel-Kader, M./Luther, R. (2008): The impact of firm characteristics on management accounting practices: A UK-based empirical analysis, in: The British Accounting Review, 40 (1), p. 2–27.

Abdel-Kader, M. G./Luther, R. (2006): Management accounting practices in the UK food and drinks industry, London (2006).

Abernethy, M. (2001): Product diversity and costing system design choice: field study evidence, in: Management Accounting Research, 12 (3), p. 261–279.

Abernethy, M. A./Bouwens, J./van Lent, L. (2010): Leadership and control system design, in: Management Accounting Research, 21 (1), p. 2–16.

Abernethy, M. A./Brownell, P. (1999): The role of budgets in organizations facing strategic change: an exploratory study, in: Accounting, Organizations and Society, 24 (3), p. 189–204.

Abrahamson, E. (1991): Managerial Fads and Fashions: The Diffusion and Rejection of Innovations, in: The Academy of Management Review, 16 (3), p. 586–612.

Adams, C./Hoque, Z./McNicholas, P. (2006): Case studies and action research, in: Hoque, Z. (ed.): Methodological issues in accounting research, London (2006), p. 361–373.

Agthe, K. (1959): Stufenweise Fixkostendeckung im System des Direct Costing, in: Zeitschrift für Betriebswirtschaft, 29 , p. 404–418.

Aguinis, H. (1995): Statistical Power with Moderated Multiple Regression in Management Research, in: Journal of Management, 21 (6), p. 1141–1158.

Aguinis, H. (2004): Regression analysis for categorical moderators, New York (2004).

Ahmed, M. N./Scapens, R. W. (2000): Cost allocation in Britain: towards an institutional analysis, in: European Accounting Review, 9 (2), p. 159–204.

Ahrens, T./Chapman, C. (2007): Management accounting as practice, in: Accounting, Organizations and Society, 32 (1-2), p. 1–27.

Ahrens, T. (1999): Contrasting involvements, Amsterdam (1999).

Ahrens, T./Chapman, C. S. (2000): Occupational identity of management accountants in Britain and Germany, in: European Accounting Review, 9 (4), p. 477–498.

Ahrens, T./Chapman, C. (1999): The Role of Management Accountants in Britain and Germany, in: Management Accounting Quarterly, 10 (1), p. 42–43.

Al Chen, Y./Romocki, T./Zuckerman, G. (1997): Examination of U.S.-based Japanese subsidiaries: Evidence of the transfer of the Japanese strategic cost management, in: The International Journal of Accounting, 32 (4), p. 417–440.

Albers, S./Hildebrandt, L. (2006): Methodische Probleme bei der Erfolgsfaktorenforschung – Messfehler, formative versus reflektive Indikatoren und die Wahl des Strukturgleichungs-Modells, in: Zeitschrift für betriebswirtschaftliche Forschung, 58 (1), p. 2–33.

Albert, H. (1980): Traktat über kritische Vernunft, 4th edn., Tübingen (1980).

Albert, M. (1996): Unrealisitische Annahmen und empirische Prüfung: Methodologische Probleme der Ökonomie am Beispiel der Außenhandelstheorie, in: Zeitschrift für Wirtschafts und Sozialwissenschaften, 116 (3), p. 451–486.

Al-Omiri, M./Drury, C. (2007): A survey of factors influencing the choice of product costing systems in UK organizations, in: Management Accounting Research, 18 (4), p. 399–424.

Al-Sayed, M./Abdel-Kader, M./Kholeif, A. (2012): ABC diffusion in the age of digital economy: the UK experience, in: International Journal of Management Accounting Research, 2 (1), p. 139–150.

Amat, O./Blake, J./Oliveras, E. (2000): Variations in National Management Accounting Approaches, UPF Economics and Business Working Paper No. 415. (2000).

Amshoff, B. (2003): Berichtswesen in Multinationalen Unternehmen, in: Holtbrügge, D. (ed.): Management multinationaler Unternehmungen, Heidelberg (2003), p. 345–362.

Anderson, S. W. (1995): A Framework for Assessing Cost Management System Changes: The Case of Activity-Based Costing Implementation at General Motors, 1986-1993, in: Journal of Management Accounting Research, 7 (1), p. 1–51.

Anderson, S. W./Young, S. M. (1999): The impact of contextual factors and process factors on the evaluation of activity-based costing systems, in: Accounting, Organizations and Society, 24 (7), p. 525–559.

Anderson, S. W./Hesford, J. W./Young, S. M. (2002): Factors influencing the performance of activity based costing teams: a field study of ABC model development time in the automobile industry, in: Accounting, Organizations and Society, 27 (3), p. 195–211.

Anderson, S. W./Young, S. M. (2001): Implementing management innovations, Boston (2001).

Angelkort, H. (2010): Integration des Rechnungswesens als Erfolgsfaktor für die Controllerarbeit, Frankfurt am Main (2010).

Ansari, S./Euske, K. (1987): Rational, Rationalizing, and Reifying Uses of Accounting Data in Organizations, in: Accounting, Organizations and Society, 12 (6), p. 549–570.

Anthony, R. N./Govindarajan, V. (2007): Management control systems, 12th edn., Boston (2007).

Armstrong, J./Overton, T. (1977): Estimating nonresponse bias in mail surveys, in: Journal of Marketing Research, 14 (3), p. 396–402.

Askarany, D./Yazdifar, H. (2012): An investigation into the mixed reported adoption rates for ABC: Evidence from Australia, New Zealand and the UK, in: International Journal of Production Economics, 135 (1), p. 430–439.

Auer, B./Rottmann, H. (2012): Statistik und Ökonometrie für Wirtschaftswissenschaftler, 2nd edn., Wiesbaden (2012).

Auer, L. v. (2011): Ökonometrie, 5th edn., Heidelberg (2011).

Aust, R. (1999): Kostenrechnung als unternehmensinterne Dienstleistung, Wiesbaden (1999).

Bach, S./Brettel, M./Grothe, M./Schäffer, U./Weber, J. (2001): Grundmodell einer dynamischen Theorie ökonomischer Akteure, in: Weber, J./Schäffer, U. (eds.): Rationalitätssicherung der Führung, Wiesbaden (2001), p. 95–111.

Backhaus, K./Erichson, B./Plinke, W./Weiber, R. (2011): Multivariate Analysemethoden, 13th edn., Berlin (2011).

Backhaus, K./Erichson, B./Weiber, R. (2013): Fortgeschrittene Multivariate Analysemethoden, 2nd edn., Berlin (2013).

Baird, K./Harrison, G./Reeve, R. (2004): Adoption of activity management practices: a note on the extent of adoption and the influence of organizational and cultural factors, in: Management Accounting Research, 15 (4), p. 383–399.

Baliga, B. R./Jaeger, A. M. (1984): Multinational Corporations: Control Systems and Delegation Issues, in: Journal of International Business Studies, 15 (2), p. 25–40.

Balke, S./Eberenz, R. (2006): Kostenrechnung als Instrument der Entscheidungssteuerung in der Praxis der Beiersdorf AG, in: Zeitschrift für Controlling und Management, 50 (Sonderheft 1), p. 105–111.

Baron, R. M./Kenny, D. A. (1986): The moderator–mediator variable distinction in social psychological research: Conceptual, strategic, and statistical considerations, in: Journal of Personality and Social Psychology, 51 (6), p. 1173–1182.

Bartlett, C. A./Ghoshal, S. (1989): Managing across borders, Boston (1989).

Bauer, M. (2002): Controllership in Deutschland, Wiesbaden (2002).

Baumann, K.-H. (1986): Das Rechnungswesen als Instrument zur Steuerung und Kontrolle von US-Tochtergesellschaften deutscher Unternehmen, in: Zeitschrift für betriebswirtschaftliche Forschung, 35 (5), p. 425–432.

Baxter, J./Chua, W. F. (2003): Alternative management accounting research - whence and whither, in: Accounting, Organizations and Society, 28 (2-3), p. 97–126.

Becker, H. P. (1984): Verwendung und Gestaltung der Kosten- und Leistungsrechnung in mittelgrossen Industrieunternehmen, Darmstadt (1984).

Becker, W./Ebner, R./Mayer, T. A./Ulrich, P. (2013): Controlling-Instrumente in mittelständischen Unternehmen, in: Controller Magazin, 38 (3), p. 58–62.

Bender, R./Lange, S./Ziegler, A. (2007): Wichtige Signifikanztests, in: Deutsche Medizinische Wochenschrift, 132 (S 01), p. e24.

Berekoven, L./Eckert, W./Ellenrieder, P. (2009): Marktforschung, 12th edn., Wiesbaden (2009).

Berens, W./Dörges, C. E./Hoffjan, A. (2000): Fundierung eines Verständnisses des Controlling multinationaler Unternehmen, in: Berens, W./Born, A./Hoffjan, A. (eds.): Controlling international tätiger Unternehmen, Stuttgart (2000), p. 1–12.

Berger, P. L./Luckmann, T. (2004): Die gesellschaftliche Konstruktion der Wirklichkeit, 20th edn., Frankfurt am Main (2004).

Bettinghaus, B./Debruine, M./Sopariwala, P. R. (2012): Idle Capacity Costs: It Isn't Just the Expense, in: Management Accounting Quarterly, 13 (2), p. 1–7.

Bhimani, A. (1999): Mapping methodological frontiers in cross-national management control research, in: Accounting, Organizations and Society, 24 (5-6), p. 413–440.

Bhimani, A. (2003): A Study of the emergence of management accounting system ethos and its influence on perceived system success, in: Accounting, Organizations and Society, 28 (523-548), p. 6.

Bhimani, A. (2004): Product Pricing and Competitive Market Pricing: Beyond economic Logic, in: Göbel, S. (ed.): Unternehmensrechnung, München (2004), p. 571–604.

Bhimani, A. (2005): International Comparative Management Accounting, in: Clubb, C. (ed.): The Blackwell encyclopedia of Accounting, Oxford (2005), p. 250–255.

Bhimani, A./Bromwich, M. (2010): Management accounting: Retrospect and Prospect, Amsterdam (2010).

Bhimani, A./Gosselin, M./Ncube, M./Okano, H. (2007): Activity-Based Costing: How far have we come internationally?, in: Cost Management, 21 (3), p. 12–17.

Bhimani, A./Pigott, D. (1992): Implementing ABC: a case study of organizational and behavioural consequences, in: Management Accounting Research, 3 (2), p. 119–132.

Birkinshaw, J./Holm, U./Thilenius, P./Arvidsson, N. (2000): Consequences of perception gaps in the headquarters–subsidiary relationship, in: International Business Review, 9 (3), p. 321–344.

Birkinshaw, J./Hood, N. (1998): Multinational Subsidiary Evolution: Capability and Charter Change in Foreign-Owned Subsidiary Companies, in: Academy of Management Review, 23 (4), p. 773–795.

Birnberg, J. G./Shields, M. D./Young, S. M. (1990): The Case for Multiple Methods in Empirical management Accounting Research (With an Illustration from Budget Setting), in: Journal of Management Accounting Research, 2 (1), p. 33.

Bisbe, J./Otley, D. (2004): The effects of the interactive use of management control systems on product innovation, in: Accounting, Organizations and Society, 29 (8), p. 709–737.

Bisbe, J./Batista-Foguet, J.-M./Chenhall, R. (2007): Defining management accounting constructs: A methodological note on the risks of conceptual misspecification, in: Accounting, Organizations and Society, 32 (7-8), p. 789–820.

Bisbe, J./Malagueño, R. (2009): The Choice of Interactive Control Systems under Different Innovation Management Modes, in: European Accounting Review, 18 (2), p. 371–405.

Bjørnenak, T. (1997): Conventional wisdom and costing practices, in: Management Accounting Research, 8 (4), p. 367–382.

Blake, J./Soldevila, P./Wraith, P. (2003): The dimensions of, and factors giving rise to, variations in national management accounting approaches, in: European Business Review, 15 (3), p. 181–188.

Blocher, E./Stout, D. E./Cokins, G. (2010): Cost management, 5th edn., Boston (2010).

Bohr, K./Obermeier, R. (2004): Grenzen der Grenzplankostenrechnung, in: Göbel, S. (ed.): Unternehmensrechnung, München (2004), p. 585–604.

Boons, A. A. M./Roberts, H. J./Roozen, F. A. (1992): Contrasting activity-based costing German/Dutch cost pool method, in: Management Accounting Research, 3 (2), p. 97–117.

Bortz, J./Lienert, G. A./Boehnke, K. (2008): Verteilungsfreie Methoden in der Biostatistik, 3rd edn., Heidelberg (2008).

Bortz, J./Schuster, C. (2010): Statistik für Human- und Sozialwissenschaftler, 7th edn., Berlin (2010).

Brewer, P. C. (1998): National Culture and activity-based costing systems: a note, in: Management Accounting Research, 9 (2), p. 241–260.

Brierley, J. A. (2008a): An Examination of the Factors Influencing the Level of Consideration for Activity-based Costing, in: International Journal of Business and Management, 3 (8), p. 58–67.

Brierley, J. A. (2008b): Toward an Understanding of the Sophistication of Product Costing Systems, in: Journal of Management Accounting Research, 20 (Special Issue), p. 61–78.

Brierley, J. A./Cowton, C. J./Drury, C. (2007): Product Costing Practice in Different Manufacturing Industries: A British Survey, in: International Journal of Management Reviews, 24 (4), p. 667–675.

Brierley, J. A./Cowton, C. J./Drury, C. (2001): Research into product costing practice: a European perspective, in: European Accounting Review, 10 (2), p. 215–256.

Briers, M. (1997): Translating activity based costing, Unpublished Doctoral Dissertation (1997).

Briers, M./Chua, W. F. (2001): The role of actor-networks and boundary objects in management accounting change: a field study of an implemenation of activity-based costing, in: Accounting, Organizations and Society, 26 (3), p. 237–269.

Brink, H.-J. (1992): Einflußfaktoren auf die Gestaltung der Kostenrechnungssysteme, in: Männel, W. (ed.): Handbuch Kostenrechnung, Wiesbaden (1992), p. 167–181.

Brislin, R. W. (1970): Back-Translation for Cross-Cultural Research, in: Journal of Cross-Cultural Psychology, 1 (3), p. 185–216.

Brown, D. A./Booth, P./Giacoobe, F. (2004): Technological and organizational influences on the adoption of activity-based costing in Australia, in: Accounting and Finance, 44 , p. 329–356.

Brown, M. B./Forsythe, A. B. (1974): Robust Tests for the Equality of Variances, in: Journal of the American Statistical Association, 69 (346), p. 364–367.

Bungenstock, C. (1995): Entscheidungsorientierte Kostenrechnungssysteme, Wiesbaden (1995).

Burchell, S./Clubb, C./Hopwood, A./Hughes, J./Nahapiet, J. (1980): The Roles of Accounting in Organizations and Society, in: Accounting, Organizations and Society, 5 (1), p. 5–27.

Burns, J./Scapens, R. W. (2000): Conceptualizing management accounting change: an institutional framework, in: Management Accounting Research, 11 (1), p. 3–25.

Burrell, G./Morgan, G. (1979): Sociological paradigms and organisational analysis, Portsmouth (1979).

Busco, C./Giovannoni, E./Riccaboni, A. (2007): Globalisation and the international convergence of management accounting, in: Hopper, T./Scapens, R./Northcott, D. (eds.): Issues in management accounting, 3rd edn., Harlow (2007), p. 65–92.

Busco, C./Frigo, M. L./Giovannoni, E./Riccaboni, A./Scapens, R. W. (2006): Integrating Global Organizations through Performance Measurement Systems: How systems of performance management helped GE and Nestlé Waters achieve cultural alignment, in: Strategic Finance, 87 (7), p. 30–35.

Busse von Colbe, W. (1996): Accounting and the business economics tradition in Germany, in: European Accounting Review, 5 (3), p. 413–434.

Cagwin, D./Bouwman, M. J. (2002): The association between activity-based costing and improvement in financial performance, in: Management Accounting Research, 13 (1), p. 1–39.

Cameron, A. C./Trivedi, P. K. (2010): Microeconometrics using Stata, College Station (2010).

Caplan, N. S./Morrison, A./Stambaugh, R. J. (1975): The use of social science knowledge in policy decisions at the national level, Ann Arbor (1975).

Cappallo, S. (2006): Funktionen und Ziele wissenschaftlichen Fortschritts aus strukturationstheoretischer Perspektive, in: Zelewski, S. (ed.): Fortschritt in den Wirtschaftswissenschaften, Wiesbaden (2006), p. 19–48.

Carruthers, B. (1995): Accounting, ambiguity, and the new institutionalism, in: Accounting, Organizations and Society, 20 (4), p. 313–328.

Chang, Y. Y./Mellahi, K./Wilkinson, A. (2009): Control of subsidiaries of MNCs from emerging economies in developed countries: the case of Taiwanese MNCs in the UK, in: The International Journal of Human Resource Management, 20 (1), p. 75–95.

Chatterjee, S./Hadi, A. S. (2012): Regression analysis by example, 5th edn., Hoboken (2012).

Cheng, H.-L./Yu, C.-M. J. (2012): Adoption of Practices by Subsidiaries and Institutional Interaction within Internationalised Small- and Medium-Sized Enterprises, in: Management International Review, 52 (1), p. 81–105.

Chenhall, R. H. (2003): Management control systems design within its organizational context: findings from contingency-based research and directions for the future, in: Accounting, Organizations and Society, 28 (2-3), p. 127–168.

Chenhall, R. H. (2004): The Role of Cognitive and Affective Conflict in Early Implementation of Activity-Based Cost Management, in: Behavioral Research in Accounting, 16 (1), p. 19–44.

Chenhall, R. H./Langfield-Smith, K. (1998): Adoption and benefits of management accounting practices: an Australian study, in: Management Accounting Research, 9 (1), p. 1–19.

Chin, W. W. (1998): The Partial Least Squares Approach for Structural Equation Modeling, in: Marcoulides, G. A. (ed.): Modern methods for business research, Mahwah (1998), p. 295–336.

Chmielewicz, K. (1994): Forschungskonzeptionen der Wirtschaftswissenschaft, 3rd edn., Stuttgart (1994).

Chow, C. W./Shields, M. D./Wu, A. (1999): The importance of national culture in the design of and preference for management controls for multi-national operations, in: Accounting, Organizations and Society, 24 (5-6), p. 441–461.

Christensen, J./Wagenhofer, A. (1997): Editorial, in: Management Accounting Research, 8 (3), p. 255–259.

Christensen, J./Demski, J. S. (1995): The classical foundations of 'modern' costing, in: Management Accounting Research, 6 (1), p. 13–32.

Chung, L. H./Gibbons, P. T./Schoch, H. P. (2000): The influence of subsidiary context and head office strategic management style on control of MNCs: the experience in Australia, in: Accounting, Auditing & Accountability Journal, 13 (5), p. 647–668.

Chung, L. H./Gibbons, P. T./Schoch, H. P. (2002): Performance metrics, parenting style and control : a study of MNC subsidiaries in four countries, in: Epstein, M. J./Manzoni, J.-F. (eds.): Performance measurement and management control: A compendium of research, Amsterdam (2002), p. 109–128.

Churchill, G. A. (1979): A Paradigm for Developing Better Measures of Marketing Constructs, in: Journal of Marketing Research, 16 (1), p. 64–73.

Clarke, P. J./Hill, N. T./Stevens, K. (1999): Activity-Based Costing in Ireland: Barriers to, and opportunities for, change, in: Critical Perspectives in Accounting, 10 (4), p. 443–468.

Clinton, D. (2007): Crisis! When will the accounting profession finally recognize the value of management accountants?, in: Strategic Finance, 88 (1), p. 14–30.

Clinton, D./White, L. (2012): The role of the Management Accountant: 2003-2012, in: Management Accounting Quarterly, 14 (1), p. 40–74.

Clinton, D./Webber, S. A. (2004): RCA at Clopay: Here's innovation in management accounting with resource consumption accounting, in: Strategic Finance, 85 (4), p. 21–26.

Coenenberg, A. G./Fischer, T. M./Günther, T. (2012): Kostenrechnung und Kostenanalyse, 8th edn., Stuttgart (2012).

Cohen, J. (2003): Applied multiple regression/correlation analysis for the behavioral sciences, 3rd edn., Mahwah (2003).

Cooper, R. B./Zmud, R. W. (1990): Information Technology Implementation Research: A Technological Diffusion Approach, in: Management Science, 36 (2), p. 123–139.

Cooper, R. (1990): Activity-Based Costing - Wann brauche ich ein Activity-Based Cost-System und welche Kostentreiber sind notwendig? (Teil 2), in: Kostenrechnungspraxis, 34 (5), p. 2271–2279.

Cooper, R./Kaplan, R. S. (1988): Measure Costs Right: Make the Right Decisions, in: Harvard Business Review, 66 (5), p. 96–103.

Cooper, R./Kaplan, R. S. (1991): Activity-Based Costing: Ressourcenmanagement at its best, in: Harvard Manager, 13 (4), p. 87–95.

Cotton, W. D./Jackman, S. M./Brown, R. A. (2003): Note on a New Zealand replication of the Innes et al. UK activity-based costing survey, in: Management Accounting Research, 14 (1), p. 67–72.

Cronbach, L. (1951): Coefficient alpha and the internal structure of tests, in: Psychometrika, 16 (3), p. 297-334.

Crönertz, O. (2010): Stoffstromorientiertes Kostenmanagement, Hamburg (2010).

Cruz, I. (2007): How might hospitality organizations optimize their performance measurement systems?, in: International Journal of Contemporary Hospitality Management, 19 (7), p. 574–588.

Cruz, I./Scapens, R. W./Major, M. (2011): The localisation of a global management control system, in: Accounting, Organizations and Society, 36 (7), p. 412–427.

Cruz, I./Major, M./Scapens, R. W. (2009): Institutionalization and practice variation in the management control of a global/local setting, in: Accounting, Auditing & Accountability Journal, 22 (1), p. 91–117.

Davila, T. (2000): An empirical study on the drivers of management control systems' design in new product development, in: Accounting, Organizations and Society, 25 (4-5), p. 383–409.

Debreu, G. (1976): Werttheorie, Berlin (1976).

Dellmann, K. (1979): Zum Stand der betriebswirtschaftlichen Theorie der Kostenrechnung, in: Zeitschrift für Betriebswirtschaft, 49 (4), p. 319–332.

Dellmann, K. (1984): Kosten- und Leistungsrechnungen, in: Baetge, J. (ed.): Vahlens Kompendium der Betriebswirtschaftslehre, München (1984), p. 271–332.

Demski, J. S./Feltham, G. A. (1976): Cost determination, Ames (1976).

Dent, J. F. (1996): Global competition: challenges for management accounting and control, in: Management Accounting Research, 7 (2), p. 247–269.

DeVellis, R. F. (2012): Scale development, 3rd edn., Thousand Oaks (2012).

Diamantopoulos, A./Souchon, A. L./Durden, G. R./Axinn, C. N./Holzmüller, H. H. (2003): Towards an understanding of cross-national similarities and differences in export information utilization: A perceptual mapping approach, in: International Marketing Review, 20 (1), p. 17–43.

Diamantopoulos, A./Souchon, A. L. (1998): Information Utilisation by Exporting Firms: Conceptualisation, Measurement, an Impact on Export Performance, in: Urban, S. M.-L./Nanopoulos, C. (eds.): Information and management, Wiesbaden (1998), p. 111–140.

Diamantopoulos, A./Winklhofer, H. M. (2001): Index Construction with Formative Indicators: An Alternative to Scale Development, in: Journal of Marketing Research, 38 (2), p. 269–277.

Diamantopoulos, A./Souchon, A. L. (1999): Measuring Export Information Use: Scale Development and Validation, in: Journal of Business Research, 46 (1), p. 1–14.

Diamantopoulos, A./Riefler, P. (2008): Formative Indikatoren: Einige Anmerkungen zu ihrer Art, Validität und Multikollinearität, in: Zeitschrift für Betriebswirtschaft, 78 (11), p. 1183-1196.

Dickmann, T. (2010): Controllingintegration nach M&A-Transaktionen, Frankfurt am Main (2010).

Dietz, D./Snyder, H. (2011): Assessing Internal Controls: Do Management and Staff Agree?, in: Management Accounting Quarterly, 12 (2), p. 35–40.

Dillman, D. A./Bowker, D. K. (2001): The Web Questionnaire Challenge to Survey Methodologists, in: Reips, U.-D./Bosnjak, M. (eds.): Dimensions of Internet science, Lengerich (2001), p. 53–71.

Dillman, D. A./Smyth, J. D./Christian, L. M. (2009): Internet, mail, and mixed-mode surveys, 3rd edn., Hoboken (2009).

DiMaggio, P. J./Powell, W. W. (1991): Introduction, in: Powell, W. W./DiMaggio, P. (eds.): The New Institutionalism in Organizational Analysis, Chicago (1991), p. 1–40.

DiMaggio, P. J./Powell, W. W. (1983): The Iron Cage Revisited: Institutional Isomorphism and Collective Rationality in Organizational Fields, in: American Sociological Review, 48 (2), p. 147–160.

Donaldson, L. (1996): The Normal Science of Structural Contingency Theory, in: Clegg, S./Hardy, C./Nord, W. R. (eds.): Handbook of organization studies, London (1996), p. 57–76.

Donaldson, L. (2001): The contingency theory of organizations, Thousand Oaks (2001).

Dopuch, N. (1993): A Perspective on Cost Drivers, in: The Accounting Review, 68 (3), p. 615–620.

Dorn, G. (1961): Die Entwicklung der industriellen Kostenrechnung in Deutschland, Berlin (1961).

Dossi, A./Patelli, L. (2008): The decision-influencing use of performance measurement systems in relationships between headquarters and subsidiaries, in: Management Accounting Research, 19 (2), p. 126–148.

Dossi, A./Patelli, L. (2010): You Learn From What You Measure: Financial and Non-financial Performance Measures in Multinational Companies, in: Long Range Planning, 43 (4), p. 498–526.

Drury, C. (2012): Management and cost accounting, 8th edn., London (2012).

Drury, C./Tayles, M. (2000): Cost System Design and Profitability Analysis in UK Companies, London (2000).

Drury, C./Braund, S./Osborne, P./Tayles, M. (1993): A survey of management accounting practices in UK manufacturing companies, London (1993).

Drury, C./Tayles, M. (2006): Profitability analysis in UK organizations: An exploratory study, in: The British Accounting Review, 38 (4), p. 405–425.

Drury, C./Tayles, M. (2005): Explicating the design of overhead absorption procedures in UK organizations, in: The British Accounting Review, 37 (1), p. 47–84.

Drury, C./Tayles, M. (1997): Evidence on the Financial Accounting Mentality Debate: A Research Note, in: British Accounting Review, 29 (3), p. 263–276.

Dugdale, D./Jones, T. C./Green, S. (2006): Contemporary management accounting practices in UK manufacturing, Oxford (2006).

Dunk, A. S. (2003): Moderated regression, constructs and measurement in management accounting: a reflection, in: Accounting, Organizations and Society, 28 (7-8), p. 793–802.

Dusemond, M. (2000): Aufbau einer Konzernkostenrechnung zur Unterstützung des internen und externen Konzernrechnungswesens, in: Sierke, B. (ed.): Zeitgerechtes Controlling, Wiesbaden (2000), p. 45–69.

Earl, M. J./Hopwood, A. G. (1980): From Management Information to Information Management, in: Lucas, H. C./Land, F. F./Lincoln, T. J./Supper, K. (eds.): The information systems environment, Amsterdam (1980), p. 3–13.

Echambadi, R./Hess, J. D. (2007): Mean-Centering Does Not Alleviate Collinearity Problems in Moderated Multiple Regression Models, in: Marketing Science, 26 (3), p. 438–445.

Eisenhardt, K. M. (1989): Building Theories from Case Study Research, in: The Academy of Management Review, 14 (4), p. 532–550.

Eisenhardt, K. M./Graebner, M. E. (2007): Theory Building from Case: Opportunities and Callenges, in: Academy of Management Journal, 50 (1), p. 25–32.

Elmar, G. (1979): Prinzipien des Konstruktivismus, in: Raffée, H./Abel, B. (eds.): Wissenschaftstheoretische Grundfragen der Wirtschaftswissenschaften, München (1979), p. 205–208.

Elsik, W. (2004): Controlling aus neoinstitutioneller Perspektive, in: Scherm, E. (ed.): Controlling, München (2004), p. 801–821.

Endenich, C./Brandau, M./Hoffjan, A. (2011): Two Decades of Research on Comparative Management Accounting - Achievements and Future Directions, in: Australian Accounting Review, 21 (4), p. 365–382.

Engelen, A. (2007): Marktorientierung junger Unternehmen, Wiesbaden (2007).

Ernst & Young (2003): 2003 Survey of Management Accounting, Available at: http://www.imanet.org/PDFs/Public/General/2003SurveyofMgtAccting%20EY.pdf, retrieved 20.12.2013.

Euske, K./Riccaboni, A. (1999): Stability to profitability: managing interdependencies to meet a new environment, in: Accounting, Organizations and Society, 24 (5-6), p. 463–481.

Ewert, R./Wagenhofer, A. (2008): Interne Unternehmensrechnung, 7th edn., Berlin (2008).

Ewert, R./Wagenhofer, A. (2006): Management Accounting Theory and Practice in German-Speaking Countries, in: Chapman, C. S./Hopwood, A. G./Shields, M. D. (eds.): Handbook of Management Accounting Research (Vol. 2), Oxford (2006), p. 1035–1069.

Fandel, G./Fey, A./Heuft, B./Pitz, T. (2009): Kostenrechnung, 3rd edn., Berlin (2009).

Fayard, D./Lee, L. S./Leitch, R. A./Kettinger, W. J. (2012): Effect of internal cost management, information systems integration, and absorptive capacity on inter-organizational cost management in supply chains, in: Accounting, Organizations and Society, 37 (3), p. 168–187.

Feldman, M. S./March, J. G. (1981): Information in Organizations as Signal and Symbol, in: Administrative Science Quarterly, 26 (2), p. 171–186.

Ferner, A. (2000): The Underpinnings of 'Bureaucratic' Control Systems: HRM in European Multinationals, in: Journal of Management Studies, 37 (4), p. 521–540.

Ferreira, A./Otley, D. (2010): Design and use of management control systems: An analysis of the interaction between design misfit and intensity of use, Draft Paper (2010).

Firth, M. (1996): The diffusion of managerial accounting procedures in the People's Republic of China and the influence of foreign partnered joint ventures, in: Accounting, Organizations and Society, 21 (7-8), p. 629–654.

Fischer, T. M./Möller, K./Schultze, W. (2012): Controlling, Stuttgart (2012).

Flacke, K. (2007): Controlling in mittelständischen Unternehmen - Ausgestaltung, Einflussfaktoren der Instrumentennutzung und Einfluss auf die Bankkommunikation, Unpublished PhD Thesis (2007).

Fligner, M. A./Policello, G. E. (1981): Robust Rank Procedures for the Behrens-Fisher Problem, in: Journal of the American Statistical Association, 76 (373), p. 162–168.

Fornell, C./Larcker, D. F. (1981): Evaluating Structural Equation Models with Unobservable Variables and Measurement Error, in: Journal of Marketing Research, 18 (1), p. 39–50.

Foster, G./Swenson, D. W. (1997): Measuring the Success of Activity-Based Cost Management and Its Determinants, in: Journal of Management Accounting Research, 9 (1), p. 109–141.

Frank, S. (2000): Erfolgreiche Gestaltung der Kostenrechnung, Wiesbaden (2000).

Frank, S./Reitmeyer, T. (1999): Gestaltung und Erfolgsfaktoren der Kostenrechnung im Mittelstand, in: Kostenrechnungspraxis, 43 (2), p. 15–25.

Franz, K.-P. (2003): Verbundbeziehungen und Komplexität im internationalen Konzern, in: Zeitschrift für betriebswirtschaftliche Forschung, 49 (Sonderheft), p. 1–12.

Franz, K.-P./Hieronimus, A. (2003): Kostenrechnung im international vernetzten Konzern, in: Schmalenbachs Zeitschrift für betriebswirtschaftliche Forschung, 49 (Sonderheft).

Frazier, P. A./Tix, A. P./Barron, K. E. (2004): Testing Moderator and Mediator Effects in Counseling Psychology Research, in: Journal of Counseling Psychology, 51 (1), p. 115–134.

Friedl, G./Hofmann, C./Pedell, B. (2013): Kostenrechnung: Eine entscheidungsorientierte Einführung, 2nd edn., München (2013).

Friedl, G./Küpper, H.-U./Pedell, B. (2005): Relevance Added: Combining ABC with German Cost Accounting, in: Strategic Finance, 85 (12), p. 56–61.

Friedl, G./Frömberg, K./Hammer, C./Küpper, H.-U./Pedell, B. (2009): Stand und Perspektiven der Kostenrechnung in deutschen Großunternehmen, in: Zeitschrift für Controlling und Management, 53 (2), p. 111–116.

Friedman, A. L./Lyne, S. R. (1999): Success and failure of activity-based techniques, London (1999).

Friedrich, R. J. (1982): In Defense of Multiplicative Terms in Multiple Regression Equations, in: American Journal of Political Science, 26 (4), p. 797–833.

Fülbier, U. (2005): Wissenschaftstheorie und Betriebswirtschaftslehre, in: Horsch, A./Meinhövel, H./Paul, S. (eds.): Institutionenökonomie und Betriebswirtschaftslehre, München (2005), p. 15–29.

Gaiser, B. (1997): International Perspectives: German Cost Management Systems, in: Journal of Cost Management, 11 (5), p. 35–41.

Gaiser, B. (1998): Prozeßkostenrechnung und Activity Based Costing (ABC), in: Horváth & Partner (ed.): Prozesskostenmanagement, 2nd edn., München (1998), p. 65–77.

Garg, A./Ghosh, D./Hudick, J./Nowacki, C. (2003): Roles and Practices in Management Accounting Today, in: Strategic Finance, 84 (1), p. 30–35.

Garner, S. P. (1976): Evolution of cost accounting to 1925, University of Alabama (1976).

Garrison, R. H./Noreen, E. W./Brewer, P. C. (2006): Managerial accounting, 11th edn., Boston (2006).

Geiger, D. R./Ittner, C. D. (1996): The influence of funding source and legislative requirements on government cost accounting practices, in: Accounting, Organizations and Society, 21 (6), p. 549–567.

Genschel, U./Becker, C. (2005): Schließende Statistik, Berlin (2005).

Gerlach, M. (2009): Controlling in einem deutsch-chinesischen Joint Venture - Ein Erfahrungsbericht, in: Zeitschrift für Controlling und Management, 53 (2), p. 94–98.

Gooderham, P. N./Nordhaug, O./Ringdal, K. (1999): Institutional and Rational Determinants of Organizational Practices: Human Resource Management in European Firms, in: Administrative Science Quarterly, 44 (3), p. 507–531.

Gordon, L. A./Miller, D. (1976): A Contingency Framework For The Design Of Accounting Information Systems, in: Accounting, Organizations and Society, 1 (1), p. 59–69.

Gordon, L. A./Narayanan, V. K. (1984): Management Accounting Systems, Perceived Environmental Uncertainty and Organisational Structure: An Empirical Investigation, in: Accounting, Organizations and Society, 9 (1), p. 33–47.

Gosselin, M. (1997): The Effect of Strategy and Organizational Structure on the Adoption and Implementation of Activity-Based Costing, in: Accounting, Organizations and Society, 22 (2), p. 105–122.

Götz, O./Liehr-Gobbers, K. (2004): Analyse von Strukturgleichungsmodellen mit Hilfe der Partial-Least-Squares(PLS)-Methode, in: Die Betriebswirtschaft, 64 (6), p. 714–738.

Götze, U. (2010): Kostenrechnung und Kostenmanagement, 5th edn., Berlin (2010).

Gould, W./Pitblado, J. S./Poi, B. (2010): Maximum likelihood estimation with Stata, College Station (2010).

Govindarajan, V. (1984): Appropriateness of accounting data in performance evaluation: An empirical examination of environmental uncertainty as an intervening variable, in: Accounting, Organizations and Society, 9 (2), p. 125–135.

Granlund, M. (2001): Towards explaining stability in and around management accounting systems, in: Management Accounting Research, 12 (2), p. 141–166.

Granlund, M./Lukka, K. (1998): It's a Small World of Management Accounting Practices, in: Journal of Management Accounting Research, 10 (1), p. 153–179.

Grasso, L. P. (2005): Are ABC and RCA Accounting Systems Compatible with Lean Management?, in: Management Accounting Quarterly, 7 (1), p. 12–27.

Grochla, E. (1976): Praxeologische Organisationstheorie durch sachliche und methodische Integration: Eine pragmatische Konzeption, in: Zeitschrift für betriebswirtschaftliche Forschung, 28 (1), p. 617–637.

Groot, T. L. (1997): Activity-Based Costing in the Food Industry: An international comparison of American and Dutch food producing companies (1997).

Groot, T./Merchant, K. (2000): Control of international joint ventures, in: Accounting, Organizations and Society, 25 (6), p. 579–607.

Guilding, C./Lamminmaki, D./Drury, C. (1998): Budgeting and Standard Costing Practice in New Zealand and the United Kingdom, in: The International Journal of Accounting, 33 (5), p. 569–588.

Gupta, P. P./Dirsmith, M. W./Fogarty, T. J. (1994): Coordination and Control in a Government Agency: Contingency and Institutional Theory Perspectives on GAO Audits, in: Administrative Science Quarterly, 39 (2), p. 264–284.

Hair, J. F. (2010): Multivariate data analysis, 7th edn., Upper Saddle River (2010).

Hardy, C. (1996): Understanding Power: Bringing about Strategic Change, in: British Journal of Management, 7 (Issue Supplement S1), p. 3–16.

Harris, J. N. (1936): What did we earn last month?, in: NACA bulletin, XVII (10), p. 501–527.

Harrison, G. L./McKinnon, J. L. (1999): Cross-cultural research in management control systems design: a review of the current state, in: Accounting, Organizations and Society, 24 (5), p. 483–506.

Hartmann, F. G./Moers, F. (1999): Testing contingency hypotheses in budgetary research: an evaluation of the use of moderated regression analysis, in: Accounting, Organizations and Society, 24 (4), p. 291–315.

Harzing, A.-W./Sorge, A. (2003): The Relative Impact of Country of Origin and Universal Contingencies on Internationalization Strategies and Corporate Control in Multinational Enterprises: Worldwide and European Perspectives, in: Organization Studies, 24 (2), p. 187–214.

Harzing, A.-W. (1999): Managing the multinationals, Cheltenham (1999).

Hax, H. (2002): Integration externer und interner Unternehmensrechnung, in: Küpper, H.-U./Wagenhofer, A. (eds.): Handwörterbuch Unternehmensrechnung und Controlling, 4th edn., Stuttgart (2002), p. 758–767.

Heenan, D. A./Perlmutter, H. V. (1979): Multinational organization development, Reading (1979).

Heimel, J./Hofmann, N./Mauthofer, S. (2012): Erfolgreiche operative Unternehmenssteuerung durch schlanke Kosten- und Ergebnisrechnung, in: CFO aktuell: Zeitschrift für Finance & Controlling, 6 (2), p. 58–60.

Heinen, E. (1968): Einführung in die Betriebswirtschaftslehre, Wiesbaden (1968).

Henri, J. (2006a): Organizational culture and performance measurement systems, in: Accounting, Organizations and Society, 31 (1), p. 77–103.

Henri, J.-F. (2006b): Management control systems and strategy: A resource-based perspective, in: Accounting, Organizations and Society, 31 (6), p. 529–558.

Hertenstein, J. H./Polutnik, L./McNair, C. J. (2006): Capacity cost measures and decisions: Two field studies, in: Journal of Corporate Accounting & Finance, 17 (3), p. 63–78.

Hilton, R. W. (2007): Managerial accounting, 7th edn., London (2007).

Hiromoto, T. (1988): Another Hidden Edge - Japanese Management Accounting, in: Harvard Business Review, 66 (4), p. 22–26.

Hirsch, B. (2007): Controlling und Entscheidungen, Tübingen (2007).

Hirsch, P. M./Lounsbury, M. (1997): Ending the Family Quarrel: Toward a Reconciliation of "Old" and "New" Institutionalisms, in: American Behavioral Scientist, 40 (4), p. 406–418.

Hirst, M. K./Baxter, J. A. (1993): A Capital Budgeting Case Study: an Analysis of a Choice Process and Roles of Information, in: Behavioral Research in Accounting, 5 (1), p. 187–210.

Ho, S.-J. K./Kidwell, L. A. (2000): A Survey of Management Techniques Implemented by Municipal Administrators, in: The Government Accountants Journal, 49 (1), p. 46–51.

Hoffjan, A. (2009): Internationales Controlling, Stuttgart (2009).

Hoffjan, A./Nevries, P./Stienemann, R. (2009): Comparative Management Accounting: Literature Review on Similarities and Differences Between Management in Germanic and

Anglophone Countries, in: Berens, W./Hoffjan, A./Burgartz, T. (eds.): Controlling in einem globalen Markt, Frankfurt am Main (2009), p. 113–146.

Hoffjan, A./Weber, J. (2007): Internationales Controlling, Weinheim (2007).

Hoffjan, A./Weide, G. (2006): Organisation des internationalen Controlling - Im Spannungsfeld zwischen Standardisierung und Differenzierung, in: Die Unternehmung, 60 (6), p. 389–406.

Hoffjan, A./Weide, G. (2009): Management control systems in multinationals: balancing global standardisation and local customisation, in: Journal for Global Business Advancement, 2 (1/2), p. 125–141.

Hofmann, S./Wald, A./Gleich, R. (2012): Determinants and effects of the diagnostic and interactive use of control systems: an empirical analysis on the use of budgets, in: Journal of Management Control, 23 (3), p. 153–182.

Hoitsch, H.-J./Lingnau, V. (2007): Kosten- und Erlösrechnung, 6th edn., Berlin (2007).

Hoitsch, H.-J./Winter, P. (2005): Japanische Kostenrechnungssysteme, Working Paper (2005).

Holtbrügge, D./Welge, M. K. (2010): Internationales Management, 5th edn., Stuttgart (2010).

Holzmüller, H. H. (1995): Konzeptionelle und methodische Probleme in der interkulturellen Management- und Marketingforschung, Stuttgart (1995).

Homburg, C. (1998): Kundennähe von Industriegüterunternehmen, 2nd edn., Wiesbaden (1998).

Homburg, C./Weber, J./Aust, R./Karlshaus, J. T. (1998): Interne Kundenorientierung der Kostenrechnung, Weinheim (1998).

Homburg, C./Baumgartner, H. (1995): Beurteilung von Kausalmodellen – Bestandsaufnahme und Anwendungsempfehlungen, in: Marketing : ZFP, 17 (3), p. 162–176.

Homburg, C./Karlshaus, J. T. (1999): Kostenrechnung in mittelständischen und großen Unternehmen - ein Vergleich, in: Kostenrechnungspraxis, 43 (Sonderheft 2), p. 73–80.

Homburg, C./Giering, A. (1996): Konzeptualisierung und Operationalisierung komplexer Konstrukte. Ein Leitfaden für die Marketingforschung, in: Marketing : ZFP, 18 (1), p. 3–24.

Homburg, C./Jensen, O./Krohmer, H. (2008): Configurations of Marketing and Sales: A Taxonomy, in: Journal of Marketing, 72 (2), p. 133–154.

Homburg, C./Klarmann, M. (2006): Die Kausalanalyse in der empirischen betriebswirtschaftlichen Forschung – Problemfelder und Anwendungsempfehlungen, in: Die Betriebswirtschaft, 66 (6), p. 727–748.

Hopper, T./Major, M. (2007): Extending Institutional Analysis through Theoretical Triangulation: Regulation and Activity-Based Costing in Portuguese Telecommunications, in: European Accounting Review, 16 (1), p. 59–97.

Hopper, T./Powell, A. (1985): Making Sense of Research into Organisational and Social Aspects of Management Accounting: A Review of its underlying Assumptions, in: Journal of Management Studies, 22 (2), p. 439–465.

Hopper, T./Koga, T./Goto, J. (1999): Cost Accounting in small and medium sized Japanese companies: an exploratory study, in: Accounting and Business Research, 30 (1), p. 73–86.

Hopwood, A. G. (1999): Situating the practice of management accounting in its cultural context: an introduction, in: Accounting, Organizations and Society, 24 (4), p. 377–378.

Hoque, Z. (2000): Just-in-time Production, Automation, Cost Allocation Practices and Importance of Cost Information: An Empirical Investigation in New Zealand-Based Manufacturing Organizations, in: The British Accounting Review, 32 (2), p. 133–159.

Hoque, Z. (2005): Linking environmental uncertainty to non-financial performance measures and performance: a research note, in: The British Accounting Review, 37 (4), p. 471–481.

Horngren, C. T./Sundem, G. L./Strattton, W. O./Burgstahler, D./Schatzberg, J. (2008): Introduction to management accounting, 14th edn., Upper Saddle River (2008).

Horngren, C. T./Foster, G./Datar, S. M. (2012): Cost accounting, 14th edn., Upper Saddle River (2012).

Horváth, P. (1993): Prozesskostenrechnung - Konzeption und Entwicklung, in: Kostenrechnungspraxis, 37 (Sonderheft 2/93), p. 15–28.

Horváth, P./Mayer, R. (1989): Prozesskostenrechnung: Der neue Weg zu mehr Kostentransparenz und wirkungsvolleren Unternehmensstrategien, in: Controlling, 11 (1), p. 215–219.

Horváth, P./Mayer, R. (1995): Konzeption und Entwicklung der Prozeßkostenrechnung, in: Männel, W. (ed.): Prozesskostenrechnung, Wiesbaden (1995), p. 59–86.

Hosmer, D. W./Lemeshow, S. (2000): Applied logistic regression, 2nd edn., New York (2000).

Howell, R. A./Brown, J. D./Soucy, S. R./Seed, A. H. (1987): Management accounting in the new manufacturing environment, Montvale (1987).

Huber, P. J. (1967): The behavior of maximum likelihood estimates under nonstandard conditions, in: Proceedings of the Fifth Berkeley Symposium on Mathematical Statistics and Probability, 1 (1), p. 221–233.

Hughes, S./Paulson Gjerde, K. A. (2003): Do Different Cost Systems Make a Difference, in: Management Accounting Quarterly, 5 (1), p. 22–30.

Hulland, J. (1999): Use of partial least squares (PLS) in strategic management research: a review of four recent studies, in: Strategic Management Journal, 20 (2), p. 195–204.

Hummel, S./Männel, W. (1986): Kostenrechnung 1 Grundlagen, Aufbau und Anwendung, Wiesbaden (1986).

Hunold, C. (2003): Kommunale Kostenrechnung, Wiesbaden (2003).

Innes, J./Mitchell, F. (1995): A Survey of activity-based costing in the U.K.'s largest companies, in: Management Accounting Research, 6 (2), p. 137–153.

Innes, J./Mitchell, F./Sinclair, D. (2000): Activity-based costing in the U.K.'s largest companies: a comparison of 1994 and 1999 survey results, in: Management Accounting Research, 11 (3), p. 349–362.

Ittner, C. D./Lanen, W. N./Larcker, D. F. (2002): The Association between Activity-Based Costing and Manufacturing Performance, in: Journal of Accounting Research, 40 (3), p. 711–726.

Jaccard, J. (2001): Interaction effects in logistic regression, Thousand Oaks (2001).

Jais, S.-D. (2007): The Successful Use of Information in Multinational Companies, New York (2007).

Järvinen, J. (2006): Institutional Pressures For Adopting New Cost Accounting Systems In Finnish Hospitals: Two Longitudinal case Studies, in: Financial Accountability & Management, 22 (1), p. 21–45.

Jarvis, C. B./MacKenzie, S. B./Podsakoff, P. M. (2003): A Critical Review of Construct Indicators and Measurement Model Misspecification in Marketing and Consumer Research, in: Journal of Consumer Research, 30 (2), p. 199–218.

Jaussaud, J./Schaaper, J. (2006): Control mechanisms of their subsidiaries by multinational firms: A multidimensional perspective, in: Journal of International Management, 12 (1), p. 23–45.

Jepperson, R. L. (1991): Institutions, Institutional Effects, and Institutionalism, in: Powell, W. W./DiMaggio, P. (eds.): The New Institutionalism in Organizational Analysis, Chicago (1991), p. 143–163.

Johnson, H. T./Kaplan, R. S. (1987): Relevance lost, Boston (1987).

Johnson, J. L./Cullen, J. B./Sakano, T./Bronson, J. W. (2001): Drivers and outcomes of parent company intervention in IJV management: a cross-cultural comparison, in: Journal of Business Research, 52 (1), p. 35–49.

Johnson, P. (1995): Towards an Epistemology For Radical Accounting: Beyond Objectivism and Relativism, in: Critical Perspectives in Accounting, 6 (6), p. 485–509.

Jones, C. (1985): An empirical study of the evidence for contingency theories of management accounting systems in conditions of rapid change, in: Accounting, Organizations and Society, 10 (3), p. 303–328.

Jones, C./Luther, R. (2005): Anticipating the impact of IFRS on the management of German manufacturing companies: some observations from a British perspective, in: Accounting in Europe, 2 (1), p. 165–193.

Jones, L. F. (1991): Product Costing at Caterpillar, in: Management Accounting, 72 (2), p. 34–42.

Jones, M. J./Munday, M./Brinn, T. (1998): Speculations on barriers to transference of Japanese management accounting, in: Accounting, Auditing & Accountability Journal, 11 (2), p. 204–215.

Jones, T. C. (1995): Accounting and the enterprise, London (1995).

Jones, T. C./Currie, W. L./Dugdale, D. (1993): Accounting and technology in Britain and Japan: learning from field research, in: Management Accounting Research, 2 (4), p. 109–137.

Jones, T. C./Dugdale, D. (2002): The ABC bandwagon and the juggernaut of modernity, in: Accounting, Organizations and Society, 27 (1-2), p. 121–163.

Jones, T. C./Luther, R. (2006): Globalization and management accounting in Germany, Paper submitted to 8th Interdisciplinary Perspective on Accounting Conference (2006).

Joseph, N./Turley, S./Burns, J./Lewis, L./Scapens, R./Southworth, A. (1996): External financial reporting and management information: a survey of U.K. management accountants, in: Management Accounting Research, 7 (1), p. 73–93.

Kajüter, P. (2000): Proaktives Kostenmanagement, Wiesbaden (2000).

Kajüter, P. (2003): Theoretische Grundlagen der Kostenrechnung im Konzern, in: Zeitschrift für betriebswirtschaftliche Forschung, 49 (Sonderheft), p. 13–18.

Kajüter, P. (2005): Kostenmanagement in der deutschen Unternehmenspraxis, in: Zeitschrift für betriebswirtschaftliche Forschung, 57 (2), p. 79–100.

Kajüter, P. (2011): Kostenrechnungssysteme im internationalen Vergleich, in: Kajüter, P./Mindermann, T./Winkler, C. (eds.): Controlling und Rechnungslegung, Stuttgart (2011), p. 89–118.

Kajüter, P. (2013): Target costing: Market-driven cost management, in: Mitchell, F./Nørreklit, H./Jakobsen, M. (eds.): The Routledge companion to cost management, Abingdon (2013), p. 82–95.

Kajüter, P./Moeschler, M. (2010): Comparative Management Accounting, Working Paper (2010).

Kaplan, R. S. (1984): The Evolution of Management Accounting, in: The Accounting Review, 59 (3), p. 390–418.

Kaplan, R. S./Anderson, S. R. (2004): Time-Driven Activity-Based Costing, in: Harvard Business Review, 82 (11), p. 131–138.

Kaplan, R. S./Cooper, R. (1998): Cost & effect, Boston (1998).

Kaplan, R. S./Anderson, S. R. (2003): Time-Driven Activity-Based Costing, White Paper presented at the First European Summit on Time-Driven Activity-Based Costing (2003).

Kaplan, R. S./Anderson, S. R. (2007): Time-driven activity-based costing, Boston (2007).

Kaplan, R. S./Atkinson, A. A. (1989): Advanced management accounting, 2nd edn., London (1989).

Karlshaus, J. T. (2000): Die Nutzung von Kostenrechnungsinformationen im Marketing, Wiesbaden (2000).

Karmarkar, U. S./Lederer, P. J./Zimmerman, J. L. (1990): Choosing Manufacturing Production Control and Cost Accounting Systems, in: Kaplan, R. (ed.): Measures for manufacturing excellence, Boston (1990), p. 353–396.

Kasuya, E. (2001): Mann–Whitney U test when variances are unequal, in: Animal Behaviour, 61 (6), p. 1247–1249.

Kellermanns, F. W./Islam, M. (2004): US and German activity-based costing: A critical comparison and system acceptability propositions, in: Benchmarking: An International Journal, 11 (1), p. 31–51.

Kennedy, T./Affleck-Graves, J. (2001): The Impact of Activity-Based Costing Techniques on Firm Performance, in: Journal of Management Accounting Research, 13 (1), p. 19–45.

Keys, D./van der Merwe, A. (2002): Gaining effective organizational control with RCA, in: Strategic Finance, 84 (5), p. 41–47.

Keys, D./van der Merwe, A. (1999): German vs. U.S. Cost Management: What Insights Does German Cost Management Have For U.S. Companies, in: Management Accounting Quarterly, 1 (1), p. 1–8.

Khandwalla, P. N. (1972): The Effect of Different Types of Competition on the Use of Management Control, in: Journal of Accounting Research, 10 (2), p. 275–285.

Kidwell, L. A./Ho, S.-J. K./Blake, J./Wraith, P./Roubi, R./Richardson, W. (2002): New Management Techniques: An International Comparison, in: The CPA Journal, 72 (2), p. 63–66.

Kieser, A. (1993): Organisationsstruktur, in: Hauschildt, J./Grün, O. (eds.): Ergebnisse empirischer betriebswirtschaftlicher Forschung: Zu einer Realtheorie der Unternehmung, Stuttgart (1993), p. 55–82.

Kieser, A. (2006): Der situative Ansatz, in: Kieser, A. (ed.): Organisationstheorien, 6th edn., Stuttgart (2006), p. 215–245.

Kieser, A./Walgenbach, P. (2010): Organisation, 6th edn., Stuttgart (2010).

Kilger, W. (1958): Die Produktions- und Kostentheorie als theoretische Grundlage der Kostenrechnung, in: Zeitschrift für handelswissenschaftliche Forschung, 10 (11), p. 553–564.

Kilger, W. (1976): Kostentheoretische Grundlagen der Grenzplankostenrechnung, in: Zeitschrift für betriebswirtschaftliche Forschung, 28 (1), p. 679–693.

Kilger, W. (1979): Die Grenzplankosten- und Deckungsbeitragsrechnung als geschlossenes Planungsmodell, in: Koch, H./Mellwig, W. (eds.): Unternehmenstheorie und Unternehmensplanung, Wiesbaden (1979), p. 69–94.

Kilger, W./Pampel, J. R./Vikas, K. (2012): Flexible Plankostenrechnung und Deckungsbeitragsrechnung, 13th edn., Wiesbaden (2012).

Kim, I./Ansari, S./Bell, J./Dan, S. (2002): Target Costing Practice in the United States, in: Controlling, 14 (11), p. 607–614.

Kim, I./Song, J. (1990): U.S., Korea, & Japan: Accounting Practices in Three Countries, in: Management Accounting: Magazine for Chartered Management Accountants (August 1990), p. 26–30.

Kirsch, H. (1998): Konzernkostenrechnung als Controllinginstrument, in: Controlling, 10 (4), p. 210–217.

Kloock, J./Sieben, G./Schildbach, T./Homburg, C. (2005): Kosten- und Leistungsrechnung, 9th edn., Stuttgart (2005).

Kloock, J./Schiller, U. (1997): Marginal costing: cost budgeting and cost variance analysis, in: Management Accounting Research, 8 (3), p. 299–323.

Kloock, J. (1992): Prozeßkostenrechnung als Rückschritt und Fortschritt der Kostenrechnung, in: Kostenrechnungspraxis, 36 (4), p. 181–193.

Knoop, R./Müller, M./Garke, C. (2006): Die integrierte Kosten- und Ergebnisrechnung (iKE) der T-Com, in: Zeitschrift für Controlling und Management, 50 (3), p. 150–157.

Knorr, K. D. (1976): Politisches System und Sozialwissenschaften: zur Plausibilität der Legitimationshypothese, in: Strasser, H./Knorr, K. D. (eds.): Wissenschaftssteuerung, Frankfurt am Main (1976), p. 81–108.

Knorr, K. D. (1977): Policymakers' Use of Social Science Knowledge: Symbolic or Instrumental, in: Weiss, C. H. (ed.): Using social research in public policy making, Lexington (1977), p. 165–182.

Kokubu, K./Silvera Campos, M. K./Furukawa, Y./Tachikawa, H. (2009): Material flow cost accounting with ISO 14051, in: ISO Management Systems, 2 (1), p. 15–18.

Kornmeier, M. (2007): Wissenschaftstheorie und wissenschaftliches Arbeiten, Heidelberg (2007).

Kosiol, E. (1964): Betriebswirtschaftslehre und Unternehmensforschung: Eine Untersuchung ihrer Standorte und Beziehungen auf wissenschaftstheoretischer Grundlage, in: Zeitschrift für Betriebswirtschaft, 34 (12), p. 743–762.

Kosmider, A. (1992): Stand und Einflussfaktoren der Kostenrechnung im Mittelstand, in: Weber, J. (ed.): Kostenrechnung im Mittelstand, Stuttgart (1992), p. 21–38.

Kostova, T. (1999): Transnational Transfer of Strategic Organizational Practices: A Contextual Perspective, in: The Academy of Management Review, 24 (2), p. 308–324.

Kostova, T./Roth, K. (2002): Adoption of an Organizational Practice by Subsidiaries of Multinational Corporations: Institutional and Relational Effects, in: The Academy of Management Journal, 45 (1), p. 215–233.

Kostova, T./Roth, K./Dacin, M. T. (2008): Institutional Theory in the Study of Multinational Corporations: A Critique and new Directions, in: Academy of Management Review, 33 (4), p. 994–1006.

Kreikebaum, H. (2002): Organisationsmanagement internationaler Unternehmen, 2nd edn., Wiesbaden (2002).

Krieger, R. G. (1995): Betriebsindividuelle Gestaltung der Kostenrechnung, Berlin (1995).

Krump, F. (2003): Diffusion prozessorientierter Kostenrechnungssysteme, Wiesbaden (2003).

Krumwiede, K. R. (1998): The Implementation Stages of Activity-Based Costing and the Impact of Contextual and Organizational Factors, in: Journal of Management Accounting Research, 10 (1), p. 239–277.

Krumwiede, K. R. (2005): Rewards and Realities of German Cost Accounting, in: Strategic Finance, 85 (10), p. 27–34.

Krumwiede, K. R./Suessmair, A./MacDonald, J. (2007): An exploratory study of the factors affecting the implementation success of German cost accounting methods, Working Paper (2007).

Krumwiede, K./Suessmair, A. (2007a): Comparing U.S. and German Cost Accounting Methods, in: Management Accounting Quarterly, 8 (3), p. 1–9.

Krumwiede, K./Suessmair, A. (2007b): Getting Down to Specifics on RCA, in: Strategic Finance, 88 (12), p. 50–55.

Kubicek, H. (1975): Empirische Organisationsforschung, Stuttgart (1975).

Kubicek, H. (1977): Heurisitische Bezugsrahmen und heuristisch angelegte Forschungsdesigns als Element einer Konstruktionsstrategie empirischer Forschung, in: Köhler, R. (ed.): Empirische und handlungstheoretische Forschungskonzeptionen in der Betriebswirtschaftslehre, Stuttgart (1977), p. 3–36.

Küpper, H.-U. (1983): Der Bedarf an Kosten- und Leistungsinformationen in Industrieunternehmen: Ergebnisse einer empirischen Erhebung, in: Kostenrechnungspraxis, 27 (4), p. 169–181.

Küpper, H.-U. (1985): Investitionstheoretische Fundierung der Kostenrechnung, in: Zeitschrift für betriebswirtschaftliche Forschung, 37 (1), p. 26–46.

Küpper, H.-U. (1990): Entwicklungslinien der Kostenrechnung als Controllinginstrument (Teil 1), in: Kostenrechnungspraxis, 34 (1), p. 11–16.

Küpper, H.-U. (1992): Theoretische Grundlagen der Kostenrechnung, in: Männel, W. (ed.): Handbuch Kostenrechnung, Wiesbaden (1992), p. 38–53.

Küpper, H.-U. (1993): Internes Rechnungswesen, in: Hauschildt, J./Grün, O. (eds.): Ergebnisse empirischer betriebswirtschaftlicher Forschung: Zu einer Realtheorie der Unternehmung, Stuttgart (1993), p. 601–631.

Küpper, H.-U. (2008): Controlling: Konzeption, Aufgaben, Instrumente, 5th edn., Stuttgart (2008).

Kurunmaki, L. (2003): Accountingization v. legitimation: a comparative study of the use of accounting information in intensive care, in: Management Accounting Research, 14 (2), p. 112–139.

Küting, K./Dusemond, M. (1994): Grundsätzliche Überlegungen zu einer eigenständigen Konzernkostenrechnung, in: Kostenrechnungspraxis, 38 (4), p. 245–252.

Kutschker, M./Schmid, S. (2011): Internationales Management, 7th edn., München (2011).

Lamminmaki, D./Drury, C. (2001): A comparison of New Zealand and British product-costing practices, in: The International Journal of Accounting, 36 (3), p. 329–347.

Lamnek, S. (1989): Methoden und Techniken, München (1989).

Lamnek, S. (2010): Qualitative Sozialforschung, 5th edn., Weinheim, Basel (2010).

Lanen, W. N./Anderson, S. W./Maher, M. (2013): Fundamentals of cost accounting, 4th edn., New York (2013).

Lange, J.-U./Schauer, B. D. (1996): Ausgestaltung und Rechenzwecke mittelständischer Kostenrechnung, in: Kostenrechnungspraxis, 40 (4), p. 202–208.

Langfield-Smith, K./Thorne, H./Hilton, R. W. (2006): Management accounting, 4th edn., North Ryde (2006).

Lapsley, I. (2001): The Accounting-Clinical Interface-Implementing Budgets for Hospital Doctors, in: ABACUS, 37 (1), p. 79–109.

Laßmann, G. (1992): Betriebsplankosten- und Betriebsplanerfolgsrechnung, in: Männel, W. (ed.): Handbuch Kostenrechnung, Wiesbaden (1992), p. 300–319.

Lattmann, C. (1993): Der Konstruktivismus und seine Bedeutung für die Betriebswirtschaftslehre, in: Management Revue, 4 (3), p. 217–241.

Lee, J. Y. (2003): Cost System Research Perspectives, in: Epstein, M. J./Lee, J. Y. (eds.): Advances in Management Accounting, Bingley (2003), p. 39–57.

Lee, N./Hooley, G. (2005): The evolution of "classical mythology" within marketing measure development, in: European Journal of Marketing, 39 (3/4), p. 365–385.

Leonhart, R. (2013): Lehrbuch Statistik, 3rd edn., Bern (2013).

Lere, J. C. (2009): Benchmarking Accounting practices in a Global Economy, in: CPA Journal, 79 (11), p. 10–12.

Levene, H. (1960): Robust tests for equality of variances, in: Olkin, I./Ghurye, S./Hoeffding, W./Madow, W./Mann, H. (eds.): Contributions to probability and statistics: Essays in honor of Harold Hotelling, Stanford (1960), p. 278–292.

Liang, H./Saaraf, N./Hu, Q./Xue, Y. (2007): Assimilation of Enterprise Systems: The Effect of Institutional Pressures and the Mediating Role of Top Management, in: Management Information Systems Quarterly, 31 (1), p. 59–87.

Liedl, R. (1999): Controlling in ausländischen Tochtergesellschaften, in: Giesel, F./Glaum, M. (eds.): Globalisierung, München (1999), p. 226–247.

Lillis, A. M./Mundy, J. (2005): Cross-Sectional field Studies in Management Accounting Research - Closing the Gaps between Surveys and Case Studies, in: Journal of Management Accounting Research, 17 (1), p. 119–141.

Littkemann, J. (2001): Beteiligungscontrolling: Organisation und Effizienz; Eine emppirische Analyse aus zentraler und lokaler Controllingperspektive, in: Zeitschrift für Betriebswirtschaft, 71 (11), p. 1283–1304.

Littkemann, J./Derfuß, K. (2004): Gestaltung von Controllingsystemen - Empirische Ergebnisse des Kontingenzansatzes des Behavioral Accounting, in: Scherm, E. (ed.): Controlling, München (2004), p. 693–727.

Littleton, A. C. (1988): Accounting evolution to 1900, New York (1988).

Lochner, S./Ayasse, P./Hummel, J. (2007): Meilensteine im Ausbau des Controlling-Instumentariums im Porsche Konzern, in: Controlling, 19 (3), p. 145–152.

Lounsbury, M. (2008): Institutional rationality and practice variation: New directions in the institutional analysis of practice, in: Accounting, Organizations and Society, 33 (4-5), p. 349–361.

Lukka, K. (1990): Ontology And Accounting: The Concepts of Profit, in: Critical Perspectives in Accounting, 1 (1), p. 239–261.

Lukka, K. (2007): Management accounting change and stability: Loosely coupled rules and routines in action, in: Management Accounting Research, 18 (1), p. 76–101.

Lukka, K./Kasanen, E. (1995): The problem of generalizability: anecdotes and evidence in accounting research, in: Accounting, Auditing & Accountability Journal, 8 (5), p. 71–90.

Luther, R./Jones, T. C./Saxl, A. (2010): Experiencing change in German controlling, Amsterdam (2010).

Lyall, D./Graham, C. (1993): Managers' Attitudes to Cost Information, in: Management Decision, 31 (8), p. 41–45.

Lynn, B./Todd, S. (2003): A Planning and Control Model Based on RCA Principles, in: Cost Management, 17 (4), p. 20–27.

MacArthur, J. B. (2006): Cultural influences on German versus US management accounting practices, in: Management Accounting Quarterly, 7 (2), p. 10–16.

Macharzina, K. (1981): Entwicklungsperspektiven einer Theorie internationaler Unternehmenstätigkeit: Modell- und Verfahrensvorschläge, in: Sieber, E. H./Wacker, W. H./Haussmann, H./Kumar, B. (eds.): Internationale Unternehmensführung, Berlin (1981), p. 33–56.

Macintosh, N. B. (1998): Management accounting in Europe: a view from Canada, in: Management Accounting Research, 9 (4), p. 495–500.

MacKenzie, S. B./Podsakoff, P. M./Jarvis, C. B. (2005): The Problem of Measurement Model Misspecification in Behavioral and Organizational Research and Some Recommended Solutions, in: Journal of Applied Psychology, 90 (4), p. 710–730.

Mackie, B. (2006): Merging GPK and ABC on the Road to RCA, in: Strategic Finance, 88 (5), p. 33–39.

Magnussen, S./Köhl, M. (2006): A better alternative to Wald's test-statistic for simple goodness-of-fit tests under one-stage cluster sampling, in: Forest Ecology and Management, 221 (1-3), p. 123–132.

Major, M./Hopper, T. (2005): Managers divided: Implementing ABC in a Portuguese telecommunication company, in: Management Accounting Research, 16 (2), p. 205–229.

Malmi, T. (1997): Towards explaining activity-based costing failure: accounting and control in a decentralized organization, in: Management Accounting Research, 8 (4), p. 459–480.

Malmi, T. (1999): Activity-based costing diffusion across organizations: an exploratory empirical analysis of Finnish firms, in: Accounting, Organizations and Society, 24 (8), p. 649–672.

March, J. G. (1987): Ambiguity and accounting: The elusive link between information and decision making, in: Accounting, Organizations and Society, 12 (2), p. 153–168.

Marginson, D. E. W. (2002): Management control systems and their effects on strategy formation at middle-management levels: evidence from a U.K. organization, in: Strategic Management Journal, 23 (11), p. 1019–1031.

Marple, R. (1967): Management Accounting Is Coming of Age, in: Management Accounting Quarterly, 48 (11), p. 3–16.

Mastilak, M. C. (2011): Cost Pool Classification and Judgment Performance, in: The Accounting Review, 86 (5), p. 1709–1729.

Mayring, P. (2010): Qualitative Inhaltsanalyse, 11th edn., Weinheim (2010).

McGowan, A. S./Klammer, T. P. (1997): Satisfaction with Activity-Based Cost Management Implementation, in: Journal of Management Accounting Research, 9 (1), p. 217–237.

McMann, P. J./Nanni, A. J. Jr. (1995): Means versus ends: a review of the literature on Japanese management accounting, in: Management Accounting Research, 6 (4), p. 313–346.

Mellewigt, T. (1995): Konzernorganisation und Konzernführung, Frankfurt am Main (1995).

Menon, A./Varadarajan, P. R. (1992): A Model of Marketing Knowledge Use within Firms, in: The Journal of Marketing, 56 (4), p. 53–71.

Merchant, K. A./Otley, D. T. (2006): A Review of the Literature on Control and Accountability, in: Chapman, C. S./Hopwood, A. G./Shields, M. D. (eds.): Handbook of Management Accounting Research (Vol. 2), Oxford (2006), p. 785–802.

Merchant, K. A./Van der Stede, W. A./Lin, T. W./Yu, Z. (2011): Performance Measurement and Incentive Compensation: An Empirical Analysis and Comparison of Chinese and Western Firms' Practices, in: European Accounting Review, 20 (4), p. 639–667.

Merchant, K. A./Shields, M. D. (1993): Commentary on When and Why to Measure Costs Less Accurately to Improve Decision Making, in: Accounting Horizons, 7 (2), p. 76–81.

Meyer, A. (1988): Einführung der Analytischen Kostenplanung in einer Produktionsstätte eines internationalen Konzerns, in: Kostenrechnungspraxis, 32 (Sonderheft 1), p. 53–60.

Meyer, J. W./Rowan, B. (1977): Institutionalized Organizations: Formal Structure as Myth and Ceremony, in: American Journal of Sociology, 83 (2), p. 340–363.

Meyer, R. E. (2004): Globale Managementkonzepte und lokaler Kontext: organisationale Wertorientierung im österreichischen öffentlichen Diskurs, Wien (2004).

Miles, R. E./Snow, C. C./Meyer, A. D./Coleman, H. J., JR (1978): Organizational Strategy, Structure, and Process, in: The Academy of Management Review, 3 (3), p. 546–562.

Miller, J./Vollmann, T. (1985): The hidden factory, in: Harvard Business Review, 63 (5), p. 142–150.

Mizruchi, M. S./Fein, L. C. (1999): The Social Construction of Organizational Knowledge: A Study of the Uses of Coercive, Mimetic, and Normative Isomorphism, in: Administrative Science Quarterly, 44 (4), p. 653–683.

Modell, S. (2001): Performance measurement and institutional processes: a study of managerial responses to public sector reform, in: Management Accounting Research, 12 (4), p. 437–464.

Modell, S. (2002): Institutional perspectives on cost allocations: integration and extension, in: European Accounting Review, 11 (4), p. 653–679.

Modell, S. (2006): Institutional and negotiated order perspectives on cost allocations: The case of the Swedish university sector, in: European Accounting Review, 15 (2), p. 219–251.

Moeschler, M. (2012): Cost Accounting in Germany and Japan: A Comparative Analysis, Frankfurt am Main (2012).

Moll, J./Burns, J./Major, M. (2006): Institutional Theory, in: Hoque, Z. (ed.): Methodological issues in accounting research, London (2006), p. 183–205.

Möller, K. (2002): Gestaltungsbeitrag der Neuen Institutionenökonomik für das Controlling, in: Gleich, R./Becker, R. (eds.): Controllingfortschritte, München (2002), p. 95–120.

Morgan, G./Smircich, L. (1980): The Case for Qualitative Research, in: Academy of Management Review, 5 (4), p. 491–500.

Mouritsen, J. (1995): Management Accounting in Global Firms, in: Ashton, D./Hopper, T./Scapens, R. W. (eds.): Issues in management accounting, 2nd edn., London (1995), p. 299–320.

Müller, H. (2001): Operative Unternehmenssteuerung global agierender Unternehmen - Konzernkostenrechnung als globale Wertschöpfungsrechnung, in: Kostenrechnungspraxis, 45 (Sonderheft 3), p. 9–13.

Müller-Jentsch, W. (2002): Organisationales Handeln zwischen institutioneller Normierung und strategischem Kalkül, in: Conrad, P./Schreyögg, G. (eds.): Theorien des Managements, Wiesbaden (2002), p. 203–209.

Mundy, J. (2010): Creating dynamic tensions through a balanced use of management control systems, in: Accounting, Organizations and Society, 35 (5), p. 499–523.

Nakajima, M. (2004): On the differences between material flow cost accounting and traditional cost accounting: in reply to the questions and misunderstandings on material flow cost accounting, in: Kansai University Review of Business and Commerce, 6 (1), p. 1–20.

Nakajima, M. (2010): Environmental Management Accounting for Sustainable Manufacturing: Establishing Management Systems of Material Flow Cost Accounting (MFCA), in: Kansai University Review of Business and Commerce, 12 (1), p. 41–58.

Naranjo-Gil, D./Hartmann, F. (2006): How Top Management Teams Use Management Accounting Systems to Implement Strategy, in: Journal of Management Accounting Research, 18 (1), p. 21–53.

Neimark, M./Tinker, T. (1986): The Social Contruction of Management Control Systems, in: Accounting, Organizations and Society, 11 (4/5), p. 369–395.

Neu, D. (1992): The social construction of positive choice, in: Accounting, Organizations and Society, 17 (3/4), p. 223–237.

Neugebauer, H. (1995): Kostentheorie und Kostenrechnung für Versicherungsunternehmen, Karlsruhe (1995).

Nguyen, H. V./Brooks, A. (1997): An Empirical Investigation of Adoption Issues Relating to Activity-Based Costing, in: Asien Review of Accounting, 5 (1), p. 1–18.

Nielsen, K. (2001): Institutionalist Approaches in the Social Sciences: Typology, Dialogue, and Future Challenges, in: Journal of Economic Issues, 35 (2), p. 505–516.

Noack, H. (2000): Struktur- und Prozeßorganisation des internationalen Controlling, in: Berens, W./Born, A./Hoffjan, A. (eds.): Controlling international tätiger Unternehmen, Stuttgart (2000), p. 343–366.

O'Donnell, S. W. (2000): Managing Foreign Subsidiaries: Agents of Headquarters, or an Interdependent Network?, in: Strategic Management Journal, 21 (5), p. 252–548.

Oliver, C. (1991): Strategic Responses to Institutional Processes, in: The Academy of Management Review, 16 (1), p. 145–179.

Oliver, C. (1992): The Antecedents of Deinstitutionalization, in: Organization Studies, 13 (4), p. 563–588.

Oliver, C. (1996): The institutional embeddedness of economic activity, in: Advances in Strategic Management, 13 (1), p. 163–186.

Otley, D. T. (1980): The Contingency Theory of Management Accounting: Achievement And Prognosis, in: Accounting, Organizations and Society, 5 (4), p. 413–428.

Pelz, D. (1978): Some Expanded Perspectives on Use of Social Science in Public Policy, in: Yinger, J. M./Yinger, J. M./Cutler, S. J. (eds.): Major Social Issues, New York (1978), p. 346–357.

Perlitz, M. (2013): Internationales Management, 6th edn., Stuttgart (2013).

Perlmutter, H. V. (1969): The Tortuous Evolution of the Multinational Corporation, in: Columbia Journal of World Business, 4 (1), p. 9–18.

Pfaff, D. (1993): Kostenrechnung, Unsicherheit und Organisation, Heidelberg (1993).

Pfaff, D. (1994): Zur Notwendigkeit einer eigenständigen Kostenrechnung: Anmerkungen zur Neuorientierung des internen Rechnungswesens im Hause Siemens, in: Zeitschrift für betriebswirtschaftliche Forschung, 46 (12), p. 1065–1084.

Pfaff, D. (1996): Kostenrechnung als Instrument der Entscheidungssteuerung: Chancen und Probleme, in: Kostenrechnungspraxis, 40 (3), p. 151–156.

Pfaff, D. (2003): Methodische Fragen einer internationalen Konzernkostenrechnung, in: Zeitschrift für betriebswirtschaftliche Forschung, 49 (Sonderheft), p. 29–46.

Picot, A. (1991): Ökonomische Theorien der Organisation: Ein Überblick über neuere Ansätze und deren betriebswirtschaftliches Anwendungspotential, in: Ordelheide, D./Rudolph, B./Büsselmann, E. (eds.): Betriebswirtschaftslehre und ökonomische Theorie, Stuttgart (1991), p. 143–172.

Pierce, B./Brown, R. (2004): An empirical study of activity-based systems in Ireland, in: The Irish Accounting Review, 11 (1), p. 33–55.

Pierce, B./O'Dea, T. (2003): Management accounting information and the needs of managers, in: The British Accounting Review, 35 (3), p. 257–290.

Pike, R. H./Tayles, M. E./Mansor, N. N. A. (2011): Activity-based costing user satisfaction and type of system: A research note, in: The British Accounting Review, 43 (1), p. 65–72.

Pizzini, M. J. (2006): The relation between cost-system design, managers' evaluations of the relevance and usefulness of cost data, and financial performance: an empirical study of US hospitals, in: Accounting, Organizations and Society, 31 (2), p. 179–210.

Plaut, H.-G. (1953a): Die Grenz-Plankostenrechnung (Erster Teil): Von der beweglichen Plankostenrechnung zur Grenz-Plankostenrechnung, in: Zeitschrift für Betriebswirtschaft, 23 (6), p. 347–363.

Plaut, H.-G. (1953b): Die Grenz-Plankostenrechnung (Zweiter Teil): Grundlagen der Grenz-Plankostenrechnung, in: Zeitschrift für Betriebswirtschaft, 23 (7), p. 402–413.

Podsakoff, P. M./MacKenzie, S. B./Lee, J.-Y./Podsakoff, N. P. (2003): Common method biases in behavioral research: A critical review of the literature and recommended remedies, in: Journal of Applied Psychology, 88 (5), p. 879–903.

Popper, K. R. (1973): Logik der Forschung, 5th edn., Tübingen (1973).

Portz, K./Lere, J. C. (2010): Cost Center Practices in Germany and the United States: Impact of Country Differences on Managerial Accounting Practices, in: American Journal of Business, 25 (1), p. 45–52.

Powel, W. W. (1991): Expanding the Scope of Institutional Analysis, in: Powell, W. W./DiMaggio, P. (eds.): The New Institutionalism in Organizational Analysis, Chicago (1991), p. 183–203.

Pratt, M. G. (2009): For the lack of a boilerplate: tips on writing up (and reviewing) qualitative research, in: Academy of Management Journal, 52 (5), p. 856–861.

Quattrone, P. (2000): Constructivism and accounting research: towards a trans-disciplinary perspective, in: Accounting, Auditing & Accountability Journal, 13 (2), p. 130–155.

Rack, O./Christophersen, T. (2009): Experimente, in: Albers, S. (ed.): Methodik der empirischen Forschung, 3rd edn., Wiesbaden (2009), p. 17–32.

Raffée, H./Abel, B. (1979): Aufgaben und aktuelle Tendenzen der Wissenschaftstheorie in den Wirtschaftswissenschaften, in: Raffée, H./Abel, B. (eds.): Wissenschaftstheoretische Grundfragen der Wirtschaftswissenschaften, München (1979), p. 1–10.

Rautenstrauch, T./Müller, C. (2007): Stand und Entwicklung des Kosten- und Erlöscontrolling in kleinen und mittleren Unternehmen, in: Der Betrieb, 60 (34), p. 1821–1826.

Rea, L. M./Parker, R. A. (2005): Designing and conducting survey research, 3rd edn., San Francisco (2005).

Reis, H. T./Judd, C. M. (2000): Handbook of research methods in social and personality psychology, New York (2000).

Reitmeyer, T. (2000): Qualität von Entscheidungsprozessen der Geschäftsleitung, Wiesbaden (2000).

Rich, R. F. (1977): Use of Social Science Information by Federal Bureaucrats: Knowledge for Action versus Knowledge for Understanding, in: Weiss, C. H. (ed.): Using social research in public policy making, Lexington (1977), p. 199–211.

Rich, R. F./Caplan, N. (1975): Selective Utilization of Social Science Related Information by Federal Policy Makers, in: Inquiry: a journal of health care organization, provision and financing / Blue Cross and Blue Shield Association, 12 (3), p. 239–245.

Riebel, P. (1959): Das Rechnen mit Einzelkosten und Deckungsbeiträgen, in: Zeitschrift für handelswissenschaftliche Forschung, 11 (5), p. 213–238.

Riesenhuber, F. (2009): Großzahlige empirische Forschung, in: Albers, S. (ed.): Methodik der empirischen Forschung, 3rd edn., Wiesbaden (2009), p. 1–16.

Robinson, C./Schumacker, R. E. (2009): Interaction Effects: Centering, Variance Inflation Factor, and Interpretation Issues, in: Multiple Linear Regression Viewpoints, 35 (2), p. 6–11.

Robinson, M. A. (1990): Contribution Margin Analysis: No Longer Relevant/Strategic Cost Management: The New Paradigm, in: Journal of Management Accounting Research, 2 , p. 1–32.

Robinson, P. A. (1996): Applying institutional theory to the study of the multinational enterprise: parental control and isomorphism among personnel practices in American manufacturers in Japan, Unpublished Dissertation (1996).

Rogers, W. H. (1993): Regression standard errors in clustered samples, in: Stata Technical Bulletin, 13 , p. 19–23.

Rosenbaum, P. R./Rubin, D. B. (1985): Constructing a Control Group Using Multivariate Matched Sampling Methods That Incorporate the Propensity Score, in: The American Statistician, 39 (1), p. 33–38.

Roth, K./Kostova, T. (2003): The Use of the Multinational Corporation as a Research Context, in: Journal of Management, 29 (6), p. 883–902.

Rusch, G. (2001): Was sind eigentlich Theorien, in: Hug, T. (ed.): Einführung in die Wissenschaftstheorie und Wissenschaftsforschung, Baltmannsweiler (2001), p. 93–116.

Ruxton, G. D. (2006): The unequal variance t-test is an underused alternative to Student's t-test and the Mann-Whitney U test, in: Behavioral Ecology, 17 (4), p. 688–690.

Sandt, J. (2004): Management mit Kennzahlen und Kennzahlensystemen, Wiesbaden (2004).

Scapens, R. W. (1996): External reporting and management decisions, London (1996).

Scapens, R. W. (2006): Understanding management accounting practices: A personal journey, in: The British Accounting Review, 38 (1), p. 1–30.

Scapens, R. W./Roberts, J. (1993): Accounting and control: a case study of resistance to accounting change, in: Management Accounting Research, 4 (1), p. 1–32.

Scarbrough, P./Nanni, A. J./Sakurai, M. (1991): Japanese management accounting practices and the effects of assembly and process automation, in: Management Accounting Research, 2 (1), p. 27–46.

Schäffer, U./Steiners, D. (2005a): Controllinginformationen für das Top-Management deutscher Industrieunternehmen - Angebot und Nutzung im Spiegel einer empirischen Erhebung, in: Zeitschrift für Controlling und Management, 49 (5), p. 209–224.

Schäffer, U./Kron, R. G./Parvis-Trevisany, N. (2005): Dynamische Theorie ökonomischer Akteure als Basis für die Modellierung von Implementierungsprozessen - Vorschläge zur Erweiterung des Akteursmodells, European Business School Working Paper on Management Accounting and Control No. 21 (2005).

Schäffer, U./Brettel, T. (2005): Ein Plädoyer für Fallstudien, in: Zeitschrift für Controlling und Management, 49 (1), p. 43–46.

Schäffer, U./Steiners, D. (2005b): Wie nutzen Geschäftsführer und Vorstände in deutschen Industrieunternehmen ihre Kostenrechnung?, in: Controlling, 17 (6), p. 321–325.

Schäffer, U./Steiners, D. (2004): Zur Nutzung von Controllinginformationen, in: Zeitschrift für Planung & Unternehmenssteuerung, 15 (4), p. 377–404.

Schäffer, U./Rehring, J./Wyszomirski, E. (2010): Performance Measurement in chinesischen Tochtergesellschaften, in: Zeitschrift für Controlling und Management, 54 (5), p. 309–313.

Schehl, M. (1994): Die Kostenrechnung der Industrieunternehmen vor dem Hintergrund unternehmensexterner und -interner Strukturwandlungen, Berlin (1994).

Scherer, A. G. (1995): Pluralismus im strategischen Management, Wiesbaden (1995).

Scherer, A. G. (2006): Kritik der Organisation oder Organisation der Kritik? Wissenschaftstheoretische Bemerkungen zum kritischen Umgang mit Organisationstheorien, in: Kieser, A. (ed.): Organisationstheorien, 6th edn., Stuttgart (2006), p. 19–61.

Scherm, E./Süß, S. (2001): Internationales Management, München (2001).

Scherm, E./Pietsch, G. (2004): Theorie und Konzeption in der Controllingforschung, in: Scherm, E. (ed.): Controlling, München (2004), p. 3–19.

Scherrer, G. (1996): Management Accounting: a German Perspective, in: Bhimani, A. (ed.): Management accounting, Oxford (1996), p. 100–122.

Schildbach, T. (1997): Cost accounting in Germany, in: Management Accounting Research, 8 (3), p. 261–276.

Schiller, U./Rossier, J.-C. (2008): Kostenmanagement in der Schweiz, Available at: http://www.pwc.ch/user_content/editor/files/publ_adv/pwc_kostenmanagement_d.pdf, retrieved 20.12.2013.

Schira, J. (2012): Statistische Methoden der VWL und BWL, 4th edn. (2012).

Schmid, S./Kretschmer, K. (2009): Performance evaluation of foreign subsidiaries: A review of the literature and a contingency framework, in: International Journal of Management Reviews, 12 (3), p. 219–258.

Schnell, R. (2012): Survey-Interviews, Wiesbaden (2012).

Schoute, M. (2009): The relationship between cost system complexity, purposes of use, and cost system effectiveness, in: The British Accounting Review, 41 (4), p. 208–226.

Schoute, M. (2011): The relationship between product diversity, usage of advanced manufacturing technologies and activity-based costing adoption, in: The British Accounting Review, 43 (2), p. 120–134.

Schreyögg, G. (2008): Organisation: Grundlagen moderner Organisationsgestaltung, 5th edn., Wiesbaden (2008).

Schweitzer, M. (2006): Die theoretische Fundierung der internen Erfolgsrechnung im Widerstreit der Ansätze, in: Seicht, G. (ed.): Unternehmensbewertung und Risiko, Internes Rechnungswesen, Bilanzierung, Bilanzreformen und Abschlussprüfung, Corporate Governance und Reporting, Controllingfragen, Varia, Wien (2006), p. 43–68.

Schweitzer, M. (1978): Wissenschafsziele und Auffassungen in der Betriebswirtschaftslehre, in: Schweitzer, M. (ed.): Auffassungen und Wissenschaftsziele der Betriebswirtschaftslehre, Darmstadt (1978), p. 1–14.

Schweitzer, M./Küpper, H.-U. (2010): Systeme der Kosten- und Erlösrechnung, 10th edn., München (2010).

Schweitzer, M./Schweitzer, M. (2008): Beiträge von Ingenieuren zur historischen Entwicklung der Kostenrechnung in Deutschland im 20. Jahrhundert, in: Spanish Journal of Accounting History, No. 8 , p. 164–182.

Scott, R. (1987): The Adolescence of Institutional Theory, in: Administrative Science Quarterly, 32 (4), p. 493–511.

Scott, W. R. (2001): Institutions and organizations, 2nd edn., Thousand Oaks (2001).

Segelod, E./Carlsson, L. (2010): The emergence of uniform principles of cost accounting in Sweden 1900–36, in: Accounting, Business & Financial History, 20 (3), p. 327–363.

Seicht, G. (1990): Cost Accounting, in: Grochla, E./Büschgen, H. E. (eds.): Handbook of German Business Management, Stuttgart (1990), p. 612–622.

Sharman, P. A. (2003a): Bring on German Cost Accounting, in: Strategic Finance, 85 (6), p. 30–38.

Sharman, P. A. (2003b): The Case for Management Accounting, in: Strategic Finance, 85 (4), p. 42–47.

Sharman, P. A./Vikas, K. (2004): Lessons Learned from German Cost Accounting, in: Strategic Finance, 85 (6), p. 28–35.

Sheridan, T. T. (1995): Management accounting in global European corporations: Anglophone and continental viewpoints, in: Management Accounting Research, 6 (3), p. 287–294.

Shields, M. D. (1995): An Empirical Analysis of Firms' Implementation Experiences with Activity-Based Costing, in: Journal of Management Accounting Research, 7 (1), p. 148–166.

Shields, M. D. (1998): Management accounting practices in Europe: a perspective from the States, in: Management Accounting Research, 9 (4), p. 501–513.

Shields, M./Chow, C./Kato, Y./Nakagawa, Y. (1991): Management Accounting Practices in the U.S. and Japan: Comparative Survey Findings and Research Implications, in: Journal of International Financial Management & Accounting, 3 (1), p. 61–77.

Siegel, S./Castellan, N. J. (1988): Nonparametric statistics for the behavioral sciences, 2nd edn., New York (1988).

Siggelkow, N. (2007): Persuasion with case studies, in: Academy of Management Journal, 50 (1), p. 20–24.

Sill, F. (2009): Controllerbereichserfolg aus Sicht des Managements, Wiesbaden (2009).

Simon, H. A./Gutzkow, H./Kozmetsky, G./Tyndall, G. (1954): Centralization Vs. Decentralisation in Organizing the Controllers' Department, New York (1954).

Simons, R. (1994): How Top Managers Use Control Systems as Levers of Strategic Renewal, in: Strategic Management Journal, 15 (3), p. 169–189.

Simons, R. (1995a): Control in an Age of Empowerment, in: Harvard Business Review, 73 (2), p. 80–88.

Simons, R. (1995b): Levers of control, Boston (1995).

Simons, R. (2000): Performance measurement & control systems for implementing strategy, Upper Saddle River (2000).

Siti-Nabiha, A./Scapens, R. W. (2005): Stability and change: an institutionalist study of management accounting change, in: Accounting, Auditing & Accountability Journal, 18 (1), p. 44–73.

Skovlund, E./Fenstad, G. U. (2001): Should we always choose a nonparametric test when comparing two apparently nonnormal distributions?, in: Journal of Clinical Epidemiology, 54 (1), p. 86–92.

Smith, C. (2005): Going for GPK, in: Strategic Finance, 85 (10), p. 36–39.

Soin, K./Seal, W./Cullen, J. (2002): ABC and organizational change: an institutional perspective, in: Management Accounting Research, 13 (2), p. 249–271.

Sopariwala, P. (2004): Cost Terminology in the 21st Century: Using Direct Labor Cost in a Costs vs. Resources Framework, in: Management Accounting Quarterly, 5 (3), p. 5–12.

StataCorp (2011): Stata user's guide, College Station, Tex (2011).

Steinbichler, G. (1990): Das Berichtswesen im internationalen Unternehmen: Gestaltungsmöglichkeiten für das Controlling, in: Controlling, 2 (3), p. 144–147.

Steiners, D. (2005): Lernen mit Controllinginformationen, Wiesbaden (2005).

Steinmann, H./Wolfram, B. (1979): Konstruktivismus und die Kritik am Wertfreiheitsprinzip, in: Raffée, H./Abel, B. (eds.): Wissenschaftstheoretische Grundfragen der Wirtschaftswissenschaften, München (1979), p. 191–203.

Stier, W. (1999): Empirische Forschungsmethoden, 2nd edn., Berlin (1999).

Stoi, R. (1999): Prozessorientiertes Kostenmanagement in der deutschen Unternehmenspraxis, München (1999).

Stratton, W./Desproches, D./Lawson, R./Hatch, T. (2009): Activity-Based Costing: Is It Still Relevant?, in: Management Accounting Quarterly, 10 (3), p. 31–40.

Sulaiman, M./Ahmad, N. N. N./Alwi, N. M. (2005): Is standard costing obsolete? Empirical evidence from Malaysia, in: Managerial Auditing Journal, 20 (2), p. 109–124.

Swenson, D. W. (1995): The Benefits of Activity-Based Cost Management to the Manufacturing Industry, in: Journal of Management Accounting Research, Fall 1995 , p. 167–181.

Tani, T./Okano, H./Shimizu, N./Iwabuchi, Y./Fukuda, J./Cooray, S. (1994): Target cost management in Japanese Companies: current state of the art, in: Management Accounting Research, 5 (1), p. 67–81.

Tani, T./Kato, Y. (1994): Target Costing in Japan, in: Dellmann, K./Franz, K. P. (eds.): Neuere Entwicklungen im Kostenmanagement, Bern (1994), p. 191–222.

Tayeb, M. (1994): Organizations and National Culture: Methodology Considered, in: Organization Studies, 15 (3), p. 429–445.

Tempel, A./Walgenbach, P. (2012): Subsidiary Managers and the Transfer of Human Resource Practices in Multinational Companies – Institutional Work at the Intersection of Multiple Institutional Frameworks, in: Schmalenbach Business Review, 64 (3), p. 230–247.

Tenenhaus, M./Vinzi, V. E./Chatelin, Y.-M./Lauro, C. (2005): PLS path modeling, in: Computational Statistics & Data Analysis, 48 (1), p. 159–205.

Tinker, A. (1982): The normative origins of positive theories: Ideology and accounting thought, in: Accounting, Organizations and Society, 7 (2), p. 167–200.

Trapp, R. (2010): Integration des internen und externen Rechnungswesens, in: Zeitschrift für Planung & Unternehmenssteuerung, 20 (3), p. 303–310.

Tse, M. S./Gong, M. Z. (2009): Recognition of idle resources in time-driven activity-based costing and resource consumption accounting models, in: Journal of Applied Management Accounting Research, 7 (2), p. 41–54.

Tuomela, T.-S. (2005): The interplay of different levers of control: A case study of introducing a new performance measurement system, in: Management Accounting Research, 16 (3), p. 293–320.

van der Merwe, A. (2004): Chapter Zero in Perspective, in: Management Accounting Quarterly, 5 (2), p. 1–6.

van der Merwe, A./Keys, D. E. (2002): The Case for Resource Consumption Accounting, in: Strategic Finance, 84 (4), p. 31–36.

Van der Stede, W. A. (2003): The effect of national culture on management control and incentive system design in multi-business firms: evidence of intracorporate isomorphism, in: European Accounting Review, 12 (2), p. 263–285.

Van der Stede, W. A./Young, S. M./Chen, C. X. (2005): Assessing the quality of evidence in empirical management accounting research: The case of survey studies, in: Accounting, Organizations and Society, 30 (7-8), p. 655–684.

van der Veeken, H. J. M./Wouters, M. J. F. (2002): Using accounting information systems by operations managers in a project company, in: Management Accounting Research, 13 (3), p. 345–370.

Vandenbosch, B. (1999): An empirical analysis of the association between the use of executive support systems and perceived organizational competitiveness, in: Accounting, Organizations and Society, 24 (1), p. 77–92.

Vandenbosch, B./Huff, S. L. (1997): Searching and Scanning: How Executives Obtain Information from Executive Information Systems, in: Management Information Systems Quarterly, 21 (1), p. 81–107.

Vellmann, K. (1990): Organisation des Controlling in einem Konzern, in: Mayer, E./Weber, J. (eds.): Handbuch Controlling, Stuttgart (1990), p. 535–563.

Vikas, K. (2006): Relevance Lost – Relevance Confirmed – Die Renaissance des German Management Accounting, in: Seicht, G. (ed.): Unternehmensbewertung und Risiko, Internes Rechnungswesen, Bilanzierung, Bilanzreformen und Abschlussprüfung, Corporate Governance und Reporting, Controllingfragen, Varia, Wien (2006), p. 27–42.

Voets, C. (2013): Kulturelle Einflüsse auf die Anwendung des Impairment-Tests nach IAS 36, Frankfurt am Main (2013).

Waeytens, D./Bruggeman, W. (1994): Barriers to succeccful implementation of ABC for continuous improvement: A case study, in: International Journal of Production Economics, 36 , p. 39–52.

Wagner, B./Nakajima, M./Prox, M. (2010): Materialflusskostenrechnung – die internationale Karriere einer Methode zu Identifikation von Ineffizienzen in Produktionssystemen, in: uwf UmweltWirtschaftsForum, 18 (3-4), p. 197–202.

Währisch, M. (1998): Kostenrechnungspraxis in der deutschen Industrie, Wiesbaden (1998).

Währisch, M. (2003): Die Berücksichtigung nationaler kostenrechnerischer Aspekt beim Aufbau einer nationalen Konzernkostenrechnung, in: Zeitschrift für betriebswirtschaftliche Forschung, 49 (Sonderheft), p. 71–80.

Walgenbach, P. (2002): Neoinstitutionalistische Organisationstheorie: State of the Art und Entwicklungslinien, in: Conrad, P./Schreyögg, G. (eds.): Theorien des Managements, Wiesbaden (2002), p. 155-202;.

Walgenbach, P. (2006): Neoinstitutionalistische Ansätze der Organisationstheorie, in: Kieser, A. (ed.): Organisationstheorien, 6th edn., Stuttgart (2006), p. 353–401.

Walker, K. B./Fleischman, G. M./Johnson, E. N. (2012): Measuring Management Accounting Service Quality, in: Management Accounting Quarterly, 13 (3), p. 15–27.

Wang, R. Y./Strong, D. M. (1996): Beyond Accuracy: What Data Quality Means to Data Consumers, in: Journal of Management Information Systems, 12 (4), p. 5–33.

Waterhouse, J./Tiessen, P. (1978): A contingency framework for management accounting systems research, in: Accounting, Organizations and Society, 3 (1), p. 65–76.

Webber, S./Clinton, D. (2004): Resource Consumption Accounting Applied: The Clopay Case, in: Management Accounting Quarterly, 6 (1), p. 1–14.

Weber, J. (1993a): Kostenrechnung im System der Unternehmensführung: Stand und Perspektiven der Kostenrechnung in den 90er Jahren, in: Weber, J. (ed.): Zur Neuausrichtung der Kostenrechnung, Stuttgart (1993), p. 1–77.

Weber, J. (1993b): Stand der Kostenrechnung in deutschen Großunternehmen: Ergebnisse einer empirischen Erhebung, in: Weber, J. (ed.): Zur Neuausrichtung der Kostenrechnung, Stuttgart (1993), p. 257–278.

Weber, J. (1994): Kostenrechnung zwischen Verhaltens- und Entscheidungsorientierung, in: Kostenrechnungspraxis, 38 (2), p. 99–104.

Weber, J. (2005): Gestaltung der Kostenrechnung, Wiesbaden (2005).

Weber, J. (2007): Das Advanced-Controlling-Handbuch Volume 2, Weinheim (2007).

Weber, J. (2010): Was unterscheidet erfolgreiche von nicht erfolgreichen Controllern?, in: Zeitschrift für Controlling und Management, 54 (2), p. 91–95.

Weber, J./Weißenberger, B. (1997): Relative Einzelkosten- und Deckungsbeitragsrechnung: a critical evaluation of Riebels approach, in: Management Accounting Research, 8 (3), p. 277–298.

Weber, J./Schäffer, U. (2011): Einführung in das Controlling, 13th edn., Stuttgart (2011).

Weber, J./Hunold, C. (2002): Gestaltung und Nutzung der kommunalen Kostenrechnung - eine empirische Studie, in: Kostenrechnungspraxis, 46 (1), p. 37–45.

Weber, J./Preis, A./Boettger, U. (2010a): Neue Anforderungen an Controller, Weinheim (2010).

Weber, J./Goretzki, L./Zubler, S. (2010b): Welche Erkenntnisse kann die empirische Controllingforschung zum Erfolg des Controllings beitragen?, in: Controlling, 22 (6), p. 322–329.

Weiss, C. H. (1977): Introduction, in: Weiss, C. H. (ed.): Using social research in public policy making, Lexington (1977), p. 1–22.

Weiss, C. H. (1979): The Many Meanings of Research Utilization, in: Public Administration Review, 39 (5), p. 426–431.

Weißenberger, B. E. (2003): Anreizkompatible Erfolgsrechnung im Konzern, Wiesbaden (2003).

Westney, D. E. (1993): Institutionalization Theory and the Multinational Corporation, in: Ghoshal, S./Westney, D. E. (eds.): Organization theory and the multinational corporation, New York (1993), p. 53–76.

White, H. (1980): A Heteroskedasticity-Consistent Covariance Matrix Estimator and a Direct Test for Heteroskedasticity, in: Econometrica, 48 (4), p. 817–838.

White, L. (2004): Why Look at German Cost Management?, in: Strategic Finance, 85 (3), p. 6–7.

White, L. (2009): Resource consumption accounting: Manager-focused management accounting, in: Journal of Corporate Accounting & Finance, 20 (4), p. 63–77.

White, L. L./Stenzel, C./Stenzel, J. (2008): Bringing RCA to market: Discussing RCA And The Newly Formed RCA Institute With The Organization's Executive Director Larry L. White, in: Journal of Cost Management, 22 (4), p. 5–13.

White, L./Clinton, D./van der Merwe, A./Cokins, G./Thomas, C./Templin, K./Huntzinger, J. (2011): Why We Need a Conceptual Framework for Managerial Costing, in: Strategic Finance, 92 (4), p. 36–42.

Widener, S. K. (2007): An empirical analysis of the levers of control framework, in: Accounting, Organizations and Society, 32 (7-8), p. 757–788.

Wild, J. (1966): Grundlagen und Probleme der betriebswirtschaftlichen Organisationslehre: Entwurf eines Wissenschaftsprogramms, Berlin (1966).

Williams, K./Mitsui, I./Haslam, C. (1991): How Far From Japan? A Case Study of Japanese Press Shop Practice and Management Calculation, in: Critical Perspectives in Accounting, 2 (1), p. 145–169.

Wolf, J. (2013): Organisation, Management, Unternehmensführung, 5th edn., Wiesbaden (2013).

Wolfsgruber, I. (2011): Kostenrechnung in international tätigen österreichischen Konzernen der Industrie, Wien (2011).

Wooldridge, J. M. (2007): Solutions Manual and Supplementary Materials for Econometric Analysis of Cross Section and Panel Data, 2nd edn., Cambridge (2007).

Wullenkord, A. (1995): Kosten- und Erfolgs-Controlling im Konzern, München (1995).

Yakhou, M./Dorweiler, V. P. (1995): Advanced Cost Management Systems: An Empirical Comparison of England, France, and the United States, in: Advances in International Accounting, 8 (1), p. 99–107.

Yazdifar, H./Tsamenyi, M. (2005): Management accounting change and the changing roles of management accountants: a comparative analysis between dependent and independent organizations, in: Journal of Accounting & Organizational Change, 1 (2), p. 180–198.

Yazdifar, H./Askarany, D. (2010a): A comparative investigation into the diffusion of management accounting innovations in the UK, Australia and New Zealand, in: CIMA - Research executive summaries series, 5 (9), p. 1–11.

Yazdifar, H./Askarany, D. (2010b): Accounting Innovations and Ownership, Working Paper (2010).

Yazdifar, H./Askarany, D. (2012): A comparative study of the adoption and implementation of target costing in the UK, Australia and New Zealand, in: International Journal of Production Economics, 135 (1), p. 382–392.

Yazdifar, H./Zaman, M./Tsamenyi, M./Askarany, D. (2008): Management accounting change in a subsidiary organisation, in: Critical Perspectives in Accounting, 19 (3), p. 404–430.

Yin, R. K. (2003): Applications of case study research, 2nd edn., Thousand Oaks (2003).

Yin, R. K. (2009): Case study research, 4th edn., Los Angeles (2009).

Zayer, E. (2005): An American Perspective on German Controlling. Unexpected Praise for German Controlling Practice. An Interview with Paul Sharman, ACMA, President CEO, IMA, in: Zeitschrift für Controlling und Management, 49 (5), p. 322–326.

Ziegler, H. (1992): Prozeßorientierte Kostenrechnung im Hause Siemens, in: Betriebswirtschaftliche Forschung und Praxis, 42 (4), p. 304–318.

Ziegler, H. (1994): Neuorientierung des internen Rechnungswesens für das Unternehmens-Controlling im Hause Siemens, in: Zeitschrift für betriebswirtschaftliche Forschung, 46 (2), p. 175–188.

Ziener, M. (1985): Controlling im multinationalen Unternehmen, Landsberg am Lech (1985).

Zirkler, B. (2001): Wesensmerkmale und Implikationen des US-amerikanischen Management Accounting, in: Kostenrechnungspraxis, 45 (Sonderheft 3), p. 15–18.

Zirkler, B. (2002): Führungsorientiertes US-amerikanisches Management-Accounting, Wiesbaden (2002).

Zitterbarth, W. (1991): Der Erlanger Konstruktivismus in seiner Beziehung zum Konstruktiven Realismus, in: Peschl, M. (ed.): Formen des Konstruktivismus in Diskussion, Wien (1991), p. 73–87.

Münsteraner Schriften zur Internationalen Unternehmensrechnung

Herausgegeben von Peter Kajüter

Band 1 Daniela Barth: Prognoseberichterstattung. Praxis, Determinanten und Kapitalmarktwirkungen bei deutschen börsennotierten Unternehmen. 2009.

Band 2 Tobias Dickmann: Controllingintegration nach M&A-Transaktionen. Eine empirische Analyse. 2010.

Band 3 Simon Esser: Produktorientiertes Kostenmanagement in der chemischen Industrie. Eine empirische Analyse. 2011.

Band 4 Christian Reisloh: Influence of National Culture on IFRS Practice. An Empirical Study in France, Germany and the United Kingdom. 2011.

Band 5 Matthias Moeschler: Cost Accounting in Germany and Japan. A Comparative Analysis. 2012.

Band 6 Martin Merschdorf: Der Management Approach in der IFRS-Rechnungslegung. Implikationen für Unternehmen und Investoren. 2012.

Band 7 Kristian Bachert: Fair Value Accounting. Implications for Users of Financial Statements. 2012.

Band 8 Daniel Blaesing: Nachhaltigkeitsberichterstattung in Deutschland und den USA. Berichtspraxis, Determinanten und Eigenkapitalkostenwirkungen. 2013.

Band 9 Christina Voets: Kulturelle Einflüsse auf die Anwendung des Impairment-Tests nach IAS 36. Eine experimentelle Untersuchung in Asien und Europa. 2013.

Band 10 Thomas Poplat: Foreign Investments in BRIC Countries. Empirical Evidence from Multinational Corporations. 2014.

Band 11 Moritz Schröder: Cost Accounting in Anglophone Subsidiaries. Empirical Evidence from Germany. 2014.

www.peterlang.com

www.ingramcontent.com/pod-product-compliance
Ingram Content Group UK Ltd.
Pitfield, Milton Keynes, MK11 3LW, UK
UKHW021830100926
8556IPUK00004B/257

9 783631 655375